Computer Graphics

Computer Graphics

Third Edition

Pradeep K. Bhatia
Associate Professor
Guru Jambheshwar University of Science and Technology
Hissar, Haryana

TECHSAR™
NEW DELHI

Published and Printed by
Techsar Pvt. Ltd.
4435-36/7, Ansari Road, Daryaganj
New Delhi-110 002 (India)
E-mail: tech_info@techsarworld.com
Website: www.techsarworld.com

ISBN: 978-93-82332-51-0

Reprint 2025

Dedicated
to
My Parents

Foreword

It is a matter of great pleasure to write a few words about the book of Pradeep Kumar Bhatia, who happens to be my Ph.D student. Computer Graphics is becoming very important and significant in the changing scenario of Information Technology. It is an effective way for communication between person and machine. This book is an attempt to provide readable material to the undergraduate and post-graduate students.

The book may be used as a text for the first course in Computer Graphics for various programmes, namely, B.Tech., MCA, BCA as well as DOEACC-B level.

This book covers the following: working of display devices, interactive devices (I/O), 2-D transformations, 3-D transformations, clipping, hidden lines and hidden surface removal, animation, multimedia, colour models, etc. The book does not require prior background of Computer Graphics. However, some knowledge of elementary algebra, geometry, trigonometry, and programming would be helpful.

The chapters of the book are organized in such a way that readers can easily grasp the contents. I am sure that this book will meet the aspirations of the readers.

Prof. Yogesh Singh

Preface to the Third Edition

Information Technology has given new dimensions to computer field and computer graphics is one of the important attributes for growth of information technology. The field of computer graphics continues to grow. New techniques are emerging everyday. This book is an attempt to organize the ideas and methods to make the concepts of computer graphics easily understandable in a concise manner.

This book provides introduction to computer graphics and their applications. This book helps the reader understand: how computer hardware interacts with computer graphics; how it draws various objects, namely, line, circle, parabola, hyperbola, etc.; how realistic images are formed; how we see pictures move; how different colors are generated from visible light.

The basic approach followed in preparation of this book is simple and elementary. At every stage, detailed experiments with suitable figures are given to make the reader understand the concepts.

This book covers syllabi of BCA, BE/BTech (CSE/IT), MCA, as well as DOEACC-B level courses.

The reader is assumed to have the knowledge of elementary algebra, geometry, trigonometry, and elementary calculus. Some exposure to vectors and matrices is also required. The reader is also expected to have experience of writing fundamental computer programs in C, C++.

About 250 unsolved problems have been given at the end of chapters in the book. There are also many solved examples and programs in C provided in the Appendices of the book.

I hope the readers will find this book interesting and useful.

Suggestions from teachers and students for improving the contents, are welcome.

Chapter 1 gives an overview of the computer graphics field. It also describes how computer hardware interacts with computer graphics.

Chapter 2 discusses working of different types of graphics display devices—soft copy display devices and hard copy display devices. Related to soft copy display devices it also explains the working of CRT (Raster Scan, Random Scan, DVST), flat panel display devices (EmissivePlasma Panel, LED and non-emissive LCD) and related hard copy display devices, working of impact printers, non-impact printers are also discussed.

Chapter 3 describes working of the input devices (mouse, light pen, joystick, touch panel, etc.).

Chapter 4 describes how images are created using scan conversion. It discusses the scan conversion algorithm of line, circle, ellipse, parabola, and hyperbola. It also discusses the various side effects of scan conversion and techniques to reduce these side effects.

Chapter 5 develops theory of transformation and describes various types of 2-D transformations (translations, rotations, scaling, flip, shear) with figures and implementation in 2-D coordinate system.

Chapter 6 describes window-to-viewport mapping and its implementation in 2-D coordinate system. It also discusses various 2-D line segment clipping algorithms against window and area filling techniques.

Chapter 7 provides overview of 3D geometry and 3-D transformations (translations, rotations, scaling, flip).

Chapter 8 helps in building realistic images using projection (parallel and perspective). It discusses various types of projections and their importance in real life.

Chapter 9 deals with 3-D viewing and clipping (direct and indirect). Cohen-Sutherland algorithm for 3-D line segment against normalized view volume is also described.

Chapter 10 deals with image surface algorithms and object-surface algorithms for removal of hidden lines and surfaces, namely, Z-buffer, Painter's Algorithm, Area subdivision, Scan line Algorithms.

Chapter 11 tells as to how to design and draw smooth curves and surfaces. The term Bezier Curve and B-spline curve is described along with rational B-spline, which leads to discussion of NURBS curves.

Chapter 12 provides an overview of animation along with its types and techniques.

Chapter 13 provides an overview of multimedia along with its type, techniques and applications.

Chapter 14 focuses on how colors are obtained from visible lights. It indicates the problems of representation of colors numerically. The CIE standard chromaticity diagram is discussed. Various types of color models, namely, RGB, CMYK, HSV, HLS are described.

Chapter 15 introduces illumination models and shading models for identifying visible surfaces.

Chapter 16 provides segmentation of graphics image and operation segmentation.

ACKNOWLEDGEMENTS

I too owe my debt to learners, and researchers especially to senior faculty including Prof. H.L.Verma, Prof. Yogesh Singh, and Prof. Dharminder Kumar who have helped, given me moral support and encouragement for completion of this task.

I am also thankful to my dear colleagues and friends, technical staff and non-technical staff of Department of Computer Science and Engineering, and of other departments and administrative block for rendering all help and co-operation necessary for completion of this book.

Thanks also to all users of previous edition who have provided me with comments and constructive criticism.

I owe my special thanks to my wife Sunita and my kids Sudhanshu and Divaynshi for sacrifices of patience. My endless gratitude goes to my mother Smt. Raj. Dulari and other family members.

Pradeep K. Bhatia

Contents

1

Introduction to Computer Graphics

1.1 INTRODUCTION

The term **graphics** refers to images, e.g., a drawing, photograph of a function.

A **photograph** (often just **photo**) is an image created by collecting and focusing electromagnetic radiation (light is a form of electromagnetic radiation).

In common usage, an **image** (from Latin *imago*) or **picture** is an artefact that reproduces the likeness of some subject — usually a physical object or a person. Images may be two-dimensional (e.g., a photograph) or three- dimensional (e.g., a statue). They are typically produced by optical devices — such as cameras, mirrors, lenses, telescopes, microscopes, etc. and natural objects and phenomena, such as the human eye or water surfaces. The word **image** is also used in the broader sense of any two-dimensional figure or illustration, e.g., a map, a graph, a pie-chart, an abstract, etc. In this wider sense, images can also be produced manually (by drawing, painting, carving, etc.) or by computer graphics technology.

A **volatile image** is one that exists only for a short period of time, e.g., the reflection of an object by a mirror, projection of the sun on a wall by a pinhole camera, a scene displayed on a cathode ray tube, etc.

A **fixed image**, also called **hard copy**, is one that has been recorded on a material object, such as paper or textile.

A **mental image** exists in someone's mind. Something one remembers or imagines).

Originally, almost all photographs were black and white. Although methods for developing colour photos were available as early as the late 19th century, they did not become widely available until the 1940s or 50s, and even till 1960s most photographs were taken in black and white. Since then, colour photography has dominated popular photography, although the black and white format remains popular for photographers and artists. Black and white film is considerably easier to develop than the colour film.

Digital photos can be stored in various file formats, of which **Joint Photographic Experts Group (JPEG)** is the most popular. Many other graphics formats are used, including **TIFF (Tagged Image File Format)**, **PNG (Portable Network Graphics)**,**GIF** (Graphics Interchange Format).

It is natural that graphical communication is the most popular method of exchanging information than verbal communication. Chinese says "*one picture is worth a thousand words*". With the introduction of computer this can be modified to "*one picture is worth many kilobytes of data*".

Computer graphics has universally penetrated our modern life, be it from the special effects in movies, gaming consoles, interactive graphics on hand-held devices or data visualization on the PC. The foundations of interactive 3D computer graphics include such various topics as graphics systems architecture, polygonal 3D modeling, illumination and shading from light, vector and matrix operations, geometric transformations, viewing in 3D, visibility and occlusion culling, clipping and screen rasterization.

1.2 THE HISTORY OF COMPUTER GRAPHICS

From the earliest text character images of a non-graphic mainframe computer to the latest photographic quality images of a high resolution personal computers, from vector displays, from 2D to 3D, computer graphics has rapid changing history.

This section describes the history of computer graphics based upon different devices, and algorithms contributed by researchers and engineers.

- 1950 Ben Laposky created the first graphics image. The image was produced by manipulating electronic beams and reading them onto high-speed film.
- 1961 Steve Russel introduced the first computer game named as Spacewars.
- 1963 Ivan Sutherland created Sketchpad. (Sketchpad allows drawing simple shapes on computer screen, save them and even recalling them later.)
- 1965 Jack Brenesham invented line drawing algorithm.
- 1966 Sutherland at MIT invented the first hand-mounted display (HMD).
- 1968 A special type of CRT produced—Tektronix.
- 1969 Hidden surface algorithm—area subdivision algorithm was introduced by John Warnock.
- 1971 Advanced computer graphics scenes appeared with the help of a separate processor known as graphics processor.
- 1974 Hidden surface algorithm—Z buffer algorithm, Texture mapping, Rendering covered surface algorithms produced by Edwin Catmull.
- 1987 VGA (Video Graphics Array) was introduced by IBM.
- 1989 SVGA (Super Video Graphics Array) was introduced by VESA.
- 1992 Open GL specifications with Silicon graphics.
- 1993 First graphics Web Browser produced.
- 1995 First full-length 3D animated and rendered motion picture was supplied.

1.3 DEFINITIONS

Computer graphics may be defined in one of the following ways:

Definition I

Computer Graphics (CG) is the discipline of producing pictures or images using a computer including modeling – creation, manipulation and storage of geometric objects and rendering – converting a scene to an image, or the process of transformation, rasterization, shading, illumination and animation of the image.

Definition II

Computer Graphics(CG) involves the generation, representation, manipulation, processing or evaluation of graphic objects by a computer as well as the association of graphic object with related non-graphic information residing in computer files.

Definition III

Computer Graphics (CG) is the field of visual computing, where one utilizes computers both to generate visual images synthetically and to integrate or alter visual and spatial information sampled from the real world.

Definition IV

Definition of program introduced by **Niklus Wirth:**
Programs = Algorithms + Data Structures
Similar definition for computer graphics:
Computer Graphics = Graphics Algorithms + Data Structures + Languages
Obviously, we should know

- data structures suitable for computer graphics.
- algorithms suitable for picture generation and transformation.
- an appropriate language construct for the generation of graphic objects.

1.4 BROAD CLASSIFICATION OF COMPUTER GRAPHICS

Non-interactive(Passive) Computer Graphics

In this type of computer graphics, the user has no control over picture. The user can only see the contents of the picture. For example, in TV monitor user has no control over picture he/she can't move picture, translate picture, rotate picture and so on.

Interactive(Active) Computer Graphics

In this type of computer graphics, the user has control over contents, structure and appearance of objects on display devices. For example, in video games a user has a lever in his hand to control level of the game.

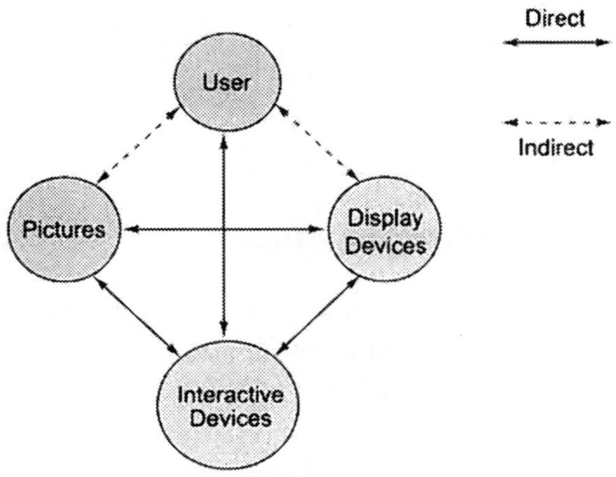

FIGURE 1.1 Interaction of User with Picture Through Other Devices

Due to control over picture by the user, we are interested to study interactive computer graphics throughout the study.

1.5 ARCHITECTURE OF INTERACTIVE COMPUTER GRAPHICS

Working of interactive computer graphics is extremely simple. Figure 1.2 illustrates the framework of interactive computer graphics. It consists of two major components:

(a) Software Level
- Application Model
- Application Program
- Graphics System

(b) Hardware Level
- Interactive Devices
- Display Devices

At hardware level, the computer receives input from interactive devices and show images on display devices.

At software level, there are three components—application program, application model and graphics system. Application program creates, stores, retrieves picture from the second component, application model. Application model represents the data or object to be pictured on the screen. Graphics system is a series of graphics commands that contain both—what is to be viewed and how it is to be viewed?

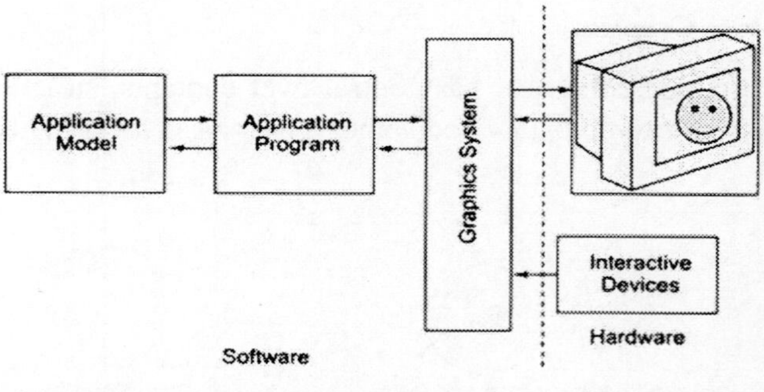

FIGURE 1.2 Framework of Interactive Computer Graphics

1.6 APPLICATIONS OF COMPUTER GRAPHICS

Computer graphics has been widely used, such as graphics presentation, paint systems, computer-aided design (CAD), image processing, simulation and virtual reality, entertainment, etc.

1.6.1 Computer-Aided Design (CAD)

It is one of the best and biggest application of computer graphics. This is particularly used in engineering applications such as building and other structural design and industrial design, design of manufacturing process, automobiles and aircraft, ships and spacecraft, very large scale-integrated

(VLSI) chips, optical systems, and telephone and computer networks. The design process involves modeling of an object or conceptual model of a process on which modification, analysis and other manipulations can be carried out. It is in this modeling aspect that computer graphics plays important role.

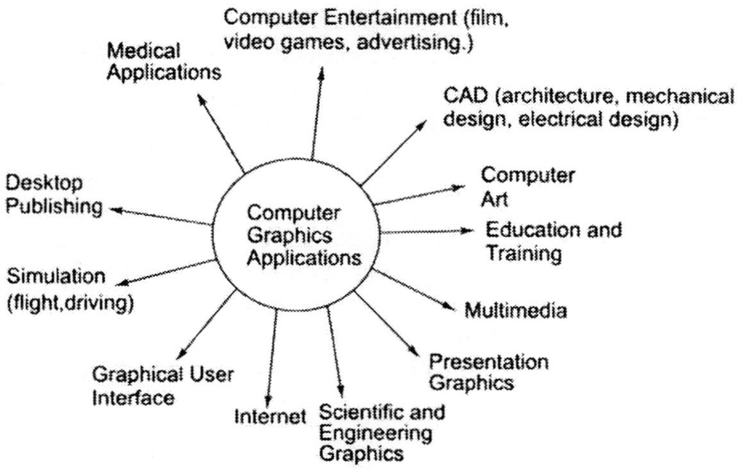

FIGURE 1.3 Applications of Computer Graphics

1.6.2 Computer Art

Computer graphics is used to produce pictures that express a message and attract attention. In professions involving artist and in other business fields, such as fashion design, architecture, these applications of computer graphics are widely used because of effective speed of computer and easy modifiability capability.

1.6.3 Education and Training

It would not be accurate to say that computer graphics has qualitatively changed the delivery of education and training as yet, although it has certainly significantly enhanced the quality of teaching. This concentration upon technique makes training much more amenable to the use of computer graphics than education. It is easy to use graphics to train someone to put together an electronic circuit, but rather harder to explain the quantum mechanics that enable the semiconductors in the circuit to work.

However, there are areas of education where graphics and multimedia can, and are, being put to good use. In the sciences and engineering, visualisation techniques, as discussed later on in this chapter, can be easily used for teaching as analysis, and in many fields images are essential to grasp fundamental concepts, for example, the structure of a molecule in chemistry, or the process of cell division in biology. The teaching of history, particularly of the 20th century, could benefit from the use of the vast amount of still and moving images in the archives, as could the teaching of Art.

Hypermedia systems can be particularly useful in higher education. As noted in the chapter on multimedia, one of the characteristics of hypertext and hypermedia is that they put the user back in control. In an educational setting, this translates to student-centred learning, where the students use *courseware*—educational software—to learn at their own pace in their own time. This fits in with modern views of learning, which place emphasis on the engagement of the student in the learning process, rather than as a passive receptacle for knowledge. A logical extension of student-centred learning is distance learning, and as recent rapid advances in telecommunications have enabled the real-time transmission of audio and video on ordinary telephone lines the science-fiction scenario of a class of students spread over hundreds or thousands of miles being addressed by one lecturer, or accessing multimedia courseware, will soon become reality.

There are a few subjects which would not benefit substantially from the use of computer graphics in their teaching: it is difficult to see how courses in such areas as English Literature, Philosophy, Music, or Religion, could be much enhanced by images whether moving or still.

1.6.4 Multimedia

Multimedia is the field concerned with the computer-controlled integration of text, graphics, drawings, still and moving images (video), animation, audio and any other media where every type of information can be represented, stored, transmitted and processed digitally.

It is clear from this definition of multimedia that if we separate multimedia from graphics, then none of the features of multimedia would be worthwhile without computer graphics. Just think for a moment a movie without video, without animation!

1.6.5 Presentation Graphics

Presentation of data in pictorial form is always preferred since it is more understood than textual data. Presentation of graphics is widely used in posters, brochures, magazines, newspapers, training purposes, etc. This presentation may be sequential still or animated on computer monitor.

1.6.6 Scientific and Engineering Visualisation

In the today's world of science, the vast volumes of data generated by modern technologies are such that visualisation is not just a means of presenting the data but is very often essential in order to extract meaning and information. Visualisation is a means of scientific enquiry and research, an analytical tool which is an integral part of the scientific process. It has had a dramatic impact on all natural sciences (and more than a few social sciences), and in some cases has actually created new fields of investigation, for example, Fractal Geometry.

1.6.7 Internet

The word internet is derived from two words *Interconnection* and *Networks*. Also referred as the Net. Internet is a worldwide system of computer networks, that is, network of networks, which allows the participants to share information on those linked computers.

Internet is a much more broader concept than entertainment. The internet would be positively boring without graphics.

1.6.8 Graphical User Interface (GUI)

Graphical User Interface is related to learning and use of packages. It is not possible to learn packages in less times without graphic items present on the screen. Mostly, software developed today must have a Graphical User Interface and interactivity.

1.6.9 Simulation and Virtual Reality

The computer graphics helps here in simulating the views that the operator would see under various circumstances. Complex, mechanical, chemical and industrial processes can be simulated in action so that persons can be trained in their operation before they handle the actual equipment. Such a practice avoids wastage of cost and time.

Simulation has now reached up to such a length that those users follow wearing some special devices on their body such as on eyes, ears, and fingers.

1.6.10 Desktop Publishing (DTP)

DTP is related to the production of journals, printing newsletters, book publishing in small organization. This technology has expanded to such an extent that many book publishers, newspapers would not be able to deliver material without DTP.

1.6.11 Medical Applications

Computer graphics has now become a very important tool of diagnosis and treatment in the hands of doctors, particularly surgeons. Two-dimensional colorful images of cross-sections of human body or specific organs and limbs are produced. These 2D images are transformed to special investigated tools; a surgeon can rehearse his operation procedure on the computerized 3D image of the patient's part of body.

1.6.12 Computer Games and Entertainment

Games are an important driving force in computer graphics. Games industries emphasis on following points at the time of development of computer games:

(a) Focus on interactivity
(b) Cost-effective solutions
(c) Avoiding computation and other tricks
(d) Games drive the baseline

Another advanced technology area is interactive cartooning. The simpler kinds of systems for producing 'flat' cartoons are becoming cost-effective in creating routine 'in-between' frames that interpolate between two explicitly specified 'key frames'. Cartoon characters will increasingly be modeled in the computer as 3D shape descriptions whose movements are controlled by computer commands, rather than by the figures being drawn manually by cartoonists.

2

Display Devices

2.1 INTRODUCTION

In the earlier days input was by means of punched cards or punched tape; perform processing and perform logic had to be checked by means of blinking lights and the accuracy of the result had to be conformed only by means of printing. When graphics became available, the same problem continued, resulting in the wastage of time and cost, with this user feel frustration. Graphics without display device could not be interactive; there could be the preview of correctness of the image until it is plotted or printed. Basically, the outputs are of following two forms:

Hard Copy: The physical form of output is known as *hard copy*. In general, it refers to the recorded information copied from a computer onto paper or some other durable surface, such as microfilm. Hard copy output is permanent and relatively stable form of output. This type of output is also highly portable. Paper is one of the most widely used hard copy output media. The principal examples are printouts, whether text or graphics, from printers. Film, including microfilm and microfiche, is also considered a hard copy output.

Soft Copy: The electronic version of an output, which usually resides in computer memory or on disk, is known as *soft copy*. Unlike hard copy, soft copy is not a permanent form of output. It is transient and is usually displayed on the screen. This kind of output is not tangible, that is, it cannot be touched. Soft copy output includes audio visual form of output, which is generated using a computer. In addition, textual or graphical information displayed on a computer monitor is also a soft copy form of output.

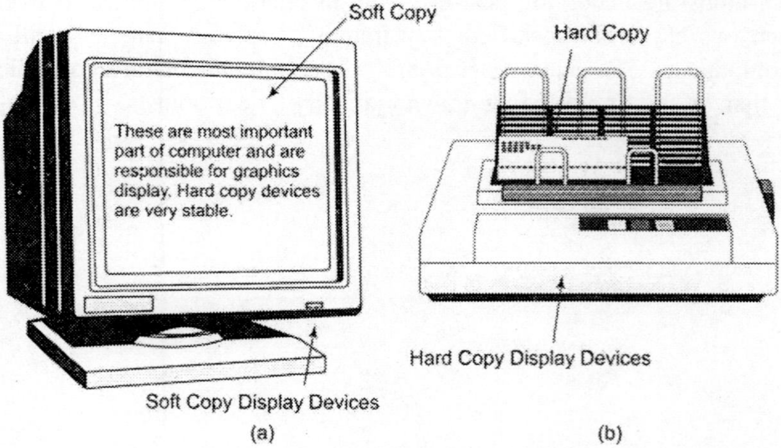

FIGURE 2.1 Two Types of Outputs

Based on the hard copy and soft copy outputs, the display devices are classified into two types: *hard copy display devices* and *soft copy display devices*. These are most important part of computer and are responsible for graphics display. Hard copy devices are very slow in operation as compared to the soft copy display devices. Both above-mentioned display devices are capable of converting computer's electrical signals into visible images at higher speeds. Over the years, a wide range of extremely effective computer display devices have emerged.

Soft Copy Display Devices

These devices are used for creating the soft copy output. Some commonly used soft copy display devices are classified into *monitors, flat Panel display devices.*

Hard Copy Display Devices

Among the wide variety of the hard copy display devices, *printers* and *plotters* are the most commonly used. A printer is used to produce printouts of the documents stored on a computer's disk drive. A plotter is a pen-based output device, which is used for producing high quality output by moving ink pens across the paper. Figure 2.2 depicts the classification of various display devices.

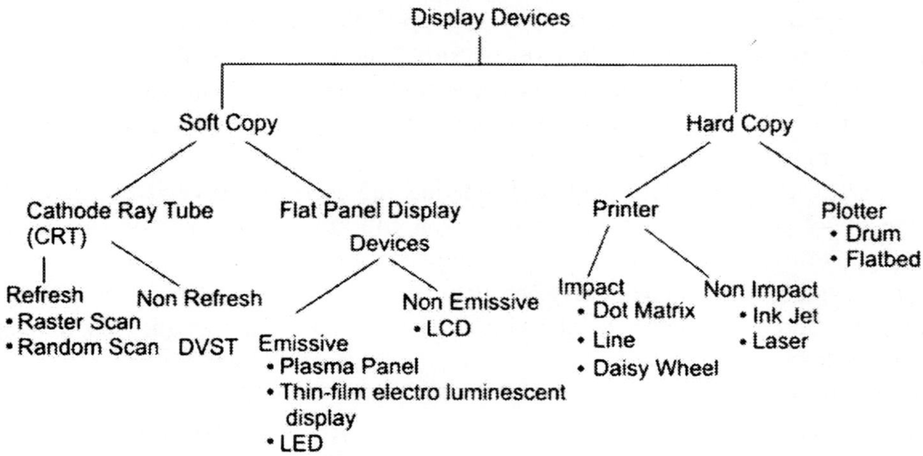

FIGURE 2.2 Classification of Display Devices

2.2 DISPLAY SYSTEM

The purpose of display system may be to display character, text, graphics and video.

However, every display system has three basic parts:

- Display controller
- Monitor
- Cable

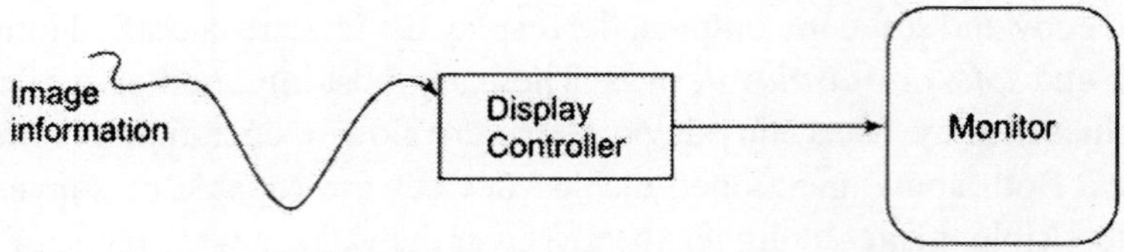

FIGURE 2.3 Display System

The display controller sits between computer and display devices, receiving information from computers and converting it into signals acceptable to device. Task done by display controllers includes voltage level conversions between computer and display devices, buffering to compensate for differences in speed of operation and generation of line segments and text characters.

Display systems do not only include your PC's monitor, but also the graphics card. Although most commercial PC packages include both a monitor and a graphics card, many people choose to upgrade their display devices. Larger, higher quality screens can improve appearance, as well as increase the viewing area. Better graphics cards can improve the speed and visual quality of many graphics applications and games.

Video Cards

Video cards (***video boards / video display boards /graphics cards /graphics adapter***) are physical hardware circuit boards that connect to the motherboard. Video cards are also now being placed onto the computer motherboard to help bring the cost down on computers. When the video card is connected to a monitor, it serves as the visual link between you and your computer, allowing you to view and manage your computer's software data.

Video cards must specify its video standards, allowing end users to know what video cards may or may not be capable of doing. With new computers, you will most likely find SVGA standard video cards, allowing you to run the majority of software applications as well as run at high resolutions.

Generally, most video cards shipped today are included with video memory. Video memory is built onto the video board and/or motherboard, allowing the video card to run at higher resolutions and run at more efficient speeds.

Video cards are most commonly found in the PCI slots; however, with the release of the Pentium II came the AGP (Advanced Graphics Port) support. This new type of slot was released on August 26, 1996. This new technology allows the card to run at 66 MHz, 32-bit bus.

With the increasing popularity of advanced gaming came a new breed of video cards known as the 3D accelerators. When originally released, these cards only had support for 3D and not 2D and commonly required an additional 2D card to fully work. Today, 3D accelerators support both 3D and 2D, contain several MB of memory and processor on the video card.

Video Card Standards

Table 2.1 depicts the most commonly found video standards in new and old computers. Within this chart, under the specifications column, you will find the types of resolutions this standard is capable of running.

TABLE 2.1 Video Standards

Display	*Specifications*	*Manufacturer*
MDA Monochrome Display Adapter	Monochrome only , text-only standard, text display at 80 × 25 Max of 720 × 350 resolution however each individual pixel is not accessible, because text-only.	Developed by IBM
CGA *Color Graphics Adapter*	Max of 640 × 200 (Monochrome) in Graphics Mode. Max of 160 × 200 (16 colors) in Graphics Mode. Max of 80 × 25 resolution in Text Mode.	Developed by IBM
EGA Enhanced Graphics Adapter	Max of 640 × 350 (16 colors, 60Hz) in Graphics Mode. Max of 80 × 25 resolution in Text Mode.	Developed by IBM in 1984
PGA Professional Graphics Adapter	Max of 640 × 400	Developed by IBM
VGA *Video Graphics Adapter*	Max of 640 × 480 (16 colors) in Graphics Mode. Max of 320 × 200 (256 colors) in Graphics Mode. Max of 720 × 400 resolution in Text Mode.	Developed by IBM in 1987
XGA *Extended graphics array*	Upgrade to the VGA video card. Max of 1,024 × 768 (256 colors) in Graphics mode.	Developed by IBM in 1990.
SVGA *No real definition* however commonly referred to as *Super Video Graphs adapter.*	Dependent upon the amount of Video memory see below chart for all available modes.	
SXGA Super XGA	Max of 1400 × 1050 in Graphics Mode	
UXGA Ultra XGA	Max of 1600 × 1200 in Graphics Mode	
WSXGA Wide SXGA	Supports resolution of 1600 × 900 pixels or 1600 × 1024 pixels	
WUXGA Wide UXGA		
WXGA Wide XGA	Max of 1366 × 768 resolution.	

Before discuss the display systems, let us first define related terms.

2.2.1 Monitors

The monitor is often referred to as *Video Monitor* or *Video Display* **Unit(VDU)** or *Display Processing* **Unit(DPU).** The most common video monitor is Raster Scan type.

The monitor is the most frequently used soft copy display device. A computer screen, that is, monitor, is a TV-like display attached to the computer on which the output can be displayed and viewed. It is the most popular input/output device used with modern computers. The computer screen can be either a monochrome display or a color display. A monochrome screen uses only one color (usually white, green, amber or black) to display text or graphics on contrasting background.

Monitors are available in various sizes like 14, 15, 17, 19 and 21 inches. Like televisions, screen sizes are normally measured diagonally (in inches), the distance from one corner to the opposite corner. CRT (cathode ray tube) monitors are the most popular type of computer display for desktop and workstation computers. Although large and bulky, CRT monitors offer many positive features not found with LCD screens. Their relatively low cost, large viewable area, and high quality picture are the main reasons for this design's popularity.

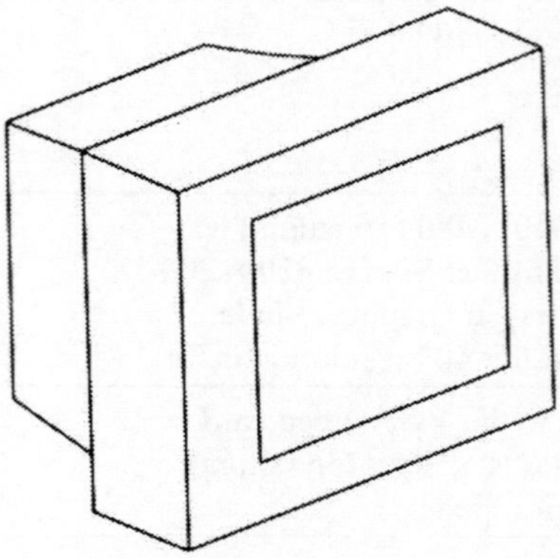

FIGURE 2.4 Monitor

Monitor Controls

Below is additional information on the likely monitor controls on monitor. Using these controls you can help improve the quality and layout of the picture on your monitor for better viewing pleasure. Please keep in mind that not all monitors will have all of the below buttons.

TABLE 2.2

Monitor Icon	*Description of icon function*
Power	**Power** - Turns the monitor on / off.
Brightness	**Brightness** - Using this button or wheel the user can increase and decrease the brightness on the screen.

(*Contd.*)

Monitor Icon	*Description of icon function*
Contrast	**Contrast:** Using this button or wheel can increase and decrease the amount of contrast on the screen.
Horizontal Size	**Horizontal Size**: Allows for the picture on the screen to be stretched to the horizontal edge of the monitor.
Vertical Size	**Vertical Size:** Allows the picture on the screen to be stretched to the vertical edges of the monitor.
Horizontal Position	**Horizontal Position:** Allows the picture to move moved horizontally, once in the centre the user can then use the Horizontal size to stretch it to have an equal amount of black border on each side.
Vertical Position	**Vertical Position**: Like the Horizontal Position, using this button or wheel the user can move the picture up or down to center the picture more appropriately.
Full Screen	**Full Screen:** Sets monitor to full screen.
Degauss	**Degauss:** This button will demagnetize the CRT, restoring possible color impurities. After this button has been pressed the degaussing circuit will be activated and then deactivated after a few seconds. Pressing and holding this button for a few seconds may cause your computer monitor to reset all data.
Corner/Trapezoid Correction Corner/Trapezoid Correction	**Corner / Trapezoid Correction:** Using this button or wheel the user can either round the edges of the picture or move the picture inward like an hour glass or outwards.
Vertical Linearity	**Vertical Linearity:** Sets the width of the vertical lines.
Moiré	**Moire:** Removes or reduces the Moire effect, if any.
OSD Controls	**OSD Controls:** If the monitor contains OSD controls, allows for the OSD menus to be adjusted.
Power Management	**Power Management:** Allows the user to define the power management settings through the monitor itself and not the software.
Monitor Status	**Monitor Status:** Displays the current monitor settings such as refresh rate and other settings.
Language	**Language:** Sets the language.

2.2.2 Pixel

The image is displayed as a collection of phosphor dots of regular shapes. These regular shapes are called *pixels(picture elements/pels)*. The pixels could be rectangles, circles, squares.

A pixel is the smallest addressable portion of an image or display that a computer is capable of printing or displaying.

Figure 2.5 illustrates each pixel as unit square area identified by the coordinates of its lower left corner. The origin of the referenced coordinate system is located at the lower left corner of the display screen.

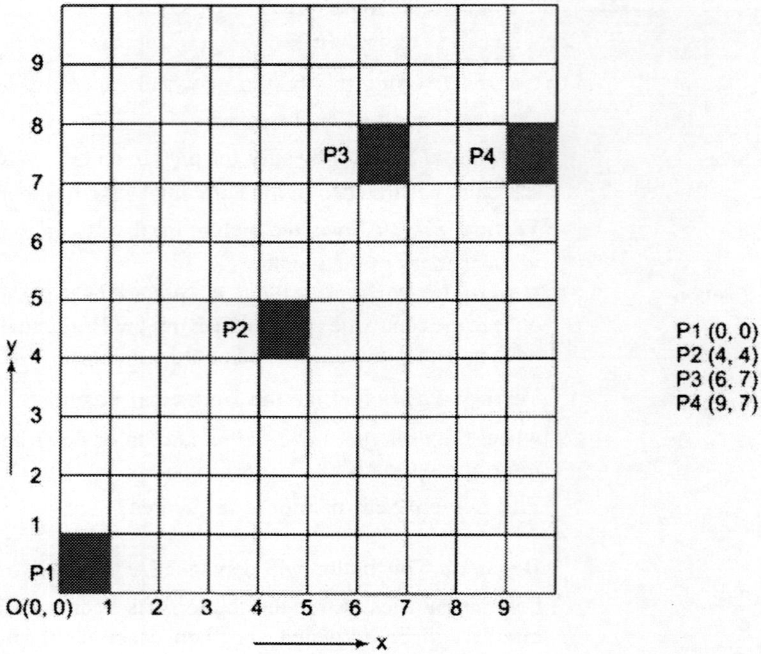

FIGURE 2.5 Grid of Pixels

Any image that is displayed on the monitor is made up of thousands of such small pixels. Each pixel has a particular color and intensity value. It is a measure of screen resolution.

Dead pixels

A dead pixel is not a common issue for monitors, however this issue can still occur. When this does occur, it is common on many monitors that an entire row or entire column of pixels to go out. Most monitor manufacturers do not have a policy or warranty for this issue and when this occurs then replace the monitor if in warranty.

2.2.3 Dot pitch

The internal surface of monitor screen is coated with red, green, and blue phosphor material that glows when struck by a stream of electrons. This coated material is arranged into an array of million of tiny cells—red, green, and blue usually called dots.

Dot pitch is the measurement of the diagonal distance between two liked-colored (red, green or blue) pixels on a display screen. It is measured in millimeter(mm). Usually monitors are available with dot pitch specification 0.25 mm to 0.40 mm. The smaller the dot pitch, the higher the resolution, sharpness and detail of the image displayed. Generally, a dot pitch of 0.31 mm will provide clear images.

2.2.4 Resolution

Image Resolution: It refers to pixel spacing i.e., the distance from one pixel to the next pixel.

Screen Resolution: It refers to number of pixels in the horizontal and vertical directions on the screen.

The information given below applies to a desktop *CRT monitor's resolution.*

Figure 2.6 shows an example of a screen running at 640 × 480 which means 640 pixels are going horizontally by 480 pixels going vertically. When increasing the resolution, the image will become smaller due to the screen displaying more pixels per inch.

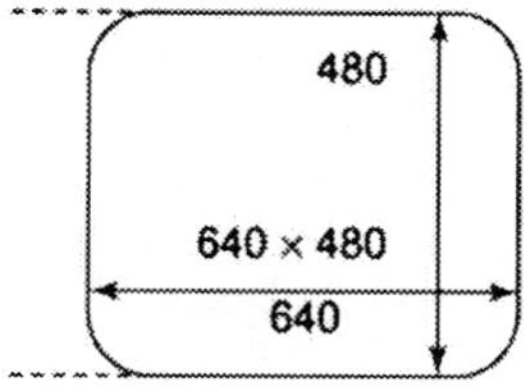

FIGURE 2.6 Screen with 640 x 480 Resolution

When setting the resolution higher you must have the needed Video RAM to support that resolution.

Minimum Resolution

Size is an important factor of the computer's running resolution. When picking the resolution, try basing it off the monitor's size for best use. Table 2.3 depicts monitors' size and their corresponding resolutions.

TABLE 2.3

Size	*Resolution*
13-inch	640 × 480
15-inch	800 × 600
17-inch	1024 × 768
21-inch	1024 × 768

Unlike the resolution on a CRT computer monitor, the LCD has a fixed amount of liquid crystal cells and can only display one set resolution defined by the LCD manufacturer. Because of this, an LCD screen which has a set resolution of 1024 × 768 can have a smaller display, however, when the screen is decreased in size it will not use the complete screen causing the image to have a black border around the image. Most new computers will have a capability of stretching this image causing the image to utilize the full screen but this degrades the display, especially noticeable on text. The size of a computer monitor is determined by going from the bottom left corner to the top right corner. However, if you have a 17" monitor, the viewable area may only be e 14.5" to 15" However, when measuring LCD panels, there is no loss of display. Generally, you will see laptop manufacturers rating the LCD in various sizes, these sizes and what they are comparable to are listed below.

TABLE 2.4

LCD	*CRT*
13.5"	15"
14.5"–15"	17"
18"	21"

2.2.5 Bit Depth

It refers to the number of bits assigned to each pixel in the image and number of colors that can be created from those bits. In other words, it specifies number of colors that a monitor can display. One byte(8 bits) per pixel represents 2^8=256 colors for each pixels.
It is also referred to as **color depth.**
Number of bits allotted to bit depth depends upon amount of memory required in display unit as illustrated in Table 2.5.

TABLE 2.5

Video Standards	*Resolution*	*Bit Depth*	*Storage Required*	*Number of Colors*
Monochrome		1		2
CGA(Color Graphics Adapter)	320 × 200	2	16000 Byte	$2^2 = 4$
EGA(Enhanced Graphics Adapter)	640 × 350	4		$2^4 = 16$
VGA(Video Graphics Array)	640 × 480	8		$2^8 = 256$
XGA(Extended Graphics Array)	800 × 600	16		$2^{16} = 65,536$
SVGA(Super Video Graphics Array)	1280 × 1024	24		$2^{24} = 16,777,216$

Display quality is quite important to many computer users because the display is one of the most used devices in your computer system. **Dot pitch, Resolution and Bit depth** are three important parameters to measure display quality.

2.2.6 Aspect Ratio

It is the ratio of the horizontal points to the vertical points necessary to produce equal-length lines in both directions on the screen i.e.,

$$\text{Aspect ratio } (l_s) = \frac{\text{No. of horizontal points}}{\text{No. of vertical points}}$$

to produce lines of equal length in both directions.
Aspect ratio is an important parameter to measure screen size.

Aspect ratio may be less than 1 or greater than 1 depending upon screen mode, horizontal format (Landscape Mode) or vertical mode(Portrait Mode).

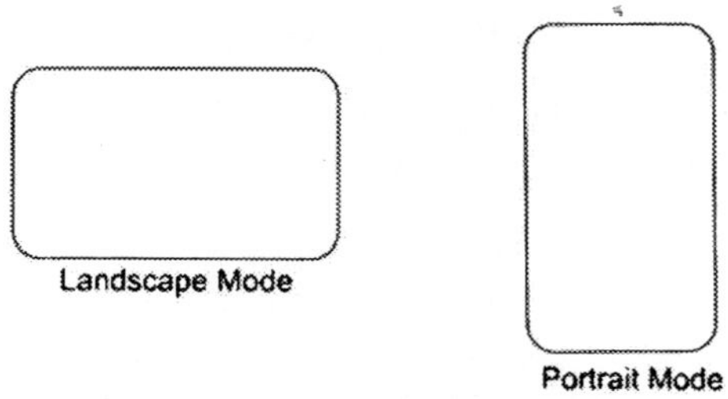

FIGURE 2.7 Screen Modes

Most computers have landscape monitors and most software is designed for that mode. Landscape monitors have aspect ratio more than 1, usually in the ratio 4:3.

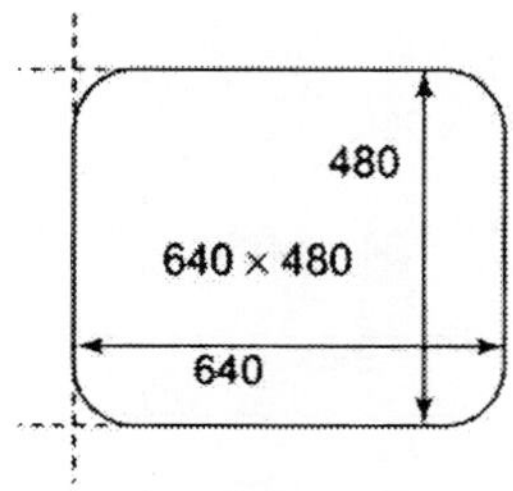

FIGURE 2.8 Screen with 640 × 480 Resolution

The aspect ratio is the viewable width divided by its height, for example, if you were determining the aspect ratio of your monitors resolution or a video size you would take the width divided by the height as shown below in the Table 2.6.

TABLE 2.6

Resolution	*Aspect Ratio*
Standard display	
640 × 480	4:3 or 1.33 :1
800 × 600	4:3 or 1.33 :1
1024 × 768	4:3 or 1.33 :1
1280 × 960	4:3 or 1.33 :1
Widescreen displays:	
1280x720	1.77
1280x768	1.66

Sometimes, it is also known as *screen aspect ratio*.

Grid Aspect Ratio

It is the width to height of each pixel and is denoted as

$$\text{Grid Aspect Ratio (l)} = \frac{\text{Size of horizontal pixel}}{\text{Size of vertical pixel}}$$

$$= \frac{\text{No. of Horizontal Pixels}}{\text{Width}} \Big/ \frac{\text{No. of vertical pixels}}{\text{Height}}$$

Number of horizontal pixels = 640
Number of horizontal divisions = 80
Number of vertical pixels = 480
Number of vertical divisions = 25
Size of each horizontal pixel = 640/80
Size of each vertical pixel = 480/25

Therefore, grid aspect ratio = $\dfrac{640}{480} \times \dfrac{25}{80}$

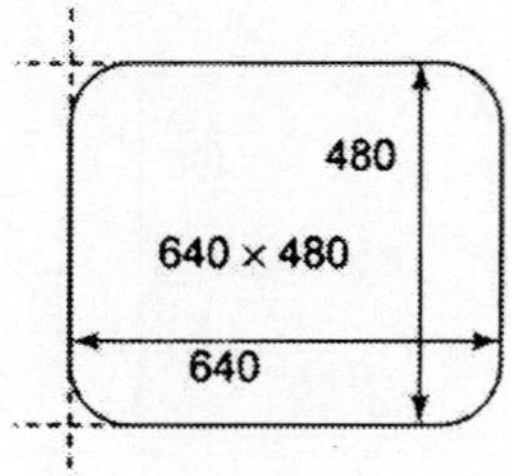

2.2.7 Display Area

In graphics mode it is less than the screen size, leaving a certain contrasting border area between the display and screen boundary. It is important to put such a gap so that user does not accidentally lose the picture from first or last column and row.

2.2.8 Refresh Rate

It is the number of times per second the pixels are recharged so that image does not flicker.

Refresh rate for a monitor is measured in Hertz(Hz), which can also be called frame rate, horizontal scan rate, refresh rate, vertical frequency, or vertical scan rate. Normally refresh rate varies form 60 to 75 Hz. A refresh rate 60 Hz means image is redrawn 60 times a second. The *higher* the refresh rate, the *lesser* is the flickering.

When setting a monitor's Hz, for example, 75 Hz, which is the Hz rate specified by Video Electronics Standard Association(VESA) for any video resolution above or equal to 640x480, means that the computer is going to redraw the screen 75 times per second. Refresh rates below 75 Hz can produce an often-imperceptible flicker that can cause eyestrain after long viewing. While some cards can support as high as 120 Hz, sometimes even higher, it is recommended you run 85-90 Hz; rates beyond 90 Hz add an unnecessary processing burden.

2.2.9 Flicker

The appearance of flickering, flashing, or unsteadiness in an image may occur on a display screen. A flicker issue can occur when the video refresh rate is too *low,* other video related issues, and in some cases, hardware issues with the monitor. Commonly, when this type of issue occurs, users feel more eyestrain.

2.2.10 Frame Buffer

It is the portion of video card memory that holds the information necessary to display a single screen image. The size of the frame buffer determines the resolution and maximum colors it is able to display.

It is the refresh storage area in the digital memory, in which the matrix of intensity values and parameters of all the pixels generating the image are stored in binary form. Thus, frame buffer is a two-dimensional table, in which every row-column entry stores information such as brightness and color values of the corresponding pixel in the screen. In a frame buffer each pixel can be represented by 1 to 24 bits.

On a black-and-white system with one bit per pixel (0 for black, 1 for white), the frame buffer is commonly called a *bilmap* as illustrated in Fig. 2.9 . For systems with multiple bits per pixel, the frame buffer is often referred to as a *pixmap or multiple frame buffer* as illustrated in Fig. 2.10.

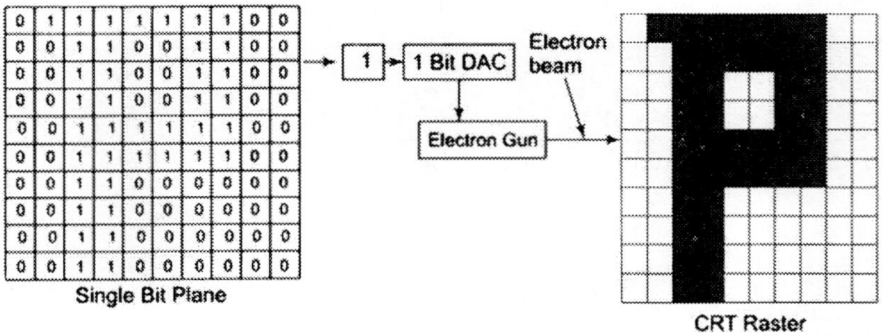

FIGURE 2.9 Display Device with Single Bit Plane Frame Buffer

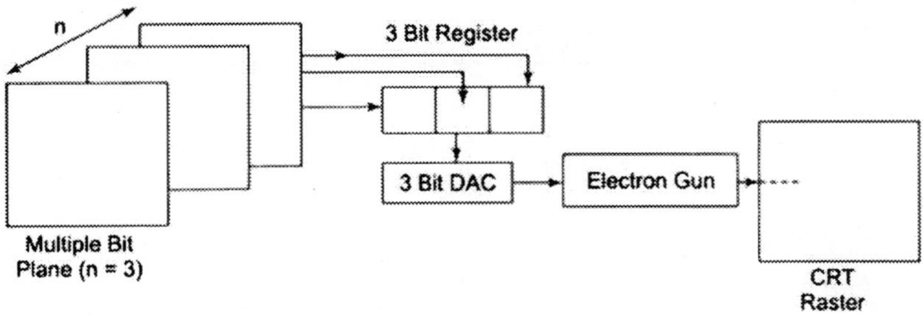

FIGURE 2.10 Display Device with Multiple bit plane Frame Buffer(n=3)

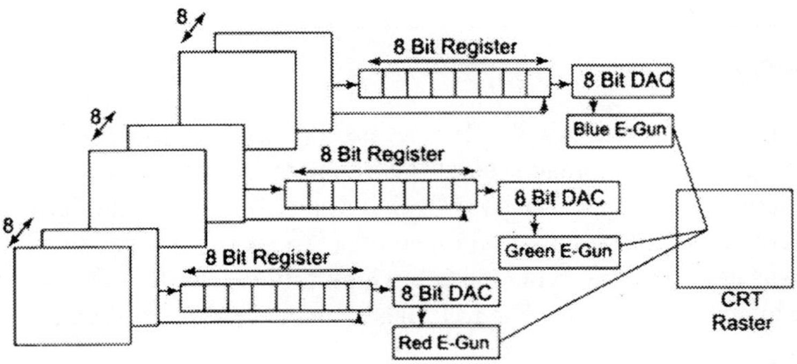

FIGURE 2.11 Display Device with 24 Bit Plane Frame Buffer(8 bits planes used for each primary color)

Colors can be achieved using additional bit planes The appearance of color of a pixel of an image depends upon intensities of three primary colors(red, blue, green) as shown in Fig. 2.11.

The more the number of bits used per pixel(bit depth), the finer is the color detail of the image. However, the increased number of bits per pixel also require significantly more memory for storage; and also more data for video process, which reduces the refresh rate.

2.2.11 Video Memory Specifications

As the video resolution and color depth increases, so do the required available resources. Table 2.7 illustrates all of the resolutions and color depths available for PC computers and the amount of memory each of them take.

TABLE 2.7

Resolution	*Bit Depth*	*No. of Colors*	*Memory Required*				
			512K	*1MB*	*2MB*	*4MB*	*6MB*
640 × 480	8-Bit	256	X	X	X	X	X
	16-Bit	65,000		X	X	X	X
	24-Bit	16.7 Million		X	X	X	X
800 × 600	8-Bit	256	X	X	X	X	X
	16-Bit	65,000		X	X	X	X
	24-Bit	16.7 Million			X	X	X
1024 × 768	8-Bit	256		X	X	X	X
	16-Bit	65,000			X	X	X
	24-Bit	16.7 Million				X	X
1152 × 1024	8-Bit	256			X	X	X
	16-Bit	65,000			X	X	X
	24-Bit	16.7 Million				X	X
1280 × 1024	8-Bit	256			X	X	X
	16-Bit	65,000				X	X
	24-Bit	16.7 Million				X	X
1600 × 1200	8-Bit	256			X	X	X
	16-Bit	65,000				X	X
	24-Bit	16.7 Million					X

2.2.12 Look Up Table (LUT)

As we have seen in the last section, number of bits per pixel (bit depth) stored in frame buffer to achieve pixel color required significantly storage space. This problem can be overcome if a storage space is introduced in between frame buffer and monitor; which is a part of display controller as shown in Fig.2.12. In this, pixel colors are not stored directly in frame buffer. An alternative way to store pixel colors in a separate table known as **color look up table (or video look table),** where frame values are now used as indices or reference into the color table. The LUT has as many entries pixel values.

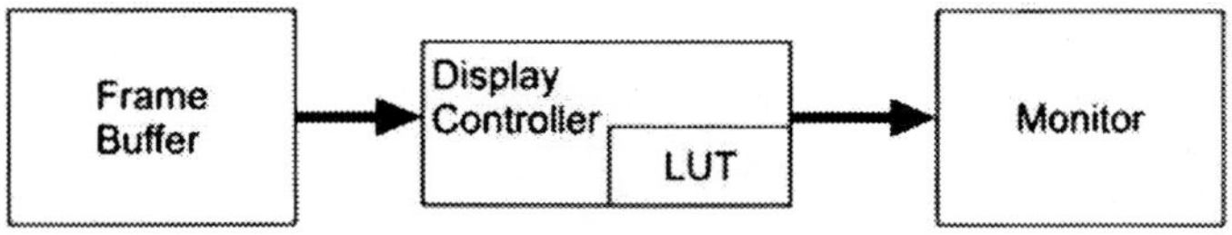

FIGURE 2.12 Display Controller with LUT

Figure 2.13 shows look up table of 256 entries with address 0 to 255. Each entry has 24-bit RGB color value.

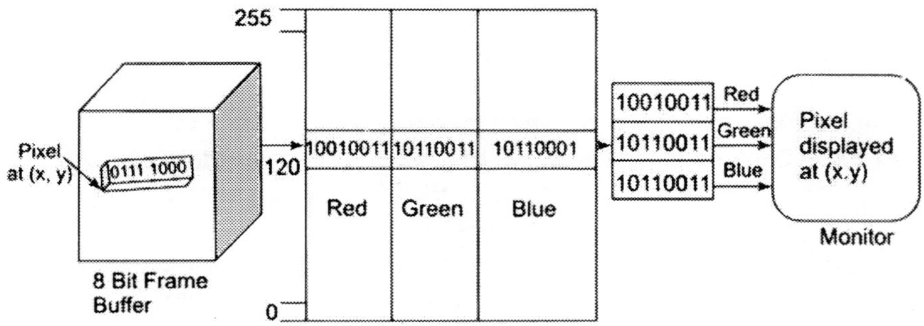

FIGURE 2.13 Organization of Look up Table for a 24-bit Color Monitor with an 8-Bit Frame Buffer

The LUT compromises at the cost of increase in memory—it allows only 8 bits of the frame buffer to be used to specify each color in an image.

Advantages

- This system provides reasonable number of simultaneous colors without large frame buffer.
- Table entries can be changed easily.

Disadvantages

- Scan conversion is slow.
- Refresh rate of the display decreases.

2.2.13 Display Processor

In the last section we have seen that if LUT is used then scan conversion becomes slow and refresh rate decreases. To avoid these problems a separate graphics processor is used that makes the main processor free from graphics burden, known as *display processor*. We now have two processors—general purpose CPU and special-purpose display processor. Display processor may use peripherals that a simple processor main CPU used (just to double the performance) or specialized for graphics operations. Most current display-processor systems use peripheral processors specialized for graphics operations.

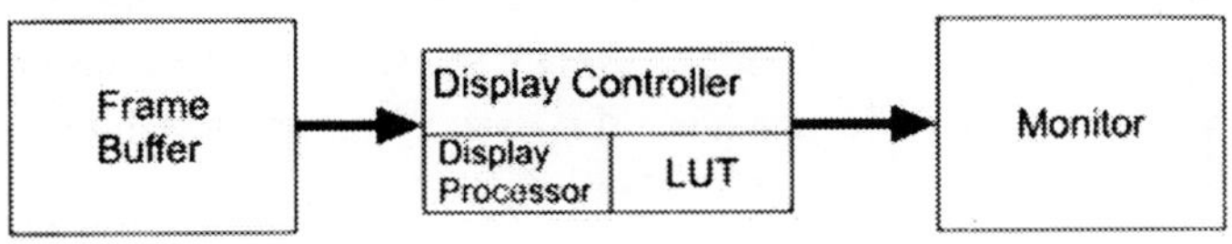

FIGURE 2.14 Display Controller with Display Processor and LUT

2.2.14 Video Specification

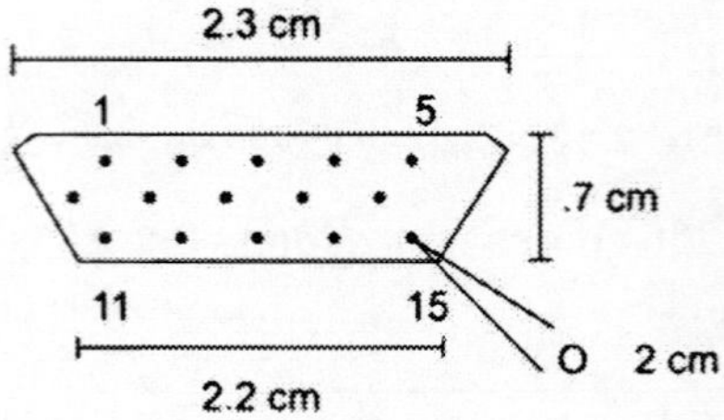

FIGURE 2.15 15 Pin Video Connection

The above picture illustrates a 15 Pin Video Port connector pin assignments as well as size dimension. Table 2.8 explains the functions of each pin of a Video Port connector.

TABLE 2.8

Pin	*Function*
1	Red Video
2	Green Video
3	Blue Video
4	Monitor ID 2
5	TTL Ground (monitor self-test)
6	Red Analog Ground
7	Green Analog Ground
8	Blue Analog Ground
9	Key (Plugged Hole)
10	Sync Ground
11	Monitor ID 0
12	Monitor ID 1
13	Horizontal Sync
14	Vertical Sync
15	Monitor ID 3

2.2.15 Ghost

If monitors, especially older CGA / EGA monitors are left on for long durations, the electron beams cause the phosphors to glow. If the electron guns continue to do this for thousands of hours refreshing the same images, this can cause the images to be burnt into the CRT surface causing a ghost image to appear. This image will become permanently displayed on your monitor for the duration of its life.

A solution to this problem are screen savers, which are programs that generate a random set of images, lines or other methods of allowing the image not to remain static while the computer is not being used. While new monitors (VGA / SVGA) do not have this issue, screen savers are still commonly used today.

2.3 CRT DISPLAY DEVICES

2.3.1 Cathode Ray Tube(CRT)

CRTs, or video monitors, are the most common input/output devices on computers today.
Figure 2.16 illustrates the basic structure of a CRT.

Components of CRT

- Electron Gun
- Control Electrode
- Focusing Electrode
- Deflection Yoke(Electrostatic deflection plate/Magnetic deflection coil)
- Phosphor Coated Screen

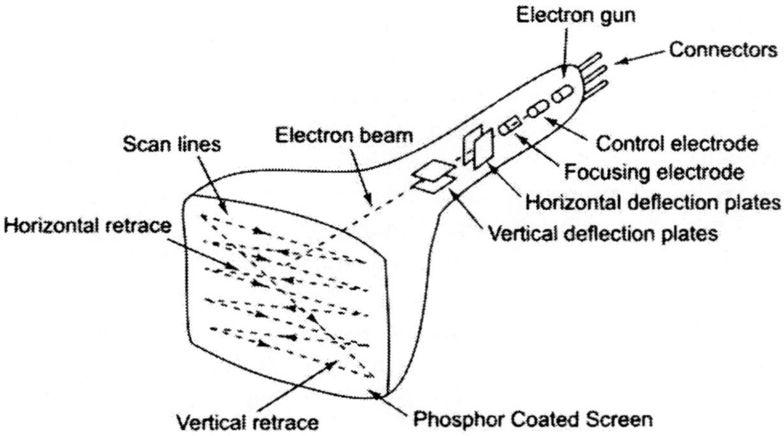

FIGURE 2.16 Structure of CRT

Electron Gun

Electron gun contains two basic parts: a heater and a cathode. Electrons are generated by a cathode heated by an electric filament, surrounding the cathode is a control grid, with a hole at one end to allow electrons to escape. The control grid is kept at a lower potential than cathode. These electrons (negatively charged) are accelerated towards the CRT screen by a high positive voltage applied near the screen or by an accelerating anode.

Control Electrode

It is used to regulate the flow of electrons. The control electrode is connected to an amplifier which, in turn, is connected to the output circuitry of the computer, thus allowing the computers to control the electron beam in turned off and on. We can modify the rate of flow of electrons, or beam current and control brightness of image.

Focusing Electrode

This system helps to converge the cloud of electrons to a small spot as it touches the CRT screen. It is used to create a clear picture by focusing the electrons into a narrow beam, in other words, it focuses the electron beam to converge into a small spot as it strikes the phosphors. Otherwise the electrons would repel each other, and beam would spread out as it approaches the screen. Focusing is accomplished with either electric or magnetic fields. *The effect of the focusing electrode on the electron beam resembles that of a glass lens on light waves.*

Electrostatic focusing is commonly used in television and computer graphics monitors. With electrostatic focusing, the electron beam passes through a positively charged metal cylinder that forms an electrostatic lens. The action of the electrostatic lens focuses the electron beam at the center of the screen, in exactly the same way that an optical lens focuses a beam of light at a particular focal distance.

Deflection Yoke

It is used to control the direction of the electron beam. The deflection yoke creates an *electric* or *magnetic* field which will bend the electron beam as it passes through the field.

When electrostatic deflection is used, two pairs of parallel plates are mounted inside the CRT envelope. One pair of plates is horizontal deflection to control the vertical deflection and other pair is mounted vertical to control horizontal deflection. In an alternative way for deflection system CRTs are constructed with magnetic deflection coils, these coils are mounted on the outside of the CRT envelope. Two pairs of coils are used. One pair is mounted on the top and bottom of the neck and other pair is mounted on opposite side to the neck. Horizontal deflection is accomplished with one pair of coils, and vertical deflection by the other pair. In a conventional CRT the yoke is connected to a sweep or scan generator. The scan generator sends out an oscillatory sawtooth current that, in turn, causes the deflection yoke to apply a varying magnetic field to the electron beam's path. The oscillatory voltage potential causes the electron beam to move across the CRT's screen in a regular pattern.

Phosphorus-coated screen

Inner surface of CRT is coated with special crystals called phosphors, which have a unique property that allows the entire system to work. Phosphors glow when they are attacked by a high-energy electron beam. They continue to glow for a distinct period of time after being exposed to electron beam. The glow given off by the phosphor during exposure to the electron is known as *fluorescence,* the continuing glow given off after the beam is removed is known as *phosphorescence* and the duration of phosphorescence is known as the phosphors *persistence.*

Lower persistence phosphors require *higher* refresh rate to maintain a picture on the screen without flicker. *Higher* persistence phosphors require *lower* refresh rate to maintain a picture on screen without flicker. A phosphor with low persistence is useful for animation. A phosphor with high persistence is useful for display highly complex picture.

Working of CRT

A CRT is an evacuated glass tube, with a heating element on one end and a phosphor coated screen on the other end. When a current flows through this heating element, called a filament, the electrons actually boil off the filament. These free electrons are attracted to a strong positive charge from the outer surface of the focusing anode cylinder (sometimes called an electrostatic lens). However, the inside of the cylinder has a weaker negative charge. Thus, when the electrons head towards the anode they are forced into a beam and accelerated by the repulsion of the inner cylinder walls in just the way that water speeds up when it flows though a smaller diameter pipe. By the time the electrons get out they are going so fast that they fly past the cathode they were heading for.

The next thing that the electrons run into are two sets of weakly charged deflection plates. These plates have opposite charges, one positive and the other negative. While their charge is not strong enough to capture the fast moving electrons they do influence the path of the beam. The first set displaces the beam up and down, and the second displaces the beam left and right. The electrons are sent flying out of the neck of the bottle, until they smash into the phosphor coating on the other end of the bottle. The impact of this collision on the outvalence bands of the phosphor compounds knocks some of the electrons to jump into another band. This causes a few photons to be generated, and results in our seeing a spot on the CRT's face.

2.3.2 Refresh Type CRT

2.3.2.1 Raster Scan Display

The most common type of graphics monitor employing a CRT is the raster-scan display, based on television technology. In this system, the electron beam is swept across the screen, one row at a time from top to bottom. As the electron beam moves across each row, the beam intensity is turned ON and OFF to create a pattern of illuminated spots. The picture definition is stored in a memory area called the *refresh buffer* or *frame buffer,* which holds the set of intensity values for all the screen points. Raster-scan system is well suited for realistic display of scenes containing shading and color patterns. Broadly speaking, a Raster Scan Systems performs following sequence of operations:

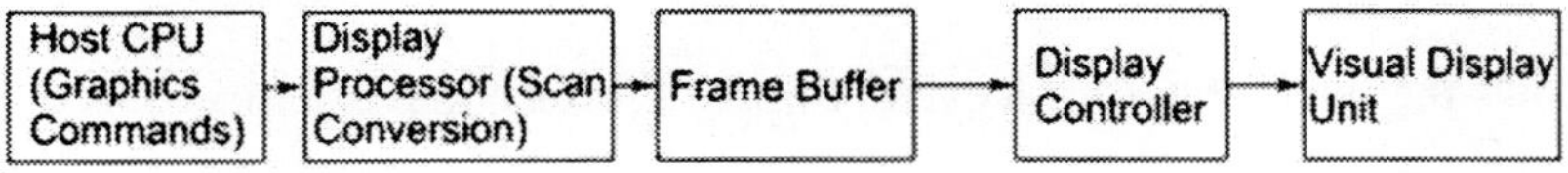

FIGURE 2.17 Block Diagram of Raster Scan System

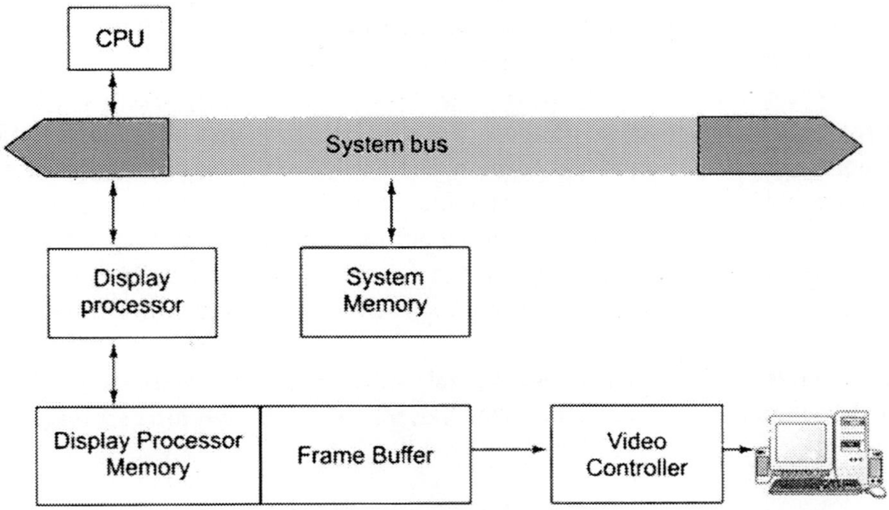

FIGURE 2.18 Architecture of Raster System with a Peripheral Display Processor

At the end of each scan line, the electron beam returns to the left side of the screen to begin displaying the next scan line. The return to the left of the screen, after refreshing each scan line, is called the *horizontal retrace* of the electron beam. At the end of each frame, the electron beam returns to the top left comer of the screen to begin the next frame. This is known as *vertical retrace,* as illustrated in figure 2.19.

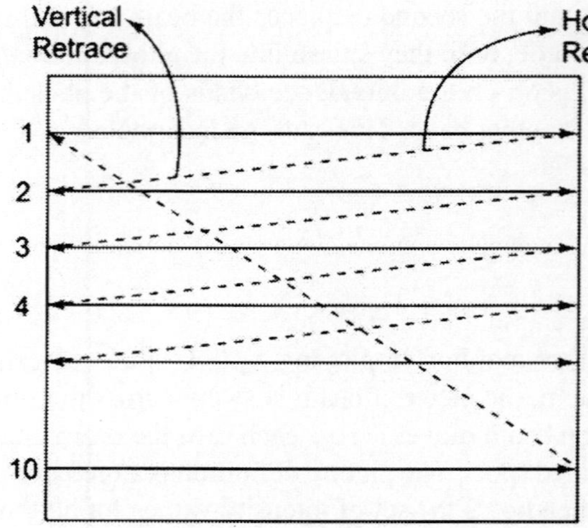

FIGURE 2.19 Raster Scan

Figure 2.19 shows the track of a refresh cycle. Suppose refresh rate is required as 60 Hz. One cycle is completed in $1/60^{th}$ sec.

Normally, refreshing on raster scan displays is carried out at the rate of 60 to 75 frames per second, although some systems are designed for higher refresh rates. Sometimes, refresh rates are described in units of cycles per second, or Hertz (Hz), where a cycle corresponds to one frame. Using these units, we would describe a refresh rate of 60 frames per second as simply 60 Hz.

In a simple black and white system, each screen point is either **on** or **off,** so only one bit per pixel is needed to control the intensity of screen positions. For a bit level system, a bit value of 1 indicates that the electron beam is to be turned **on** at that position, and a value of 0 indicates that the beam intensity is to be **off.** Additional bits are needed when color and intensity variations can be displayed. Up to 24 bits per pixel are included in high-quality systems, which can require several megabytes of storage for the frame buffer, depending on the resolution of the system. A system with 24 bits per pixel and a screen resolution of 1024 by 1024 requires $((1024 \times 1024) \times 24)/8 = 3$ MB storage for the frame buffer.

On a black and white system with one bit per pixel, the frame buffer is commonly called a *bitmap.* For systems with multiple bits per pixel, the frame buffer is often referred to as *apixmap.*

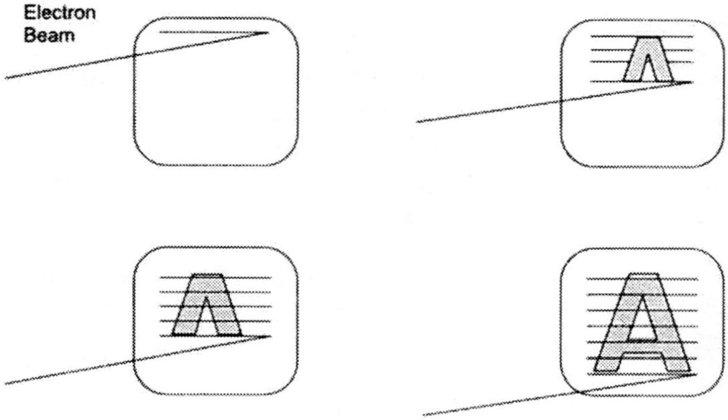

FIGURE 2.20 Raster Scan Display

Home television sets and printers are examples of using raster scan methods.

Interlacing

On some raster scan systems each frame is displayed in two passes using an interlaced refresh procedure. In the first pass, the beam sweeps (odd scan lines) across every other scan line from top to bottom. Then after the vertical re-trace, the beam sweeps out the remaining (even scan lines). Interlacing of the scan lines in this way allows us to see the entire screen displayed in one-half the time it would have taken to sweep across all the scan lines at once from top to bottom. Interlacing is primarily used with slower refreshing rates.

Suppose we have refresh rate 30 Hz for non-interlaced display, some flicker is noticeable. But with interlacing, each of the two passes can be accomplished in 1/60th of a second, which brings the refresh rate nearer to 60 frames per second as illustrated in Fig. 2.21(a) and 2.21(b). This is an effective technique for avoiding flicker, providing that adjacent scan lines contain similar display information.

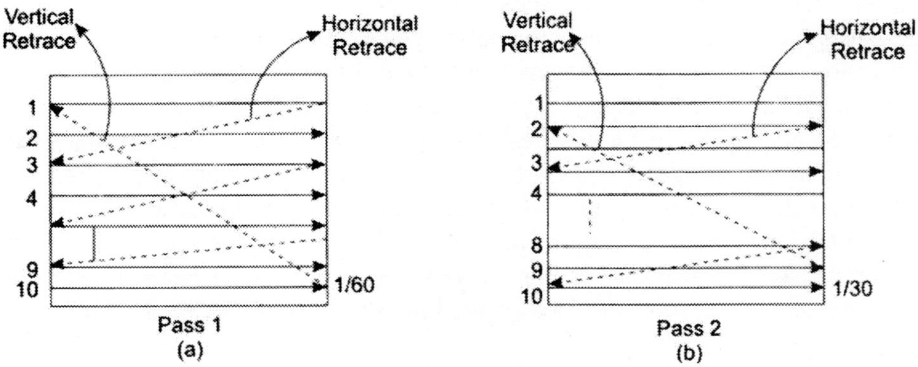

FIGURE 2.21 Interlacing scan lines on a raster scan display. First, all points on the odd-numbered scan lines are displayed (Pass 1); then all points along the even-numbered lines are displayed (Pass 2).

2.3.2.2 Random Scan Displays

In random scan display system, the electron beam is directed to the particular point of the screen where the image is to be drawn. It generates the image by drawing set of straight lines in a similar way as the pen plotting an image on paper. This is why this technique is also referred to as **vector displays** (or **stroke-writing** or **calligraphic displays).** The component lines of a picture can be drawn and refreshed by a random scan system in any specified order.

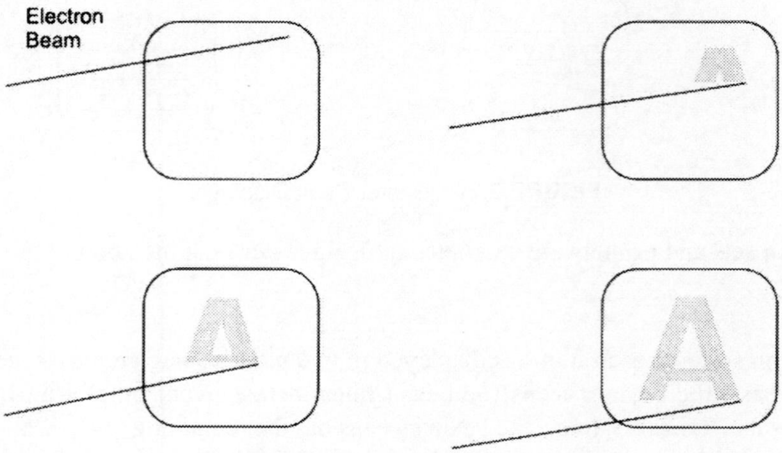

FIGURE 2.22 Random Scan Display.

Random scan system does not consist of bit planes containing mapped values. Picture definition is stored as a set of line drawing commands in an area of memory referred to as the *refresh display file* (also known as *display list, display program,* or simply *refresh buffer).* To display a specified picture, the system cycles through the set of commands in the display file, drawing each component line in turn. After all line-drawing commands have been processed, the system cycles back to the first line command in the list. Refresh rate on a random scan system depends on the number of lines to be displayed. Random scan displays are designed to draw all the component lines of a picture 30 to 60 times each second.

High-quality vector systems are capable of handling approximately 1,00,000 "short" lines at this refresh rate. When a small set of lines is to be displayed, each refresh cycle is delayed to avoid refresh rates greater than 60 frames per second. Otherwise, faster refreshing of the set of lines could burn out the phosphor.

Random scan systems are designed for line-drawing applications and can't display realistic shaded scenes. Since, picture definition is stored as a set of line-drawing instructions and not as a set of intensity values for all screen points, vector displays generally have higher resolution than raster systems. Also, vector displays produce smooth line drawings because the CRT beam directly follows the line path. A raster system, in contrast, produces jagged lines that are plotted as discrete point sets.

Differences between Raster Scan Displays and Random Scan Displays

(a) Random displays can work at higher resolution than raster displays.
(b) Random displays produce sharp images and have smooth edges whereas raster displays produce jagged edges and lines.
(c) Random displays have images with lack in real colors due to absence of color depth unlike the raster scan displays.

(d) Random scan systems are designed for line-drawing applications and can't display realistic shaded scenes.

2.3.3 Color Display on a CRT

A CRT monitor displays color pictures by using a combination of phosphors that emit different colored light. The two basic techniques for producing color displays with a CRT are the *beam penetration* method and the *shadow-mask* method.

2.3.3.1 Beam Penetration

This method for displaying color pictures has been used with random scan monitors.

The arrangement of beam penetotion CRT is similar to normal CRT, except that of multilayer phosphor in which a layer of red phosphor is deposited behind the initial layer of green phosphor.

The displayed color depends on how far the electron beam penetrates into the phosphor layers. A beam of slow electrons excites only the outer red layer while a beam of very fast electrons penetrates through the red layer and excites the inner green layer. At intermediate beam speeds, combinations of red and green light are emitted to show two additional colors, orange and yellow. The speed of the electrons, and hence the screen color at any point, is controlled by the beam-acceleration voltage. The beam-penetration method for displaying color pictures is commonly used with random scan displays.

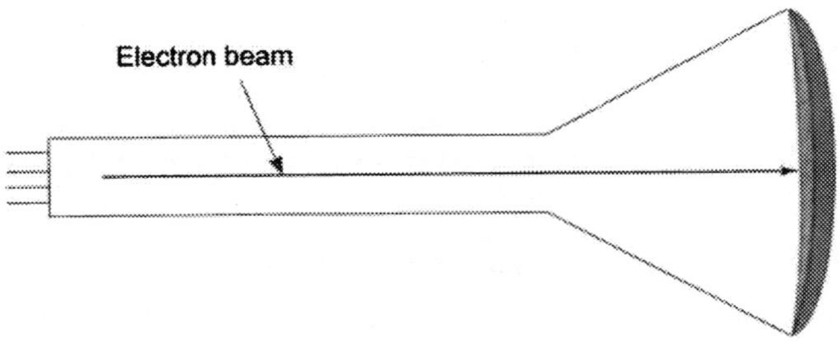

FIGURE 2.23 Beam Penetration Method

The speed of electrons, and hence the screen color at any point, is controlled by the beam acceleration voltage. It requires significant amount of adjustment in order to switch colors.

- A beam of *slow* electrons excites only outer *red* layer.
- A beam of very *fast* electrons penetrates through the red layer and excites the inner *green* layer.
- At intermediate beam speeds, combinations of red and green light are emitted to show two additional colors, orange and yellow.

However, only four colors are possible, and the quality of pictures is not as good as compared to other methods. Beam penetration is an inexpensive way to produce color on random scan monitors.

2.3.3.2 Shadow-mask Method

A shadow-mask CRT has three phosphor color dots at each pixel position. One phosphor dot emits a red light, another emits a green light, and the third emits a blue light (three primary colors red, blue, green).

This type of CRT has three electron guns, one for each color dot, and a shadow-mask grid just behind the phosphor-coated screen. The deflection system of CRT operates on three electron beams simultaneously, bringing all these to the same point of focus on the shadow mask, and strike the phosphor. The three electron beams are deflected and focused as a group onto the shadow mask, which contains a series of holes aligned with the phosphor-dot patterns. When the three beams pass through a hole in the shadow mask, they activate a dot triangle, which appears as a small color spot on the screen. The phosphor dots in the triangles are arranged so that each electron beam can activate only its corresponding color dot when it passes through the shadow mask.

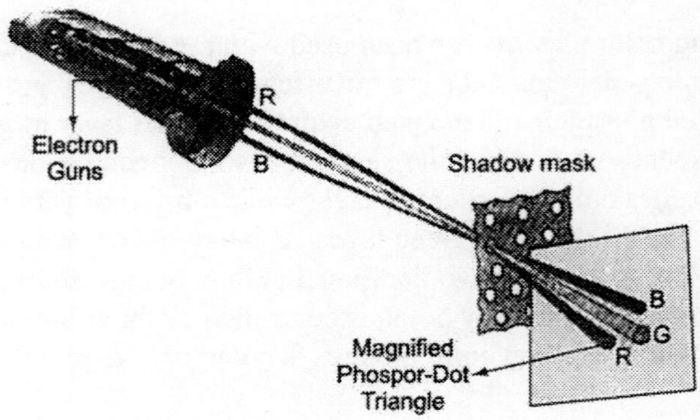

FIGURE 2.24 Shadow-mask Method

Color variations in a shadow-mask CRT can be obtained by varying the intensity levels of the three electron beams. For example, a white (or grey) area is the result of activating all three dots with equal intensity i.e.,

White (or Grey) = Red + Green + Blue each with equal intensity.

Shadow-mask method is commonly used in raster scan systems; they produce a much wider range of colors than the beam-penetration method.

Another configuration for the three electron guns is an in-line arrangement in which the three electron guns and the corresponding red-green-blue color dots on the screen are aligned along one scan line instead of in a triangular pattern. This in-line arrangement of electron guns is easier to keep in alignment and is commonly used in high-resolution color CRTs.

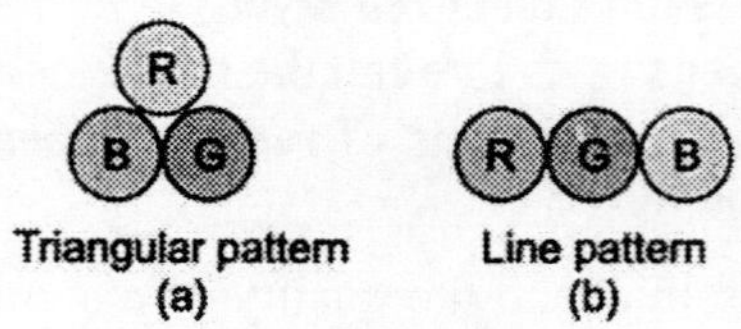

FIGURE 2.25

Problem with shadow mask CRTs is that of convergence. It is extremely difficult to adjust three guns and deflection system so that electron beams are deflected exactly together, all converging on same hole in shadow mask. Where they fail to converge, the three component colors appear to spread in a manner reminiscent of a poorly aligned color printing process. Often it is possible to achieve adequate convergence over only a limited area of screen. Another problem is relatively poor resolution of shadow mask CRT.

2.3.4 Non-Refresh Type CRT

Inherent Memory Devices

Refresh line drawing displays based on CRT have disadvantage of high cost and tendency to flicker, so inherent memory storage devices were developed. Most widely used of these is DVST (direct-view storage tube), others are plasma panel and laser scan display.

Direct View Storage Tube

Both in the raster scan and random scan system the screen image is maintained by redrawing or re-freshing the screen many times per second and picture data is stored in refresh buffer. An alternative method for maintaining a screen image is to store the picture information inside the CRT instead of refreshing the screen.

In DVST there is no refresh buffer, image is stored as a distribution of charges in the inside surface of the screen. A direct-view storage tube (DVST) stores the pictures information as a charge distribution just behind the phosphor-coated screen.

Two electron guns are used in a DVST—*flood gun* and *electron gun.*

The electron gun deposits the electrostatic charge on *a fine-mesh* wire (storage mesh) grid instead of directly on phosphor coated screen. This pattern of +ve charge is transferred to phosphor by a continuous flood of electrons from a flood gun. Just behind the storage mesh there is a *collector*, the purpose of collector is to smooth out the flow of flood electrons.

Differences between DVST and Refresh CRT

Unlike CRT, DVST has storage tube and this tube retains the picture until it is erased. Thus no refreshing is necessary, complex pictures can be displayed at very high resolutions without flicker.

Performance of DVST is somewhat inferior to refresh CRT.

DVST has no refresh buffer thus to eliminate a picture section, the entire screen must be erased and to modified.

DVST behaves like a CRT with an extremely long persistence phosphor.

DVS Tcreates bright picture.

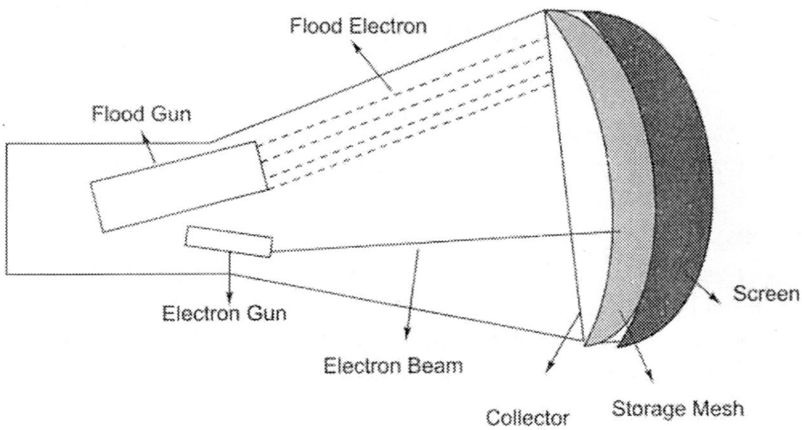

FIGURE 2.26 Direct View Storage Tube

2.4 FLAT PANEL DISPLAY DEVICES

The term flat-panel display refers to a class of video devices that have reduced *volume weight, volume, size,* and *less power requirements* compared to a CRT.

A significant feature of flat-panel display is that they are the smaller, lighter, and thinner than conventional CRT, and we can hang them on walls or wear them on wrists and thus termed as flat-panel display devices (FPD). Current uses for flat-panel displays include small TV monitors, calculators, pocket video games, laptop computers and graphic displays in applications requiring rugged, portable monitors. We can even write on flat panel displays.

We ran categorize flat-panel displays into two categories.

(a) Emissive displays (emitters)

Such flat-panel display devices are based upon *"Converts electrical energy into light principle"*.

- Plasma panels.
- Thin-film electro luminescent display
- Light-emitted diode (LED)

(b) Non-emissive displays (ammeters)

Such flat-panel display devices based upon principle *"Uses optical effects to convert some or light from other sources into graphic patterns"*.

- Liquid-crystal device.

2.4.1 Plasma Panels

It is also called gas-discharge display. Plasma panel consists of layer of gas (usually neon gas), sandwiched between two glass plates.

The basic components of a plasma and related display are as follows:

(a) Conductors

(i) Cathodes

A series of vertical ribbons is placed in one glass plate which delivers –ve voltage to the gas cells.

(ii) Anodes

A series of horizontal ribbons is placed on the other glass plate which delivers the +ve voltage to the gas cells.

(b) Glass plates

Plates that act as capacitors in DC plasma displays and monitors voltages to ensure that a cell will continue to glow after the cell has received a single burst of power. To remain lit, alternating current plasma displays must supply a background voltage.

(c) Fluorescent cells

Small pockets of gas, liquids or solids are excited when a voltage is applied. In the excited state the substance emits light.

By applying high voltage to a pair of electrodes, a small section of neon gas at the intersection of electrodes breaks down onto glowing plasma of electrons and ions. Thus, each electron can set ON state or OFF state by adjusting the voltage in the appropriate pair of wires. State of an electron remains unchanged until it is disturbed by adjusting the voltage applied to its pair of electrodes. Due to this no refreshing is required.

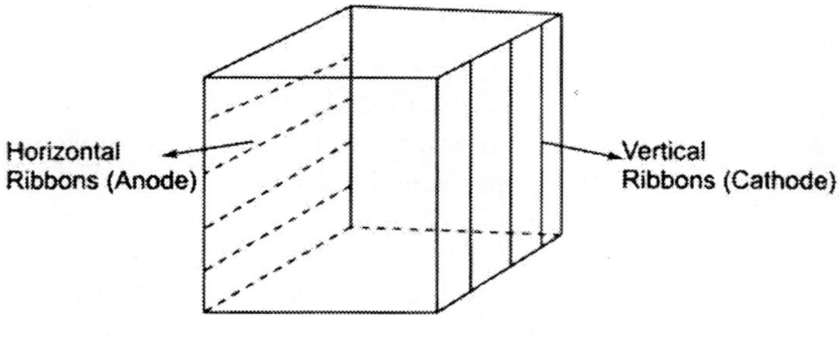

FIGURE 2.27 Plasma Panel

Each point remains bright after it has been intensified. So it is similar in function to DVST. Plasma panel produces a very steady image, totally free of flicker, and is a less bulky device than a CRT of compatible screen size.

Plasma panel has excellent brightness, contrast, and is often used for large display. Plasma panel are attractive. Color plasma panel display devices are also popular due to low production cost.

Its main disadvantage is relatively poor resolution, of about 60 dpi and complex addressing and writing requirements.

Gas-plasma displays are sometimes found with older portable computers. However, because of advances in portable LCD technologies and the power requirements, gas-plasma displays are often used for large displays. These displays can range anywhere from 42 to 60 inches and can cost anywhere from \$8,000 to \$30,000 and higher.

Difference between PPD and CRT

(a) PPD is less bulky than CRT but cost of construction is very high.
(b) Wiring is complex in PPD than CRT.
(c) PPD provides excellent brightness than CRT.
(d) PPD is used for comparatively large display than CRT.
(e) PPD has poor resolution relative to CRT.

2.4.2 Thin-Film Electroluminescent

These are similar in construction to a plasma panel. The only difference is that the enfilment of the region between the glass plates is with a phosphor, such as zinc sulfide doped with manganese, instead of a gas.

Likewise plasma panels, they resemble a sandwich of polarizer and ultra thin grid wires. Instead of neon gas there are liquid crystal layers as shown in figure 2.28.

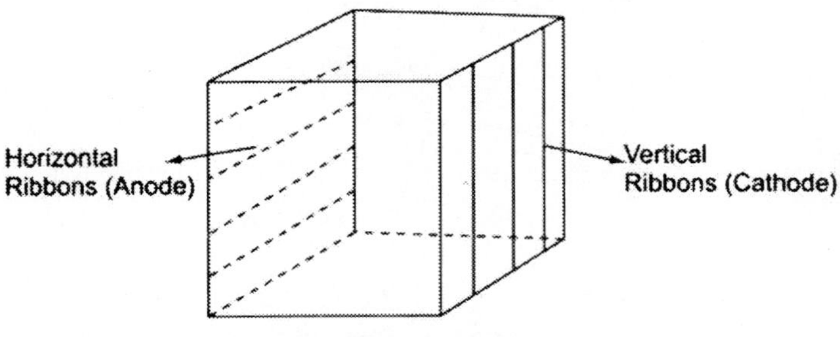

FIGURE 2.28 Thin-film Electroluminescent

2.4.3 Light-Emitting Diode (LED)

A matrix of diode is arranged to form the pixel positions in the display, and picture definition is stc in refresh buffer. Information is read from the refresh buffer and converted to voltage levels that applied to the diodes to produce the light patterns in the display.

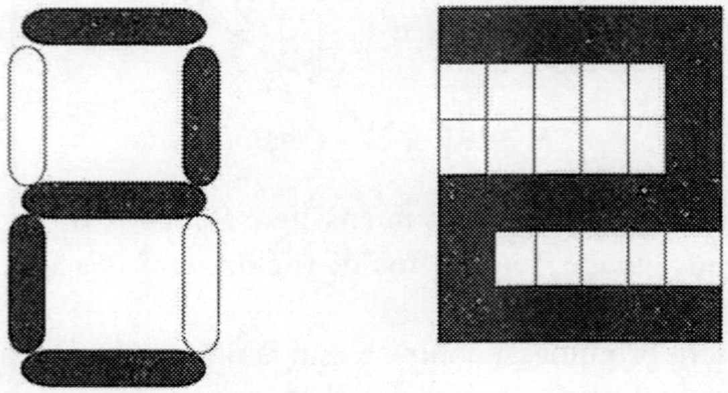

(a) Seven Segment Display

(b) Matrix of Diode Dispaly

FIGURE 2.29 LED

2.4.4 Liquid Crystal Device (LCD)

LCDs, in particular, are most suitable for laptop computers but are expensive. They are commc used in small systems, such as calculators and portable, laptop computer pictures. These non-emis: devices produce picture by passing polarized light from the surrounding or from an internal light sou through a liquid-crystal material that can be aligned to either block or transmit the light.

LCD consists of six layers. The front layer is a vertical polarizer plate followed by vertical g wires, then liquid crystal layer (about 0.0005 inch), horizontal grid wires, then a horizontal polari and finally a reflector.

Liquid crystal material is made up of crystalline molecules and these molecules are arrange spiral shape such that light passing through these molecules is rotated 90°. Light entering through front layer is polarized vertical and then turns to the horizontal due to spherical nature of molecu These rays are polarized by horizontal polarizer layer and which, in turn, are reflected back by flected layer and retrace the path as long as crystalline molecules retain a spherical shape. When tl spherical shapes are disturbed, then dark spots appear since light is reflected back.

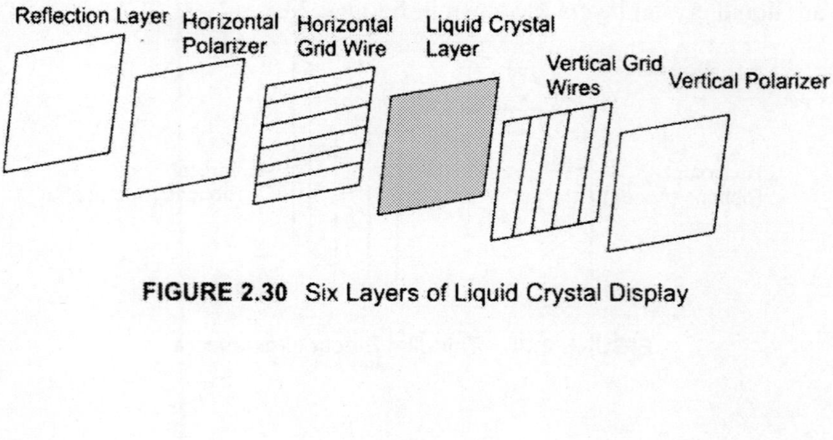

FIGURE 2.30 Six Layers of Liquid Crystal Display

When the crystals are in an electric field, they all live up and thus have no polarizing effect. Hence, crystals in the electric fields do not change the polarization of the transmitted light, so the light remains vertically polarized and does not pass through the rear polarizer. The light is absorbed so that viewer sees a dark spot on the display. A LCD having such type of arrangement is known as *passive LCD* i.e., to apply voltage and then drawing it to make the pixel spot bright.

A LCD panel that has transistor at (x, y) grid point is known as *active LCD panel.* It is also referred to as *active* matrix *Thin Film Transistor (TFT)* display. Transistors are used to change the state of crystal quickly and to control the degree to which the state has been changed; these transistors actively control the brightness of pixels. Transistors provide memory for the state of a cell.

Advantages

- Low GSI
- Low weight
- Low power consumption
- LCDs are "flat".

Liquid crystal displays are temperature dependent (operating temperatures are typically between 0 and 70° Celsius).

2.5 PROJECTORS

Like monitors, projectors are used to produce soft copy output. Projector display is commonly used for classroom training or conference room or presentation. Projectors are mainly of two types *LCD Projectors* and *DLP Projectors.*

2.5.1 LCD Projectors

LCD is the acronym for Liquid Crystal Display. It is the established technology used by most of the leading manufacturers. Most of today's LCD projectors contain three separate LCD glass panels, one each for red, green, and blue components of the image signal being fed into the projector. As light passes through the LCD panels, individual pixels can be opened to allow light to pass through, or closed to block the light. This activity modulates the light and produces the image that is projected onto the screen.

2.5.2 DLP Projectors

DLP is the acronym for Digital Light Processing. It is a proprietary technology developed by Texas Instruments. DLP uses a single Digital Mirror Device (DMD) chip that has thousands of tiny mirrors, each representing a single pixel. These mirrors tilt back and forth, directing the light either into the lens path to turn the pixel ON, or away from the lens path to turn it OFF and create the image. DLP is a newer technology than LCD and is used on some of the smallest, lightest projectors currently available. DLP projectors handle video images extremely well.

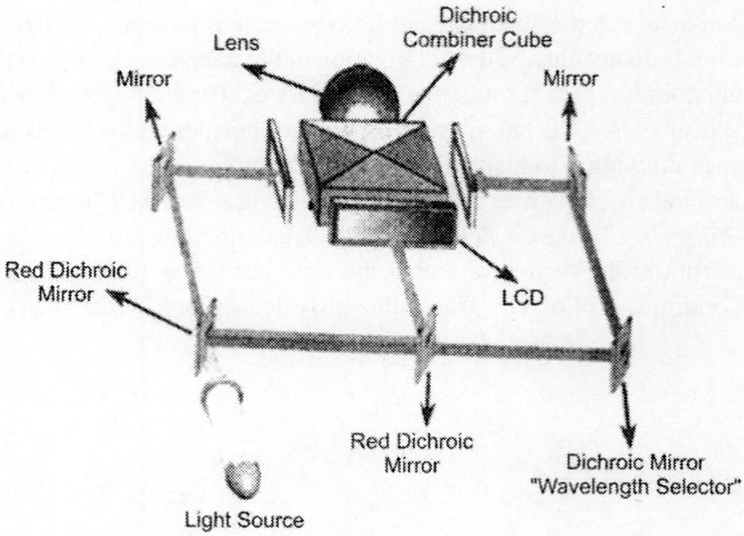

FIGURE 2.31 LCD Projector

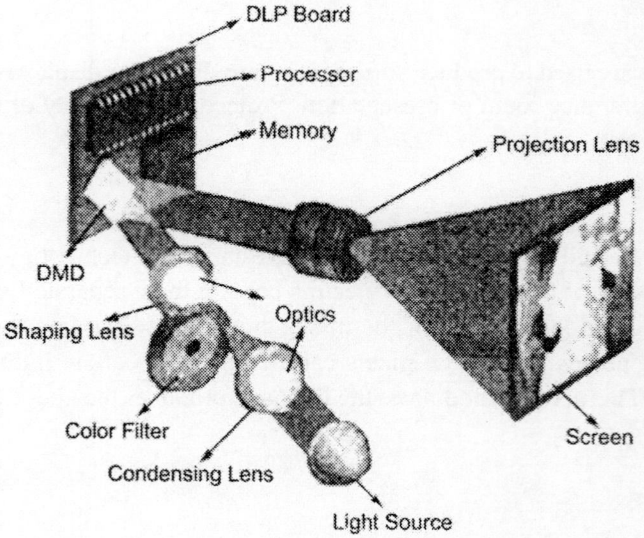

FIGURE 2.32 DLP Projector

LCD versus DLP

- LCD controls red, green and blue independently through three separate LCD panels. As a result, the user can adjust the brightness and contrast of each color channel individually. In most single chip DLP projectors, color is fixed.

- LCD delivers a sharper image than DLP at any given resolution. However, it does not mean that DLP is fuzzy.
- LCD is more light-efficient. LCD projectors produce significantly higher lumen outputs than DLP projectors do with the same wattage lamp.
- The DLP light engine consists of a single chip rather than three LCD panels. Hence, DLP projectors tend to be more compact.

2.6 HARD COPY OUTPUT DEVICES

Output which is produced on a paper is known as Hard Copy output. They are permanent in nature. Among the wide variety of the hard copy output devices, *printers* and *plotters* are the most commonly used. A printer is used to produce printouts of the documents stored on a computer's disk drive. A plotter is a pen-based output device, which is used for producing high quality output by moving ink pens across the paper.

2.6.1 Impact Printers

As their names specify, impact printers work by physically striking a head or needle against an ink ribbon to make a mark on the paper. Impact printers are the oldest printers and are still in use. Impact printers can print only one character at a time while some impact printers can print an entire line. The three most commonly used impact printers are *dot matrix printers, daisy wheel printers* and *drum printers.*

The printer that prints the characters by striking the ribbon and onto the paper, are called impact printers. These printers are of two types, (i) Character and (ii) Line printers.
Characteristics of impact printers:

- In impact printers, there is physical contact with the paper to produce an image.
- They have relatively low consumable costs. The primary recurring costs for these printers are the ink ribbons and paper.
- Due to being robust and low cost, they are useful for bulk printing.
- They can withstand dusty environment, vibrations and extreme temperature.
- Impact printers are ideal for printing multiple copies (that is, carbon copies) because they can easily print through many layers of paper.
- Due to its striking activity, impact printers are very noisy.
- Since they are mechanical in nature, they tend to be slow.
- Impact printers do not support transparencies.

2.6.1.1 Dot Matrix Printer (DMP)

A dot matrix printer (also known as the *wire matrix printer)* uses the oldest printing technology and it prints one character at a time. Usually, dot matrix printers can print any shape of character, which a user can specify. This allows the printer to print many special characters, different sizes of print and enables it to print graphics, such as charts and graphs. The speed of dot matrix printers is measured in *characters per second* (cps). Most dot matrix printers offer different speeds depending on the quality of print desired. The speed can vary from about 200 to over 500 cps. The print quality is determined by the number of pins (the mechanisms that print the dots), which can vary from 9 to 24. The more pins per inch, the higher the print resolution. The best dot matrix printers (24 pins) can produce near letter quality type image.

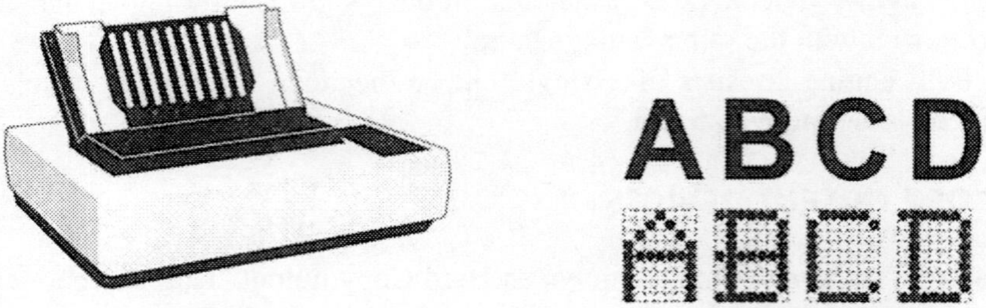

(a) Dot Matrix Printer (b) Dot Matrix characters

FIGURE 2.33

Dot matrix printers are inexpensive and have low operating costs. These printers are able to use different types of fonts, different line densities, and different types of paper. Many dot matrix printers are bi-directional, that is, they can print the characters from both the directions, left or right. These printers are limited to situations where carbon copies are needed and the quality is not too important.

The major limitation of a dot matrix printer is that it prints only in black and white. The image printing ability is also very limited. These printers may not be able to print graphic objects adequately. Dot matrix printers are commonly used in low-cost, low-quality applications, like cash registers. DMP prints text in near letter Quality mode. They can't print in pure letter quality.

DMPs are available in two sizes as 80 col. and 132 col. Many vendors are supplying them i.e., WIPRO, TVSE, EPSON, etc. printing speed varies from 200 to 360 characters per second.

Advantages

- Inexpensive
- Widely used
- Other language characters can be printed.

Disadvantages

- Slow speed
- Poor quality

2.6.1.2 Daisy Wheel

Head is lying on a wheel and pins corresponding to characters are like petals of a daisy, that is why it is called Daisy Wheel Printer. A motor spins the wheel at a very fast speed. The daisy wheel is a disk made of plastic or metal on which characters stand out in relief along the outer edge. To print a character, the printer rotates the disk until the desired letter is facing the paper. Then a hammer strikes the disk, forcing the character to hit an ink ribbon, leaving an impression of the character on the paper. You can change the daisy wheel to print different fonts. The output is same as Letter Quality Printing, is as good as that of a high-quality typewriter.

These printers have very slow speed of the order of 10 to 50 characters per second. Quality of printing is very good. These printers are generally used for word processing in offices which require a few letters to be sent here and there with very nice quality representation.

Daisy wheel printers produce high-resolution output and are more reliable than dot matrix printers. They can have speeds up to 90 cps. These printers are also called *smart printers* because of its bidirectional printing and built-in microprocessor control features.

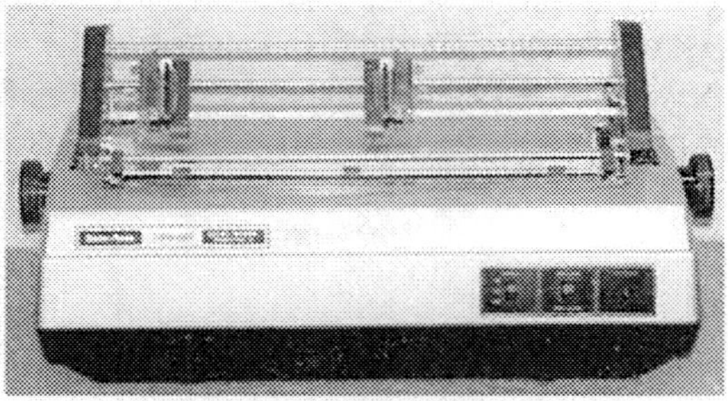

FIGURE 2.34 Daisy Wheel Printer

However, daisy wheel printers give only alphanumeric output. They cannot print graphics and cannot change fonts unless the print wheel is physically replaced. These printers are usually very slow because of the time required to rotate the print wheel for each character desired. Daisy wheel printers are slower and more expensive than dot matrix printers.

Advantages

- More reliable than DMPs
- Better quality
- The fonts of characters can easily be changed.

Disadvantages

- Slower than DMPs
- Noisy
- More expensive than DMPs

2.6.1.3 Line Printers

Line printers are printers which print one line at a time. These are impact printers for producing very large volume paper output. They are very fast and speed varies from a range of 300 to 3000 lines per minute. Two most commonly used printers in this category are: Drum Printer and Chain Printer.

Drum Printer

This line printer consists of a drum. The surface of the drum is divided into tracks. Total tracks are equal to size of paper i.e., for a paper width of 132 characters, the drum will have 132 tracks. A characters sets is embossed on track. Character set is not of character that printer will support. Different characters sets are available in the market, 48 character set, 64 and 96 characters set. Drum is made to rotate at a very fast speed. Paper is wrapped in drum and each track has a hammer attached to it. Ribbon is sandwiched between paper and hammer. Say if letter 'j' is to be printed. As soon as 'j' comes in front of hammer attached to jth track, it is fired. Thus, 'j' is embossed on paper.

In this way one character is printed, but we need a whole line to be printed at once. For that a buffer is used, which has storage capacity equal to size of paper. All character in a line are stored in buffer and as soon as all come in front of hammers, all hammers are fired at once. It is very important that all hammers should be fired at once and thus a line is printed. If synchronization is not achieved in firing of hammers, then wavy output will occur.

One rotation of drum prints one line. Drum printers are fast in speed and speed is between 300 to 2000 lines per minute. All printing features are available in this line printer.

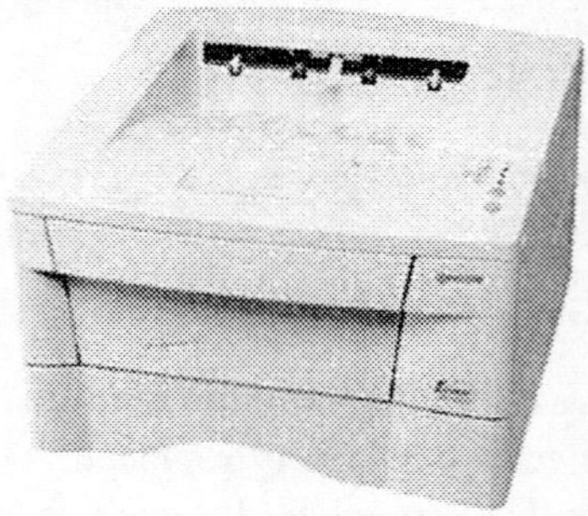

FIGURE 2.35 Drum Printer

Working of a Drum Printer

The basics of a line printer like drum printer are similar to those of a serial printer, except that multiple hammers strike multiple type elements against the paper almost simultaneously, so that an entire line is printed in one operation. A typical arrangement of a drum printer involves a large rotating drum mounted horizontally and positioned in front of a very wide, inked ribbon, which in turn is positioned in front of the paper itself. The drum contains characters molded onto its surface in columns around its circumference; each column contains a complete set of characters (letters, digits, etc.) running around the circumference of the drum. The drum spins continuously at high speed when the printer is operating. In order to print a line, hammers positioned behind the paper ram the paper against the ribbon and against the drum beyond it at exactly the right instant; such that the appropriate character is printed in each column, as it spins past on the drum. Once every column has been printed, the paper is advanced upward so that the next line can be printed.

Advantages

- Very high speed.

Disadvantages

- Very expensive.
- Characters, fonts cannot be changed.
- As the strike should be very precise, the mistiming causes wavy printing.

Chain Printer

They are also line printers, because of use of a chain of character sets, they are called Chain Printers. They can be thought of as a type wound on two spools with a character set repeated, three or four times. A standard character set may have 48, 64 and 96 characters.

In addition to the chain, the printer has a set of hammer mounted in front of the chain in a manner that an inked ribbon and paper can be placed between the hammer and the chain. The total number of hammers is equal to the total number of print positions. Therefore, if there are 132 print positions, the printer will have 132 hammers.

The chain rotates at a high speed, and a character at a print position is printed by activating the appropriate hammer, when the character embossed on the chain passes below it. Because character set is repeated three to four times, speed of chain printer increases, it is not necessary to wait for a whole cycle as in drum for a particular character to come in front of hammer. Speed varies from 400 to 3000 LPM (lines per minute).

Advantages

- Character fonts can easily be changed.
- The problem of wavy printing does not arise as the chain rotates horizontally where a drum rotates vertically.
- Different scripts (languages) can be used with the same printer.

Disadvantages

- The timing of hammer strike is very critical.
- Do not have the ability to print any shape of characters, different sizes of prints and graphics.
- Noisy in operation.

2.6.2 Non-Impact Printers

The printers that print the characters without striking against the ribbon and onto the paper are called Non-impact Printers. These printers print a complete page at a time, therefore, also called Page Printers. Unlike impact printers, a non-impact printer forms characters and images without making direct physical contact between printing mechanism and paper. In this printer, the print head does not make contact with the paper, and no inked ribbon is required. Ink can be sprayed against the paper and then heat and pressure are used to fuse a fine black powder into the shape of a character. They use techniques other than physically striking the page to transfer ink onto the page. The major technologies competing in the non-impact market are *ink-jet* and *laser*. Page printers are of three types:(i) Laser Printers, (ii) Ink Jet Printers and (iii) Thermal Printers.

Characteristics of Non-impact Printers

- Non-impact printers are faster than impact printers.
- They are quieter than impact printers because there is no striking mechanism involved and only few moving parts are used.
- They possess the ability to change typefaces automatically.
- These printers produce high-quality graphics.
- These printers usually support the transparencies.
- These printers cannot print multipart forms because no impact is being made on the paper.

2.6.2.1 *Ink-Jet Printer*

It is the most commonly used printer. Being a non-impact it does not touch the paper while creating an image. It uses a series of nozzles to spray onto the paper. Originally it was made black and white only.

However, the print head has now been expanded and the nozzle accommodates CMYK. The combination of these four colors will be the resultant color.

These printers are costlier than the dot matrix printers, but the quality is much better. Ink-jet printers typically print with a resolution of 600 dpi or more. Due to the high resolution, these printers produce high quality graphics and text printouts. They are also affordable, which appeals to small businesses and home-users. These printers print documents at a medium pace, but slow down if printing a document in multicolor. These printers can print about 6-15 pages per minute. Moreover, they can also be programmed to print unusual symbols such as Japanese or Chinese characters.

FIGURE 2.36 Ink-Jet Printer

Working of an ink-jet Printer

An ink-jet printer has a print cartridge with a series of tiny electrically heated chambers. These cartridges are attached to print heads with a series of small nozzles that spray ink onto the surface of the paper. As print head moves back and forth across the page, software gives instructions regarding the type and the quantity of colors. It also tells the position where the dots of ink should be 'sprayed'. There are two main ways to drop the ink droplets, namely, the *bubble-jet* and *piezoelectric* technology.

Bubble-jet printers use heat to fire ink onto the paper. Piezoelectric technology uses a piezo crystal at the back of the ink reservoir.

2.6.2.2 Laser Printers

These are non-impact printers. They use laser lights to produce the dots needed to form the character to be printed on a page and hence are known as laser printers. A laser printer provides the highest quality text and images for personal computers today, operates on the same principle as that of a photocopy machine. They are also known as *page printers* because they process and store the entire page before they actually print it.

The output is generated in following steps:

Step 1: The bits of data sent by processing unit act as triggers to turn the laser beam on and off.

Step 2: The output device has a drum which is cleared and is given a positive electric charge. To print a page the modulated laser beam passing from the laser, scans back and forth the surface of the drum. The positive electric charge on the drum is stored on just those parts of the charges on the exposed drum surface.

Step 3: The laser exposed parts of the drum attract an ink powder known as toner.

Step 4: The attracted ink powder is transferred to paper.

Step 5: The ink particles are permanently fixed to the paper by using either heat or pressure technique.

Step 6: The drum rotates back to the cleaner where a rubber blade cleanse off the excess ink and prepares the drum to print the next page.

Characteristics of Laser printer:

- It is a very fast printer.
- It can print text and graphics with a very high quality resolution from 300 to 1200 dpi.
- It can print in different fonts, that is, type styles and sizes.
- It is more expensive to buy and maintain than the other printers.

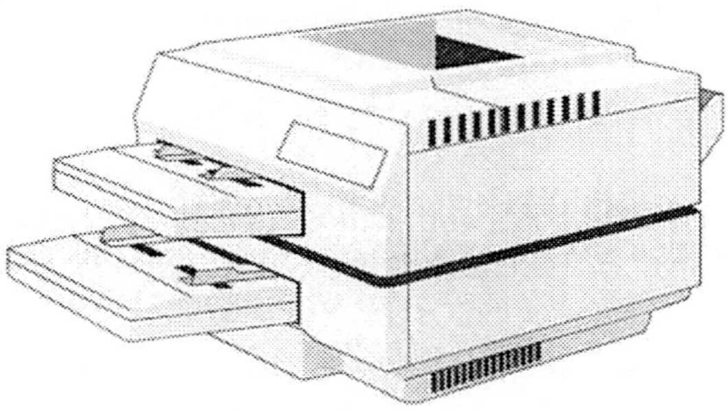

Laser Printer

FIGURE 2.37 Laser Printer

Working of a Laser Printer

The core component of laser printing system is the *photoreceptor drum*. A rotating mirror inside the printer causes the beam of a laser to sweep across the photoconductive drum. Initially, the beam of laser charges the photoconductive drum positively. When the charged photoconductor is exposed to an optical image through a beam of light to discharge, a latent or invisible image is formed. At the point where the laser strikes the surface of drum, it creates a dot of positive charge. These points are represented by a black dot, which will be printed on the paper. After this, the printer coats the drum with a container, which contains a black powder called *toner*. This toner is negatively charged, and so it clings to the positive areas of the drum surface. When the powder pattern gets fixed, the drum is rotated and the paper is fed into the drum surface via a pressure roller. This pressure roller transfers the black toner onto the paper. Since, the paper is moving at the same speed as the drum, the paper picks up the image pattern precisely. Finally, the printer passes the paper through the fuser, a pair of heated rollers. As the paper passes through these rollers, the loose toner powder gets melted and fuses with the fibers in the paper.

Advantages

- Very high speed.
- Very high quality output.
- Give good graphics quality.
- Support many fonts and different character size.

Disadvantages

- Expensive.
- Cannot be used to produce multiple copies of a document in a single printing.

2.6.3 Plotters

A plotter is a pen-based output device that is attached to a computer for making vector graphics, that is, images created by a series of many straight lines. It is used to draw high-resolution charts, graphs, blueprints, maps, circuit diagrams, and other line-based diagrams. Plotters are used to print high quality graphics and drawings. Plotters are generally used for printing drawing graphical images such as charts, drawings, maps, etc. of engineering and scientific applications. Some important types of plotters are: *Drum Plotters* and *Flatbed Plotters*.

2.6.3.1 Drum Plotters

In drum plotters, the paper on which the design is to be made is placed over a drum. These plotters consist of one or more pen(s) that are mounted on a carriage and this carriage is horizontally placed across the drum. The drum can rotate in either clockwise or anticlockwise direction under the control of plotting instructions sent by the computer. Drum plotters are used to produce continuous output, such as plotting earthquake activity, or for long graphic output, such as tall building structures. The drum plotters are generally the least expensive.

2.6.3.2 Flatbed Plotters

Flatbed plotters consist of a stationary horizontal plotting surface on which paper is fixed. The pen is mounted on a carriage, which can move horizontally, vertically, leftwards or rightwards to draw line. In flatbed plotters, the paper does not move, the pen-holding mechanism provides all the motion. These plotters are instructed by the computer on the movement of pens in the X-Y coordinates on the page. These plotters are capable of working on any standard, that is, from A4 size paper to some very big beds. Depending on the size of the flatbed surface, these are used in designing of ships, aircraft, buildings, etc. The size of these automated drafting tables can range upto roughly 5ft. (1.5m) by 20ft. (6.1m) with plotting accuracies approaching ±0.001 in. (±0.025 mm).

The major disadvantage of this plotter is that it is a slow output device and can take hours to complete a complex drawing. The flatbed plotter is also more expensive.

Drum Plotter

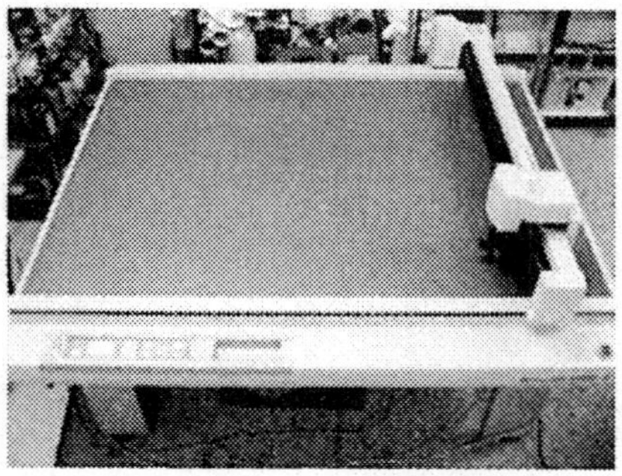

Flatbed Plotter

FIGURE 2.38 Plotters

Comparison between Plotters and Printers

Plotters are similar to printers, but they draw lines using a pen. As a result, they can produce continuous lines, whereas printers can only simulate lines by printing a closely spaced series of dots. Multicolor plotters use different-colored pens to draw different colors. Color plots can be made by using four pens (cyan, magenta, yellow, and black) and need no human intervention to change them. Plotters are relatively expensive as compared to printers but can produce more printouts than standard printers. They are mainly used for Computer Aided Design (CAD) and Computer Aided Manufacturing (CAM) applications such as printing out plans for houses or car parts. These are also used with programs like AUTO CAD (computer assisted drafting) to give graphic outputs.

SOLVED PROBLEMS

Problem 2.1 A raster system has resolution 640 × 480. Compute the size of frame buffer (in byte) to store 24 bits per pixel.

Solution

Resolution of the screen = 640 × 480

or Total number of pixels on the screen = 640 × 480

Number of bits per pixel = 24

Total number of bits in frame buffer = 640 × 480 × 24

or Size of frame buffer = 640 × 480 × 24 bits

= 640 × 480 × 3 bytes

Problem 2.2 Consider a screen has size 12 × 12 inch with resolution 50 pixels per square inch. How much storage (in byte) do we need for frame buffer if we need for frame buffer if we want to store 16 bits per pixel.

Solution:

Size of the screen = 12 × 12 inch

Resolution per square inch = 50

Therefore resolution of the screen = 12 × 12 × 50

or Total number of pixels on the screen = 12 × 12 × 50

Number of bits per pixel = 16

Total number of bits in frame buffer = 12 × 12 × 50 ×16

or Size of frame buffer = 12 × 12 × 50 × 16 bits

= 12 × 12 × 50 × 2 bytes

Problem 2.3 A frame buffer has a size 1024 × 1024 with 10 bits per pixel. Compute the time required to load it if transferred rate is 10 bits per sec.

Solution:

Resolution of the screen = 1024 × 1024

or Total number of pixels on the screen = 1024 × 1024

Number of bits per pixel = 10

Total number of bits in frame buffer = 1024 × 1024 × 10

or Size of frame buffer = 1024 × 1024 × 10 bits

Number of bits loaded per sec. = 10

or Time required to load 10 bits = 1 sec.

Time required to load 1024 × 1024 × 10 bits = 1024 × 1024 sec.

Problem 2.4 A raster system has resolution 1024 × 768 and refresh rate 60 Hz. How many pixels could be accessed per second.

Solution:

Resolution of the screen = 1024 × 768

or Total number of pixels on the screen = 1024 × 768

Refresh rate = 60 Hz

This implies each pixel on the screen refreshed 60 times within one sec.

or 1024 × 768 pixels refreshed 60 times within one sec.

Total number of pixels accessed in one sec. = 1024 × 768 × 60

Problem 2.5 A raster system has resolution 1024 × 1024 and refresh rate 60 Hz., horizontal retrace time is 4 μsec. and vertical retrace time 400 μsec. Compute the time spent to retrace of the electron beam per frame.

Solution:

$$\text{Horizontal retrace time} = 4\ \mu\text{sec}$$

$$\text{Vertical retrace time} = 400\ \mu\text{sec}$$

$$\text{Total retrace time} = 4 + 400\ \mu\text{ sec}$$

$$\text{Refresh rate} = 60\text{ Hz}$$

This implies number of frames buffers refreshed in one sec. = 60

Time required to retrace one frame buffer = 404/60 sec.

Problem 2.6 A screen has 1024 scan lines with aspect ratio 4:3 and bit depth 16, how many bits per sec. are required to show 60 frames per sec.

Solution:

$$\text{Number of scan lines} = 1024$$

$$\text{Aspect ratio} = 4:3$$

$$\text{Therefore resolution of the screen} = 1024 \times 4 \times 3$$

or $$\text{Total pixels on the screen} = 1024 \times 4 \times 3$$

$$\text{Bit depth} = 16$$

$$\text{Number of bits per pixel} = 16$$

$$\text{Therefore total number of bits} = 1024 \times 4 \times 3 \times 16$$

$$\text{Refresh rate} = 60$$

$$\text{Number of bits per sec. required} = 1024 \times 4 \times 3 \times 16 \times 60$$

Problem 2.7 Calculate the time spent in scanning each row of pixels in a raster system of resolution 680 × 420 and a refresh rate of 50 frames per second.

Solution:

$$\text{Resolution of the screen} = 640 \times 420$$

$$\text{Refresh rate} = 50\text{ Hz}$$

$$\text{Time required to refresh 50 frames} = 1\text{ sec.}$$

$$\text{Time required to refresh 1 frame} = 1/50\text{ sec.}$$

Each frame has 680 columns and 420 rows.

Therefore time required to scan each row = 1/(50*420) sec.

EXERCISES

1. Explain the architecture of Raster Scan Display.
2. Give the logical organization of a Video Controller and explain its importance in Raster Scan Display.
3. With a logical organization, explain the role of Look Up Table. Create organization of LUT with 24 bit entry and 4 bit per pixel frame buffer.

4. Differentiate between monochrome CRT and color CRT.
5. Explain the working of LCD with a neat diagram.
6. Compare various characteristics of LCD over other flat panel display devices.
7. Compare storage type CRT and refresh type CRT display.
8. Compare the Rater Scan Display and Flat-panel Display with their merits and demerits.
9. Differentiate between Shadow mask and Beam Penetration technique.
10. What is frame buffer? Identify its contents.
11. Define aspect ratio. Explain its importance in graphics.
12. How color depth and resolution of an image effect on video memory requirement?
13. Explain the role of Display Processor in Raster Scan System.
14. Define the terms System memory, Display Processor Memory, Frame Buffer.
15. In what scene Soft copy devices introduce interactivity in computer graphics?
16. Compare and contrast the operating characteristics of DMP, Laser Printer, Ink-jet Printer.
17. What are the basic differences between impact printers and non-impact printers?
18. A raster system has resolution 1024×1024. Compute the size of frame buffer(in byte) to store 12 bits per pixel.
19. Consider a screen has a size 8×10 inch with resolution 100 pixels per square inch. How much storage (in byte) do we need for frame buffer if we want store 8 bits per pixel?
20. Suppose a fame buffer has a size 640×480 with 10 bits per pixel. Compute the time required to load it if transferred rate is 10^2 bits per sec.
21. Consider a screen with resolution 640×480. If refresh rate is 60Hz, how many pixels could be accessed per second?
22. A RGB monitor with full-color has frame buffer size 1024×1024. How many distinct color choices would we be available?
23. A raster system has resolution 1024×1024 and refresh rate 60 Hz, horizontal retrace time 2 μ sec and vertical retrace time 200 μ sec. Compute the time spent to retrace of the electron beam per frame.
24. A screen has 525 scan lines with aspect ratio 4:3 and bit depth is 8, how many bits per sec are required to show 60 frames per sec?

3

Interactive Devices

3.1 INTRODUCTION

A computer accepts (input) information and manipulates (processes) it to get desired result (output) on a sequence of instructions. In computer terminology devices can be referred as a unit of hardware, which is capable of providing input to the computer or receiving output or both. An input device captures information and translates into the form that is understandable by computer and output devices (discussed in chapter 2) translate information into the form that is understandable by human beings as shown in fig 3.1. Through input devices users talk to the computer; through output devices, the computer communicates with the users.

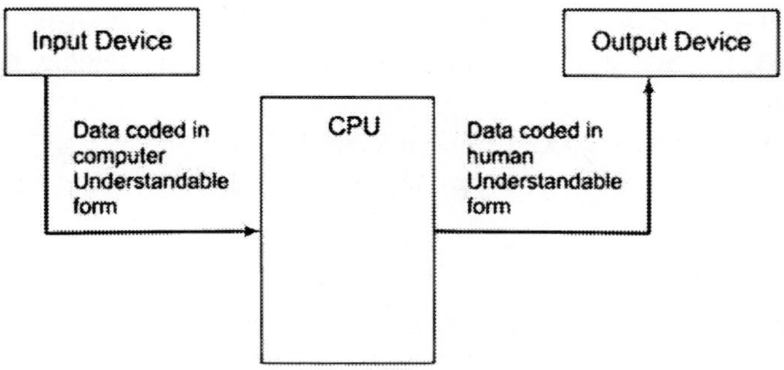

FIGURE 3.1 Interrelationship between Input Device, CPU and Output Device

The common input devices are *keyboards* and *mouse*. The common output devices are *monitors* and *printers*. In the chapter 2 we have discussed various soft copy and hard copy display devices.

Most display terminals provide the user with an alphanumeric keyboard with which to type commands and enter data for the program. For some applications, however, the keyboard is inconvenient or inadequate. For example, the user may wish to indicate one of a number of symbols on the screen, in order to erase the symbol. If each symbol is labeled, he can do so by typing the symbol's name; by pointing at the symbol, however, he may be able to erase more rapidly.

Another problem arises if the user has to add lines or symbols to the picture on the screen. Although he can identify an item's position by typing coordinates he or she can do so even better by pointing at the screen, particularly if what matters most is the item's position relative to the rest of the picture.

These two examples illustrate the two basic types of graphical interaction: *pointing at items already on the screen* and *positioning new items.* The need to interact in these ways requires the development of a number of different types of graphical input devices, classified into *positioning devices* and *pointing devices.*

Ideally a graphical input device should have properties both to pointing and to positioning. In reality there are no devices with this versatility. Most devices are much better at positioning than at pointing; one device, the light pen, is the exact opposite. Fortunately, however we can supplement the deficiencies of these devices by software and in this way produce hardware-software system that has both capabilities. Nevertheless the distinction between pointing and positioning capability is extremely important.

Another important distinction is between devices that can be used directly on the screen surface and devices that cannot. The latter might appear to be less useful, but this is far from true.

Input devices can be broadly classified into two categories: *positioning* and *pointing*.

3.2 POINTING AND POSITIONING DEVICES

Various devices are available for data input on graphics workstations. Most systems have a keyboard and one or more additional devices specially designed for interactive input. These include a mouse, trackball, joystick, digitizers, light pen, tablet, data gloves, touch panels.

Pointing Devices

In some applications, keyboard is not convenient. For example, if the user wants to select an item from a list, the user can identify items position by selecting it through the keyboard. However, this action could be performed quickly by pointing at correct position. Pointing devices are used to select the items already on the screen. Some of the commonly used pointing devices are mouse, trackball, joystick, light pen and touch panel.

Pointing devices are sometimes also known as *selectors*.

Pointing refers to location of items already on the screen. Pointing is also known as selection.

Positioning Devices

These are the devices used to add new items on the screen. These devices give position information. These devices provide the coordinate of a point.

Positioning devices are also known as *locators.*

Positioning refers to location of new items. Positioning is sometimes known as locating.

Pointing and positioning are two basic types of graphical interactions.

3.2.1 Keyboard

A keyboard is designed to resemble a regular typewriter with a few additional keys. A keyboard is the most common data entry device. Using a keyboard, the user can type text and execute commands. Data is entered into a computer by simply pressing various keys. The layout of a keyboard comes in various styles such as QWERTY, DVORAK, AZERTY but the most common layout is the QWERTY. It is named so because the first six keys on the top row of letters are *Q, W E, R, T,* and *Y.* The number of keys on a typical keyboard varies from 82 keys to 108 keys. Portable computers such as laptops quite often have custom keyboards that have slightly different key arrangements than a standard keyboard. In addition, many system manufacturers add special buttons to the standard layout. A keyboard is the easiest input device, as it does not require any special skill, it is supplied with a computer so no additional cost is incurred. The maintenance and operation cost of keyboard is also less. However, using a keyboard for data entry may be a slow process.

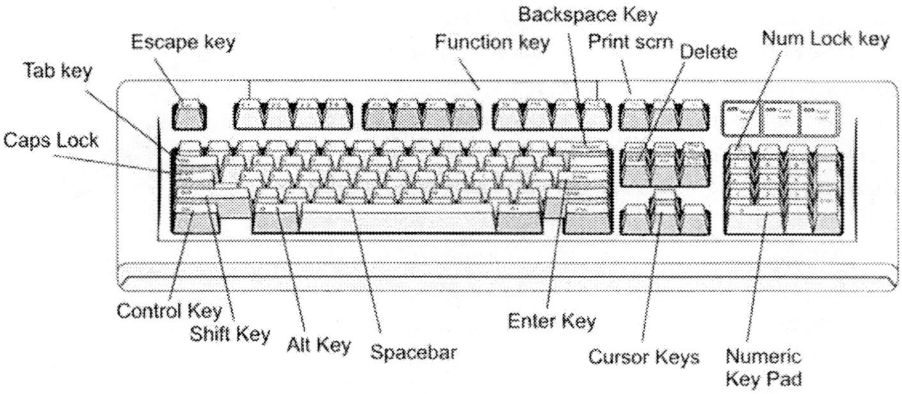

FIGURE 3.2 Keyboard

Layout of the Keyboard

The layout of the keyboard can be divided into the following five sections:

Typing Keys: These keys include the letter keys (1, 2, A, B, etc.), which are generally laid out in the same style that was common for typewriters.

Numeric Keypad: Numeric keys are located on the right hand side of the keyboard. Generally, it consists of a set of 17 keys that are laid out in the same configuration used by most adding machines and calculators.

Function Keys: The functions keys (F1, F2, F3, etc.) are arranged in a row along the top of the keyboard and could be assigned specific commands by the current application or the operating system.

Control Keys: These keys provide cursor and screen control. It includes four directional arrows(← ↑ → ↓). These keys allow the user to move the cursor on the display area one space at a time in either an up, down, left or right direction. Control keys also include *Home, End, Insert, Delete, Page Up, Page Down, Control (Ctrl), Alternate (Alt),* and *Escape (Esc).*

Special Purpose Keys: Apart from the above-mentioned keys, a keyboard contains some special purpose keys such as *Enter, Shift, Caps Lock, Num Lock, Spacebar, Tab* and *Print Screen.*

Working of a Keyboard

A keyboard is series of switches connected to a small keyboard microprocessor. When the user presses a key, it causes a change in the amount of current flowing through the circuit associated specifically with that key. The keyboard microprocessor detects this change in current flow. By doing this, the processor can tell when a key has been pressed and when it is being released. The processor generates the associative code, known as *scan code,* of the key and sends it to the operating system. A copy of this code is also stored in the keyboard's memory.

3.2.2 Mouse

It was invented by Douglas Englebart of Standard Institute in 1963. A mouse is small hand-held box *pointing* device used to position the screen cursor with a rubber ball or wheel embedded at its lower side and buttons on the top. Usually a mouse contains two or three buttons, which can be used to input commands or information. Figure 3.3 shows a mouse with three buttons.

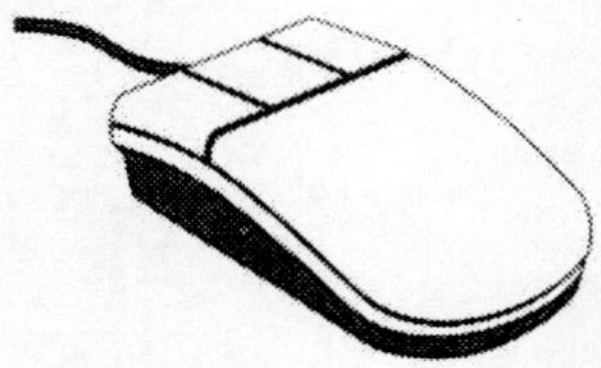

FIGURE 3.3 Mouse

The mouse may be classified as a *mechanical* mouse or an *optical* mouse, based on technology it uses.

A *mechanical mouse* uses a rubber ball at the bottom surface, which rotates as the mouse is moved along a flat surface, to move the cursor. Mechanical mouse is the most common and least expensive pointing device. Microsoft, IBM and Logitech are some well-known manufacturers of the mechanical mouse.

An *optical mouse* uses a light beam instead of a rotating ball to detect movement across a specially patterned mouse pad. As the user rolls the mouse on a flat surface, the cursor on the screen also moves in the direction of the mouse's movement.

An optical mouse has the following benefits over the mechanical mouse:

- No moving part means less wear and a lower chance of failure.
- Dirt cannot get inside the mouse and hence no interference with the tracking sensors.
- They do not require a special surface such as a mouse pad.

The cursor of the mouse can be *text cursor* or *graphic cursor*. The text cursor(I) is used for text while the graphic cursor(↖)is used for pointing and drawing.

A mouse allows us to create graphic elements on the screen, such as lines, curves, and freehand shapes. Since it is an intuitive device, it is much easier and convenient to work as compared to the keyboard. Like keyboard, usually it is also supplied with a computer; therefore, no additional cost is incurred. The mouse cannot easily be used with laptop, notebook or palmtop computers. These need a track ball or a touch sensitive pad called a touch pad.

Working of a Mouse

A mechanical mouse has a rubber ball in the bottom. When the user moves the mouse, the ball rolls along the surface of the mouse pad, and the mouse keeps track of how far the ball rolls. This allows it to tell how far it has moved. Inside the bottom of the mouse are three rollers. These rollers are mounted at a 90° angle to the one other, one roller measures how fast the ball is turning horizontally, and the other measures how fast it is turning vertically. When the ball rolls, it turns these two rollers. The rollers are connected to axles, and the axles are connected to a small sensor that measures how fast the axle is turning. Both sets of information are passed to the electronics inside the mouse. This little processor, usually consisting of little more than a single chip, uses the information to determine how fast the mouse itself is Processor Chip moving, and in what direction. This information is passed to the computer via mouse cord, where the operating system then moves the pointer accordingly.

The optical mouse uses an infrared light and special mouse pads with fine grid lines to measure the rotation of the axle. The axle in optical mouse is connected to a little photo-interrupter wheel with a number of tiny holes in it. In front of this wheel is a light and on the other side of the wheel is a light meter. As the wheel turns, the light flashes through the holes in the wheel. By measuring how often these flashes occur, the light sensor can measure how fast the wheel is turning and sends the corresponding coordinates to the computer. The computer moves the cursor on the screen based on the coordinates received from the mouse. This happens hundreds of times each second, making the cursor appear to move very smoothly.

3.2.3 Joystick

Joystick is a device that moves in all directions and controls the movement of the cursor. The joystick offers three types of control: *digital, glide* and *direct.*

Digital control allows movement in a limited number of directions such as *up, down, lef* and *right.*

Glide and direct control allow movements in all directions (360 degrees). Direct control joysticks have the added ability to respond to the distance and speed. A joystick is generally used to control the velocity of the screen cursor movement rather than its absolute position. Joysticks are mainly used for computer games, for other applications, which include controlling machines such as elevators, cranes, trucks, and powered wheelchairs; and flight simulators, training simulators, CAD/CAM systems, and for controlling industrial robots.

Joystick elements: 1. Stick 2. Base 3. Trigger 4. Extra buttons 5. Auto fire switch 6. Throttle 7. Hat Switch (POV Hat) 8. Suction Cup

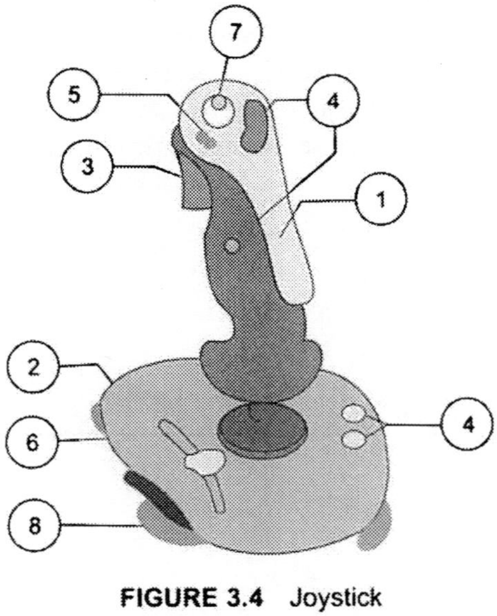

FIGURE 3.4 Joystick

3.2.4 Trackball

Trackball is another *pointing device* that resembles a ball nestled in a square cradle and serves as an alternative to a mouse. It has a ball, which can be rotated by fingers or palm of the hand in any direction, the cursor moves accordingly. In order to measure the direction of rotation a potentiometer is attached to ball. The trackballs are mounted on keyboard or Z mouse.

The size of the ball of the trackball varies from as large as a cue ball, to as small as a marble. Since, it is a static device so rather than rolling the mouse on the top of the table, the ball on the top is moved by using fingers, thumbs, and palms.

FIGURE 3.5 Trackball

3.2.5 Light Pen

It is a pen-like device, which is connected to the machine by a cable. A light pen (sometimes called a *mouse pen*) is a hand-held electro-optical pointing device which when touched to or aimed closely at a connected computer monitor, will allow the computer to determine where on that screen the pen is aimed. *It actually does not emit light; its light sensitive-diode would sense the light coming from the screen.*

They are sensitive to the short burst of light emitted from the phosphor coating at the instant the electron beam strikes a particular point. Other light sources, such as the background light in the room, are usually not detected by a light pen.

An activated light pen, pointed at a spot on the screen as the electron beam lights up that spot, causes the photocell to respond by generating an electrical pulse. This electric pulse response is transmitted to the processor that identifies the position to which the light pen is pointing. As with cursor-positioning devices, recorded light-pen coordinates can be used to position an object or to select a processing option.

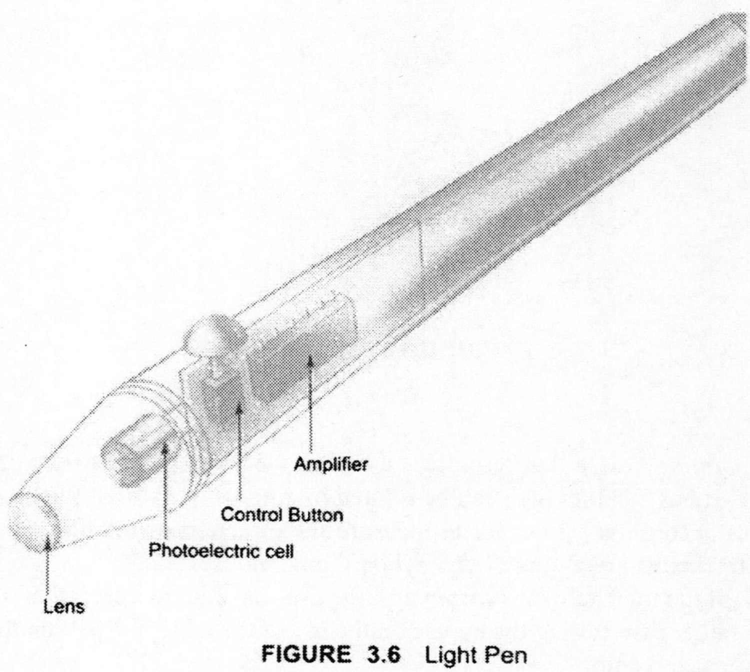

FIGURE 3.6 Light Pen

It facilitates drawing images and selects objects on the display screen by directly pointing the objects with the pen.

Although light pens are still with us, they are not as popular as they once were since they have several disadvantages compared to other input devices that have been developed.

- A light pen is pointed at the screen; part of the screen image is obscured by the hand and pen.
- Prolonged use of the light pen can cause arm fatigue. Also, light pens require special implementation for some applications because they cannot detect positions within black areas. To be able to select positions in any screen area with a light pen, we must have some non-zero intensity assigned to each screen pixel.
- Light pens sometime give false readings due to background lighting in a room.

3.2.6 Touch Sensitive Screens (TSS)

Perhaps the easiest way to enter data is with the touch of a finger. Touch screens enable the user to select an option by pressing a specific part of the screen. Touch screens are commonly used in grocery stores, fast-food restaurants and information kiosks.

As the name implies, touch panels allow displayed objects or screen positions to be selected with the touch of a finger. Touch input can be recorded using optical, electrical, or acoustical methods.

They are not too reliable or accurate but easy to use.

3.2.6.1 Optical Touch Sensitive Screens

Optical touch panels employ a line of infrared light-emitting diodes (LEDs) along one vertical edge and along one horizontal edge of the frame. The opposite vertical and horizontal edges contain light detectors. These detectors are used to record the beams which are interrupted when the panel is touched. The two crossing beams that are interrupted identify the horizontal and vertical coordinates of the screen position selected. Positions can be selected with an accuracy of about an inch. With closely spaced LEDs, it is possible to break two horizontal or two vertical beams simultaneously. In this case, an average position between the two interrupted beams is recorded. The LEDs operate at infrared frequencies, so that the light is not visible to a user.

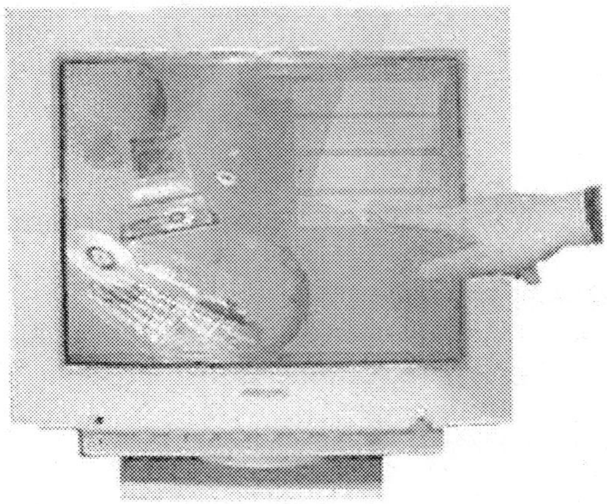

FIGURE 3.7 Optical Touch Sensitive Screen

3.2.6.2 Electrical Touch Sensitive Screens

An electrical touch panel is constructed with two transparent plates separated by a small distance. One of the plates is coated with a conducting material, and the other plate is coated with a resistive material. When the outer plate is touched, it is forced into contact with the inner plate. This contact creates a voltage drop at the point touched point, from which the position may be determined.

3.2.6.3 Acoustic Touch Sensitive Screens

In acoustical touch panels, high-frequency sound waves are generated in the horizontal and vertical directions across a glass plate. Touching the screen causes parts of each wave to be reflected from the finger to the emitters. The screen position at the point of contact is calculated from a measurement of the time interval between the transmission of each wave and its reflection to the emitter.

3.2.6.4 Electro-Mechanical Touch Sensitive Screens

A plastic or glass sheet with strain gagues placed around the edges records the positions by the relative magnitude of the deformations of the slightly bent plates.

3.2.7 Graphics Tablets

A tablet is used to input two-dimensional coordinates by activating a hand cursor or stylus at selected positions on a flat surface. A hand cursor contains cross hairs for sighting positions, while a stylus is a pencil-shaped device that is pointed at positions on the tablet. It is also referred to as a data tablet. Tablet size varies from 12 × 12 inches for desktop models to 44 × 60 inches. Graphics tablets provide a highly accurate method for selecting coordinate positions, with an accuracy that varies from about 0.2 mm on desktop models to about 0.05 mm or less on larger models.

FIGURE 3.8 The NotePad Tablet with Stylus

These devices are more accurate than light pens.

Based on the mechanism used to find two-dimensional coordinates on a flat surface, there are two types of tablets: *Electromagnetic Field and Acoustic tablet*.

3.2.7.1 Electromagnetic Field or Voltage Tablet

These types of tablets are constructed with a rectangular grid of wire embedded in the tablet surface, with different voltages or magnetic fields corresponding to different coordinates. Electromagnetic pulses are generated in sequence along the wires, and an electric signal is induced in a wire coil in an activated stylus or hand cursor to record a tablet position. Depending on the technology, and their signal strength, coded pulses, or phase shifts can be used to determine the position on the tablet.

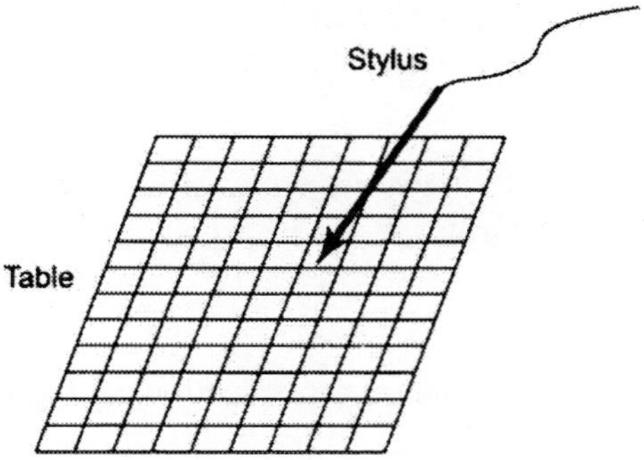

FIGURE 3.9 Electromagnetic Tablet

3.2.7.2 Acoustic or Sonic Tablet

Acoustic tablet designed by the Science Acessories Corporation works on an acoustic principle suggested by Brenner.

This type of tablet uses sound waves to detect a stylus position. The stylus has a small piece of ceramic mounted at its tip; a small spark is generated across the surface of the ceramic between two electrodes. The sound of the spark is picked up by the strip microphones along the edges of the tablet as shown in Fig 3.10. The perpendicular distances of the stylus tip from the axes is proportional to time intervals of sound created and received at destination.

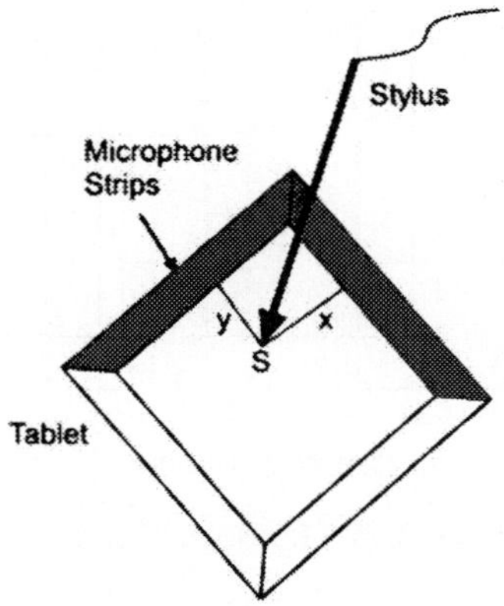

FIGURE 3.10 Acoustic Tablet

An advantage of two-dimensional acoustic tablets is that the microphones can be placed on any surface to form the "tablet" work area.

Disadvantage of this method is that inbuilt noisiness as well as weakness in noise to intervention from other noise.

Three-dimensional digitizers use sonic or electromagnetic transmissions to record positions. One electromagnetic transmission method is similar to that used in the data glove: A coupling between the transmitter and receiver is used to compute the location of a stylus as it moves over the surface of an object.

3.3 POSITIONING CONSTRAINTS

In many graphical applications the user must align input information with other information already available on the screen. This is a very difficult task for the user without some assistance from the computer. However steady user's hand there is always jittering to throw off. We therefore use computer to achieve accurate positioning.

Constraint: A constraint is a rule for altering input-coordinates values to produce a specified orientation or alignment of the displayed coordinates.

3.3.1 Modular Constraint

This constraint forces the input point to the nearest intersection on a grid. This can be applied both to symbols and line end-points.

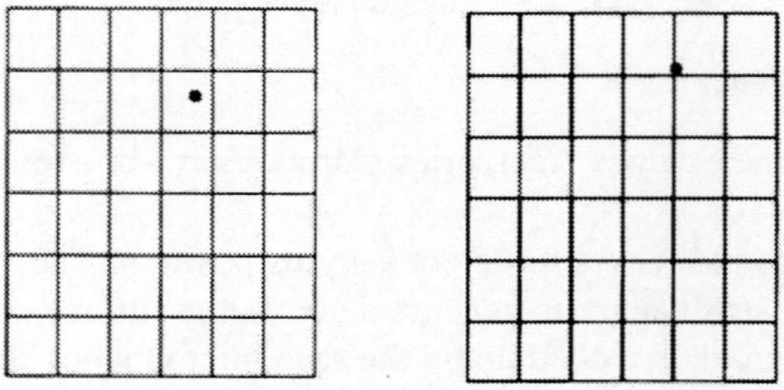

(a) Implemented to Point

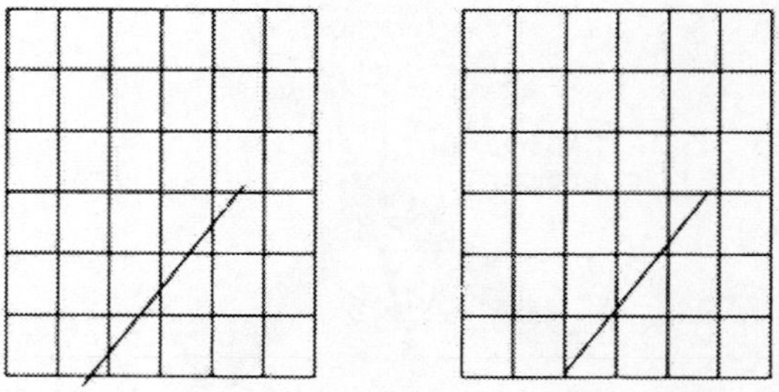

(b) Implemented to Line

FIGURE 3.11 Modular Constraint

3.3.2 Gravity-field Effect

This constraint provides the effect of gravitational field around a line or an object. This effect introduced gravitational pull between two or more pictures on the screen so that realistic picture is produced. This technique depends upon amount of gravity-field around the primitives to be attached. Fig. 3.12(a), 3.12(b), 3.12(c), 3.12(d) show gravity field around a line, rectangle, circle, respectively. In figures dotted lines show line drawn by hand via mouse, deviating from desired line. The solid lines show respective location produced by gravity-field constraint.

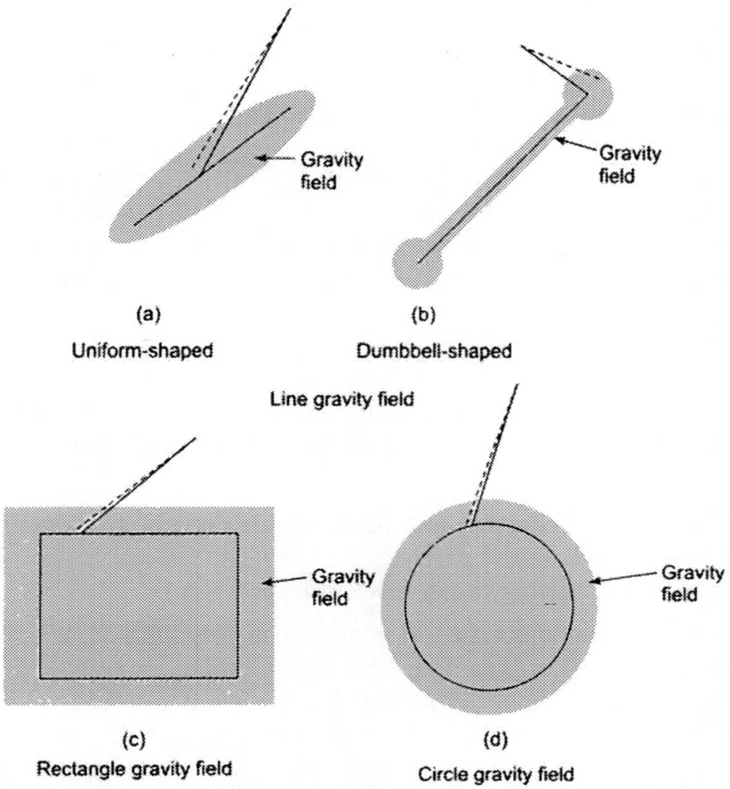

FIGURE 3.12 Demonstration of Line, Rectangle and Circle Gravity field

3.3.3 Directional Constraint

Directional constraint can be applied to lines only to straight lines along certain standard direction. It is relatively simple constraint.

Many applications use only horizontal and vertical lines. The user specifies two end points; the program detects whether the line specified is more nearly horizontal or vertical or any enabled direction 45°. Then software draws a line from first point, towards the second point in exactly horizontal, vertical or specified direction.

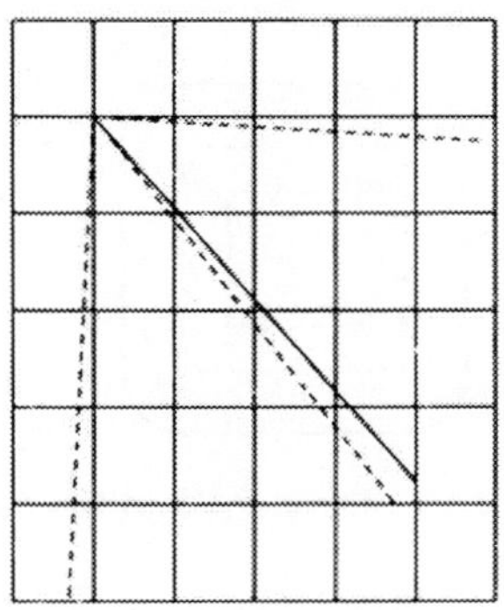

FIGURE 3.13 Directional Constraint

In figure 3.13 dotted lines show line drawn by hand via mouse, deviating from desired line. The solid lines show respective location produced by directional constraint.

3.3.4 Proportion Constraint

This is another very useful constraint in which software provides a shift key to constraint a general geometric figure to a specific configuration. For example, a rectangle command can be used to generate a square by pressing down the shift key during the drawing process; an ellipse command can be used to generate a circle by pressing down the shift key during the drawing process.

3.4 RUBBER BAND TECHNIQUE (RBT)

In positioning technique a line is drawn to indicate one end-point and then the other end-point, until a second end-point is not specified, a line is not drawn between two specified points as illustrated in the figures.

RBT is one step forward from positioning technique that also involves feedback. Thus, RBT is a combination of positioning technique and feedback.

Rubber band technique = Positioning Technique + Feedback

When a user clicks a mouse, the starting position of the line is established. When the mouse button is released, the endpoint of the line is fixed. Fig. 3.14 shows a rubber band line drawing sequence. It should be noted that rubber band technique is active only when a button is held down. When the user is satisfied with the final position, the pressed button is released and the line is drawn between the start and the last position. Rubber band technique methods are useful to construct and position other objects, besides straight lines.

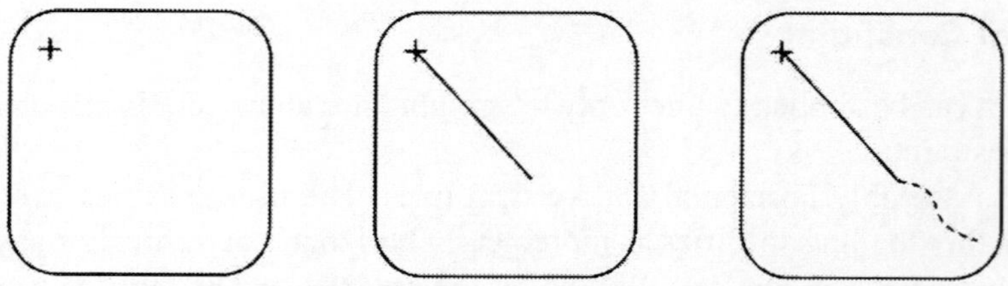

FIGURE 3.14 Rubber Band Line Drawing

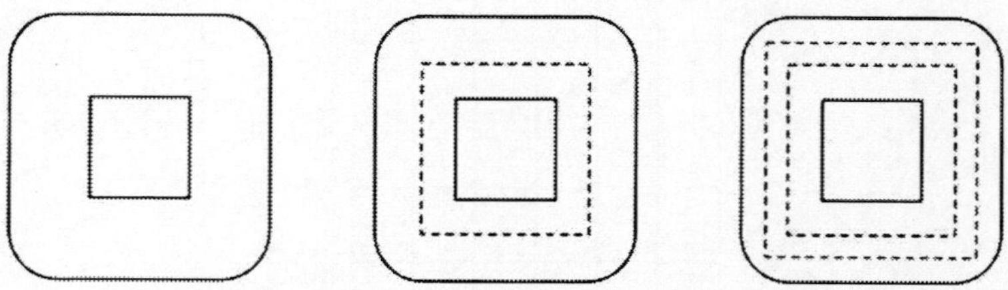

FIGURE 3.15 Rubber Band Rectangle

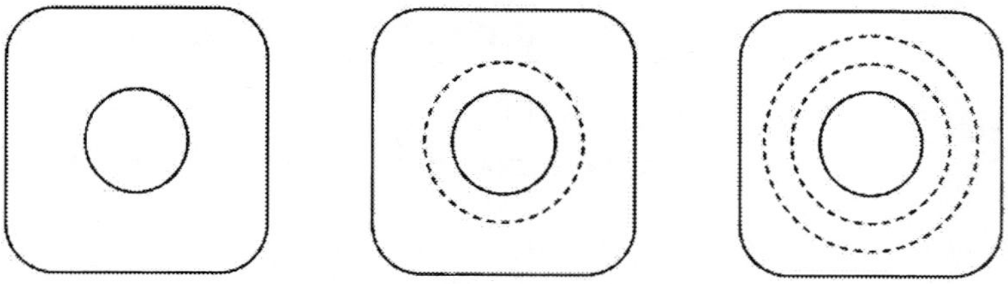

FIGURE 3.16 Rubber Band Circle

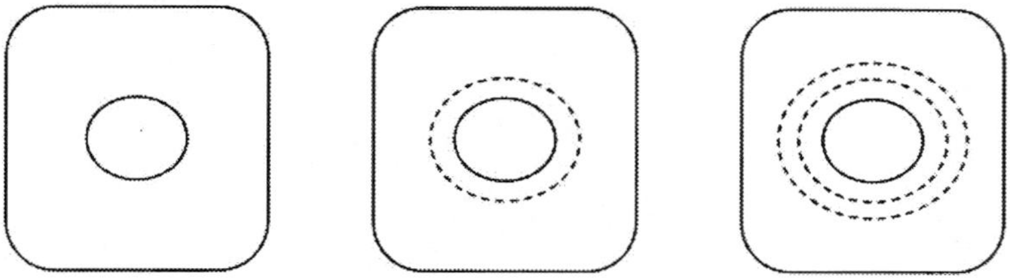

FIGURE 3.17 Rubber Band Ellipse

Advantages and Disadvantages of RBT

The most useful feature of RBT is that the user is continuously aware of what is going on and has control on whatever is happening. When the line or other image follows his hand movement through the mouse then decision making process is easier.

RBT requires computational resources likewise software and CPU speed. Thus, it puts extra cost burden.

There are some more input devices besides the above-mentioned input devices like: Digital Camera, Scanners (Hand-Held Scanner, Flat-Bed scanner), Optical Scanners (Optical Character Recognition (OCR) Optical Mark Recognition (OMR) Magnetic-Ink Character Recognition (MICR) Bar Code Reader)

Dragging

Dragging moves a selected symbol or object from one position to another position under the control of mouse button. Dragging is the sequence of following operations:

Above sequence may also be called as *click-and-drag*.

Dynamic rotation of a symbol or object can also be performed with the help of above sequence of operations; we have to identify point or axis of rotation.

Scaling of an object can also be performed with the help of above sequence of operations; we have to identify fixed point.

EXERCISES

1. Why would someone choose a trackball over a mouse?
2. What do you mean by constraint? Explain various positioning constraints. Why these constraints are required?
3. Explain the importance of *Rubber-band Technique* in interactive graphics.
4. Compare Positioning and Pointing techniques with suitable examples.
5. Explain the working principle of following interactive devices:

   (a) Light pen (b) Joystick (c) Tablet(s) (d) Touch Sensitive Screen(s) (e) Mouse

4

Scan Conversion

4.1 INTRODUCTION

The process of representing continuously graphic objects as a collection of discrete pixels is called scan conversion. In other words, we can say that scan conversion is continuous-to-discrete transformation.

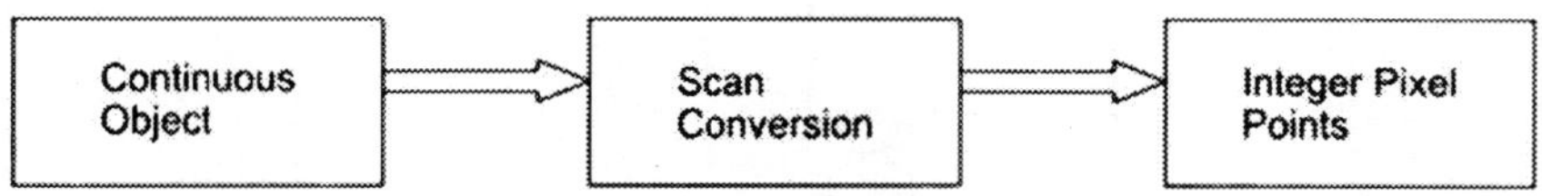

FIGURE 4.1 Continuous-to-Discrete Transformation

The most used graphic objects are the lines, the sectors, the arcs, the ellipses, the rectangles, and the polygons. In this book we will discuss only simple primitives, i.e., straight lines and few simple curves such as circle, ellipse, parabola and hyperbola. The motivation of a scan conversion algorithm is not only to produce primitive but also to produce it rapidly and satisfactorily.

On the monitor screen, let origin actually be at the top left-hand corner; x coordinate increases from left-to-right and y coordinate increases in downward direction. Such a system is left-handed coordinate system, Fig. 4.2(a). However, in this chapter and onward we will consider origin at lower left-hand corner where x coordinate increases from left-to-right and y coordinate increases in upward direction. Such a system is called right-handed coordinate system, Fig. 4.2(b).

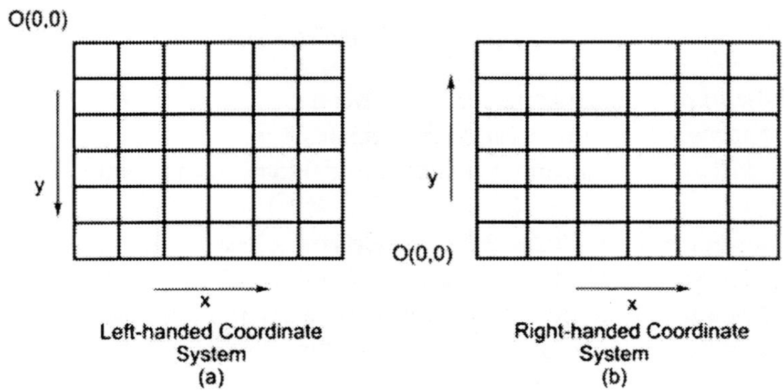

FIGURE 4.2

4.2 PIXEL PLOTTING

Definition

Pixel (Picture element): It is the smallest addressable screen element.

We consider each pixel as unit square area identified by the coordinates of its lower left corner, as shown in Fig. 4.3. The origin of the referenced coordinate system is located at the lower left corner of the display screen.

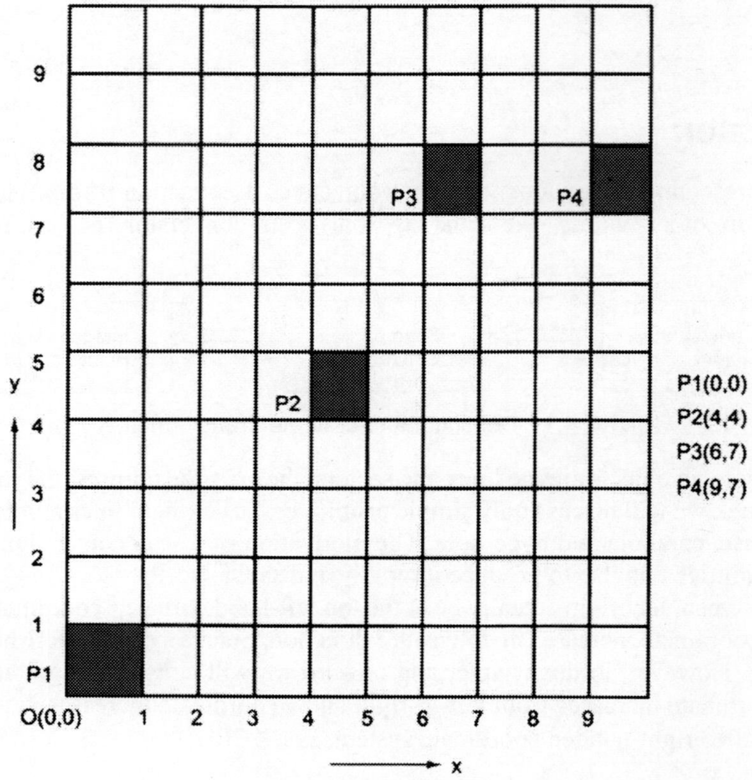

FIGURE 4.3 Grid of Pixels

Here are some of the important concepts related to pixel:

1. Each pixel is accessed by non-negative coordinates(x,y).
2. The x values start at the origin and increase from left to right and y values increase from bottom to top.
3. Floating values of pixel coordinators are rounded off to nearest integer, i.e., a coordinate position (2.1,1) is represented by $P(2,1)$ whereas (2.6,2) is represented by (3,2).
4. Any image that is displayed on the monitor is made up of thousands of such small pixels.
5. Each pixel has a particular color and intensity value.

4.3 SCAN CONVERSION OF LINES

Characteristics of a good line drawing algorithm:

- Lines should appear straight.
- Lines should have constant density.
- Lines should be drawn rapidly.
- Lines should start and terminate accurately.

We have lines with different slopes. Algorithms of lines vary with slope of lines as shown in Fig.4.4. We will consider lines in the first quadrant only with slope $0 < m \leq 1$ and $m > 1$.

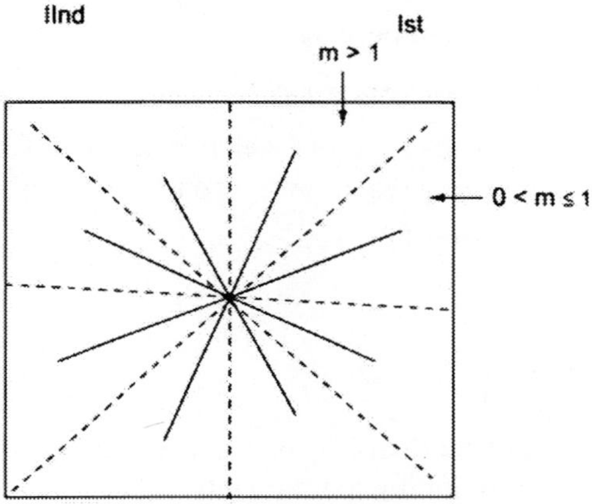

FIGURE 4.4 Lines in Four Quadrants

4.3.1 Digital Differential Analyzer (DDA)

This method is referred by this name because this method is very similar to the numerical differential equations. The DDA is a mechanical device that solves differential equations by numerical methods. There are two DDA techniques for straight-line, namely:

1. Simple DDA
2. Symmetrical DDA

4.3.1.1 Simple DDA for Straight Line

In this method, the x or y increment is set to 1 in the direction of x-axis or y-axis, as the case may be, depending upon the slope of line (if $m \leq 1$ increment is set to 1 in x otherwise increment is set to 1 in y). Then the increment in other direction (y or x) is calculated by the equation:

$$y = mx + b$$

Let us consider a straight line connecting from A(xs,ys) to $B(xe,ye)$ and the equation of the line as:

$$y = mx + b$$

where, m represents the slope of the line and b is the intercept made by the line on positive direction of y-axis. Then m can be expressed as:

$$m = \frac{ye - ys}{xe - xs}$$

Case I (m ≤ 1)

Two conjunctive points (x_i, y_i) and (x_{i+1}, y_{i+1}) lying on this line segment should satisfy the equation:

$$m = \frac{y_{i+1} - y_i}{x_{i+1} - x_i}$$

or,
$$m = \frac{\Delta y}{\Delta x}$$

or
$$\Delta y = \Delta x * m$$

If $\Delta x = 1$ i.e., $x_{i+1} = x_i + 1$ then $\Delta y = m$, which implies

$$y_{i+1} = y_i + m \quad \text{when } x_{i+1} = x_i + 1$$

Thus, a unit change in x along x-axis changes y by m which is constant for a given line.

Note that m being slope of line it may be a real number (positive or negative), so the calculated value of y must be rounded off to the nearest integer.

Case II (m>1)

$$m = \frac{\Delta y}{\Delta x}$$

It means increment in y will make it greater than 1 on unit increment in x, which is not desirable. In that case we reverse the role of x and y by sampling at unit y interval as:

$$\Delta y = 1$$

$$\frac{\Delta y}{\Delta x} = m$$

This implies,

$$\frac{1}{\Delta x} = m$$

or,
$$x_{i+1} = x_i + \frac{1}{m}$$

TABLE 4.1

$m \le 1$	X	xs	$xs + 1$	$xs + 2$	....	xe
	Y	ys	$ys + m$	$ys + 2m$	....	ye
$m > 1$	X	xs	$xs + \frac{1}{m}$	$xs + \frac{2}{m}$	....	xe
	Y	ys	$ys + 1$	$ys + 2$	....	ye

Algorithm 4.1 Plot of Straight Line with Simple DDA method

Input *xs, ys, xe, ye*

If (abs(*ye* – *ys*) > abs(*xe* – *xs*)) : Checks whether $m \le 1$ or $m > 1$

length = abs($ye - ys$)
else
length = abs($xe - xs$)
end if

$xinc = \dfrac{xe - xs}{\text{length}}$: Compute x increment $(m > 1)$

$yinc = \dfrac{ye - ys}{\text{length}}$: Compute y increment $(m \leq 1)$

$x = xs$:Initialize x, y pixel coordinates with xs, ys

$y = ys$

while ($x \leq xe$):Continue loop till **xend** and **yend** is reached

plotpixel(round(x), round (y)),1)

$x = x + xinc$

$y = y + yinc$

end while
stop

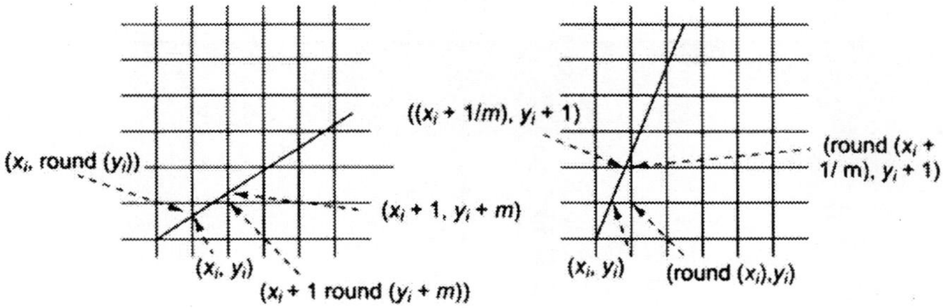

(a) $m < 1$ (b) $m >= 1$

FIGURE 4.5 Choosing Pixels in Simple DDA Method

Table 4.2 shows all possible cases to plot straight line in different quadrant with different slopes.

TABLE 4.2

Quadrant	$m \leq 1$	$m > 1$
First	$x = x + 1$ $y = y + m$	$x = x + \dfrac{1}{m}$ $y = y + 1$
Second	$x = x - 1$ $y = y + m$	$x = x - 1/m$ $y = y + 1$
Third	$x = x - 1$ $y = y - m$	$x = x - 1/m$ $y = y - 1$
Fourth	$x = x + 1$ $y = y - m$	$x = x + 1/m$ $y = y - 1$

Example 4.1

Plot straight line from (5,10) to (15,30) by Simple DDA method.

Solution

Slope of the line (m) = $(y2 - y1)/(x2 - x1)$ = 20/10 >1

Therefore, we implement the algorithm with y increment unit direction i.e., $y = y + 1$ and $x = x + 1/m$ [Table 4.1].

xinc= 1/m = 10/20 = 0.5

$$y = y + 1 \tag{4.1(a)}$$

$$x = x + 1/0.5 \tag{4.1(b)}$$

Results from equations 4.1(a) and 4.1(b) are listed in Table 4.3.

4.3.1.2 Symmetrical DDA Method for Straight Line

In this method instead of choosing increment with unit direction in one direction x or y, the increments in each direction are chosen at *small convenient values* to satisfy this relationship. *Small convenient value should not exceed 0.5 the pixel dimension.* For this binary arithmetic is used as follows:

TABLE 4.3 Points on Straight Line

Point	*xcal*	*ycal*	*xplot= round(xcal)*	*yplot = round(ycal)*
1	5.0	10	5	10
2	5.5	11	6	11
3	6.0	12	6	12
4	6.5	13	7	13
5	7.0	14	7	14
6	7.5	15	8	15
7	8.0	16	8	16
8	8.5	17	9	17
9	9.0	18	9	18
10	9.5	19	10	19
11	10.0	20	10	20
12	10.5	21	11	21
13	11.0	22	11	22
14	11.5	23	12	23
15	12.0	24	12	24
16	12.5	25	13	25
17	13.0	26	13	26
18	13.5	27	14	27
19	14.0	28	14	28
20	14.5	29	15	29
21	15.0	30	15	30

Figure 4.6 depicts the pixels for the line from the Table 4.3.

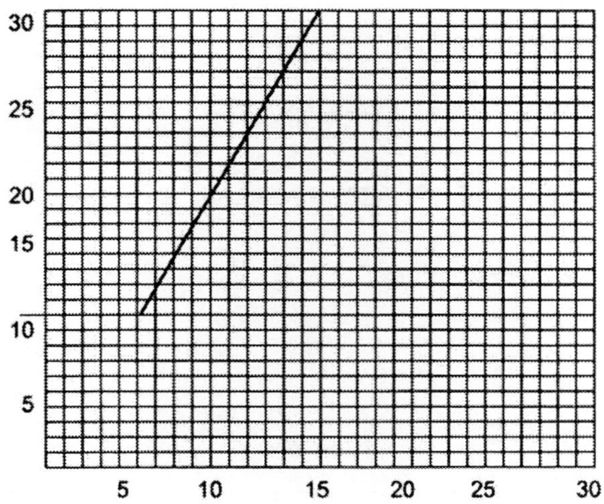

FIGURE 4.6 Plot of Straight Line by Simple DDA Method

Step (a) Find the smallest integer value n such that:

$$2^n \geq \text{largest of abs } (ye - ys) \text{ OR abs } (xe - xs)$$

or,
$$n \geq \log_2 (\text{length})$$

where,
$$\text{length} = \text{largest of abs } (ye - ys) \text{ OR abs } (xe - xs)$$

or,
$$n \geq \frac{\log(\text{length})}{\log 2} \quad \text{since} \quad \log_n m = \frac{\log m}{\log n}$$

Step (b) Set the increment factor

$$xinc = \frac{xe - xs}{2^n}$$

$$yinc = \frac{ye - ys}{2^n}$$

Algorithm 4.2 Plot of Straight Line with Symmetrical DDA method

Input xs, ys, xe, ye

If (abs ($ye - ys$) > abs ($xe - xs$)) : Checks whether $m \leq 1$ or $m > 1$

length = abs ($ye - ys$)

else

length = abs ($xe - xs$)

end if

$$n = \frac{\log(\text{length})}{\log 2}$$

$xinc = \dfrac{xe - xs}{2^n}$: Compute x increment

$yinc = \frac{ye-ys}{2^n}$: Compute y increment

$x = xs$: Initialize x, y pixel coordinates with xs, ys

$y = ys$

while ($x \le xe$) :Continue loop till **xend** and **yend** is reached

plotpixel(round(x),round(y))

$$x = x + \text{xinc}$$

$$y = y + \text{yinc}$$

end while

stop

TABLE 4.4

x	xs	xs + $x$inc	xs + 2$x$inc	xe
y	ys	ys + $y$inc	ys + 2$y$inc...............	ye

Where

$$\text{xinc} = \frac{xe-xs}{2^n} \quad \text{and} \quad \text{yinc} = \frac{ye-ys}{2^n}$$

Example 4.2

Plot straight line from (5,10) to (15,30) by Symmetrical DDA method.

Solution

$$\text{length } x = xe - xs = 15 - 5 = 10$$

$$\text{length } y = ys - ye = 30 - 10 = 20$$

$$\text{Larger value (length)} = 20$$

$$n = \frac{\log(\text{length})}{\log 2} = \frac{\log(20)}{\log 2} = 4.321928$$

Take $n = 5$

$$\text{xinc} = \frac{xe-xs}{2^n} = 0.3125$$

$$\text{yinc} = \frac{ye-ys}{2^n} = 0.625$$

$$x = xs$$

$$y = ys$$

$$x = x + \text{xinc} \quad \text{......} \quad 4.2(a)$$

$$y = y + \text{yinc} \quad \text{......} \quad 4.2(b)$$

Results from equations 4.2(a) and 4.2(b) are listed in table 4.5.

TABLE 4.5 Points on Straight Line by Symmetrical Method

Point	*Xcal*	*ycal*	*xplot = round(xcal)*	*Yplot = round(xcal)*
1	5	10	5	10
2	5.3125	10.625	5	11
3	5.625	11.25	6	11
4	5.9375	11.875	6	12
5	6.25	12.5	6	13
6	6.5625	13.125	7	13
7	6.875	13.75	7	14
8	7.1875	14.375	7	14
9	7.5	15	8	15
10	7.8125	15.625	8	16
11	8.125	16.25	8	16
12	8.4375	16.875	8	17
13	8.75	17.5	9	18
14	9.0625	18.125	9	18
15	9.375	18.75	9	19
16	9.6875	19.375	10	19
17	10	20	10	20
18	10.3125	20.625	10	21
19	10.625	21.25	11	21
20	10.9375	21.875	11	22
21	11.25	22.5	11	23
22	11.5625	23.125	12	23
23	11.875	23.75	12	24
24	12.1875	24.375	12	24
25	12.5	25	12	25
26	12.8125	25.625	13	26
27	13.125	26.25	13	26
28	13.4375	26.875	13	27
29	13.75	27.5	14	28
30	14.0625	28.125	14	28
31	14.375	28.75	14	29
32	14.6875	29.375	15	29
33	15	30	15	30

Figure 4.7 depicts the pixels for the line from the Table 4.5.

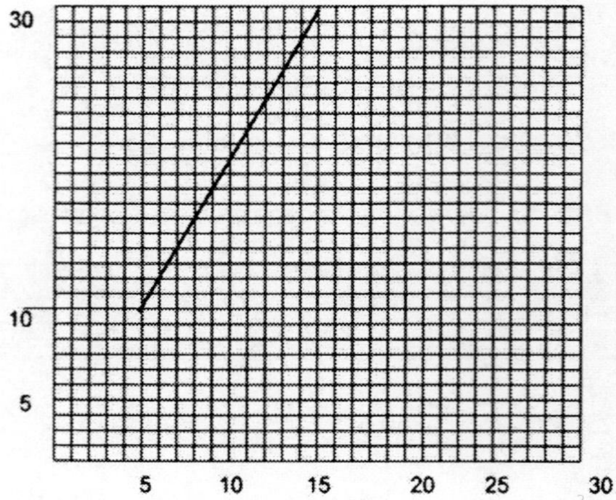

FIGURE 4.7 Plot Straight Line by Symmetrical DDA Method

4.3.2 Bresenham's Algorithm for Straight Line

One serious drawback of DDA algorithm is that it is very time-consuming as it deals with a rounding operation and floating point arithmetic. It would take too much time and too much memory space. On the other side integer computations are much faster and take much less memory space. With this motivation, in 1965 Jack Bresenham introduced simple scan conversion straight line technique.

This algorithm is more accurate and efficient because it scans lines using only incremental integer and avoids the use of round function and floating point arithmetic.

Working of the algorithm

In this algorithm, the x or y increment is set to 1 in the direction of x-axis or y-axis respectively depending upon the slope of line ($m \leq 1$ increment is set to 1 in x otherwise increment is set to 1 in y) and the increment in other direction (y or x) is calculated by selecting the closest pixel from the true line at each position of x or y based upon the value of decision variable, as shown in Fig. 4.8.

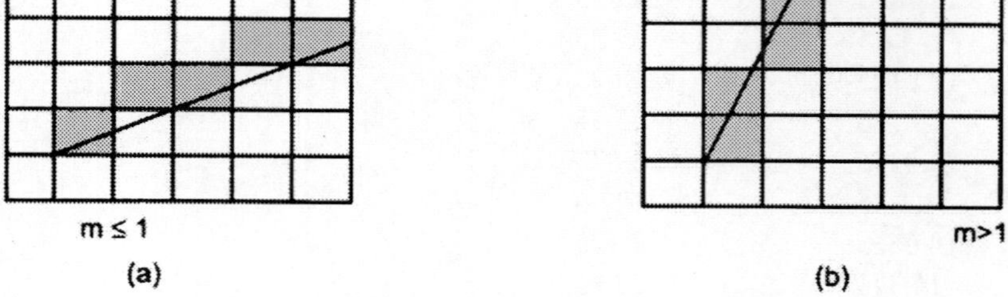

FIGURE 4.8 Line is Plotted using Bresenham's Method

Case I (Slope lies between 0° to 45°;m ≤ 1)

$$\text{Slope of line } m = \frac{y}{x}$$

or, $y = m*x$

this implies $y \leq 1$ iff $x = 1$ and $m \leq 1$

Which further implies that line is sampled at unit interval in x-direction.

Now we require some criteria to decide which pixel to plot at next sampling position i.e., at $x_s + 1$ grid line. From fig. 4.9 we have two choices at sampling position, pixels at $U(x_s + 1, y_s + 1)$ and $L(x_s + 1, y_s)$. Let $M(x_s + 1, y')$ be the point of intersection of the true line with grid line $xs + 1$.

According to Bresenham principle, the difference between the vertical distance(du) of U to M and distance(dl) of L to M and is computed and sign of the difference is used to select the upper or lower pixel.

d = Distance of L from M(dl) - Distance of U from M(du)

$$\text{Value of d}\begin{cases} <0 & dl < du \text{ select lower pixel(L)} \\ >0 & dl > du \text{ select upper pixel(U)} \\ =0 & dl = du \text{ hence, we can select either lower pixel (L) or upper pixel(U)} \end{cases}$$

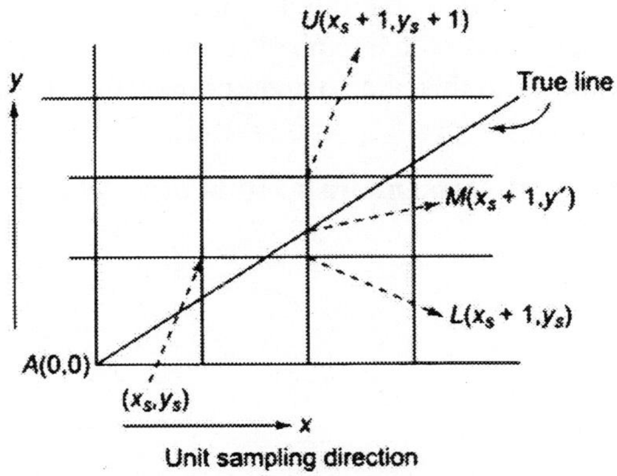

FIGURE 4.9 Choosing Pixels in Bresenham's Line Algorithm

$$\begin{aligned} d &= dl - du \\ &= (y' - y_s) - ((y_s + 1) - y') \\ &= 2y' - 2y_s - 1 \\ &= 2((x_s+1)\, m + b) - 2y_s - 1 \end{aligned} \tag{4.3}$$

(i) Initial value of d

Since, $y_s - mx_s - b = 0$ and $m = \Delta y/\Delta x$, then we have initial value of d

$$d = 2\Delta y - \Delta x \qquad \text{[From 4.3]}$$

(ii) Selection of Point and Updation of Decision Variable

Substituting $m = \Delta y/\Delta x$ and using a new variable d_i, which has same sign as $(dl - du)$, since Δx is positive always, we have

$$d_i = 2\Delta y^*x_i - 2\Delta x^*y_i + C, \text{ where } C = 2\Delta y - 2\Delta x(2b-1)$$

Similarly, we can write the decision variable d_{i+1} for the next step as

$$d_{i+1} = 2\Delta y^* x_{i+1} - 2\Delta x^* y_{i+1} + C$$

Then,

$$d_{i+1} - d_i = 2\Delta y(x_{i+1}) - x_i) - \Delta x(y_{i+1} - y_i) \qquad (4.4)$$

Since, $x_{i+1} = x_i + 1$, we have

$$d_{i+1} = d_i + 2\Delta y - 2\Delta x(y_{i+1} - y_i)$$

If the chosen pixel is the upper pixel U ($d_i \geq 0$) then $y_{i+1} = y_i + 1$ and so

$$d_{i+1} = d_i + 2(\Delta y - \Delta x) \qquad \text{(From 4.4)}$$

On the other hand, if the chosen pixel is the lower pixel $L(d_i < 0)$, then $y_{i+1} = y_i$ and so

$$d_{i+1} = d_i + 2\Delta y \qquad \text{(From 4.4)}$$

Hence, we have

$$d_{i+1} = \begin{cases} d_i \; + 2(\Delta y - \Delta x) \text{ if } d_i \geq 0 \\ d_i \; + 2\Delta y \qquad \text{if } d_i < 0 \end{cases}$$

This process is continued till the endpoint of the line is reached.

Thus, we see that algorithm chosen between two pixels is based on the sign of the decision parameter calculated in the previous iteration. With this, it also updates the value of decision parameter simply by incrementing the old value by a factor depending upon the choice of the pixel.

Algorithm 4.3 Plot straight line with Bresenham's Method(m ≤ 1)

```
Input xs, ys, xe, ye
dy = ye – ys
dx = xe – xs
incl = 2*dy
inc2 = 2*(dy – dx)
d = incl – dx
if(dx < 0)
            x = xe
            y = ye
         xend = xs
else
            x = xs
            y = ys
         xend = xe
endif
while (x < = xend)
plotpixel (x, y)
if (d ≥ 0) then
            y = y +1   /*upper pixel
            d = d + inc2
```

else

$d = d + \text{inc1}$ /* lower pixel

end if
$x = x + 1$
end while
stop

Case II

When magnitude of the slope is greater than 1 (line lies between 45° to 90°; m > 1)

In this algorithm we step along y direction (instead of x) in unit steps and calculate the successive value of x using the Bresenham's Principle (closest pixel), as shown in Fig. 4.10.

Slope m > 1

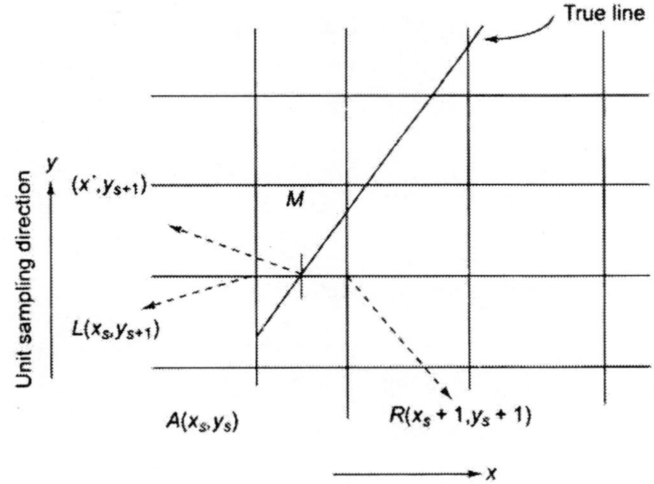

FIGURE 4.10 Choosing Pixels in Bresenham's Line Algorithm(m>1)

Algorithm 4.4 Plot straight line with Bresenham's Method(m > 1)

Input xs, ys, xe, ye
$dy = xe - xs$
$dx = ye - ys$
$\text{inc1} = 2*dy$
$\text{inc2} = 2*(dy - dx)$
$d = \text{inc1} - dx$
$x = xs$
$y = ys$
if($dx < 0$)

$x = xe$
$y = ye$
$\text{xend} = xs$

```
else
                x = xs
                y = ys
             xend = xe
endif
while (x ≤ x end)
plotpixel (x, y)
if(d ≥ 0) then
                x = x +1    /* Select Right pixel
                d = d + inc2
else
                d = d + inc1    /* Select Left pixel
endif
y = y + 1
end while
stop
```

Example 4.3

Plot a line from (1,1) to (8,5) using Bresenham's Method.

Solution

$$dx = xe - xs = 8 - 1 = 7$$

$$dy = ye - ys = 5 - 1 = 4$$

Slope of the line $(m) = dy/dx = 4/8 = 1/2 < 1$

$$\text{inc1} = 2*dy = 8$$

$$\text{inc2} = 2*(dy - dx) = -6$$

$$d = \text{inc1} - dx = 8 - 7 = 1$$

TABLE 4.6 Point on Straight Line by Bresenham's Method

Point	*X*	*Y*	*d*
1	1	1	
2	2	2	1 + inc2 = –5
3	3	2	–5 + inc1 = 3
4	4	3	3 + inc2 = –3
5	5	3	–3 + inc1 = 5
6	6	4	5 + inc2 = –1
7	7	4	–1 + inc1 = 7
8	8	5	7 + inc2 = 1

Figure 4.11 depicts the pixels for the line from the Table 4.6.

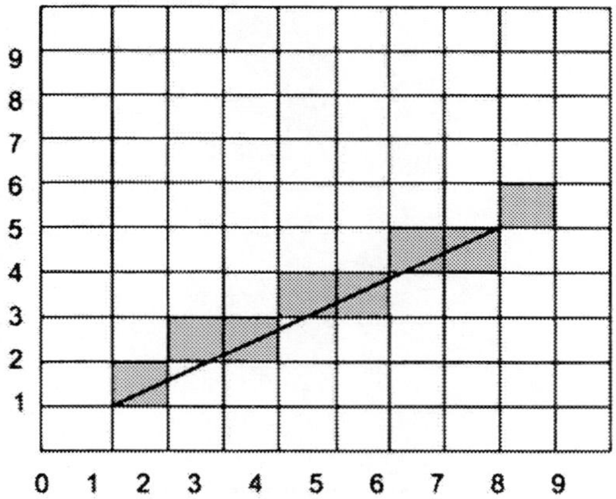

FIGURE 4.11 Plot Straight Line by Bresenham's Method ($m \leq 1$)

Example 4.4

Plot a line from (0,0) to (6,10) using Bresenham's Method.

Solution

Slope of line (m) = $\dfrac{10-0}{6-0} = 10/6 > 1$

Therefore, take $dx = ye - ys = 10 - 0 = 10$

and,
$$dy = xe - xs = 6 - 0 = 6$$
$$\text{inc1} = 2{*}dy = 12$$
$$\text{inc2} = 2{*}(dy - dx) = -8$$
$$d = \text{inc1} - dx = 12 - 10 = 2$$

TABLE 4.7 Point on Straight Line by Bresenham's Method

Point	*X*	*Y*	*d*
1	0	0	
2	1	1	2 − 8 = − 6
3	1	2	− 6 + 12 = 6
4	2	3	6 − 8 = − 2
5	2	4	− 2 + 12 = 10
6	3	5	10 − 8 = 2
7	4	6	2 − 8 = −6
8	4	7	− 6 + 12 = 6
9	5	8	6 − 8 = − 2
10	5	9	− 2 + 12 = 10
11	6	10	

Figure 4.12 depicts the pixels for the line from the Table 4.7.

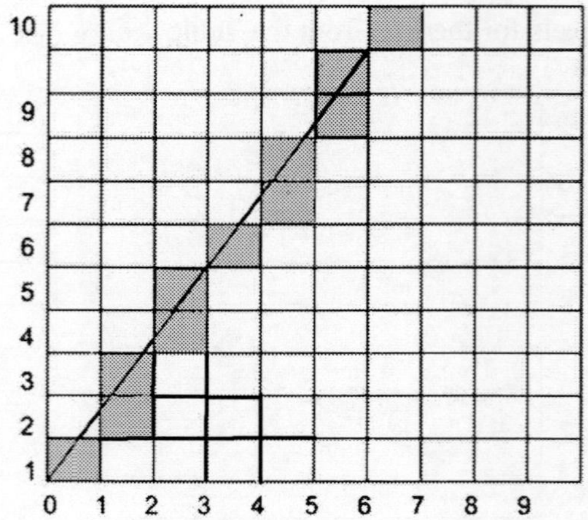

FIGURE 4.12 Plot Straight Line by Bresenham's Method(m>1)

Case III When negative slopes

The procedure is similar except that one coordinate decreases and other increases from start to end-point of such lines, as shown in Fig. 4.13.

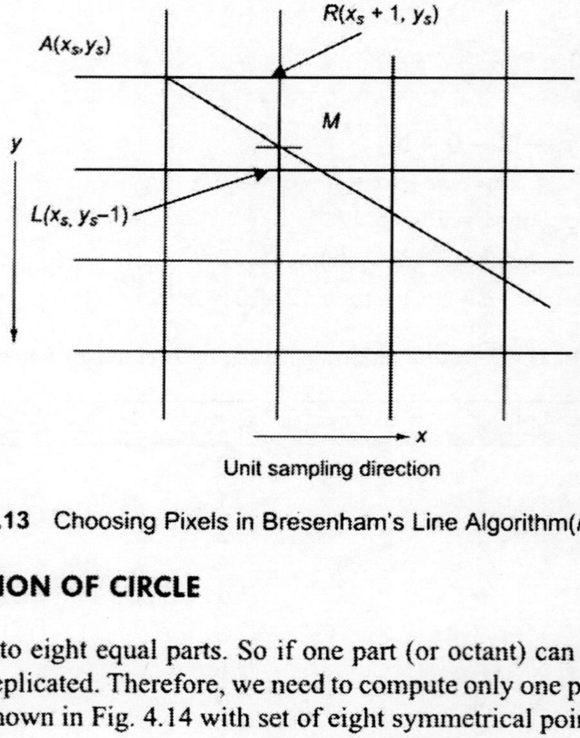

FIGURE 4.13 Choosing Pixels in Bresenham's Line Algorithm(*m* is -ve)

4.4 SCAN CONVERSION OF CIRCLE

A circle can be divided into eight equal parts. So if one part (or octant) can be generated then other seven parts can be easily replicated. Therefore, we need to compute only one part (octant) to determine the circle completely, as shown in Fig. 4.14 with set of eight symmetrical points.

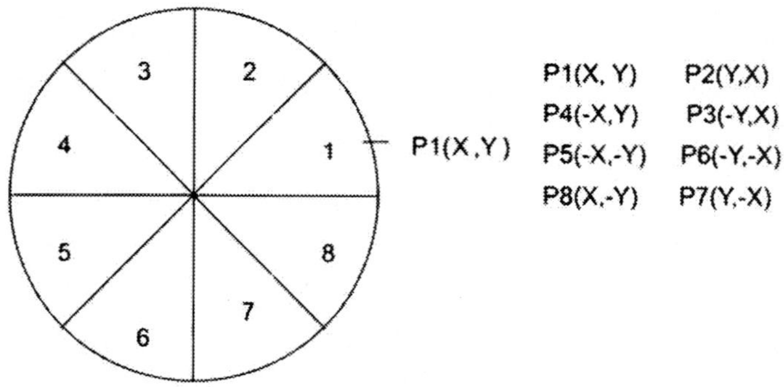

FIGURE 4.14 Eight-way Symmetry of Circle

4.4.1 Digital Differentials Analyzer (DDA)

There are two DDA techniques for scan conversion of circle, namely:

1. Direct or Polynomial Approach
2. Parametric or Trigonometric Approach

4.4.1.1 Direct or Polynomial Approach

A circle can be represented as second degree polynomial equation :

$$(x - h)^2 + (y - k)^2 = r^2 \tag{4.5}$$

Where, (h,k) centre of circle
r radius of circle

The equation (4.5) can be simplified as:

$$y = k \pm \sqrt{r^2 - (x-h)^2}$$

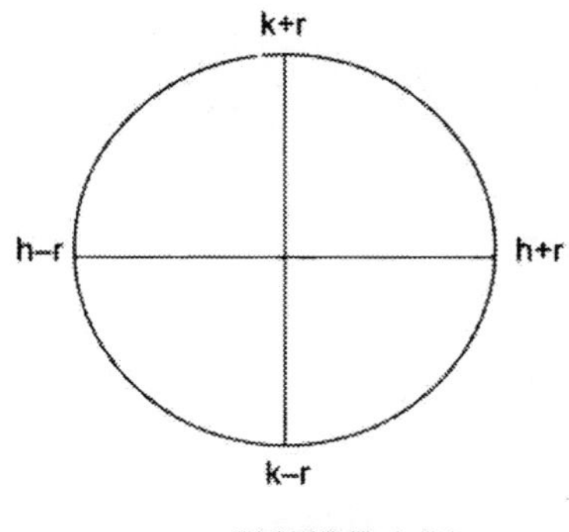

FIGURE 4.15

To draw a circle, value of x is incremented in units of 1 from $h - r$ to $h + r$. The equation (4.5) is used to solve the value of y. This method is time-consuming since multiplications and square-root operations are involved at each step. However, we can improve the process by taking advantage of symmetry in a circle. Therefore, we need to compute only second octant to determine the circle completely, as shown in Fig. 4.14. With this method plots are generated from 90° to 45°, each x coordinate in the sector 90° to 45°, is found by incremented x by 1 from 0 to $r/\sqrt{2}$ and each value of y is found by evaluating $\sqrt{r^*r-x^*x}$.

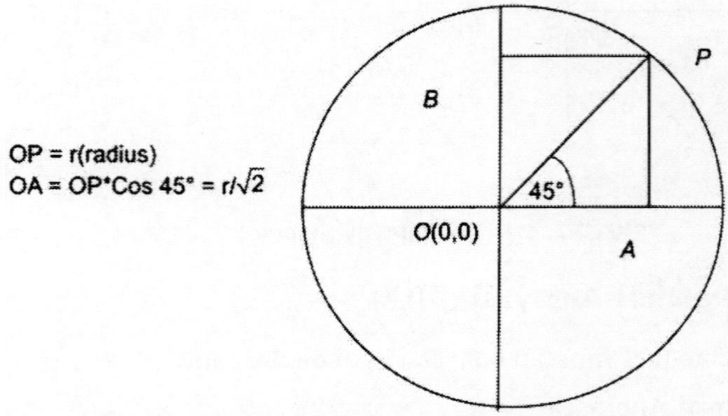

FIGURE 4.16 Circle with Polynomial Approach

Algorithm 4.5 Plot Circle with Polynomial Approach

Input (h,k) , r (h,k) : Centre of circle
r : Radius of Circle

$x = 0$

$y = r$

xend $= \dfrac{r}{1.414}$

while ($x \le$ xend)

y = square root of $(r^*r - x^*x)$

plotpixel $(x + h, y + k)$ /* Plot eight points; each point
plotpixel $(-x + h, y + k)$ corresponding to one octant.
plotpixel $(x + h, -y + k)$
plotpixel $(-x + h, -y + k)$
plotpixel $(y + h, x + k)$
plotpixel $(-y + h, x + k)$
plotpixel $(y + h, -x + k)$
plotpixel $(-y + h, -x + k)$

$x = x + 1$

end while
stop

4.4.1.2 *Parametric or Trigonometric Approach*

Parametric polar representation of a circle is

$$x = h + r\cos(\theta) \tag{4.6}$$

$$y = k + r\sin(\theta) \tag{4.7}$$

where, (h, k) centre of the circle, r the radius and θ is measured in radian 0 to 2π.

In this method value of θ is incremented from 0 to 2π; then values of x and y are calculated from equations (4.6) and (4.7), respectively. This method is time- consuming since multiplications and trigonometric functions are involved at each step. We can improve the process by taking the advantage of symmetry in a circle.

As arc length(s) are proportional to θ i.e.,

$$\text{Arc}(s) = r*\theta.$$

Fixed increment of θ i.e., $\Delta\theta$ results in equal spacing Δs between successively plotted points.

Let us assume $\Delta s = 1$, i.e.,

$$\Delta s = 1$$

or,

$$r*\Delta\theta = 1$$

$$\Delta\theta = 1/r$$

Therefore, we need to compute only first octant to determine the circle completely, as shown in Fig.4.17. With this method, plots are generated from 0° to 45°. Each x coordinate in the first octant is found by incremented thetainc by $1/r$ from 0° to 45° and each value of x and y is found by evaluating from equations (4.6) and (4.7), respectively.

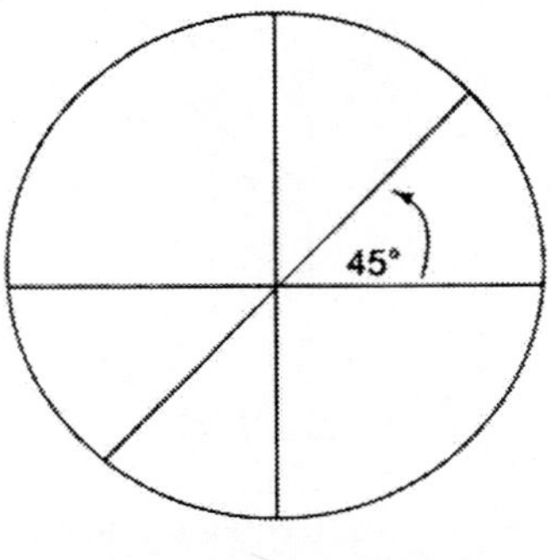

FIGURE 4.17 Circle with Trigonometric Approach

Algorithm 4.6 Plot of Circle with Trigonometric Approach

Input (h,k) , r (h,k) : Centre of circle

r : Radius of circle

$$\text{temp} = \frac{3.141}{180}$$

$$\text{thetainc} = \frac{1}{r}$$

theta = 0

```
thetaend = 45
while (theta < = thetaend)
                        angle = temp*theta
                            x = r*cos(angle)
                            y = r*sin(angle)
            plotpixel (x + h,y + k)    /*Plot eight points-each point
            plotpixel (– x + h, y + k)   corresponding to one octant
            plotpixel (x + h, –y + k)
            plotpixel (– x + h,– y + k)
            plotpixel (y + h, x + k)
            plotpixel (– y + h, x + k)
            plotpixel (y + h,– x + k)
            plotpixel (– y + h, –x + k)
            theta = theta + thetainc
end while
stop
```

Note : This method is very useful to draw an arc with starting angle thetastart (θ_1) to thetaend (θ_2) in figure 4.18.

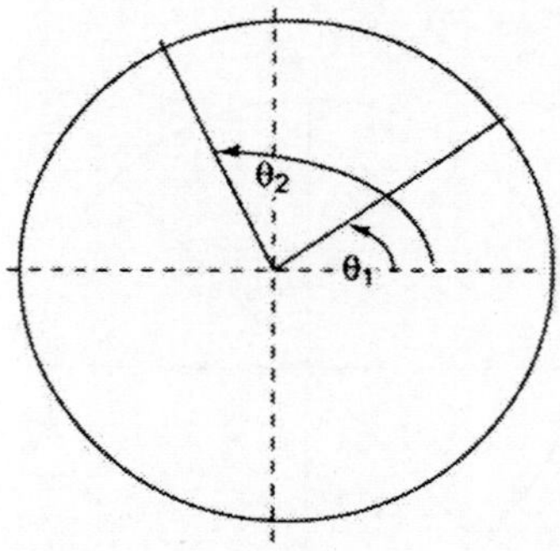

FIGURE 4.18 Arc with Trigonometric Approach

4.4.2 Bresenham's Algorithm

In 1977, Jack Bresenham applied the principle used to plot a straight line, to develop the circle. No doubt this algorithm can also be applied to the entire circle, but for simplicity and to avoid the time of calculation, points of the other seven octants can be found by symmetry. This method is more accurate and efficient than above two methods (polynomial and parametric methds) because it can convert circle using only incremental integer and avoids the use of trigonometric and square root calculation.

"The best approximation of true circle will be described by those pixels in the raster that fall the least distance from the true circle".

Points are generating from 90° to 45°, moves will be made from increment in x and decrease in y, as shown in Fig 4.19.

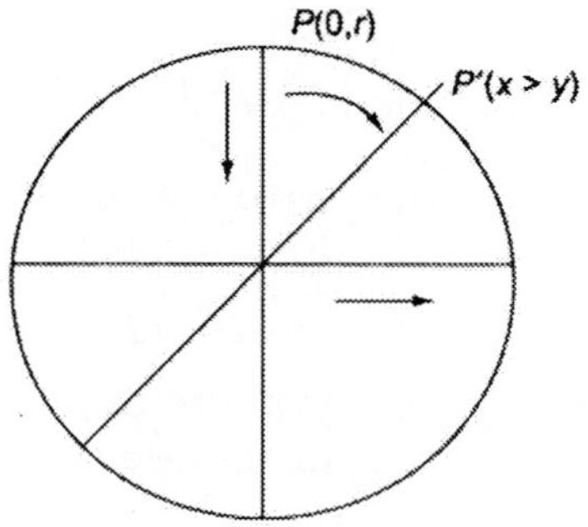

FIGURE 4.19 Circle with Bresenham's Method

Working of the Algorithm

For simplicity we will analyse the algorithm for a circle with centre at O (0,0). Scan converting a circle using Bresenham's method works as follows:

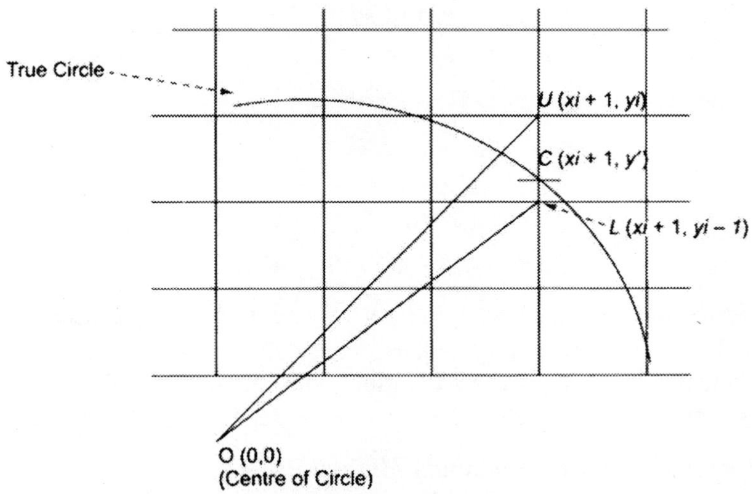

FIGURE 4.20 Choosing Pixels with Bresenham's Method

$$du = (\text{Distance from the origin to pixel U})^2 - (\text{ radius of circle})^2$$

$$dl = (\text{radius of circle})^2 - (\text{Distance from the origin to pixel L})^2$$

du will always be positive, since it lies outside the circle and *dl* will always be negative since it lies inside the circle. Therefore,

$$d = du - (+dl) = du - dl$$

$$\text{Value of } d \begin{cases} < 0 & dl > du \quad \text{select} \quad \text{upper pixel(U)} \\ > 0 & dl < du \quad \text{select} \quad \text{lower pixel(L)} \\ = 0 & dl = du \quad \text{hence we can select either lower} \\ & \qquad\qquad \text{pixel (L) or upper pixel(U)} \end{cases}$$

Therefore,

$$d_i = 2(x_i + 1)^2 + y^2_i + (y_i - 1)^2 - 2r^2$$

(i) Initial value of d

We set (0, r) to be the starting pixel coordinates and computes the initial value of d from the original definition of d_i:

$$d = 2(0+1)^2 + r^2 + (r-1)^2 - 2r^2 = \mathbf{3 - 2r}$$

(ii) Selection of Point and Updation of decision parameter

We can also write the decision variable d_{i+1} for the next step:

$$d_{i+1} = (2x_{i+1} + 1)^2 + y^2_{i+1} + (y_{i+1} - 1)^2 - 2r^2$$

Hence,

$$d_{i+1} - d_i = 2(x_{i+1} + 1)^2 + y^2_{i+1} + (y_{i+1} - 1)^2 - 2(x_i+1)^2 - y^2_i - (y_i - 1)^2$$

Since, $x_{i+1} = x_i+1$, we have

$$d_{i+1} = d_i + 4x_i + 2(y^2_{i+1} - y^2_i) - 2(y_{i+1} - y_i) + 6 \quad (4.8)$$

If U is the chosen pixel ($d_i < 0$), then $y_{i+1} = y_i$ and so

$$\mathbf{d_{i+1} = d_i + 4x_i + 6} \quad \text{(From 4.8)}$$

If L is the chosen pixel ($d_i \geq 0$) then $y_{i+1} = y_i - 1$ and so

$$\mathbf{d_{i+1} = d_i + 4(x_i - y_i) + 10} \quad \text{(From 4.8)}$$

Hence, we have

$$d_{i+1} = \begin{cases} d_i + 4x_i + 6 & \text{if } d_i < 0 \\ d_i + 4(x_i - y_i) + 10 & \text{if } d_i \geq 0 \end{cases}$$

This process is continued till the end point(P' in fig 4.15 where $x > y$) of the second octant is reached.

Thus, we see that algorithm chooses intermediate pixels between two pixels based on the sign of the decision parameter calculated in the previous iteration; with this it also updates the value of decision parameter simply by incrementing the old value by a factor depending upon the choice of the pixel.

Algorithm 4.7 Plot of circle with Bresenham's Method

Input (*h*,*k*) and *r* where (*h*,*k*): centre of circle
r : radius of circle

```
x = 0
y = r
d = 3–2*r
while(x ≤ y)
   plotpixel (x + h,y + k)        /* Plot eight points; each point
   plotpixel (– x + h,y + k)      corresponding to one octant
   plotpixel (x + h,–y + k)
   plotpixel (– x + h,– y + k)
   plotpixel (y + h,x + k)
   plotpixel (–y + h, x + k)
   plotpixel (y + h,–x + k)
   plotpixel (–y + h,– x + k)
```

```
if(d < 0) then
            d = d + 4*x + 6            /* upper pixel
else
            d = d + 4*(x – y) + 10     /* lower pixel
            y = y – 1
end if
x = x + 1
end while
stop
```

Example 4.5

Find out the pixel location approximating the second octant of circle having centre at O(0,0) and radius 8.

Solution

$$x = 0, y = r = 8$$

$$d = 3 - 2*r = 3 - 2*8 = -13$$

TABLE 4.8 Points on Second Octant of Circle by Bresenham's Method

Point	*x*	*y*	d_{i+1}
1	0	8	
2	1	8	– 13 + 4x + 6 = –7
3	2	8	– 7 + 4x + 6 = 3
4	3	7	3 + 4 (x – y) + 10 = –11
5	4	7	– 11 + 4x + 6 = 7
6	5	6	7 + 4 (x – y) + 10 = 5
7	6	5	

Figure 4.21 depicts the pixels for the circle from the Table 4.8.

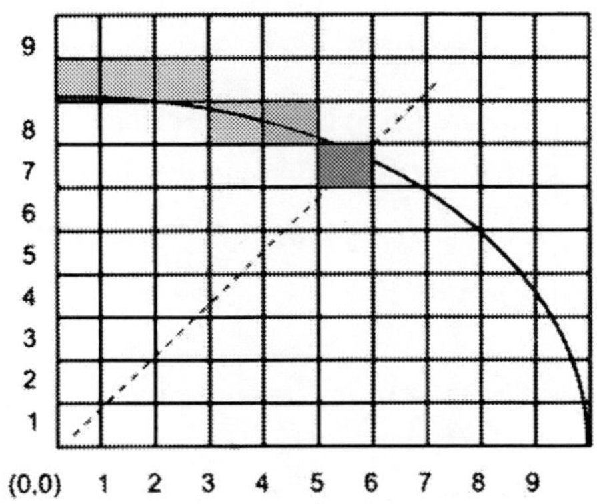

FIGURE 4.21 Plot Second Octant of Circle with Bresenham's Method

4.4.3 Mid-point Circle Algorithm

Likewise Bresenham' algorithm this algorithm is better than above two methods (Polynomial and Parametric method) because it avoids trigonometric and square root calculation by adopting only integer operation. This algorithm can also be applied to the entire circle, but for simplicity and to avoid the time of calculation, points of the other seven octants can be found by symmetry.

We consider only second octant of the circle from $x = 0$ to $x \leq y$ and use the concept eight-way symmetry to plot the entire circle as in this algorithm to select which of the 2 pixels ($U(x_i+1, y_i)$, $L(x_i + 1, y_i - 1)$) is closer to the true circle by evaluating the mid-point between the two pixels. In the second octant if pixel $Pi(x_i, y_i)$ is the previous plotted pixel choice of next pixel between $U(x_{i+1}, y_i)$ and $L(x_{i+1}, y_{i-1})$. $M(x_{i+1}, (y_i + y_{i-1})/2)$ is mid-point of L and U.

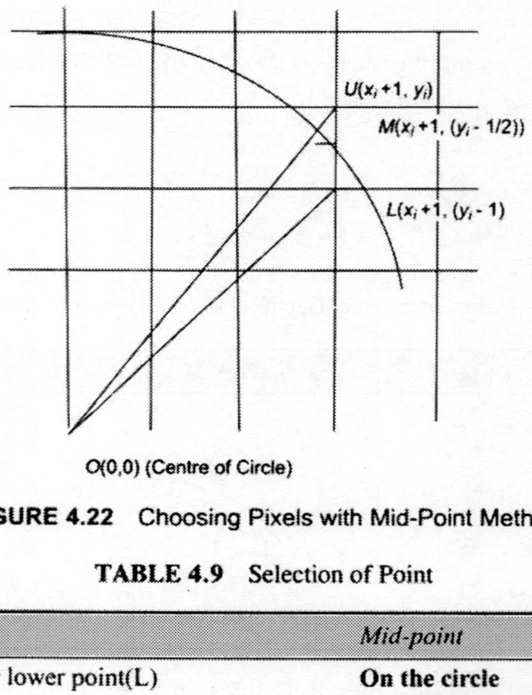

FIGURE 4.22 Choosing Pixels with Mid-Point Method

TABLE 4.9 Selection of Point

Select	*Mid-point*
Either upper point(U) or lower point(L)	**On the circle**
Upper point(U)	**Outside the circle**
Lower point(L)	**Inside the circle**

$$F(x,y) = x^2 + y^2 - r^2 \begin{cases} 0 \text{ point } (x, y) \text{ lies on the circle} \\ > 0 \text{ point } (x, y) \text{ lies outside the circle} \\ < 0 \text{ point } (x, y) \text{ lies inside the circle} \end{cases}$$

(i) Initial value of *d*

We consider only second octant of the circle, starting pixel lies on $(0, r)$.

The next mid-point lies on $(1, r-1/2)$, therefore,

$$d = F(1, r-1/2) = 1^2 * (r-1/2)^2 - r^2 = \mathbf{5/4 - r}$$

Now consider the coordinates of the point halfway between lower pixel L and upper pixel U in Fig. 4.18. $M(x_i + 1, y_i - ½)$. We use it to define a decision parameter:

$$d_i = f\left(x_i + 1, y_i - \frac{1}{2}\right) = (x_i + 1)^2 + \left(y_i - \frac{1}{2}\right)^2 - r^2$$

If *di* is negative, the mid-point is inside the circle, and we choose pixel L. On the other hand, if *di* is positive (or equal to zero), the midpoint is outside the circle (or on the circle), and we choose pixel U. Similarly, the decision parameter for the next step is:

$$d_{i+1} = (x_{i+1} + 1)^2 + \left(y_{i+1} - \frac{1}{2}\right)^2 - r^2$$

Since, $x_{i+1} = x_i + 1$, we have

$$d_{i+1} - d_i = [(x_{i+1}) + 1]^2 - (x_i + 1)^2 + \left(y_{i+1} - \frac{1}{2}\right)^2 \left(y_i - \frac{1}{2}\right)^2$$

Hence,

$$d_{i+1} = d_i + 2(x_i + 1) + 1 + (y^2_{i+1} - y^2_i) - (y_{i+1} - y_i)$$

If pixel L is chosen ($d_i < 0$), we have $y_{i+1} = y_i$. On the other hand, if pixel U is chosen ($d_i \geq 0$), we have $y_{i+1} = y_i - 1$. Thus,

$$d_{i+1} = \begin{cases} d_i + 2(x_i + 1) + 1 & \text{if } d_i < 0 \\ d_i + 2(x_i - 1) + 1 - 2(y_i - 1) & \text{if } d_i \geq 0 \end{cases}$$

We can continue to simplify this in terms of (x_i, y_i) and get

$$d_{i+1} = \begin{cases} d_i + 2x_i + 3 & \text{if } d_i < 0 \\ d_i + 2(x_i - y_i) + 5 & \text{if } d_i \geq 0 \end{cases}$$

Or,
we can write it in terms of (x_{i+1}, y_{i+1}) and have

$$d_{i+1} = \begin{cases} d_i + 2x_{i+1} + 1 & \text{if } d_i > 0 \\ d_i + 2(x_{i+1} - y_{i+1}) + 1 & \text{if } d_i \geq 0 \end{cases}$$

One can see that this is not really integer computation. However, when r is an integer we can simply set $d = 1 - r$. The error of being ¼ less than the precise value does not prevent d from getting the appropriate sign. It does not affect the rest of the scan-conversion process either, because the decision variable is only updated with integer increments in subsequent steps.

Algorithm 4.7 Plot of circle with Mid-point Method
Input (h,k) and r where (h,k): centre of circle
r : radius of circle

$x = 0$

$y = r$

$d = 1 - r$

```
while (x ≤ y)
    plotpixel (x + h, y + k)          /* Plot eight points—each point
    plotpixel (– x + h,y + k)         corresponding to one octant
    plotpixel (x + h, – y + k)
    plotpixel (– x + h, – y + k)
    plotpixel (y + h, x + k)
    plotpixel (– y + h,x + k)
    plotpixel (y + h, – x + k)
    plotpixel (– y + h, – x + k)
If(d < 0), then
                    d = d + 2*x + 3        /* upper pixel
else
                    d = d + 2*(x – y)+5    /* lower pixel
                    y = y – 1
end if
x = x + 1
end while
stop
```

4.5 ELLIPSE

An ellipse can be divided into four equal parts. So if one part (or quadrant) can be generated then other three parts can be easily replicated. Therefore, we need to compute only one part (or quadrant) to determine the ellipse completely, as shown in Fig. 4.23 with set of four symmetrical points.

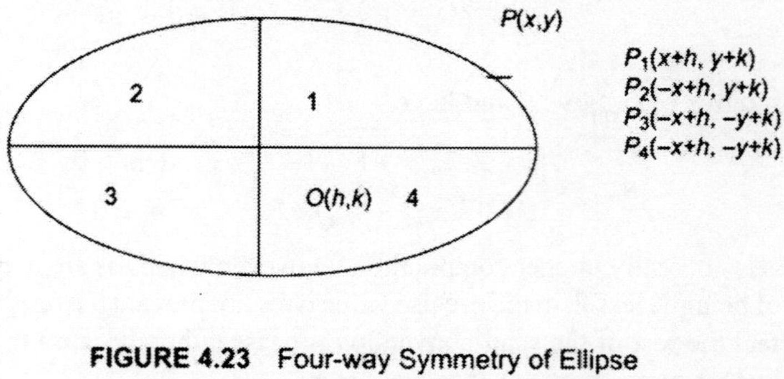

FIGURE 4.23 Four-way Symmetry of Ellipse

4.5.1 Digital Digitizer Analyzer (DDA)

There are two DDA techniques for scan conversion of ellipse, namely:

1. Direct or Polynomial Approach
2. Parametric or Trigonometric Approach

4.5.1.1 *Direct or Polynomial Approach*

An ellipse can be represented as second degree polynomial equation

$$\frac{(x-h)^2}{a^2} + \frac{(y-k)^2}{b^2} = 1 \tag{4.9}$$

The equation (4.9) can be simplified as:

$$y = k \pm b\sqrt{1 - \frac{(x-h)^2}{b^2}}$$

To draw an ellipse value of x is incremented in units of 1 from $h-a$ to $h+a$, the equation 4.9 is used to solve the value of y. This method is time-consuming, since multiplications and square-root operations are involved at each step. However, we can improve the process by taking advantage of symmetry in an ellipse. Therefore, we need to compute only first quadrant to determine the ellipse completely, as shown in Fig. 4.23. With this method plots are generated from 0° to 45°, each x coordinate is incremented by 1 from 0 to a and each value of y is found by evaluating $b\sqrt{1 - \frac{x*x}{a*a}}$.

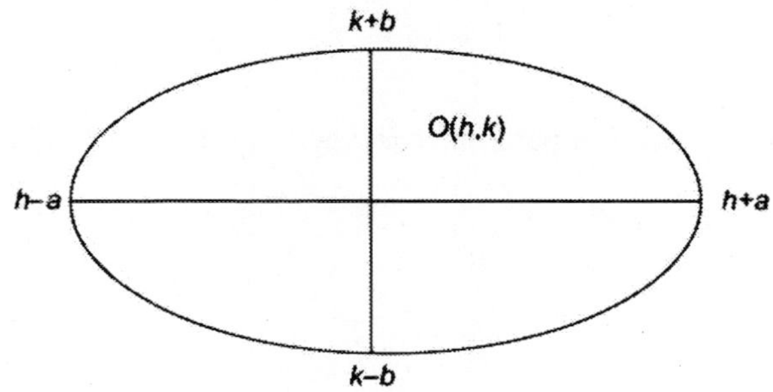

FIGURE 4.24

Algorithm 4.8 Plot of Ellipse with Polynomial Approach

Input (h,k), $a, b(h,k)$: Centre of ellipse
$2a$: Length of Major axis
$2b$: Length of Minor axis

```
xstart = 0
xend = a
while (x ≤ xend)
   y = b * square root of (1 – x*x/a*a)
   plotpixel (x + h, y + k)
   plotpixel (– x + h, y + k)
   plotpixel (x + h,– y + k)
   plotpixel (– x + h,– y + k)
```

$x = x + 1$

end while

stop

4.5.1.2 *Parametric or Trigonometric Approach*

Parametric polar representation of an ellipse

$$x = h + a\cos(\theta) \tag{4.10}$$

$$y = k + b\sin(\theta) \tag{4.11}$$

where, (h, k) centre of the ellipse, $2a$ be the length of major axis and $2b$ be the length of minor axis, and θ is measured in radian 0 to 2π.

In this method value of θ is incremented from 0 to 2π, then values of x and y are calculated from equations 4.10 and 4.11, respectively. This method is time- consuming since multiplications and trigonometric functions are involved at each step. However, we can improve the process by taking advantage of symmetry in an ellipse. Therefore, we need to compute only first quadrant to determine the ellipse completely, as shown in Fig. 4.23. With this method plots are generated from 0° to 45°, each x and y value is computed by evaluated equations 4.10 and 4.11, respectively with theta *incerment thetainc* (say).

Calculation of Thetainc

As x range is 0 to **a**, we shall divide the parameter θ range of 0 to 1.571(π/2) into **a** parts i.e.,

$$a^*\Delta\theta = \frac{\pi}{2}$$

or,

$$\Delta\theta = \frac{\pi}{2a}$$

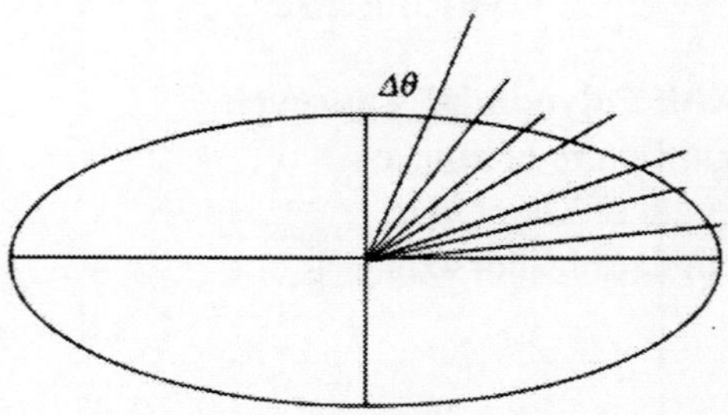

FIGURE 4.25 Division of Range 0 to1.571(π/2) into *a* Parts

Algorithm 4.9 (When angular increment is counter clockwise)
Plot of Ellipse with Trigonometric Approach

Input (h,k) , a, b (h,k) : Centre of ellipse

$2a$: Length of major axis

$2b$: Length of minor axis

$\text{temp} = \dfrac{3.141}{180}$

$\text{thetainc} = \dfrac{1.571}{a}$: $\dfrac{\pi}{2} = 1.571$

theta = 0

thetaend = 90

while(theta ≤ thetaend)

angle = temp*theta

$x = a$*cos (angle)

$y = b$*sin (angle)

```
plotpixel (x + h, y + k)     \*Plot four points; each point
plotpixel (– x + h, y + k)   corresponding to one quadrant
plotpixel (x + h, – y + k)
plotpixel (– x + h,– y + k)
theta = theta + thetainc
```

end while
stop

Note: If the increment is in clockwise direction, thetainc is taken to be *negative.*

4.5.2 Mid-point Method

Ellipse is described by the equation:

$$\frac{x^2}{a^2} + \frac{y^2}{b^2} = 1$$

where, $2a$ = length of major axis.
$2b$ = length of minor axis.

The mid-point technique applied to line and circle can also be applied to ellipse. To simplify the analysis of the algorithm, we consider only arc of ellipse with centre at O(0,0) that lies in first quadrant, since the other three quadrants can be drawn by symmetry.

From coordinate geometry, we get

$$F(x,y) = b^2x^2 + a^2y^2 - a^2b^2 \begin{cases} < 0 & \text{point } (x, y) \text{ lies inside the ellipse.} \\ = 0 & \text{point } (x, y) \text{ lies on the ellipse.} \\ > 0 & \text{point } (x, y) \text{ lies outside the ellipse.} \end{cases}$$

Working of the Method

First quadrant is temporarily divided into two regions:

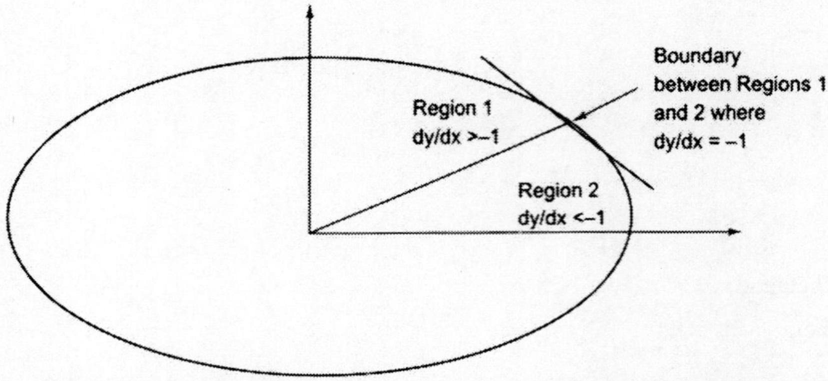

FIGURE 4.26 Representation of Two Regions in First Quadrant

Region 1

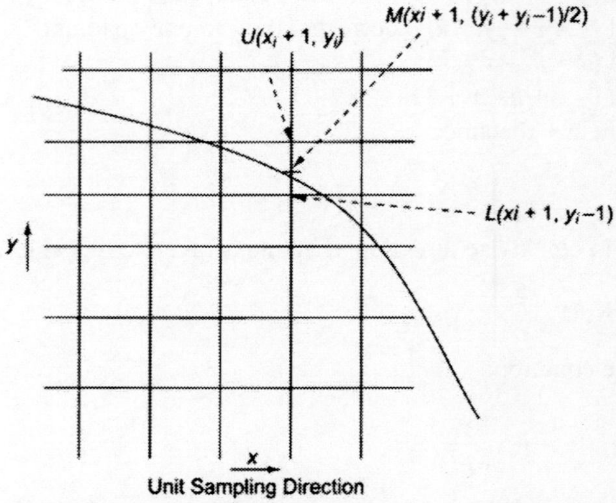

FIGURE 4.27 Choosing Pixels in Region 1 with Mid-Point Method

Region 2

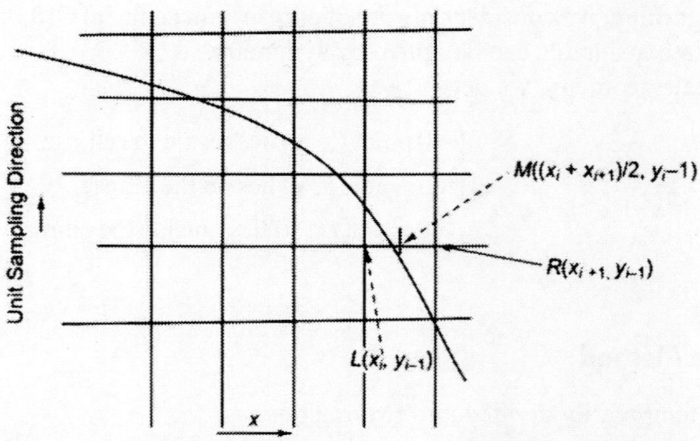

FIGURE 4.28 Choosing Pixels in Region 2 with Mid-Point Method

The checking is done by evaluating $f(x_i + 1, y_i - 1/2)$ and checking the sign.

Let, $$di = f\left(x_i + 1, y_i - \frac{1}{2}\right) = b^2(x_i + 1)^2 + a^2\left(y_i - \frac{1}{2}\right) - a^2b^2$$

Similarly, $$d_{i+1} = f\left(x_{i-1} + 1, y_{i+1} - \frac{1}{2}\right) = b^2(x_{i+1} + 1)^2 + a^2\left(y_{i+1} - \frac{1}{2}\right)^2 - a^2b^2$$

$$\Rightarrow\ d_{i+1} - d_i = b^2\,[(x_{i+1} + 1)^2 - (x_i + 1)^2 - (x_i + 1)^2] + a^2\left[\left(y_{i+1} - \frac{1}{2}\right)^2 - \left(y_i - \frac{1}{2}\right)^2\right]$$

$$\Rightarrow\ d_{i+1} - d_i = b^2[(x_{i+1} + 1)^2 - (x_i + 1)^2 - (x_i + 1)^2] + a^2\left[\left(y_{i+1} - \frac{1}{2}\right)^2 - \left(y_i - \frac{1}{2}\right)^2\right] \qquad 4.12$$

If $d_i < 0$, midpoint is inside ellipse, hence $y_{i+1} = y_i$

$\therefore$ $$d_{i+1} = d_i + 2b^2 x_{i+1} + b^2, \text{ where } x_{i+1} = x_i + 1 \qquad \text{[From 4.12]}$$

If $di \geq 0$, midpoint is outside or on ellipse, hence $y_{i+1} = y_i - 1$

$\therefore$ $$d_{i+1} = d_i + 2b^2 x_{i+1} + b^2 - 2a^2 y_{i+1}, \text{ where } x_{i+1} = x_i + 1 \qquad \text{[From 4.12]}$$

As soon as we reach the boundary between regions 1 and 2 (i.e., when $f_x = f_y$) we start sampling at unit steps in the (–)ve Y direction and the midpoint is now taken between two horizontal pixels. The choice between the candidate pixels (x_j, y_{j-1}) and $(x_{j+1}\ y_{j-1})$ is made by evaluating and checking the sign of f(candidate mid-point) i.e., $f(x_j + 1/2, y_j - 1)$.

Let

$$d_j = f\left(x_j + 1, y_j - \frac{1}{2}\right) = b^2(x_j + \frac{1}{2})^2 + a^2(y_i - 1) - a^2b^2$$

Similarly,

$$d_{j+1} = f\left(x_{j+1} + \frac{1}{2}, y_{j+1} - 1\right) = b^2(x_{j+1} + \frac{1}{2})^2 + a^2(y_{i+1} - 1)^2 - a^2b^2$$

$$\Rightarrow\ d_{j+1} - d_j = b^2\left[\left(x_{j+1} + \frac{1}{2}\right)^2 - \left(x_j + \frac{1}{2}\right)^2\right] + a^2\left[(y_{j+1} - 1)^2 - (y_j - 1)^2\right]$$

$$\Rightarrow\ P_{j+1} = P_j + b^2\left[\left(x_{j+1} + \frac{1}{2}\right)^2 - \left(x_j + \frac{1}{2}\right)^2\right] + a^2\left[(y_{j+1} - 1)^2 - (y_j - 1)^2\right] \qquad (4.13)$$

If $d_j < 0$, midpoint is inside ellipse, hence $x_{j+1} = x_j + 1$

$\therefore$ $$d_{j+1} = d_j + 2b^2x_{j+1} - 2a^2y_{j+1} + a^2, \text{ where } y_{j+1} = y_j - 1 \qquad \text{[From 4.13]}$$

If $d_j \geq 0$, midpoint is outside or on ellipse, hence $x_{j+1} = x_j$

$\therefore$ $$d_{j+1} = d_j - 2a^2y_{j+1} + a^2 \text{ where } y_{j+1} = y_j - 1 \qquad \text{[From 4.13]}$$

The starting value of d_j is obtained using the last point (x_i, y_i), calculated in Region 1.

$\therefore$ $$d_{j-1} = b^2(x_i + 1/2)^2 + a^2(y_i - 1)^2 - a^2b^2$$

Algorithm 4.10 Plot of Ellipse with Mid-point method

```
Input (h,k), a, b                 (h,k) : Centre of ellipse
                                  2a : Length of major axis
                                  2b : Length of minor axis
x = 0
y = b
d1 = b^2 - a^2 b + 0.25a^2      /* Region 1
while ( a^2(y - 0.5) < b^2 (x + 1))
if( d1 < 0 )
                    d1 = d1 + b^2(2*x + 3)
else
                    d1 = d1 + b^2(2*x + 3) + a^2(-2y + 2)
                    y = y - 1
end if
x = x + 1
end of while                              /* Region 1
/*-----------------------------------------------
d2 = b^2 (x + 0.5)^2 + a^2(y - 1)^2 - a^2 b^2   /*Region 2
while (y > 0)
if (d2 < 0)
                d2 = d2 + b^2 (2x + 2) + a^2(- 2y + 3)    /* Select pixel R
else                x = x + 1
                d2 = d2 + a^2 (-2y + 3)
end if
y = y - 1                           /* Select pixel L
end of while                              /* Region 2
end of mid-point ellipse algorithm
```

4.6 PARABOLA

Parabola may be drawn by

1. Direct Method
2. Parametric Method

Parabola is not a closed curve like circles or ellipses.

4.6.1 Polynomial Approach

Common polynomial equations of parabolas with their representations are shown as follows: Parabola is not a closed curve, an upper limit for x or y must be set.

4.6.2 Parametric Equation

Parametric equation of parabola corresponds to $y^2 = 4ax$ is:

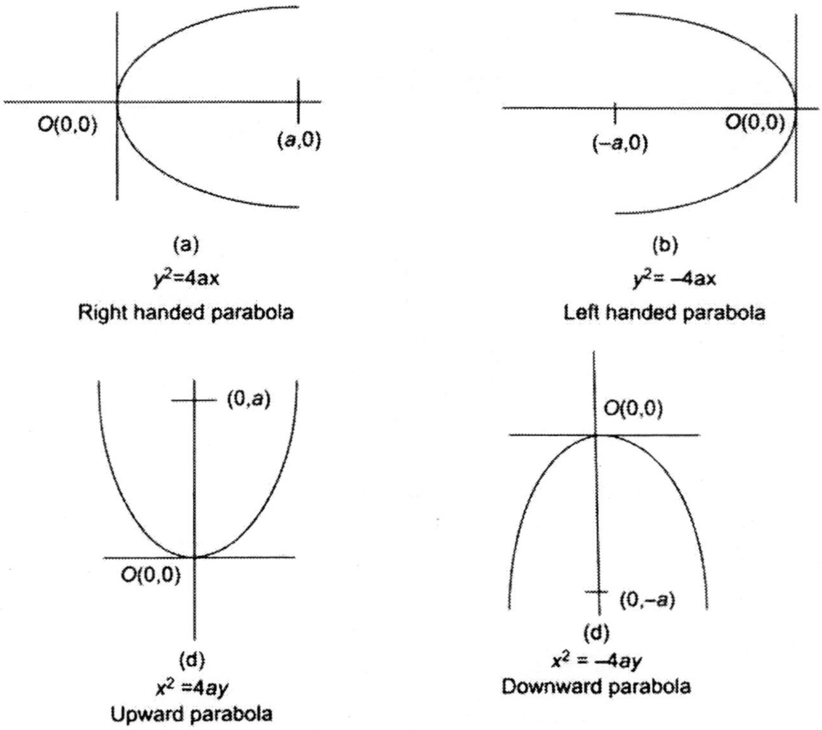

FIGURE 4.29 Various Representations of Parabolas

$$x = a.\ u^2$$
$$y = 2a\ u$$

where, value of u from 0 to ∞.

4.7 HYPERBOLA

Hyperbola is not a closed curve like circles or ellipses.
Hyperbola may be drawn by

1. Direct Method or Polynomial Approach
2. Parametric Approach

4.7.1 Polynomial Approach

General equation of hyperbola is

$$\frac{x^2}{a^2} - \frac{y^2}{b^2} = 1$$

where,

b/a represents slope of asymptote to the hyperbola.

$$y = \pm b\sqrt{\frac{x * x}{a * a} - 1}$$

Hyperbola is not a closed curve, to draw a hyperbola an upper limit for x or y must be set.

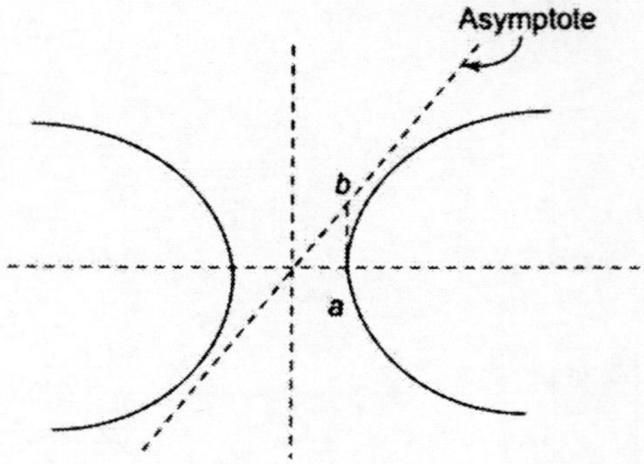

FIGURE 4.30 Representation of Hyperbola

4.7.2 Parametric Equation

Parametric equation of hyperbola corresponds to $\frac{x^2}{a^2} - \frac{y^2}{b^2} = 1$ is:

$$x = a \cosh(u)$$

$$y = b \cosh(u)$$

where, u varies from 0 to $\propto$.

Example 4.6

Scan convert upper half of the parabola $y^2 = 20x$, x varies from 0 to 5 by

(a) Direct Method.

(b) Parametric Method.

Solution

Equation of parabola

$$y^2 = 20x \tag{4.14}$$

therefore,

$$4a = 20$$

or,

$$a = 5$$

(a) Direct Approach

From the equation (4.14)

$$y = \pm\sqrt{20x} \tag{4.15}$$

Results from equation 4.15 are listed in table 4.10 (considered only + ve sign).

TABLE 4.10 Points on Parabola by Direct Approach

Point	x_{cal}	y_{cal}	x_{plot} = round(x_{cal})	x_{plot} = round(x_{cal})
1	0	0	0	0
2	1	4.472136	1	4
3	2	6.324555	2	6
4	3	7.745967	3	8
5	4	8.944272	4	9
6	5	10	5	10

Figure 4.31 depicts the pixels for the straight from the Table 4.10.

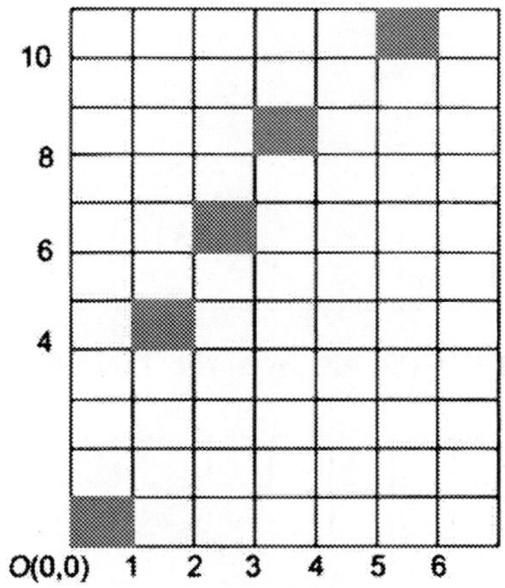

FIGURE 4.31 Plot of Upper Half of Parabola by Direct Approach

(b) Parametric Approach

Equation of parabola corresponding to $y^2 = 4ax$ is

$$x = au^2 \qquad 4.16(a)$$

$$y = 2au \qquad 4.16(b)$$

From the equations 4.16(a) and 4.16(b) for the specified range 0 to 5 for x the corresponding ranges for u is 0 to 1 and for y is 0 to 10.

Slope of the parabola

$$\frac{dy}{dx} = \frac{2a}{\sqrt{x}} > 1 \quad \text{when } x \text{ varies from 0 to 5.}$$

This implies increment in y is performed by unity to get continuous pixels. That is,

$$\begin{aligned}\Delta y &= y_{new} - y_{old} \\ &= 2au_{new} - 2au_{old} \\ &= 2a(\Delta u)\end{aligned}$$

or,

$$\Delta u = 1/2a \quad \text{(since } \Delta y \text{ is unity)}$$
$$= 1/10 = 0.1$$

Results from equations 4.16(a) and 4.16(b) are listed in table 4.12.

TABLE 4.11 Points on Parabola by Parametric Approach

Point	*u*	x_{cal}	y_{cal}	x_{plot} = round(x_{cal})	y_{plot} = round(x_{cal})
1	0	0	0	0	0
2	0.1	0.05	1	0	1
3	0.2	0.2	2	0	2
4	0.3	0.45	3	0	3
5	0.4	0.8	4	1	4
6	0.5	1.25	5	1	5
7	0.6	1.8	6	2	6
8	0.7	2.45	7	2	7
9	0.8	3.2	8	3	8
10	0.9	4.05	9	4	9
11	1	5	10	5	10

Figure 4.32 depicts the pixels for the straight from the Table 4.11.

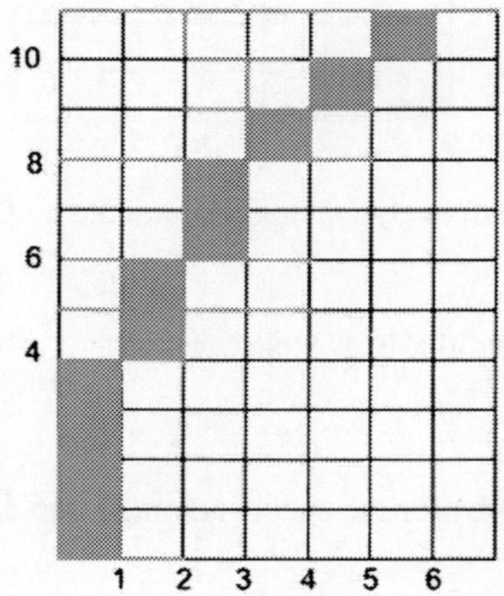

FIGURE 4.32 Plot of Upper Half of Parabola by Parametric Approach

4.8 SIDE EFFECTS OF SCAN CONVERSION

In the pervious sections we have discussed the scan conversion algorithms for plotting straight line, circle, ellipse, etc. These algorithms cannot generate accurate objects since there are some side effects in scan conversion. Following are the some standard side effects of scan conversion:

- Overstriking
- Unequal Intensity
- Aliasing

These side effects can be minimized but cannot be removed completely.

4.8.1 Overstriking

During the scan conversion algorithms discussed so far, we have seen that the same pixel is unnecessarily 'ON' multiple times. This concept is known as overstriking. Thus, overstriking:

- degrades the speed because time is spent in scan-converting the same point two or more times.
- a part of an object appears brighter than its other parts.

This can be avoided by checking each pixel to see weather it has been already whether plotted or not.

4.8.2 Unequal Intensity

Unequal Intensity of pixels is another drawback of unequal brightness of an object during scan conversion. The reason of this problem is that screen has not thoroughly equal density of pixels. Screen with resolution 1024 × 768 has 1024 pixels along horizontal direction and 768 pixels along vertical direction. So, horizontal line has more dense pixels as compared to vertical line i.e., distance between two conjunctive pixels along vertical direction is more than distance between two conjunctive pixels along horizontal direction. Further, distance between two conjunctive pixels along diagonal line is more than the distance between two conjunctive pixels along vertical direction as well as horizontal direction. As shown in figure 4.33 wherein horizontal and vertical pixels are considered at equal distance.

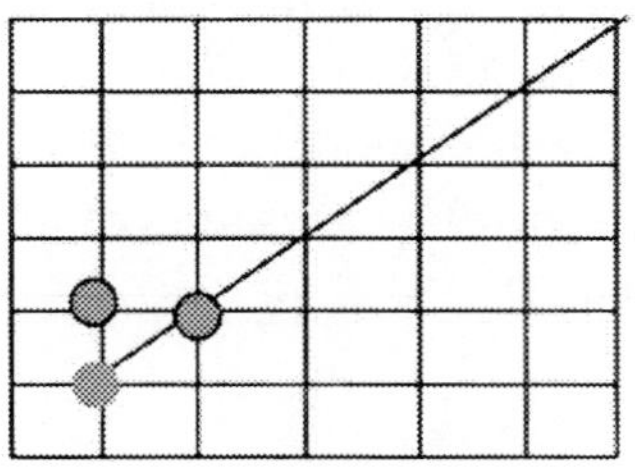

FIGURE 4.33 Effect of Unequal Intensity

4.8.3 Aliasing

There is problem of discontinuity of lines and object, because scanning is restricted at integer values. This causes that straight lines and curves do not look smooth but look jagged when viewed on a monitor, these gaps are called jaggies.

Let $y = 0.3x + 2$ be a straight line equation.

Point A(2,3) is an alias location of B(2,2.6)

This phenomenon of shifting is called aliasing (alias means a substitution or alternative).

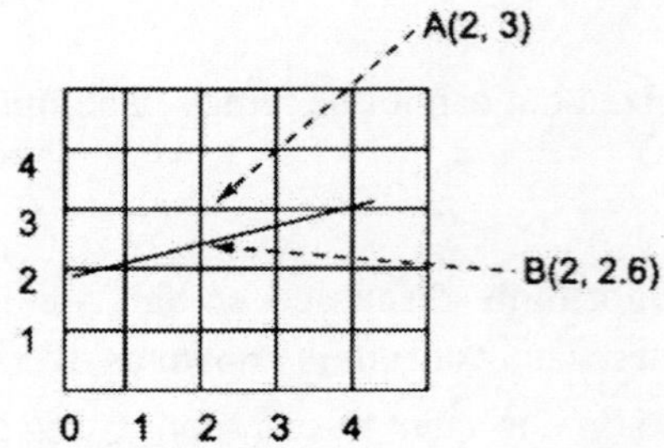

FIGURE 4.34 Effect of Aliasing

Restriction to integer values leads the following problems:

- Non-integer value points shift to the nearest integer value location; causing deviation of the line.
- There are steps of sudden jumps from one integer value to the next.

Out of the above-mentioned side effects of scan conversions, aliasing is a typical image quality problem in all pixel devices, including computer screen.

Antialiasing

Aliasing is an inherent part of any discrete process, which cannot be eliminated but can be minimized. This process of minimization of aliasing is called antialiasing.

Following are the techniques of antialiasing:

- **To increase the number of resolution**
  The size of stair step error is never larger than the size of actual size pixel. Thus, screen with high resolution minimizes the effect of aliasing. But the cost of image production becomes higher with increased resolution. It is not feasible.
- **Dithering:** Display two or more pixels around the computed location at very intensities.
- **Pixel phasing technique**: Shift the pixel by a fraction of dimension.

Above techniques are implemented in the following two antialiasing approaches:

Super sampling

In this approach we subdivide each pixel into sub pixels. Thus, every pixel area in the display surface is assumed to be subdivided into a grid of smaller sub pixels (super samples) screen is treated as *higher resolution* than what actually it is. The intensity value of pixel is the average of the intensity values of all the sampled sub pixels within the pixel.

Each pixel is subdivided into a 3×3 area; the maximum number of subpixel units covered by the line within each pixel will be 3; the minimum will be 0. This allows up to 4 different levels of gradation in intensity to be defined, rather than just 2.

$$\text{Color of Pixel } (x,y) = \frac{\text{Sum of intentsities of subpixels within pixel}(x, y)}{\text{Sum of the weights of the subpixels}}$$

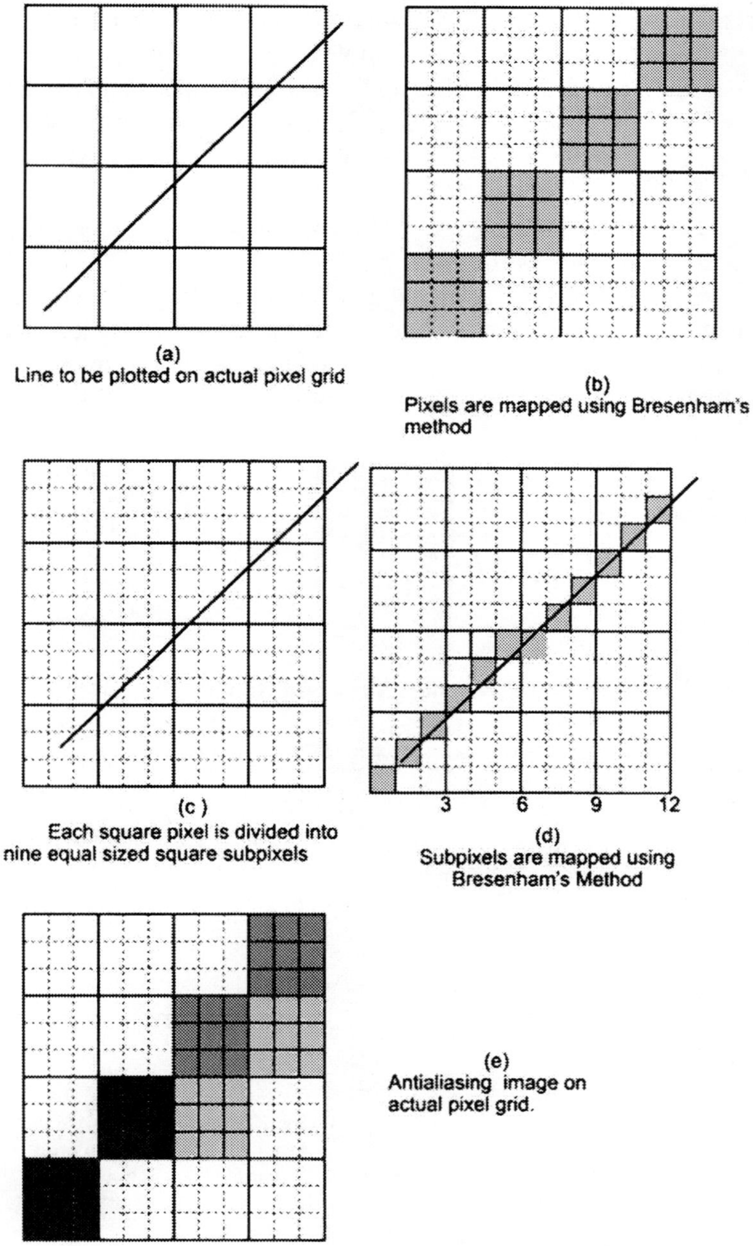

FIGURE 4.35 Super Sampling Process

1	1	1
1	1	1
1	1	1

FIGURE 4.36 3 × 3 Pixel Weighted Mask with Uniform Weights

This method is also known as *post filtering* because filtering is carried out after sampling. Filtering means eliminating the higher frequencies i.e., combining the supersamples to compute a pixel color. This type of filtering is known as unknown filtering because each super sample in a pixel has given an equal weight irrespective of the position. Thus, unweighted filter gives unweighted average.

Weighted filter(Weighted averages)

Non-uniform weighting can be used when the values are combined, to give more weight to the subpixel samples that are closest to the center of the pixel.

In such type of filtering process each super sample is multiplied by its corresponding weight and products are summed to produce a weighted average, which is used as a pixel color. Weights to each super sample are given based upon its distance from the centre of the pixel. The centre sample within a pixel has a maximum weight. An array of containing weights of subpixels is referred to as pixel-weighted mask.

1	2	1
2	4	2
1	2	1

3x3

1	2	2	1
2	4	4	2
2	4	4	2
1	2	2	1

4x4

1	2	3	2	1
2	3	4	3	2
3	4	5	4	3
2	3	4	3	2
1	2	3	2	1

5x5

FIGURE 4.37 Pixel Weighted Mask with Non-uniform Weights

$$\text{Color of Pixel }(x,y) = \frac{(w_1 x\, I_1 + w_2 x I_2 + \ldots\ldots w_k x\, I_k\ )\text{within pixel}(x,y)}{w_1 + w_2 + \ldots . w_k}$$

$$= \frac{\sum_{i=1}^{k} w_i x\, I_i}{\sum_{i=1}^{k} w_i} \text{ within pixel } (x,y)$$

where, w_i is the weight of ith subpixel.
and, I_i is the intensity of ith subpixel.

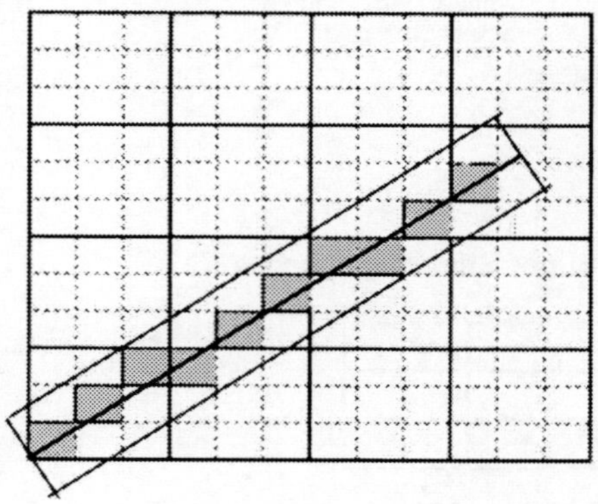

FIGURE 4.38

Area Sampling(Prefiltering)

This approach treats pixel as an area. For each pixel area that intersects the object, we calculate the percentage of overlap by the object. This percentage determines the portion of the overall intensity value of the corresponding pixel that is due to the object's contribution.

- Area sampling works by defining the intensity of each pixel to be proportional to the area of the pixel that is covered by a primitive.
- Primitives must be defined as having a finite (non-zero) thickness area sampling.

Let us consider area sampling for a straight line. The line can be treated as rectangle as shown in fig. 4.38.

Resultant Intensity of pixel (x,y) = % age of area of pixel overlap with rectangle x Maximum intensity of pixel (x,y)

$$= \frac{\text{Total no. subpixels overlap with rectangle}}{\text{Total no. of subpixels}} x$$

Maximum intensity of pixel (x,y)

Weighted area approach used same approach as discussed in previous section, but greater weight is given to area near the center of the pixel.

1	2	1
2	4	2
1	1	1

FIGURE 4.39 3 × 3 Weighted Array Mask

Resultant Intensity of Pixel (x,y) =

$$\frac{\text{Sum of weights of subpixels overlap with rectangle}}{\text{Total weights of subpixels}} \times \text{Maximum intensity of pixel } (x, y)$$

$$= \frac{(\sum_{i=1}^{k} w_i)\text{of subpixels overlap with rectangle}}{\sum_{i=}^{n} w_i} \times \text{Maximum intensity of pixel } (x,y)$$

In case of pixels (1,1)

(a) Uniform
Resultant intensity of pixel(1,1) = 7/9 * maximum intensity of pixels (1,1)
= 80% intensity of the pixel (1,1)

(b) Non-uniform
Resultant intensity of pixel (1,1) = 14/16 * maximum intensity of pixels (1,1)
= 90% intensity of the pixel (1,1)

There are other methods besides Raytracing, Adaptive sampling, Stochastic sampling.

SOLVED PROBLEMS

Problem 4.1 Plot straight line from (6, 3) to (20, 10) by Simple DDA method.

Solution:

Slope of the line $(m) = (y2 - y1)/(x2 - x1) = 7/14 < 1$

Therefore we will implement the algorithm with x increment unit direction i.e. $x = x + 1$ and $y = y + m$ [from Table 4.2]

$$yinc = m = 7/14 = 0.5$$

$$x = x + 1 \quad \text{.......... (1)}$$

$$y = y + 0.5 \quad \text{.......... (2)}$$

Results from equations (1) and (2) are listed in the following table.

Point	*xcal*	*ycal*	*xplot = Round(xcal)*	*yplot= round(ycal)*
1	6	3	6	3
2	7	3.5	7	4
3	8	4	8	4
4	9	4.5	9	5
5	10	5	10	5
6	11	5.5	11	6
7	12	6	12	6
8	13	6.5	13	7
9	14	7	14	7
10	15	7.5	15	8
11	16	8	16	8
12	17	8.5	17	9
13	18	9	18	9
14	19	9.5	19	10
15	20	10	20	10

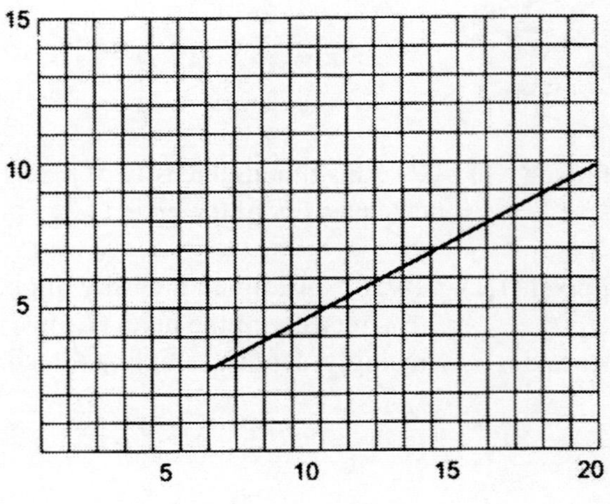

Problem 4.2 Plot straight line from (–6, 3) to (–20, 10) by simple DDA method.

Solution:

Here the line lies in 2nd quadrant.

Slope of the line $(m) = (y2 - y1)/(x2 - x1) = 7/14 < 1$

Since the line lies in 2nd quadrant and $m<1$, therefore we will implement the algorithm with x decrement unit direction i.e. $x = x - 1$ and $y = y + m$ [from table 4.2].

$$yinc = m = 7/14 = 0.5$$

$$x = x - 1 \quad \text{.......... (1)}$$

$$y = y + 0.5 \quad \text{.......... (2)}$$

Results from equations (1) and (2) are listed in the following table.

Point	*xcal*	*ycal*	*xplot = Round(xcal)*	*yplot= round(ycal)*
1	– 6	3	– 6	3
2	– 7	3.5	– 7	4
3	– 8	4	– 8	4
4	– 9	4.5	– 9	5
5	– 10	5	– 10	5
6	– 11	5.5	– 11	6
7	– 12	6	– 12	6
8	– 13	6.5	– 13	7
9	– 14	7	– 14	7
10	– 15	7.5	– 15	8
11	– 16	8	– 16	8
12	– 17	8.5	– 17	9
13	– 18	9	– 18	9
14	– 19	9.5	– 19	10
15	– 20	10	– 20	10

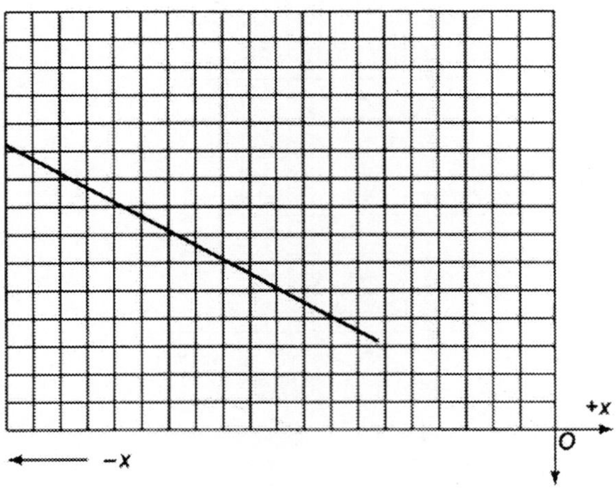

Problem 4.3 Plot straight line from (–5, 2) to (–14, 20) by simple DDA method.

Solution:

Here the line lies in 2nd quadrant.

Slope of the line $(m) = (y2 - y1)/(x2 - x1) = 18/9>1$

Since the line lies in 2nd quadrant and $m > 1$, therefore we implement the algorithm with y increment unit direction i.e. $y = y + 1$ and $x = x - 1/m$ [Table 4.2 of the Chapter 4].

$$xinc = 1/m = 9/18 = 0.5$$

$$y = y + 1 \qquad \text{......(1)}$$

$$x = x - 0.5 \qquad \text{......(2)}$$

Point	*xcal*	*ycal*	*xplot= round(xcal)*	*yplot= round(ycal)*
1	–5	2	–5	2
2	–5.5	3	–6	3
3	–6	4	–6	4
4	–6.5	5	–7	5
5	–7	6	–7	6
6	–7.5	7	–8	7
7	–8	8	–8	8
8	–8.5	9	–9	9
9	–9	10	–9	10
10	–9.5	11	–10	11
11	–10	12	–10	12
12	–10.5	13	–11	13
13	–11	14	–11	14
14	–11.5	15	–12	15
15	–12	16	–12	16
16	–12.5	17	–13	17
17	–13	18	–13	18
18	–13.5	19	–14	19
19	–14	20	–14	20

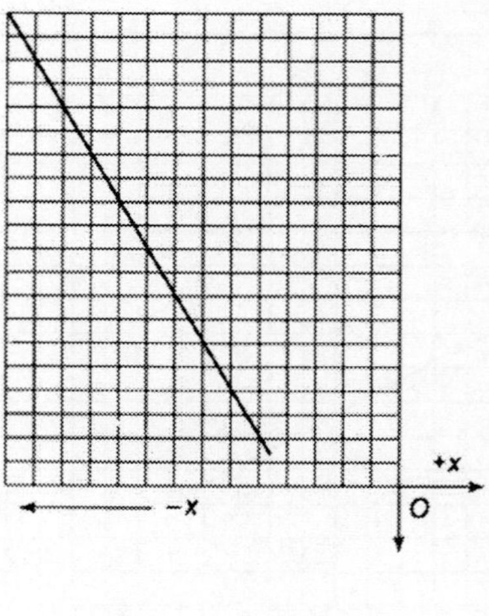

Note: Similar cases may also be considered for 3rd and 4th quadrant.

Problem 4.4 Plot straight line from (6, 3) to (20, 10) by Symmetrical DDA method.

Solution:

$$\text{Length } y = abs(xe - xs) = 20 - 6 = 14$$

$$\text{Length } x = abs(ye - ys) = 10 - 3 = 7$$

$$\text{Larger value (length)} = 14$$

$$n = \frac{\log(\text{length})}{\log 2} = \frac{\log(14)}{\log 2} = 3.807355$$

$$\text{Take } n = 4$$

$$xinc = \frac{xe - xs}{2^n} = 0.875$$

$$yinc = \frac{ye - ys}{2^n} = 0.4375$$

$$x = xs$$

$$y = ys$$

$$x = x + xinc \quad \text{.......... (1)}$$

$$y = y + yinc \quad \text{.......... (2)}$$

Results from equations (1) and (2) are listed in the following table.

Point	*Xcal*	*ycal*	*xplot= round(xcal)*	*Yplot= round(xcal)*
1	6	3	6	3
2	6.875	3.4375	7	3
3	7.75	3.875	8	4
4	8.625	4.3125	9	4
5	9.5	4.75	10	5
6	10.375	5.1875	10	5
7	11.25	5.625	11	6
8	12.125	6.0625	12	6
9	13	6.5	13	7
10	13.875	6.9375	14	7
11	14.75	7.375	15	7
12	15.625	7.8125	16	8
13	16.5	8.25	17	8
14	17.375	8.6875	17	9
15	18.25	9.125	18	9
16	19.125	9.5625	19	10
17	20	10	20	10

Note: This method may also be implemented for 2nd, 3rd, and 4th quadrant.

Example 4.5 Find out the pixel location approximating the second octant of circle having centre at $C(2,2)$ and radius 8 using Bresenham's Method.

Solution: $x = 0 \quad y = r = 8$

$d = 3 - 2*r = 3 - 2*8 = -13$

Points on second octant of circle

Point	*x+2*	*y+2*	d_{i+1}
1	2	10	
2	3	10	$-13 + 4x + 6 = -1$
3	4	10	$-1 + 4x + 6 = 17$
4	5	9	$17 + 4(x - y) + 10 = 3$
5	6	9	$11 + 4x + 6 = 7$
6	7	8	$7 + 4(x - y) + 10 = 5$
7	8	7	

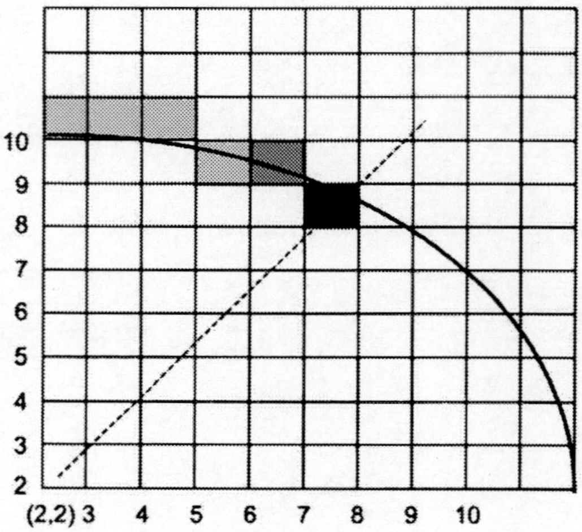

Example 4.6 Find out the pixel location approximating the second octant of circle having centre at $C(0,0)$ and radius 8 using Mid point Method.

Solution: $x = 0 \quad y = r = 8$

$d = 1 - r = 1 - 8 = -7$

Points on second octant of circle

Point	*X*	*Y*	d_{i+1}
1	0	8	
2	1	8	$-7 + 2x + 3 = -4$
3	2	8	$-4 + 2x + 3 = 1$
4	3	7	$1 + 2(x - y) + 5 = -6$
5	4	7	$-6 + 2x + 3 = 3$
6	5	6	$3 + 2(x - y) + 5 = 2$
7	6	5	

EXERCISES

1. Explain how rasterization accuracy is preserved with scan conversion algorithm.
2. What are the steps required to plot a line using Simple DDA Method?
3. What are the steps required to plot a line using Symmetrical DDA Method?
4. What are the steps required to plot a line using Bresenham's Method regardless of slope of the line?
5. What are the steps required to plot a dashed line using Bresenham's Method.
6. Compare advantages and disadvantages of the Bresenham's line drawing algorithm with those of the DDA algorithm.
7. State and justify the circumstances in which we prefer unit X interval or unit Y interval.
8. What are the steps required to plot a circle using Bresenham's Method?
9. What are the steps required to plot a circle using Mid-point Method?
10. What are the steps required to plot an arc with initial angle θ_1 and final angle θ_2 using parametric approach?
11. What are the major adverse side effects of scan conversion ? Explain.
12. Compare the result obtained from the use of unweighted and weighted anti-aliasing with a suitable example.
13. Define the term aliasing and antialiasing. What are the various techniques for antialiasing? Explain briefly.
14. Explain with example why weighted supersampling generates better results than unweighted supersampling.
15. Explain with example why weighted area sampling generates better results than unweighted area sampling.
16. Explain why horizontal and vertical lines have better quality than diagonal lines.
17. Scan convert a straight line whose end points are (5,10) and (10,25) using:
    a. Simple DDA Method
    b. Symmetrical DDA Method
    c. Bresenham's Method
18. Scan convert one quadrant of circle of radius 12 units and centre at O (0,0) by
    a. Direct Application
    b. Bresenham's Approach
19. Scan convert one quadrant of ellipse.
20. $\frac{x^2}{4}+\frac{y^2}{16}=1$ by Direct Method.
21. Scan convert upper half of parabola $y^2=24x$ from $x = 0$ to 6 by Direct Method.

5

2-D Transformations

5.1 INTRODUCTION

The purpose of computer graphics is not to simply display a picture on monitor screen or plot it on a piece of paper just once. An effective computer graphics manipulates the initially created image and to display the modified image, without redrawing it every time. This manipulation is referred to as transformation. This chapter describes various transformations viz., translation, rotation, scaling, reflection, and shearing.

5.2 CLASSIFICATIONS OF TRANSFORMATIONS

Transformations can be broadly classified as:

1. Geometric Transformations
2. Coordinate Transformations

5.2.1 Geometric Transformations

In such transformations the object itself is transformed relative to stationary coordinate system or background, Fig 5.1(a).

5.2.2 Coordinate Transformations

In such transformations the object is held stationary while the coordinate system is transformed relative to the object, Fig.5.1(b).

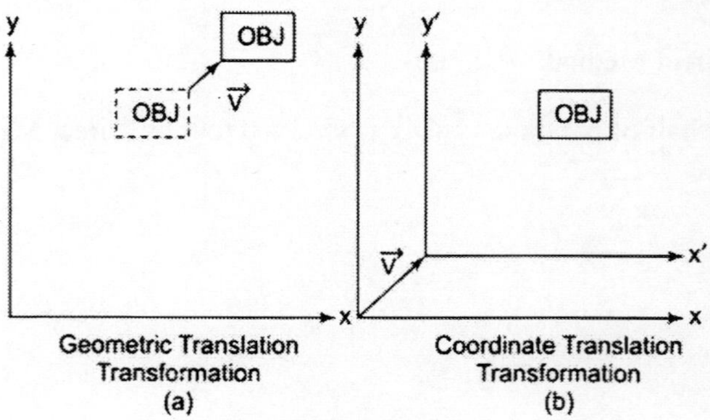

FIGURE 5.1

5.3 TYPES OF TRANSFORMATIONS

The modifications that are commonly required for an image are as follows:

1. Translate or Move or Shift
2. Rotate
3. Scale or Zoom
4. Reflect or Flip
5. Shear or Twist or Torque or Tilt

This chapter covers all the above five types of transformations.

Transformations may be done to the object in world coordinates as shown in Fig. 5.2(a) or they may be applied to the image in viewport coordinates, Fig 5.2(b). The former transformation is generally preferred because if we manipulate the image in the viewport, the part of the modified image may go out of the viewport.

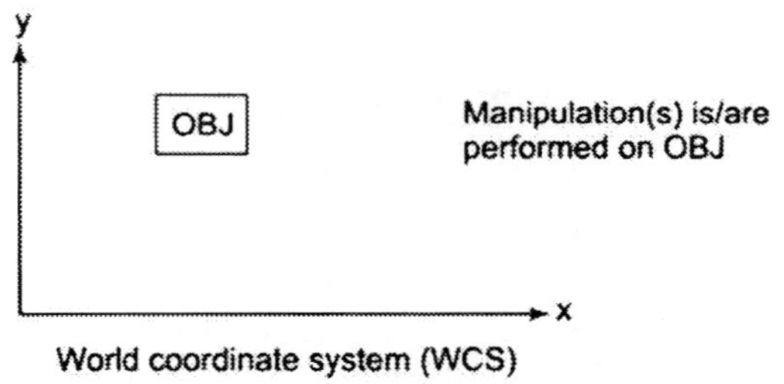

FIGURE 5.2(a) Transformations in WCS

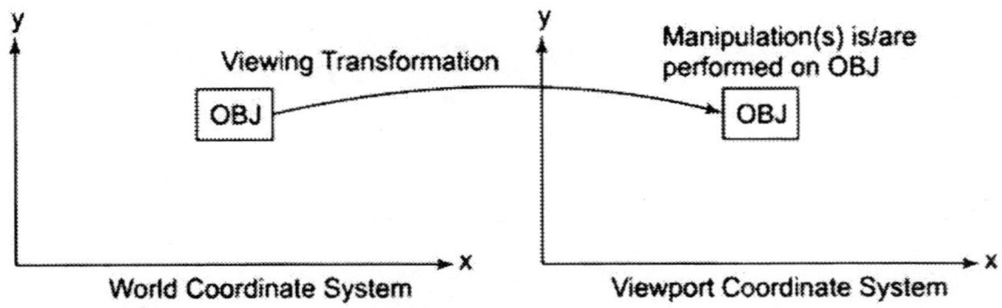

FIGURE 5.2(b) Transformations in Viewport Coordinate System

These transformations change either position or orientation or size or shape of graphics objects like curve, circle, ellipse, rectangle, etc. These are known as 2D transformations.

5.4 REPRESENTATION OF POINT AND OBJECT

5.4.1 Representation of a Point

A point coordinate can be expressed as elements of a matrix. Two matrix formats are used:

- Row matrix
- Column Matrix

Row Matrix format of point $P(x, y)$ is a $[x\ y]$.

Column Matrix format of point $P(x, y)$ is a $\begin{bmatrix} x \\ y \end{bmatrix}$.

In this book, we will follow column matrix format since the column matrix format is standard mathematical notation, and since many graphics packages, for example Graphics Kernel System (GKS) and Programmer's Hierarchical Interactive Graphics Standard (PHIGS), also use this representation.

5.4.2 Representation of an Object

All objects are built with finite number of points, each such object can be uniquely represented by an optimum number of definition points lying on the object. Column matrix format of line between points $A(x_1,y_1)$ and $B(x_2,y_2)$ is

$$\begin{bmatrix} x_1 & x_2 \\ y_1 & y_2 \end{bmatrix}$$

Column matrix format of triangle $A(x_1, y_1)$, $B(x_2, y_2)$ and $C(x_3, y_3)$ is

$$\begin{bmatrix} x_1 & x_2 & x_3 \\ y_1 & y_2 & y_3 \end{bmatrix}$$

Example 5.1

Column matrix format of

Line L $\begin{bmatrix} 2 & 6 \\ 3 & 7 \end{bmatrix}$

Rectangle $ABCD$ $\begin{bmatrix} 3 & 8 & 8 & 3 \\ 4 & 4 & 8 & 8 \end{bmatrix}$

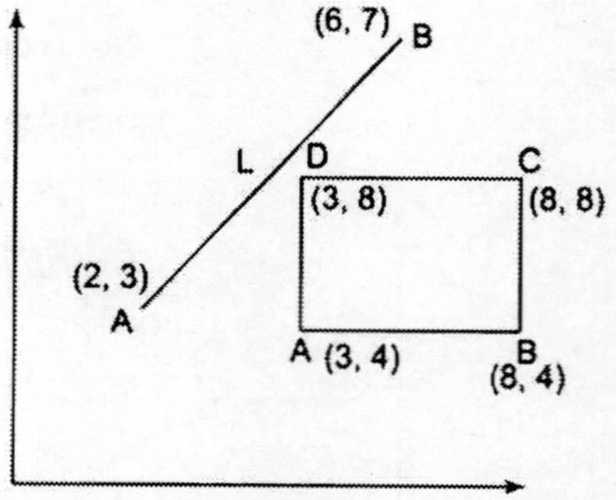

FIGURE 5.3

Row matrix format of

Line L $\begin{bmatrix} 2 & 3 \\ 6 & 7 \end{bmatrix}$

Rectangle $ABCD$ $\begin{bmatrix} 3 & 4 \\ 8 & 4 \\ 8 & 8 \\ 3 & 8 \end{bmatrix}$

5.5 GEOMETRIC TRANSFORMATIONS

5.5.1 Translation

(a) Translation of a Point

Let us consider that a point $P(x, y)$ is translated to $P'(x', y')$ by vector $\bar{v} = t_{x\hat{i}} + t_{y\hat{j}}$, t_x and t_y represent translation factors along x-axis and y-axis respectively, as shown in Fig. 5.4. The translation distance pair (t_x, t_y) is also called a translation vector or shift vector.
Algebraically,

$$x' = x + t_x \quad 5.1(a)$$

$$y' = y + t_y \quad 5.1(b)$$

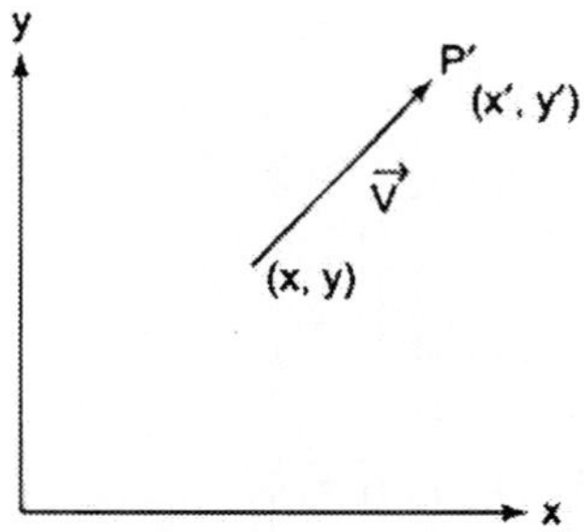

FIGURE 5.4 Translation of a Point

In column matrix format, above equations 5.1(a) and 5.1(b) can be expressed as,

$$\begin{bmatrix} x' \\ y' \\ 1 \end{bmatrix} = \begin{bmatrix} 1 & 0 & t_x \\ 0 & 1 & t_y \\ 0 & 0 & 1 \end{bmatrix} \begin{bmatrix} x \\ y \\ 1 \end{bmatrix}$$

$$P' = T_{txty} \cdot P$$

T_{txty} is called translation transformation matrix, where t_x and t_y are translation factors along x-axis and y-axis, respectively.

(b) Translation of an Object

Translation is a rigid body transformation that moves objects without distortion. Every point on the object is translated by the same amount and there exists a one-to-one correspondence between the transformed points and original points.

Consider the triangle, shown in Fig. 5.5(a). If we have to apply equal translations to each vertex of the triangle, then translated object is shown in fig. 5.5(b).

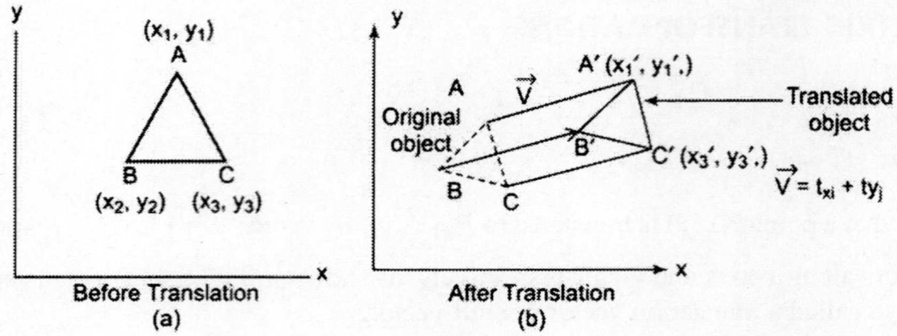

FIGURE 5.5

$$A' = T_{tx,ty} \cdot A$$
$$B' = T_{tx,ty} \cdot B$$
$$C' = T_{tx,ty} \cdot C$$

$$\begin{bmatrix} x_1' \\ y_1' \\ 1 \end{bmatrix} = \begin{bmatrix} 1 & 0 & t_x \\ 0 & 1 & t_y \\ 0 & 0 & 1 \end{bmatrix} \begin{bmatrix} x_1 \\ y_1 \\ 1 \end{bmatrix} \quad 5.2(a)$$

$$\begin{bmatrix} x_2' \\ y_2' \\ 1 \end{bmatrix} = \begin{bmatrix} 1 & 0 & t_x \\ 0 & 1 & t_y \\ 0 & 0 & 1 \end{bmatrix} \begin{bmatrix} x_2 \\ y_2 \\ 1 \end{bmatrix} \quad 5.2(b)$$

$$\begin{bmatrix} x_3' \\ y_3' \\ 1 \end{bmatrix} = \begin{bmatrix} 1 & 0 & t_x \\ 0 & 1 & t_y \\ 0 & 0 & 1 \end{bmatrix} \begin{bmatrix} x_3 \\ y_3 \\ 1 \end{bmatrix} \quad 5.2(c)$$

Combining these three 5.2(a), 5.2(b), 5.2(c), we have

$$\begin{bmatrix} x_1' & x_2' & x_3' \\ y_1' & y_2' & y_3' \\ 1 & 1 & 1 \end{bmatrix} = \begin{bmatrix} 1 & 0 & t_x \\ 0 & 1 & t_y \\ 0 & 0 & 1 \end{bmatrix} \begin{bmatrix} x_1 & x_2 & x_3 \\ y_1 & y_2 & y_3 \\ 1 & 1 & 1 \end{bmatrix}$$

$$A'B'C' = T_{tx,\,ty} ABC$$

A straight line segment is translated by adding the translation vector to the coordinate position of each vertex and redrawing the line between the new end point positions as shown in Fig. 5.6(a) and Fig. 5.6(b).

Similar methods are used for curved objects. To translate circle or ellipse, we translate its centre coordinate and redraw. Figure 5.7(b) shows the translation of a circle.

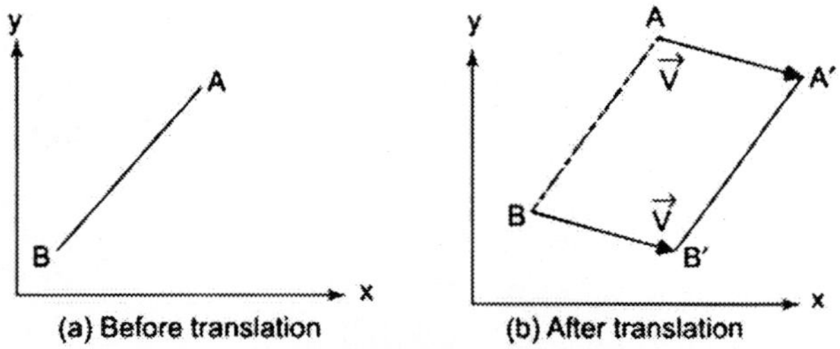

FIGURE 5.6 Translation of a Line

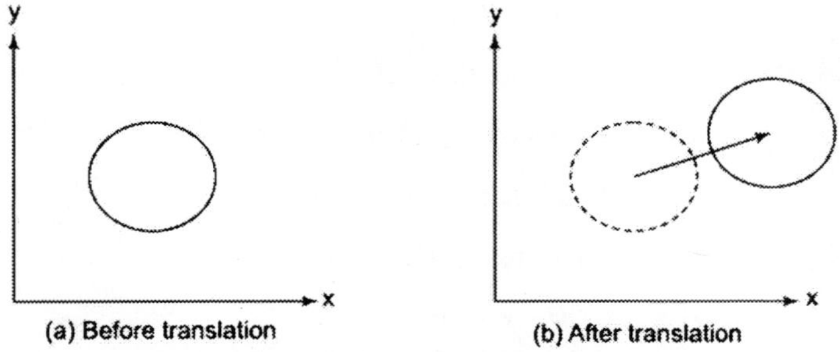

FIGURE 5.7 Translation of a Circle

In general, $OBJ' = T_{tx,\, ty} \cdot OBJ$

5.5.2 Rotation

This transformation is used to rotate objects about any point in a 2-D plane. To accomplish rotation, we specify

- rotation angle (θ)
- rotation point (pivot point)

Positive value of rotation angle defines that rotation is in anticlockwise or counter-clockwise direction, negative value of rotation defines that rotation is in clockwise direction. Rotation may be performed in counter-clockwise or clock-wise. By default, word rotation means counter-clockwise, otherwise we mentioned the direction of rotation.

(a) Rotation of a Point About Origin

Consider a figure 5.8 wherein a point $P(x, y)$ is rotated by an angle θ about $O(0, 0)$.

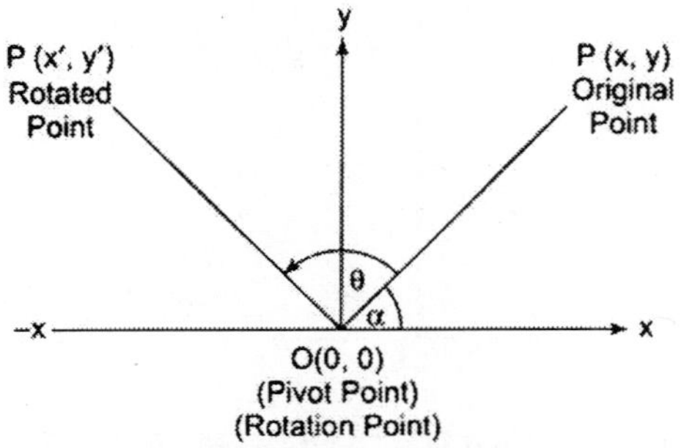

FIGURE 5.8 Rotation of a Point about Origin

Let us suppose
$OP = r$ (radius vector)
$P(x, y)$ can be represented as:

$$x = r \cos \alpha \tag{5.3(a)}$$

$$y = r \sin \alpha \tag{5.3(b)}$$

Where, (r, α) is the polar coordinate of point P.
Similarly, $P'(x', y')$ can be represented as:

$$x' = r(\cos(\theta + \alpha)) \tag{5.4(a)}$$

$$y' = r(\sin(\theta + \alpha)) \tag{5.4(b)}$$

Rewriting equations 5.4(a) and 5.4(b) using the laws of sins and cosines,

$$x' = r \cos\theta \cos\alpha - r \sin\theta \sin\alpha \tag{5.5(a)}$$

$$y' = r \sin\theta \cos\alpha - r \cos\alpha \sin\theta \tag{5.5(b)}$$

Using 5.3(a) and 5.3(b) in 5.5(a) and 5.5(b), respectively, we get

$$x' = x \cos\theta - y \sin\theta \tag{5.6(a)}$$

$$y' = x \sin\theta + y \cos\theta \tag{5.6(b)}$$

In column matrix format, above equations 5.6(a) and 5.6(b) can be expressed as

$$\begin{bmatrix} x' \\ y' \end{bmatrix} = \begin{bmatrix} \cos\theta & -\sin\theta \\ \sin\theta & \cos\theta \end{bmatrix} \begin{bmatrix} x \\ y \end{bmatrix}$$

$$P' = R_\theta \cdot P \tag{5.7}$$

R_θ is called rotational transformation matrix, when point P is rotated in counter clockwise direction about origin by an angle θ.

(b) Rotation of a Point About an Arbitrary Pivot Point

Equation (5.7) is applicable only for rotation about the origin. But in many applications pivot point will not be the origin. It may be any point outside the object or on the object in 2D plane. For example : (a) like cases when we want to rotate a line about its mid-point. (b) rotate a triangle about its one of the vertex (c) rotation of an object along the circumstance of a circle i.e., about its centre.

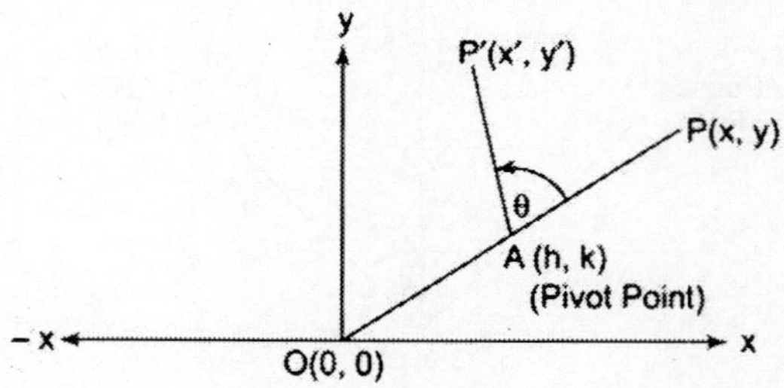

FIGURE 5.9 Rotation of a Point About an Arbitrary Point

Let us suppose point $P(x, y)$ is rotated by an angle θ about an arbitrary pivot point $A(h, k)$. Process involves three steps:

Step 1: Translate $A(h, k)$ to $O(0,0)$ $(T\vec{v})$.

Step 2: Perform rotation of θ degree about the origin (R_θ).

Step 3: Translate A back to (h, k) $(T-\vec{v})$.

Combining these three matrices in the order in which these are performed

$$R_{\theta,A} = \overleftarrow{T-\vec{v}\cdot R_\theta\cdot T\vec{v}}$$

$$= \begin{bmatrix} 1 & 0 & h \\ 0 & 1 & k \\ 0 & 0 & 1 \end{bmatrix} \begin{bmatrix} \cos\theta & -\sin\theta \\ \sin\theta & \cos\theta \end{bmatrix} \begin{bmatrix} 1 & 0 & -h \\ 0 & 1 & -k \\ 0 & 0 & 1 \end{bmatrix}$$

$$= \begin{bmatrix} 1 & 0 & h \\ 0 & 1 & k \\ 0 & 0 & 1 \end{bmatrix} \begin{bmatrix} \cos\theta & -\sin\theta & 0 \\ \sin\theta & \cos\theta & 0 \\ 0 & 0 & 1 \end{bmatrix} \begin{bmatrix} 1 & 0 & -h \\ 0 & 1 & -k \\ 0 & 0 & 1 \end{bmatrix}$$

$$R_{\theta,A} = \begin{bmatrix} \cos\theta & -\sin\theta & -h\cos\theta + k\sin\theta + h \\ \sin\theta & \cos\theta & -h\sin\theta - k\cos\theta + k \\ 0 & 0 & 1 \end{bmatrix}$$

Column matrix format of above rotational transformation is:

$$\begin{bmatrix} x' \\ y' \\ 1 \end{bmatrix} = \begin{bmatrix} \cos\theta & -\sin\theta & -h\cos\theta + k\sin\theta + h \\ \sin\theta & \cos\theta & -h\sin\theta - k\cos\theta + k \\ 0 & 0 & 1 \end{bmatrix} \begin{bmatrix} x \\ y \\ 1 \end{bmatrix}$$

Algebraically,

$$x' = x\cos\theta - y\sin\theta - h\cos\theta + k\sin\theta + h \qquad 5.8(a)$$

$$y' = x\sin\theta + y\cos\theta - h\sin\theta - k\cos\theta + k \qquad 5.8(b)$$

Equations 5.8(a) and 5.8(b) generate new coordinates (x', y') after rotation in counter-clockwise by an angle θ of a point (x, y) about an arbitrary point (h, k).

$$x' = x\cos(-\theta) - y\sin(-\theta) - h\cos(-\theta) + k\sin(-\theta) + h \qquad 5.9(a)$$

$$y' = x\sin(-\theta) + y\cos(-\theta) - h\sin(-\theta) - k\cos(-\theta) + k \qquad 5.9(b)$$

Equations 5.9(a) and 5.9(b) generate new coordinates (x', y') after rotation in clockwise by an angle θ of a point (x, y) about an arbitrary point (h, k).

(c) Rotation of an Object

As with translation, rotations are rigid body transformations that rotate the object without distortion. Every point on an object is rotated through the same angle. A straight line is rotated by displaying each vertex through the specified rotation angle and redrawing the line.

(i) About Origin

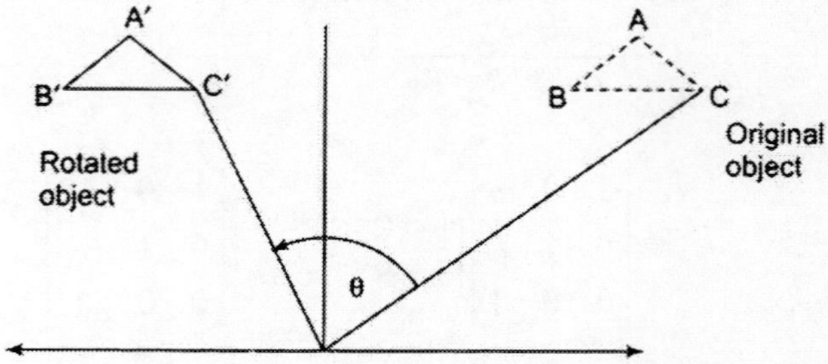

FIGURE 5.10 Rotation of an Object About Origin

(ii) About an Arbitrary Pivot Point

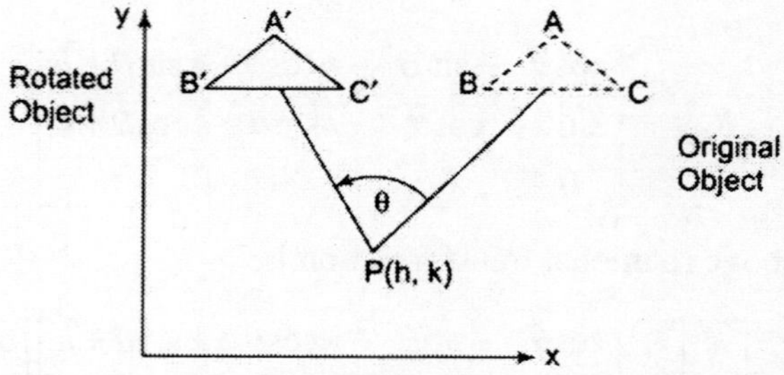

FIGURE 5.11 Rotation of an Object About Origin

$$A' = R_{\theta, P} \cdot A$$

$$B' = R_{\theta, P} \cdot B$$

$$C' = R_{\theta, P} \cdot C$$

Combining these three,

$$A'\,B'\,C' = R_{\theta, P} \cdot ABC$$

In general,

$$\text{OBJ}' = R_{\theta, P} \cdot \text{OBJ} \qquad 5.10$$

5.5.3 Scaling

Scaling is a transformation that changes the size or shape of an object.

(a) Scaling of a Point w.r.t. Origin

Scaling w.r.t origin of a point can be carried out by multiplying the coordinate values (x, y) by scaling factors sx and sy, respectively to produce the coordinates (x', y').

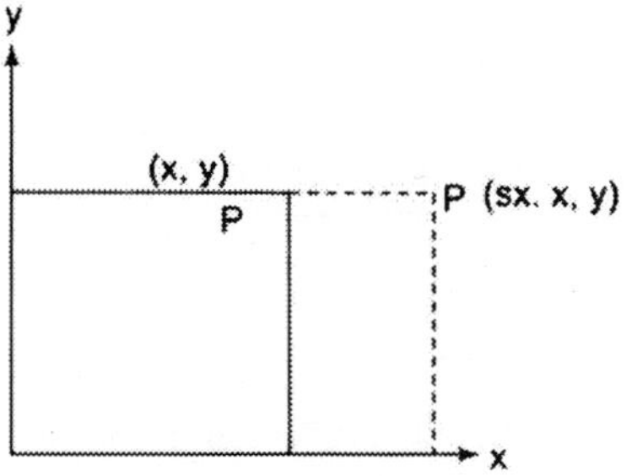

FIGURE 5.12 Scaling of a Point

$$OP' = sx \cdot OP$$

$$x' = sx \cdot x$$

Similarly,

$$y' = sy \cdot y$$

In column matrix format

$$\begin{bmatrix} x' \\ y' \end{bmatrix} = \begin{bmatrix} sx & 0 \\ 0 & sy \end{bmatrix} \begin{bmatrix} x \\ y \end{bmatrix}$$

$$P' = S_{sx,\,sy} \cdot P \qquad 5.11$$

Where, $S_{sx,sy}$ represents scaling transformation matrix, when scaling carried out w.r.t. origin and sx, sy are scaling factors along x-axis and y-axis, respectively.

Following table 5.1 shows various types of scaling operations depending upon the different values of sx and sy.

TABLE 5.1

Value of Scaling factors	*Remarks*
sx = sy > 1	Uniform extension
sx = sy < 1	Uniform reduction
sx = sy = 1	No change
sx ≠ sy	Distortion in shape
sx = sy = 0	Collapse
sx = sy < 0	No meaning in practical terms.

(b) Scaling of a Point w.r.t. any Arbitrary Point

Equation (5.11) is applicable only for scaling w.r.t. origin. But in many applications fixed point will not be origin. It may be any point outside the object in 2D plane or on the object. For example, like cases when we want to scale a rectangle about its mid-point as shown in fig. 5.13 , scale a circle about its centre as shown in fig. 5.14.

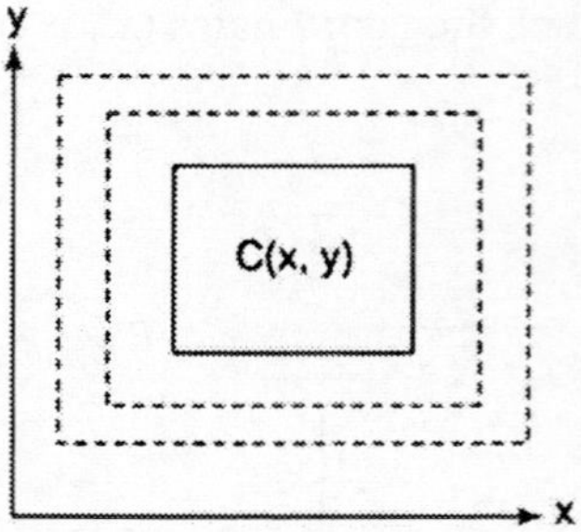

FIGURE 5.13 Scaling of a Rectangle w.r.t. its Mid-point

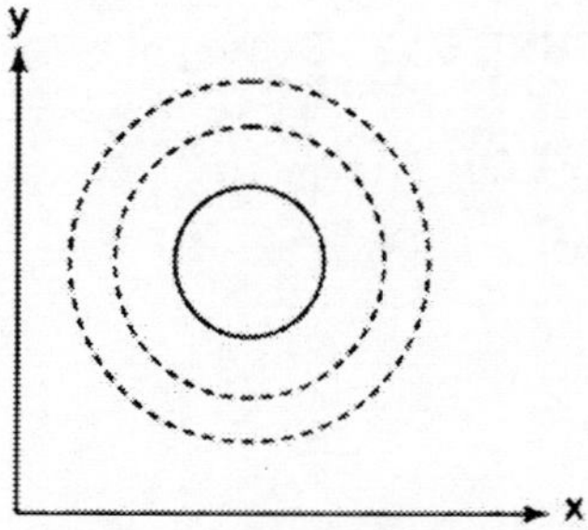

FIGURE 5.14 Scaling of a Circle w.r.t. its Centre

The process of scaling w.r.t. any point A(h,k) involves three steps:

Step 1: Translate $A(h, k)$ to $O(0, 0)$ $(T\vec{v})$.

Step 2: Perform scaling w.r.t. $O(S_{sx,\,sy})$.

Step 3: Translate A back to (h, k) $(T-\vec{v})$

$$T\text{-}\vec{v} = \begin{bmatrix} 1 & 0 & h \\ 0 & 1 & k \\ 0 & 0 & 1 \end{bmatrix} \quad S_{sx,sy} = \begin{bmatrix} sx & 0 \\ 0 & sy \end{bmatrix} \quad T\vec{v} = \begin{bmatrix} 1 & 0 & -h \\ 0 & 1 & -k \\ 0 & 0 & 1 \end{bmatrix}$$

Combining these three matrices in the order in which these are performed:

$$S_{sx,\,sy,\,A} = \overleftarrow{T-\vec{v}\cdot S_{sx,sy}\cdot T\vec{v}}$$

$$S_{sx,\,sy,\,A} = \begin{bmatrix} 1 & 0 & h \\ 0 & 1 & k \\ 0 & 0 & 1 \end{bmatrix} \begin{bmatrix} sx & 0 \\ 0 & sy \end{bmatrix} \begin{bmatrix} 1 & 0 & -h \\ 0 & 1 & -k \\ 0 & 0 & 1 \end{bmatrix}$$

$$= \begin{bmatrix} 1 & 0 & h \\ 0 & 1 & k \\ 0 & 0 & 1 \end{bmatrix} \begin{bmatrix} sx & 0 & 0 \\ 0 & sy & 0 \\ 0 & 0 & 1 \end{bmatrix} \begin{bmatrix} 1 & 0 & -h \\ 0 & 1 & -k \\ 0 & 0 & 1 \end{bmatrix}$$

$$= \begin{bmatrix} sx & 0 & -hsx + h \\ 0 & sy & -ksy + k \\ 0 & 0 & 1 \end{bmatrix}$$

Column matrix format

$$\begin{bmatrix} x' \\ y' \\ 1 \end{bmatrix} = \begin{bmatrix} sx & 0 & -hsx + h \\ 0 & sy & -ksy + k \\ 0 & 0 & 1 \end{bmatrix} \begin{bmatrix} x \\ y \\ 1 \end{bmatrix}$$

$$P' = S_{sx,\, sy, A} \cdot P$$

Algebraically,

$$x' = sx.\ x - hsx + h \qquad 5.12(a)$$

$$y' = sy \cdot y - ksy + k \qquad 5.12(b)$$

Equations 5.12(a) and 5.12(b) generate new coordinates (x', y') after scaling with scaling factors sx and sy along x-axis and y-axis, respectively of a point (x, y) w.r.t. an arbitrary point (h, k).

(c) Scaling of an Object

(i) w.r.t. origin

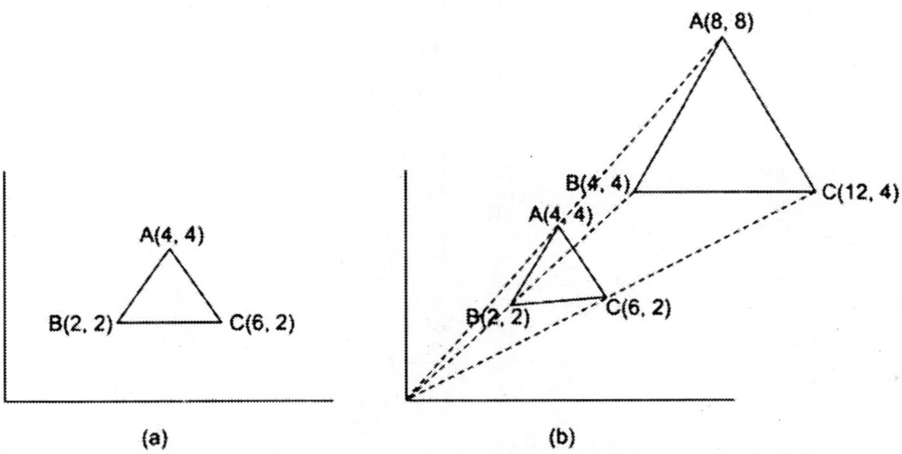

FIGURE 5.15 Scaling w.r.t. Origin

(ii) w.r.t. fixed point B(2,2)

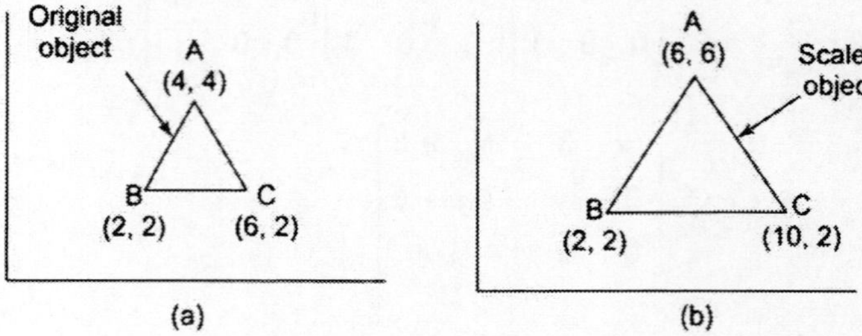

FIGURE 5.16 Scaling w.r.t. Fixed Point *B*(2,2)

In general, $$\text{OBJ}' = S_{sx,\,sy} \cdot \text{OBJ} \qquad 5.13$$

5.5.4 Reflection

A reflection is a transformation that produces a mirror image of an object. In 2D reflection, we consider a line in 2D plane as the mirror. The original object and reflected object are both in the same plane of the mirror line.

The mirror image for a 2D reflection is generated relative to an axis of rotation by rotating the object 180° about the reflection axis.

The basic principles of reflection transformation are:

1. The image of an object is formed on the side opposite to where the object is lying.
2. The perpendicular distance of reflected object from mirror line is identical to the original object from mirror line.

(a) Reflection about x-axis

Consider Fig. 5.17 wherein point $P(x, y)$ and triangle ABC reflected about x-axis.

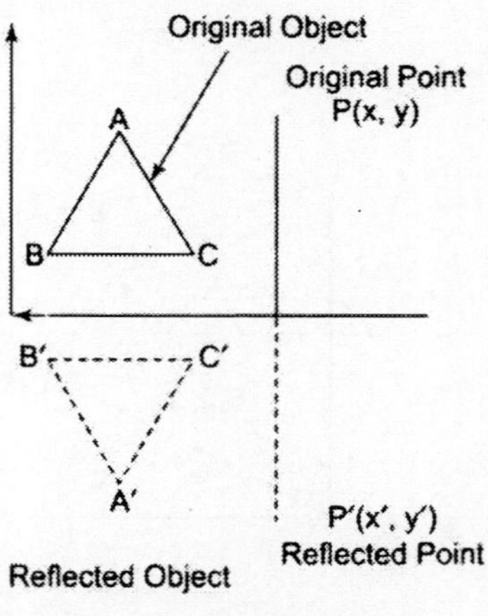

FIGURE 5.17 Reflection about *x*-axis

Relationship between $P(x, y)$ and $P'(x', y')$

$$\left.\begin{array}{l} x' = x \\ y' = -y \end{array}\right\}$$ keeps x values the same but flips the y values.

Column matrix format

$$\begin{bmatrix} x' \\ y' \end{bmatrix} = \begin{bmatrix} 1 & 0 \\ 0 & -1 \end{bmatrix} \begin{bmatrix} x \\ y \end{bmatrix}$$

$$P' = M_x \cdot P$$

(b) Reflection about y-axis

Consider Fig. 5.18 wherein point $P(x, y)$ and triangle ABC reflected about y-axis.

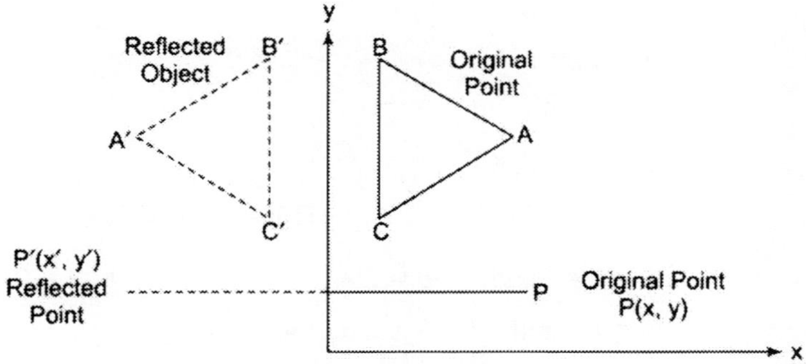

FIGURE 5.18 Reflection about *y*-axis

Relationship between $P(x, y)$ and $P'(x', y')$ is

$$\left.\begin{array}{l} x' = -x \\ y' = y \end{array}\right\}$$ Keeps y values the same but flips the x values.

Column Matrix format

$$\begin{bmatrix} x' \\ y' \end{bmatrix} = \begin{bmatrix} -1 & 0 \\ 0 & 1 \end{bmatrix} \begin{bmatrix} x \\ y \end{bmatrix}$$

$$P' = My \cdot P$$

(c) Reflection about line y = x

We have,

$$PM = P'M$$

$$\angle PMO = \angle P'MO \qquad \text{(each } 90^\circ\text{)}$$

$$OM = OM \qquad \text{(Common side)}$$

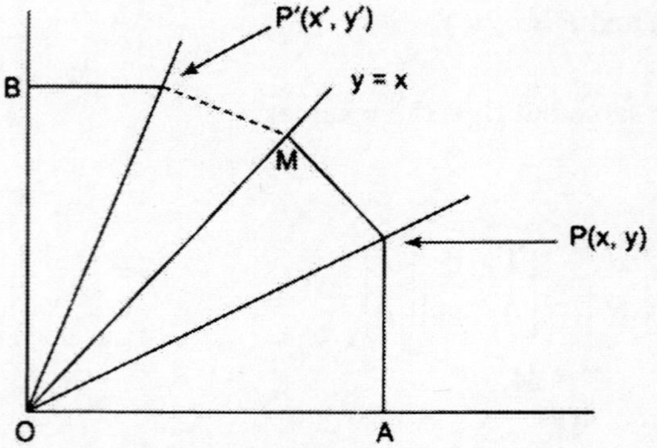

FIGURE 5.19 Reflection about Line $y = x$

From simple geometry,

$$\Delta POM \cong \Delta P'OM$$

$\therefore$ $OP = OP'$

and,

$$\angle POM = \angle P'OM$$

$\Rightarrow$ $\angle POA = \angle P'OB$ [Line $y = x$ is x-axis and y axis]

So $PB = PA$ and $OB = OA$

But $OA = x$ and $PA = y$, therefore

$$OB = y' = x$$

$$P'B = x' = y$$

Column matrix format

$$\begin{bmatrix} x' \\ y' \end{bmatrix} = \begin{bmatrix} 0 & 1 \\ 1 & 0 \end{bmatrix} \begin{bmatrix} x \\ y \end{bmatrix}$$

$$P' = M_{y=x} \cdot P$$

Alternative Method

We can drive this matrix by concatenating a sequence of the following rotation and reflection matrixes.

1. Rotate $y = x$ clockwise with an angle 45° so that it becomes x-axis ($R - 45°$).
2. Perform reflection about x-axis (M_x) so that
3. Rotate counter-clockwise with an angle 45° ($R_{45°}$)

Combining these three matrices in the order in which these are performed:

$$M_{y=x} = \overleftarrow{R_{45°}\, Mx\, R_{-45°}}$$

(d) Reflection about the Straight Line $y = -x$

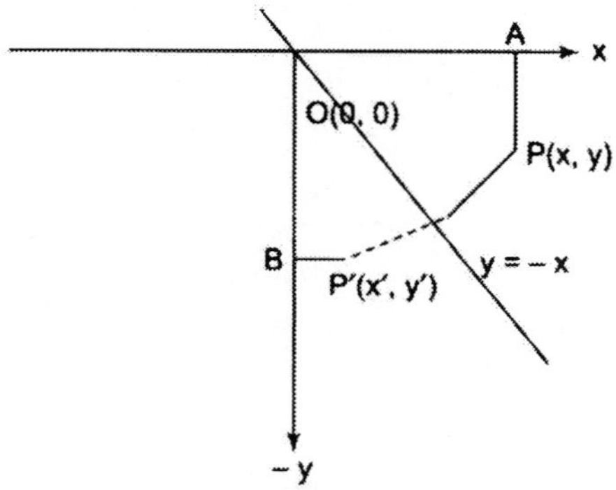

FIGURE 5.20 Reflection about Line $y = -x$

Similar to fig. 5.19, we can prove

$$PA = P'B$$
$$OA = OB$$

But here the points $P(x, y)$ and $P'(x', y')$ both being in the 4th quadrant and x and x' are +ve where as y and y' are – ve. So keeping in view this fact,

$$x' = -y$$
$$y' = -x$$

$$\begin{bmatrix} x' \\ y' \end{bmatrix} = \begin{bmatrix} 0 & -1 \\ -1 & 0 \end{bmatrix} \begin{bmatrix} x \\ y \end{bmatrix}$$

$$P' = M_y = -x \cdot P$$

Alternative Method

We can drive this matrix by concatenating a sequence of the following rotation and reflection matrixes.

1. Rotate $y = -x$ clockwise with 45° so that it becomes y-axis (R –45°).
2. Perform reflection about y-axis (M_y).
3. Rotate counter-clockwise with an angle 45° ($R_{45°}$).

Combining these three matrices in the order in which these are performed:

$$M_{y=-x} = \overleftarrow{R_{45} M_y R_{-45}}$$

(e) Reflection Relative to the Origin

In this case mirror line as the axis perpendicular to the xy plane and passing through origin as shown in Fig. 5.21 Relationship between $P(x, y)$ and $P'(x', y')$ from simple geometry.

$OP = OP'$

$\angle OAP = \angle OBP'$ (each angle is 90°)

$\angle AOP = \angle BOP'$ (alternative angles)

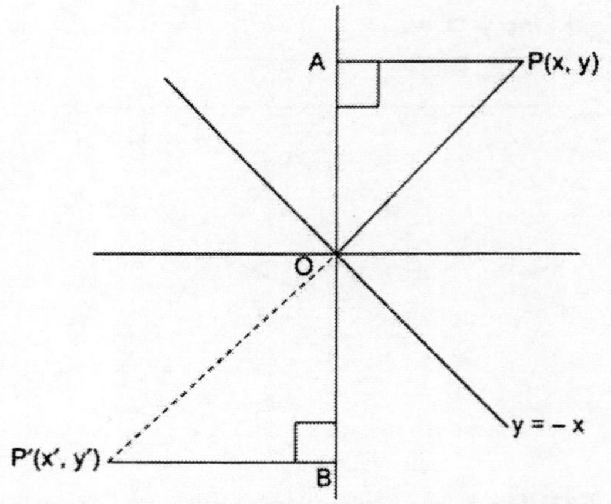

FIGURE 5.21 Reflection Relative to the Origin

Hence,

$$AP = BP'$$
$$OA = OB$$
$$x' = -x$$
$$y' = -y$$
$$\begin{bmatrix} x' \\ y' \end{bmatrix} = \begin{bmatrix} -1 & 0 \\ 0 & -1 \end{bmatrix} \begin{bmatrix} x \\ y \end{bmatrix}$$
$$P' = M_{y=x=0} P$$

Alternative Method

The reflection matrix is rotation matrix R_θ with $\theta = 180°$

$$P' = R_{180°} \cdot P$$
$$= \begin{bmatrix} \cos(180°) & -\sin(180°) \\ \sin(180°) & \cos(180°) \end{bmatrix} \begin{bmatrix} x \\ y \end{bmatrix}$$
$$\begin{bmatrix} x' \\ y' \end{bmatrix} = \begin{bmatrix} -1 & 0 \\ 0 & -1 \end{bmatrix} \begin{bmatrix} x \\ y \end{bmatrix}$$

(f) Reflection about an Arbitrary Axis

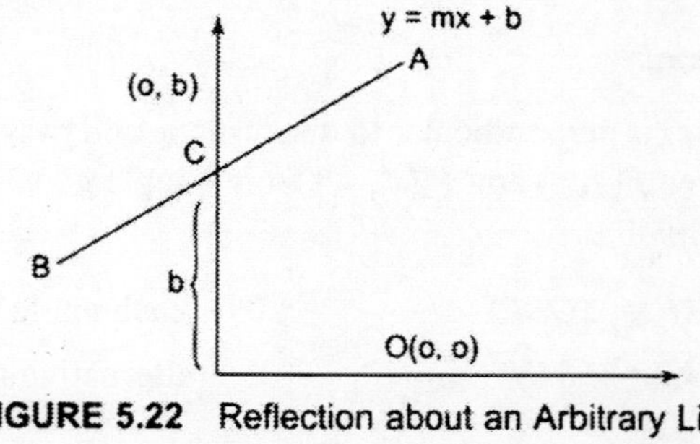

FIGURE 5.22 Reflection about an Arbitrary Line

Process involved following steps:

Step 1: Translate the line and object so that the line passes through O(0,0) ($T\vec{v}$). [Fig. 5.23(a)]

Step 2: Rotate the line and object about the origin in clockwise direction until the line coincides with x-axis ($R_{-\theta}$). [Fig. 5.23(b)]

Step 3: Reflect the object about x-axis (M_x). [Fig. 5.23(c)]

Step 4: To the object, apply the converse rotation about the origin (R_θ) [Fig. 5.23(d)]

Step 5: Translate object back to the original location ($T-\vec{v}$). [Fig. 5.23(e)]

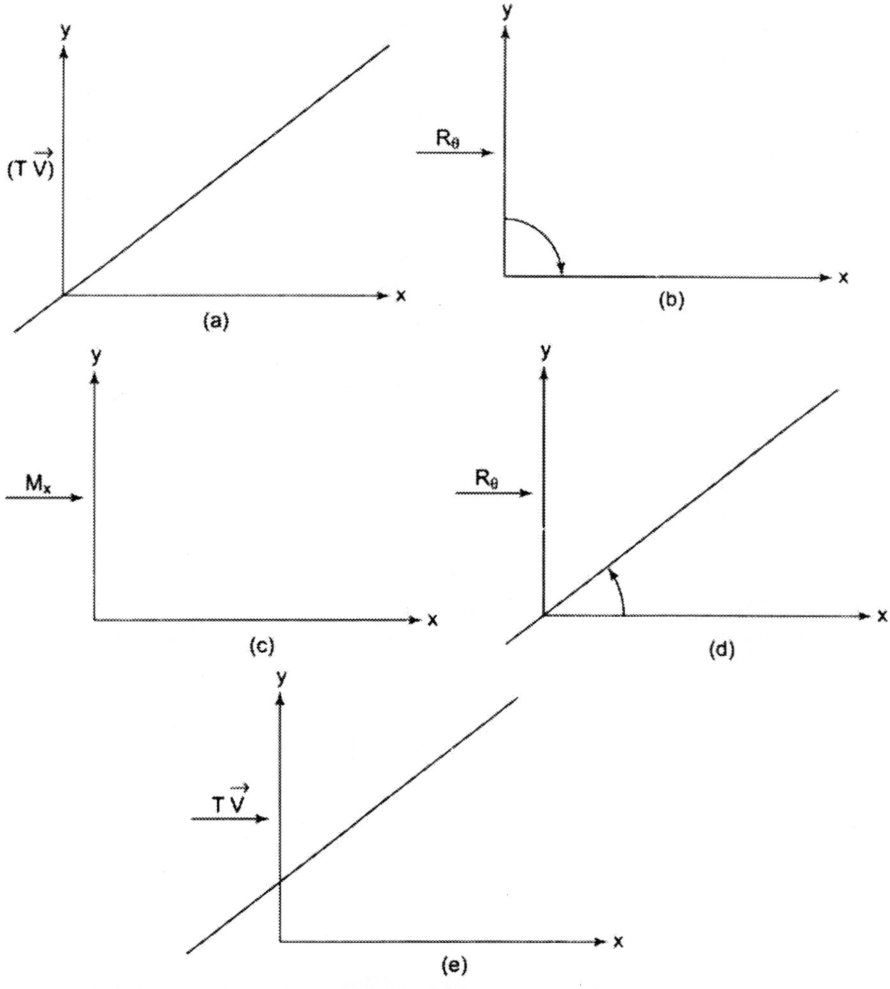

FIGURE 5.23 Stages During Reflection about an Arbitrary Axis

Combining these five transformations in the order these are performed:

$$M_{AB} = \overleftarrow{T\text{-}\vec{v}\ R\theta M_x R{-\theta}\ T\text{-}\vec{v}}$$

Now if $\tan\theta = m$

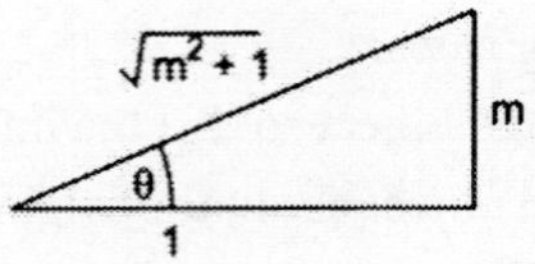

$$\sin\theta = \frac{m}{\sqrt{m^2+1}}$$

$$\cos\theta = \frac{1}{\sqrt{1+m^2}}$$

$$M_{AB} = \begin{bmatrix} 1 & 0 & 0 \\ 0 & 1 & b \\ 0 & 0 & 1 \end{bmatrix} \begin{bmatrix} \cos\theta & -\sin\theta & 0 \\ \sin\theta & \cos\theta & 0 \\ 0 & 0 & 1 \end{bmatrix} \begin{bmatrix} 1 & 0 & 0 \\ 0 & -1 & 0 \\ 0 & 0 & 1 \end{bmatrix}$$

$$\begin{bmatrix} \cos\theta & \sin\theta & 0 \\ -\sin\theta & \cos\theta & 0 \\ 0 & 0 & 1 \end{bmatrix} \begin{bmatrix} 1 & 0 & 0 \\ 0 & 1 & -b \\ 0 & 0 & 1 \end{bmatrix}$$

$$= \begin{bmatrix} \dfrac{1-m^2}{m^2+1} & \dfrac{2m}{m^2+1} & \dfrac{-2bm}{m^2+1} \\ \dfrac{2m}{m^2+1} & \dfrac{m^2-1}{m^2+1} & \dfrac{2b}{m^2+1} \\ 0 & 0 & 1 \end{bmatrix}$$

where, m is slope of line.
b is intercept made by line on positive direction of y-axis.

5.5.5 Shear

The shear transformation causes the image to slant. It is also called twist or torque or tilt transformation, more commonly named as shear transformation. Common shearing transformations are:

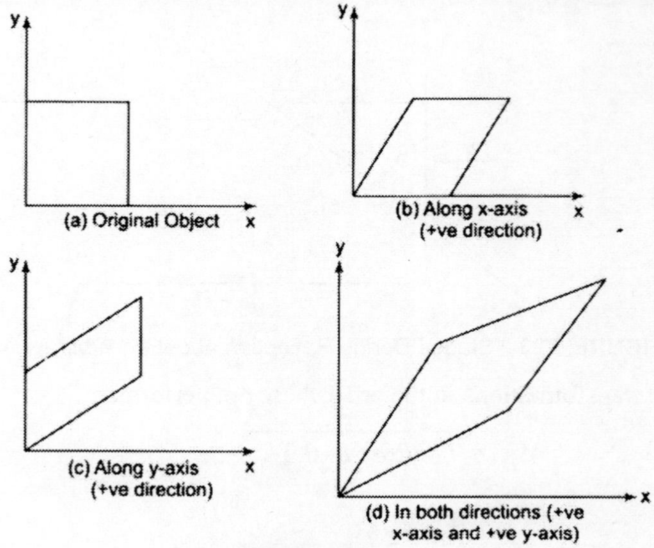

FIGURE 5.24

(a) Shearing of an object along x-axis relative to x-axis

Let us consider that a point $P(x, y)$ is sheared horizontally by a factor sh_x being the lateral movement for unit distance. Then,

$$PP' = shx \cdot AP$$
$$= shx \cdot y$$

Figure 5.25 (b) shows shearing of a point.
Therefore, relationship between $P'(x', y')$ and $P(x, y)$ is

$$x' = x + sh_x \cdot y$$
$$y' = y$$

$$\begin{bmatrix} x' \\ y' \end{bmatrix} \begin{bmatrix} 1 & sh_x \\ 0 & 1 \end{bmatrix} \begin{bmatrix} x \\ y \end{bmatrix}$$

Negative value of sh_x shifts coordinate positions to the left, fig.5.25(d) and fig. 5.25(e).

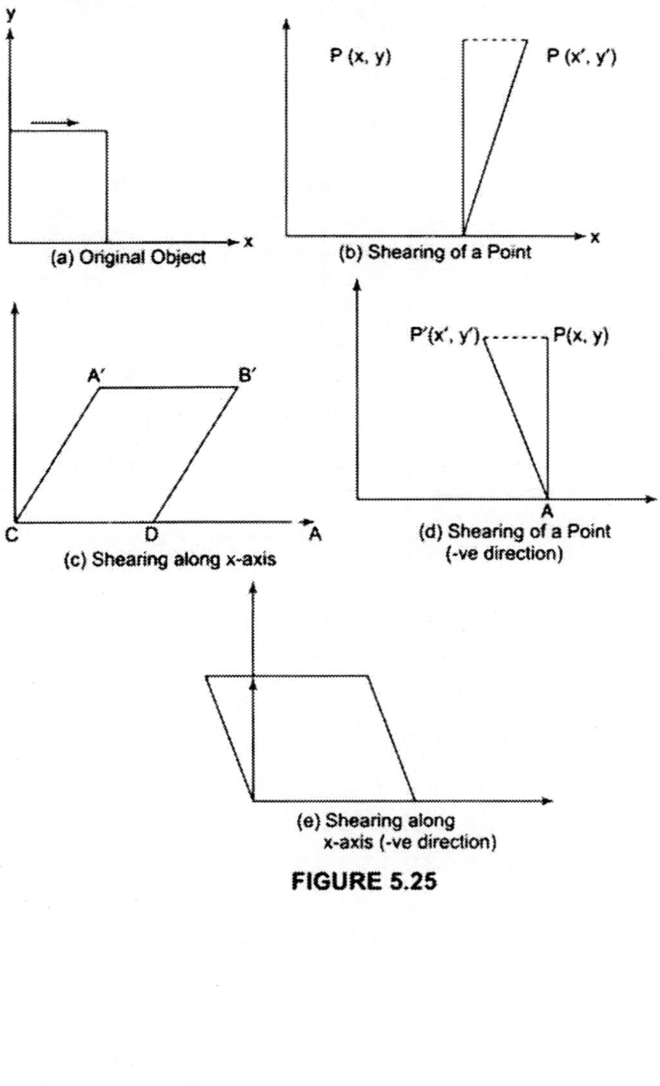

FIGURE 5.25

(b) Shearing of an object along y-axis relative to y-axis

Similarly consider fig.5.26(b) wherein point $P(x, y)$ is sheared by a factor sh_y, being the lateral movement per unit distance. Then,

$$PP' = sh_y \cdot BP$$
$$= sh_y \cdot x$$

Therefore, relationship between $P(x, y)$ and $P'(x', y')$ is $x' = x$

$$y' = y + sh_y \cdot x$$

Negative value of sh_y shifts coordinate positions downward, Fig. 5.26(c) and Fig 5.26(d).

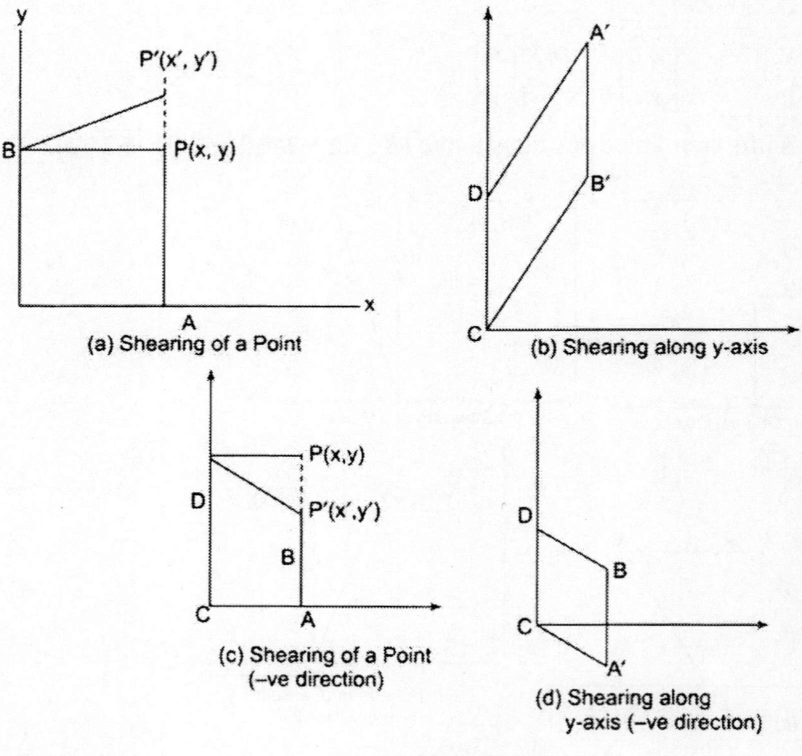

FIGURE 5.26

$$\begin{bmatrix} x' \\ y' \end{bmatrix} = \begin{bmatrix} 1 & 0 \\ sh_y & 1 \end{bmatrix} \begin{bmatrix} x \\ y \end{bmatrix}$$

(c) Shearing in both directions

Let us consider that a point $P(x, y)$ is shared to $P'(x', y')$ in both directions with shearing factors sh_x and sh_y respectively, fig 5.28(a). Then

$$x' = x + sh_x \cdot y$$

$$y' = y + sh_y \cdot x$$

$$\begin{bmatrix} x' \\ y' \end{bmatrix} \begin{bmatrix} 1 & sh_x \\ sh_y & 1 \end{bmatrix} \begin{bmatrix} x \\ y \end{bmatrix}$$

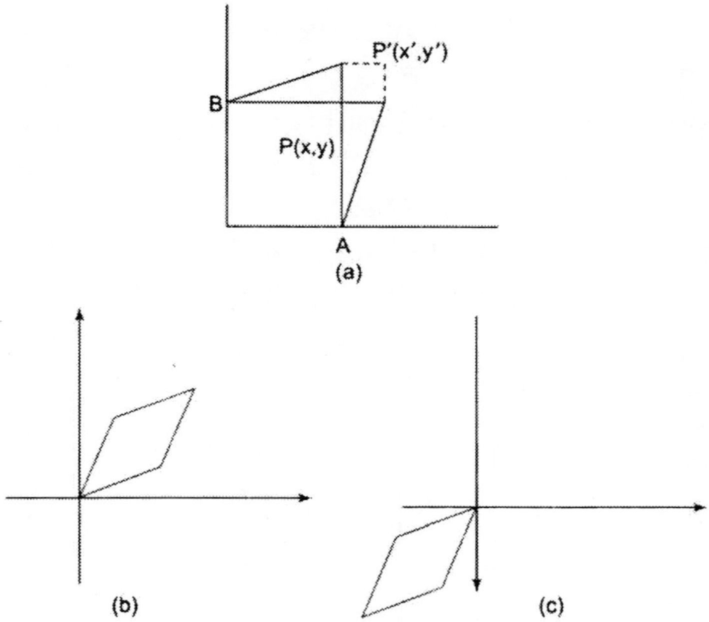

FIGURE 5.27 Shearing of Point in both Directions

Table 5.2 depicts various values of shearing factors and their corresponding effects.

TABLE 5.2

Values of Shearing factors	*Remarks*
$sh_x > 0$ $sh_y > 0$	Shearing in positive direction
sh_x, $sh_y < 0$	Shearing in negative direction
$sh_x = sh_y = 0$	No shearing
$sh_x = sh_y = 1.0$	Unrealistic distortion

Note: In general sh_x and sh_y should be less than 1.

(d) Shearing relative to other reference lines (parallel to x-axis or y-axis)

We can introduce x-direction or y-direction shear relative to other reference line parallel to x-axis or y-axis.

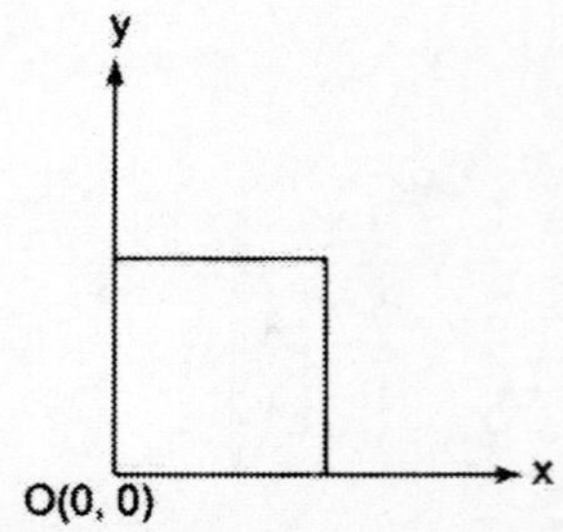

FIGURE 5.28(a) Original Object

(i) Shearing along y-axis relative to a line $x = x_{ref}$

Consider fig. 5.29(a) wherein a rectangle shown with its lower left corner at O(0,0).

$$x' = x$$
$$y' = y + sh_y\,(x - x_{ref})$$

$$\begin{bmatrix} x' \\ y' \\ 1 \end{bmatrix} = \begin{bmatrix} 1 & 0 & 0 \\ sh_y & 1 & -sh_y \cdot x_{ref} \\ 0 & 0 & 1 \end{bmatrix} \begin{bmatrix} x \\ y \\ 1 \end{bmatrix}$$

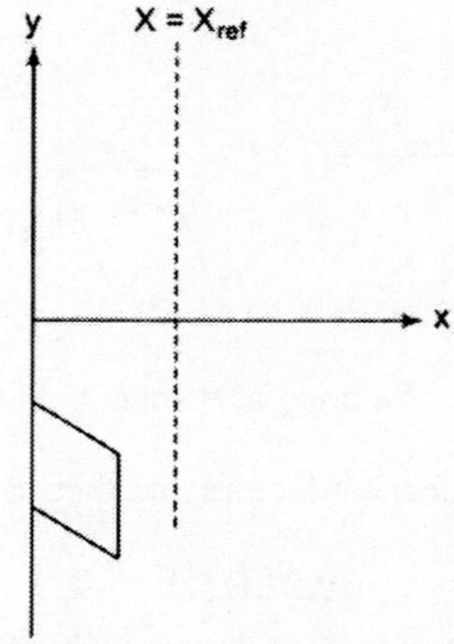

FIGURE 5.28(b) Shearing Along *y*-axis Relative to a Line $x = x_{ref}$

(ii) Shearing along y-axis relative to a line $x = -x_{ref}$

$$x' = x$$
$$y' = y + sh_y\,(x + x_{ref})$$

$$\begin{bmatrix} x' \\ y' \\ 1 \end{bmatrix} = \begin{bmatrix} 1 & 0 & 0 \\ sh_y & 1 & sh_y \cdot x_{ref} \\ 0 & 0 & 1 \end{bmatrix} \begin{bmatrix} x \\ y \\ 1 \end{bmatrix}$$

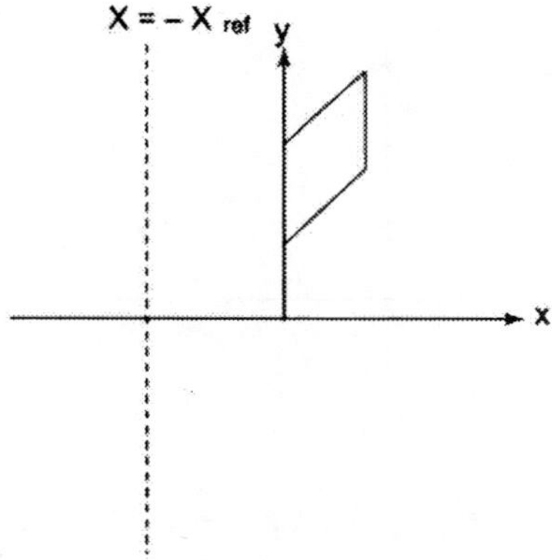

FIGURE 5.28(c) Shearing Along y-axis Relative to a Line $x = -x_{ref}$

(iii) Shearing along x-axis relative to a line $y = y_{ref}$

$$x' = x + sh_x(y - y_{ref})$$
$$y' = y$$

$$\begin{bmatrix} x' \\ y' \\ 1 \end{bmatrix} = \begin{bmatrix} 1 & sh_x & -sh_x \cdot y_{ref} \\ 1 & 0 & 0 \\ 0 & 0 & 1 \end{bmatrix} \begin{bmatrix} x \\ y \\ 1 \end{bmatrix}$$

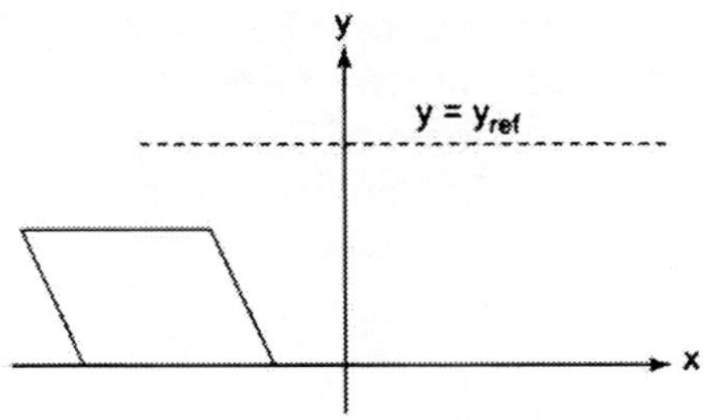

FIGURE 5.28(d) Shearing Along x-axis Relative to a Line $y = y_{ref}$

(iv) Shearing along x-axis relative to a line $y = -y_{ref}$

$$x' = x + sh_x(y + y_{ref})$$
$$y' = y$$

$$\begin{bmatrix} x' \\ y' \\ 1 \end{bmatrix} = \begin{bmatrix} 1 & sh_x & sh_x \cdot y_{ref} \\ 1 & 0 & 0 \\ 0 & 0 & 1 \end{bmatrix} \begin{bmatrix} x \\ y \\ 1 \end{bmatrix}$$

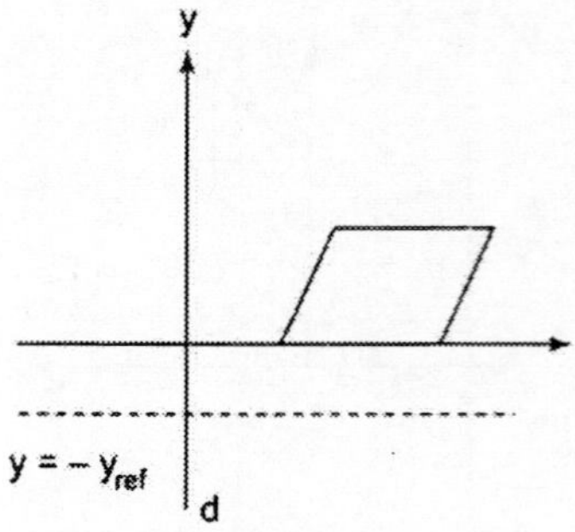

FIGURE 5.28(e) Shearing along *x*-axis relative to a Line $y = -y_{ref}$

5.6 COORDINATE TRANSFORMATIONS

So far we have discussed geometric transformations of 2D objects which are defined with respect to World Coordinate System (WCS), also called the *Global Coordinate System*. Generally, the user is interested to defined object with respect to User Coordinate System (UCS), also called the *model coordinate system* or *local coordinate system*.

UCS may vary as per convenience whereas the WCS remains fixed for a given display system.

Once we have coordinates of a point w.r.t. WCS, we can find its coordinates w.r.t. UCS, if we have location of origin of UCS and angle of rotation of UCS. Such transformations are known as global-to-local transformations.

Likewise, if we have the coordinates of a point from local coordinate system to global coordinate system, such transformation is known as local-to-global system transformations. In general, the term we use for both the above types of transformations is known as coordinate transformation. Coordinate transformation helps us to find the coordinates of a point or object from one coordinate system to another coordinate system, if location of origin of S' and angle of location of S' is known to us. If we have two coordinate systems say S and S', coordinate transformation helps to find coordinate of a point in S' if we have coordinates in S. For this, we require location of origin of S' and angle of rotation of S'.

5.6.1 Translate

If the xy coordinate system is displaced to new position $x'y'$, $\vec{v} = tx\hat{i} + ty\hat{j}$ is displacement vector. Mathematically,

$$x' = x - tx$$

$$y' = y - ty$$

$$\begin{bmatrix} x' \\ y' \\ 1 \end{bmatrix} = \begin{bmatrix} 1 & 0 & -tx \\ 0 & 1 & -ty \\ 0 & 0 & 1 \end{bmatrix} \begin{bmatrix} x \\ y \\ 1 \end{bmatrix}$$

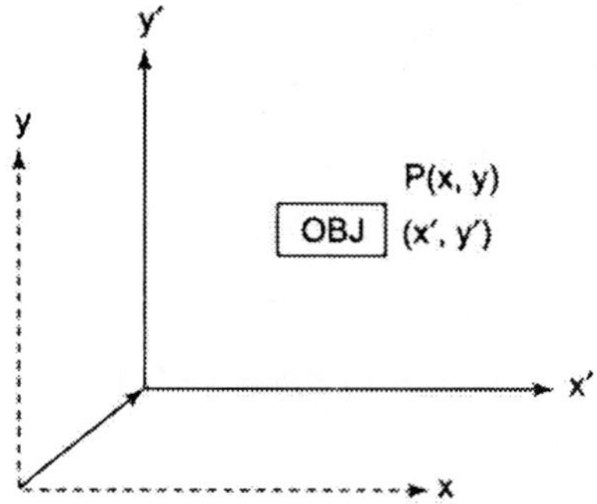

FIGURE 5.29 Coordinate Translation of an Object

$\overline{T_{tx,ty}}$ is coordinate translation transformation matrix, where tx, ty are displacement factors along x-axis and y-axis, respectively.

5.6.2 Rotation about the Origin

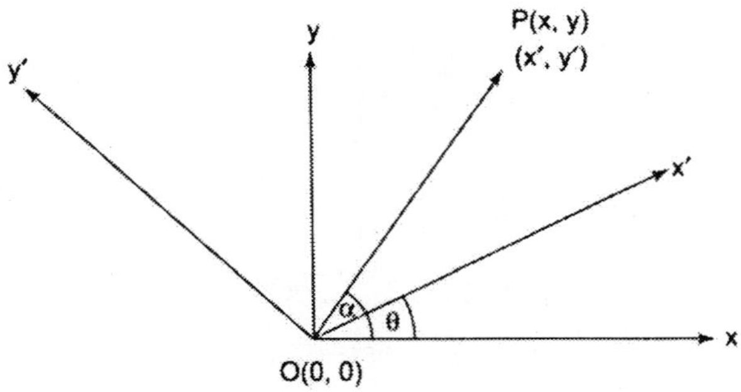

FIGURE 5.30 Coordinate Rotation of a Point

Consider fig. 5.30 wherein point $P(x, y)$ is represented. Let us suppose coordinate axis is rotated by an angle $\theta°$ about the origin.
Let us suppose
(x, y) coordinates of P w.r.t. xy coordinate system.
(x',y') coordinates of P w.r.t. $x' y'$ coordinate system.
$OP = r$ (radius vector)

$P(x, y)$ and $P(x', y')$ can be expressed as:

$$x = r\cos\alpha \quad 5.14(a)$$

$$y = r\sin\alpha \quad 5.14(b)$$

$$x' = r\cos(\alpha - \theta) \quad 5.15(a)$$

$$y' = r\sin(\alpha - \theta) \quad 5.15(b)$$

Rewriting 5.15(a) and 5.15(b) using laws of sines and cosines

$$x' = r(\cos\theta\cos\alpha + \sin\theta\sin\alpha) \quad 5.16(a)$$

$$y' = r(\sin\alpha\cos\theta - \sin\theta\cos\alpha) \quad 5.16(b)$$

Using 5.14(a) and 5.14(b) in 5.16(a) and 5.16(b) respectively, we get

$$x' = x\cos\theta + y\sin\theta$$

$$y' = -x\sin\theta + y\cos\theta$$

$$\begin{bmatrix} x' \\ y' \end{bmatrix} = \begin{bmatrix} \text{Cos}\theta & \text{Sin}\theta \\ -\text{Sin}\theta & \text{Cos}\theta \end{bmatrix} \begin{bmatrix} x \\ y \end{bmatrix}$$

$\bar{R}_\theta$ is rotational transformation matrix when coordinate axis is rotated in counter-clockwise direction by an angle θ.

Relationship between Coordinate Rotation Transformation and Geometric Rotation Transformation

$\bar{R}_{-\theta}$ represents rotation transformation matrix when coordinate axis is rotated in clockwise direction and is given by

$$\bar{R}_{-\theta} = \begin{bmatrix} \cos(-\theta) & \sin(-\theta) \\ -\sin(-\theta) & \cos(-\theta) \end{bmatrix} = \begin{bmatrix} \cos\theta & -\sin\theta \\ \sin\theta & \cos\theta \end{bmatrix} = R_\theta \text{ (By def.)}$$

$$\bar{R}_\theta = \begin{bmatrix} \cos\theta & \sin\theta \\ -\sin\theta & \cos\theta \end{bmatrix}$$

$$R_\theta = \begin{bmatrix} \cos\theta & -\sin\theta \\ \sin\theta & \cos\theta \end{bmatrix}$$

$$R_{-\theta} = \begin{bmatrix} \cos(-\theta) & -\sin(-\theta) \\ \sin(-\theta) & \cos(-\theta) \end{bmatrix}$$

$$= \begin{bmatrix} \cos(\theta) & \sin(\theta) \\ -\sin(\theta) & \cos(\theta) \end{bmatrix}$$

$$= \bar{R}_\theta = R_\theta^{-1}$$

$$\bar{R}_\theta = R_\theta^{-1}$$

Further

$$R_\theta = \begin{bmatrix} \cos\theta & -\sin\theta \\ \sin\theta & \cos\theta \end{bmatrix}$$

$\therefore$

$$R_\theta^{-1} = \begin{bmatrix} \cos\theta & \sin\theta \\ -\sin\theta & \cos\theta \end{bmatrix} = \bar{R}_\theta$$

Thus,

$$R_{-\theta} = R_\theta^{-1} = \bar{R}_\theta$$

and,

$$\bar{R}_{-\theta} = R_\theta$$

5.6.3 Scaling with respect to Origin

Consider Fig 5.31 wherein a point $P(x, y)$ is represented. Let us suppose, a new coordinate axis is obtained by scaling sx units along the x-axis and sy along the y-axis. Then we will have
$P(x, y)$ coordinate of P w.r.t. xy coordinate system
$P(x', y')$ coordinate of P w.r.t. $x'y'$ coordinate system
Relationship between $P(x, y)$ and $P(x', y')$ is given by

$$x = sx \cdot x'$$

$$y = sy\,'\,y'$$

or,

$$x' = 1/sx \cdot x$$

$$y' = 1/sy \cdot y$$

$$\begin{bmatrix} x' \\ y' \end{bmatrix} = \begin{bmatrix} 1/sx & 0 \\ 0 & 1/sy \end{bmatrix} \begin{bmatrix} x \\ y \end{bmatrix}$$

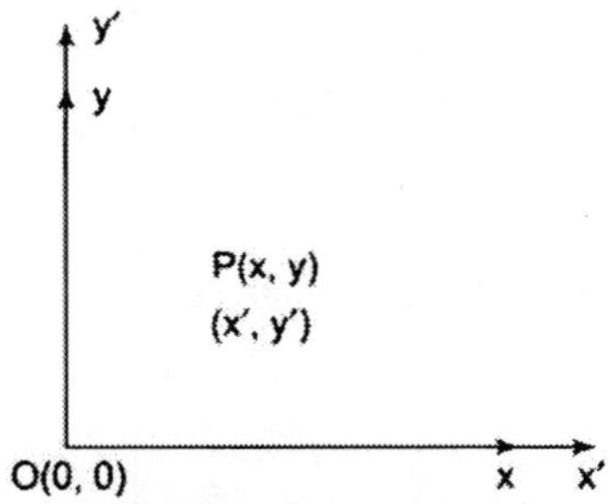

FIGURE 5.31 Scaling of a Point

$\bar{S}_{sx \cdot sy} = \begin{bmatrix} 1/sx & 0 \\ 0 & 1/sy \end{bmatrix}$ is coordinate scaling transformation, where sx and sy represent scaling factors along x-axis and y-axis, respectively.

Relationship between Coordinate and Geometric Scaling Transformations

$$\bar{S}_{sx,sy} = \begin{bmatrix} 1/sx & 0 \\ 0 & 1/sy \end{bmatrix}$$

$$= S_1/sx,\ 1/sy \quad \text{[by def.]}$$

$$= S^{-1}_{sx,sy}$$

Thus,

$$\bar{S}_{sx,sy} = S_{1/sx,1/sy} = S^{-1}_{sx,sy}$$

Table 5.3 depicts the Geometric and Coordinate transformations for all types of transformations discussed so far.

TABLE 5.3

S. No.	Type of Transformation	Geometric(Forward) Transformation	Coordinate(Backward) Transformation
1.	Translate	$T_{tx,ty} = \begin{bmatrix} 1 & 0 & t_x \\ 0 & 1 & t_y \\ 0 & 0 & 1 \end{bmatrix}$	$\bar{T}_{tx,ty} = \begin{bmatrix} 1 & 0 & -t_x \\ 0 & 1 & -t_y \\ 0 & 0 & 1 \end{bmatrix}$
2.	Rotate	$R_\theta = \begin{bmatrix} \cos\theta & -\sin\theta \\ \sin\theta & \cos\theta \end{bmatrix}$	$\bar{R}_\theta = \begin{bmatrix} \cos(\theta) & \sin(\theta) \\ -\sin(\theta) & \cos(\theta) \end{bmatrix}$
3.	Scale	$S_{sx,sy} = \begin{bmatrix} sx & 0 \\ 0 & sy \end{bmatrix}$	$\bar{S}_{sx,sy} = \begin{bmatrix} 1/sx & 0 \\ 0 & 1/sy \end{bmatrix}$
4.	Flip		
	a. About x-axis	$M_x = \begin{bmatrix} 1 & 0 \\ 0 & -1 \end{bmatrix}$	$\bar{M}_x = \begin{bmatrix} 1 & 0 \\ 0 & -1 \end{bmatrix}$
	b. About y-axis	$M_y = \begin{bmatrix} -1 & 0 \\ 0 & 1 \end{bmatrix}$	$\bar{M}_y = \begin{bmatrix} -1 & 0 \\ 0 & 1 \end{bmatrix}$
	c. About Origin	$M_o = \begin{bmatrix} -1 & 0 \\ 0 & -1 \end{bmatrix}$	$\bar{M}_o = \begin{bmatrix} -1 & 0 \\ 0 & -1 \end{bmatrix}$
	d. About line $y = x$	$M_{y=x} = \begin{bmatrix} 0 & 1 \\ 1 & 0 \end{bmatrix}$	$\bar{M}_{y=x} = \begin{bmatrix} 0 & 1 \\ 1 & 0 \end{bmatrix}$
5.	Shear	$S_{shx,shy} = \begin{bmatrix} 1 & sh_x \\ sh_y & 1 \end{bmatrix}$	$\bar{S}_{shx,shy} = \begin{bmatrix} 1 & sh_x/d \\ sh_y/d & 1 \end{bmatrix}$ where, $d = 1 - sh_x \cdot sh_y$

Product of Geometric transformation matrix[T] and its corresponding coordinate transformation matrix[$\bar{T}$] is always the identity matrix[I]. That is,

$$T \cdot \bar{T} = I$$

Or,

$$T = \bar{T}^{-1}$$

This mathematical result interprets physically that if an object or a point is moved by a certain amount and then coordinate system is moved by the same amount, then the object or point would be at the same position and vice versa.

5.7 INVERSE TRANSFORMATIONS

Each geometric and coordinate transformation has an inverse which describes just the opposite operation performed by the original transformation as shown in fig. 5.32.

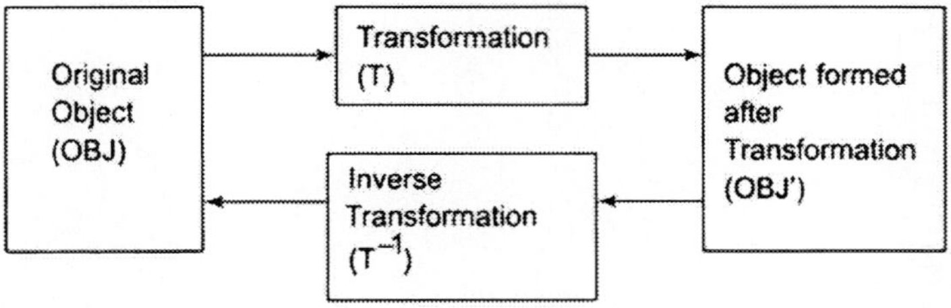

FIGURE 5.32 Relationship Between Transformation and Inverse Transformation.

5.7.1 Geometric Inverse Transformations

Each geometric inverse transformation is equal to opposite geometric transformation.

(i) Translation

$$T\bar{v}^{-1} = T_{-v}$$

$$\text{OBJ} \left\{ \begin{matrix} T_v^{-1} \\ T_{-v} \end{matrix} \right\} \longrightarrow \text{OBJ}'$$

(ii) Rotation

$$R_\theta^{-1} = R_{-\theta}$$

$$\text{OBJ} \left\{ \begin{matrix} R_\theta^{-1} \\ \mathrm{R}_{-\theta} \end{matrix} \right\} \longrightarrow \text{OBJ}'$$

(iii) Scaling

$$S_{sx,sy}^{-1} = S_{1/sx,1/sy}$$

$$\text{OBJ} \left\{ \begin{matrix} S_{sx,sy}^{-1} \\ S_{1/sx,1/sy} \end{matrix} \right\} \longrightarrow \text{OBJ}'$$

(iv) Mirror reflection

$$M_x^{-1} = M_x$$

$$M_y^{-1} = M_y$$

$$\text{OBJ} \left\{ \begin{matrix} M_x^{-1} \\ M_x \end{matrix} \right\} \longrightarrow \text{OBJ}'$$

5.7.2 Coordinate Inverse Transformations

(i) Translation

$$\overline{T\bar{v}}^{-1} = \overline{T_{-v}}$$

$$\text{OBJ}\left\{\begin{matrix}\overline{T\bar{v}}^{-1}\\ \overline{T_{-v}}\end{matrix}\right\}\longrightarrow \text{OBJ}'$$

(ii) Rotation

$$\overline{R_{\theta}^{-1}} = \overline{R_{-\theta}}$$

$$\text{OBJ}\left\{\begin{matrix}\overline{R_{\theta}^{-1}}\\ \overline{R_{-\theta}}\end{matrix}\right\}\longrightarrow \text{OBJ}'$$

(iii) Scaling

$$\overline{R}_{sx,sy}^{-1} = \overline{S}_{1/sx,1/sy}$$

$$\text{OBJ}\left\{\begin{matrix}\overline{R}_{sx,sy}^{-1}\\ \overline{S}_{1/sx,1/sy}\end{matrix}\right\}\longrightarrow \text{OBJ}'$$

(iv) Mirror reflection

$$\overline{M_x}^{-1} = \overline{M}_x$$

$$\overline{M_y}^{-1} = \overline{M}_y$$

$$\text{OBJ}\left\{\begin{matrix}\overline{M_x}^{-1}\\ \overline{M_y}^{-1}\end{matrix}\right\}\longrightarrow \text{OBJ}'$$

5.8 CONCATENATION OF SIMILAR TRANSFORMATIONS

In this section we will consider multiplication of some similar transformations and hence prove that concatenation of similar transformations produces practicable combinations. The resultant matrix is called *composite transformation matrix.*

5.8.1 Translation Combination

Two consecutive translation transformations T_1 and T_2 are additive.

Let us suppose (t_{x1}, t_{y1}) are the components of the first translation(T_1) and (t_{x2}, t_{y2}) are the components of the second translation (T_2).

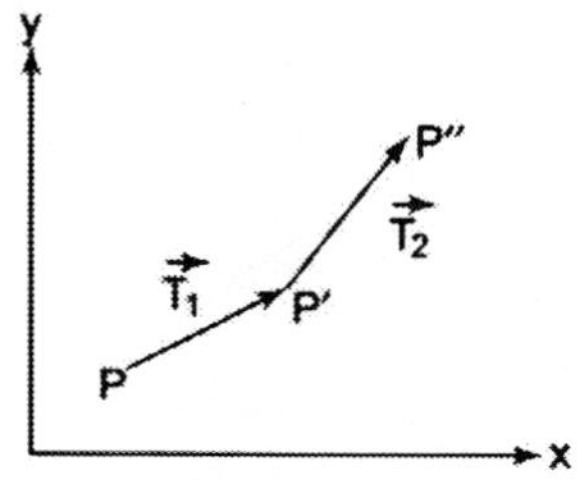

FIGURE 5.33 Two Consecutive Translations on a Point

Then their concatenation gives:

$$T_1 \cdot T_2 = \begin{bmatrix} 1 & 0 & tx_1 \\ 0 & 1 & ty_1 \\ 0 & 0 & 1 \end{bmatrix} \begin{bmatrix} 1 & 0 & tx_2 \\ 0 & 1 & ty_2 \\ 0 & 0 & 1 \end{bmatrix} = \begin{bmatrix} 1 & 0 & tx_1 + tx_2 \\ 0 & 1 & ty_1 + ty_2 \\ 0 & 0 & 1 \end{bmatrix}$$

Order to first and second translation does not matter.

5.8.2 Scale Concatenation

Two consecutive scale transformations are multiplicative.

sx_1, sy_1 are scaling factors of first scaling (S_1)

sx_2, sy_2 are scaling factors of second scaling (S_2)

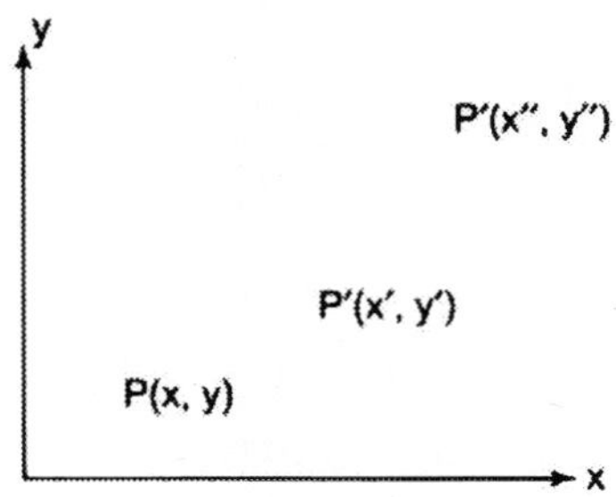

FIGURE 5.34 Two Consecutive Scaling on a Point

Then their concatenation gives:

$$S_1 \cdot S_2 = \begin{bmatrix} sx_1 & 0 & 0 \\ 0 & sy_1 & 0 \\ 0 & 0 & 0 \end{bmatrix} \begin{bmatrix} sx_2 & 0 & 0 \\ 0 & sy_2 & 0 \\ 0 & 0 & 0 \end{bmatrix} = \begin{bmatrix} sx_1 \cdot sx_2 & 0 & 0 \\ 0 & sy_1 \cdot sy_2 & 0 \\ 0 & 0 & 0 \end{bmatrix}$$

Order of first and second scaling does not matter i.e., if we increase size of a picture 4 times first then again by 2 times, final picture will be 8 times the original size.

5.8.3 Rotation Concatenation

Two consecutive rotate transformations are additive.

If θ_1 is the angle of first rotation θ_2 is the angle of second rotation.

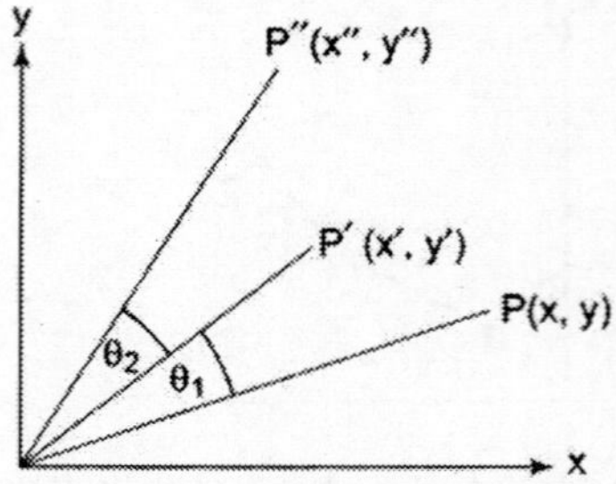

FIGURE 5.35 Two Consecutive Rotations on Point

Then their concatenation gives:

$$R_{\theta 1} \times R_{\theta 2} = \begin{bmatrix} \sin\theta_1 & -\cos\theta_1 \\ \sin\theta_1 & \cos\theta_1 \end{bmatrix} \begin{bmatrix} \cos\theta_2 & -\sin\theta_2 \\ \sin\theta_2 & \cos\theta_2 \end{bmatrix} = \begin{bmatrix} \cos(\theta_1+\theta_2) & -\sin(\theta_1+\theta_2) \\ \sin(\theta_1+\theta_2) & \cos(\theta_1+\theta_2) \end{bmatrix}$$

$$= R_{\theta_1+\theta_2}$$

Order of rotation does not matter i.e., if we rotate an object by 20° and then by 30°, we would have rotated it by 50°.

5.8.4 Shear Concatenation

sh_{x1} and sh_{y1} are the components of the first shear Sh_1, shx_2 and shy_2 are the components of the second shear Sh_2, then

$$Sh_1 \cdot Sh_2 = \begin{bmatrix} 1 & sh_{x1} & 0 \\ sh_{y1} & 1 & 0 \\ 0 & 0 & 1 \end{bmatrix} \begin{bmatrix} 1 & sh_{x2} & 0 \\ sh_{y2} & 1 & 0 \\ 0 & 0 & 1 \end{bmatrix}$$

$$= \begin{bmatrix} 1 + sh_{x1} \cdot sh_{y2} & sh_{x2} + sh_{x1} & 0 \\ sh_{y1} + sh_{y2} & sh_{x2} \cdot sh_{y1} + 1 & 0 \\ 0 & 0 & 1 \end{bmatrix}$$

which is not easy to interpret physically.

5.8.5 Mirror Concatenation

Two consecutive flips about x-axis simply cancel each other .
Object comes back.

$$M_x \cdot M_x = \begin{bmatrix} 1 & 0 & 0 \\ 0 & -1 & 0 \\ 0 & 0 & 1 \end{bmatrix} \begin{bmatrix} 1 & 0 & 0 \\ 0 & -1 & 0 \\ 0 & 0 & 1 \end{bmatrix} = \begin{bmatrix} 1 & 0 & 0 \\ 0 & 1 & 0 \\ 0 & 0 & 1 \end{bmatrix}$$

Same thing happens with two flips about y-axis and along the origin.

5.9 HOMOGENEOUS COORDINATE

5.9.1 Composite Transformation

We have seen that in some cases a desired transformation matrix may receive more than one transformation to be applied successively to get a desired transformation matrix.
For example,
Rotation transformation about a point requires some basic transformations.

$$R_{\theta,A} = 0 \begin{bmatrix} 1 & 0 & h \\ 0 & 1 & k \\ 0 & 0 & 1 \end{bmatrix} \begin{bmatrix} \cos\theta & -\sin\theta \\ \sin\theta & \cos\theta \end{bmatrix} \begin{bmatrix} 1 & 0 & -h \\ 0 & 1 & -k \\ 0 & 0 & 1 \end{bmatrix}$$

This process of calculating the product of a number of different transformations in a sequence is known as concatenation or combination of transformations and the resultant product matrix is referred to as composite or concatenated transformation matrix. *We must be extremely careful about the order in which transformations actively take place and the order we follow while multiplying the corresponding transformation matrices.*

TABLE 5.4

Matrix format	*Order of multiplication*
Column matrix	Right -to -left
Row matrix	Left -to -Right

5.9.2 Homogeneous Coordinates

Problem of homogeneity of transformation is involved. We must be able to represent the basic transformations as 3 × 3 homogeneous coordinate matrices do as to be compatible with the transformation matrix. This can be accomplished with the following procedure:

Representation of a point (x, y) in 2D Cartesian system is $(x, y, 1)$ in homogenous coordinate system. Further any point (x, y, w) when $w \neq o$ is in homogeneous coordinate corresponding to the point $(x/w, y/w)$ in 2D Cartesian system. Likewise there can be infinite number of revivalist homogeneous representations of any given point, as shown below.

$$\begin{bmatrix} x \\ y \end{bmatrix} = \begin{bmatrix} xw \\ yw \\ w \end{bmatrix} = w\begin{bmatrix} x \\ y \\ 1 \end{bmatrix} \quad w \text{ is known as weight.}$$

If $w = 1$ then table $(x, y, 1)$ represents homogeneous coordinate for representation of point positions (x, y) in xy-plane.

Advantages of Representation in Homogeneous Coordinates

(a) It allows us to represent all geometric transformation equations informally.
(b) It allows us to avoid floating point arithmetic. For example, a point (1/3,1/4) in 2D can be represented as homogeneous coordinates (4,3, 12).

Homogeneous coordinate representation of

$$R_{\theta A} = \begin{bmatrix} 1 & 0 & h \\ 0 & 1 & k \\ 0 & 0 & 1 \end{bmatrix} \begin{bmatrix} \cos\theta & -\sin\theta \\ \sin\theta & \cos\theta \end{bmatrix} \begin{bmatrix} 1 & 0 & -h \\ 0 & 1 & -k \\ 0 & 0 & 1 \end{bmatrix}$$

is

$$R_{\theta,A} = \begin{bmatrix} 1 & 0 & h \\ 0 & 1 & k \\ 0 & 0 & 1 \end{bmatrix} \begin{bmatrix} \cos\theta & -\sin\theta & 0 \\ \sin\theta & \cos\theta & 0 \\ 0 & 0 & 1 \end{bmatrix} \begin{bmatrix} 1 & 0 & -h \\ 0 & 1 & -k \\ 0 & 0 & 1 \end{bmatrix}$$

$$y' = y + shy\,(x - x_{ref})$$

SOLVED PROBLEMS

Problem 5.1 A triangle with vertices $A(2,2)$, $B(5,2)$, and $C(5,5)$ is rotated by an angle 45° about

(a) Point A(2,2)

(b) Point G (where G is the point of intersection of bisectors passing through mid points of edges of the triangle).

Find the transformed triangle in both the cases.

Solution:

In general transformation matrix for rotation about any point $P(h, k)$ is

$$R\theta_{,p} = \begin{bmatrix} \text{Cos}\,\theta & -\text{Sin}\,\theta & -h\text{Cos}\,\theta + k\text{Sin}\,\theta + h \\ \text{Sin}\,\theta & \text{Cos}\,\theta & -h\text{Sin}\,\theta - k\text{Cos}\,\theta + k \\ 0 & 0 & 1 \end{bmatrix}$$

(a) About $A(2,2)$

$$R45°,A = \begin{bmatrix} \frac{1}{\sqrt{2}} & -\frac{1}{\sqrt{2}} & 2 \\ \frac{1}{\sqrt{2}} & \frac{1}{\sqrt{2}} & 2(1-\sqrt{2}) \\ 0 & 0 & 1 \end{bmatrix} \begin{bmatrix} 2 & 5 & 5 \\ 2 & 2 & 5 \\ 1 & 1 & 1 \end{bmatrix}$$

$$= \begin{bmatrix} 2 & 3+\sqrt{2} & 2 \\ 2 & 3+2\sqrt{2} & 5\sqrt{2} \\ 1 & 1 & 1 \end{bmatrix}$$

(b) About point G

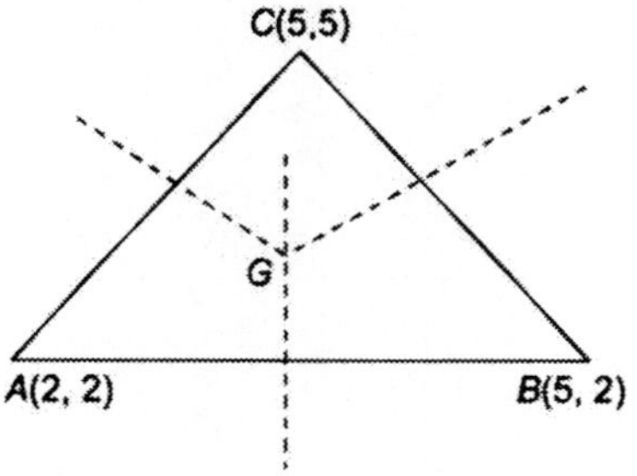

$$G\left(\frac{2+5+5}{3}, \frac{2+2+5}{3}\right) = G(4,3)$$

Now we will proceed similar to part (a) of the problem.

Problem 5.2 A diamond with vertices $A(10,0)$, $B(0,10)$, $C(-10,0)$, and $D(0,-10)$ and origin at the mid point is scaled twice uniformly w.r.t. $O(0,0)$. Find the co-ordinates of transformed diamond and sketch the transformed diamond.

Solution:

Transformation matrix for scaling w.r.t $O(0,0)$ is

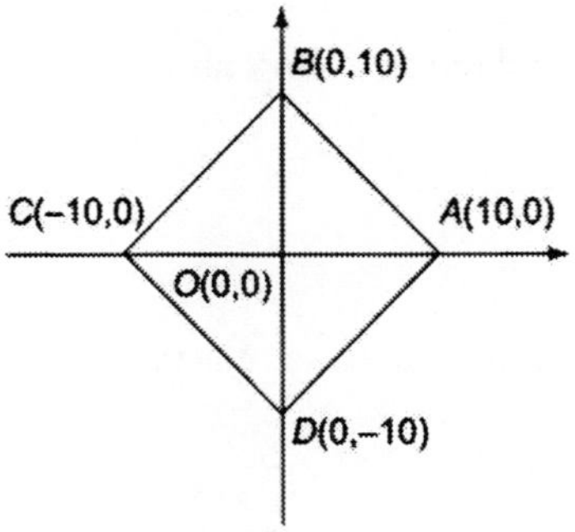

$$S_{sx,sy} = \begin{bmatrix} sx & 0 & 0 \\ 0 & sy & 0 \\ 0 & 0 & 1 \end{bmatrix}$$

$$sx = 2 \text{ and } sy = 2$$

$$S_{2,2} = \begin{bmatrix} 2 & 0 & 0 \\ 0 & 2 & 0 \\ 0 & 0 & 1 \end{bmatrix}$$

$$A'B'C'D' = \begin{bmatrix} 2 & 0 & 0 \\ 0 & 2 & 0 \\ 0 & 0 & 1 \end{bmatrix} \overset{\begin{matrix} A & B & C & D \end{matrix}}{\begin{bmatrix} 10 & 0 & -10 & 0 \\ 0 & 10 & 0 & -10 \\ 1 & 1 & 1 & 1 \end{bmatrix}}$$

$$= \begin{bmatrix} 20 & 0 & -20 & 0 \\ 0 & 20 & 0 & -20 \\ 1 & 1 & 1 & 1 \end{bmatrix}$$

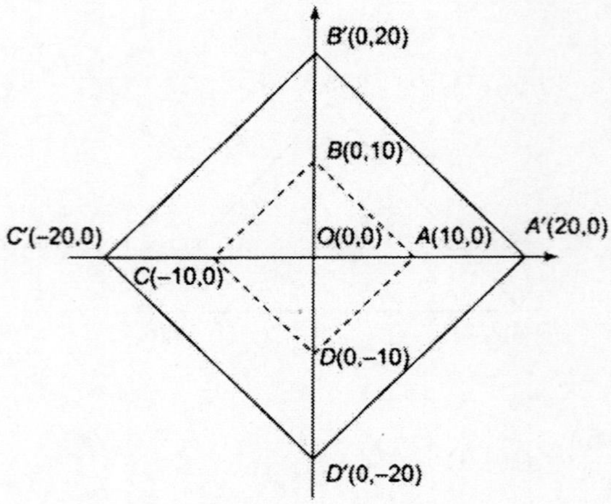

Problem 5.3 Prove that reflection along the line $y = x$ is equivalent to reflection along the x-axis followed by counter clockwise rotation by 90°.

Solution:

The reflection matrix about the line $y = x$ is

$$M_{y=x} = \begin{bmatrix} 0 & 1 & 0 \\ 1 & 0 & 0 \\ 0 & 0 & 1 \end{bmatrix}$$

The reflection matrix about the line x-axis or $y = 0$ is

$$M_{y=0} = \begin{bmatrix} 1 & 0 & 0 \\ 0 & -1 & 0 \\ 0 & 0 & 1 \end{bmatrix}$$

The transformation matrix for rotation w.r.t. θ

$$R_\theta = \begin{bmatrix} \text{Cos}\,\theta & -\text{Sin}\,\theta & 0 \\ \text{Sin}\,\theta & \text{Cos}\,\theta & 0 \\ 0 & 0 & 1 \end{bmatrix}$$

$$R_{90°} = \begin{bmatrix} 0 & -1 & 0 \\ 1 & 0 & 0 \\ 0 & 0 & 1 \end{bmatrix}$$

$$T = \overleftarrow{\begin{bmatrix} 0 & -1 & 0 \\ 1 & 0 & 0 \\ 0 & 0 & 1 \end{bmatrix} \begin{bmatrix} 1 & 0 & 0 \\ 0 & -1 & 0 \\ 0 & 0 & 1 \end{bmatrix}}$$

$$= \begin{bmatrix} 0 & 1 & 0 \\ 1 & 0 & 0 \\ 0 & 0 & 1 \end{bmatrix}$$

Clearly

$$T = M_{y=x}$$

Hence the result.

Problem 5.4 Show that the order in which transformations are performed is important by applying the transformations of the triangle $A(1,0)$, $B(0,1)$, $C(1,1)$ by

(i) Rotated 45° about the origin and then translating in the direction of the vector$(1,0)$.
(ii) Translating first and then rotating by 45° about the origin.

Solution:

In general transformation matrix for rotation about any point $P(h,k)$ is

$$R\theta_{,P} = \begin{bmatrix} \text{Cos}\,\theta & -\text{Sin}\,\theta & -h\,\text{Cos}\,\theta + k\,\text{Sin}\,\theta + h \\ \text{Sin}\,\theta & \text{Cos}\,\theta & -h\,\text{Sin}\,\theta - k\,\text{Cos}\,\theta + k \\ 0 & 0 & 1 \end{bmatrix}$$

Here $\theta = 45°$ and $(h,k) = (0,0)$

$$R_{45°,O} = \begin{bmatrix} \frac{1}{\sqrt{2}} & -\frac{1}{\sqrt{2}} & 0 \\ \frac{1}{\sqrt{2}} & \frac{1}{\sqrt{2}} & 0 \\ 0 & 0 & 1 \end{bmatrix}$$

Translate transformation matrix with direction vector $<tx,ty>$ is

$$T_{tx,ty} = \begin{bmatrix} 1 & 0 & tx \\ 0 & 1 & ty \\ 0 & 0 & 1 \end{bmatrix}$$

$$T_{1,0} = \begin{bmatrix} 1 & 0 & 1 \\ 0 & 1 & 0 \\ 0 & 0 & 1 \end{bmatrix}$$

$$T2 = R_{45°,O}\,T_{1,o} = \begin{bmatrix} \frac{1}{\sqrt{2}} & -\frac{1}{\sqrt{2}} & 0 \\ \frac{1}{\sqrt{2}} & \frac{1}{\sqrt{2}} & 0 \\ 0 & 0 & 1 \end{bmatrix} \begin{bmatrix} 1 & 0 & 1 \\ 0 & 1 & 0 \\ 0 & 0 & 1 \end{bmatrix}$$

$$= \begin{bmatrix} \frac{1}{\sqrt{2}} & -\frac{1}{\sqrt{2}} & \frac{1}{\sqrt{2}} \\ \frac{1}{\sqrt{2}} & \frac{1}{\sqrt{2}} & \frac{1}{\sqrt{2}} \\ 0 & 0 & 1 \end{bmatrix}$$

$$T1 = T_{1,o}\, R_{45°,O} = \begin{bmatrix} 1 & 0 & 1 \\ 0 & 1 & 0 \\ 0 & 0 & 1 \end{bmatrix} \begin{bmatrix} \frac{1}{\sqrt{2}} & -\frac{1}{\sqrt{2}} & 0 \\ \frac{1}{\sqrt{2}} & \frac{1}{\sqrt{2}} & 0 \\ 0 & 0 & 1 \end{bmatrix}$$

$$= \begin{bmatrix} \frac{1}{\sqrt{2}} & -\frac{1}{\sqrt{2}} & 1 \\ \frac{1}{\sqrt{2}} & \frac{1}{\sqrt{2}} & 0 \\ 0 & 0 & 1 \end{bmatrix}$$

Clearly,

$$T1 \neq T2$$

Hence *translation* and *rotation* are not commutative.

Problem 5.5 Shear a unit square whose opposite vertices are at (0,0) and (2,2) by

(a) 2 units along x-axis and reference line $y = 0$
(b) 3 units along y-axis and reference line $x = 0$.
(c) 2 units along x-axis and 3 units along y-axis w.r.t. principal axis.
(d) 2 units along x-axis and reference line $y = -1$
(e) 3 units along y-axis and reference line $x = -1$.

Solution:

Part (a)

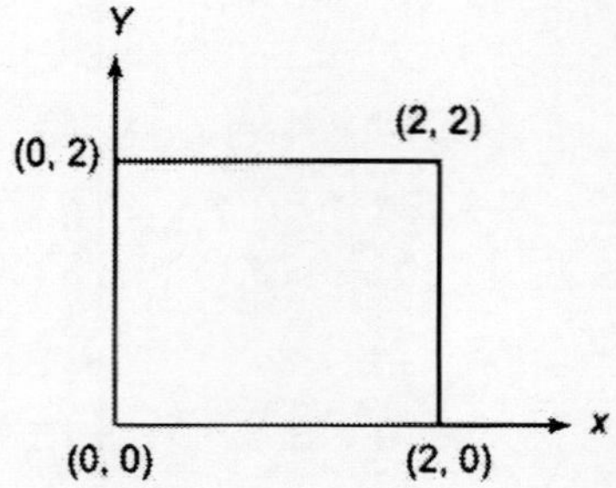

$$\begin{bmatrix} x^1 \\ y^1 \end{bmatrix} = \begin{bmatrix} 1 & shx \\ 0 & 1 \end{bmatrix} \begin{bmatrix} x \\ y \end{bmatrix}$$

Here $shx = 2$

$$\begin{bmatrix} x^1 \\ y^1 \end{bmatrix} = \begin{bmatrix} 1 & 2 \\ 0 & 1 \end{bmatrix} \begin{bmatrix} x \\ y \end{bmatrix}$$

$$A'B'C'D' = \begin{bmatrix} 1 & 2 & 0 \\ 0 & 1 & 0 \\ 0 & 0 & 1 \end{bmatrix} \begin{bmatrix} 0 & 2 & 2 & 0 \\ 0 & 0 & 2 & 2 \\ 1 & 1 & 1 & 1 \end{bmatrix}$$

$$= \begin{bmatrix} 0 & 2 & 6 & 4 \\ 0 & 0 & 2 & 2 \\ 1 & 1 & 1 & 1 \end{bmatrix}$$

Part (b)

$$\begin{bmatrix} x' \\ y' \end{bmatrix} = \begin{bmatrix} 1 & 0 \\ sh_y & 1 \end{bmatrix} \begin{bmatrix} x \\ y \end{bmatrix}$$

$$\begin{bmatrix} x' \\ y' \end{bmatrix} = \begin{bmatrix} 1 & 0 \\ 3 & 1 \end{bmatrix} \begin{bmatrix} x \\ y \end{bmatrix}$$

$$A'B'C'D' = \begin{bmatrix} 1 & 0 & 0 \\ 3 & 1 & 0 \\ 0 & 0 & 1 \end{bmatrix} \begin{bmatrix} 0 & 2 & 2 & 0 \\ 0 & 0 & 2 & 2 \\ 1 & 1 & 1 & 1 \end{bmatrix}$$

$$= \begin{bmatrix} 0 & 2 & 2 & 0 \\ 0 & 6 & 8 & 2 \\ 1 & 1 & 1 & 1 \end{bmatrix}$$

Part (c)

$$\begin{bmatrix} x^1 \\ y^1 \end{bmatrix} = \begin{bmatrix} 1 & sh_x \\ sh_y & 1 \end{bmatrix} \begin{bmatrix} x \\ y \end{bmatrix}$$

$$\begin{bmatrix} x^1 \\ y^1 \end{bmatrix} = \begin{bmatrix} 1 & 2 \\ 3 & 1 \end{bmatrix} \begin{bmatrix} x \\ y \end{bmatrix}$$

$$A'B'C'D' = \begin{bmatrix} 1 & 2 & 0 \\ 3 & 1 & 0 \\ 0 & 0 & 1 \end{bmatrix} \begin{bmatrix} 0 & 2 & 2 & 0 \\ 0 & 0 & 2 & 2 \\ 1 & 1 & 1 & 1 \end{bmatrix}$$

$$= \begin{bmatrix} 0 & 2 & 6 & 4 \\ 0 & 6 & 8 & 2 \\ 1 & 1 & 1 & 1 \end{bmatrix}$$

Part (d)

$$\begin{bmatrix} x' \\ y' \\ 1 \end{bmatrix} = \begin{bmatrix} 1 & sh_x & -sh_x \cdot y_{ref} \\ 0 & 1 & 0 \\ 0 & 0 & 1 \end{bmatrix} \begin{bmatrix} x \\ y \\ 1 \end{bmatrix}$$

$$\begin{bmatrix} x' \\ y' \\ 1 \end{bmatrix} = \begin{bmatrix} 1 & 2 & -2.(-1) \\ 0 & 1 & 0 \\ 0 & 0 & 1 \end{bmatrix} \begin{bmatrix} x \\ y \\ 1 \end{bmatrix}$$

$$A'B'C'D' = \begin{bmatrix} 1 & 2 & 2 \\ 0 & 1 & 0 \\ 0 & 0 & 1 \end{bmatrix} \begin{bmatrix} 0 & 2 & 2 & 0 \\ 0 & 0 & 2 & 2 \\ 1 & 1 & 1 & 1 \end{bmatrix}$$

$$= \begin{bmatrix} 2 & 4 & 8 & 6 \\ 0 & 0 & 2 & 2 \\ 1 & 1 & 1 & 1 \end{bmatrix}$$

Part (e)

$$\begin{bmatrix} x' \\ y' \\ 1 \end{bmatrix} = \begin{bmatrix} 1 & 0 & 0 \\ sh_y & 1 & -sh_y.x_{ref} \\ 0 & 0 & 1 \end{bmatrix} \begin{bmatrix} x \\ y \\ 1 \end{bmatrix}$$

$$\begin{bmatrix} x' \\ y' \\ 1 \end{bmatrix} = \begin{bmatrix} 1 & 0 & 0 \\ 3 & 1 & 3 \\ 0 & 0 & 1 \end{bmatrix} \begin{bmatrix} x \\ y \\ 1 \end{bmatrix}$$

$$A'B'C'D' = \begin{bmatrix} 1 & 0 & 0 \\ 3 & 1 & 3 \\ 0 & 0 & 1 \end{bmatrix} \begin{bmatrix} 0 & 2 & 2 & 0 \\ 0 & 0 & 2 & 2 \\ 1 & 1 & 1 & 1 \end{bmatrix}$$

$$= \begin{bmatrix} 0 & 2 & 2 & 1 \\ 3 & 9 & 11 & 5 \\ 1 & 1 & 1 & 1 \end{bmatrix}$$

Problem 5.6 Prove that generally successive scaling transformation and rotation transformation are not commutative.

Solution:
Scaling transformation matrix w.r.t $O(0, 0)$ is

$$S_{sx,sy} = \begin{bmatrix} sx & 0 & 0 \\ 0 & sy & 0 \\ 0 & 0 & 1 \end{bmatrix}$$

Rotation transformation matrix w.r.t $O(0,0)$ is

$$R_\theta = \begin{bmatrix} \text{Cos}\,\theta & -\text{Sin}\,\theta & 0 \\ \text{Sin}\,\theta & \text{Cos}\,\theta & 0 \\ 0 & 0 & 1 \end{bmatrix}$$

$$T1 = S_{sx,sy} x R_\theta = \begin{bmatrix} sx & 0 & 0 \\ 0 & sy & 0 \\ 0 & 0 & 1 \end{bmatrix} \begin{bmatrix} \text{Cos}\,\theta & -\text{Sin}\,\theta & 0 \\ \text{Sin}\,\theta & \text{Cos}\,\theta & 0 \\ 0 & 0 & 1 \end{bmatrix}$$

$$= \begin{bmatrix} sx\text{Cos}\,\theta & -sx\text{Sin}\,\theta & 0 \\ sy\text{Sin}\,\theta & sy\text{Cos}\,\theta & 0 \\ 0 & 0 & 1 \end{bmatrix}$$

$$T2 = R_{\theta\,x} S_{sx,sy} = \begin{bmatrix} \text{Cos}\,\theta & -\text{Sin}\,\theta & 0 \\ \text{Sin}\,\theta & \text{Cos}\,\theta & 0 \\ 0 & 0 & 1 \end{bmatrix} \begin{bmatrix} sx & 0 & 0 \\ 0 & sy & 0 \\ 0 & 0 & 1 \end{bmatrix}$$

$$= \begin{bmatrix} sx\text{Cos}\,\theta & -sy\text{Sin}\,\theta & 0 \\ sx\text{Sin}\,\theta & sy\text{Cos}\,\theta & 0 \\ 0 & 0 & 1 \end{bmatrix}$$

Clealy

$$T1 \neq T2$$

Hence *scaling* and *rotation* are not commutative.

Special Cases

Case I In case of uniform scaling i.e. $sx = sy$, we have

$$T1 = T2$$

Case II

$\theta = n\pi$, where n is any integer, $\sin\theta = 0$ and $\cos\theta = 1$, we have

$$T1 = T2$$

Problem 5.7 Prove that successive translation transformation and rotation transformation are not commutative.

Solution:

Similar to problem 5.5.

Problem 5.8 A unit square with origin at one of the vertex of the square is scaled twice along one of diagonal of the square. Find the co-ordinates of the transformed square and sketch the transformed square.

Solution:

In this case direction of scaling is not parallel to principal axis, therefore we proceed as follows:

(a) Rotate x-axis by 45° so that it aligns with the diagonal $\left(\overline{R_{45^\circ}}\right)$

(b) Perform scaling $(S_{2,2})$

(c) Rotate back by 45° so that points return to original position $\left(\overline{R_{-45^\circ}}\right)$

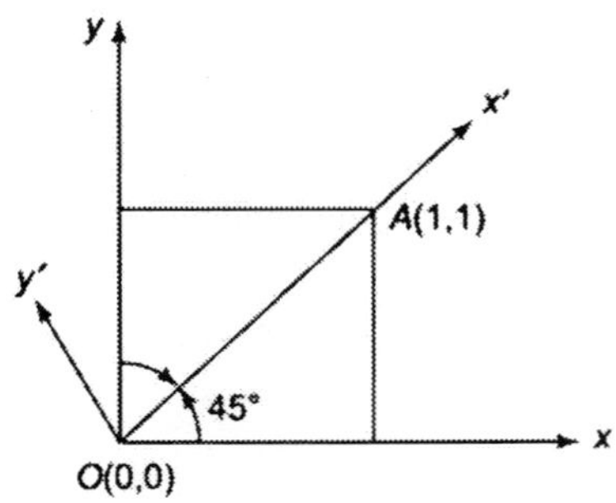

$$T = \overleftarrow{\left(\overline{R_{-45^\circ}}\right)(S_{2,2})\left(\overline{R_{45^\circ}}\right)}$$

$$T = \begin{bmatrix} \frac{1}{\sqrt{2}} & -\frac{1}{\sqrt{2}} & 0 \\ \frac{1}{\sqrt{2}} & \frac{1}{\sqrt{2}} & 0 \\ 0 & 0 & 1 \end{bmatrix} \begin{bmatrix} 2 & 0 & 0 \\ 0 & 2 & 0 \\ 0 & 0 & 1 \end{bmatrix} \begin{bmatrix} \frac{1}{\sqrt{2}} & \frac{1}{\sqrt{2}} & 0 \\ -\frac{1}{\sqrt{2}} & \frac{1}{\sqrt{2}} & 0 \\ 0 & 0 & 1 \end{bmatrix} \quad [\overline{R_\theta} = R_{-\theta}]$$

$$T = \begin{bmatrix} \frac{1}{\sqrt{2}} & -\frac{1}{\sqrt{2}} & 0 \\ \frac{1}{\sqrt{2}} & \frac{1}{\sqrt{2}} & 0 \\ 0 & 0 & 1 \end{bmatrix} \begin{bmatrix} \frac{\sqrt{2}}{1} & \frac{\sqrt{2}}{1} & 0 \\ -\frac{\sqrt{2}}{1} & \frac{\sqrt{2}}{1} & 0 \\ 0 & 0 & 1 \end{bmatrix}$$

$$T = \begin{bmatrix} 2 & 0 & 0 \\ 0 & 2 & 0 \\ 0 & 0 & 1 \end{bmatrix}$$

$$\begin{matrix} & & & A & B & C & D \end{matrix}$$

$$A'B'C'D' = \begin{bmatrix} 2 & 0 & 0 \\ 0 & 2 & 0 \\ 0 & 0 & 1 \end{bmatrix} \begin{bmatrix} 0 & 1 & 1 & 0 \\ 0 & 0 & 1 & 1 \\ 1 & 1 & 1 & 1 \end{bmatrix}$$

$$= \begin{bmatrix} 0 & 2 & 2 & 0 \\ 0 & 0 & 2 & 2 \\ 1 & 1 & 1 & 1 \end{bmatrix}$$

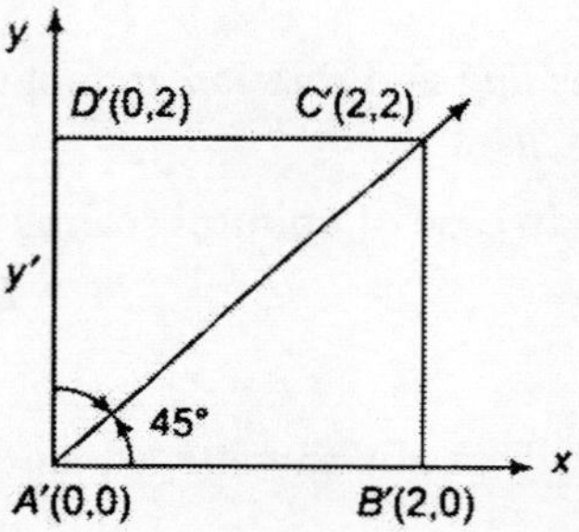

Problem 5.9 Obtain the reflection of the triangle formed by the vertices $A(0,3)$, $B(1,4)$, $C(0,5)$ about the line passes through points (1,3) and (–1,–1).

Solution:

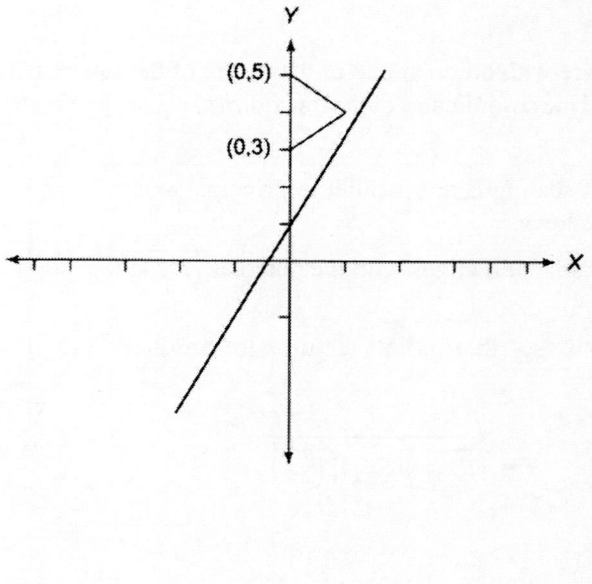

In general reflection transformation matrix about line $y = mx + b$

$$M_L = \begin{bmatrix} \frac{1-m^2}{m^2+1} & \frac{2m}{m^2+1} & \frac{-2bm}{m^2+1} \\ \frac{2m}{m^2+1} & \frac{m^2-1}{m^2+1} & \frac{2b}{m^2+1} \\ 0 & 0 & 1 \end{bmatrix}$$

Here

Slope of the line$(m) = \dfrac{3+1}{1+1} = 2$

Since this line passes through (1,3), therefore

$$b = y - mx$$
$$= 3 - 2*1 = 1$$

$$M_L = \begin{bmatrix} \frac{-3}{5} & \frac{4}{5} & \frac{-4}{5} \\ \frac{4}{5} & \frac{3}{5} & \frac{2}{5} \\ 0 & 0 & 1 \end{bmatrix}$$

$$A'B'C' = \begin{bmatrix} \frac{-3}{5} & \frac{4}{5} & \frac{-4}{5} \\ \frac{4}{5} & \frac{3}{5} & \frac{2}{5} \\ 0 & 0 & 1 \end{bmatrix} \overset{\quad A \;\; B \;\; C}{\begin{bmatrix} 0 & 1 & 0 \\ 3 & 4 & 5 \\ 1 & 1 & 1 \end{bmatrix}}$$

$$= \begin{bmatrix} \frac{8}{5} & \frac{-3}{5} & \frac{16}{5} \\ \frac{11}{5} & \frac{18}{5} & \frac{17}{5} \\ 1 & 1 & 1 \end{bmatrix}$$

Problem 5.10 Describe the form of transformation matrix for line (–2,3) to (6,7) reflection about and arbitrary line with equation $y = 4x + 2$.

Solution:

Here $m = 4$

$b = 2$

Similar to problem 5.9.

Problem 5.11 A square with vertices with (0,0), (0,2), (2,0), and (2,2) is rotated by an angle of 45° (anticlockwise) about the vertices (2,2). Determine co-ordinates of the vertices after rotation of the figure. Will figure remain square?

Solution:

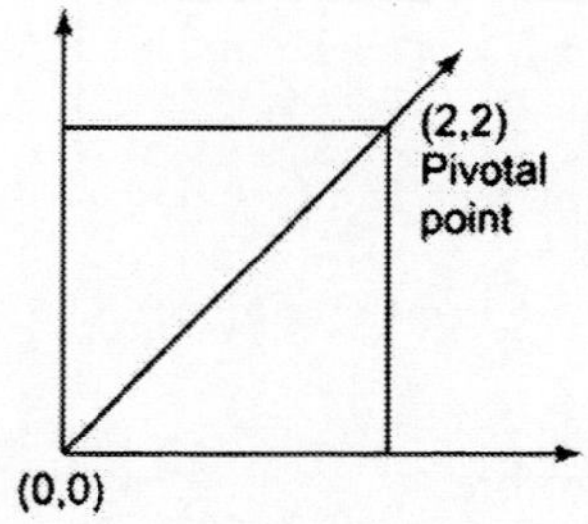

In general rotational transformation matrix w.r.t. $P(h,k)$ is

$$R_{\theta,P} = \begin{bmatrix} \text{Cos}\theta & -\text{Sin}\theta & -h\text{Cos}\theta + k\,\text{Sin}\theta + h \\ \text{Sin}\theta & \text{Cos}\theta & -h\text{Sin}\theta - k\,\text{Cos}\theta + k \\ 0 & 0 & 1 \end{bmatrix}$$

$$A'B'C'D' = \begin{bmatrix} \frac{1}{\sqrt{2}} & -\frac{1}{\sqrt{2}} & 2 \\ \frac{1}{\sqrt{2}} & \frac{1}{\sqrt{2}} & 2(1-\sqrt{2}) \\ 0 & 0 & 1 \end{bmatrix} \overset{\begin{matrix} A & B & C & D \end{matrix}}{\begin{bmatrix} 0 & 2 & 2 & 0 \\ 0 & 0 & 2 & 2 \\ 1 & 1 & 1 & 1 \end{bmatrix}}$$

$$= \begin{bmatrix} 2 & \sqrt{2}\left(1+\sqrt{2}\right) & +2 & -\sqrt{2}\left(1-\sqrt{2}\right) \\ \sqrt{2}\left(1-\sqrt{2}\right) & \sqrt{2}\left(1-\sqrt{2}\right) & 2 & \sqrt{2}\left(1-\sqrt{2}\right) \\ 1 & 1 & 1 & 1 \end{bmatrix}$$

EXERCISES

1. What is the difference between Geometric and Coordinate Transformations? Explain why the product of transformation matrices of these two is an identity matrix.
2. The reflection along $y = x$ is equivalent to the reflection along x-axis followed by counter-clockwise rotation by θ degree. Find the value of θ.
3. Prove that scaling and rotation is commutative.
4. Prove that rotation and translation is commutative.
5. A unit square is scaled by a factor 2 units along one of its diagonals. Find transformation matrix required to achieve this transformation.
6. Derive general form of scaling matrix with respect to fixed point $P(h, k)$.
7. Derive general form of rotation matrix with respect to fixed point $P(h, k)$.

8. Compress the square $A(0,0)$, $B(0,1)$, $C(1,1)$ and $D(1,0)$ half its size.
9. Scale the triangle with vertices $A(0,0)$, $B(2,2)$ and $C(5,3)$ to 2.5 times its size, keeping A fixed in position.
10. Translate a triangle with vertices up a plane with slope 45° and 4 units up.

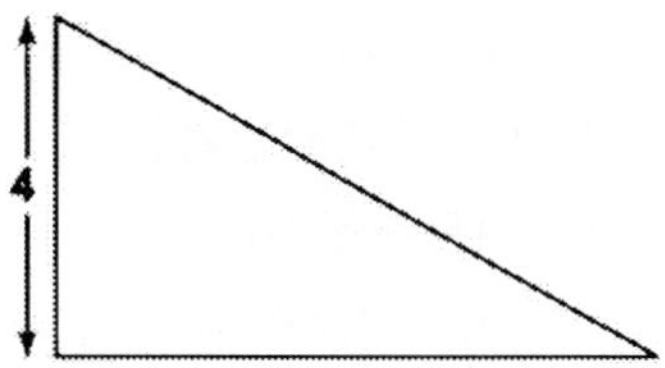

11. A line $A(10,5)$, $B(50,20)$ is rotated about its mid-point by an angle 90°. Find the coordinates of transformed point.
12. A triangle $A(2,2)$, $B(4,2)$ and $C(4,4)$ is rotated by an angle 90°. Find the transformed coordinates.
13. A rectangle is scaled twice along x-axis and four times along y-axis. Find the transformed coordinates.
14. Find the transformed coordinates of polygon $A(80,50)$, $B(60,10)$, $C(100,10)$ when it is reflected about a line parallel to y-axis passing through $P(30,10)$.
15. Derive relationship between following coordinate and geometric transformations:
    $R_\theta, R_{-\theta}\, \bar{R}_\theta, \bar{R}_{-\theta}\, R_\theta^{-1}, \bar{R}_\theta^{-1}$
16. Derive relationship between the following coordinate and geometric transformations:
    $S_{sx,sy}, S_{1/sx,1/sy}, \bar{S}^{-1}_{1/sx,1/sy}, \bar{S}_{sx,sy}, S^{-1}_{1/sx,1/sy}, S_{1/sx,1/sy}$
17. Prove that two consecutive translations are additive i.e.,
    $Tv_1 \cdot Tv_2 = Tv_2 \cdot Tv_1 = T_{v1} + v_2$
18. Prove that two consecutive rotations are additive i.e.,
    $R_{\theta 1} \cdot R_{\theta 2} = R_{\theta 2} \cdot R_{\theta 1} = R_{\theta 1+\theta 2}$
    Prove that two consecutive scale transformations are multiplicative. i.e.,
    $Ssx_1, sy_1 \cdot S\,sx_2\,.\,sx_2 = S\,sx_2 \cdot sx_2 \cdot S\,sx_1, sy_1$
    $= S\,sx_1 \cdot sx_2, sy_1 \cdot sy_2$
19. Prove that the multiplication of transformation matrices for each of the following sequences of transformations is commutative:
    a. Two successive translations
    b. Two successive rotations
    c. Two successive scalings
20. Prove that the reflection along $y = x$ is equivalent to the reflection about x-axis followed by counter-clockwise rotation by 90°.
21. Prove that the reflection along $y = -x$ is equivalent to the reflection about y-axis followed by counter-clockwise rotation by 90°.
22. For a the unit $ABCD$ square with coordinates $A(0,0)$, $B(0,1)$, $C(1,1)$, and $D(1,0)$, apply the following shearing transformations:
    a. $shx = 1/2$ and reference line $y = 0$
    b. $shx = 1/2$ and reference line $y = -1$
    c. $shy = 1/2$ and reference line $x = 0$
    d. $shy = 1/2$ and reference line $x = -1$

6

2-D Viewing Transformation and Clipping

6.1 INTRODUCTION

In this chapter we concentrate on viewing transformation, clipping and filling. Mostly, we have to draw objects whose dimensions are given incompatible with screen coordinate system. In order to take care of such problems we will introduce the concept of window-to-viewport transformation. Further, it may be possible that object may be seen totally or partially or completely outside the viewing area. Here we take the help of clipping process. For the viewing transformation we want to display only those picture parts that are within the window area. Clipping algorithms are applied, so that only the contents of the window interior are mapped to viewport.

Before we go into the detail, let us define some related terms.

6.2 WINDOW

Window frame outlines and defines the portion of the scene or object.

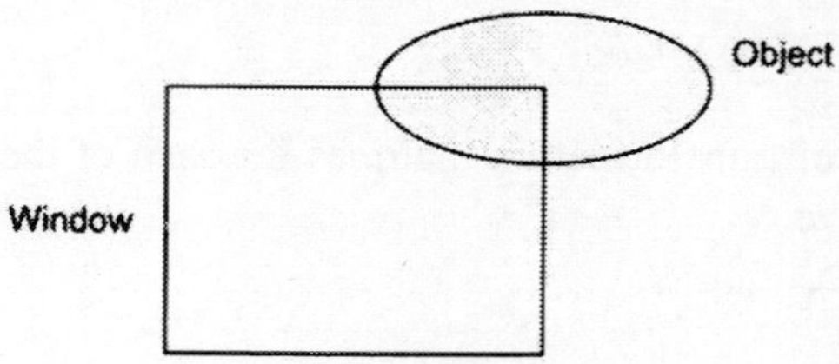

FIGURE 6.1

6.3 VIEWPORT

Viewport is the zone of the monitor screen within which we wish to view the selected object.

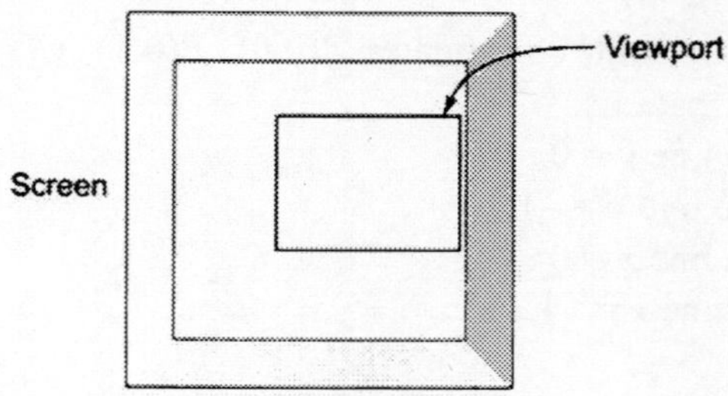

FIGURE 6.2

Thus, window selects a point of an object; viewport displays the selected part at desired location on the display area. Thus, we can say that significance of window is what we want to see and significance of viewport is where we want to display.

Window or viewport can be general polygon-shaped or circular. For simplicity here we will consider rectangular window and rectangular viewport, with edges of the rectangles being parallel to the coordinate axis.

6.4 VIEWING TRANSFORMATION

The process that helps an object or portion of an object is mapped from window to viewport. It is also referred to as window-viewport mapping.

Viewing transformation may use the following four coordinate systems:

- World Coordinate System (WCS)
- Normalized Coordinate System (NCS)
- Screen Coordinate System (SCS)
- Physical Device Coordinate System (PDCS)

WCS is referred to as window and the other three coordinate systems refer to the viewport.

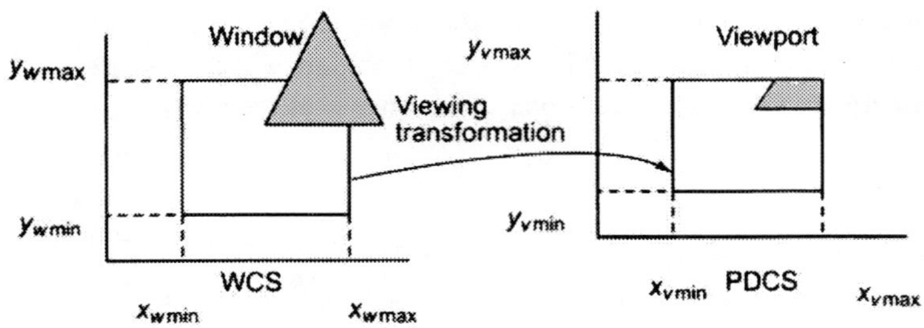

FIGURE 6.3 Viewing Transformation

6.5 NORMALIZED TRANSFORMATION

It is a special type of window-viewport transformation that maps world coordinates to normalized coordinates.

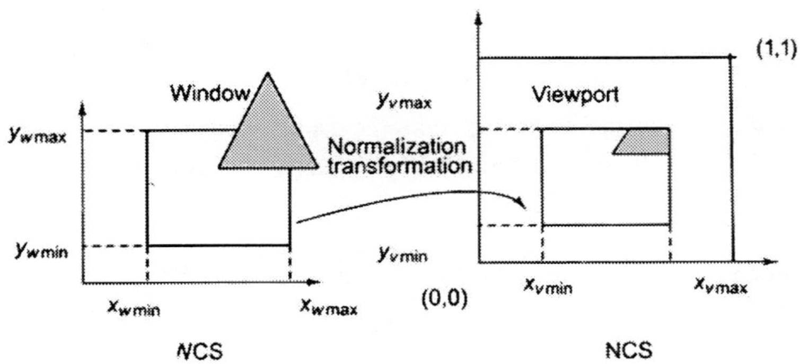

FIGURE 6.4 Normalized Transformation

6.6 WORKSTATION TRANSFORMATION

It is a special type of window-viewport transformation that maps normalized coordinates to physical device coordinates. It is dependent on the resolution; aspect ratio; size of display device.

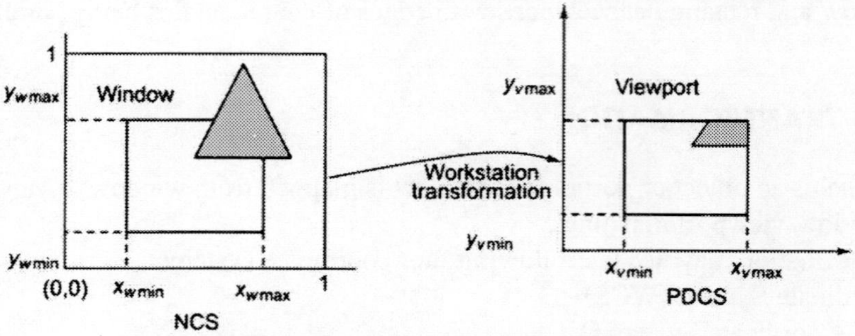

FIGURE 6.5 Workstation Transformation

6.7 NORMALIZED SCREEN COORDINATE

Monitor sizes differ from one system to another; so a device-independent system is introduced in between world coordinates and screen coordinates. This system is called *normalized device coordinate system* (NDCS) in which unit square is used whose lower left corner is at the origin of the coordinate system.

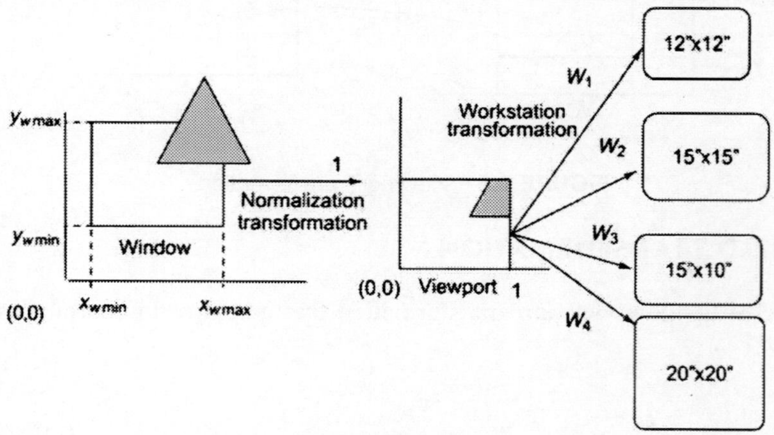

FIGURE 6.6

A major benefit of such normalization is that the same value can be used for monitors of different sizes, aspect ratios and resolutions. Fig. 6.6 depicts this fact

$$x_s = x_n \cdot b$$
$$y_s = y_n \cdot h$$

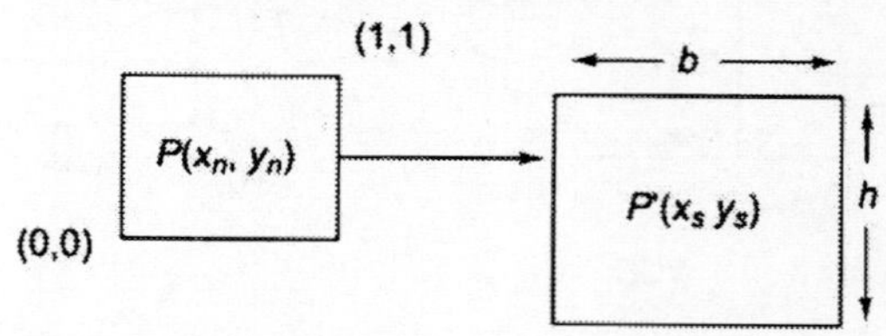

Figure 6.7

where,

(x_s, y_s) are known as screen coordinates.
(x_n, y_n) are known as normalized coordinates.
b is the breadth of the screen.
h is the height of the screen.

6.8 CLIPPING

Any procedure that identifies positions of a picture which are either inside or outside of a specified region is known as *clipping algorithm* or *clipping*.

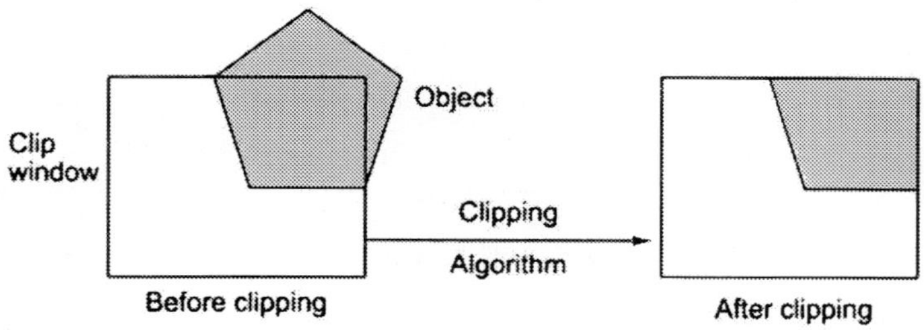

FIGURE 6.8 Clipping Process

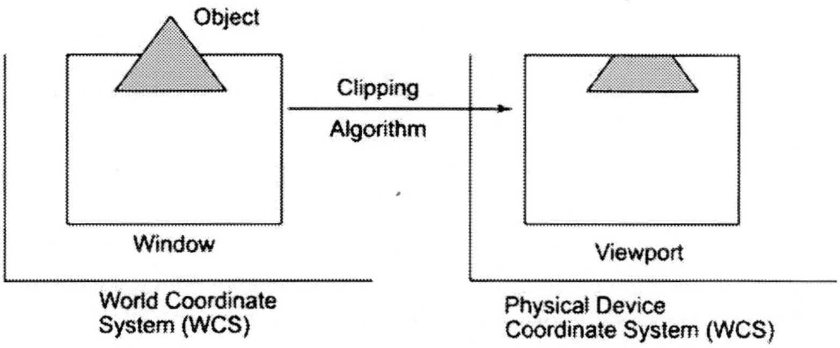

FIGURE 6.9

The above process may be preceded with two methods(each involves two stages):

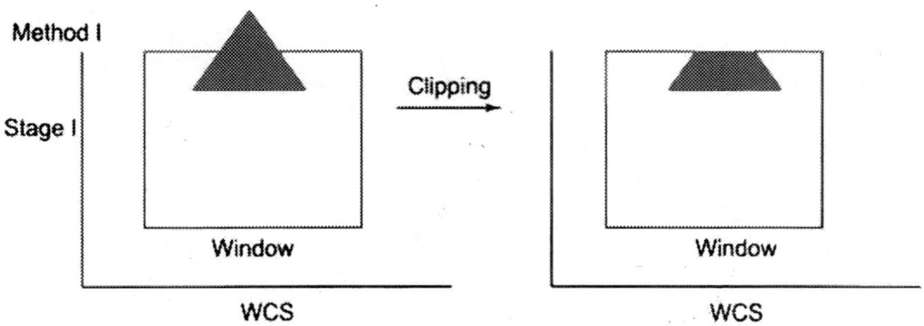

FIGURE 6.10(a)

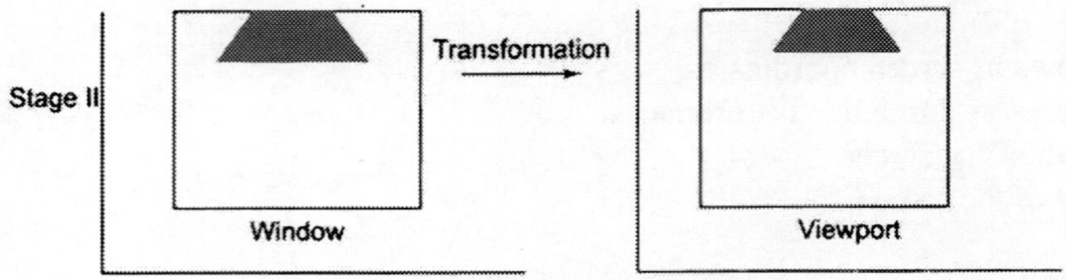

FIGURE 6.10(b)

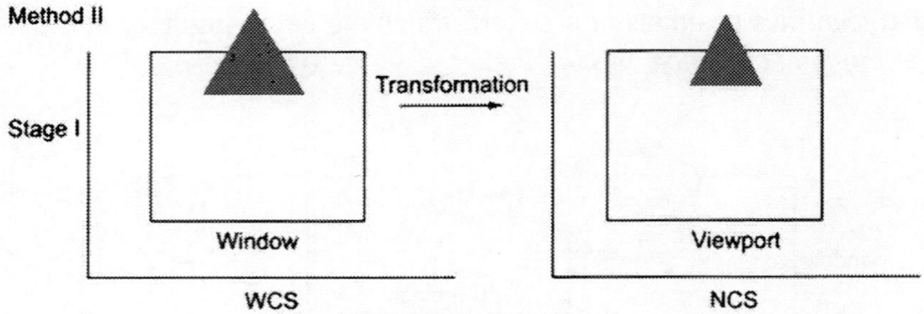

FIGURE 6.11(a)

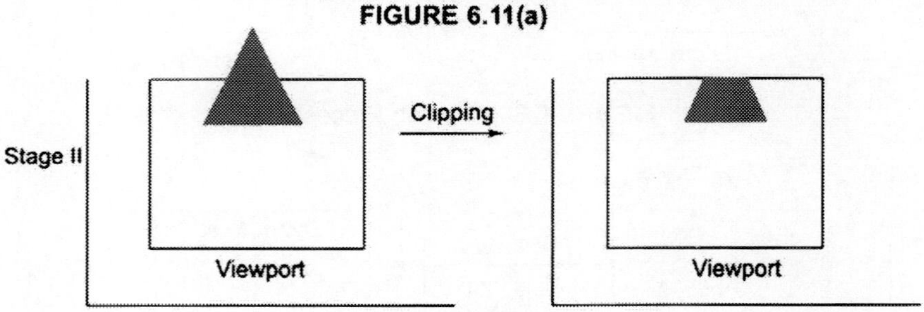

FIGURE 6.11(b)

For the viewing transformation, we want to display only those picture parts that are within the window area. Clipping algorithms can be applied in world coordinates, so that only the contents of the window interior are mapped to device coordinates Fig. 6.10(a) and 6.10(b). In contrast, the complete world coordinate picture can be mapped first to device coordinate system (DCS) or normalized device coordinate (NCS) and then clipped against the viewport boundaries Fig. 6.11(a) and 6.11(b). Generally, first one is more preferable since it removes those primitives outside the window, thus eliminating unnecessary processing effort to transform those primitives to device space.

To explore viewing transformation in between the window and the viewport, let us assume (xw_{min}, yw_{min}) and (xw_{max}, yw_{max}) are the lower left corner and upper right corner of window and if(xv_{min}, yv_{min}) and (xv_{max}, yv_{max}) are those of lower left corner and upper right corner of viewport. i.e.,

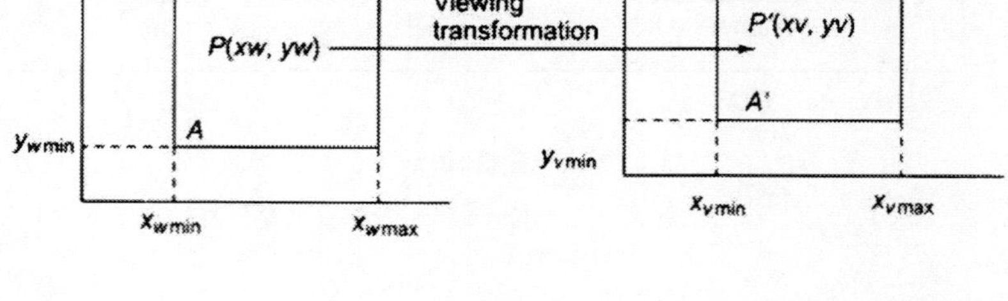

To maintain the same relative placement of the point in the viewport as in the window, we require

$$\frac{xv - xv_{min}}{xv_{max} - xv_{min}} = \frac{xw - xw_{min}}{xw_{max} - xw_{min}} \tag{6.1}$$

and also,

$$\frac{yv - yv_{min}}{yv_{max} - yv_{min}} = \frac{yw - yw_{min}}{yw_{max} - yw_{min}} \tag{6.2}$$

From eq. 6.1 $$\frac{xv - xv_{min}}{xw - xw_{min}} = \frac{xv_{max} - xv_{min}}{xw_{max} - xw_{min}}$$

or, $$xv = xv_{min} + (xw - xw_{min}) \frac{xv_{max} - xv_{min}}{xw_{max} - xw_{min}} \tag{6.3}$$

Similarly, from equation 6.2

$$yv = yv_{min} + (yw - yw_{min}) \frac{yv_{max} - yv_{min}}{yw_{max} - yw_{min}} \tag{6.4}$$

Equations 6.3 and 6.4 may be written as

$$xv = xv_{min} + (xw - xw_{min})s_x \tag{6.5}$$

$$yv = yv_{min} + (yw - yw_{min})s_y \tag{6.6}$$

where, $s_x = \frac{xv_{max} - xv_{min}}{xw_{max} - xw_{min}}$ and $s_y = \frac{yv_{max} - yv_{min}}{yw_{max} - yw_{min}}$ are known as window to viewport scaling factors along x-axis and y-axis, respectively.

Alternative Method

Equations 6.5 and 6.6 can also be derived with the help of following sequence of transformations:

Step 1: Scaling the window area to the size of the viewport with scale factors s_x and s_y w.r.t. a fixed point (xw_{min}, yw_{min}) (Ssx, sy, A).

$$Ssx, sy, A = \begin{bmatrix} sx & 0 & xw_{min}(1 - s_x) \\ 0 & sy & yw_{min}(1 - s_y) \\ 0 & 0 & 1 \end{bmatrix}$$

Step 2: Translating the scaled window to the position of the viewport $(T_{\vec{v}})$.

$$\Delta x = xv_{min} - xw_{min} \text{ and}$$

$$\Delta y = yv_{min} - yw_{min} \text{ and}$$

$$T_{\vec{v}} = \begin{bmatrix} 1 & 0 & \Delta x \\ 0 & 1 & \Delta y \\ 0 & 0 & 1 \end{bmatrix}$$

Combining these matrices in the order these are performed, we get

$$N = \overline{Ssx, sy, A.T_{\vec{v}}} = \begin{bmatrix} sx & 0 & \Delta x + xw_{min}(1 - s_x) \\ 0 & sy & \Delta y + yw_{min}(1 - s_y) \\ 0 & 0 & 1 \end{bmatrix}$$

Replacing the values of Δx and Δy in the above transformation matrix, we finally get

$$N = \begin{bmatrix} sx & 0 & -s_x.xw_{min} + xv_{min} \\ 0 & sy & -s_y.yw_{min} + yv_{min} \\ 0 & 0 & 1 \end{bmatrix}$$

The aspect ratio of a rectangular window or viewport

In general, aspect ratio is defined as

$$\text{Aspect ratio} = \frac{x_{max} - x_{min}}{y_{max} - y_{min}}$$

$$\text{Aspect ratio of viewport } (a_v) = \frac{xv_{max} - xv_{min}}{yv_{max} - yv_{min}}$$

$$\text{Aspect ratio of window } (a_w) = \frac{xw_{max} - xw_{min}}{yw_{max} - yw_{min}}$$

If $\quad a_v = a_w \Rightarrow \dfrac{xv_{max} - xv_{min}}{yv_{max} - yv_{min}} = \dfrac{xw_{max} - xw_{min}}{yw_{max} - yw_{min}}$

$$\Rightarrow \frac{xv_{max} - xv_{min}}{xw_{max} - xw_{min}} = \frac{yv_{max} - yv_{min}}{yw_{max} - yw_{min}}$$

$$\Rightarrow s_x = s_y$$

If $\quad s_x = s_y$ or $a_v = a_w$, then No distortion

$s_x \neq s_y$ or $a_v \neq a_w$, then Geometric distortion

6.9 CLIPPING ALGORITHMS

We will study the algorithms for clipping the following types of primitives:

(1) Point clipping, (2) Line clipping, a. Cohen-Sutherland Algorithm, b. Mid-point Subdivision Algorithm, c. The Liang-Barsky Algorithm, (3) Polygon (Area) clipping

6.9.1 Point Clipping

Before we discuss clipping lines, let us first discuss about clipping of a point. Assuming, the clip window is a rectangle in standard position. A point $P(x, y)$ is *inside* the window if following four inequalities are satisfied:

$$x \geq x_{wmin}$$
$$x \leq x_{wmax}$$
$$y \geq y_{wmin}$$
$$y \leq y_{wmax}$$

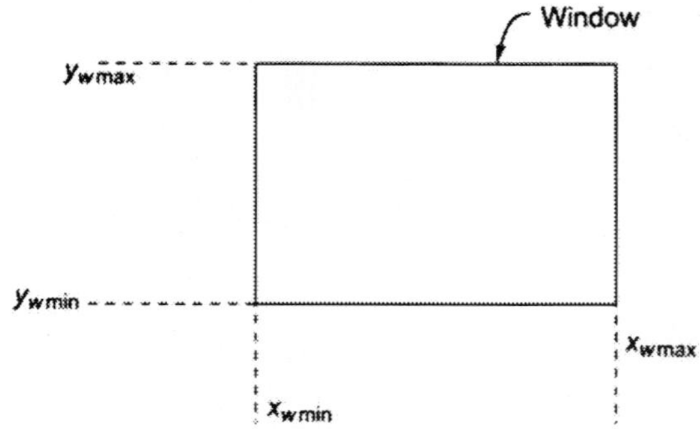

FIGURE 6.12

Equal sign indicates that points are on the window boundary and included within the window. If any one of the above inequality does not hold, the point is *outside* the window.

6.9.2 Line Clipping

To clip a line we need to consider only its end points, not its infinitely many interior points. To determine the visibility of a line w.r.t. a rectangular window, a line may belong to any one of the following three categories:

(a) Visible: If both end points of the line lie inside the window, line lies inside the clip rectangle. For example, line MN is visible in Fig. 6.13.

(b) Non-visible: If both end points are to the right (line UV) or to the left (line ST) or above (line CD) or below (line JK) of the window as in Fig. 6.13, the line definitely lies outside the window.

In other words, a line $A(x_1,y_1)$ to $B(x_2,y_2)$ is definitely non-visible if any *one* of following four inequalities are satisfied:

$x_1, x_2 > x_{wmax}$	Right
$x_1, x_2 < x_{wmin}$	Left
$y_1, y_2 > y_{wmax}$	Above
$y_1, y_2 < y_{wmin}$	Below

(c) Clipping Candidate: Lines which fail these two tests are partially visible (line PQ) in Fig. 6.13. In case of partially visible we must compute intersection point(s).

If both end points are outside the clip rectangle, the line may or may not intersect the clip rectangle and **we need to perform process to check whether there are any intersects** and if there are, we must compute the intersection point(s). For example, *EF*, *AB*, *XY* intersect the clip rectangle and JK and ST do not intersect the clip rectangle.

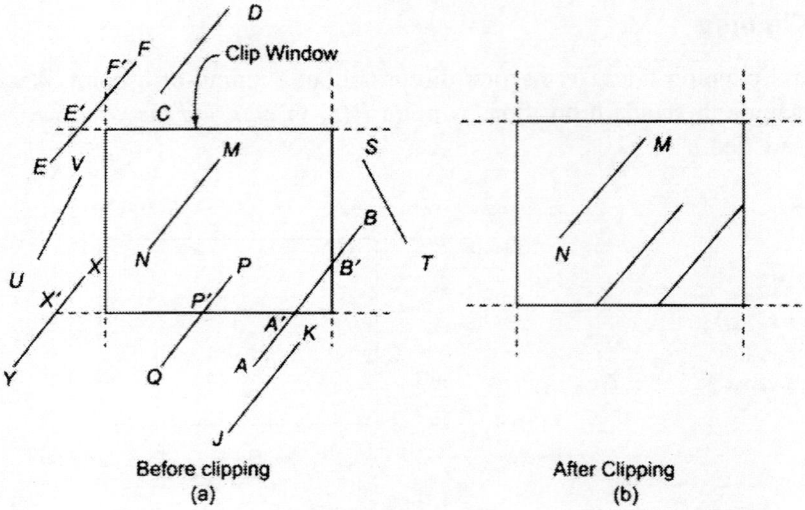

FIGURE 6.13

(a) The Cohen–Sutherland Algorithm

The Cohen-Sutherland line clipping algorithm quickly detects and dispenses with two common and trivial cases (visible and non-visible). In other words, this algorithm performs initial tests on a line to determine whether intersection calculations can be avoided.

The Cohen-Sutherland algorithm uses a divide-and-conquer strategy. The line segment's end-points are tested to see if the line can be trivially accepted or rejected. If the line cannot be trivially accepted or rejected, an intersection of the line with a window edge is determined and the trivial reject/accept test is repeated. This process is continued until the line is accepted. To perform the trivial acceptance and rejection tests, we extend the edges of the window to divide the plane of the window into the nine regions— the eight "outside" regions and the one "inside" region. Each of the nine regions associated with the window is assigned a 4-bit code to identify the region. Each end-point of the line segment is then assigned the code of the region in which it lies.

This algorithm divides the process into the following three phases:

Stage I: Identify the totally visible lines and draw.

Stage II: Identify the totally non-visible lines and ignore.

Stage III: Identify those lines which intersect the window and compute intersection point(s).

Algorithm 6.1 Cohen-Sutherland Algorithm for Line Segment clipping

Step 1 Input x_{wmin}, x_{wmax}, Y_{wmin}, Y_{wmax}, $A(x_1, y_1)$, $B(x_2, y_2)$.

Step 2 Each end-point of the line segment is assigned a four bit code, called a region code.

Least Significant Bit (LSB)	Bit 1 = 1 If point (x, y) lies above the window i.e., $(y - y_{wmax}) > 0$
	Bit 2 = 1 If point (x, y) lies below the window i.e., $-(y - y_{wmin}) > 0$
Most Significant Bit (MSB) ↓	Bit 3 = 1 If point (x, y) lies right to the window i.e., $(x - x_{wmax}) > 0$
	Bit 4 = 1 If point (x, y) lies left to the window i.e., $-(x - x_{wmin}) > 0$

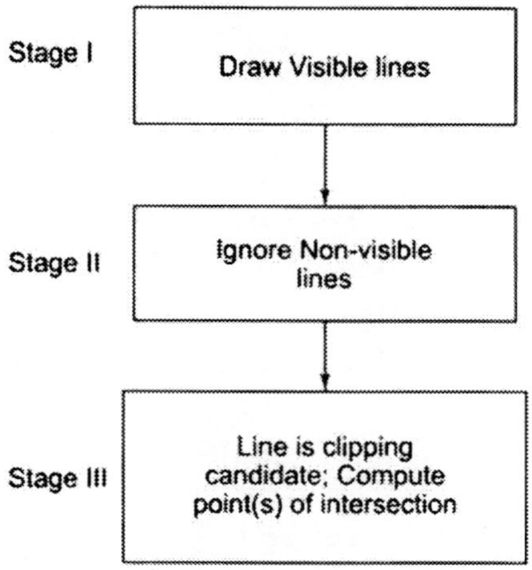

FIGURE 6.14

Thus, four bit code is

$$\text{CODE} = 2^3 \times \text{Bit4} + 2^2 \times \text{Bit3} + 2^1 \times \text{Bit2} + 2^0 \times \text{Bit1}$$

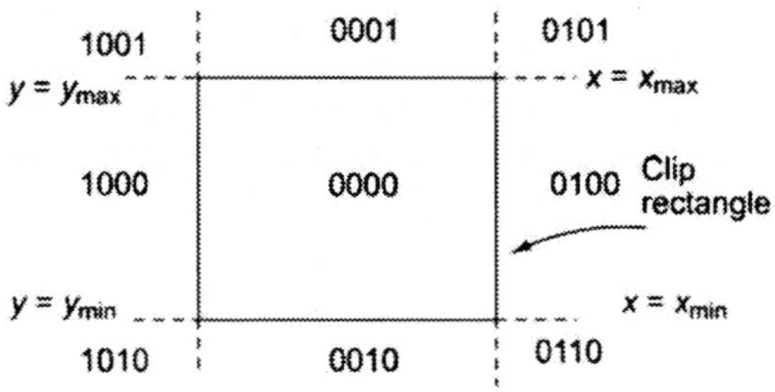

FIGURE 6.15

Step 3

(a) Visible:
If codes of both end-points are equal to 0000, then draw line (totally visible).

(b) Non-visible:
If logical AND of 4 bit code of both end-points is not equal to 0000, then ignore line (totally invisible).

(c) Clipping candidate (partially visible):
If logical AND of 4 bit code of both end-points is equal to 0000, then line is clipping candidate. Such lines may or may not cross into the window interior as shown in Fig. 6.16. In such a case algorithm breaks the line segments into smaller sub-segments by finding intersection with appropriate window edges. Lines *AA'*, *A'B'*, *B'B* are the sub-segments of line *AB* and *MM'* and *M'N* are sub- segments of line *MN*, and *CC'*, *C'D'*, and *D'D* are the sub segments of line *CD*. Steps 2 and 3 are repeated for these sub-segments.

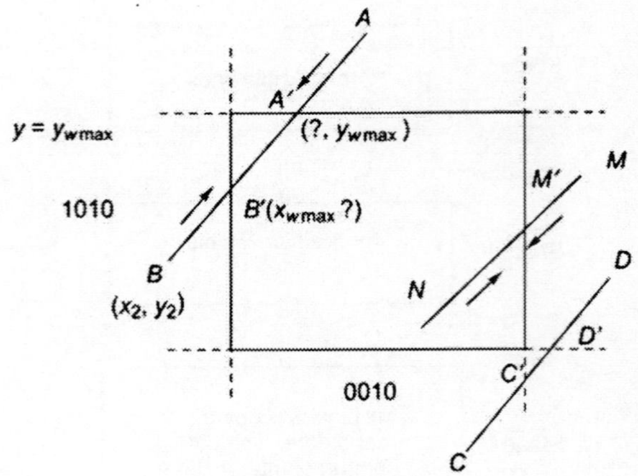

FIGURE 6.16

For line belonging to clipping candidate category, we proceed to find point (s) of intersection, as follows:

If 4-bit code of end-point of line segment has,

Bit 1 = 1 Line intersects line $y = y_{wmax}$
Bit 2 = 1 Line intersects line $y = y_{wmin}$
Bit 3 = 1 Line intersects line $x = x_{wmax}$
Bit 4 = 1 Line intersects line $x = x_{wmin}$

To illustrate the point of intersections of clipping candidate lines against rectangular boundaries using Cohen-Sutherland algorithm, we consider the lines *AB* and *CD*, as shown in Fig.6.16.

Method I

The parametric representation of line *AB* is

$$x = x_1 + u\,(x_2 - x_1) \qquad 6.7(a)$$
$$y = y_1 + u\,(y_2 - y_1) \qquad 6.7(b)$$

where, $0 \le u \le 1$,

Since, *AB* intersects $y = y_{wmax}$, therefore from equation 6.7(b) value of *u* is computed. That value of *u* is used in equation 6.7(a) to compute the value of *x* coordinate of *A′*(in question).

Similarly, *y* coordinate of *B′* can be calculated from *x* coordinate which is already known to us.

If the value of *u* lies in the range $0 \le u \le 1$, then the line crosses clip window and if it lies outside the range 0 and 1, the line does not enter interior of the clip window. For example, for the line *AB* value of *u* lies inside the range 0 and 1; and for line *CD* value of *u* lies outside the range 0 and 1.

Method II

Intersection points with a clipping boundary can also be calculated using the slope intersect form and the line equation. If a line has two end-points $A\,(x_1, y_1)$ and $B\,(x_2, y_2)$, then *y* coordinates of the intersection point with vertical boundary are obtained as:

$$\frac{y - y_1}{x - x_1} = m \quad \text{or} \quad y = y_1 + m\,(x - x_1)$$

where, $x = x_{wmax}$ or x_{wmin}
x coordinate of the intersection point with horizontal boundary is obtained as:

$$\frac{x-x_1}{y-y_1} = \frac{1}{m} \quad \text{or} \quad x = x_1 + \frac{y-y_1}{m}$$

where, $y = y_{wmax}$ or y_{wmin}.
Slope of line is calculated as:

$$m = \frac{y_2-y_1}{x_2-x_1}$$

(b) Mid-point Subdivision

This algorithm is based upon "*divide-and-conquer*" strategy.

Initially, we test a line for clipping as discussed in Cohen-Sutherland algorithm. If the line belongs to clipping candidate category i.e., partially visible or totally invisible, divide such line into two equal segments by finding the mid-point (AM_1, M_1B as sub segments of AB). The two resultant lines are preceded similarly through test and we find out line (s) belonging to category 3 (clipping candidate). Lines belonging to category 1(visible) and 2 (non-visible) are ignored. This bisection and testing procedure is continuing until the intersection with a window edge is formed up to specified accuracy. Refer figure 6.17(a) and 6.17(b).

The mid-point subdivision algorithm, if implemented in hardware works very fast, because hardware addition and division by 2 are very fast.

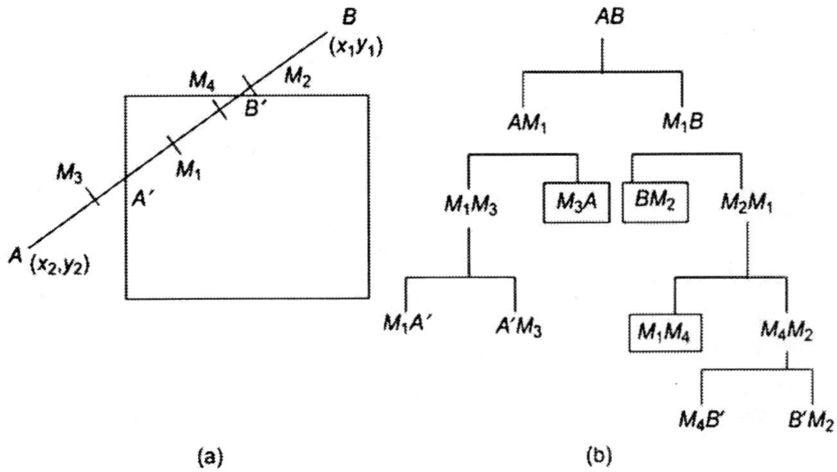

FIGURE 6.17 Demonstration of Mid-point Subdivision Algorithm (sub-segments enclosed in rectangular box are ignored)

Algorithm 6.2 Mid-point subdivision algorithm for line segment clipping.

Step 1: Input x_{wmin}, x_{wmax}, Y_{wmin}, Y_{wmax}, $A(x_1, y_1)$, $B(x_2, y_2)$.

Step 2: Each end-point of the line segment is assigned a four bit code, called a region code (similar to Step 2 of Cohen-Sutherland Algorithm).

Step 3

(a) Visible: Codes of both end-points are equal to 0000, and then draw line (totally visible).

(b) Non-visible: If logical AND of 4 bit code of both end-points is not equal to 0000, then ignore line (totally invisible).

(c) Clipping Candidate: If logical AND of 4 bit code of both end-points is equal to 0000, then line is clipping candidate.

Step 4: If line is clipping candidate, then find mid-point M1 of *A* and *B* i.e.,

$$M1 = \frac{A+B}{2} \text{ ; code assigned to M1.}$$

Step 5: If code (M1) <> 0, then
If code (*A*) AND code (M1)<>0 then
A = M1 goto step 4
else
If code (*B*) AND code (M1)<>0 then
B = M1 goto step 4
end if

Step 6: If code (M1) = 0, then
If code (*A*), code (M1) both = 0 then
Consider BM1
ELSE if code (*B*), code (M1) both = 0 then
Consider AM1
End if
End if

Step 7: do /* considering AM1 segment

$$M3 = \frac{A+M1}{2} \text{ ; assigned 4-bit code to M3}$$

If (code (M3) <> 0) then
A = M3
Else
M1 = M3
End if
While (M1.x <> x_{wmin} and M1.x <> x_{wmax} and
M1.y <> y_{wmin} and M1.y <> y_{wmax})
/*end while
A = M1

Step 8 do /* considering BM1 segment

$$M2 = \frac{B+M1}{2} \text{ ; assigned 4-bit code to M2}$$

If (code (M2) <> 0), then
B = M2
else
M1 = M2
Endif

While (M1.x <> x_{wmin} and M1.x <> x_{wmax} and
M1.y <> y_{wmin} and M1.y <> y_{wmax})
/*end while

B = M1

Step 9 Draw AB

Step 10 End

(c) The Liang-Barsky Algorithm

In 1978, Cyrus and Back have been developed an algorithm based upon parametric equations that is generally more efficient approach to line clipping than the Cohen-Sutherland Algorithm. Later in 1984, Liang and Barsky independently developed even more efficient parametric line clipping algorithm.

Let us assume a line segment with end points $A(x_1, y_1)$, $B(x_2, y_2)$ and window with lower left corner (x_{wmin}, y_{wmin}) and upper right corner (x_{wmax}, y_{wmax}) as depicted in Fig. 6.18(a) and 6.18(b).

Express the line segment $A(x_1, y_1)$, $B(x_2, y_2)$ in parametric form

$$x = x_1 + m(x_2 - x_1)$$
$$y = y_1 + m(y_2 - y_1)$$

where $0 \le m \le 1$

or

$$x = x_1 + m.dx \qquad 6.8(a)$$
$$y = y_1 + m.dy \qquad 6.8(b)$$

when $m = 0$ then $x = x_1$ $y = y_1$

and $m = 1$ then $x = x_2$ $y = y_2$

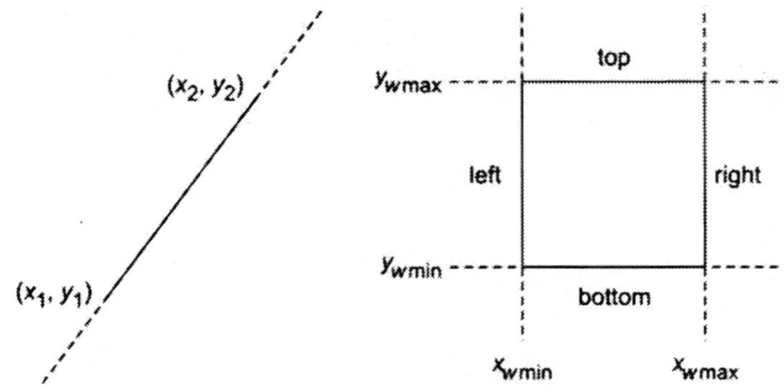

(a) Line Segment (b) Window

FIGURE 6.18

Any point $P(x, y)$ on line segment which is inside window (x_{wmin}, y_{wmin}) to (x_{wmax}, y_{wmax}) satisfies:

$$x_{wmin} \le x \le x_{wmax} \qquad 6.9(a)$$
$$y_{wmin} \le y \le y_{wmax} \qquad 6.9(b)$$

If $x = x_{wmin}$ ⇒ An intersection on the line with ***left*** boundary

If $x = x_{wmax}$ ⇒ An intersection on the line with ***right*** boundary

If $y = y_{wmin}$ ⇒ An intersection on the line with ***bottom*** boundary
If $y = y_{wmax}$ ⇒ An intersection on the line with ***up*** boundary

Equations 6.9(a) and 6.9(b) can be rewritten after using equations 6.8(a) and 6.8(b) respectively

$$x_{wmin} \le x_1 + m.dx \le x_{wmax} \quad 6.10(a)$$
$$y_{wmin} \le y_1 + m.dy \le y_{wmax} \quad 6.10(b)$$

Equation 6.10(a) can be rewritten as

$$-dx.\ m \le x_1 - x_{wmin} \text{ (left boundary)} \quad 6.11(a)$$
$$dx.\ m \le x_{wmax} - x_1 \text{ (right boundary)} \quad 6.11(b)$$

Equation 6.10(b) can be rewritten as

$$-dy.m \le y_1 - y_{wmin} \text{ (bottom boundary)} \quad 6.11(c)$$
$$dy.m \le y_{wmax} - y_1 \text{ (top boundary)} \quad 6.11(d)$$

Equations 6.11(a), 6.1 l(b), 6.11(c), 6.1l(d) all of the form

$$P_i m < Q_i$$

where $i = 1, 2, 3, 4$
and

$$P_1 = -dx \qquad Q_1 = x_1 - x_{wmin}$$
$$P_2 = dx \qquad Q_2 = x_{wmax} - x_1$$
$$P_3 = -dy \qquad Q_3 = y_1 - y_{wmin}$$
$$P_4 = dy \qquad Q_4 = y_{wmax} - y_1$$

Now note that if line is parallel to ***left/right*** boundary then

$$dx = 0 \qquad P_1 = 1 \qquad \text{and} \qquad P_2 = 0$$

If line is parallel to **top/bottom** boundary then

$$dy = 0 \qquad P_3 = 0 \qquad \text{and} \qquad P_4 = 0$$

Case I

Now if $\quad P_1 = 0$
and $\quad Q_1 < 0$
or $\quad x_1 - x_{wmin} < 0$
or $\quad x_1 < x_{wmin}$

⇒ ***line lies completely outside of window then reject***

Similarly, if $\quad P_2 = 0$
and $\quad Q_2 < 0$
or $\quad x_{wmax} - x_1 < 0$
or $\quad x_{wmax} < x_1$

⇒ ***line lies completely outside of window then reject***

if $\quad P_3 = 0$
and $\quad Q_3 < 0$
or $\quad y_1 - y_{wmin} < 0$
or $\quad y_1 < y_{wmin}$

⇒ line lies completely outside of window then reject

if $P_4 = 0$
and $Q_4 < 0$
or $y_{wmax} - y_1 < 0$
or $y_{wmax} < y_1$

⇒ line lies completely outside of window then reject

In general,
If $P_i = 0$ and $Q_i < 0$ reject the line $i = 1, 2, 3, 4$ otherwise retain the line

Case II

If

$$P_1 < 0$$
$$-dx < 0$$
$$-(x_2 - x_1) < 0$$
$$x_1 < x_2$$

so if extend line segment it goes from left to right or from outside of left boundary to inside (Fig. 6.19(a))

If

$$P_2 < 0$$
$$dx < 0$$
$$(x_2 - x_1) < 0$$
$$x_2 < x_1$$

so if extend line segment it goes from right to left or from outside of right boundary to inside (Fig. 6.19(b))

if

$$P_3 < 0$$
$$-dy < 0$$
$$-(y_2 - y_1) < 0$$
$$y_1 < y_2$$

so if extend line segment it goes from bottom to top or from outside of bottom boundary to inside (Fig. 6.19(c))

if

$$P_4 < 0$$
$$dy < 0$$
$$(y_2 - y_1) < 0$$
$$y_2 < y_1$$

so if extend line segment it goes from top to bottom or from outside of top boundary to inside (Fig. 6.19(d)).

In general,
if $P_i < 0$ extended line proceeds from the outside to inside of the corresponding boundary line and $m_i = Q_i/P_i$, calculate the point of intersection, i = 1, 2, 3, 4.

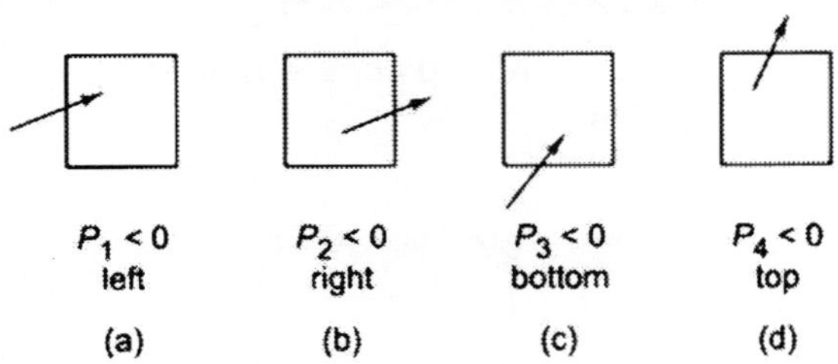

FIGURE 6.19

Case III

Similarly, in general

If $P_i > 0$ extended line proceeds from the inside to outside of the corresponding boundary line and $m_i = Q_i/P_i$, calculate the point of intersection, i = 1, 2, 3, 4 as depicted in Fig. 6.20(a), 6.20(b), 6.20(c) and 6.20(d).

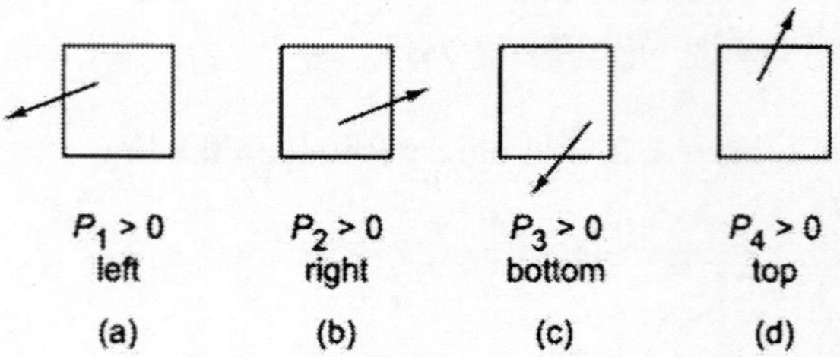

FIGURE 6.20

Since $0 \leq m \leq 1$

For case $P_i < 0$ i.e. **outside to inside**

$$m_1 = \text{Max}\{(Q_i/P_i | P_i < 0, i = 1, 2, 3, 4)\}$$

For case $P_i > 0$ i.e. **inside to outside**

$$m_2 = \text{Min}\{(Q_i/P_i | P_i > 0, i = 1, 2, 3, 4)\}$$

So if $m_1 > m_2$ reject line

Else visible segment corresponds to the parametric interval

$$m_1 \leq m \leq m_2 \quad \text{and} \quad m_1 \leq m_2$$

then compute visible endpoint from m_1 and m_2.

Algorithm

Step 1 If $P_i = 0$ and $Q_i < 0$ for any $i = 1, 2, 3, 4$ reject the line and go to step 5

Step 2 If $P_i < 0$ calculate Q_i/P_i for all $i = 1, 2, 3, 4$ and find the largest from the set consisting of 0 and these four values, i.e.

$$m_1 = \text{Max}\{0, (Q_i/P_i), i = 1, 2, 3, 4)\}$$

Step 3 If $P_i > 0$ calculate Q_i/P_i for all $i = 1, 2, 3, 4$ and find the smallest from the set consisting of 1 and these four values, i.e.

$$m_2 = \text{Min}\{1, (Q_i/P_i), i = 1, 2, 3, 4)\}$$

Step 4 If $m_1 > m_2$ reject line else line is visible and clipped line (P_1P_2) is calculated from parametric equations of the line using m_1 and m_2, thus

Coordinates of point P_1 are

$$(x_1 + dx.\ m_1, y_1 + dy.m_1)$$

and coordinates of point P_2 are

$$(x_1, dx.m_2, y_1 + dy.m_2)$$

Step 5 Stop

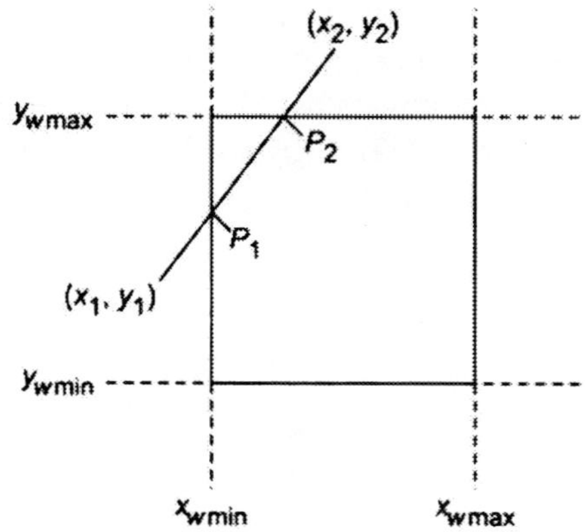

FIGURE 6.21 Clipped line P_1P_2 of line segment *AB*

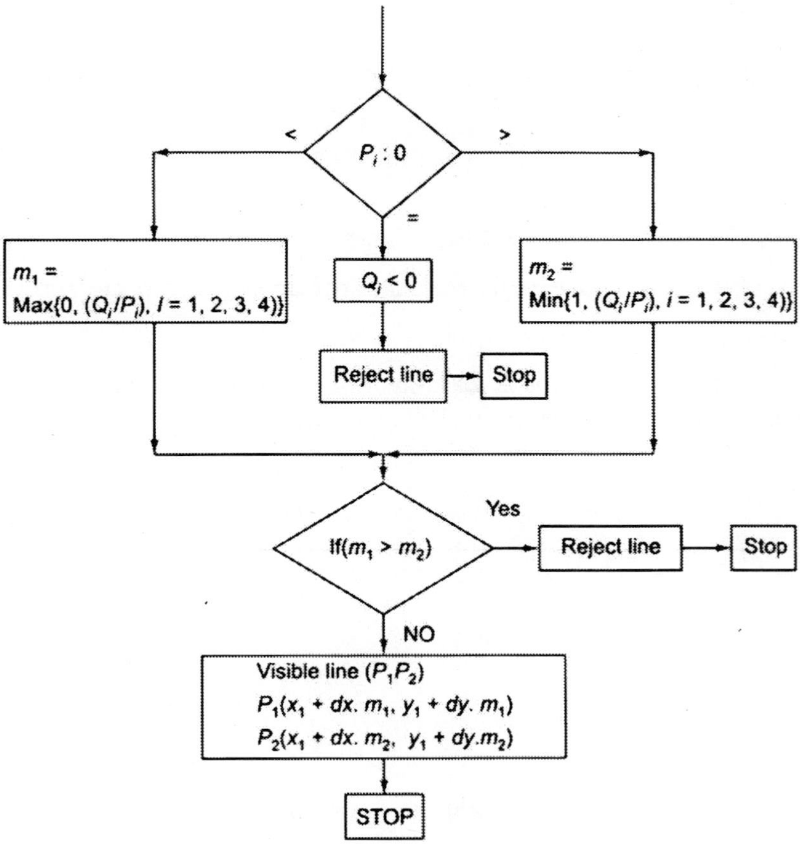

FIGURE 6.22 Flow Chart Represents the Working of Liang-Barsky Method

Comparison between Liang Barsky and Cohen-Sutherland Algorithm

1. Liang Barsky is more efficient than Cohen-Sutherland algorithm, since intersection calculations are reduced. Each update of parameters require only one division and window intersection of lines are calculated once, when final values have been computed. In Cohen-Sutherland algorithm repeatedly

calculate intersections along a line path, even though the line may be completely outside the clip window. And each intersection calculation requires both a multiplication and a division.

2. Cohen-Sutherland line clipping algorithm is based on 4-bit codes. If the point of line lies outside the window it is assigned 1 otherwise 0 bit is assigned. But Liang-Barsky algorithm involves the parametric equation of line. We have.to derive equations to check whether the line is inside or outside the clipping window.

6.9.3 POLYGON CLIPPING

Polygon

An object with more than two vertices is called a polygon.

Convex Polygon

A polygon is called a convex if a line obtained after joining two interior points of the polygon lies *completely inside* the polygon.

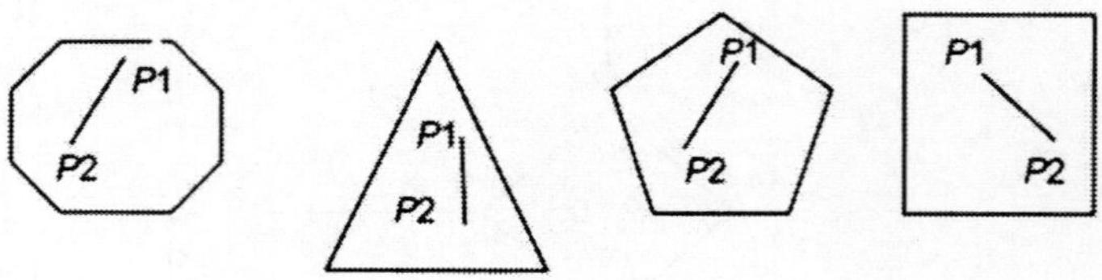

FIGURE 6.23(a) Convex Polygons

All symmetrical polygons likewise triangle, rectangle, pentagon, hexagon, etc. are convex polygons.

Concave Polygon

A polygon is called a concave if there is at least one pair of points such that line joining the points belong to polygon that does not lie completely inside the polygon.

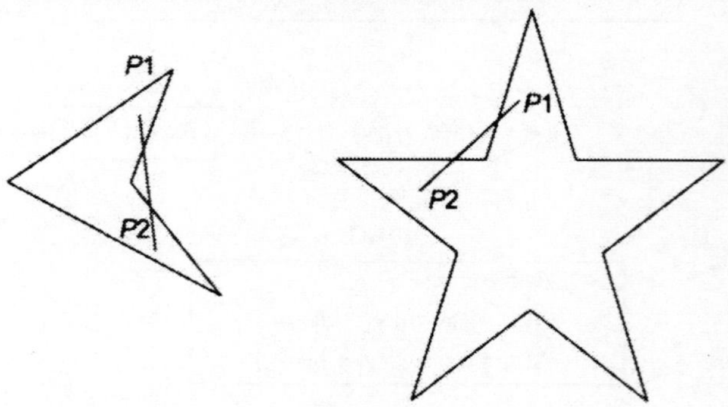

FIGURE 6.23(b) Concave Polygons

Positive Oriented Convex Polygon

A convex polygon with vertices $v1, v2, \ldots\ldots vn$ $(n \geq 3)$ is said to be positive oriented convex polygon if the vertices $v1 \rightarrow v2 \rightarrow v3 \rightarrow v4 \rightarrow \ldots\ldots \rightarrow vn (n \geq 3)$ produce a counter-clockwise circuit.

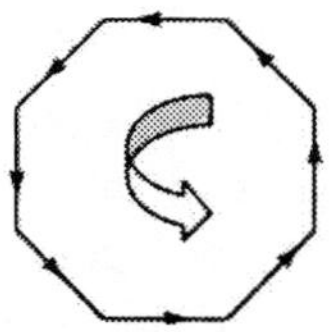

FIGURE 6.24

Negative Oriented Convex Polygon

A convex polygon with vertices $v1, v2 \ldots\ldots vn$ $(n \geq 3)$ is said to be negative oriented convex polygon if the vertices $v1 \rightarrow v2 \rightarrow v3 \rightarrow v4 \rightarrow .. \rightarrow vn$ $(n \geq 3)$ produce a clockwise circuit.

We may use the following simple rule to determine that a point $P(x,y)$ lies towards *left*, *right* or *on* a directed line $A(x1,y1)$ to $B(x2,y2)$ iff

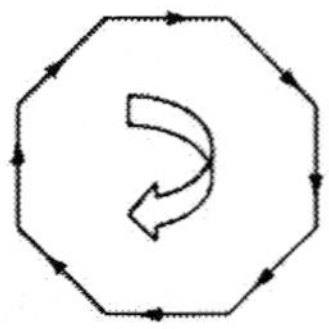

FIGURE 6.25

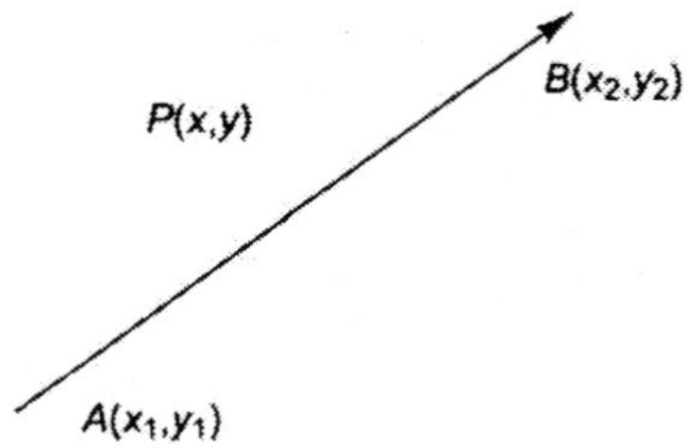

$$E = (y - y1)(x2 - x1) - (y2 - y1)(x - x1)$$

$$\begin{cases} > 0 & \text{point } P(x, y) \text{ lies towards left of line } A \text{ to } B \\ < 0 & \text{point } P(x, y) \text{ lies towards right of line } A \text{ to } B \\ = 0 & \text{point } P(x, y) \text{ lies on the line } A \text{ to } B \end{cases}$$

Value of E	*Point (x,y)*
Positive	Left of line
Negative	Right of line
Zero	On the line

This rule helps us to check whether a point lies inside or outside a polygon.

(Rule A) If a point $P(x, y)$ is to the *left* of *every* edge of positive oriented convex (counter-clockwise) polygon, then it is *inside* the polygon otherwise outside the polygon. It interprets that if a point $P(x, y)$ is to the left of any *one edge* of a positive oriented convex(counter-clockwise)polygon, then it may be inside or outside the polygon.

Polygon clipping algorithms against a positive convex window based upon rule A.

(Rule B) If a point $P(x, y)$ is to the *right* of *every* edge of negative oriented convex(clockwise) polygon, then it is *inside* the polygon otherwise outside the polygon. It interprets that if a point $P(x, y)$ is to the *right* of any *one edge* of a negative oriented convex (clockwise) polygon, then it may be inside or outside the polygon.

Polygon clipping algorithms against a negative convex window based upon rule B.

Polygon	*Point is Inside*	*Point may or may not be inside the polygon*	*Point is Outside*
Positive oriented convex	Left of every edge	Left of any one edge	Right of any one edge
Negative oriented convex	Right of every edge	Right of any one edge	Left of any one edge

Sutherland-Hodgman

An algorithm that clips a polygon must deal with many different cases. The case is particularly noteworthy in that the concave polygon is clipped into two separate polygons. All in all, the task of clipping seems rather complex. Each edge of the polygon must be tested against each edge of the clip rectangle; new edges must be added, and existing edges must be discarded, retained, or divided. Multiple polygons may result from clipping a single polygon. We need an organized way to deal with all these cases.

In 1974, Sutherland and Hodgman developed a technique for clipping the portions of a polygon within window. Sutherland-Hodgman algorithm is used for clipping convex or concave polygon against any convex polygonal clipping windows. As a particular case we will consider rectangular convex clip window.

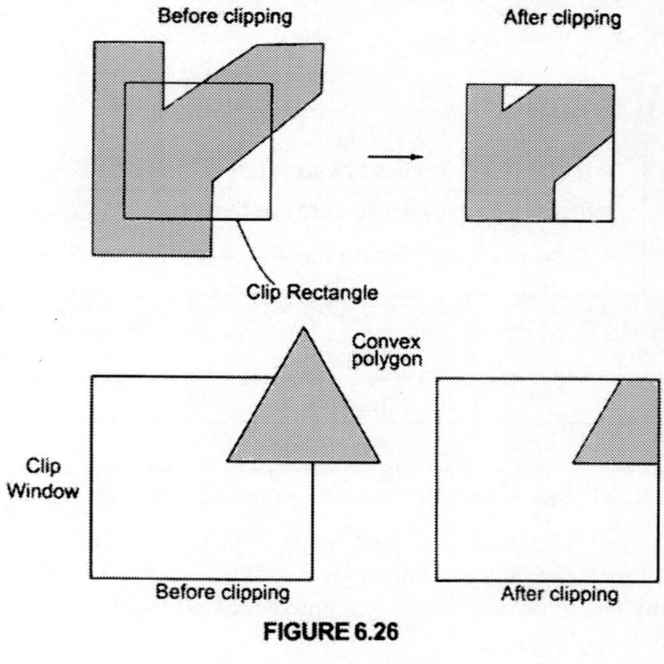

FIGURE 6.26

Basic principle of this algorithm is that it decomposes the problem of polygon clipping against a clip window into identical sub-problems. Sutherland-Hodgman follows the *divide-and-conquer* strategy. A sub-problem is to clip all polygon edges successively against a single clip edge. The outputs of the sub-problem (clipping edges or parts of the vertices) are considered input to the next sub-problem of clipping against the second window edge. This process is repeated for third window edge and fourth window edge.

This algorithm involves following four stages:

Step 1: Clip the polygon against edges of the *right* rectangle boundary to produce a new sequence of vertices.

Steps 2: The new sequence of vertices so formed (in step 1) is passed through the polygon against the *bottom* rectangle boundary to produce a new sequence of vertices.

Steps 3: The new sequence of vertices so formed (in step 2) is passed through the polygon against the *left* rectangle boundary to produce a new sequence of vertices.

Steps 4: The new sequence of vertices so formed (in step 3) is passed through the polygon against the *top* rectangle boundary to produce a new sequence of vertices.

The output of a polygon clipper should be a sequence of vertices that defines the clipped polygon boundaries. At each stage zero, one or two vertices are added.

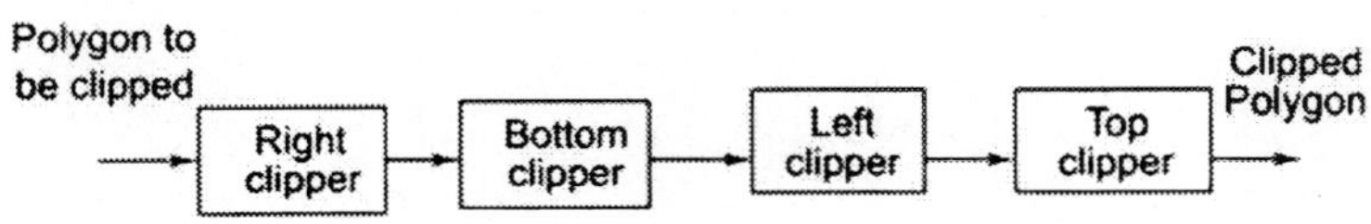

When processing vertices in sequence, following four cases may arise:

Case I First vertex is outside the window boundary and second vertex is inside.

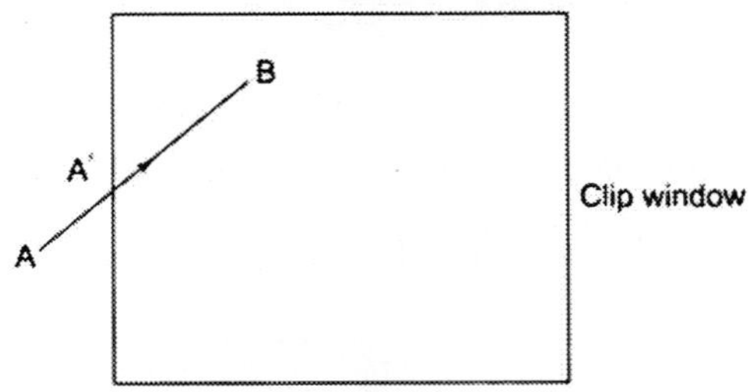

Save A′, B

FIGURE 6.27(a)

Case II If both input vertices are inside the window boundary.

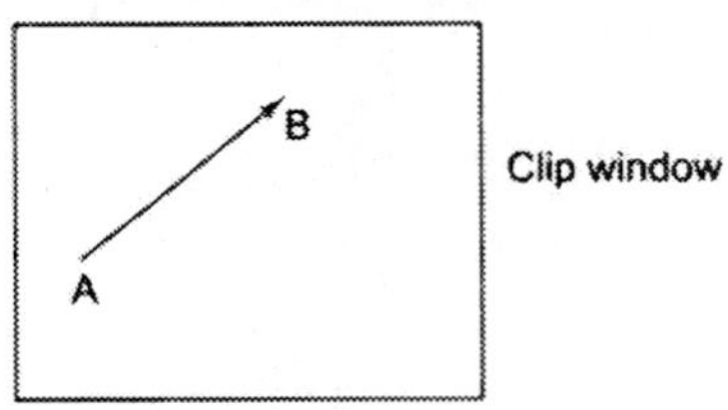

Save B

FIGURE 6.27(b)

Case III

If first vertex is inside the window boundary and the second vertex is outside.

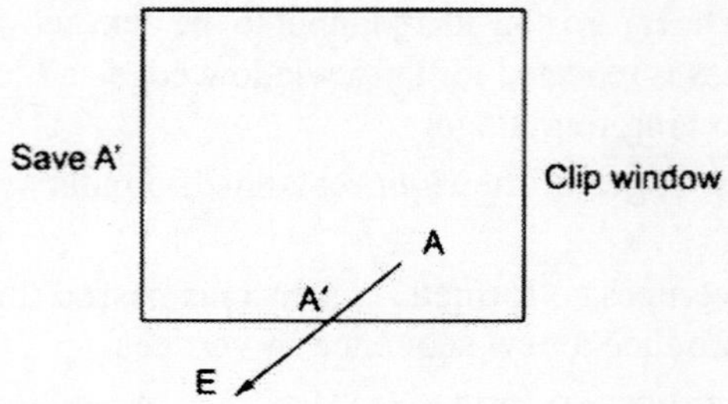

FIGURE 6.27(c)

Case IV

If both input vertices are outside the window boundary, nothing is added to output list.

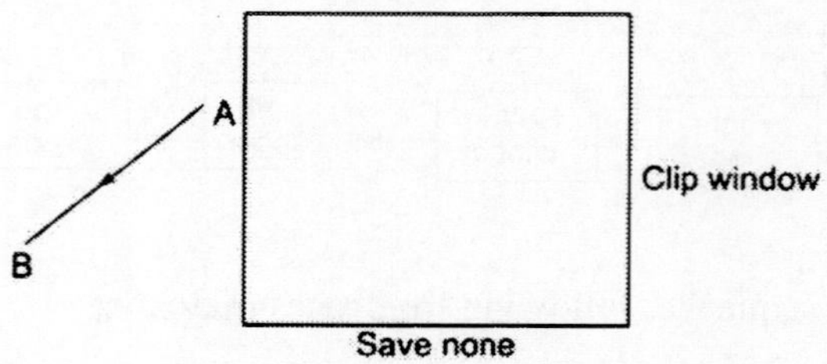

FIGURE 6.27(d)

Now let us see what exactly happens while clipping a 4-point star (concave polygon) against a rectangular clip window using the above mentioned rules.

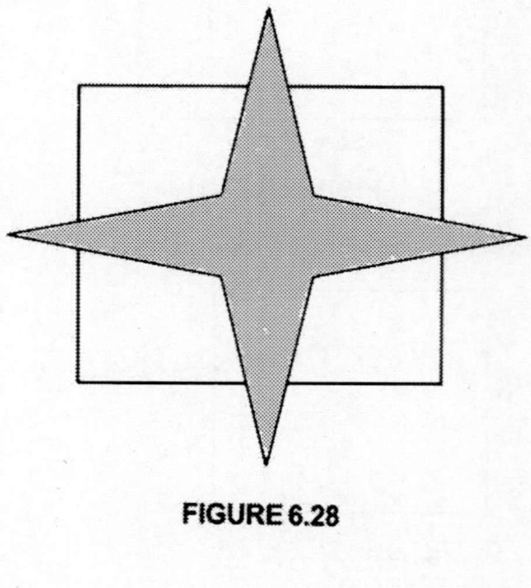

FIGURE 6.28

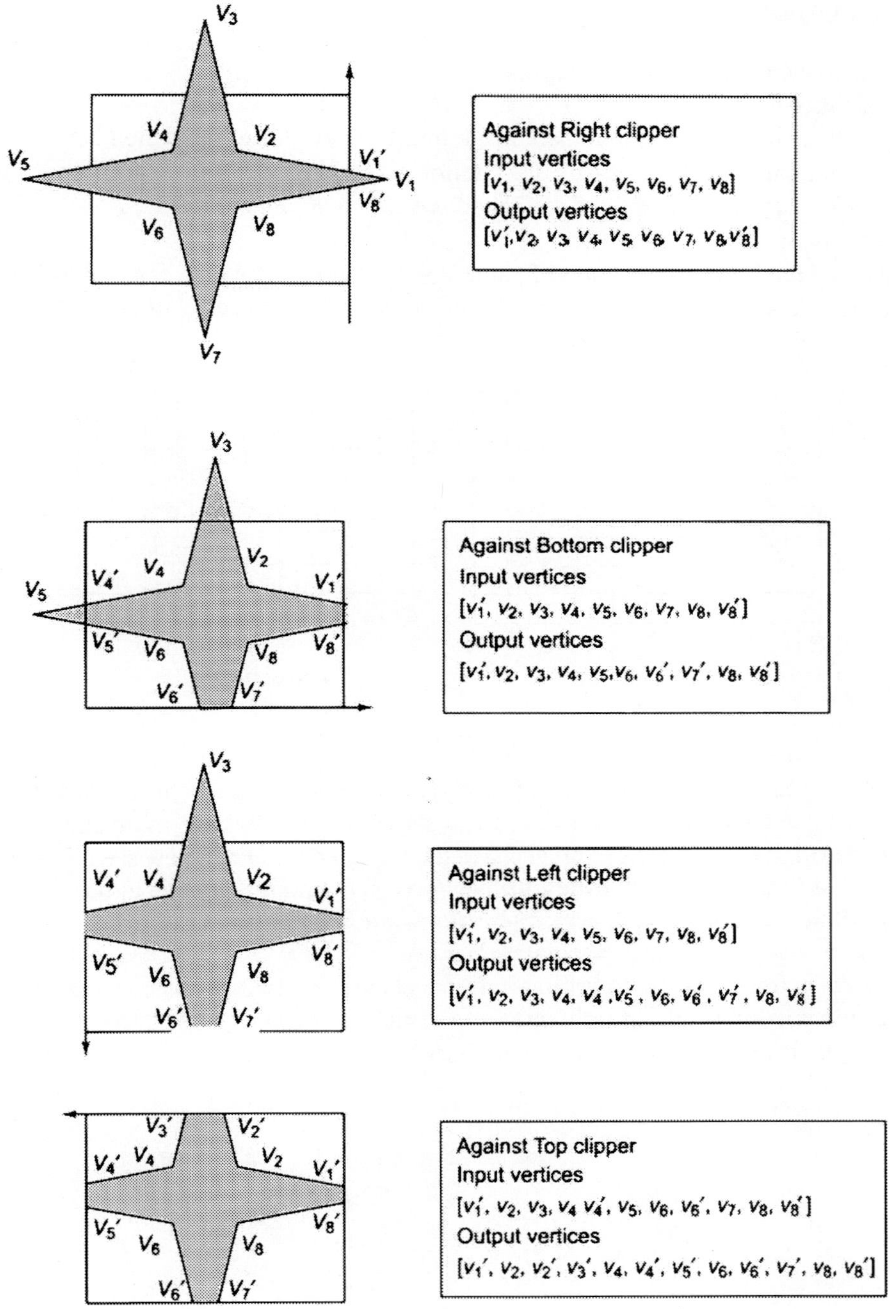

V_3
V_4
V_2
V_5
V_1'
V_1
V_8'
V_6
V_8
V_7
Against Right clipper
Input vertices
$[v_1, v_2, v_3, v_4, v_5, v_6, v_7, v_8]$
Output vertices
$[v_1', v_2, v_3, v_4, v_5, v_6, v_7, v_8, v_8']$
Against Bottom clipper
Input vertices
$[v_1', v_2, v_3, v_4, v_5, v_6, v_7, v_8, v_8']$
Output vertices
$[v_1', v_2, v_3, v_4, v_5, v_6, v_6', v_7', v_8, v_8']$
Against Left clipper
Input vertices
$[v_1', v_2, v_3, v_4, v_5, v_6, v_7, v_8, v_8']$
Output vertices
$[v_1', v_2, v_3, v_4, v_4', v_5', v_6, v_6', v_7', v_8, v_8']$
Against Top clipper
Input vertices
$[v_1', v_2, v_3, v_4, v_4', v_5, v_6, v_6', v_7, v_8, v_8']$
Output vertices
$[v_1', v_2, v_2', v_3', v_4, v_4', v_5', v_6, v_6', v_7', v_8, v_8']$

FIGURE 6.29

6.10 AREA FILLING

Basically, we have two types of areas or regions:

- Boundary-defined
  Boundary-defined region pixels that mark the boundary or outline of the region have a unique color that is not same as the color of the interior pixels. Fig. 6.30(a). Algorithms that are used to fill boundary-defined regions are called *boundary-fill algorithms*.
- Interior-defined
  Interior-defined region is a collection of same color continuous pixels. Fig. 6.30(b). Pixels exterior to region have different colors. Algorithms that are used to fill interior-defined regions are called *flood-fill algorithms*.

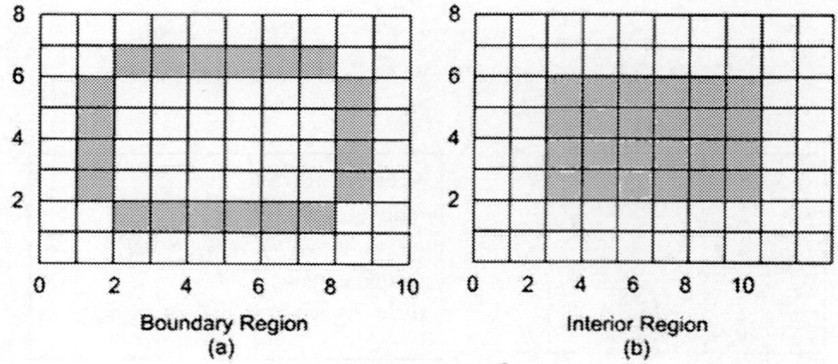

FIGURE 6.30

Sometimes both these algorithms are called *seed-fill algorithms*, since both are started from a pixel within region. You plant a seed (the pixel where you start), and, recursively, more and more seeds are planted around the original seed if those pixels have the correct color. Each new seed is responsible for coloring the pixel at its position, and testing for new pixels around it that have to be colored.

Seed fill algorithms based upon the principle that to start at a *sample pixel* (called seed pixel) from the area , *fill color value*, and *boundary color value*.

A region is a collection of pixels. A region is 4-connected if every 2-pixels be joined by a sequence of pixels using only up, down, left, or right moves. A region is 8- connected if every 2-pixels be joined by four diagonal pixels are also enclosed as neighbors.

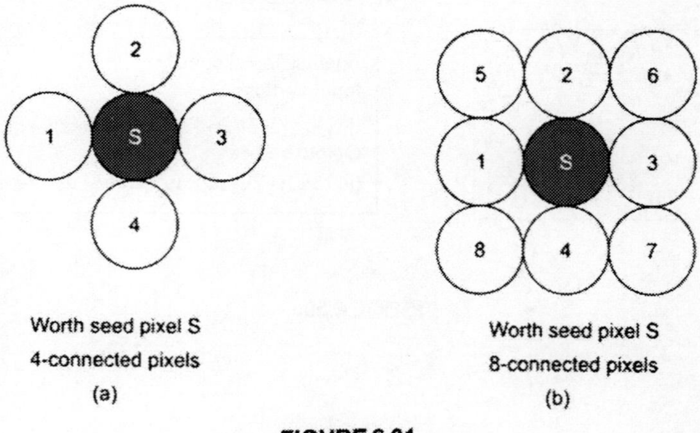

FIGURE 6.31

6.10.1 Flood-fill vs Boundary fill Algorithms

The purpose of Flood-fill algorithm is to color an entire area of connected pixels with the same color and leaving its borders and the pixels outside intact. On the other side, there also exists Boundary Fill Algorithms, these are very similar to Flood-fill, but will color an area with pixels of a certain color as boundary. The algorithms for boundary fill are very similar apart from the conditions in the tests for planting new seeds.

When dealing with images in which the boundary pixels have already been defined, the interior of an arbitrary region delimited by a closed boundary can be filled using a recursive algorithm that starts from a seed point in the interior and fills 4-connected or 8-connected neighboring points that are not already filled (by either the fill color or the boundary color).

Here we will discuss two approaches for each (Boundary-fill, Flood-fill) algorithm:

- Recursive Approach
- Stack-Based Approach

6.10.2 Boundary fill Algorithms

6.10.2.1 *Recursive Approach*

Following is the boundary fill algorithm using 8-connected fill method. It is a recursive procedure with fill color specified by, '*fill*' and boundary color specified by '*boundary*'.

Algorithm 6.3 Boundary fill using 8-connected fill method

```
Input seed_pixel (x, y), fill, boundary
Procedure boundary_fill (x, y, fill, boundary)
If (Get pixel x, y) < > fill and Get Pixel (x, y) < > boundary) then
Set pixel (x, y fill)
boundary_fill (x + 1, y, fill, boundary)
boundary_fill (x – 1, y, fill, boundary)
boundary_fill (x, y + 1, fill boundary)
boundary_fill (x, y – 1, fill boundary)
boundary_fill (x + 1, y + 1, fill boundary)
boundary-fill (x – 1, y + 1, fill boundary)
boundary_fill (x – 1, y – 1, fill boundary)
boundary_fill (x + 1, y –1, fill boundary)
End of Procedure
```

6.10.2.2 *Stack-based Approach*

Following is the boundary fill algorithm using 4-connected fill method. It is a stacked-based approach with fill color specified by '*fill*' and boundary color specified by '*boundary*'.

Algorithm 6.4 Boundary fill using 4-connected fill method

```
Input seed pixel (x, y), fill, boundary
PUSH pixel (x, y)
While (stack not empty)
POP pixel (x, y)
```

```
Set pixel (x, y, fill)
if (Get pixel (x + 1, y) < > fill and get pixel (x + 1, y) < > boundary) then
PUSH pixel (x + 1, y)
If Get pixel (x – 1, y) < >fill and get pixel (x – 1, y) < > boundary) then
PUSH pixel (x – 1, y)
If Get pixel (x, y + 1) < >fill and get pixel (x, y + 1) < > boundary) then
PUSH pixel (x, y + 1)
If Get pixel (x, y –1) < >fill and get pixel (x, y –1) < > boundary) then
PUSH pixel (x, y –1)
end of while
```

Above algorithm can also be extended for 8-connected method.

6.10.3 Flood fill algorithms

6.10.3.1 *Recursive Approach*

This is the simplest algorithm to make, but also the slowest. Also, since it uses a recursive function, the recursion stack may overflow making it crash when filling larger areas.

The recursion works like this: at the start position, you "plant a seed". Each seed gives the pixel at its position the new color, and then plants a new seed at its 4 neighbors. Each of these new seeds will draw a pixel again and plant even more seeds, but only if fulfils the following conditions:

- The pixel is inside the screen: edges of the screen also count as edges of the area to be filled.
- The pixel has old_Color: if it hasn't, it's either a border of the area we're filling, or a pixel that has already been given the fill_Color.
- The pixel doesn't have fill_Color: this condition is only needed if old_Color is the same as old_Color, otherwise it'll keep running forever since newly drawn pixels will again have old_Color and thus seeds will be planted again and again forever.

Following is the flood fill algorithm using 4-connected fill method. It is a recursive approach with old fill color specified by, '*old_color*' and new color specified by '*fill_color*'.

Algorithm 6.5 Flood fill algorithm using 4-connected fill method

```
Input seed_pixel (x, y), fill_color, old_color
procedure Flood_fill (x, y, fill_color, old_ color)
 if (Get pixel (x, y) = old_color) then
Set pixel (x, y, fill_color)
Flood_fill (x + 1, y, fill_color, old_color)
Flood_fill (x, y,+1, fill_color, old_color)
Flood_fill (x–1, y), fill_color, old_color)
Flood_fill (x, y-1, fill_color, old_color)
end of procedure
```

Algorithm 6.6 Flood-fill algorithm using 8-connected fill method

This algorithm is pretty similar to the previous one, except it doesn't test 4 neighbors, but 8. This means, that this version of the floodfill algorithm will leak through sloped edges of 1 pixel thick:Both red pixels are now a neighbor of each other, so the algorithm will continue behind the sloped black line, as shown in Fig. 6.32. The code is very similar to the 4-way one:

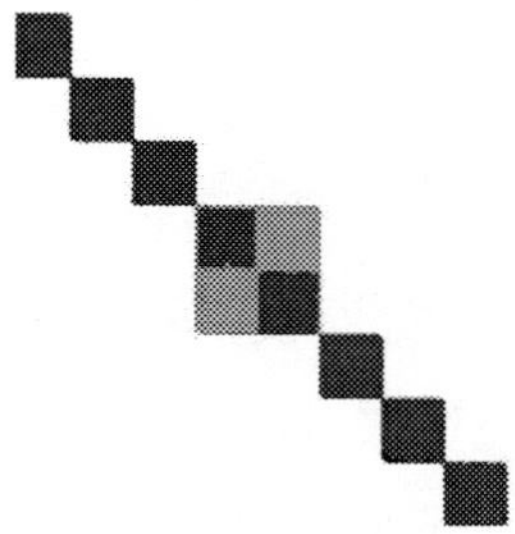

FIGURE 6.32

Algorithm

Input seed_pixel (x, y), fill_color, old_color
procedure Flood_fill (x, y, fill_color, old_ color)
if (Get pixel (x, y) = old_color) then
Set pixel (x, y, fill_color)
Flood_fill (x + 1, y, fill_color, old_color)
Flood_fill (x, y,+1, fill_color, old_color)
Flood_fill (x–1, y), fill_color, old_color)
Flood_fill (x, y–1, fill_color, old_color)
Flood_fill (x +1, y +1, fill_color, old_color)
Flood_fill (x–1, y–1, fill_color, old_color)
Flood_fill (x–1, y +1, fill_color, old_color)
Flood_fill (x +1, y–1, fill_color, old_color)
end of procedure

6.10.3.2 Stack-based Approach

4-Way Method With Stack (floodFill4Stack)

This algorithm does exactly the same as the one with recursion, only it uses a while loop that loops until the stack is empty, and you push new positions to the stack instead of starting another recursion. So, the only difference is that we're using our own stack routines now, instead of the ones used for recursive functions. This means we can control the size of the stack, and properly stop the floodfill algorithm if the stack overflows, instead of just letting the program crash. There are also a few other minor differences in the implementation.

Algorithm 6.7 4-Way Method With Stack-based approach

```
void floodFill4Stack(int x, int y, int newColor, int oldColor)
{
 if(newColor == oldColor) return; //avoid infinite loop
    emptyStack();

    if(!push(x, y)) return;
    while(pop(x, y))
    {
        screenBuffer[x][y] = newColor;
        if(x + 1 < w && screenBuffer[x + 1][y] == oldColor)
```

```
        {
            if(!push(x + 1, y)) return;
        }
        if(x - 1 >= 0 && screenBuffer[x - 1][y] == oldColor)
        {
            if(!push(x - 1, y)) return;
        }
        if(y + 1 < h && screenBuffer[x][y + 1] == oldColor)
        {
            if(!push(x, y + 1)) return;
        }
        if(y - 1 >= 0 && screenBuffer[x][y - 1] == oldColor)
        {
            if(!push(x, y - 1)) return;
        }
    }
}
```

This algorithm goes a bit faster than the recursive version.

Algorithm 6.8 8-Way Method With Stack (floodFill8Stack)

This is the 8-way version of the previous function, and only differs because it has 4 extra neighbor test conditions:

```
void floodFill4Stack(int x, int y, int newColor, int oldColor)
{
    if(newColor == oldColor) return; //avoid infinite loop
    emptyStack();
    if(!push(x, y)) return;
    while(pop(x, y))
    {
     screenBuffer[x][y] = newColor;
     f(x + 1 < w && screenBuffer[x + 1][y] == oldColor)
      {
      if(!push(x + 1, y)) return;
      }
      if(x - 1 >= 0 && screenBuffer[x - 1][y] == oldColor)
      {
      if(!push(x - 1, y)) return;
      }
      if(y + 1 < h && screenBuffer[x][y + 1] == oldColor)
      {
      if(!push(x, y + 1)) return;
      }
     if(y - 1 >= 0 && screenBuffer[x][y - 1] == oldColor)
     {
     if(!push(x, y - 1)) return;
     }
  if(x + 1 < w && y + 1 < h && screenBuffer[x + 1][y + 1] == oldColor)
        {
            if(!push(x + 1, y + 1)) return;
        }
```

```
if(x + 1 < w && y - 1 >= 0 && screenBuffer[x + 1][y - 1] == oldColor)
        {
            if(!push(x + 1, y - 1)) return;
        }
if(x - 1 >= 0 && y + 1 < h && screenBuffer[x - 1][y + 1] == oldColor)
        {
            if(!push(x - 1, y + 1)) return;
        }
if(x - 1 >= 0 && y - 1 >= 0 && screenBuffer[x - 1][y - 1] ==oldColor)
        {
            if(!push(x - 1, y - 1)) return;
        }
    }
}
```

6.10.4 Scan Line Seed Fill Algorithm

The seed fill algorithm makes the stack quite large because in every loop the algorithm pushes at most 4 to 8 pixels into the stack. The stack may also contain duplicate pixels. In contrast scan line seed fill algorithm minimize stack size by pushing to the stack only one pixel instead of proceeding along 4-connected and 8-connected pixels. This algorithm proceeds as follows:

Step 1: A seed pixel on a scan line within the area is popped from a stack containing the seed pixel.

Step 2: The line or span containing the seed pixel is filled to the right and left of the seed pixel including the seed pixel itself until a boundary is found.

Step 3: The extreme left and extreme right unprocessed pixel in the scan are saved as x_{left} and x_{right}, respectively.

Step 4: In the range of x_{left} and x_{right} the scan lines immediately above the current scan lines and immediately below the current scan line are examined to see if they completely contain boundary pixels or previously filled pixel, then in the range of x_{left} and x_{right} the extreme right pixel in each span is marked as a seed pixel and pushed onto the stack.

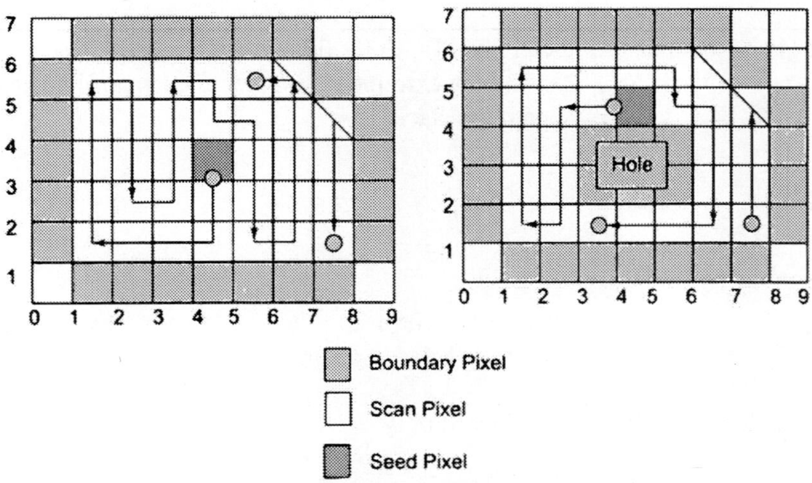

FIGURE 6.33 Demonstration of Scan Line Seed Fill Algorithm

Algorithm 6.9 Scan line Seed fill Algorithm

```
Input : Pixel (x, y) as the seed pixel, fill as fill color and boundary as boundary colour
Push pixel (x, y)                          : Initialise stack with seed pixel
while (stack not empty)
Pop pixel (x, y)                           : Get the seed pixel
Setpixel (x, y,fill)                       : Set it to fill color
save x = x                                 : Save the x & y coordinates of seed pixel
save y = y
x = x +1
while (Get pixel (x,y) <> boundary
setpixel (x,y,fill)                        : Fill the span to the right of the seed pixel
x = x + 1
end while
x_right = x - 1                            : Save the extreme right pixel of the span in the current scan
                                             line
x = save x                                 : Again come back to the seed pixel position
x = x - 1
while Get pixel (x,y) <> boundary)
Set pixel (x, y, fill)                     : fill the span to the left of the seed pixel
x = x - 1
end while
x_left = x +1                              : Save the extreme left pixel of the span in the current scan line
x = x_left, y = save y + 1
while (x < = x right)
if Get (pixel (x,y) = boundary or Get pixel (x, y) = fill
                                           : check the scan line immediately above the current can line
                                             for filled pixel span or boundary filled span
                                           : Simply cross over such span, if found
x = x + 1
else
while (Get pixel (x,y) <> boundary and Get pixel (x, y) <> fill and x < = x_right)
x = x + 1                                  : find the extreme right pixel of each unfilled span and push it
                                             onto the stack
end while
Push pixel (x - 1, y)
x = x + 1
end if
end while
x = x_left y = save y - 1                  : Move to the scan line immediately below the scan line con-
                                             taining the seed pixel.
while ( < = x_right)
check the scan line below and stack pixels accordingly
end while
end while
```

SOLVED PROBLEMS

Problem 6.1 Find complete viewing transformation that maps a window in world co-ordinates with x-extent 1 to 5 and y-extent 1 to 10 onto:

(a) normalized viewport
(b) onto viewport whose opposite corners are at (1,1) and (4,4).

Solution:

In general viewing transformation matrix is

$$N = \begin{bmatrix} sx & 0 & -s_x \cdot xw_{min} + xv_{min} \\ 0 & sy & -s_y \cdot yw_{min} + yv_{min} \\ 0 & 0 & 1 \end{bmatrix}$$

where

$$sx = \frac{xv_{max} - xv_{min}}{xw_{max} - xw_{min}}$$

$$sy = \frac{yv_{max} - yv_{min}}{yw_{max} - yw_{min}}$$

Part (a)

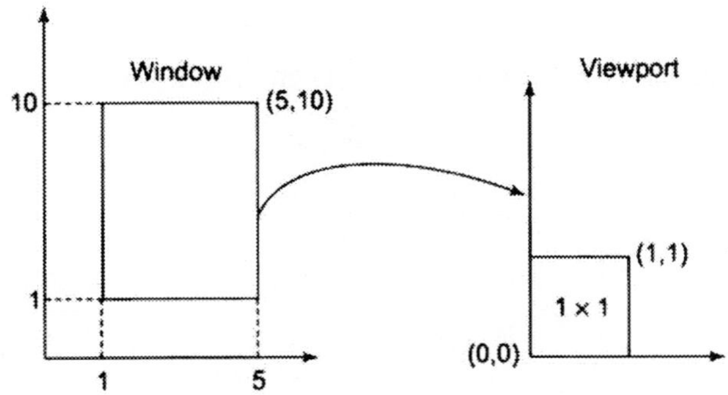

$$sx = \frac{xv_{max} - xv_{min}}{xw_{max} - xw_{min}} = \frac{1-0}{5-1} = \frac{1}{4}$$

$$sy = \frac{yv_{max} - yv_{min}}{yw_{max} - yw_{min}} = \frac{1-0}{10-1} = \frac{1}{9}$$

therefore

$$N = \begin{bmatrix} 1/4 & 0 & -1/4 \\ 0 & 1/9 & -1/9 \\ 0 & 0 & 1 \end{bmatrix}$$

Part (b)

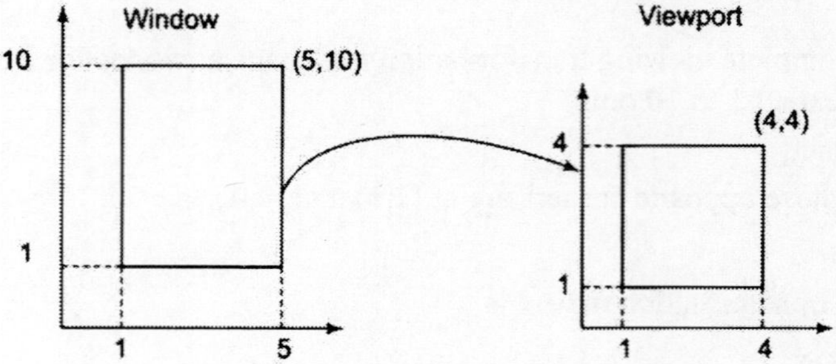

$$sx = \frac{xv_{max} - xv_{min}}{xw_{max} - xw_{min}} = \frac{4-1}{5-1} = \frac{3}{4}$$

$$sy = \frac{yv_{max} - yv_{min}}{yw_{max} - yw_{min}} = \frac{4-1}{10-1} = \frac{3}{9}$$

$$N = \begin{bmatrix} 3/4 & 0 & 1/4 \\ 0 & 3/9 & 2/3 \\ 0 & 0 & 1 \end{bmatrix}$$

Problem 6.2 Find complete viewing transformation of a triangle with vertices $A(2,2)$, $B(4,2)$, and $C(3,6)$ that maps from window in world co-ordinates with x-extent 1 to 5 and y-extent 1 to 10 onto viewport:

(a) normalized viewport
(b) onto viewport whose opposite corners are at (1,1) and (4,4).

Solution:

Part (a)

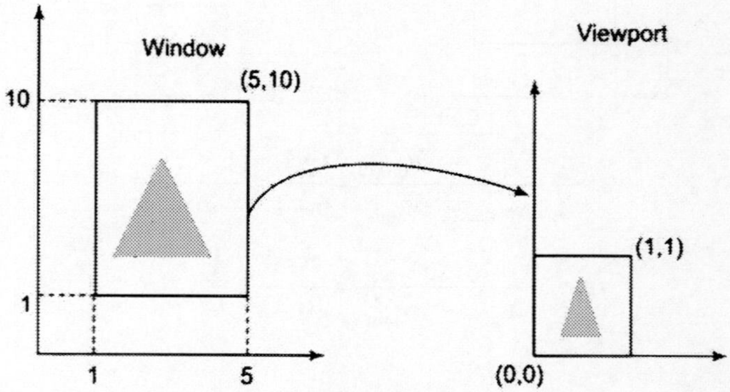

Viewing transformation matrix from window with opposite corners ((1,1), (5,10)) to viewport with opposite corners ((0,0), (1,1)) is

$$N = \begin{bmatrix} 1/4 & 0 & -1/4 \\ 0 & 1/9 & -1/9 \\ 0 & 0 & 1 \end{bmatrix} \quad \text{[from Problem 6.1(a)]}$$

$$A'B'C' = \begin{bmatrix} 1/4 & 0 & -1/4 \\ 0 & 1/9 & -1/9 \\ 0 & 0 & 1 \end{bmatrix} \begin{bmatrix} \overset{A}{2} & \overset{B}{4} & \overset{C}{3} \\ 2 & 2 & 6 \\ 1 & 1 & 1 \end{bmatrix}$$

$$= \begin{bmatrix} 1/4 & 3/4 & 1/2 \\ 1/9 & 1/9 & 5/9 \\ 1 & 1 & 1 \end{bmatrix}$$

Part (b)

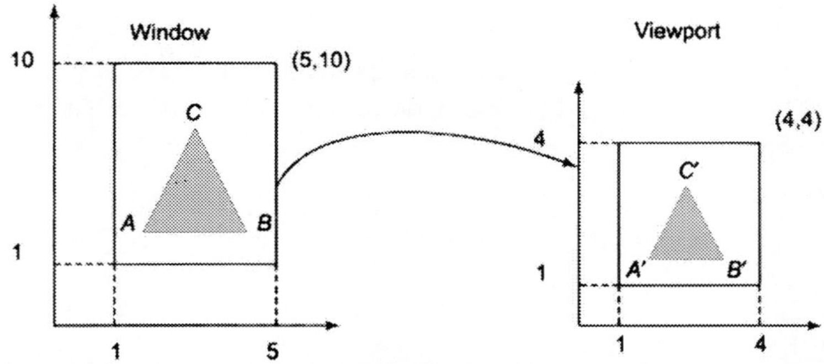

Viewing transformation matrix from window with opposite corners ((1,1), (5,10)) to viewport with opposite corners ((1,1), (4,4)) is

$$N = \begin{bmatrix} 3/4 & 0 & -3/4 \\ 0 & 3/9 & -3/9 \\ 0 & 0 & 1 \end{bmatrix} \quad \text{[from Problem 6.1(b)]}$$

$$A'B'C' = \begin{bmatrix} 3/4 & 0 & -3/4 \\ 0 & 3/9 & -3/9 \\ 0 & 0 & 1 \end{bmatrix} \begin{bmatrix} \overset{A}{2} & \overset{B}{4} & \overset{C}{3} \\ 2 & 2 & 6 \\ 1 & 1 & 1 \end{bmatrix}$$

$$A'B'C' = \begin{bmatrix} \frac{3}{4} & \frac{9}{4} & \frac{6}{4} \\ 3/9 & 3/9 & 15/9 \\ 1 & 1 & 1 \end{bmatrix}$$

Problem 6.3 Find the normalization transformation which uses an ellipse with major axis 6 units and minor axis 4 units and centre (2,2) as a window and an ellipse with major axis 4 units and minor axis 2 units and centre (1,1) as a viewport.

Solution:

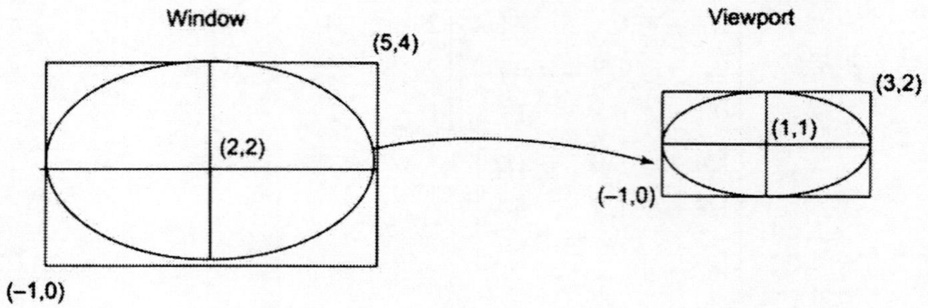

Now proceed similar to problem 6.1.

Problem 6.4 Suppose R be the window which has its lower left corner at (–3,1) and upper right corner at (2,6) for each of the following line segments, state whether it is visible, invisible or partially visible.

(i) (–4,2) to (–1,7)
(ii) (–1,5) to (3,8)
(iii) (–2,3) to (1,2)
(iv) (1,–2) to (3,3)
(v) (–4,7) to (–2,10)

In case of partially visible find the points of intersection with window.

Solution:

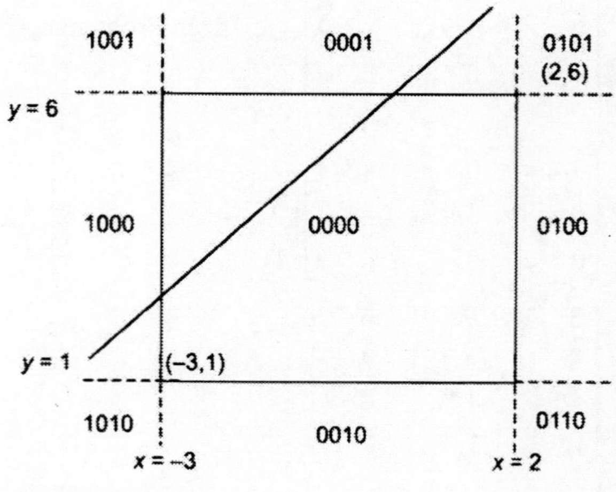

Rules to assigned 4 bits code as follows:

Last significant Bit 1 = 1 If point (x,y) lies above the window i.e. $(y - y_{wmax})>0$

Bit (LSB) Bit 2 = 1 If point (x,y) lies below the window i.e. $-(y - y_{wmin}) > 0$

Most significant Bit 3 = 1 If point (x,y) lies right the window i.e. $(x - x_{wmax}) > 0$

Bit (MSB) Bit 4 = 1 If point (x,y) lies left the window i.e. $-(x - x_{wmin}) > 0$

Then using these rules, we have

	Line segment	*4-bit code*		*Logical AND*	*RESULT*	*Point(s) of intersections*
a)	(–4, 2) to (–1, 7)	1000(–4, 2)	0001(–1, 7)	0000	Partially Visible	(–3, ?) bit 4 is 1 (?,6) bit 1 is 1
b)	(–1, 5) to (3, 8)	0000(–1, 5)	0101(3, 8)	0000	Partially Visible	
	(–2, 3) to (1, 2)	0000(–2, 3)	0000(1, 2)	0000	Visible	....
c)	(1, –2) to (3, 3)	0010(1, –2)	0100(3, 3)	0000	Partially Visible	(?,1) bit 2 is 1 (2,?) bit 3 is 1
	(–4, 7) to (–2, 10)	1001(–4, 7)	0001(–1, 10)	0001	Non-Visible	....

If a line having two end points $A(x1, y1)$ and $B(x2, y2)$, then y co-ordinates of the intersection point with vertical boundary are obtained as:

$$\frac{y - y_1}{x - x_1} = m \text{ or } y = y_1 + m(x - x_1) \qquad .....(i)$$

where $x = x_{wmax}$ or x_{wmin}

x co-ordinate of the intersection point with horizontal boundary is obtained as:

$$\frac{x - x_1}{y - y_1} = \frac{1}{m} \text{ or } x = x_1 + \frac{y - y_1}{m} \qquad .....(ii)$$

where $y = y_{wmax}$ or y_{wmin}

(a) Line(–1,5) to (3,8)

$$m = \frac{8-5}{3-(-1)} = \frac{3}{4}$$

From equation (i)

$$\frac{y-5}{x-(-1)} = m \text{ or } y = 5 + \frac{3}{4}(x+1)$$

When $x = 2 \quad y = \frac{29}{4}$

From equation (ii)

$$x = -1 + \frac{(y-3)4}{3}$$

When $y = 6 \quad x = 3$

Thus, line (–1,5) to (3,8) intersects the window at points $(2, \frac{29}{4})$, and (3,6).

(b) Line (1, –2) to (3,3)

$$m = \frac{3-(-2)}{3-1} = \frac{5}{2}$$

From equation (i)

$$\frac{y-3}{(x-3)} = m \text{ or } y = 3 + \frac{5}{2}(x-3)$$

When $x = 2 \quad y = \frac{1}{2}$

From equation (ii)

$$x = 1 + \frac{(y-(-2))2}{5}$$

When $y = 1 \quad x = \frac{11}{5}$

Thus, line (1, –2) to (3,3) intersects the window at points $(2, \frac{1}{2})$, and $(\frac{11}{5}, 1)$.

Problem 6.5 A 10 × 10 square is centered at co-ordinates (50,50) in WCS. Assuming that square has been defined as segments:

(i) Translate the centre at (20,20)
Then
(ii) Double the size of the square w.r.t. its centre.

Solution:

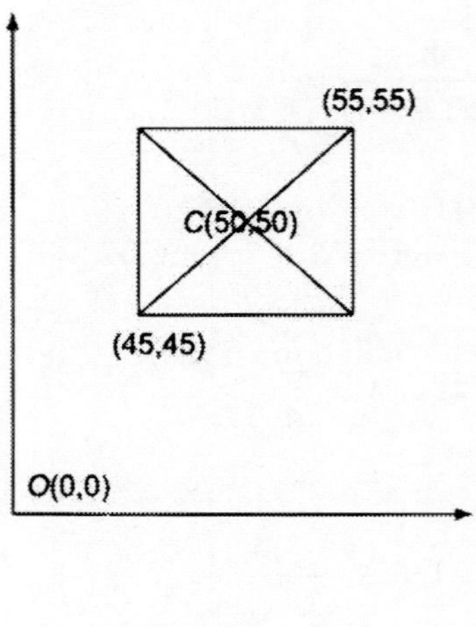

Transformation matrix when a point (x,y) translating to $(x + tx, y + ty)$

$$T_{tx,,ty} = \begin{bmatrix} 1 & 0 & tx \\ 0 & 1 & ty \\ 0 & 0 & 1 \end{bmatrix}$$

Scaling transformation matrix w.r.t. $P(h,k)$ is

$$S_{sx,sy,P} = \begin{bmatrix} sx & 0 & -hsx + h \\ 0 & sy & -ksy + k \\ 0 & 0 & 1 \end{bmatrix}$$

Transformation matrix when (50,50) is translating to (20,20) is

$$T_{-30,\,-30} = \begin{bmatrix} 1 & 0 & 20-50 \\ 0 & 1 & 20-50 \\ 0 & 0 & 1 \end{bmatrix}$$

$$= \begin{bmatrix} 1 & 0 & -30 \\ 0 & 1 & -30 \\ 0 & 0 & 1 \end{bmatrix}$$

Scaling w.r.t. (20,20) is

$$S_{2,2,C} = \begin{bmatrix} 2 & 0 & -20x2+20 \\ 0 & 2 & -20x2+20 \\ 0 & 0 & 1 \end{bmatrix}$$

$$= \begin{bmatrix} 2 & 0 & -20 \\ 0 & 2 & -20 \\ 0 & 0 & 1 \end{bmatrix}$$

$$A'B'C'D = \begin{bmatrix} 2 & 0 & -20 \\ 0 & 2 & -20 \\ 0 & 0 & 1 \end{bmatrix} \begin{bmatrix} 1 & 0 & -30 \\ 0 & 1 & -30 \\ 0 & 0 & 1 \end{bmatrix} \begin{matrix} \text{A} & \text{B} & \text{C} & \text{D} \\ \end{matrix} \begin{bmatrix} 45 & 55 & 55 & 45 \\ 45 & 45 & 55 & 55 \\ 1 & 1 & 1 & 1 \end{bmatrix}$$

$$= \begin{bmatrix} 5 & 30 & 30 & 5 \\ 5 & 5 & 30 & 30 \\ 1 & 1 & 1 & 1 \end{bmatrix}$$

EXERCISES

1. Differentiate between:
   a. Window and Viewport
   b. Clipping and Scissoring
2. Explain Cohen-Sutherland Algorithm for line segment clipping.
3. Describe a Cohen-Sutherland algorithm for line segment clipping against a circular window.
4. Describe a Mid-Point algorithm for line segment clipping against a circular window.
5. Contrast the efficiency of clipping between Sutherland-Cohen and Mid-Point algorithm.
   Describe Sutherland-Hodgeman algorithm for polygon clipping. Explain why this algorithm works for convex polygons.
7. Describe the flood-fill algorithm and boundary-fill algorithm.
8. Differentiate between flood-fill algorithm and boundary-fill algorithm.
9. Consider a convex polygon with n vertices being clipped against a clip rectangle. What is the maximum number and minimum number of vertices in the resulting clipped polygon?
10. Derive the window-to- viewport transformation matrix:
    a. First translating window to viewport then scaling the window to the size of the viewport.
    b. First scaling the window to the size of the viewport then translating window to viewport.
11. Explain the importance of normalized coordinate system in viewing transformation.
12. Derive workstation transformation matrix clip the triangle ABC with coordinates (15,7), (30,7), and (30,27) against the window with parameters:

Lower Left Corner	Upper Right Corner
(i) (10,5)	(25,15)
(ii) (15,10)	(31,42)
(iii) (5,8)	(25,20)

13. Find the normalization transformation which uses a circle of radius 2 units and centre (1, 1) as a window and a circle of radius 1/2 and centre (1/2, 1/2) as a viewport.
14. Find a normalization transformation from the window whose lower left corner is at (0, 0) and upper right corner is at (4,3) on the normalized device screen so that aspect ratios are preserved.
15. How can we decide whether a point $P(x, y)$ lies towards the right, left, or on a line segment joining the points $A(x_1, y_1)$ to $B(x_2, y_2)$?
16. Find the normalized transformation from the window whose lower left corner is at (0, 0) and upper right corner is at (8, 6) on the normalized viewport.
17. A clipping window whose lower left corner is at (0,0) and upper right corner is at (40, 40). Check whether two lines $P(-20, 70)$, $Q(20, 30)$ and $R(50, 10)$, $S(70, 70)$ are totally invisible or partially visible. In case of partially visible, find out the visible portions of the lines.
18. The following set of vertices describes the polygons:
    (1, 1), (3, 1), (3, 4), (5, 1), (5, 6), (3, 6), (3, 8), (1, 6)
    what pixels are filled by the scan line fill algorithm on lines $y = 3$, $y = 4$, $y = 6$, $y = 7$? Explain in detail how you derive your answer and what rules are applied.
19. Using the scan line oriented seed fill algorithm, fill the polygon with exterior vertices at (2, 1), (2, 6), (8, 6), (8, 5), (10, 5), (10, 4), (11, 4), (11, 1). Given seed as (6, 4).
20. A clipping window whose lower left corner is at (–1, –1) and upper right is corner at (1, 1). Find the portion of the line $A(-3/2, 1)$, $B(3/2, 2)$ lying outside the window.

7

3-D Transformations

7.1 INTRODUCTION

So far we have discussed two-dimensional (zero thickness) graphic objects. The concept of three-dimensional space is very old and very simple. By observation one can notice that the world around us is comprehensible by simply watching at it. Although there is a material existence of objects (molecules, atoms, etc.) nonetheless it is enough to use our eyes to locate objects. We do not have to physically touch objects to locate them. The eye is a piece of glass where rays from the real world are projected. Therefore, we can distinguish two systems: a three-dimensional **world system** and a **projection system**. In this chapter we will concentrate on 3-D geometry and 3-D transformations viz., translation, rotation, scaling reflection, and shear and projection system is taken in the next chapter.

7.2 3-D GEOMETRY

3-D is an extension of 2-D in the sense that it takes the coordinate perpendicular to x-axis and y-axis. Thus,
Thus, x, y and z axes are mutually perpendicular lines, as shown in Fig. 7.1.

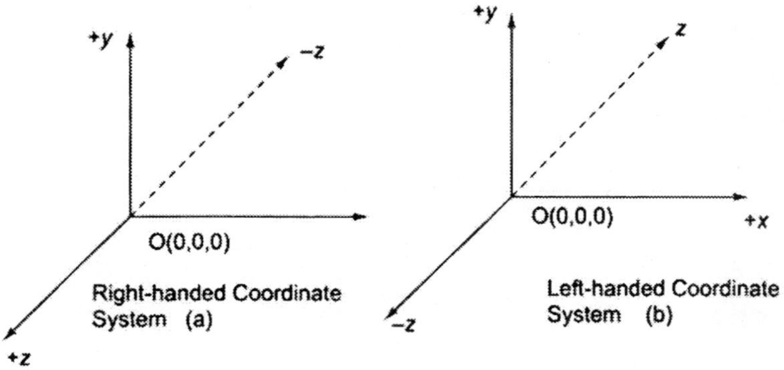

FIGURE 7.1

Further xy plane, zx plane and yz plane are three mutually perpendicular planes and their equations are $z = 0$, $y = 0$ and $x = 0$, respectively, as shown in Fig. 7.2.

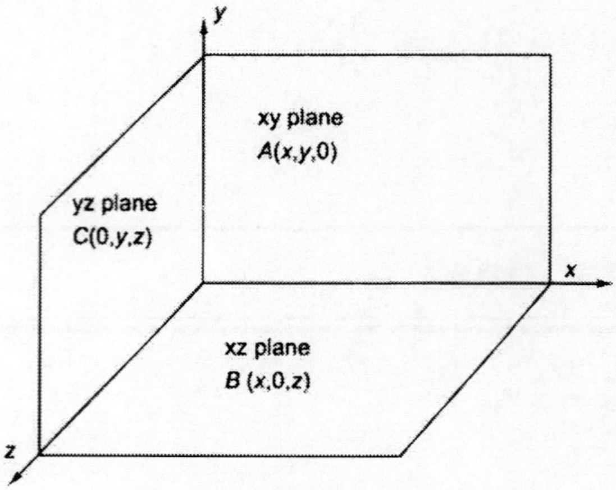

FIGURE 7.2

Representation of a point in 3-D

Figure 7.3 illustrates the representation of a point in 3-D.

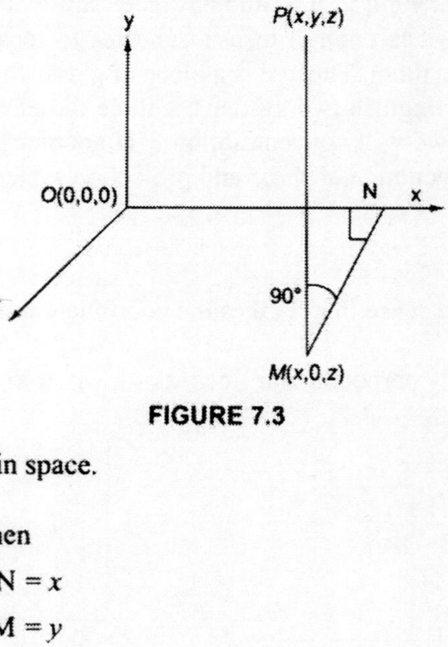

FIGURE 7.3

Let us consider a point $P(x,y,z)$ in space.
Let PM ⊥ to xz plane
MN ⊥ to x-axis or || to z-axis, then

$$\text{ON} = x$$

$$\text{PM} = y$$

$$\text{MN} = z$$

7.3 3-D TRANSFORMATION

7.3.1 Translation

Translation is another word for moving an object to a new position. It is also sometimes called **offsetting.** Basically, it is the change of location of the object in space as shown in the figure 7.4.

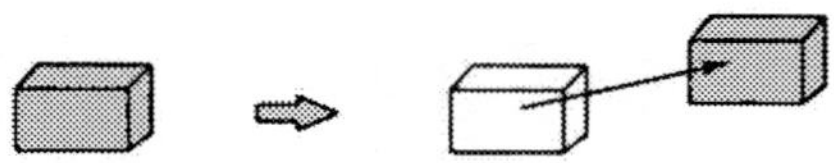

FIGURE 7.4

If a point $P(x,y,z)$ in 3D is moved to $P'(x',y',z')$ by translated vector = $<t_x, t_y, t_z>$, tx, ty, tz are the displacements of P along three principal directions x, y, z, respectively. Algebraically,

$$x' = x + t_x$$
$$y' = y + t_y$$
$$z' = z + t_z$$

Above equations can be expressed in column matrix format as

$$\begin{pmatrix} x' \\ y' \\ z' \\ 1 \end{pmatrix} = \begin{pmatrix} 1 & 0 & 0 & t_x \\ 0 & 1 & 0 & t_y \\ 0 & 0 & 1 & t_z \\ 0 & 0 & 0 & 1 \end{pmatrix} \begin{pmatrix} x \\ y \\ z \\ 1 \end{pmatrix}$$

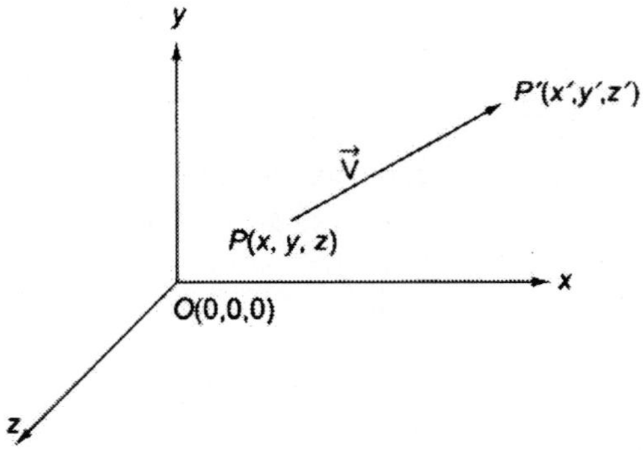

FIGURE 7.5 Translation of a Point

7.3.2 Scaling

Scale (or sizing) either reduces or enlarges an object. Objects are scaled by specifying a percentage of scaling, the direction, and a pivot point. Then simple multiplication of each coordinate determines the new position.

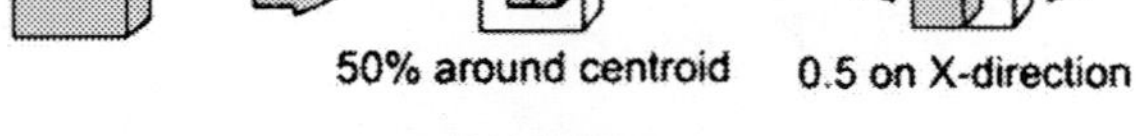

FIGURE 7.6

Likewise in 2-D Scaling in 3-D can be carried out by multiplying the coordinate values (x,y,z) by scaling factors sx, sy, and sz respectively to produce the coordinates (x', y', z).

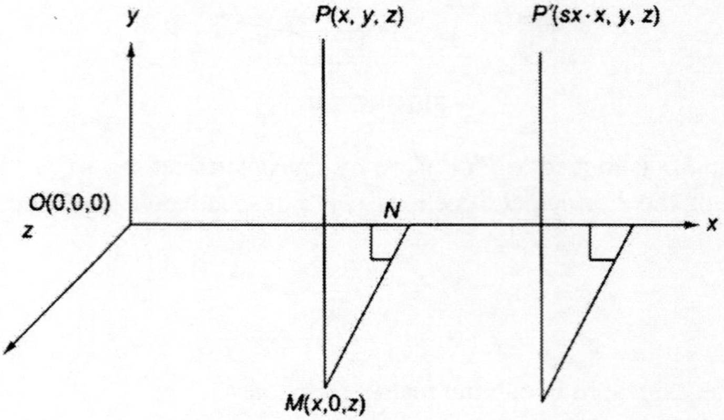

FIGURE 7.7 Scaling of a Point along x-axis

(a) Scaling w.r.t. Origin

Figure 7.3 illustrates the scaling of a point $P(x,y,z)$ along x-axis by scaling factor sx.
Then,

$$x' = sx\,.\,x \qquad 7.1(a)$$

$$y' = sy.\,y \qquad 7.1(b)$$

$$z' = sz\,.\,z \qquad 7.1(c)$$

Where s_x, s_y, s_z are scale factors in x, y and z direction, respectively.

Above equations 7.1(a), 7.1(b) and 7.1(c) can be expressed in column matrix format as

$$\begin{pmatrix} x' \\ y' \\ z' \end{pmatrix} = \begin{pmatrix} sx & 0 & 0 \\ 0 & sy & 0 \\ 0 & 0 & sz \end{pmatrix} \begin{pmatrix} x \\ y \\ z \end{pmatrix}$$

$$P' = S_{sx,\,sy,\,sz}\,.\,P \qquad 7.2$$

(b) Scaling of a point w.r.t. any arbitrary point $A(x_p, y_p, z_p)$

Equation (7.2) is applicable only for scaling w.r.t. origin. But in many applications fixed point will not be origin. It may be any point outside the object or on the object in 3D plane.

The process of scaling w.r.t. any point $A(x_p, y_p, z_p)$ involves following three steps:

Step 1: Translate $A(x_p, y_p, z_p)$ to $O(0,0,0)$ $(T\overline{V})$

Step 2: Perform scaling w.r.t. O $(S_{sx,\,sy,\,sz})$

Step 3: Translate A back to (x_p, y_p, z_p) $(T\text{-}\overline{V})$

$$T\overline{V} = \begin{pmatrix} 1 & 0 & 0 & tx \\ 0 & 1 & 0 & ty \\ 0 & 0 & 1 & tz \\ 0 & 0 & 0 & 1 \end{pmatrix} \quad S_{sx.sy,sz} = \begin{pmatrix} sx & 0 & 0 \\ 0 & sy & 0 \\ 0 & 0 & sz \end{pmatrix} \quad \mathrm{T}\overline{V} = \begin{pmatrix} 1 & 0 & 0 & -tx \\ 0 & 1 & 0 & -ty \\ 0 & 0 & 1 & -tz \\ 0 & 0 & 0 & 1 \end{pmatrix}$$

Combining these three matrices in the order in which these are performed:

$S_{sx,\, sy,\, sz\; A} = \xleftarrow[T_{-\vec{V}} \cdot S_{sx,sy,sz} \cdot T_{\vec{V}}]{}$

$$S_{sx,\, sy,\, sz\; A} = \begin{pmatrix} 1 & 0 & 0 & x_p \\ 0 & 1 & 0 & y_p \\ 0 & 0 & 1 & z_p \\ 0 & 0 & 0 & 1 \end{pmatrix} \begin{pmatrix} sx & 0 & 0 \\ 0 & sy & 0 \\ 0 & 0 & sz \end{pmatrix} \begin{pmatrix} 1 & 0 & 0 & -x_p \\ 0 & 1 & 0 & -y_p \\ 0 & 0 & 1 & -z_p \\ 0 & 0 & 0 & 1 \end{pmatrix}$$

$$= \begin{bmatrix} sx & 0 & 0 & -x_p\, sx + x_p \\ 0 & sy & 0 & -y_p\, sy + y_p \\ 0 & 0 & sz & -z_p sz + z_p \\ 0 & 0 & 0 & 1 \end{bmatrix}$$

Column matrix format

$$\begin{bmatrix} x' \\ y' \\ z' \\ 1 \end{bmatrix} = \begin{bmatrix} sx & 0 & 0 & -x_p\, sx + x_p \\ 0 & sy & 0 & -y_p\, sy + y_p \\ 0 & 0 & sz & -z_p sz + z_p \\ 0 & 0 & 0 & 1 \end{bmatrix} \begin{bmatrix} x \\ y \\ z \\ 1 \end{bmatrix}$$

$P' = S_{sx,\, sy,\, sz\; A} \cdot P$

Algebraically,

$$x' = sx.x + (1 - sx)\, x_p \qquad 7.3(a)$$

$$y' = sy.y + (1 - sy\,)\, y_p \qquad 7.3(b)$$

$$z' = sz.z + (1 - sz)\, y_p \qquad 7.3\ (c)$$

Equations 7.3(a), 7.3(b) and 7.3(c) generate new coordinates (x', y', z') after scaling with scaling factors sx, sy and sz along x-axis, y-axis and z-axis, respectively of a point (x,y,z) w.r.t. an arbitrary point (x_p, y_p, z_p).

7.3.3 Rotation

A rotation specifies a pivoting, or angular displacement about an axis. Objects are rotated by specifying an angle of rotation and a pivot point. Then trigonometric functions are used to determine the new position.

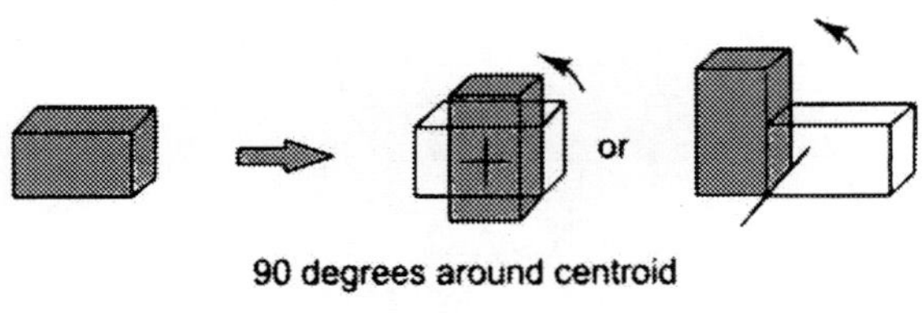

90 degrees around centroid

FIGURE 7.8

In 2-D rotation, we have seen that any 2-D rotation transformation is defined by specifying:

> a centre of rotation (pivot point)
> an amount of angular rotation

But these two parameters do not uniquely define a rotation in 3D space because an object can rotate along different circular paths. 3-D rotation transformation is defined by specifying:

> an axis of rotation .
> an angle of rotation is always perpendicular to the axis of rotation.

Canonical rotation: A 3-D rotation is called canonical rotation when one of the positive *x*, *y* or *z* coordinate axis is chosen as the axis of rotation. Figures 7.9 (a), 7.9(b) and 7.9(c) represent canonical rotations. By convention positive rotation angles(counter-clockwise) are taken but negative rotation angles (clockwise) may also be taken.

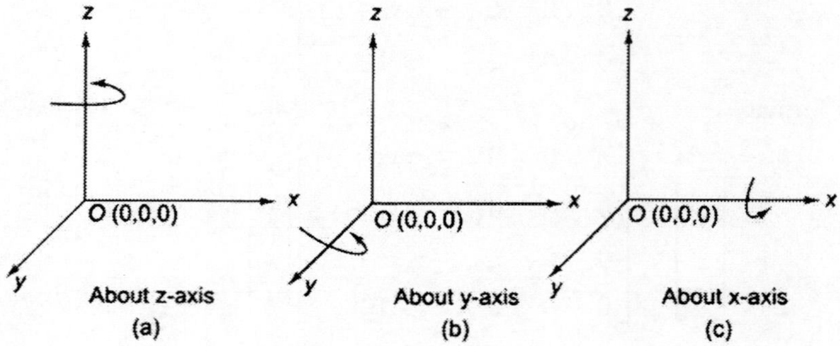

FIGURE 7.9 Canonical Rotations

(a) Rotation about z-axis

If the rotation is carried out about the z-axis, the *z* coordinates remains unchanged (because rotation occurs in planes perpendicular to the z-axis) while *x* and *y* coordinates behave exactly the same way as in two dimensions, as shown in Fig. 7.10.

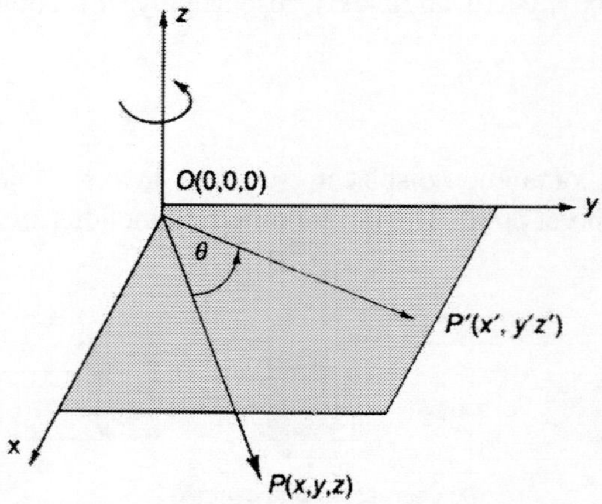

FIGURE 7.10 Rotation about z-axis

Rotation of any point $P(x,y,z)$ about z-axis by an amount θ is represented by

$$\left.\begin{aligned} x' &= x\cos\theta - y\sin\theta \\ y' &= x\sin\theta + y\cos\theta \\ z' &= z \end{aligned}\right\} \qquad 7.4$$

The corresponding transformation matrix in 4×4 form is,

$$R_{\theta,\hat{k}} = \begin{pmatrix} \cos\theta & -\sin\theta & 0 & 0 \\ \sin\theta & \cos\theta & 0 & 0 \\ 0 & 0 & 1 & 0 \\ 0 & 0 & 0 & 1 \end{pmatrix}$$

$R_{\theta,\hat{k}}$ represents rotational transformation matrix about z-axis, $\hat{k}$ is the unit vector along z-axis.

$R_{-\theta,\hat{k}}$ represents rotational transformation matrix about z-axis when rotation is taken in clockwise, $\hat{k}$ is the unit vector along z-axis.

(b) Rotation about x-axis

Here rotation takes place in the planes perpendicular to x-axis, hence x coordinate doesn't change after rotation while y and z coordinates are transformed. The expression can be derived similarly as before if we replace the z-axis in Fig. 7.11 with x-axis and the other two axes accordingly, maintaining right-handed coordinate system.

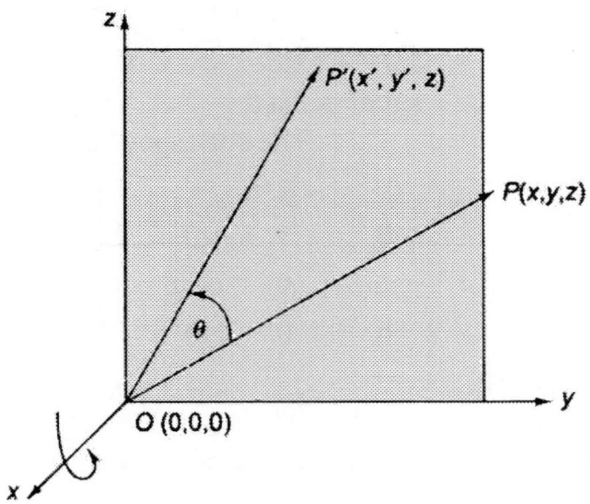

FIGURE 7.11 Rotation about x-axis

Rotation of any point $P(x,y,z)$ about x-axis by an amount θ is represented by

$$\left.\begin{aligned} y' &= y\cos\theta - z\sin\theta \\ z' &= y\sin\theta + z\cos\theta \\ x' &= x \end{aligned}\right\}$$

The corresponding tranformation matrix is in 4 × 4 form is

$$R_{\theta}\hat{i} = \begin{pmatrix} 1 & 0 & 0 & 0 \\ 0 & \cos\theta & -\sin\theta & 0 \\ 0 & \sin\theta & \cos\theta & 0 \\ 0 & 0 & 0 & 1 \end{pmatrix}$$

$R_{\theta}\hat{i}$ represents rotational transformation matrix about *x*-axis, $\hat{i}$ is the unit vector along *x*-axis.

$R_{-\theta}\hat{i}$ represents rotational transformation matrix about *x*-axis when rotation is taken in clockwise, $\hat{i}$ is the unit vector along *x*-axis.

(c) Rotation about Y Axis

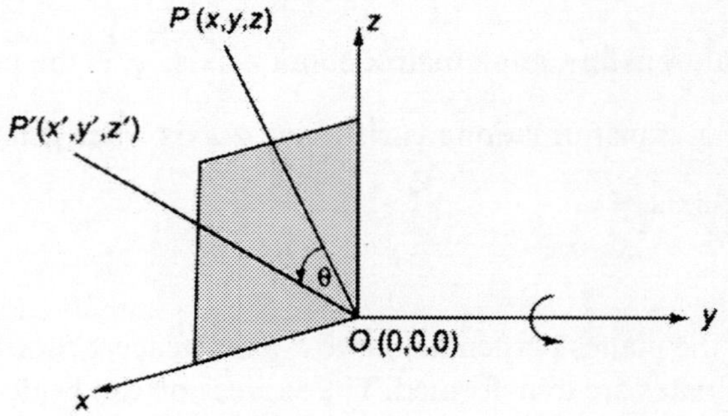

FIGURE 7.12 Rotation about *y*-axis

Rotation of any point $P(x,y,z)$ about *y*-axis by an amount θ is represented by

$$z' = z\cos\theta - x\sin\theta$$
$$x' = y\sin\theta + x\cos\theta$$
$$y' = y$$

The corresponding tranformation matrix in 4 × 4 form is

$$R_{\theta}\hat{j} = \begin{pmatrix} \cos\theta & \sin\theta & 0 & 0 \\ 0 & 1 & 0 & 0 \\ -\sin\theta & 0 & \cos\theta & 0 \\ 0 & 0 & 0 & 1 \end{pmatrix}$$

$R_{\theta}\hat{j}$ represents rotational transformation matrix about *y*-axis, $\hat{j}$ is the unit vector along *y*-axis.

$R_{-\theta}\hat{j}$ represents rotational transformation matrix about *y*-axis when rotation is taken in clockwise, $\hat{j}$ is the unit vector along *y*-axis.

(d) Rotation about any Arbitrary Axis in space

To perform rotation about an arbitrary line that is not parallel to one of the coordinate axes we first need to align the line with one of the coordinate axes through some intermediate transformations. Then the actual specified rotation is performed about that coordinate axis, the expressions for which are known standards.

Let us assume an arbitrary axis in space passing through the point $P(xp, yp, zp)$ and having direction cosines (dx, dy, dz). Process of rotation about this axis involves the following steps:

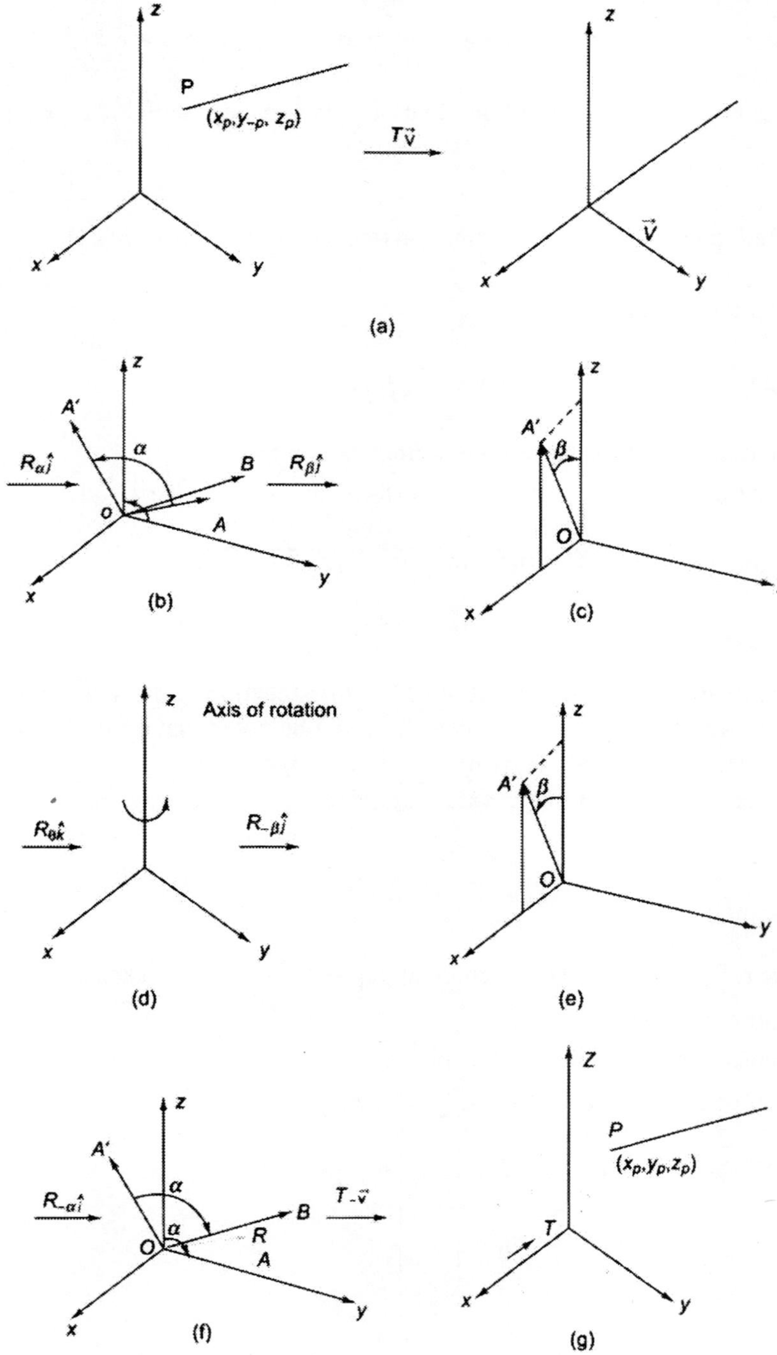

FIGURE 7.13 Stages of Rotation about any Arbitrary Axis

Step 1: Translate so that the point (*xp*, *yp*, *zp*) is at the origin of the coordinate system.$(T_{\bar{V}})$. [Fig. 7.13(a)]

Step 2: Perform rotation about *x*-axis until the rotation axis is in the *zx* plane $R_{\alpha\hat{i}}$. [Fig. 7.13(b)]

Step 3: Perform rotation about *y*-axis until the rotation axis coincides with the z-axis $\left(R_{\beta\hat{j}}\right)$ [Fig. 7.13(c)]

Step 4: Perform rotation about *z*-axis by the angle θ (the axis of rotation) $\left(R_{-\theta k}\right)$. [Fig. 7.13(d)]

Step 5: Reverse the rotation about y-axis $\left(R_{-\beta\hat{j}}\right)$. [Fig. 7.13(e)]

Step 6: Reverse the rotation about x-axis plane $\left(R_{-\alpha\hat{i}}\right)$. [Fig. 7.13(f)]

Step 7: Reverse the transformation carried out in Step 1.$(T_{-\bar{V}})$. [Fig. 7.13(g)]

Combine these matrices in the order these are performed:

$$R_{\theta,L} = \overleftarrow{(T_{-\bar{V}})(R_{-\alpha\hat{i}})(R_{-\beta\hat{j}})(R_{-\theta\hat{i}})(R_{\beta\hat{j}})(R_{\alpha\hat{i}})(T_{\bar{V}})}$$

(e) Rotation about more than one axis

Rotation about more than one axis may be obtained by concatenation of the matrices of the individual matrix in the order in which these are performed. It should be noted that matrix multiplication is not commutative. Therefore, the order of the rotation would be significant.

Rotation about *x*-axis, *y*-axis, and then *z*-axis is given as:

$$R_{\theta} = \overleftarrow{R_{\theta x\hat{i}} \cdot R_{\theta y\hat{j}} \cdot R_{\theta z\hat{k}}}$$

7.3.4 Flip

Flip in 3D would be reflection about specified plane rather than specified axes as in 2D.

(a) Reflection about zx plane.

Figure 7.14 illustrates reflection about *zx* plane.

$$x' = x, y' = -y, z' = z$$

$$M_{xy} = \begin{bmatrix} 1 & 0 & 0 & 0 \\ 0 & -1 & 0 & 0 \\ 0 & 0 & 1 & 0 \\ 0 & 0 & 0 & 1 \end{bmatrix}$$

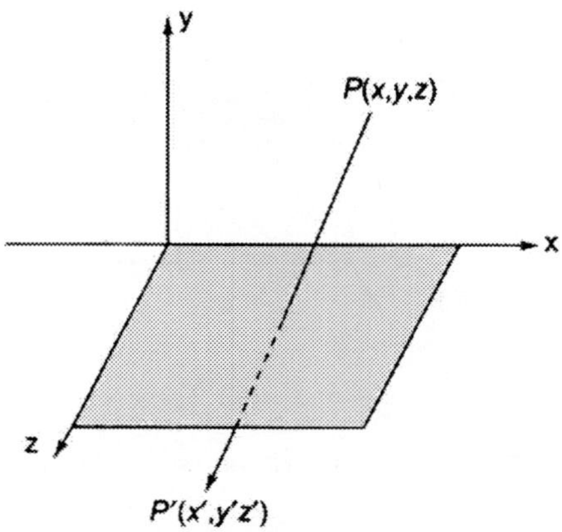

FIGURE 7.14 Reflection about *zx* plane ($y = 0$)

(b) Reflection about yz plane (x = 0)

Figure 7.16 illustrates reflection about *yz* plane.

$$x' = -x,\ y' = y,\ z' = z$$

$$M_{yz} = \begin{bmatrix} -1 & 0 & 0 & 0 \\ 0 & 1 & 0 & 0 \\ 0 & 0 & 1 & 0 \\ 0 & 0 & 0 & 1 \end{bmatrix}$$

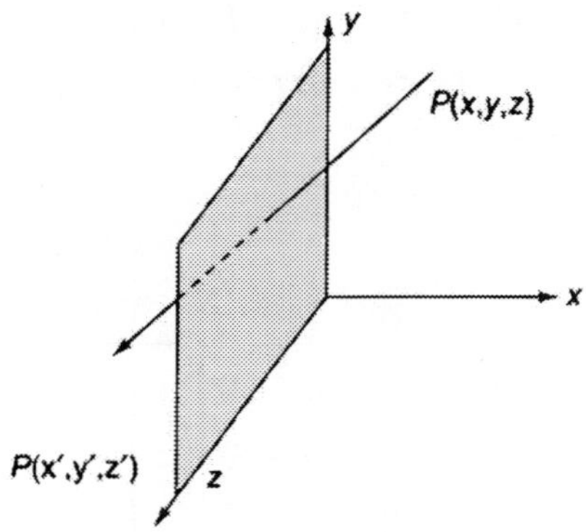

FIGURE 7.15 Reflection about *yz* plane ($x = 0$)

(c) Reflection about xy plane (z = 0)

Figure 7.17 illustrates reflection about *xy* plane.

$$x' = -x,\ y' = y,\ z' = z$$

$$M_{yz} = \begin{bmatrix} 1 & 0 & 0 & 0 \\ 0 & 1 & 0 & 0 \\ 0 & 0 & -1 & 0 \\ 0 & 0 & 0 & 1 \end{bmatrix}$$

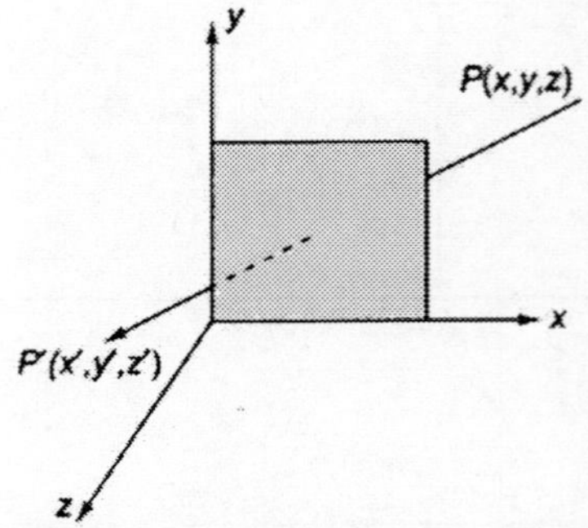

FIGURE 7.16 Reflection about *xy* plane (*z* = 0)

7.3.5 Shear Transformation

Twist in 3D graphics takes place along any one of the axis perpendicular to other two axes.

(a) Along x-axis, perpendicular to y-axis and z-axis : (sh_{xy}, sh_{xz})

$$x' = y.sh_{xy} + z.sh_{xz}$$
$$y' = y$$
$$z' = z$$

$$\begin{bmatrix} x' \\ y' \\ z' \\ 1 \end{bmatrix} = \begin{bmatrix} 0 & sh_{xy} & sh_{xz} & 0 \\ 0 & 1 & 0 & 0 \\ 0 & 0 & 1 & 0 \\ 0 & 0 & 0 & 1 \end{bmatrix} \begin{bmatrix} x \\ y \\ z \\ 1 \end{bmatrix}$$

(b) Along y-axis, perpendicular to the z-axis and x-axis : (sh_{yz}, sh_{yx})

$$x' = x$$
$$y' = x.sh_{yz} + z.sh_{yx}$$
$$z' = z$$

$$\begin{bmatrix} x' \\ y' \\ z' \\ 1 \end{bmatrix} = \begin{bmatrix} 0 & 0 & 0 & 0 \\ sh_{yx} & 0 & sh_{yz} & 0 \\ 0 & 0 & 1 & 0 \\ 0 & 0 & 0 & 0 \end{bmatrix} \begin{bmatrix} x \\ y \\ z \\ 1 \end{bmatrix}$$

(c) Along z-axis, perpendicular to the x-axis and y-axis : (sh_{zx}, sh_{zy})

$$x' = x$$
$$y' = y$$
$$z' = x.sh_{zx} + y.sh_{zy}$$

$$\begin{bmatrix} x' \\ y' \\ z' \\ 1 \end{bmatrix} = \begin{bmatrix} 1 & 0 & 0 & 0 \\ 0 & 1 & 0 & 0 \\ sh_{zx} & sh_{zy} & 0 & 0 \\ 0 & 0 & 0 & 1 \end{bmatrix} \begin{bmatrix} x \\ y \\ z \\ 1 \end{bmatrix}$$

7.4 COORDINATE TRANSFORMATIONS

Effect of translation, scaling and rotation can also be performed when action is taken on coordinate axes instead of object. Such type of transformation is called coordinate transformation.

7.4.1 Translation

Figure 7.17 illustrates the displacement of coordinate system by vector $\vec{V} = <t_x, t_y, t_z>$.

$P(x,y,z)$ coordinate of P w.r.t. coordinate system xyz.
$P(x',y',z')$ coordinate of P w.r.t. coordinate system $x'y'z'$.

Algebraically

$$x' = x - t_x$$
$$y' = y - t_y$$
$$z' = z - t_z$$

In column matrix format

$$\begin{pmatrix} x' \\ y' \\ z' \\ 1 \end{pmatrix} = \begin{pmatrix} 1 & 0 & 0 & -t_x \\ 0 & 1 & 0 & -t_y \\ 0 & 0 & 1 & -t_z \\ 0 & 0 & 0 & 1 \end{pmatrix} \begin{pmatrix} x \\ y \\ z \\ 1 \end{pmatrix}$$

$\bar{T}\, t_x, t_y, t_z = \begin{bmatrix} 1 & 0 & 0 & -t_x \\ 0 & 1 & 0 & -t_y \\ 0 & 0 & 1 & -t_z \\ 0 & 0 & 0 & 1 \end{bmatrix}$ is called coordinate translation transformation matrix.

Similar coordinate transformation matrices for rotation and scaling can be derived.

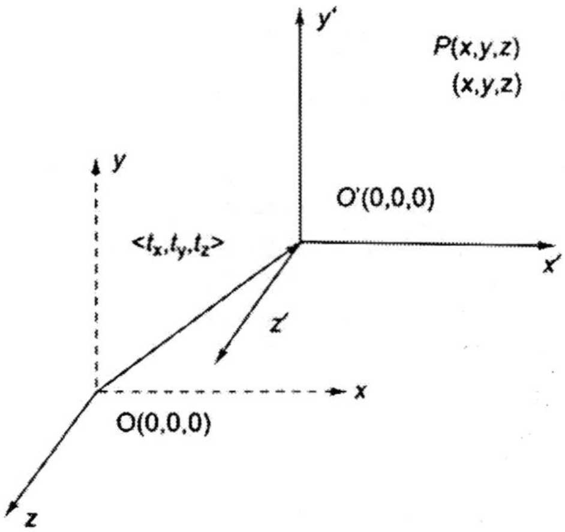

FIGURE 7.17 Translation of Coordinate System

7.5 RELATIONSHIP BETWEEN GEOMETRIC AND COORDINATE TRANSFORMATION MATRICES

Likewise 2D, in 3D product of Geometric transformation matrix $[T]$ and Coordinate transformation matrix $[\bar{T}]$ is always the identity matrix $[I]$. That is,

$$T \cdot \bar{T} = I$$

Or,

$$T = \bar{T}^{-1}$$

This mathematical result interprets physically that if an object or a point is moved by a certain amount and then coordinate system is moved by the same amount, then the object or point would be at the same position and vice versa.

SOLVED PROBLEMS

Problem 7.1 Derive transformation matrix to scale a unit cube twice *uniformly* w.r.t. origin. Find the coordinates of transformed cube.

Solution:

$$\begin{pmatrix} x' \\ y' \\ z' \end{pmatrix} = \begin{pmatrix} sx & 0 & 0 \\ 0 & sy & 0 \\ 0 & 0 & sz \end{pmatrix} \begin{pmatrix} x \\ y \\ z \end{pmatrix}$$

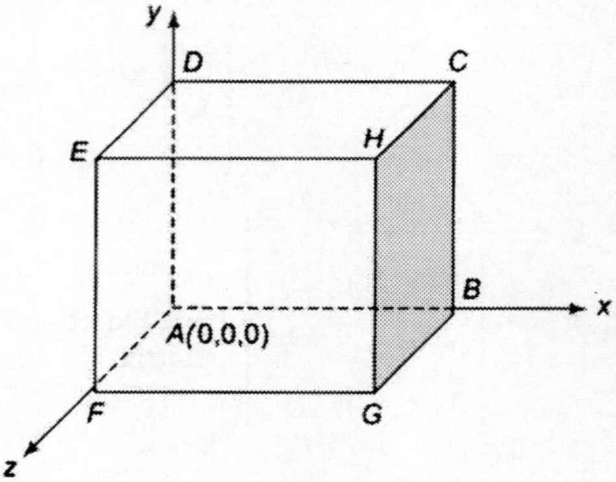

Coordinates of all vertices of the cube are
$A(0,0,0)$ $B(1,0,0)$
$C(1,1,0)$ $D(0,1,0)$
$E(0,1,1)$ $F(0,0,1)$
$G(1,0,1)$ $H(1,1,1)$

$$A'B'C'D'E'F'G'H' = \begin{bmatrix} 2 & 0 & 0 \\ 0 & 2 & 0 \\ 0 & 0 & 2 \end{bmatrix} \overset{\begin{matrix} A & B & C & D & E & F & G & H \end{matrix}}{\begin{bmatrix} 0 & 1 & 1 & 0 & 0 & 0 & 1 & 1 \\ 0 & 0 & 1 & 1 & 1 & 0 & 0 & 1 \\ 0 & 0 & 0 & 0 & 1 & 1 & 1 & 1 \end{bmatrix}}$$

Problem 7.2 Derive transformation matrix to scale a unit cube twice uniformly w.r.t. origin and origin of the coordinate system lies at the centre of the cube. Find the coordinates of transformed cube.

Solution:

Co-ordinates of the vertices of the cube
$A(1/2, -1/2, 1/2)$ $B(1/2, 1/2, 1/2)$
$C(1/2, 1/2, -1/2)$ $D(-1/2, 1/2, -1/2)$
$E(-1/2, 1/2, 1/2)$ $F(-1/2, -1/2, 1/2)$
$G(1/2, -1/2, 1/2)$ $H(-1/2, -1/2, -1/2)$

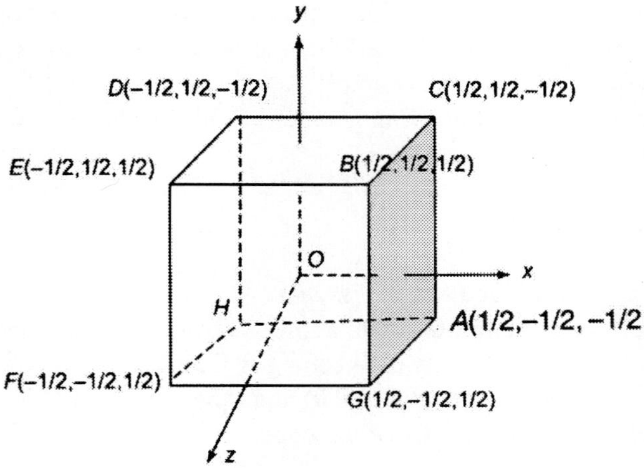

$$A'B'C'D'E'F'G'H' = \begin{bmatrix} 2 & 0 & 0 \\ 0 & 2 & 0 \\ 0 & 0 & 2 \end{bmatrix} \begin{bmatrix} \overset{A}{1/2} & \overset{B}{1/2} & \overset{C}{1/2} & \overset{D}{-1/2} & \overset{E}{-1/2} & \overset{F}{-1/2} & \overset{G}{1/2} & \overset{H}{-1/2} \\ -1/2 & 1/2 & 1/2 & 1/2 & 1/2 & -1/2 & -1/2 & -1/2 \\ -1/2 & 1/2 & -1/2 & -1/2 & 1/2 & 1/2 & 1/2 & -1/2 \end{bmatrix}$$

EXERCISES

1. Derive transformation matrix to scale a unit cube twice uniformly w.r.t. origin. Find the coordinates of transformed cube.
2. Derive 3D-transformation matrices to find reflection of a $P(x,y,z)$ about xy plane, yz plane, and zx plane.
3. Derive the transformation matrix to rotate a 3D object by an angle θ about an arbitrary line in space.
4. Differentiate between rotation in 2D plane and in 3D(space).
5. Prove that multiplication of transformation matrices for the following sequence of operations is commutative:
   a. Any two successive translations
   b. Any two successive scaling operations
   c. Any two successive rotations about any one of the coordinate axes.

6. Derive general 3D scaling transformation matrix w.r.t. any arbitrary point.
7. Explain physical significance between 3D Geometric transformation system and 3D Coordinate transformation system with suitable example.
8. Find the relationship between following geometric and coordinate transformations:
   a. $R_\theta, \overline{R}_\theta, R_\theta^1$
   b. $T_{\bar{v}}, \overline{T}_{\bar{v}}, T_{\bar{v}}^{-1}, \overline{T}_{\bar{v}}^{-1}$
   c. $S sx,sy,sz$, $\overline{S}\ sx,sy,sz$, $S^{-1} sx,sy,sz$, $\overline{S}^{-1} sx,sy,sz$
9. Derive the transformation matrix to rotate a line *AB* by 45° counter-clockwise about *x*-axis then scale the line in *Y* direction by 2.5 while keeping A fixed.
10. Given a unit cube with one corner at O(0,0,0) and other corner at (1,1,1), derive transformation matrix to translate the origin at centre of the cube.

8

Projection

8.1 INTRODUCTION

3D objects or scenes which are defined and manipulated using actual physical units of measurements in a 3D space, has to be transformed at one stage from a 3D representation to 2D. Because, finally the image is viewed on a 2*D* plane of the display device. Such 3D-to-2D transformation is called projection.

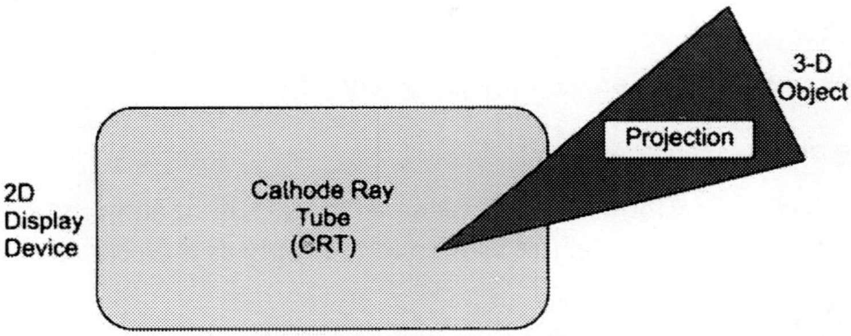

FIGURE 8.1 Projection

In general, projection transforms a N dimension points to $(N - 1)$ dimension points.

2D projected images are formed by intersection of projection rays (Projectors) with a plane called the Projection plane(View plane). Projectors are lines or curves starting from an arbitrary point called the centre of projection passes through each vertex of an object, as illustrated in Fig. 8.2(a) and Fig. 8.2(b).

Thus, for projection we specify,

- 3D object (to be projected)
- View plane
- Centre of projection

It is clear from the figures if we change the position of centre of projection then we have different projections of same 3D object on same view plane. Thus, we can say that we have several projections of a 3D object on same view plane for different centre of projections. We will prove this statement mathematically later on in this chapter.

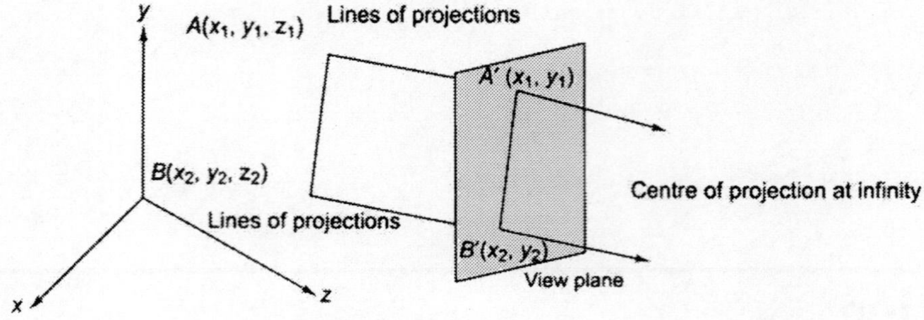

FIGURE 8.2(a) Parallel Projection

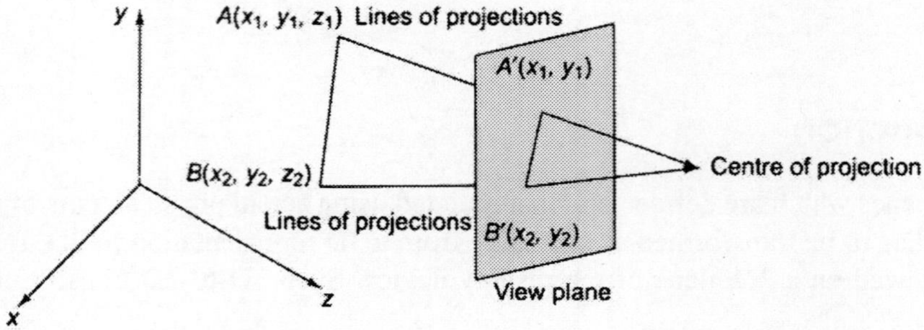

FIGURE 8.2(b) Perspective Projection

Based upon shape of projectors, projections can be classified into:

(a) Planar Geometric Projection

Such type of projections are performed onto a plane with the help of straight lines (lines of projections). Planar geometric projection hereafter is referred to simply as *projections.*

(b) Cartographic Projection

Such type of projections are performed onto a curved surface with the help of curved projectors.

8.2 CLASSIFICATION OF 3D TO 2D PROJECTIONS

There are different categories of projections depending on the directions of projectors and also the relative position of the centre of projection and plane of projection. Following figure 8.3 classifies the most common projections used to represent 3D geometry on a *2D* surface. Each projection type has a brief comment describing its unique characteristic.

8.2.1 Parallel Projection

When the centre of projection is situated at infinite distance such that the projectors are parallel to each other, the type of projection is called *parallel projection.* The parallel projection is so named because centre of projection on infinity distant, the projectors are parallel. A parallel projection is formed by extending parallel lines in a fixed direction from each vertex on the object until they intersect the view plane.

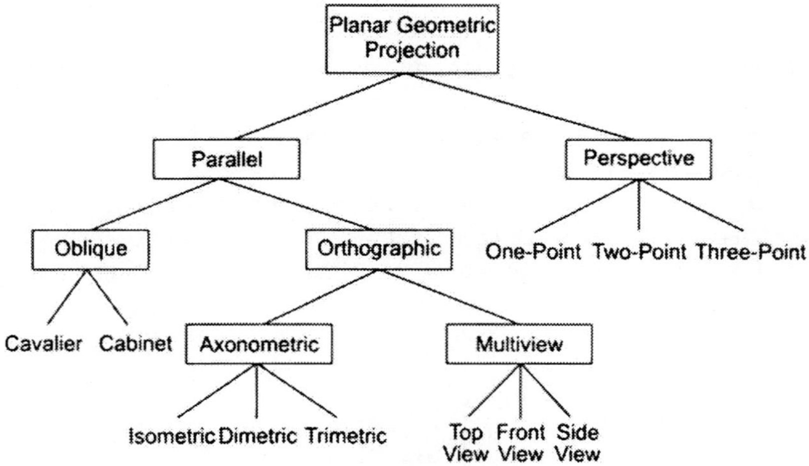

FIGURE 8.3 Subclasses of Planar Projection

Thus, in parallel projection, images points are found at the intersection of the view plane with parallel projectors drawn from the object points in a fixed direction. *Different parallel projections of the same object results on the same view plane for different direction of projectors.*

When defining a parallel projection, we specify

- View plane
- Direction of projection

Figure 8.4 shows the projection of line *AB* to the viewplane. In this case, the measurement of line *AB* is maintained in the projected line *A ′ B′*. While the measurements of an object are not preserved in all parallel projections, the parallel nature of projectors maintains the proportion of an object along a major axis. Therefore, parallel projections are useful in applications requiring the relative proportions of an object to be maintained. Parallel projection is a less realistic view as compared to perspective projection due to lack of foreshortening. It can be used for applications where exact measurement is required. For example, architectures use such projection to represent a building and designers use such projection to represent machine parts.

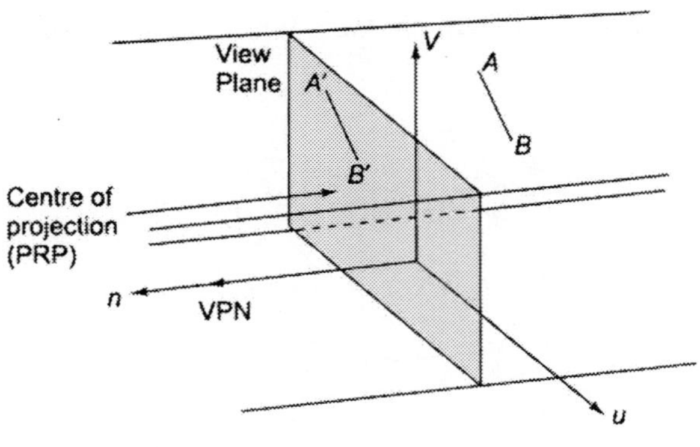

FIGURE 8.4 Parallel Projection

8.2.2 Perspective Projection

Like parallel projections, perspective projections define a major subclass of planar geometric projections. Divisions within perspective projections are consistent in that the center of projection (PRP) is placed at a finite distance from the view plane. Because of this finite distance between the camera and the view plane, projectors are no longer parallel.

To obtain a perspective projection of a 3D object we transform points along projection lines which are not parallel to each other and converge to meet at a finite point known as the projection reference point or the center of projection. The projected view is obtained by calculating the intersection of the projection lines with the view plane.

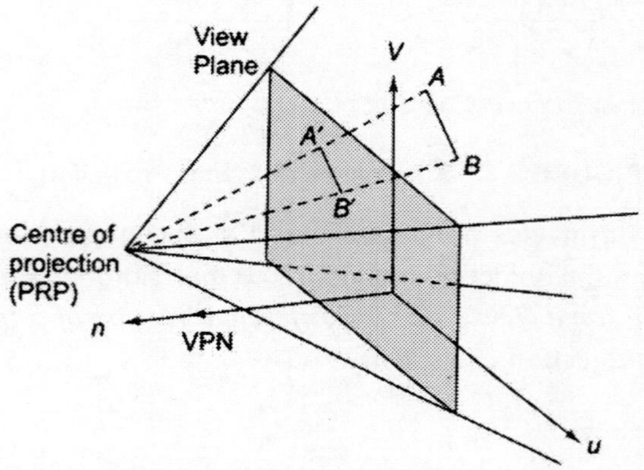

FIGURE 8.5 Perspective Projection

When defining a perspective projection, we specify

- View plane
- Centre of projection

By varying the position of projection reference point and the projection plane ,we will study different standard cases of perspective projection.

A perspective projection whose centre is at infinity becomes a parallel projection.

Perspective projection resembles with that of photographic systems and of the human visual system.

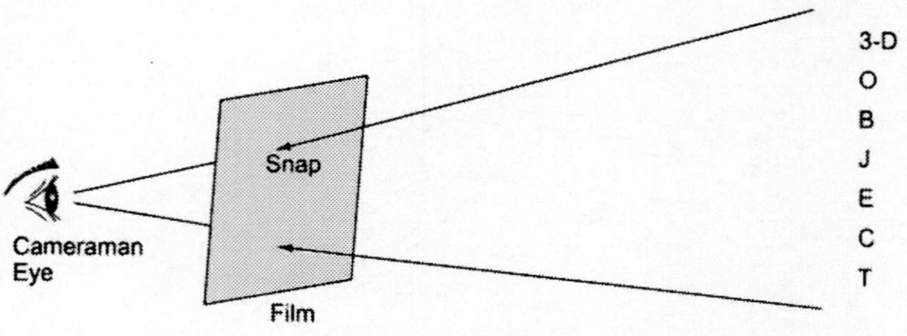

FIGURE 8.6 Illustration of Perspective Projection

By comparing the view plane of a perspective projection with the view seen from the lens of a camera, the underlying principles of a perspective projection can be easily understood. Like the view from a camera, lines in a perspective projection not parallel to the view plane converge to a distant point (called a vanishing point) in the background. When the eye or camera position is close to the object, perspective foreshortening occurs with distant objects appearing smaller in the view plane than closer objects of the same size.

The size of the perspective projection of an object varies inversely with the distance of that object from the centre of projection is known as foreshortening.

It is more realistic than parallel projection because of the existence of foreshortening, but it cannot be used for exact measurement and exact shape of the object.

8.3 BASIC DEFINITIONS OF THE SUBCLASSES OF THE PARALLEL AND PERSPECTIVE PROJECTIONS

8.3.1 Orthographic Projection and Oblique Projection

(a) Orthographic Projections

Orthographic projections are one of two parallel projection types. In addition to being parallel, projectors in an orthographic projection (shown in Figure 4) are also perpendicular to the view plane i.e.,orthographic projection occurs when the direction of projection is perpendicular to the plane of projection. Refer Fig. 8.7.

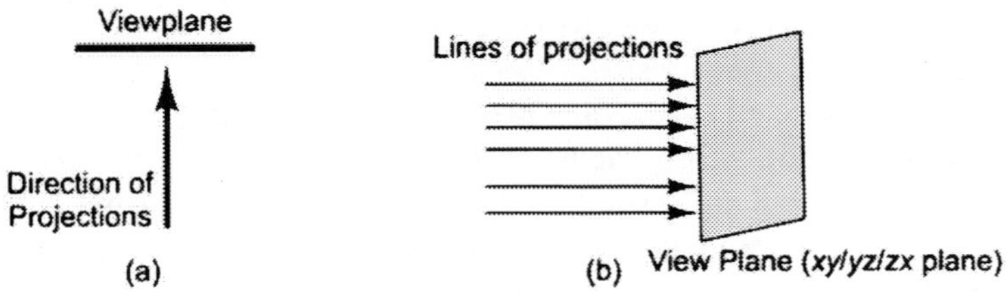

FIGURE 8.7 Orthographic Projections

Figure 8.7(b) shows particular case of orthographic projection in which projection plane is any one of the three principal planes *xy*, *yz* and *zx*. In other words, lines of projections are perpendicular to all three principal planes or parallel to normal to the all three principal planes.

Orthographic projections are further catorgorized as either **multiview** or **axonometric** projections, which are described below.

(b) Multiview Projections

A multiview projection displays a single face of a three-dimensional object. Common choices for viewing an object in two dimensions include the **front**, **side**, and **top** or planar view. The view plane normal differs in the world coordinate system axis it is placed along for each of the multiview projections. In the top view, the view plane normal is parallel with the positive *y*-axis in a right-handed system. Figure 8.8(a) illustrates a top or planar view of the three-dimensional building shown in Figure 8.8(b). To project the top view of the 3-D object, the *y*-coordinates are discarded and the *x*- and *z*-coordinates for each point are mapped to the view plane.

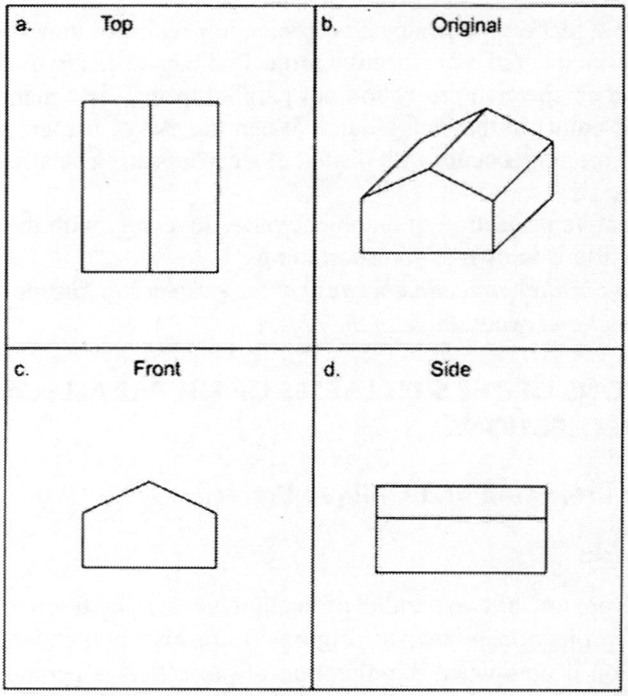

FIGURE 8.8 Two- and Three-dimensional Projections; (a) Top or Planar View; (b) Three-dimensional View for Reference; (c) Front view; and (d) Side View.

Likewise, a front view is projected to the view plane normal to the positive z-axis and selecting the x- and y-coordinates for each point, a front view is projected to the view plane (Figure 8.8(c)).

Likewise, a side view (Figure 8.8(d)) results when the view plane normal is directed along the positive x-axis and the y-and z-coordinates of a three-dimensional object are projected to the view plane. These projections are often used in engineering and architectural drawings. While they do not show the three-dimensional aspects of an object, multiview projections are useful because the angles and dimensions of the object are maintained.

(c) Axonometric Projections

Axonometric projections are orthographic projections in which the directions of projection are not parallel to any of the three principal axes or perpendicular to any of the three principal planes.

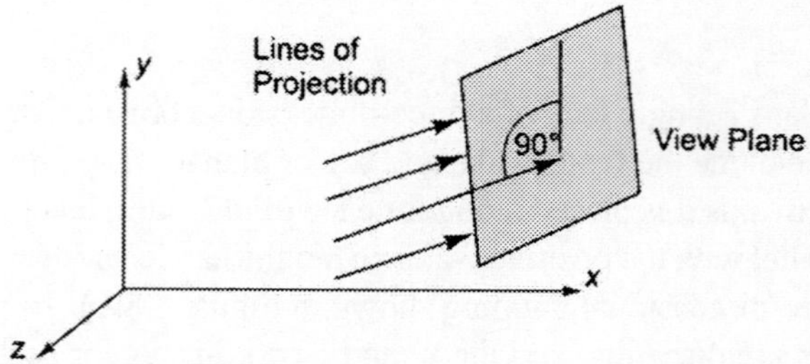

Figure 8.9 Axonometric Projections

Unlike multivew projections, axonometric projections allow the user to place the view plane normal in any direction such that three adjacent faces of a "cube-like" objects are visible. To avoid duplication of views displayed by multiview projections, the view plane normal for an axonometric view is usually not placed parallel with a major axis. The increased versatility in the direction of the view plane normal positions the view plane such that it intersects at least two of the major axes. Lines of a three-dimensional object that are parallel in the world coordinate system are likewise projected to the view plane as parallel lines. In addition, the length of a line, or line preservation, is maintained for lines parallel to the view plane. Other receding lines maintain only their proportion and are foreshortened equally with lines along the same axes.

Axonometric projections are further divided into three classes that depend upon the number of major axes which are foreshortened equally. These axonometric views are defined as **isometric dimetric** or **trimetric** projections.

The sub-categories of axonometric projections are:

Isometric projection: The direction of projection makes *equal* angles with all three principal axes.

It is a commonly used axonometric projection. In this view, all three of the major axes are foreshortened equally since the view plane normal makes equal angles with the principal axes. To satisfy this condition, the view plane normal $\mathbf{n} = (n_x, n_y, n_z)$ has the requirement that $|n_x| = |n_y| = |n_z|$. This limitation restricts **n** to only eight directions. Figure 8.10 shows an isometric projection of a cube. Isometric projections scale lines equally along each axis, which is often useful since lines along the principal axes can be measured and converted using the same scale.

Dimetric projection: The direction of projection makes equal angles with exactly *two* of the principal axes.

Thus, in the class of projections, $\mathbf{n} = (n_x, n_y, n_z)$ is set so that it makes equal angles with two of the axes. Valid settings for a dimetric projection allow $n_x = |n_y|$, $n_x = |n_z|$, or $n_y = |n_z|$ (Hill, 1990). In this class, only lines drawn along the two equally foreshortened axes are scaled by the same factor. Figure 8.11 shows a dimetric projection of a cube. When the view plane normal is set so that the view plane is parallel to a major axis, line measurements are maintained in the projection for lines which are parallel to this axis.

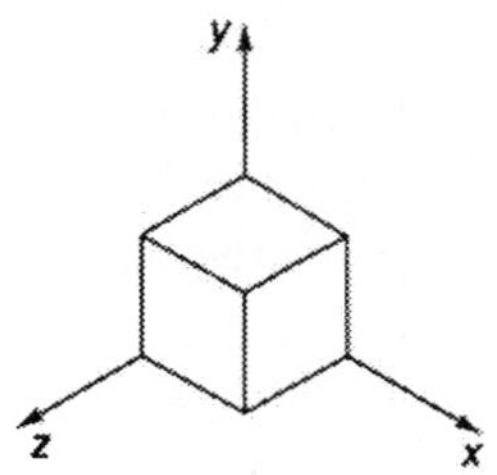

FIGURE 8.10 Isometric Projection

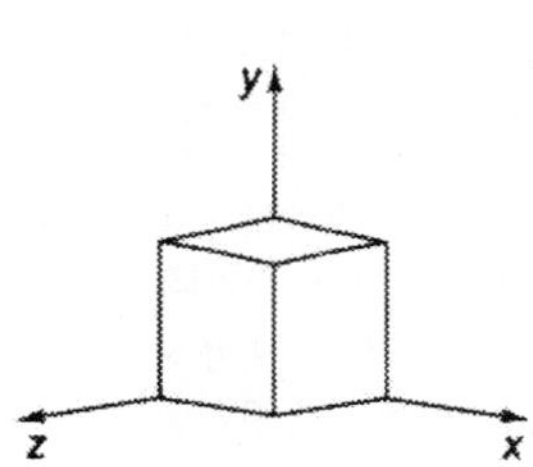

FIGURE 8.11 Dimetric Projection

Trimetric projection: The direction of projection makes *unequal* angles with the three principal axes. This type of axonometric projection allows the viewer the most freedom in selecting the components of *n*. In this class, the view plane normal makes differing angles with each major axis, since no two components of **n** have the same value. As with a dimetric view, a trimetric view displays different orientations by placing differing amounts of emphasis on the faces. Trimetric projections have a potential disadvantage in that measurement of lines along the axes is difficult because of a difference in scaling factors. Figure 8.12, a trimetric view of a cube, shows how this unequal-foreshortening characteristic affects line measurements along different axes. While disadvantageous in maintaining measurements, a trimetric projection, with the correct orientation, can offer a realistic and natural view of an object.

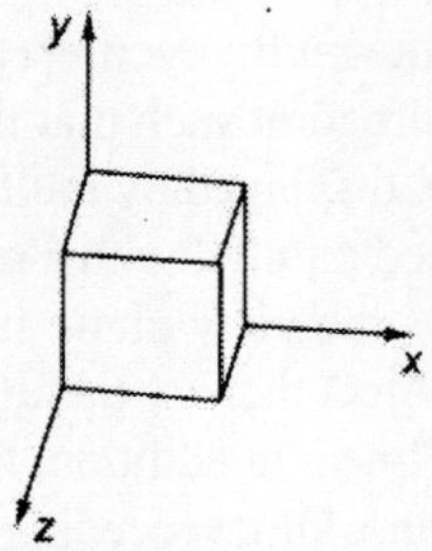

FIGURE 8.12 Trimetric Projection

(d) Oblique Projections

Oblique projections represent the second category of parallel projections.

Oblique Projection occurs when the angle between the projectors and the plane of projection is not equal to 90°. Refer to 8.13(b).

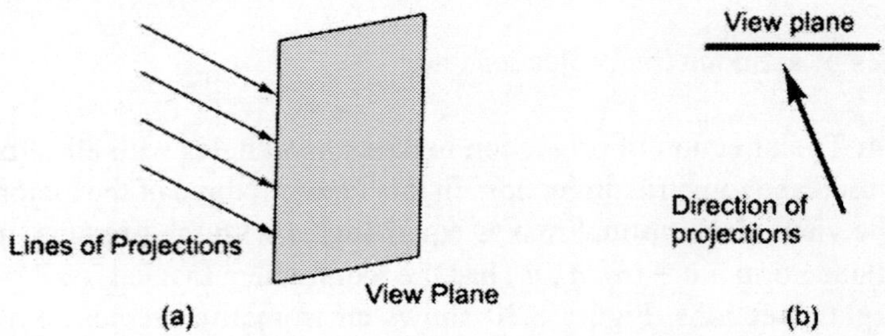

FIGURE 8.13 Oblique Projection

As in an orthographic view, this class of projections uses parallel projectors but the angle between the projectors and the view plane is no longer orthogonal. Figure 8.13(a) shows an example of the direction of the projectors in relation to the view plane.

Oblique views are useful, since they combine the advantageous qualities of both multiview and axonometric projections. Like an axonometric view, this class presents an object's 3D appearance. Similar to a multiview projection, oblique views display the exact shape of one face.

Oblique projections are further defined as either **cavalier** or **cabinet** projections.

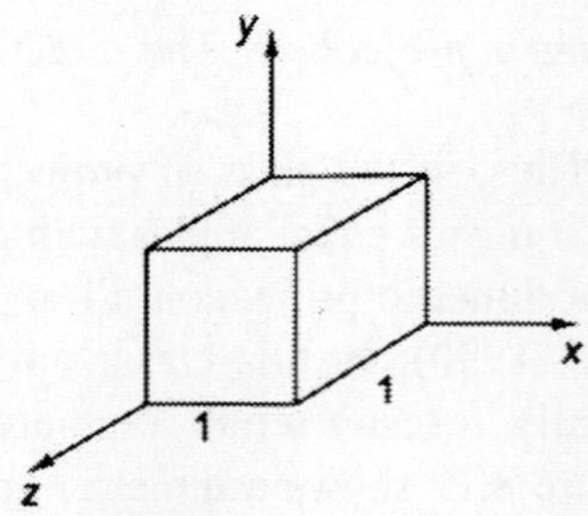

FIGURE 8.14 Cavalier Projection

Cavalier projection: The direction of projection is so chosen that makes an angle with the projection plane, so that lines perpendicular to the projection plane have same length as the line itself, Fig. 8.14. *Thus, there is no foreshortening.*

Cabinet projection: The direction of projection is so chosen that makes an angle of with the plane of projection so that lines perpendicular to the projection plane project at one-half their actual length. Fig. 8.15. *Thus, there is foreshortening of lines perpendicular to projection plane.* Cabinet projections are little bit realistic than cavalier projection.

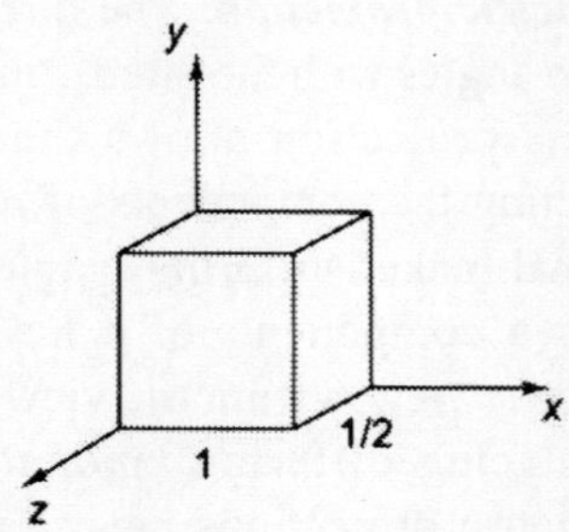

FIGURE 8.15 Cabinet Projection

An oblique projection is obtained by projecting points along parallel lines that are not perpendicular to the projection plane. Fig. 8.16 shows an oblique projection of a point $P(x, y, z)$ on the $z = 0$ plane. $P_{ob}(x_p, y_p)$ is oblique projection of the point P and $P_{or}(x, y)$ is the orthographic projection of P on the $z = 0$ plane. Let L be the length of the line joining points $P_{ob}(x_p, y_p)$ and $P_{or}(x, y)$, being the angle made by the line L with X axis.

Cavalier and cabinet projections differ by the value used for the angle *alpha*. Angle *alpha* is defined as the angle between the oblique projection line from (x, y, z) to (x_p, y_p) and the line on the view plane from (x_p, y_p) to (x, y) (see Figure 8.16). Two commonly used values for $\alpha = 45°$, and $\alpha = 63.4°$.

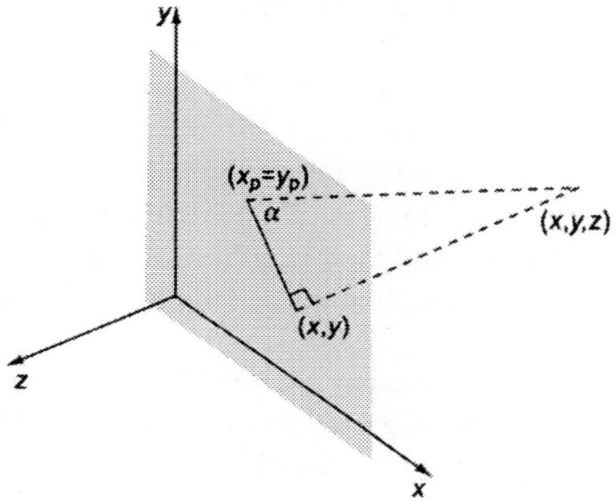

FIGURE 8.16 Projection of Point (x, y, z) to the Position (x_p, y_p) on the View plane for an Oblique Projection

Then, x_p and y_p can be expressed as:

$$x_p = x + L\cos\theta$$

$$x_p = y + L\sin\theta$$

Here the length L is a function of z coordinate. If a is the direction of projection, i.e., the angle made by the projector with the projection plane, then

$$\tan\alpha = \frac{z}{L}$$

Thus, $$L = \frac{L}{\tan\alpha}$$

$$= \quad zL_1\left(\text{where } L_1 = \frac{1}{\tan\alpha}\right)$$

When $$z = 1,\ L_1 = L$$

$$x_p = x + z(L_1\cos\theta)$$

$$y_p = y + z(L_1\sin\theta)$$

Considering $z_p = 0$, we get

$$\begin{pmatrix} x_p \\ y_p \\ z_p \\ 1 \end{pmatrix} = \begin{pmatrix} 1 & 0 & L_1 \cos\theta & 0 \\ 0 & 1 & L_1 \sin\theta & 0 \\ 0 & 0 & 1 & 0 \\ 0 & 0 & 0 & 1 \end{pmatrix} \begin{pmatrix} x \\ y \\ z \\ 1 \end{pmatrix}$$

This is the standard matrix expression for oblique projection onto $z = 0$ plane.

When $L_l = 0$ (implying $\alpha = 90°$) it will represent an orthographic projection on $z = 0$ plane (see eqn.) (6)

Commonly used values for angle θ are 30° and 45°. Two commonly used values of α are those for which $\tan \alpha = 1$ and $\tan \alpha = 2$. For the first case, $\alpha = 45°$ and the views obtained are called cavalier projections. All lines perpendicular to the projection plane are projected with no change in length.

For $\tan \alpha = 2$, $\alpha = 63.4°$ and the resulting view is called a cabinet projection. All lines perpendicular to the viewing surface are projected at one half their lengths. Cabinet projections appear more realistic than cavalier projections because of the reduction in the length of perpendiculars (i.e., depths of objects).

When $\alpha = 45°$ as in Figure 8.16, the projection is a **cavalier** projection. In this projection, a cube will be displayed with all sides maintaining equal lengths (see Figure 8.16). This property is often advantageous, since edges can be measured directly. However, the cavalier projection can make an object look too elongated.

In the second case, when $\alpha = 63.4°$, the projection is labeled as a **cabinet** projection. For this angle, lines perpendicular to the view plane are displayed one-half the actual length (see Figure 8.16). Because of the reduction of length in lines perpendicular to the view plane, cabinet projections appear more realistic than cavalier projections (Hearn & Baker, 1996).

Foreshortening factors: The projected length divided by the actual length is called foreshortening factor. The lines or edges, which are perpendicular to the plane of projection, suffer different shortening in lengths for different values of α. In Fig. 8.16, the length of the perpendicular PP_{ob} is z. As the oblique projection of P is P_{ob}, the projected length of z is PP_{ob} i.e., L. Here the foreshortening factors is $\frac{L}{z} = \frac{1}{\tan \alpha}$. For $\alpha = 45°$ foreshortening factor $1/\tan\alpha = 1$and for = 63.4, foreshortening factor 1/tan $\alpha = 1/2$. In case of orthographic projection ($\alpha = 90$) foreshortening factor is 0 as in this case the projected length (L) is equal to 0. In all the above cases value of may θ vary.

8.3.2 Types of Perspective Projection

(a) Vanishing Point

It is one of the characteristics features of the perspective projection. It is the illusion that after projection certain sets of parallel lines appear to meet at some point on the projection plane. Sometimes this phenomenon is also called 'fanning'. These points are called *vanishing points*. For each set of such parallel lines, we get a vanishing point if they are not parallel to view plane. It means we have infinite number of vanishing points.

The railway track is the common real life example which appears to meet at the vanishing point.

(b) Principal Vanishing Point

The vanishing point for any set of parallel lines that are parallel to any of the three principal axes *X*, *Y*, or *Z* of an object is referred to as principal vanishing point. The number of principal vanishing point one, two, or three is determined by the number of principal axes intersected by the view plane and perspective projections are accordingly classified as:

- One-point projection
- Two-point projection
- Three-point projection

Each class differs in the orientation of the view plane and the number of vanishing points the unit cube has.

In a **one-point** perspective, lines of a three-dimensional object along a major axis converge to a single vanishing point while lines parallel to the other axes remain horizontal or vertical in the view plane (Hill, 1990). To create a one-point perspective view, the view plane is set parallel to one of the principal planes in the world coordinate system. The view plane normal is set parallel to a major axis and the view plane normal vector **n** is initialized such that two of its three components are zero. Figure 8.16 shows a one-point perspective view of a cube. In this projection, the view plane is positioned in front of the cube and parallel to the *x*- and *y*-plane.

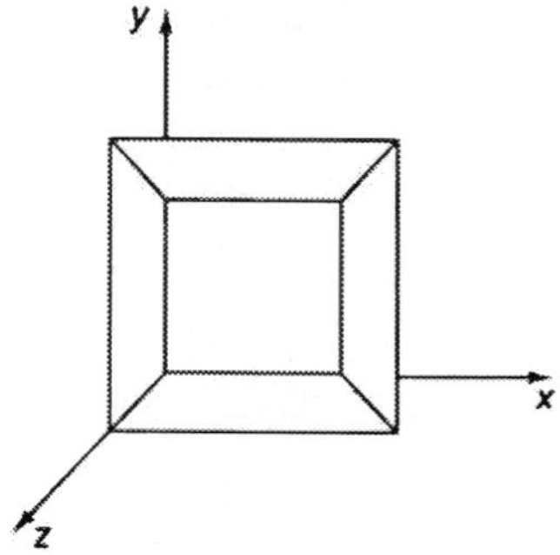

FIGURE 8.17 One-point Perspective Projection

A **two-point perspective** projects an object to the view plane such that lines parallel to two of the major axes converge into two separate vanishing points. To create a two-point perspective, the view plane is set parallel to a principal axis rather than a plane. In satisfying this condition, the view plane normal vector **n** should be set perpendicular to one of the major world coordinate system axes. In this case, two of the components of $\mathbf{n} = (n_x, n_y, n_z)$ are non-zero, while the third is zero. Figure 8.17 shows a two-point perspective view of a cube. In this figure, lines parallel to the *x*-axis converge to vanishing point VP_1 while lines parallel to the *z*-axis converge to vanishing point VP_2. Two-point perspective views often provide additional realism in comparison to other projection types, therefore, they are commonly used in architectural engineering, industrial design, and in advertising drawings.

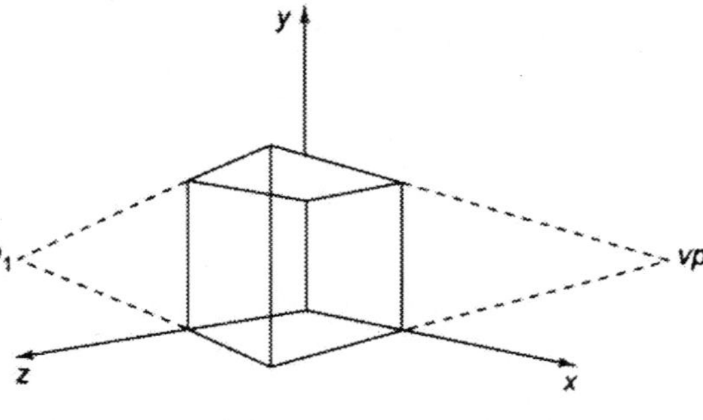

FIGURE 8.18 Two-point Perspective Projection

A **three-point** perspective has three vanishing points. In this case, the view plane is not parallel to any of the major axes. To position the view plane, each component of the view plane normal is set to a non-zero value so that the view plane intersects the three major axes. Vanishing points are often used by artists for highlighting features or increasing dramatic effects.

8.4 PROJECTIONS BASED UPON LOCATION OF CENTRE OF PROJECTION AND VIEW PLANE

Figures 8.2(a) and 8.2(b) depict that if

- we change the position of centre of projection, then we have different projections (parallel or perspective) of same 3D object on same view plane.
- we change the equation of view plane, then we have different projections (parallel or perspective) of same 3D object for same centre of projection.

In this section, we take different cases of projections (parallel or perspective) on different centre of projection and view plane.

Case I : Equation of parallel projection onto the XY plane in the direction of projection $V = x_p i + y_p j + z_p k$.

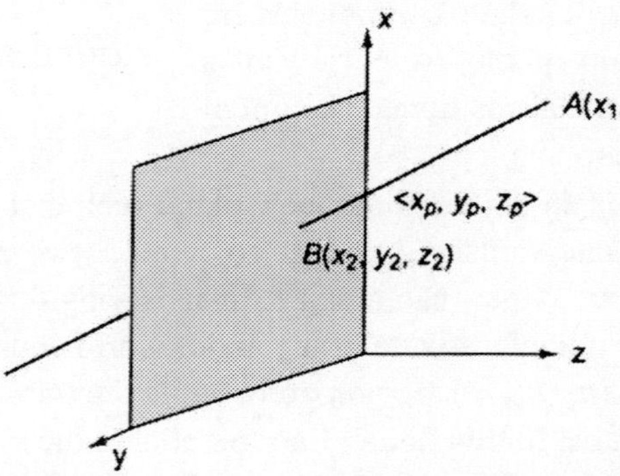

FIGURE 8.19 Parallel Projection on XY Plane in the Direction $V = x_p i + y_p j + z_p k$

Let $A(x_1, y_1, z_1)$ be any point and B (x_2, y_2, z_2) is the parallel projection of A on XY plane in lines of direction $V = x_p i + y_p j + z_p k$.

The parametric equation of line AB passing through A (x_1, y_1, z_1) having direction cosines $<x_p, y_p, z_p>$.

$$x = x_1 + ux_p \qquad 8.1(a)$$

$$y = y_1 + uy_p \qquad 8.1(b)$$

$$z = z_1 + uz_p \qquad 8.1(c)$$

Line AB intersects xy plane ($z = 0$) where $z = 0$. Therefore, we have from 8.1(c)

$$u = -\frac{z_1}{z_p}$$

Putting the value of u in 8.1(a) and 8.1(b), we have

$$x_2 = x_1 - \frac{z_1}{z_p} x_p \qquad 8.2(a)$$

$$y_2 = y_1 - \frac{z_1}{z_p} y_p \qquad 8.2(b)$$

Column matrix format is

$$\begin{bmatrix} x_2 \\ y_2 \end{bmatrix} = \begin{bmatrix} 1 & 0 & -\frac{x_p}{z_p} \\ 0 & 1 & -\frac{y_p}{z_p} \end{bmatrix} \begin{bmatrix} x_1 \\ y_1 \\ z_1 \end{bmatrix}$$

$$B = \text{Par}_{z=0} \cdot A$$

$$\text{Par}_{z=0} = \begin{bmatrix} 1 & 0 & -\frac{x_p}{z_p} \\ 0 & 1 & -\frac{y_p}{z_p} \end{bmatrix} \qquad 8.3$$

is known as parallel projection matrix when projection is taken on $xy(z=0)$ plane in the lines of direction $\boldsymbol{V} = x_p\boldsymbol{i} + y_p\boldsymbol{j} + z_p\boldsymbol{k}$.

From equations 8.2(a) and 8.2(b), it is clear that x_2 and y_2 depend upon $<x_p, y_p, z_p>$ and x_1, y_1, z_1. Thus, for a given point we have a number of projected points in different directions of projections on same view plane.

Similarly, we can draw transformation matrices for projections on yz, zx view planes.

$$\text{Par}_{x=0} = \begin{bmatrix} 1 & 0 & -\frac{y_p}{x_p} \\ 0 & 1 & -\frac{z_p}{x_p} \end{bmatrix} \text{ for } yz \text{ view plane.} \qquad 8.4$$

$$\text{Par}_{y=0} = \begin{bmatrix} 1 & 0 & -\frac{z_p}{y_p} \\ 0 & 1 & -\frac{x_p}{y_p} \end{bmatrix} \text{ for } zx \text{ view plane.} \qquad 8.5$$

Orthographic Projection

As we have already discussed in section 8.3.1, an orthographic projection always shows the true size and shape of a single plane face (of an object) parallel to a projection plane. Transformation matrices and corresponding expressions for orthographic projection on to the coordinate planes given below are special cases of the transformation matrix discuss above.

Orthographic Projection when View Plane is xy Plane(z = 0)

In this case lines of directions are perpendicular to xy plane i.e., parallel to normal to xy plane. This specifies that $\boldsymbol{v}$ = **<0, 0, 1>**. Replace the components <xp, yp, zp> in transformation matrix $\text{Par}_{z=0}$ with <0, 0, 1>, we have orthographic transformation matrix

$$\text{Par}_{z=0} = \begin{pmatrix} 1 & 0 & 0 & 0 \\ 0 & 1 & 0 & 0 \\ 0 & 0 & 0 & 0 \\ 0 & 0 & 0 & 1 \end{pmatrix} \text{ for } xy \text{ view plane}(z=0)$$

$$\text{For } z=0 \text{ plane} \begin{pmatrix} x_p \\ y_p \\ z_p \\ 1 \end{pmatrix} = \begin{pmatrix} 1 & 0 & 0 & 0 \\ 0 & 1 & 0 & 0 \\ 0 & 0 & 0 & 0 \\ 0 & 0 & 0 & 1 \end{pmatrix} \begin{pmatrix} x \\ y \\ z \\ 1 \end{pmatrix}$$

Orthographic Projection when View Plane is yz Plane(x = 0)

In this case lines of directions are perpendicular to yz plane i.e., parallel to normal to yz plane. This specifies that $\boldsymbol{v}$ = **<1, 0, 0>**. Replace the components <xp, yp, zp> in transformation matrix $\text{Par}_{x=0}$ with <1, 0, 0>, we have

$$\text{For } x=0 \text{ plane} \begin{pmatrix} x_p \\ y_p \\ z_p \\ 1 \end{pmatrix} = \begin{pmatrix} 0 & 0 & 0 & 0 \\ 0 & 1 & 0 & 0 \\ 0 & 0 & 1 & 0 \\ 0 & 0 & 0 & 1 \end{pmatrix} \begin{pmatrix} x \\ y \\ z \\ 1 \end{pmatrix}$$

Orthographic Projection when View Plane is zx Plane (y = 0)

In this case lines of directions are perpendicular to xy plane i.e., parallel to normal to xy plane. This specifies that $\boldsymbol{v}$ = **<0, 1, 0>** . Replace the components <xp, yp, zp> with we have

$$\text{For } y=0 \text{ plane} \begin{pmatrix} x_p \\ y_p \\ z_p \\ 1 \end{pmatrix} = \begin{pmatrix} 1 & 0 & 0 & 0 \\ 0 & 0 & 0 & 0 \\ 0 & 0 & 1 & 0 \\ 0 & 0 & 0 & 1 \end{pmatrix} \begin{pmatrix} x \\ y \\ z \\ 1 \end{pmatrix}$$

Using the above-mentioned equations, we can get the projected images of the planes (object faces) which are parallel to the coordinate planes. So instead of a single orthographic projection multiple orthographic projections (i.e., multiview orthographic projection) are necessary to show the true shape and size of different faces of an object. By combining multiple views like top and bottom view, front and rear view, right side and left side view of the same object, the whole object can be visually reconstructed.

The front, side and top views are obtained by orthographic projection onto the $z = 0$, $x = 0$ and $y = 0$ coordinate planes from centers of projection and infinity on the (+)ve Z, (+)ve X and (+)ve Y axes, respectively. Similarly, the rear, left side and bottom views are obtained by orthographic projection onto the $z = 0$, $x = 0$ and $y = 0$ planes from centers of projections at infinity on the (–)ve Z, (–)ve X and (–)ve Y axes, respectively.

Case II: General equation of parallel projection onto a given view plane in the direction of a given projector $V = ai + bj + ck$. The view plane is defined by a reference point $R(x_0, y_0, z_0)$ and normal vector $N = n_1 i + n_2 j + n_3 k$.

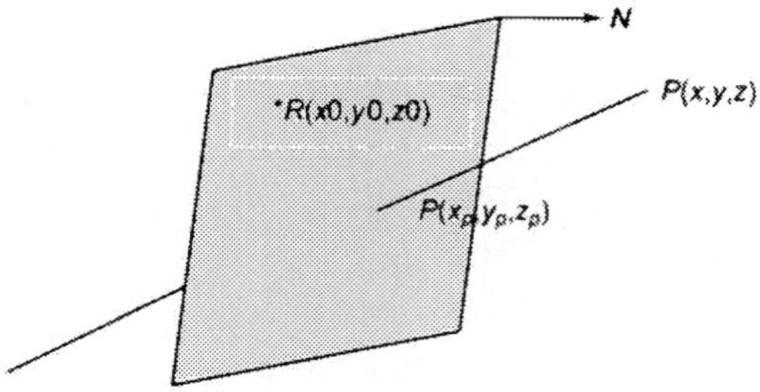

FIGURE 8.20 Parallel Projection on any Plane in Direction of Projection $V = ai + bj + ck$

Here we align the view plane with one of the principal planes (xy or yz or zx plane). then we perform the projection in the given lines of direction.

Let $P(x_p, y_p, z_p)$ point of parallel projection of point $P(x, y, z)$.

Process involves the concatenating the sequence of following matrices:

Step 1: First we have to give a translation so that the reference point $R(x_0, y_0, z_0)$ becomes the origin.(T_V).

Step 2: Rotate the view plane such that the normal vector N becomes parallel to the Z axis. Refer Fig. 8.20. This process involves the following sequence of two rotations:

(a) Rotation about X axis. $(R_{\alpha x})$

(b) Rotation about Y axis. $(R_{-\beta y})$

Step 3: Project the transformed point $P(x, y, z)$ on the XY plane in the direction of $V = ai + bj + ck$, let the transformed $P(x, y, z)$ point be $P'(x', y', z')$ and then $P'(x', y', z')$ projected to $P_p(x_p, y_p, z_p)$.$(Par_{z=0})$

Step 4: Inverse the rotations correspond to step 2.$(R_{-\beta y} \cdot R_{-\alpha X})$

Step 5: Inverse the translation correspond to step 1.(T_{-V})

Now we will proceed to Derive Values of Individual Matrices text type:

(i) The transformation matrix for translation of reference point is:

$$[Tv] = \begin{pmatrix} 0 & 0 & 0 & -x_0 \\ 0 & 1 & 0 & -y_0 \\ 0 & 0 & 1 & -z_0 \\ 0 & 0 & 0 & 1 \end{pmatrix}$$

(ii) The transformation matrix for rotation about the X axis is:

$$N = n_1 i + n_2 j + n_3 k$$

$$N = \frac{N}{|N|} = \frac{n_1 i + n_2 j + n_3 k}{\sqrt{n_1^2 + n_2^2 + n_3^2}}$$

$$= \frac{n_1}{n'} i + \frac{n_2}{n'} j + \frac{n_3}{n'} k \quad \text{where } n' = \sqrt{(n_1^2 + n_2^2 + n_3^2)}$$

$$= C_x i + C_y j + C_z k$$

where, C_x, C_y, C_z are the direction cosines of the normal and

$$C_x = \frac{n_1}{n'}, C_y = \frac{n_2}{n'} C_z = \frac{n_3}{n'}$$

Let

$$d = \sqrt{\left(C_y^2 + C_z^2\right)} = \frac{\sqrt{(n_2^2 + n_3^2)}}{\sqrt{(n_1^2 + n_2^2 + n_3^2)}}$$

$$R_{ax} = \begin{pmatrix} 1 & 0 & 0 & 0 \\ 0 & \cos\alpha & -\sin\alpha & 0 \\ 0 & \sin\alpha & \cos\alpha & 0 \\ 0 & 0 & 0 & 1 \end{pmatrix}$$

$$= \begin{pmatrix} 1 & 0 & 0 & 0 \\ 0 & \frac{C_z}{d} & -\frac{C_y}{d} & 0 \\ 0 & \frac{C_y}{d} & \frac{C_z}{d} & 0 \\ 0 & 0 & 0 & 1 \end{pmatrix}$$ where, α is the rotation angle about X axis

(iii) The transformation matrix for rotation about the y axis is

$$R_{\beta y} = \begin{pmatrix} \cos(-\beta) & 0 & \sin\alpha(-\beta) & 0 \\ 0 & 1 & 0 & 1 \\ -\sin(-\beta) & 0 & \cos(-\beta) & 0 \\ 0 & 0 & 0 & 1 \end{pmatrix}$$

$$= \begin{pmatrix} d & 0 & -C_x & 0 \\ 0 & 1 & 0 & 0 \\ C_x & 0 & d & 0 \\ 0 & 0 & 0 & 1 \end{pmatrix}$$ Where B is the rotation angle about Y axis

(iv) Transformation matrix for projection on xy plane

Since $PP_p \parallel V$

$\therefore \quad (x_p - x')\boldsymbol{i} + (y_p - y')\boldsymbol{j} + (z_p)\boldsymbol{k} = t(a\boldsymbol{i} + b\boldsymbol{j} + c\boldsymbol{k})$, where t is a scalar multiple.

Comparing LHS and RHS, we have

$$x_p - x' = at \qquad 8.6(a)$$

$$y_p - y' = bt \qquad 8.6(b)$$

$$z_p - z' = ct \qquad 8.6(c)$$

since, $z_p = 0$ [as the point lies on XY plane]

From 8.6 (c) , we have

$$\therefore \qquad t = \frac{-z'}{c}$$

Substituting the value of t in equ. 8.6 (a) and 8.6(b), we have

$$x_p = x - \frac{az'}{c}$$

$$y_p = y' - \frac{bz'}{c}$$

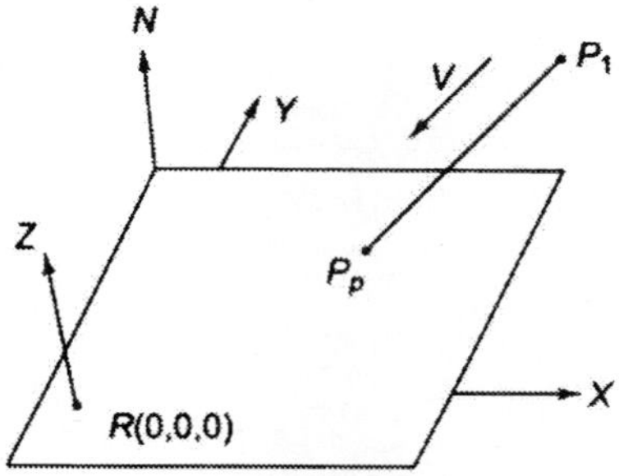

FIGURE 8.21

$$\begin{pmatrix} x_p \\ y_p \\ z_p \\ 1 \end{pmatrix} = \begin{pmatrix} 1 & 0 & \frac{-a}{c} & 0 \\ 0 & 1 & \frac{-b}{c} & 0 \\ 0 & 0 & 0 & 0 \\ 0 & 0 & 0 & 1 \end{pmatrix} \begin{pmatrix} x' \\ y' \\ z' \\ 1 \end{pmatrix}$$

(v) Inverse transformation matrix for rotation about the X axis is:

$$R_{\beta y}^{-1} = R_{-\beta y} = \begin{pmatrix} d & 0 & C_x & 0 \\ 0 & 1 & 0 & 0 \\ -C_x & 0 & d & 0 \\ 0 & 0 & 0 & 1 \end{pmatrix}$$

(vi) Inverse transformation matrix for rotation about the Y axis is:

$$R_{\alpha x}^{-1} = R_{-\alpha x} = \begin{pmatrix} 1 & 0 & 0 & 0 \\ 0 & \frac{C_z}{d} & \frac{C_y}{d} & 0 \\ 0 & \frac{-C_y}{d} & \frac{C_z}{d} & 0 \\ 0 & 0 & 0 & 1 \end{pmatrix}$$

(vii) Inverse transformation matrix for translation of reference point:

$$T_v^{-1} = T_{-v} = \begin{pmatrix} 1 & 0 & 0 & x_0 \\ 0 & 1 & 0 & y_0 \\ 0 & 0 & 1 & z_0 \\ 0 & 0 & 0 & 1 \end{pmatrix}$$

Concatenating all the matrices in the sequence, these are performed, we get

$$T = \overline{T_{-v} \cdot R_{-\alpha x} \cdot R_{\beta y} \cdot Par_{z=0} \cdot R_{-\beta y} \cdot R_{\alpha x} \cdot Tv}$$

$$= \begin{pmatrix} 1 & 0 & 0 & x_0 \\ 0 & 1 & 0 & y_0 \\ 0 & 0 & 1 & z_0 \\ 0 & 0 & 0 & 1 \end{pmatrix} \begin{pmatrix} 1 & 0 & 0 & 0 \\ 0 & \frac{C_z}{d} & \frac{C_y}{d} & 0 \\ 0 & \frac{-C_y}{d} & \frac{C_z}{d} & 0 \\ 0 & 0 & 0 & 1 \end{pmatrix} \begin{pmatrix} d & 0 & C_x & 0 \\ 0 & 1 & 0 & 0 \\ -C_x & 0 & d & 0 \\ 0 & 0 & 0 & 1 \end{pmatrix}$$

$$\begin{pmatrix} 1 & 0 & \frac{-a}{c} & 0 \\ 0 & 1 & \frac{-b}{c} & 0 \\ 0 & 0 & 0 & 0 \\ 0 & 0 & 0 & 1 \end{pmatrix} \begin{pmatrix} d & 0 & -C_x & 0 \\ 0 & 1 & 0 & 0 \\ C_x & 0 & d & 0 \\ 0 & 0 & 0 & 1 \end{pmatrix} \begin{pmatrix} 1 & 0 & 0 & 0 \\ 0 & \frac{C_z}{d} & \frac{-C_y}{d} & 0 \\ 0 & \frac{-C_y}{d} & \frac{C_z}{d} & 0 \\ 0 & 0 & 0 & 1 \end{pmatrix}$$

$$\begin{pmatrix} 1 & 0 & 0 & -x_0 \\ 0 & 1 & 0 & -y_0 \\ 0 & 0 & 1 & -z_0 \\ 0 & 0 & 0 & 1 \end{pmatrix} \qquad 8.7$$

∴ The projected point is

$$\begin{pmatrix} x_p \\ y_p \\ z_p \\ 1 \end{pmatrix} = [T] \begin{pmatrix} x \\ y \\ z \\ 1 \end{pmatrix}$$

Case III: Center of projection is any point and plane of projection is *xy* plane ($z = 0$).
In Fig. 8.22 $A(x, y, z)$ is any point and $C(x_c, y_c, z_c)$ is the center of projection. $B(x_p, y_p, z_p)$ is the perspective projection of A on $z = 0$ plane. We have to find the projection matrix.

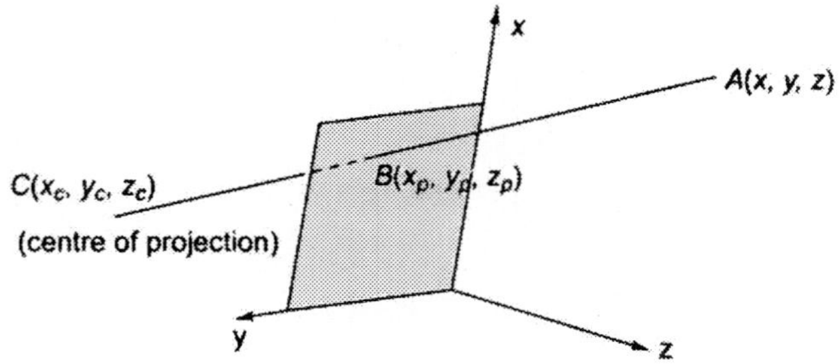

FIGURE 8.22 Perspective Projection on *xy* Plane

Any point $D(x', y', z')$ on the line AC is given by

$$x' = x + (x_c - x)t \quad 8.8\ (a)$$

$$y' = y + (y_c - y)t \quad 8.8\ (b)$$

$$z' = z + (z_c - z)t \quad 8.8\ (c)$$

where, t is the parameter.

Equation (8.8) is the parametric equation.

For $t = 0$; $x' = x$; $y' = y$; $z' = z$

For $t = 1$; $x' = x_c$; $y' = y_c$; $z' = z_c$

We have to find out for what value of t, $x' = x_p$, $y' = y_p$ and $z' = z_p$.

Standard Perspective Projection

We assume a special case, where C is on the any one of the (–)ve principal axis at a distance d(*say*) from the origin and view plane is the corresponding principal plane. Fig. 8.23 shows such type of transformation. It is called *standard perspective transformation*. Hence, for *xy* plane (z=0), and $C(0,0,-d)$ we can write,

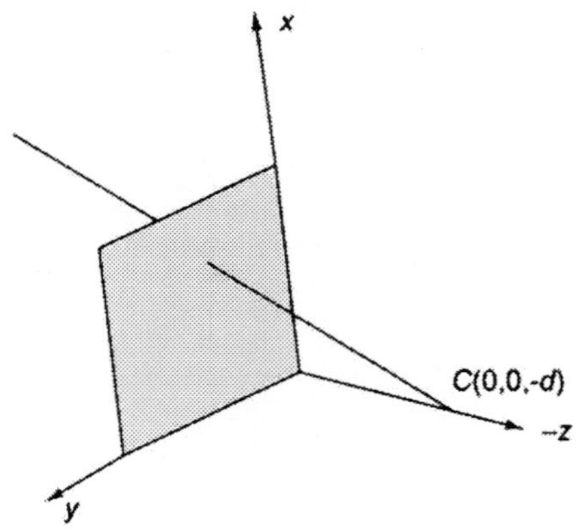

FIGURE 8.23 Standard Perspective Projection

$$x_c = 0, y_c = 0, z_c = -d$$

Putting $z' = z_c$ and $z_c = -d$ in eqn. (8.8)

$$z' = z_p = z + (z_c - z)t$$

$$\Rightarrow \quad z_p = z + (-d - z)t = z - (z + d)t$$

$$\Rightarrow \quad t = \frac{z - z_p}{z + d}$$

As z_p is on XY plane $z_p = 0$ i.e., $t = \dfrac{z}{z+d}$

Putting this value of t in equation (8.8), we have

$$x_p = x' = x + (x_c - x)t$$

$$= \quad x + (x_c - x)\frac{z}{z+d}$$ But $x_c = 0$ in this case, as C is on the Z axis

So,

$$x_p = x - \frac{xz}{z+d} = \frac{xd}{z+d} = \frac{x}{\left(1+\dfrac{z}{d}\right)}$$

Similarly, putting the value of t in equation (8.8) for the value of y_p, we have

$$y_p = y' = y + (y_c - y)t$$

$$= y = (y_c - y)\frac{z}{z+d}$$

Here also $y_c = 0$ as C *is* on the Z axis.

So,

$$y_p = y - \frac{yz}{z+d} = \frac{yd}{z+d} = \frac{y}{\left(1+\dfrac{z}{d}\right)}$$

Thus, we have

$$x_p = \frac{x}{\left(1+\dfrac{z}{d}\right)}$$

$$y_p = \frac{y}{\left(1+\dfrac{z}{d}\right)}$$

$$z_p = 0$$

So, the transformation equation involved when the point (x, y, z) is projected on the xy plane($z = 0$) with C(centre of projection) at distance d from origin on the $-ve$ Z axis.

$$\begin{pmatrix} x_h \\ y_h \\ z_h \\ 1 \end{pmatrix} = \begin{pmatrix} x_p \\ y_p \\ z_p \\ z+d \end{pmatrix} = \begin{pmatrix} d & 0 & 0 & 0 \\ 0 & d & 0 & 0 \\ 0 & 0 & 0 & 0 \\ 0 & 0 & 1 & d \end{pmatrix} \begin{pmatrix} x \\ y \\ z \\ 1 \end{pmatrix}$$

$$P_{er\hat{k}} = \begin{pmatrix} d & 0 & 0 & 0 \\ 0 & d & 0 & 0 \\ 0 & 0 & 0 & 0 \\ 0 & 0 & 1 & d \end{pmatrix}$$

is known as standard perspective transformation matrix. (view plane xy plane and centre of projection $(0, 0, -d)$).

Here h is homogeneous factor and is equal to $z + d$.

x_p, y_p and z_p can be found by $x_p = \frac{x_h}{h}$, $y_p = \frac{y_h}{h}$ and $z_p = \frac{z_h}{h}$.

Similarly, we can derive $P_{er\hat{i}}$, $P_{er\hat{j}}$

$$P_{er\hat{i}} = \begin{pmatrix} 0 & 0 & 0 & 0 \\ 0 & d & 0 & 0 \\ 0 & 0 & d & 0 \\ 1 & 0 & 0 & d \end{pmatrix}$$

is known as standard perspective transformation matrix. (when view plane is yz plane centre of projection $(-d,0,0)$.

$$P_{er\hat{j}} = \begin{pmatrix} d & 0 & 0 & 0 \\ 0 & 0 & 0 & 0 \\ 0 & 0 & d & 0 \\ 0 & 1 & 0 & d \end{pmatrix}$$

is known as standard perspective transformation matrix. (view plane is zx plane and centre of projection $(0,-d,0)$)

Case IV : Center of Projection is $(0, 0, -d)$ and Plane of Projection is parallel to xy plane($z = k$).

Same as case III, only difference being the view plane to principal plane.

Figure 8.23 illustrates the perspective projection of any point $P(x, y, z)$ onto the $z = k$ plane with reference to the centre of projection $C(0, 0, -d)$. We have to find the transformation matrix.

We know that for $z = 0$ plane of projection transformation matrix involved is

$$P_{er\hat{k}} = \begin{pmatrix} d & 0 & 0 & 0 \\ 0 & d & 0 & 0 \\ 0 & 0 & 0 & 0 \\ 0 & 0 & 1 & d \end{pmatrix}$$

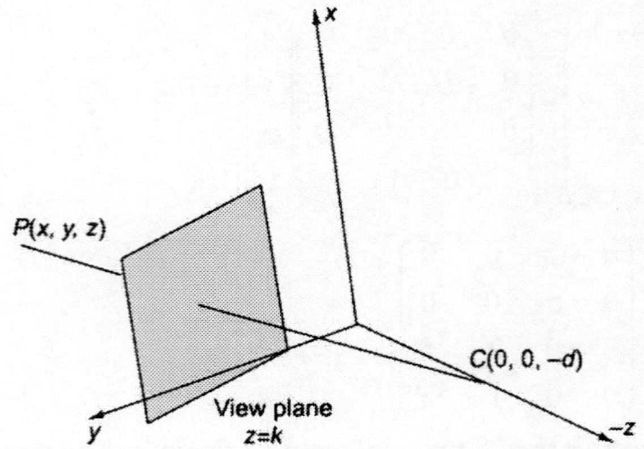

FIGURE 8.24 Perspective Projection on View Plane Parallel to xy Plane

In this problem the plane of projection involved is the $z = k$ plane which is parallel to $z = 0$ plane. We adopt a similar technique as we have done when the plane of projection was $z = 0$ plane(Case III). The position of C is unchanged.

If (x', y', z') is any point lying on the PC, then

$$x' = x + (0 - x)t$$
$$y' = y + (0 - y)t$$
$$z' = z + (-d - z)t$$

or,

$$x' = x - xt$$
$$y' = y - yt$$
$$z' = z - (z + d)t$$

Here t is the parameter.

Now when $z' = z_p$ then,

$\Rightarrow$ $$z_p = k = z - (z + d)t$$

$\Rightarrow$ $$t = \frac{z - k}{z + d}$$

Now, $$x_p = x' \text{ for } t = \frac{z-k}{z+d}$$

$\therefore$ $$x_p = x\left\{1 - \frac{z-k}{z+d}\right\} = x\frac{d+k}{z+d}$$

Similarly, $$y_p = y' \text{ for } t = \frac{z-k}{z+d}$$

$\therefore$ $$y_p = y\left\{1 - \frac{z-k}{z+d}\right\} = y\frac{d+k}{z+d}$$

Here transformation matrix can be found by

$$x_p = \frac{x_h}{h} = x\frac{d+k}{z+d}$$

$$y_p = \frac{y_h}{h} = y\frac{d+k}{z+d}$$

$$z_p = \frac{z_h}{h} = k\frac{z+d}{z+d} = k$$

where $h = z + d$

$$\therefore \quad \text{Per}_{z=k} = \begin{pmatrix} d+k & 0 & 0 & 0 \\ 0 & d+k & 0 & 0 \\ 0 & 0 & k & kd \\ 0 & 0 & 1 & d \end{pmatrix}$$

Case V : Center of Projection is (0,0,0) and Plane of Projection is any plane

The plane of projection is defined by a reference point $R(x0, y0, z0)$ lying on that plane and a vector normal to that plane $\boldsymbol{N} = n_1\boldsymbol{i} + n_2\boldsymbol{j} + n_3\boldsymbol{k}$, the centre of projection is at origin $O(0, 0, 0)$. Refer figure 8.25.

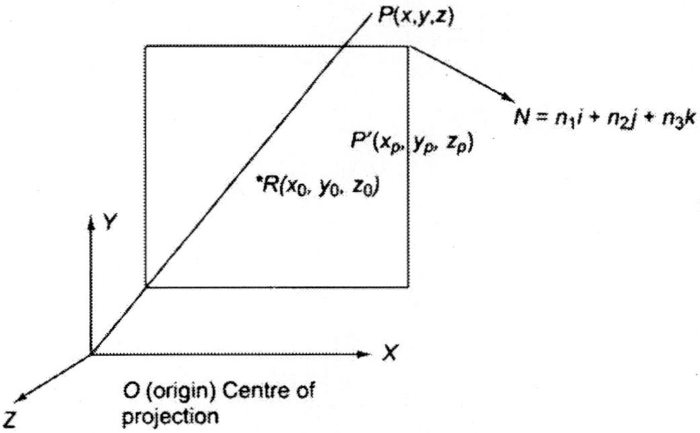

FIGURE 8.25 Perspective Projection when view Plane is any Plane

The point $P(x, y, z)$ is to be projected.

Any point x', y', z' lying on the PC is given by

$$x' = 0 + (x - 0)t$$

$$y' = 0 + (y - 0)t$$

$$z' = 0 + (z - 0)t$$

or, $x' = xt,\ y' = yt,\ z' = zt$

Let $x' = x_p = xt,\ y' = y_p = yt,\ z' = z_p = zt$

The vector passing through the points $P(x_p, y_p, z_p)$ and $R(x_0, y_0, z_0)$ [as both of them lie on the plane of projection] is given by

$$v = (x_p - x_0)i + (y_p - y_0)j + (z_p - z_0)k$$

The normal vector N is perpendicular to the vector v, hence, $v.N = 0$

i.e.,
$$n_1(x_p - x_0) + n_2(y_p - y_0) + n_3(z_p - z_0) = 0$$

Now replacing the values of (x_p, y_p, z_p) in the above equation, we get

$$n_1(xt - x_0) + n_2(yt - y_0) + n_3(zt - z_0) = 0$$

$$\Rightarrow \quad t(n_1x + n_2y + n_3z) = n_1x_0 + n_2y_0 + n_3z_0$$

$$\Rightarrow \quad t = \frac{n_1x_0 + n_2y_0 + n_3z_0}{n_1x + n_2y + n_3z}$$

This is the value of t for which x' becomes x_p, y' becomes y_p and z' becomes z_p

so, $t = \dfrac{d_0}{n_1x + n_2y_0 + n_3z}$ Where, $d_0 = (n_1x_0 + n_2y_0 + n_3z_0)$

since,
$$x_p = x' = xt \text{ for } t = \frac{d_0}{n_1x + n_2y + n_3z}$$

so,
$$x_p = \frac{xd_0}{n_1x + n_2y + n_3z}$$

Similarly,
$$y_p = \frac{yd_0}{n_1x + n_2y + n_3z}$$

$$z_p = \frac{zd_0}{n_1x + n_2y + n_3z}$$

So, the transformation matrix is

$$T = \begin{pmatrix} d_0 & 0 & 0 & 0 \\ 0 & d_0 & 0 & 1 \\ 0 & 0 & d_0 & 0 \\ n_1 & n_2 & n_3 & 0 \end{pmatrix}$$

where,
$$d_0 = (n_1x_0 + n_2y_0 + n_3z_0)$$

Case VI: Center of Projection is (a, b, c) and Plane of Projection is any plane

Same as **case V**, only difference being the centre of projection is not at origin but at (a, b, c) this is the most generalized case of perspective transformation.

Figure 8.25 illustrates the perspective projection $P'(x_p, y_p, z_p)$ of point $P(x, y, z)$ with reference to the centre of projection $C(a, b, c)$ and view plane with normal vector N and reference point $\boldsymbol{R}$.

Any point (x', y', z') passing through line joining PC is given by

$$x' = a + (x - a)t$$

$$y' = b + (y - b)t$$

$$z' = c + (z - c)t$$

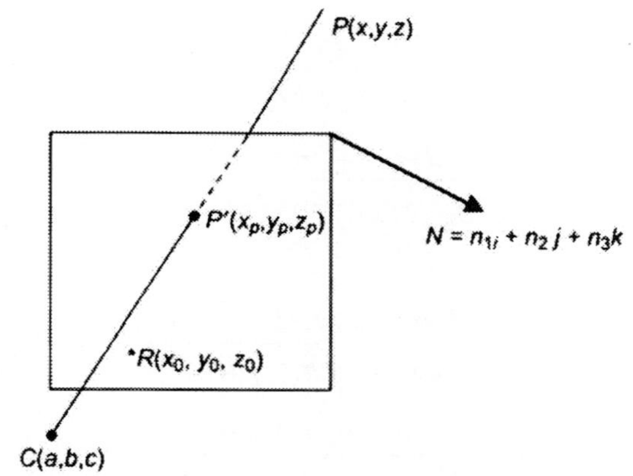

FIGURE 8.26 Perspective Projection when View Plane is any Plane and Centre of Projection is any Point.

Any vector $\boldsymbol{v}$ passing through $P'(x_p, y_p, z_p)$ and $R(x_0, y_0, z_0)$ as they lie on the same plane of projection is given by

$$\boldsymbol{v} = (x_p - x_0)\boldsymbol{i} + (y_p - y_0)\boldsymbol{j} + (z_p - z_0)\boldsymbol{k}$$

Now since $\boldsymbol{N}$ is perpendicular to $\boldsymbol{v}$ so $\boldsymbol{N}.\boldsymbol{v} = 0$.

$$\text{So } (x_p - x_0)n_1 + (y_p - y_0)n_2 + (z_p - z_0)n_3 = 0.$$

Considering $x_p = x'$, $y_p = y'$ and $z_p = z'$ for a particular value of t and substituting the value in the above equation, we get

$$[\{a+(x-a)t\} - x_0]n_1 + [\{b + (y-b)t\} - y_0]n_2 + [\{c + (z-c)t\} - z_0]n_3 = 0$$

$$\Rightarrow \quad (x-a)n_1t + (y-b)n_2t + (z-c)n_3t = (x_0 - a)n_1 + (y_0 - b)n_2 + (z_0 - c)n_3$$

$$\Rightarrow \quad t = (x_0n_1 - an_1 + y_0n_2 - bn_2 + z_0n_3 - cn_3)\{(x-a)n_1 + (y-b)n_2 + (z-c)n_3\}$$

Let $\quad d_0 = x_0n_1 + y_0n_2 + z_0n_3$

$\quad d_1 = an_1 + bn_2 + cn_3$

and, $\quad d = d_0 - d_1 = x_0n_1 - an_1 + y_0n_2 - bn_2 + z_0n_3 - cn_3$

$$\therefore \quad t = \frac{d}{(n_1x + n_2y + n_3z) - d_1}$$

Now $\quad x_p = x'$ for $t = \dfrac{d}{(n_1x + n_2y + n_3z) - d_1}$

Similarly, $y_p = y'$ and $z_p = z'$ for the same value of t

$$x_p = x' = a + (x-a)\,t$$

$$= a + \frac{(x-a)d}{(n_1x + n_2y + n_3z) - d_1}$$

$$= \frac{(n_1x + n_2y + n_3z - d_1)a + (x-a)d}{n_1x + n_2y + n_3z - d_1}$$

$$= \frac{x(n_1 a + d) + a n_2 y + a n_3 z - a d_1 - a d}{n_1 x + n_2 y + n_3 z - d_1}$$

$$x_p = \frac{x(n_1 a + d) + a n_2 y + a n_3 z - a d_0}{n_1 x + n_2 y + n_3 z - d_1}$$

Proceeding, similarly for y_p and z_p, we have,

$$y_p = \frac{b n_1 x + (b n_2 + d) y + b n_3 z - a d_0}{n_1 x + n_2 y + n_3 z - d_1}$$

$$y_p = \frac{c n_1 x + c n_2 + (c n_3 + d) z - a d_0}{n_1 x + n_2 y + n_3 z - d_1}$$

$$\therefore \qquad T = \begin{pmatrix} (a n_1 + d) & a n_2 & a n_3 & -a d_0 \\ b n_1 & (b n_2 + d) & b n_3 & -b d_0 \\ c n_1 & c n_2 & (c n_3 + d) & -c d_0 \\ n_1 & n_2 & n_3 & -d_1 \end{pmatrix}$$

where, $\qquad d_0 = x_0 n_1 + y_0 n_2 + z_0 n_3$

$\qquad\qquad d_1 = a n_1 + b n_2 + c n_3$

and, $\qquad d = d_0 - d_1$

Table 8.1 depicts the summary of projection transformation matrices based upon location of centre of projection and position of view plane.

TABLE 8.1

Type of projection	*View plane*	*Direction vector*	*Transformation matrix*
Parallel	*XY*	$V = x_p i + y_p j + z_p k$	$\text{Par}_{z=0} = \begin{bmatrix} 1 & 0 & -\frac{x_p}{z_p} \\ 0 & 1 & -\frac{y_p}{z_p} \end{bmatrix}$
	YZ	$V = x_p i + y_p j + z_p k$	$\text{Par}_{x=0} = \begin{bmatrix} 1 & 0 & -\frac{y_p}{x_p} \\ 0 & 1 & -\frac{z_p}{x_p} \end{bmatrix}$

(Contd.)

Type of projection	*View plane*	*Direction vector*	*Transformation matrix*
	ZX	$\boldsymbol{V} = x_p\boldsymbol{i} + y_p\boldsymbol{j} + z_p\boldsymbol{k}$	$\text{Par}_{y=0} = \begin{bmatrix} 1 & 0 & -\dfrac{z_p}{y_p} \\ 0 & 1 & -\dfrac{x_p}{y_p} \end{bmatrix}$
	Any plane with reference point $R(x_0, y_0, z_0)$ and normal vector $\boldsymbol{N} = n_1\boldsymbol{i} + n_2\boldsymbol{j} + n_3\boldsymbol{k}$	$\boldsymbol{V} = x_p\boldsymbol{i} + y_p\boldsymbol{j} + z_p\boldsymbol{k}$	Refer to transformation matrix 8.6
Perspective	XY	On –ve z-axis $C(0, 0, -d)$	$P_{er\,\hat{k}} = \begin{pmatrix} d & 0 & 0 & 0 \\ 0 & d & 0 & 0 \\ 0 & 0 & 0 & 0 \\ 0 & 0 & 1 & d \end{pmatrix}$
	YZ	On –ve x-axis $C(-d, 0, 0)$	$P_{er\,\hat{i}} = \begin{pmatrix} 0 & 0 & 0 & 0 \\ 0 & d & 0 & 0 \\ 0 & 0 & d & 0 \\ 1 & 0 & 0 & d \end{pmatrix}$
	ZX	On –ve y-axis $C(0, -d, 0)$	$P_{er\,\hat{j}} = \begin{pmatrix} d & 0 & 0 & 0 \\ 0 & 0 & 0 & 0 \\ 0 & 0 & d & 0 \\ 0 & 1 & 0 & d \end{pmatrix}$
	Parallel to principal plane($z = k$)	On –ve z-axis $C(0, 0, -d)$	$\text{Per}_{z=k} = \begin{pmatrix} d+k & 0 & 0 & kd \\ 0 & d+k & 0 & 0 \\ 0 & 0 & k & kd \\ 0 & 0 & 1 & d \end{pmatrix}$
	$X = k$	On –ve x-axis	$\text{Per}_{x=k} = \begin{pmatrix} k & 0 & 0 & kd \\ 0 & d+k & 0 & 1 \\ 0 & 0 & d+k & 0 \\ 1 & 0 & 0 & d \end{pmatrix}$

(Contd.)

Type of projection	*View plane*	*Direction vector*	*Transformation matrix*
	$Y = k$	On −ve y-axis $C(0,-d,0)$	$\text{Per}_{y=k} = \begin{pmatrix} d+k & 0 & 0 & 0 \\ 0 & k & 0 & kd \\ 0 & 0 & d+k & 0 \\ 0 & 1 & 0 & d \end{pmatrix}$
	Any plane with reference point $R(x_0, y_0, z_0)$ & normal vector $N = n_1 i + n_2 j + n_3 k$	At origin $C(0,0,0)$	$T = \begin{pmatrix} d_0 & 0 & 0 & 0 \\ 0 & d_0 & 0 & 1 \\ 0 & 0 & d_0 & 0 \\ n_1 & n_2 & n_3 & 0 \end{pmatrix}$ where, $d_0 = (n_1 x_0 + n_2 y_0 + n_3 z_0)$
	Any plane with reference point and $R(x_0, y_0, z_0)$ & normal vector $N = n_1 i + n_2 j + n_3 k$	Any 3D point $C(a, b, c)$	$T = \begin{pmatrix} (an_1 + d) & an_2 & an_3 & -ad_0 \\ bn_1 & (bn_2 + d) & bn_3 & -bd_0 \\ cn_1 & cn_2 & (cn_3 + d) & -cd_0 \\ n_1 & n_2 & n_3 & -d_1 \end{pmatrix}$ where, $d_0 = x_0 n_1 + y_0 n_2 + z_0 n_3$ $d_1 = an_1 + bn_2 + cn_3$ and, $d = d_0 - d_1$

SOLVED PROBLEMS

Problem 8.1 A unit cube is projection onto the XY plane under the parallel projection whose direction projection is (1,1,1). Obtain the projection of the cube and draw it.

Solution:

Parallel transformation matrix on XY plane direction $\langle x_p, y_p, z_p \rangle$

$$\text{Par} = \begin{bmatrix} 1 & 0 & -\dfrac{x_p}{z_p} \\ 0 & 1 & -\dfrac{y_p}{z_p} \end{bmatrix}$$

$A(0,0,0)$ $B(1,0,0)$

$C(1,1,0)$ $D(0,1,0)$

$E(0,1,1)$ $F(0,0,1)$

$G(1,0,1)$ $H(1,1,1)$

In this case

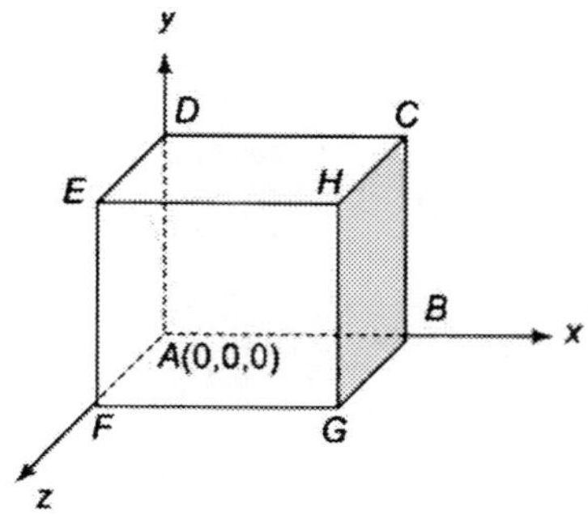

$$\text{Par} = \begin{bmatrix} 1 & 0 & -\frac{1}{1} \\ 0 & 1 & -\frac{1}{1} \end{bmatrix}$$

$A'B'C'D'E'F'G'H' =$

$$\begin{bmatrix} 1 & 0 & -\frac{1}{1} \\ 0 & 1 & -\frac{1}{1} \end{bmatrix} \begin{array}{c} \begin{matrix} A & B & C & D & E & F & G & H \end{matrix} \\ \begin{bmatrix} 0 & 1 & 1 & 0 & 0 & 0 & 1 & 1 \\ 0 & 0 & 1 & 1 & 1 & 0 & 0 & 1 \\ 0 & 0 & 0 & 0 & 1 & 1 & 1 & 1 \end{bmatrix} \end{array}$$

$$A'B'C'D'E'F'G'H' = \begin{bmatrix} 0 & 1 & 1 & 0 & -1 & -1 & -1 & -1 \\ 0 & 0 & 0 & 0 & -1 & -1 & -1 & -1 \end{bmatrix}$$

Problem 8.2 Find the standard perspective projection of a line joining points $A(-1,1,-2)$ to $B(2,-2,0)$ when centre of projection at (0,0,–4).

Solution:

$$P_{er\hat{k}} = \begin{pmatrix} d & 0 & 0 & 0 \\ 0 & d & 0 & 0 \\ 0 & 0 & 0 & 0 \\ 0 & 0 & 1 & d \end{pmatrix}$$

Here $d = 4$

$$P_{er\hat{k}} = \begin{pmatrix} 4 & 0 & 0 & 0 \\ 0 & 4 & 0 & 0 \\ 0 & 0 & 0 & 0 \\ 0 & 0 & 1 & 4 \end{pmatrix}$$

$$\begin{pmatrix} 4 & 0 & 0 & 0 \\ 0 & 4 & 0 & 0 \\ 0 & 0 & 0 & 0 \\ 0 & 0 & 1 & 4 \end{pmatrix} \begin{array}{c} \begin{matrix} A & B \end{matrix} \\ \begin{pmatrix} -1 & 2 \\ 1 & -2 \\ -2 & 0 \\ 1 & 1 \end{pmatrix} \end{array}$$

$$= \begin{pmatrix} -4 & 8 \\ 4 & -8 \\ 0 & 0 \\ 2 & 4 \end{pmatrix}$$

Therefore,

$$A'B' = \begin{pmatrix} -2 & 2 \\ 2 & -2 \\ 0 & 0 \\ 1 & 1 \end{pmatrix}$$

Problem 8.3 A unit cube is viewed from (0,10,20). Obtain the perspective projection of cube on the *xy* plane.

Solution:
$A(x,y,z)$ is any point and $C(0,10,20)$ is the centre of projection. $B(x_p, y_p, z_p)$ is the perspective projection of A on xy ($z = 0$) plane.

Then B is given by:

$$x_p = x + (0 - x)t \qquad \text{.....(1)}$$
$$y_p = y + (10 - y)t \qquad \text{.....(2)}$$
$$z_p = z + (20 - z)t$$

where, t ($0 \le t \le 1$) is the parameter.

Here $z_p = 0$ since the plane of projection is the xy plane.

Therefore,

$$t = \frac{z}{z - 20}$$

substituting the value of t in equations (1) and (2)

$$x_p = x + -x\frac{z}{z-20} = \frac{-20x}{z-20}$$

$$y_p = y + (10 - y)\frac{z}{z-20}$$

$$= \frac{-20y + 10z}{z - 20}$$

$$\begin{bmatrix} x_p \\ y_p \\ z_p \\ 1 \end{bmatrix} = \frac{1}{z-20}\begin{bmatrix} -20 & 0 & 0 & 0 \\ 0 & -20 & 10 & 0 \\ 0 & 0 & 0 & 0 \\ 0 & 0 & 1 & -20 \end{bmatrix}\begin{bmatrix} x \\ y \\ z \\ 1 \end{bmatrix}$$

$$
\begin{array}{c} \\ \begin{bmatrix} -20 & 0 & 0 & 0 \\ 0 & -20 & 10 & 0 \\ 0 & 0 & 0 & 0 \\ 0 & 0 & 1 & -20 \end{bmatrix} \end{array}
\begin{array}{c} \begin{matrix} A & B & C & D & E & F & G & H \end{matrix} \\ \begin{bmatrix} 0 & 1 & 1 & 0 & 0 & 0 & 1 & 1 \\ 0 & 0 & 1 & 1 & 1 & 0 & 0 & 1 \\ 0 & 0 & 0 & 0 & 1 & 1 & 1 & 1 \\ 1 & 1 & 1 & 1 & 1 & 1 & 1 & 1 \end{bmatrix} \end{array}
$$

$$
= \begin{bmatrix} 0 & -20 & -20 & 0 & 0 & 0 & -20 & -20 \\ 0 & 0 & -10 & -20 & -10 & 10 & 10 & -10 \\ 0 & 0 & 0 & 0 & 0 & 0 & 0 & 0 \\ -20 & -20 & -20 & -20 & -19 & -19 & -19 & -19 \end{bmatrix}
$$

Therefore

$$
A'B'C'D'E'F'G'H' = \begin{bmatrix} 0 & 1 & 1 & 0 & 0 & 0 & 20/19 & 20/19 \\ 0 & 0 & 1/2 & 1 & 10/19 & -10/19 & -10/19 & 10/19 \\ 0 & 0 & 0 & 0 & 0 & 0 & 0 & 0 \\ 1 & 1 & 1 & 1 & 1 & 1 & 1 & 1 \end{bmatrix}
$$

Problem 8.4 Find the standard perspective projection of a point in the plane $z = d$ when centre of projection at (0,0,0).

Solution

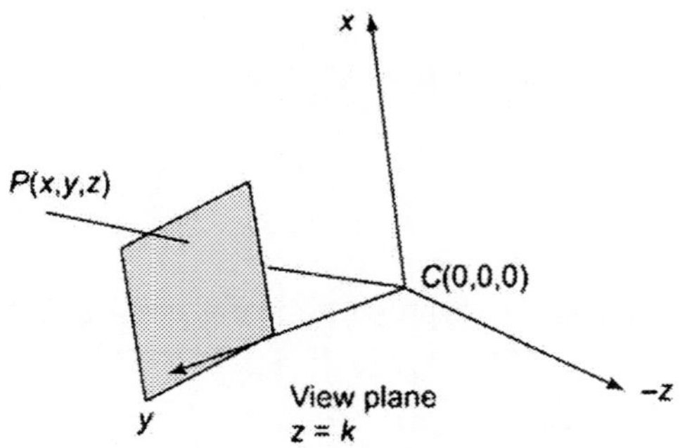

Any point $D(x',y',z')$ on the line PC is given by

$$x' = x + (0 - x)t \qquad .....1(a)$$

$$y' = y + (0 - y)t \qquad .....1(b)$$

$$z' = z + (0 - z)t \qquad .....1(c)$$

where t $(0 \le t \le 1)$ is the parameter.

Equation (1) is the parametric equation of 3-D line.

For $t = 0;\ x' = x;\ y' = y;\ z' = z$

For $t = 1;\ x' = 0\ ;\ y' = 0\ ;\ z' = 0$

We have to find out for what value of t, $x' = x_p$, $y' = y_p$ and $z' = z_p$.

$$x' = x(1-t) \quad .....(2)$$

$$y' = y(1-t) \quad .....(3)$$

$$z' = z(1-t) \quad .....(4)$$

from equation (4)

$$t = 1 - \frac{d}{z} = \frac{z-d}{z}$$

Substitute value of t in equations (2) and (3), we have

$$x_p = x + (0-x)\,\frac{z-d}{z} = \frac{xd}{z}$$

$$y_p = y + (0-y)\,\frac{z-d}{z} = \frac{yd}{z}$$

$$z_p = z + (0-z)\,\frac{z-d}{z} = d$$

$$\begin{pmatrix} x_p \\ y_p \\ z_p \\ 1 \end{pmatrix} = \begin{pmatrix} d & 0 & 0 & 0 \\ 0 & d & 0 & 0 \\ 0 & 0 & d & 1 \\ 0 & 0 & 1 & 0 \end{pmatrix} \begin{pmatrix} x \\ y \\ z \\ 1 \end{pmatrix}$$

Problem 8.5 Find the standard perspective projection of a point in the plane $x = d$ when centre of projection at (0,0,0).

Solution:

Similar to problem 8.4.

Problem 8.6 Find the standard perspective projection of a point in the plane $y = d$ when centre of projection at (0,0,0).

Solution:

Similar to problem 8.4.

EXERCISES

1. Define the terms view plan, foreshortening factor and depth cueing.
2. Compare parallel and perspective projections with reference to real life.
3. What is oblique projection? Provide some examples of oblique projection.
4. What is orthographic projection? Provide some examples of orthographic projection.
5. Define the terms vanishing point and principal vanishing point. What is the physical significance of vanishing point?
6. Find the standard perspective projection of a point in the plane $z = -d$ when centre of projection at $(0, 0, -d)$.

7. Find the standard perspective projection of a line joining points $A(-1,1,-2d)$ to $B(2,-2,0)$ when centre of projection is at $(0, 0, -d)$.
8. Obtain the projection of point $P(x, y, z)$ on
   a. yz plane
   b. $x + 4 = 0$ plane

   when it is viewed from point (20, 0, 0).
9. A unit cube is projection onto the XY plane under the parallel projection whose direction projection is (1,1,1). Obtain the projection of cube and draw it.
10. A unit cube is viewed from (0,10,20). Obtain the perspective projection of cube and draw it.
11. Differentiate between cabinet and cavalier projection. Why cabinet projection is more realistic than cavalier projection? Explain.
12. State and explain the anomalies of perspective projection.

9

3-D Viewing and Clipping

9.1 INTRODUCTION

As we have seen in two-dimensional viewing and clipping objects are clipped against window is then mapped to the viewport for display. Refer to Fig. 9.1.

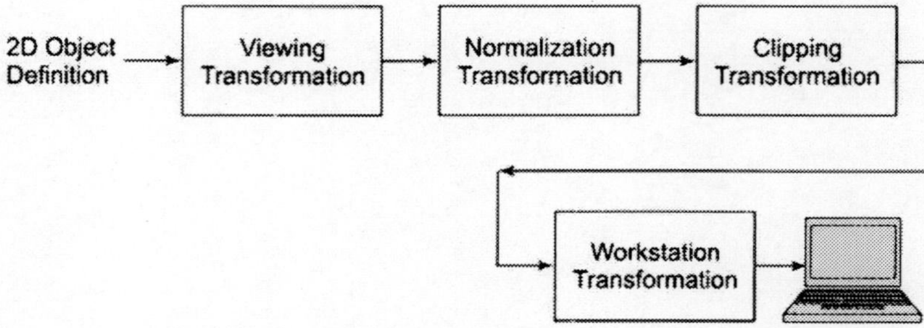

FIGURE 9.1 2D Viewing and Clipping

Unlike 2D, 3D objects are clipped against view volume and projected on the projection plane (view plane or projection window) is then mapped to the viewport for display. Only those objects within the view volume will appear on a display device—all others are clipped away from the display. Projection operation can take place before view volume clipping or after view volume clipping. Refer to Fig. 9.2(a) and 9.2(b).

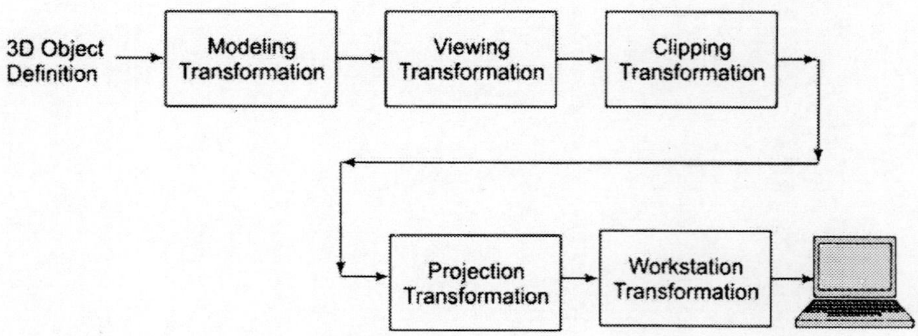

FIGURE 9.2 (a) 3D Viewing and Clipping (Clipping before Projection)

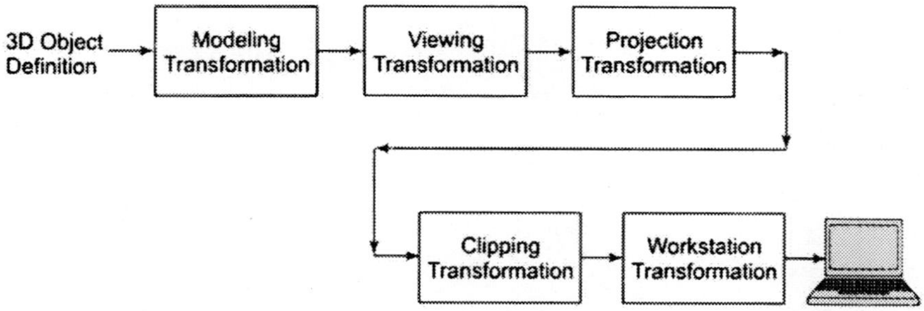

FIGURE 9.2 (b) 3D Viewing and Clipping (Clipping after Projection)

Lines and polygons surfaces in real world (three-dimensional) can be clipping against view volume boundaries with the same methodology as used in 2D, except that objects are now clipped against planes instead of clipping edges. Curved surfaces are clipped using the defining equations for the surface boundary and locating the intersection lines with parallelepiped planes.

9.2 3D VIEWING

The shape of view volume depends upon the type of projection (parallel or perspective). In any case, four sides (top, bottom, left, right) of view volume are planes that pass through the edges of the window. For a parallel projection, these four sides of view volume form an infinite parallelepiped, as shown in Fig. 9.3(a). For perspective projection, the view volume is a pyramid with apex at the projection reference point, as shown in Fig. 9.3(b)

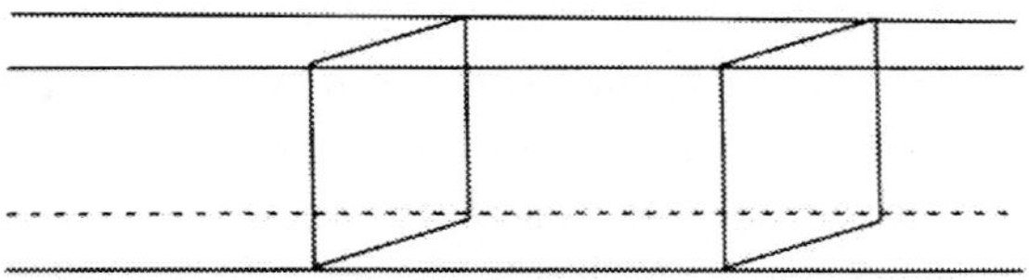

FIGURE 9.3(a) Infinite Parallelepiped

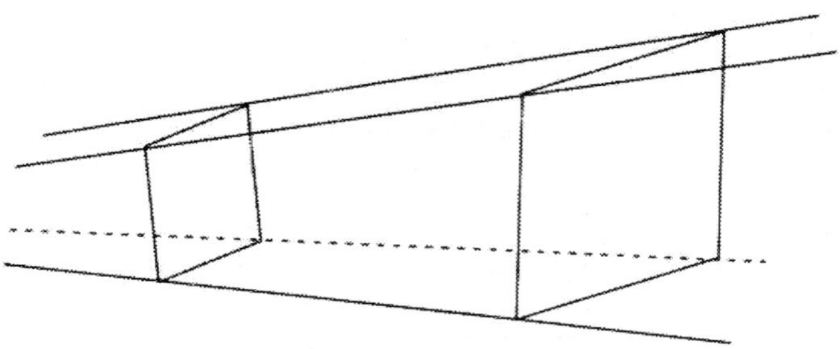

FIGURE 9.3(b) Pyramid

9.2.1 Size of View Volume

In either case (parallel or perspective) view volume four sides of view volume intersects with view plane that formed the edges of window. Thus, size of view volume depends upon the size of the window, as shown in Fig. 9.4(a) and 9.4(b).

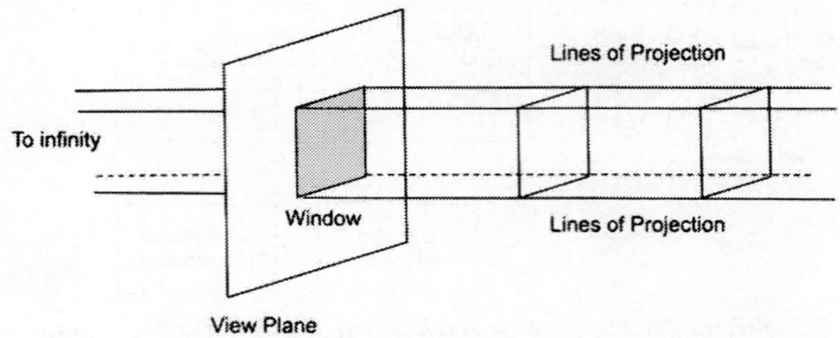

FIGURE 9.4(a) Window in Parallel Projection

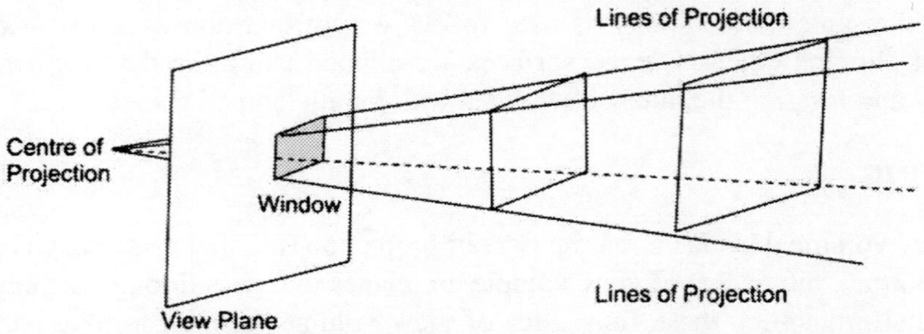

FIGURE 9.4(b) Window in Perspective Projection

9.2.2 Finite View Volume

A finite view volume is obtained by limiting the extent of the volume in the z_v direction. This is performed if two additional boundary planes parallel to view plane are introduced. These planes are referred as the front plane (near plane or hitler) and back plane(far plane or yon) of the view volume. The front and back planes are parallel to view plane at a specified position. *Both planes must be on the same side of the projection reference point in such a way that back plane must be farther from the projection point than front plane.*

In orthographic parallel projection, the six planes form a **rectangular parallelepiped**. In perspective projection front and back clipping planes truncated the infinite pyramid view volume to form ***frustum.*** In both cases front and back clipping planes allow us to see parts of objects based on depth. Thus, we

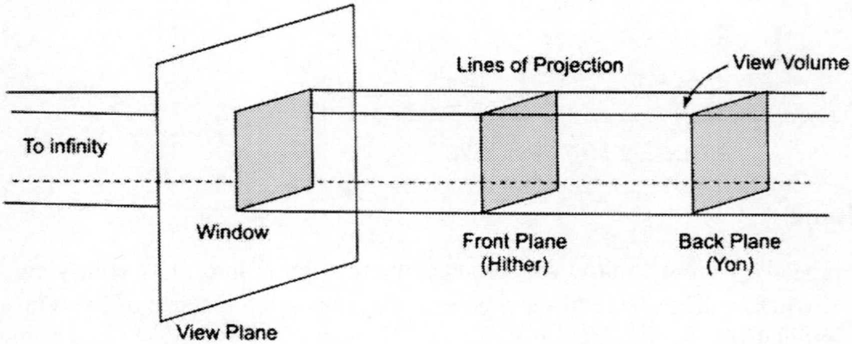

FIGURE 9.5(a) Finite Parallel View Volume (Rectangular parallelepiped)

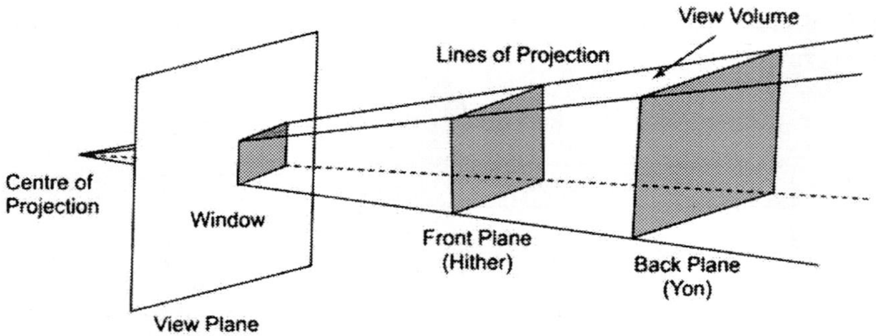

FIGURE 9.5(b) Finite Perspective View Volume (Frustum)

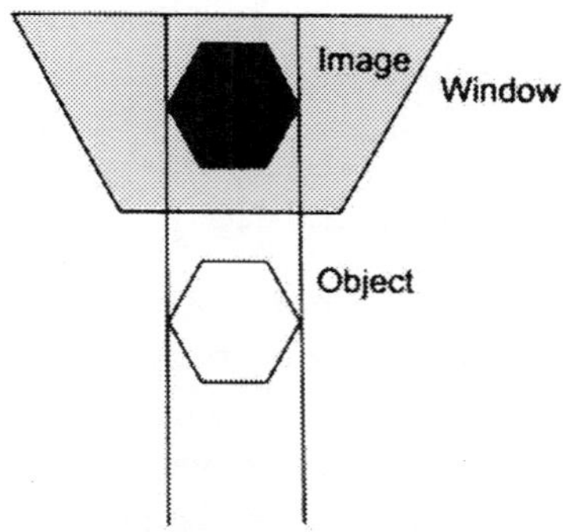

FIGURE 9.6

can select parts of objects in depth that we would like to view and exclude on adjusting the position of front and back clipping plane. Thus, selection of parts of objects depends upon placement of view plane and the front and back clipping plane. For a given view volume selection of parts of objects depends upon position of view plane. A view plane can be position along z_v–axis except that it cannot contain the projection reference point. Orthographic parallel projection is not affected by the view plane positioning. Oblique parallel projection may be affected by view plane positioning, depending on the direction of projection, as shown in Fig. 9.6. In contrast perspective projection depends on the positioning of the projection reference point relative to the view plane. If projection reference point is close to view plane, then objects will appear much larger than more distant objects of the same size. As we move reference point farther from the view plane, the size of the object goes on decrease. The projected size of an object is also affected by the position of the object and the view plane. If the view plane is in front of the object i.e., the nearer the reference point, the projected size is smaller, as shown in Fig. 9.7(a). On the other side, if view plane is moved away from reference point, the projected size goes on increasing, as shown in Fig. 9.7(b).

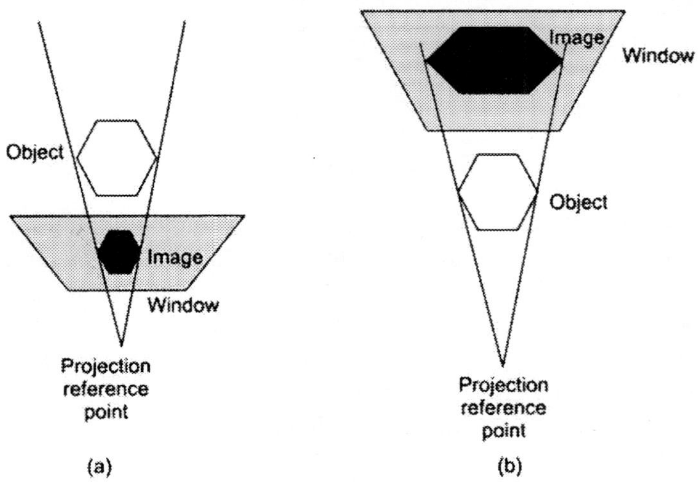

FIGURE 9.7

Distances of front plane and back plane are measured relative to view reference point(VRP) and along view plane normal(VPN).

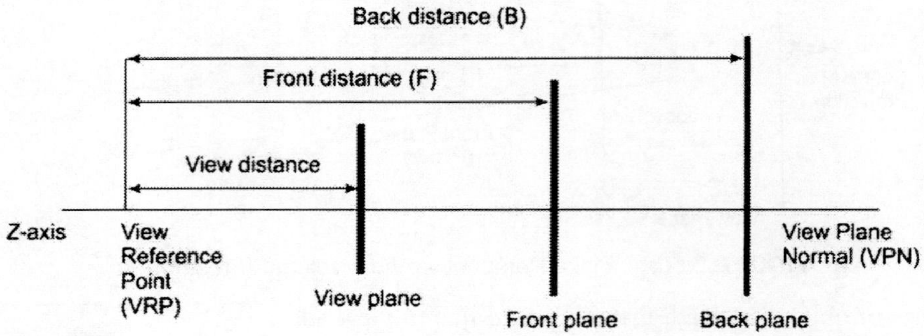

FIGURE 9.8

9.3 3D CLIPPING

Clipping in two-dimensional is performed against rectangular window whose sides are parallel to co-ordinate axes or aligned with *x* and *y* axes. Unlike 2D, 3D clipping is performed against view volume. Clipping in three dimensions can be accomplished using extensions of two-dimensional clipping methodology. In 3D, an object is clip against the boundary planes of view volume instead of clipping against straight-line window boundaries in 2D, as shown in Fig. 9.9(a) and 9.9(b).

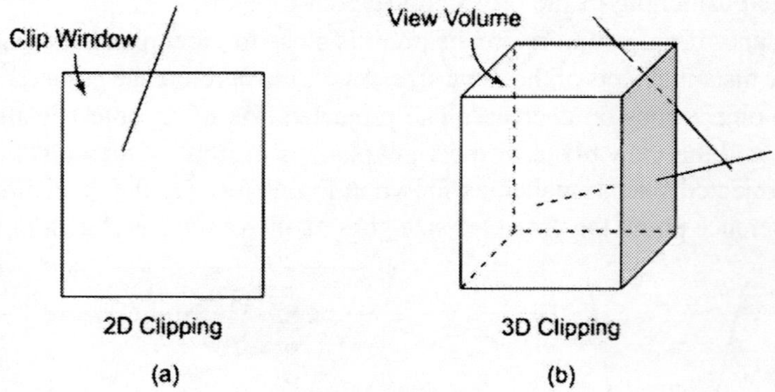

FIGURE 9.9 Clipping

Clipping in three-dimensional is performed against view volume clipping boundaries and these boundaries are planes whose orientation depends on the *type of projection*, *the projection window* and *the position of projection reference point*.

Projection operations can take place before the view volume clipping or after view volume clipping. Contents of the view volume are mapped to projection window. Finally, the contents of the window are transforming to a two-dimensional viewport.

In three-dimensional space the concept can be extended to a *clipping volume* or *view volume*. This is a three-dimensional region or box. Objects within the view volume may be seen, while those outside are not displayed. Objects crossing the boundary are cut, and only the portion within the view volume is shown. A view volume may clip the front or back of an object as well as its sides. There can be any arbitrary clipping region formed with six planes. But following two view volume shapes are usually used because it is easy to work with these two view volumes:

(a) View volume based upon parallel projection.
(b) View volume based upon perspective projection.

Projection operations can take place before the view volume clipping or after view volume clipping. Contents of the view volume are mapped to projection window. Finally, the contents of the window are transforming to a two-dimensional viewport, as already shown in Fig. 9.2(a) and 9.2(b).

9.3.1 Direct Clipping

In this method, as the name suggests clipping is done against the view volume.

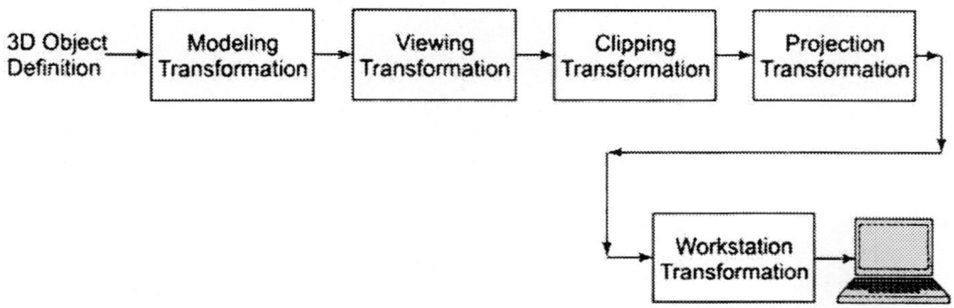

FIGURE 9.10 Direct Clipping Process

9.3.2 Canonical Clipping

In this method, normalized transformations are applied which transform the original view volume into canonical view volume. Clipping is then performed against the *canonical view volume* (normalized view volume).

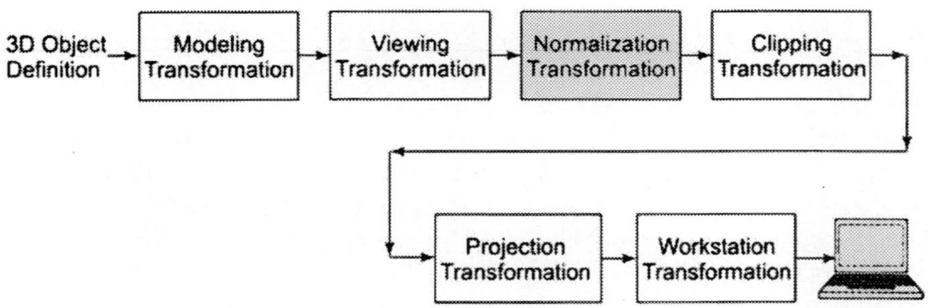

FIGURE 9.11 Canonical Clipping Process

Canonical view volume for parallel projection is unit cube whose faces are defined by the planes $x = 0, x = 1, y = 0, y = 1, z = 0, z = 1$.

Canonical view volume for perspective projection is the truncated pyramid whose faces are defined by the planes $x = z, x = -z, y = z, y = -z, z = z_f, z = 1$.

Advantages to clip against Normalized View Volume:

- It provides a standard shape for representing any sized view volume.
- Clipping procedures are simplified.
- Depth cuing and visible-surface determination are simplified, since the z-axis always points towards the viewer.

9.3.3 Point Clipping

The methods remain basically the same. The difference lies in the test to see whether or not a point is inside the visible region. Instead of comparing the point against a line, we now must compare the point against a plane.

A point $P(x,y,z)$ inside a parallel view volume if following inequalities satisfy:

$$x_{wmin} \le x \le x_{wmax}$$
$$y_{wmin} \le y \le y_{wmax}$$
$$z_{wmin} \le z \le z_{wmax}$$

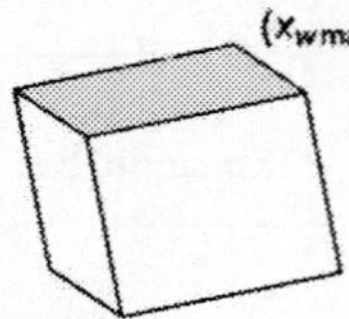

In case of canonical parallel view volume

$$x_{wmin} = y_{wmin} = z_{wmin} = 0 \text{ and } x_{wmax} = y_{wmax} = z_{wmax} = 1$$

A point $P(x,y,z)$ inside a perspective view volume if following inequalities satisfy:

$$-z \le x \le z$$
$$-z \le y \le z$$
$$z_f \le z \le 1$$

$Ax + By + Cz + D = 0$ is one of the boundary planes of a view volume, then a point $P(x1,y1,z1)$

(a) lies on the plane if $Ax1 + By1 + Cz1 + D = 0$

or,

(b) lies on one side of the plane if $Ax1 + By1 + Cz1 + D > 0$

or,

(c) lies on other side of the plane if $Ax1 + By1 + Cz1 + D < 0$

We can, therefore, tell a line segment *visible* or *non-visible* or *clipping candidate* by checking the sign of the expression obtained from the equations of boundary planes for both end points of line segment and from all six boundary planes. In case, line intersects with any one of the boundary plane then point of the intersection(s) can be computed by solving line of the equation and plane of the equation.

9.3.4 Line Clipping

A line segment is *completely outside* or *inside* or *partially visible* w.r.t. a view volume according to the following strategies:

9.3.4.1 *Cohen-Sutherland Algorithm*

This algorithm provides an efficient procedure for finding the category (visible, non-visible, clipping candidate) of a line segment against normalized view volume (parallel or perspective).

Algorithm

Step 1: (a) Input $A(x1, y1, z1)$, $B(x2, y2, z2)$ /* End points of line segment

(b) $x = 0, x = 1, y = 0, y = 1, z = 0, z = 1$ /* Six planes of canonical parallel view volume

(c) $x = z, x = -z, y = z, y = -z, z = 1, z = z_f$ /* Six planes of canonical perspective view volume

Step 2: Each end point of the line segment is assigned a six bit code, called a region code.

(a) Parallel view volume:

Least Significant Bit (LSB)	Bit1 = 1 end point is above the view volume i.e., $(y-1) > 0$
	Bit2 = 1 end point is below the view volume i.e., $(-y) > 0$
	Bit3 = 1 end point is in right of the view volume i.e., $(x-1) > 0$
	Bit4 = 1 end point is in left of the view volume i.e., $(-x) > 0$
Most Significant Bit (MSB) ↓	Bit5 = 1 end point is behind the view volume i.e., $(z-1) > 0$
	Bit6 = 1 end point is behind the view volume i.e., $(-z) > 0$

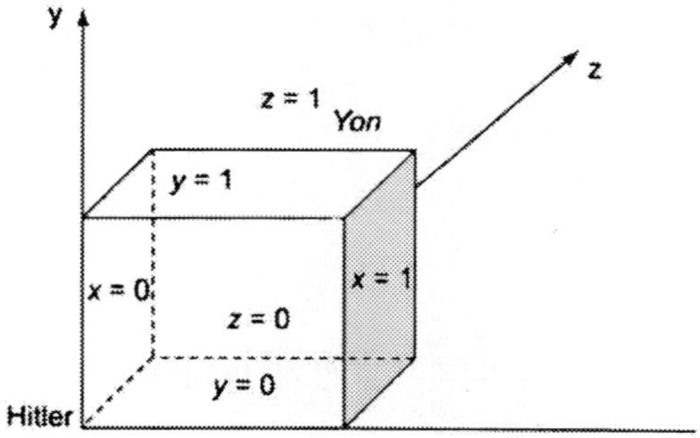

FIGURE 9.12 Canonical Parallel View Volume

(b) Perspective view volume:

Least Significant Bit (LSB)	Bit1 = 1 end point is above the view volume i.e., $(y - z) > 0$
	Bit2 = 1 end point is below the view volume i.e., $(-z - y) > 0$
	Bit3 = 1 end point is right of the view volume i.e., $(x - z) > 0$
	Bit4 = 1 end point is left of the view volume i.e., $(-z - x) > 0$
Most Significant Bit (MSB) ↓	Bit5 = 1 end point is behind the view volume i.e., $(z - 1) > 0$
	Bit6 = 1 end point is behind the view volume i.e., $(z_f - z) > 0$

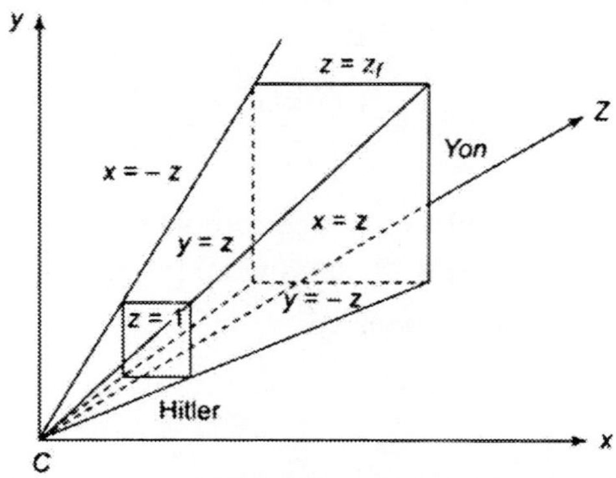

FIGURE 9.13 Canonical Perspective View Volume

Thus, six bit code is

$$\text{CODE} = 2^5 \times \text{Bit6} + 2^4 \times \text{Bit5} + 2^3 \times \text{Bit4} + 2^2 \times \text{Bit3} + 2^1 \times \text{Bit2} + 2^0 \times \text{Bit1}$$

Step 3

(a) Visible:
Codes of both end points are equal to 0000, and then draw line (totally visible).

(b) Non-visible:
If logical AND of 6 bit code of both end points is not equal to 0000, and then ignore line (totally invisible).

(c) Clipping candidate (partially visible):
If logical AND of 6 bit code of both end points is equal to 0000, then line is clipping candidate.

In case the line intersects the view volume we are interested to compute the point of intersection(s). The process of point of intersection uses the parametric equation of the line from $A(x1,y1,z1)$ to $B(x2,y2,z2)$:

$$x = x1 + u(x2 - x1) \quad 9.1(a)$$

$$y = y1 + u(y2 - y1) \quad 9.1(b)$$

$$z = z1 + u(z2 - z1) \quad 9.1(c)$$

where, u varies from 0 to 1.

As the u varies from 0 to 1, the three equations give all the points on the line, from A to B.

To compute the point of intersection of the line

(a) Canonical parallel view volume with the $y = 1$ plane of the view volume, simplify the equation 9.1(b) for u after replacing the value of y with 1.

If u lies outside the range 0 and 1, the line does not intersect the view volume. If the value of u lies in the range $0 \le u \le 1$, then the line crosses the view volume and that value of u is used in equations 9.1(a) and 9.1(c) to compute the values of x and z coordinates of point of intersection (in question).

From 9.1(a), we have $$x = x1 + \frac{(x2 - x1)(1 - y1)}{y2 - y1}$$

From 9.1(c), we have $$z = z1 + \frac{(z2 - z1)(1 - y1)}{y2 - y1}$$

Therefore, point of intersection with $y = 1$ plane is

$$\left(x1 + \frac{(x2 - x1)(1 - y1)}{y2 - y1}, 1, z1 + \frac{(z2 - z1)(1 - z1)}{z2 - z1} \right)$$

Likewise point of intersection with other planes can be computed.

(b) To compute point of intersection with the canonical perspective view volume:

With plane $y = z$ plane for the view volume, we have

$$y1 + u(y2 - y1) = z1 + u(z2 - z1)$$

Simplifying for u, we have

$$u = \frac{z1 - y1}{(y2 - y1) - (z2 - z1)}$$

Putting that value of u in equations 9.1(a) and 9.1(b) to compute the value of x and y.

$$x = x1 + \frac{(z1 - y1)(x2 - x1)}{(y2 - y1) - (z2 - z1)}, \quad y = y1 + \frac{(z1 - y1)(y2 - y1)}{(y2 - y1) - (z2 - z1)}$$

Since $y = z$, therefore

$$z = y = y1 + \frac{(z1 - y1)(y2 - y1)}{(y2 - y1) - (z2 - z1)}$$

Therefore, point of intersection with $y = z$ plane is

$$\left\{x1 + \frac{(z1 - y1)(x2 - x1)}{(y2 - y1) - (z2 - z1)}, y1 + \frac{(z1 - y1)(y2 - y1)}{(y2 - y1) - (z2 - z1)}, y1 + \frac{(z1 - y1)(y2 - y1)}{(y2 - y1) - (z2 - z1)}\right\}$$

EXERCISES

1. Define View Plane, View Volume, Clipping, Window, Front, Back Plane.
2. Is projection and clipping are interchangeable? If yes, which sequence is more efficient? Explain.
3. How do you check whether a point P is inside or outside a view volume?
4. Differentiate between 2D clipping and 3D clipping.
5. What are the various stages involved in mapping a 3D object on 2D view plane? Explain briefly.
6. Differentiate between *direct clipping* and *normalized clipping*. Which is easy to perform? Explain.
7. Describe Cohen-Sutherland algorithm to clip a 3D line against a normalized view volume.
8. Sketch parallel view volume and perspective view volume. Write equations of planes for normalized parallel view volume and normalized perspective view volume.
9. Explain the importance of normalized view volume.
10. Why there are two types of view volumes – parallel and perspective?
11. Is position of window effects on size of image so formed on it? If yes, Justify it.
12. Find points of intersection of a 3D line $A(6,10,3)$ to $B(-3, -5, 2)$ when it intersects with normalized parallel view volume and normalized perspective view volume.

10

Hidden Lines and Hidden Surfaces

10.1 INTRODUCTION

Whenever 3D objects are projected on 2D view plane, lines and surfaces that are closer to viewer block the lines and surfaces that are far from the viewer. The blocked or hidden surfaces must be removed in order to render a realistic image. The identification and removal of those surfaces is called hidden surface problem. The solution involves the determination of depth and visibility for all the points/lines/surfaces in the picture. Further, it may be possible that hidden lines/hidden surfaces may occur when a 3D object is viewed directly.

We are interested to determine which lines or surfaces of the objects are visible, along the lines of projection in case of parallel projection or from centre of projection in case of perspective projection, so that we can display only *visible lines* or *surfaces*. This process is called **visible line/visible surface determination**, or **hidden line/hidden-surface elimination.**

A number of algorithms have been derived for identification of visible objects based upon different applications. Some methods are more efficient requiring more memory and more processing time. Some of these are applicable to special type of objects, but none of them is the best.

Based upon whether to deal with objects directly or with their project images, visible-surface algorithms are broadly classified as:

Object-space Method

These methods are implemented on physical coordinate system in which the object is described. These methods are independent of display devices. Effort required for implementation of such methods is a function n^2, where n is the number of objects.

Image-space Method

These methods are implemented on screen coordinate system. These methods depend on the resolution of display devices. The effort is function of $n.N$, where N is the number of pixels in the display and n is the number of objects.

Generally, $n.N$ is larger than n^2 . Most visible surface algorithms used image-surface algorithms. These methods are more efficient than object-space method because it is easier to take advantage of coherence in a raster scan implementation of an image space algorithm.

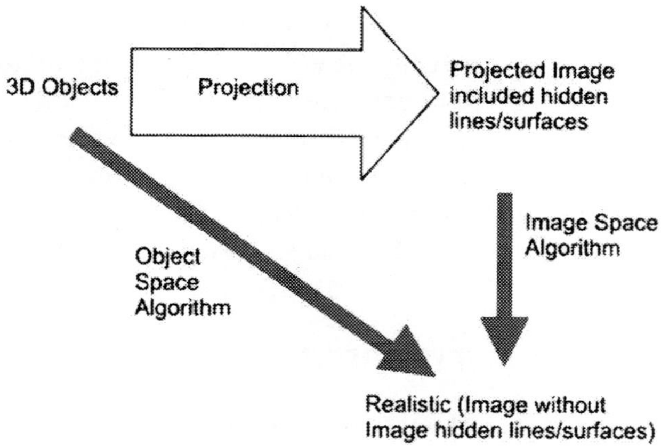

FIGURE 10.1 Illustration to Achieve Realistic Image after Removal hidden lines/hidden Surfaces Through Image Space Algorithm and Object Space Algorithm

Principle of Hidden-surface Elimination Methods

All hidden lines/surface elimination methods based upon principle whenever a picture contains opaque object and surfaces, those that are closer to the eye and in the line of sight of other objects will block those object from view.

Given two points $P1(x1, y1, z1)$ and $P2(x2, y2, z2)$. To check either point obscures the other? In case $P1$ and $P2$ are on same projection line i.e., for an orthographic projection on to the xy plane, and if $z1<z2$, then $P1$ obscures $P2$, as shown in Fig. 10.2(a). In case of perspective projection, 10.2(b), the calculations are more complex. Here we can take the help of perspective to parallel transformation.

FIGURE 10.2 Depth Comparison

All hidden line/hidden surface algorithms involve sorting. The order in which sorting of the geometric coordinates occur is generally immaterial to the efficiency of the algorithms. The principal sort is based on the geometric distance of a volume, surface, edge or point from the viewpoint. After establishing the distance or depth priority, it remains to sort laterally and vertically to determine whether in fact an object is observed by those closer to the viewpoint. The efficiency of a hidden line/ hidden surface algorithm depends significantly on the efficiency of the sorting process. Coherence i.e., the tendency for the characteristics of a scene to be locally constant, is used to increase the efficiency of the sort.

10.2 Z-BUFFER ALGORITHM (DEPTH BUFFER ALGORITHM)

The z-buffer is one of the simplest algorithms of the hidden surface removal. The technique was originally proposed by Catmull and is an image space method. The z-buffer is a simple extension of the frame buffer idea. A frame buffer is used to store the attributes (intensity) of each pixel in image space. The z-buffer is a separate depth buffer used to store the z-coordinate or depth of every visible pixel in image space as illustrated in Fig. 10.3(a) and 10.3(b).

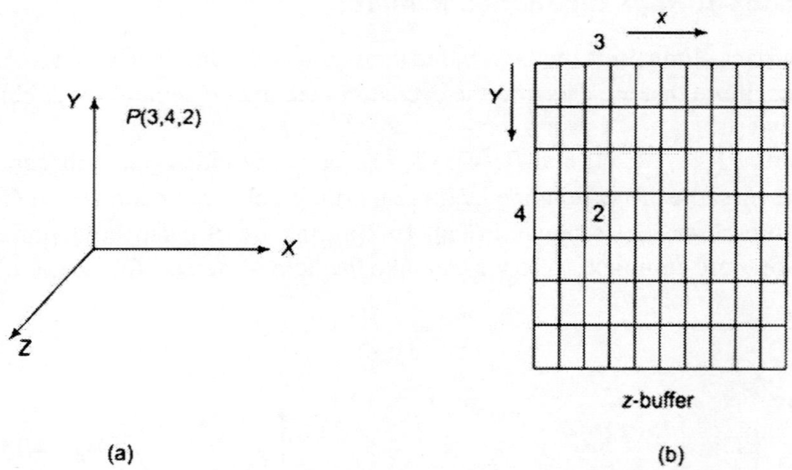

FIGURE 10.3 Representation of a 3D point in z-buffer

The depth or z-value of a new pixel to be written to a frame buffer is compared to the depth or z-value of the pixel already stored in the z-buffer. If the comparison indicates that the z-value of the new pixel is greater than z-value already stored in the z-buffer, then z-buffer is updated with the new z-value and intensity of new pixel is written in frame buffer, otherwise no action is taken.

Figure 10.4 depicts the triangle XYZ covering some portion of rectangle ABCD.

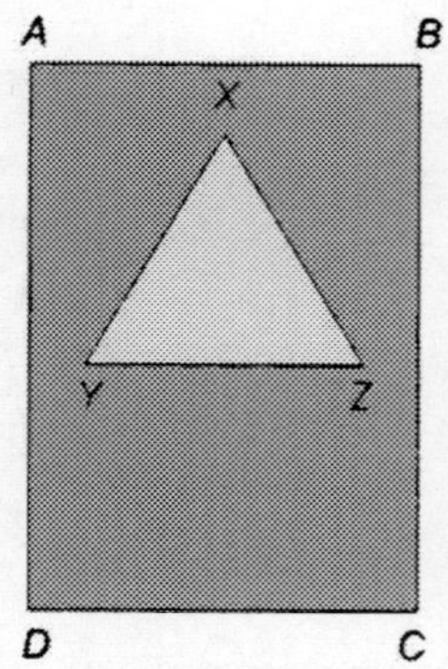

FIGURE 10.4

0	0	0	0	0	0	0	0	0	0	0	0	0
0	0	0	0	0	0	0	0	0	0	0	0	0
0	1	1	1	1	1	1	1	1	1	1	1	0
0	1	1	1	1	1	1	1	1	1	1	1	0
0	1	1	1	1	1	1	1	1	1	1	1	0
0	1	1	1	1	1	1	1	1	1	1	1	0
0	1	1	1	1	1	1	1	1	1	1	1	0
0	1	1	1	1	1	1	1	1	1	1	1	0
0	1	1	1	1	1	1	1	1	1	1	1	0
0	1	1	1	1	1	1	1	1	1	1	1	0
0	1	1	1	1	1	1	1	1	1	1	1	0
0	1	1	1	1	1	1	1	1	1	1	1	0
0	1	1	1	1	1	1	1	1	1	1	1	0
0	0	0	0	0	0	0	0	0	0	0	0	0
0	0	0	0	0	0	0	0	0	0	0	0	0

Frame buffer of Rectangle

(a)

0	0	0	0	0	0	0	0	0	0	0	0	0
0	0	0	0	0	0	0	0	0	0	0	0	0
0	6	6	6	6	6	6	6	6	6	6	6	0
0	6	6	6	6	6	6	6	6	6	6	6	0
0	6	6	6	6	6	6	6	6	6	6	6	0
0	6	6	6	6	6	6	6	6	6	6	6	0
0	6	6	6	6	6	6	6	6	6	6	6	0
0	6	6	6	6	6	6	6	6	6	6	6	0
0	6	6	6	6	6	6	6	6	6	6	6	0
0	6	6	6	6	6	6	6	6	6	6	6	0
0	6	6	6	6	6	6	6	6	6	6	6	0
0	6	6	6	6	6	6	6	6	6	6	6	0
0	6	6	6	6	6	6	6	6	6	6	6	0
0	0	0	0	0	0	0	0	0	0	0	0	0
0	0	0	0	0	0	0	0	0	0	0	0	0

Z-buffer of Rectangle

(b)

0	0	0	0	0	0	0	0	0	0	0	0	0
0	0	0	0	0	0	0	0	0	0	0	0	0
0	0	0	0	0	0	2	0	0	0	0	0	0
0	0	0	0	0	2	2	2	0	0	0	0	0
0	0	0	0	2	2	2	2	2	0	0	0	0
0	0	0	2	2	2	2	2	2	2	0	0	0
0	0	2	2	2	2	2	2	2	2	2	0	0
0	0	0	0	0	0	0	0	0	0	0	0	0
0	0	0	0	0	0	0	0	0	0	0	0	0
0	0	0	0	0	0	0	0	0	0	0	0	0
0	0	0	0	0	0	0	0	0	0	0	0	0
0	0	0	0	0	0	0	0	0	0	0	0	0
0	0	0	0	0	0	0	0	0	0	0	0	0
0	0	0	0	0	0	0	0	0	0	0	0	0

Frame buffer of Triangle

(c)

0	0	0	0	0	0	0	0	0	0	0	0	0
0	0	0	0	0	0	0	0	0	0	0	0	0
0	0	0	0	0	0	8	0	0	0	0	0	0
0	0	0	0	0	8	8	8	0	0	0	0	0
0	0	0	0	8	8	8	8	8	0	0	0	0
0	0	0	8	8	8	8	8	8	8	0	0	0
0	0	8	8	8	8	8	8	8	8	8	0	0
0	0	0	0	0	0	0	0	0	0	0	0	0
0	0	0	0	0	0	0	0	0	0	0	0	0
0	0	0	0	0	0	0	0	0	0	0	0	0
0	0	0	0	0	0	0	0	0	0	0	0	0
0	0	0	0	0	0	0	0	0	0	0	0	0
0	0	0	0	0	0	0	0	0	0	0	0	0
0	0	0	0	0	0	0	0	0	0	0	0	0

Z-buffer of Triangle

(d)

0	0	0	0	0	0	0	0	0	0	0	0	0
0	0	0	0	0	0	0	0	0	0	0	0	0
0	1	1	1	1	1	1	1	1	1	1	1	0
0	1	1	1	1	1	2	1	1	1	1	1	0
0	1	1	1	1	2	2	2	1	1	1	1	0
0	1	1	1	2	2	2	2	2	1	1	1	0
0	1	1	2	2	2	2	2	2	2	1	1	0
0	1	2	2	2	2	2	2	2	2	2	1	0
0	1	1	1	1	1	1	1	1	1	1	1	0
0	1	1	1	1	1	1	1	1	1	1	1	0
0	1	1	1	1	1	1	1	1	1	1	1	0
0	1	1	1	1	1	1	1	1	1	1	1	0
0	1	1	1	1	1	1	1	1	1	1	1	0
0	0	0	0	0	0	0	0	0	0	0	0	0
0	0	0	0	0	0	0	0	0	0	0	0	0

Frame buffer of Fig. 10.4
(e)

0	0	0	0	0	0	0	0	0	0	0	0	0
0	0	0	0	0	0	0	0	0	0	0	0	0
0	6	6	6	6	6	6	6	6	6	6	6	0
0	6	6	6	6	6	8	6	6	6	6	6	0
0	6	6	6	6	8	8	8	6	6	6	6	0
0	6	6	6	8	8	8	8	8	6	6	6	0
0	6	6	8	8	8	8	8	8	8	6	6	0
0	6	8	8	8	8	8	8	8	8	8	6	0
0	6	6	6	6	6	6	6	6	6	6	6	0
0	6	6	6	6	6	6	6	6	6	6	6	0
0	6	6	6	6	6	6	6	6	6	6	6	0
0	6	6	6	6	6	6	6	6	6	6	6	0
0	6	6	6	6	6	6	6	6	6	6	6	0
0	0	0	0	0	0	0	0	0	0	0	0	0
0	0	0	0	0	0	0	0	0	0	0	0	0

Z-buffer of Fig.10.4
(f)

FIGURE 10.5 Demonstration of Z-Buffer Method

Algorithm: Z-Buffer Algorithm for Hidden lines/Hidden Surface Removal

Step 1: Set the frame buffer to the background intensity color.

$$\text{frame\_buffer}(x,y) = I_{\text{background}}$$

Step 2: Set the z buffer to the minimum value. $Z_{\text{buffer}}(x,y)=0$

Step 3: For each pixel (x,y) in the polygon, calculate the depth $z(x,y)$ at that pixel.

Step 4: Compare the depth $z(x,y)$ with the value stored in the z-buffer at that location, $Z_{\text{buffer}}(x,y)$ to determine the visibility.

If $z(x,y) > Z_{\text{buffer}}(x,y)$, then write the polygon attributes (intensity, color, etc.) to the frame buffer at pixel location(x,y) and replace $Z_{\text{buffer}}(x,y)$ with $z(x,y)$ otherwise no action is taken i.e.,

$$Z_{\text{buffer}}(x,y) = z(x,y)$$

$$\text{frame\_buffer}(x,y) = I_{\text{proj}}(x,y)$$

where, $I_{proj}(x,y)$ is the projected intensity value for the surface at pixel position (x,y).

Step 5: Repeat steps 3 to 4 for all polygons in arbitrary order.

Step 6: Finally when all the polygons have been processed, the depth buffer contains depth value for the visible surfaces and the frame buffer contains the corresponding intensity values for those surfaces.

10.3 THE PAINTER'S ALGORITHM (DEPTH SORT OR PRIORITY ALGORITHM)

It was developed by Nowell, Nowell and Sancha.

The Painter's algorithm based upon the principle that more distance polygons are painted first, and over it the next farther polygon, totally or partially obscuring them from view, and so on, as depicted in

Fig. 10.6. Now the basic problem is to find priority ordering of the polygons in order to determine which polygons are to be painted first (scan-converted). This determination is made by comparing x-extent, y-extent and z-extents of the various polygons.

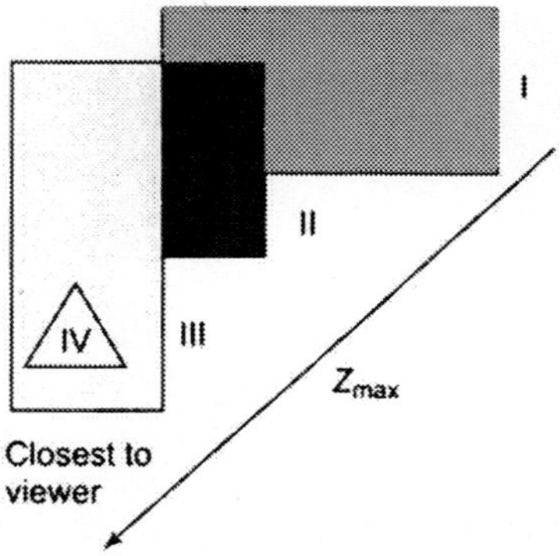

0	0	0	0	0	1	1	1	1	1
0	0	3	3	3	2	2	1	1	1
0	0	3	3	3	2	2	1	1	1
0	0	3	3	3	2	2	0	0	0
0	0	3	4	3	2	2	0	0	0
0	0	4	4	4	0	0	0	0	0
0	0	3	3	3	0	0	0	0	0
0	0	0	0	0	0	0	0	0	0
0	0	0	0	0	0	0	0	0	0
0	0	0	0	0	0	0	0	0	0

Frame Buffer

FIGURE 10.6 Illustration of Painter's Algorithm (when Polygons are parallel to each other)

Tests whether *P* obscures Q

Polygon *P* does not obscure polygon *Q* if any one of the following tests, applied in sequential order, is ture. Alternatively, *P* obscures *Q* if all of the following tests are found to be true.

Test 0: The *Z* extent of *P* and *Q* do not overlap and Z_{Qmax} of *Q* is smaller than Z_{Pmin} of *P*.

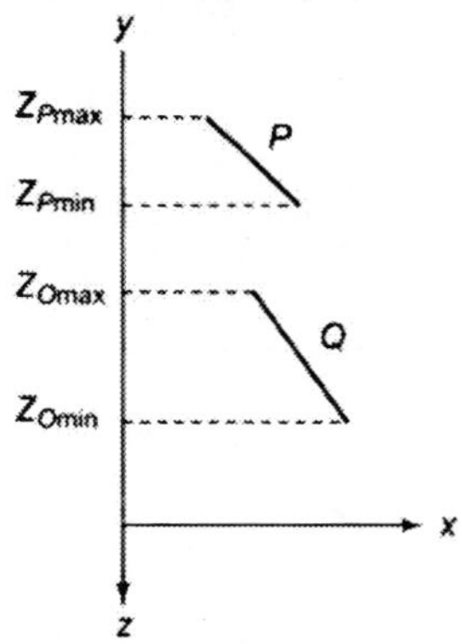

Test 1: The *Y* extent of *P* and *Q* do not overlap and Y_{Qmax} of *Q* is smaller than Y_{Pmin} of *P*.

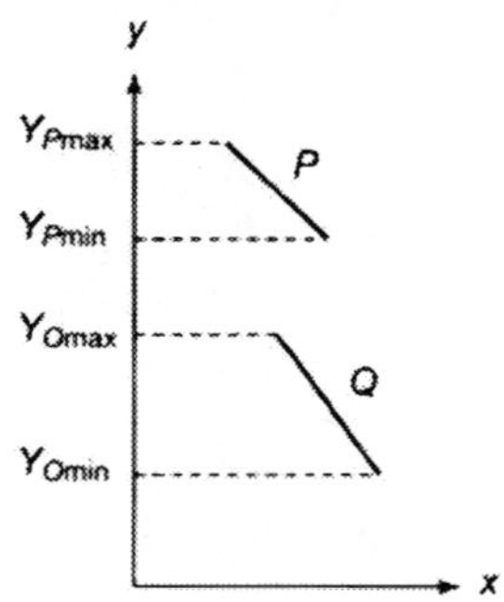

Test 2: The X extent of P and Q do not overlap and X_{Qmax} of Q is smaller than X_{Pmin} of P.

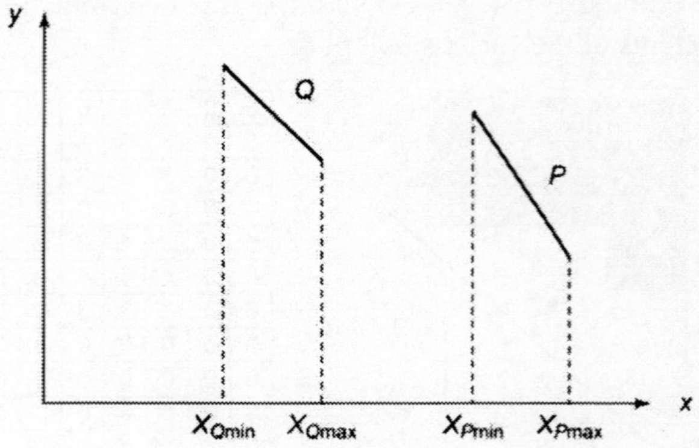

Test 3: All the vertices of P lie on that side of the plane containing Q which is farthest from the viewpoint.

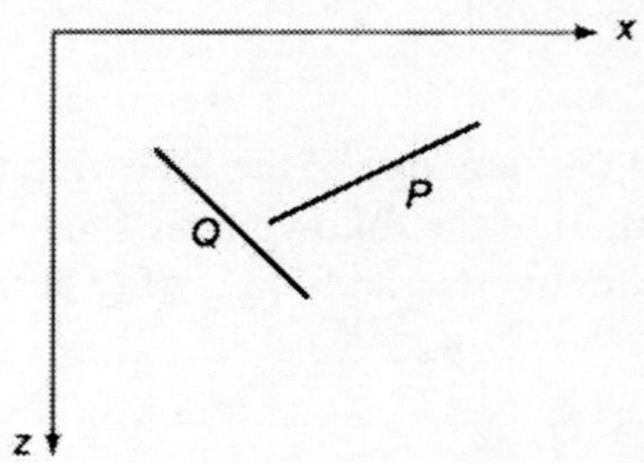

Test 4: All the vertices of Q lie on that side of the plane containing P which is closest to the viewpoint.

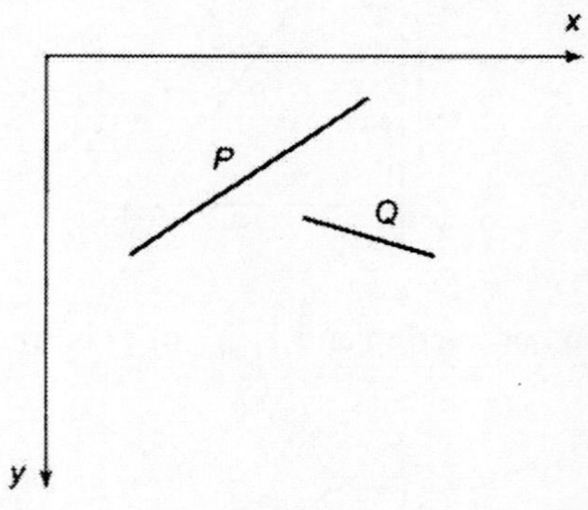

Test 5: The projection of the polygons P and onto the xy screen does not overlap. This is checked by comparing each edge of one polygon against each edge of the other polygon to search for interactions.

Algorithm

Step 1: Sort all polygons into a polygon list according to Z_{max}. Starting from the end of the list, assign priorities for each polygon P.

Step 2: Find all polygons (preceding P) in the polygon list whose Z extents overlap that of P(test 0 is false).

Step 3: For each Q, perform tests 1 through 5.
   (a) If every Q, test 1 to test 5 true, P does not obscure Q, scan convert polygon P.
   (b) If false for some Q, swap P and Q on the list tag Q as swapped, if Q has already been tagged, use the plane containing polygon P to divide polygon Q into two polygons, Q_1 and Q_2. The polygon-clipping techniques can be used to perform the division. Remove Q from the list and place Q_1 and Q_2 on the list, in sorted order.

10.4 AREA-SUBDIVISION ALGORITHM

The area-subdivision algorithm was developed by Warnock. This algorithm follows the "***divide-and-conquer***" strategy.

This algorithm based on two steps:

1 First decide which polygons are visible in area, they are displayed.

2 Otherwise the area is divided into four equal areas, on each area those polygons are further tested to determine which ones should therfore be displayed. If a visibility descision cannot be made, this second area, is further subdivided either until a visibility decision can be made or until the screen area is a single pixel.

This method is also termed **Quadtree Method.**

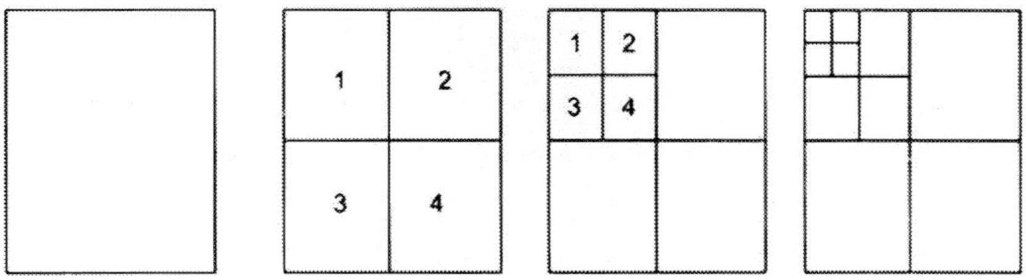

(a) Initial Area (b) First Subdivision (c) Second Subdivision (d) Third Subdivision

FIGURE 10.7

To check the visibility of a polygon within the viewport, its x-extent and y-extent are compared with the horizontal and vertical spans of the viewports, and classified as one of the following categories:

(a) Surrounding: A polygon surrounds a viewport if it completely encloses or covers the viewport. Refer to Fig. 10.8(a).

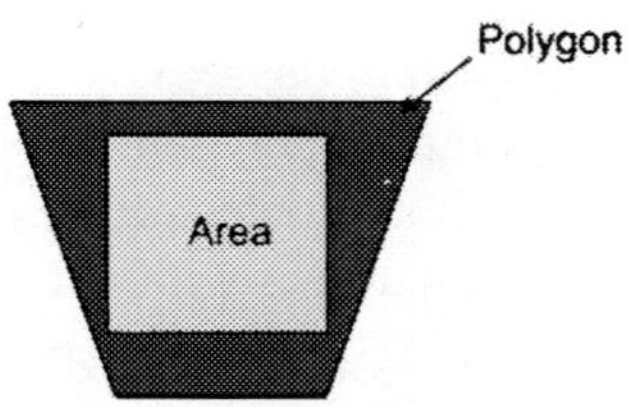

FIGURE 10.8(a) Surrounding

(b) Contained: A polygon is contained in a viewport if no part of it is outside any of the edges of the viewport. Refer to Fig. 10.8(b).

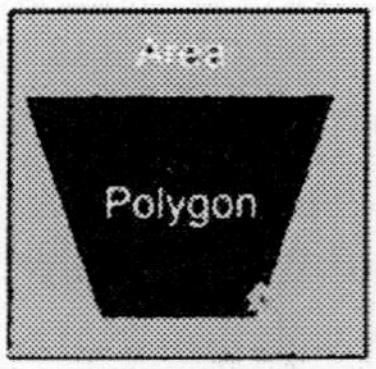

FIGURE 10.8(b) Contained

(c) Disjoint: A polygon is disjoint from the viewport if the x-extent and y-extents of the polygon do not overlap the viewport anywhere. Refer Fig. 10.7(c).

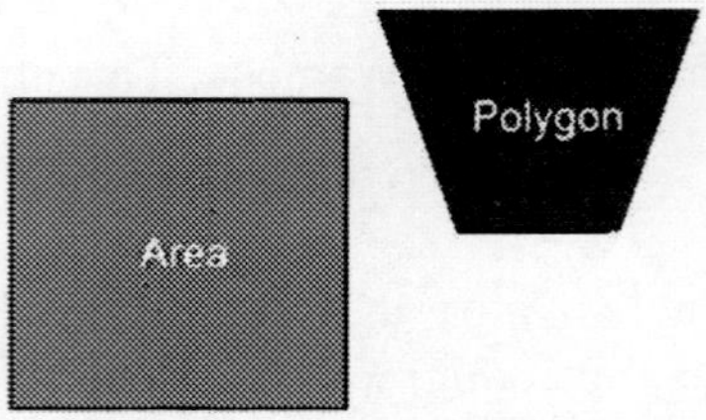

FIGURE 10.8(c) Disjoint

(d) Overlapping or Intersecting: A polygon overlaps or intersects the current background if any of its side cuts the edges of viewport. Refer to Fig. 10.8(d).

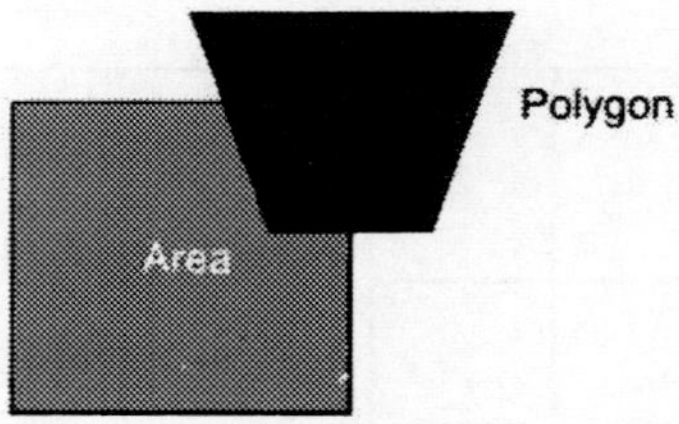

FIGURE 10.8(d) Intersecting

Disjoint polygons have no effect on area of interest. The part of intersecting polygon that is outside the area is also irrelevant, whereas the part of an intersecting polygon inside the interior to the area is the same as a contained polygon.

Algorithm

Step 1: Initialize the area to be the whole screen.
Step 2: Area does not need to be further subdivided if one of the following conditions is true:

a. All the polygons are **outside** with respect to the area.
b. There is only **one intersecting** or **contained** polygon.
c. There is **single surrounding** polygon, but no intersecting or contained polygon.
d. Surrounding surface **obscures** all other surfaces within the area boundaries.

Step 3: For any remaining polygon, the viewport is divided into four quarters, and each viewport segment is evaluated for step 2. We continue this process until the subdivisions are easily analysed as belonging to single surface or until they are reduced to the size of a single pixel. A viewing area with resolution 1024 × 1024 could be required up to 10 subdivisions.

Step 4: If area is the pixel (x,y), compute $z(x,y)$ at (x,y) of all polygons. Set color of pixel with smallest z coordinate.

10.5 SCAN LINE ALGORITHM

Scan line algorithms, first developed by Wylie, Romnef, Evans and Erdahl, Birkright and Watkins.

It is an extension of the polygon scan conversion algorithm.. The difference is that here we deal with a set of polygons.

The following data structures are created:

(a) Edge Table (ET)

It consists of all non-horizontal edges of all polygons projected on the view plane, horizontal edges are ignored. Each entry of the edge table contains the following informations:

(i) The x coordinate of the end of the edge with the smaller y coordinate.

(ii) The y coordinate of the edge's other end (y_{max}).

(iii) The x increment, $\Delta x = \frac{1}{m}$ used in stepping in increment one scan line to next.

(iv) The polygon identification number, indicating the polygon to which the edge belongs.

ET entry

x	y_{max}	Δx	ID

Figure 10.9 depicts the rule to construct edge table (ET).

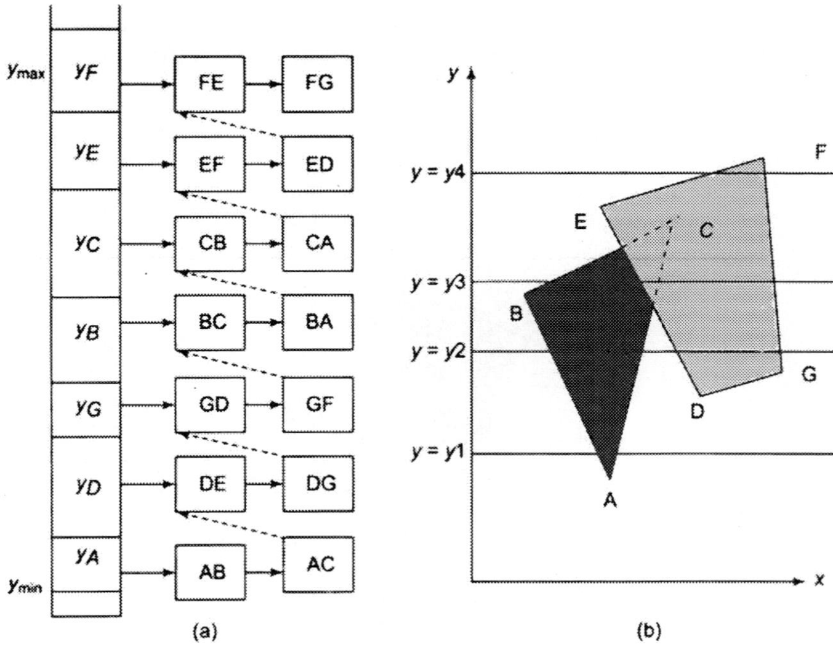

ET : AB → AC → DE → DG → GF → BC → EF → FE

(After removing the repeated edges)

FIGURE 10.9

(b) Polygon Table (PT)

It contains the following information for each polygon:

(i) The coefficient of the plane equation. This helps us to compute the z value(depth) at (x,y).
(ii) Color information for the polygon.
(iii) In-out Boolean *flag,* initialized to false and used during scan-line processing. This flag helps us to check whether a scan line in or out a polygon.

PT Entry	ID	Equation of polygon	Color	Status(IN/OUT)

(c) Active Edge Table (AET)

The AET contains only edges that cross the current scan line, sorted in order of increment x.

Scan line	*Entries*
$y = y1$	*AB,AC*
$y = y2$	*AB,AC, DE,FG*
$y = y3$	*BC,DE, AC, FG*
$Y=y4$	*EF,FG*

Algorithm

Step 1: Initialize each screen pixel to the background color.

Step 2: Activate edges whose $y = y_{min}$. Sort activates edges in order of increasing x.

Step 3: Process from left-to-right, each active edge list.

(a) *AEL* for scan line $y = y1$ contains edges entries *AB* and *AC* in that order. The edges are processed from left to right. In this case, only the flag for polygon *ABC* becomes true; thus, the Scan is "**in**" the polygon *ABC*. Therefore, no depth calculations are required. Intensity information for polygon *ABC* accessed from its *PT* as shown in Fig. 10.10.

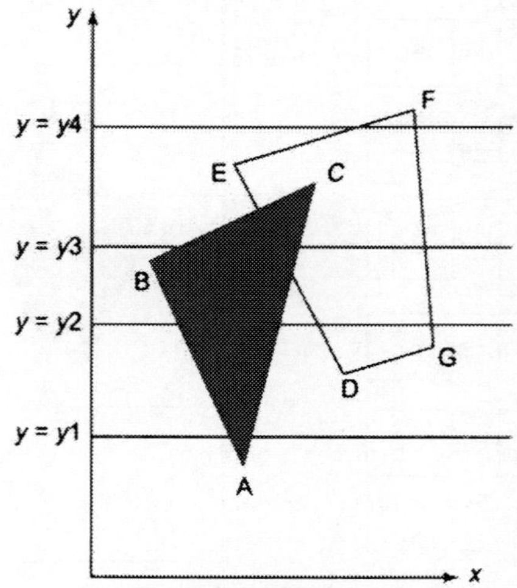

FIGURE 10.10

(b) *AEL* for scan line $y = y2$ contains edges entries *AB*, *AC*, *DE* and *FG* in that order. The edges are processed from left to right. In this case, processing precedes much as before. There are two polygons on the scan line, but the scan is "**in**" only one polygon at a time.

In between the edges *AB* and *AC*, flag for polygon *ABC* becomes true; thus, the scan is "**in**" for the polygon *ABC*. Therefore, no depth calculations are required. Intensity information for polygon *ABC* accessed from its *PT*. Now because the scan is "**in**" only one polygon (*ABC*), it must be visible, so the shading for *ABC* is applied to the span from edge *AB* to the next edge in the *AET*, edge *AC*, at this edge flag for *ABC* is inverted to false, so that scan is no longer "**in**", as shown in Fig. 10.10(a).

Similarly, between the edges *DE* and *FG*, flag for only polygon *DEFG* becomes true; thus, the Scan is "**in**" for the polygon *DEFG*. Therefore, no depth calculations are required. Intensity information for polygon *DEFG* accessed from its *PT* as shown in Fig. 10.11(b).

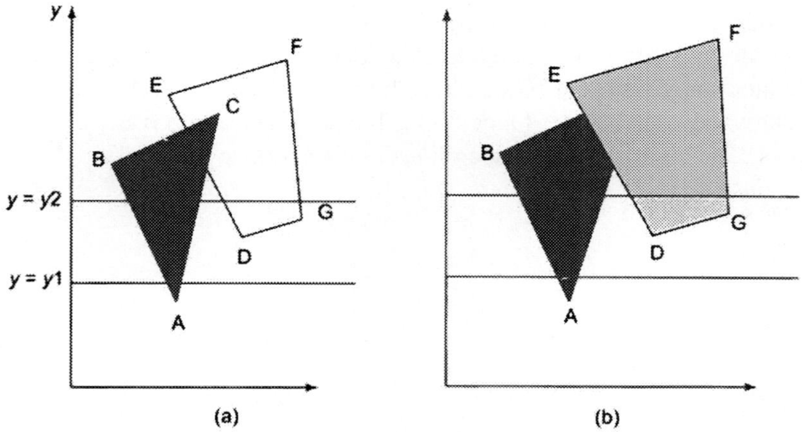

FIGURE 10.11

(c) *AEL* for scan line $y = y3$ contains edges entries *BC*, *DE*, *AC*, *FG* in that order. When this scan line entering polygon *ABC*, its flag becomes true. *ABC*'s shade is used for span up to the next edge, *DE*. At this point, the flag for *DEFG* also becomes true, so the scan line "**in**" two polygons simultaneously. Thus, we have seen that between the edges *ED* and *AC* the flags for both polygons are true. In this interval depth calculations must be made using the plane equations. On the basis of depths, we will decide whether *ABC* or *DEFG* is closer to the viewer. In this example we assume *DEFG* is closer to viewer. Therefore, the shading for *DEFG* is used for the span to edge *CB*, at which point *ABC*'s flag becomes false and the scan is again "**in**" only one polygon *DEFG* whose shade continues to be used up to edge *FG* as shown in Fig. 10.12.

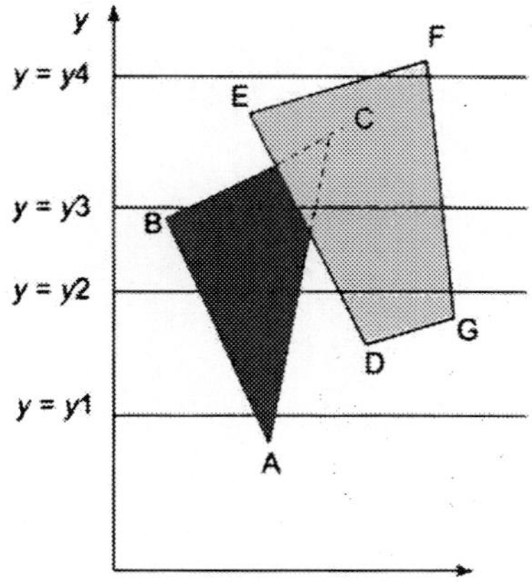

FIGURE 10.12

EXERCISES

1. What is the importance of hidden lines/hidden surfaces removal?
2. Explain the basic principle for removal of hidden lines/hidden surfaces.
3. Differentiate between image-space method and object-space method for hidden lines/hidden surface removal. Which is easier to implement? Why?
4. How does scan-line algorithm help to reduce computation?
5. Why are non-horizontal lines stored in the edge list of the scan-list algorithm?
6. Is it possible that two polygons have the same z value? What happens when two polygons have the same z value and the Z-buffer algorithm is used?
7. Describe Z-buffer algorithm for hidden lines/hidden surface removal.
8. Describe Painter's algorithm for hidden lines/hidden surface removal.
9. Describe Subdivision Method for hidden lines/hidden surface removal.
10. Describe Scan Line algorithm for hidden lines/hidden surface removal.

11

Bezier Curves and B-Splines

11.1 INTRODUCTION

Given a set of discrete coordinate points a function is obtained that best fits the designated points. Splines are examples of this class of curves and surfaces. Curves and surface equations can be expressed in parametric or non-parametric equation. One of the objectives of computer graphics is modeling of objects. Curve surfaces allow constructing modeling.

In historic days, splines were specified mechanically by systems such as flexible strips of wood or metal that were tied into position to record a desired curve. These mechanical systems were difficult to work and they could not use to give permanent reproducible description of a curve. Nowadays, mathematical descriptions are more useful and permanent. In 1970s, a French engineer, Pierre Bezier developed a method of fitting of polynomial curve. Bezier curves were first developed by automobile designers to describe the shape of exterior car panels.

11.2 PRELIMINARY DEFINITIONS

11.2.1 Convex Plane

A subset *S* of the plane is called *convex* if and only if for every pair of points *p*,*q* in *S*, the line segment pq is completely contained in *S*.

11.2.2 Convex Hull

Definition #1: The convex hull *CH*(*S*) of a set *S* is the smallest convex set that contains *S*.

Definition #2: The convex hull *CH*(*S*) of a set *S* is the intersection of all convex sets that contain *S*.

Definition #3: The convex hull *CH*(*S*) of a set *S* is the unique convex polygon which contains *S* and all of whose vertices are points from *S*.

11.2.3 Spline

Splines are smooth curves passing through given set of points.

Splines can be either closed or open.They are the basic 2D shapes which will later be used to make 3D objects.

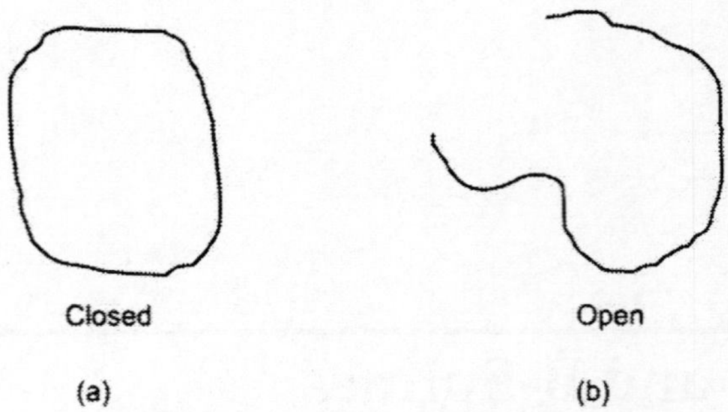

FIGURE 11.1 Spline Curves

Cubic splines are popular because they are simpler to compute, provide continuity of the curve, its slope, if necessary its curvature at appoint. Any curve may be built of a series of cubic segments.

The general equation of 2-D cubic spline is:

$$y = a_0 + a_1 t + a_2 t^2 + a_3 t^3 \tag{11.1}$$

where, a_0, a_1, a_2, and a_3 are constants to be computed, thus we require four boundary conditions to evaluate four unknowns.

Parametric form of 2-D cubic spline is:

$$x = a_0 + a_1 u + a_2 u^2 + a_3 u^3$$
$$y = b_0 + b_1 u + b_2 u^2 + b_3 u^3$$

where, the parameter u lies between minimum and maximum values to cover the desired range of the curve.

Parametric form of 3D spline is

$$x = f(t) \quad , \quad y = g(t) \quad , \quad z = h(t)$$

where, (x,y,z) is a point on the curve corresponding to a unique value of $t(0 \le t \le 1)$.

In general, the function

$x = f(t)$ is polynomial function of degree n in t and is given by:

$$f(t) = a_0 + a_1 t + a_2 t^2 + a_3 t^3 + a_4 t^4 \ldots a_{n-1} t^{n-1} + a_n t^n$$

Similarly for $y = g(t)$ and $z = h(t)$.

The nature and shape of curve varies with value of n. We get straight line when $n = 1$; quadratic plane curve when $n = 2$; cubic space curve when $n = 3$; a quadratic space curve when $n = 4$, and so on.

Parametric form of 3D cubic spline is

$$x = a_0 + a_1 u + a_2 u^2 + a_3 u^3$$
$$y = b_0 + b_1 u + b_2 u^2 + b_3 u^3$$
$$z = c_0 + c_1 u + c_2 u^2 + c_3 u^3$$

where, the parameter u lies between minimum and maximum values to cover the desired range of the curve.

Depending on the type of polynomials used and set of boundary conditions satisfied, spline curves classified into following categories:

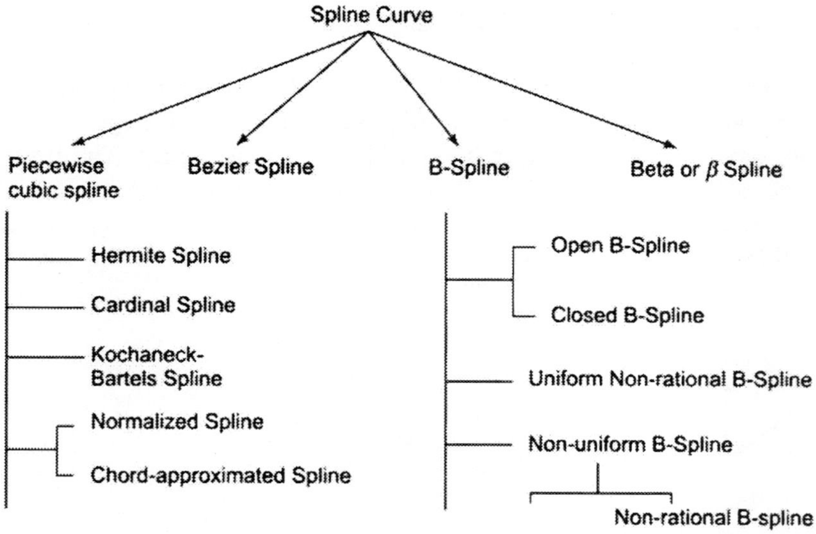

FIGURE 11.2 Classification of Spline Curves

Above-mentioned spline curves can be put into following two basic categories depending on how they fit the given set of data points (control points):

11.2.4 Interpolated Spline

When curve passes through ***each*** control point, the resulting curve is said to interpolated spline.

FIGURE 11.3 Interpolated Curve

11.2.5 Approximated Spline

When curve need not necessarily passing through each control point, it approximates the shape of the control polygon, the resulting curve is said to approximated spline.

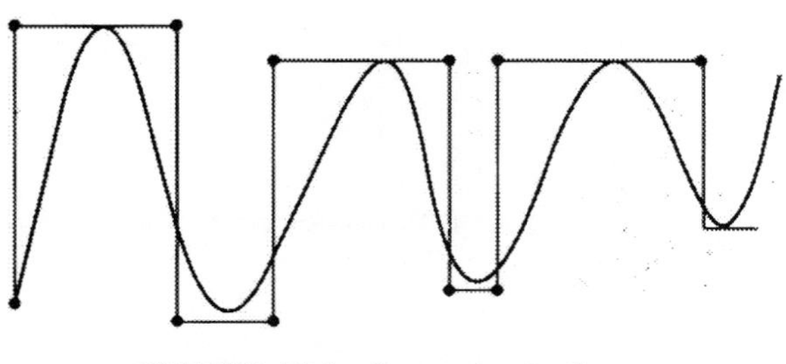

FIGURE 11.4 Approximate Curve

11.3 BEZIER CURVE AND BEZIER SURFACE

In 1970s, French Engineer, Pierre Bezier developed a method of fitting of polynomial curve. Bezier curves useful in innovative geometric deign of cars, planes, architectural shape, etc.

In chapter 2, we have specified a line by the position of its end points. The Bresenham or anti-aliased algorithm simply draws a straight line between the two points. A Bezier curve allows you to specify, not only the end points of the line, but also the direction of the line as it passes through the end points. The algorithm draws a curve that passes through the end points at an angle parallel to the specified ***direction.***

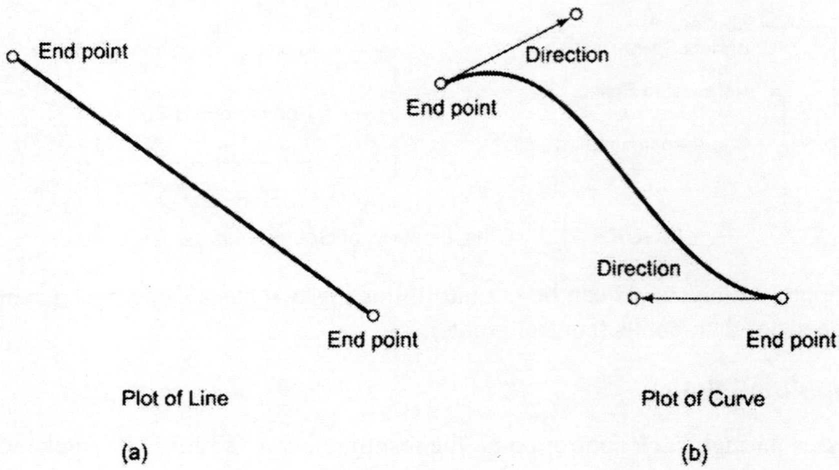

FIGURE 11.5

All sorts of curves can be specified with different direction vectors at the end points (Refer to Fig. 11.6(a)). Reflex curves appear when you set the vectors in opposite directions(Refer to Fig. 11.6(b)). Even loops can also be made(Refer to Fig. 11.6(c)).

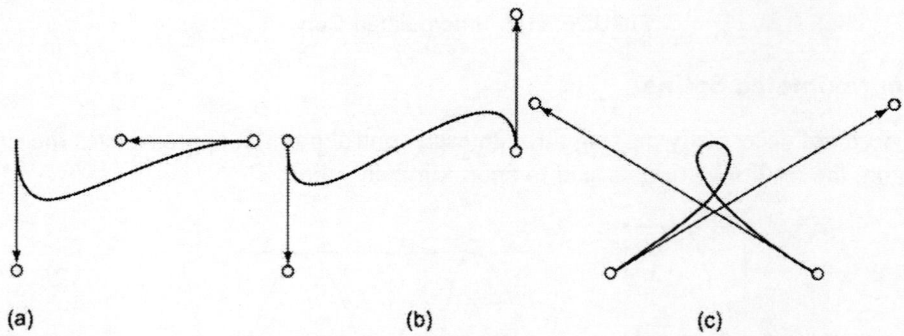

FIGURE 11.6 Different Types of Curves Based on Direction of Tangent

11.3.1 Bezier Curve

Definition

Given a set of $(n+1)$ control points $P_0, P_1, P_2, \ldots P_n$, a parametric Bezier curve (Bernstein-Bezier curve) segment is a weighted sum of $n + 1$ control points $P_0, P_1 P_1 P_2, \ldots P_n$ that will fit to those points is mathematically defined by:

$$P(t) = \sum_{i=0}^{n} P_i B_{i,n}(t)$$

where, $B_{i,n}(t)$ are the Bezier blending function, also known as Bernstein Basis functions (weights) defined as follows:

$$B_{i,n}(t) = C\{n,_i)t^i (1-t)^{n-i}$$

$$C(n,i) = \frac{n!}{i!(n-i)!}$$

Thus, a Bezier curve can be seen as a weighted average of all of its control points. Because all of the weights are positive, and because the weights sum to one, the Bezier curve is guaranteed to lie within the convex hull of its control points.

The Bezier curve of order $n + 1$ (degree n) has $n + 1$ control points. Following are the first three orders of Bezier curve definitions:

Linear $P(t) = (1-t)P_0 + tP_1$

Quadratic $P(t) = (1-t)^2 P_0 + 2(1-t)\, tP_1 + t^2 P_2$

Cubic $P(t) = (1-t)^3 P_0 + 3(1-t)^2 tP_1 + 3(1-t)\, t^2 P_2 + t^3 P_3$

$\boldsymbol{B(u)}$ is a continuous function in 3 space defining the curve with N discrete control points P_k. $u = 0$ at the first control point ($k = 0$) and $u = 1$ at the last control point ($k = N$).

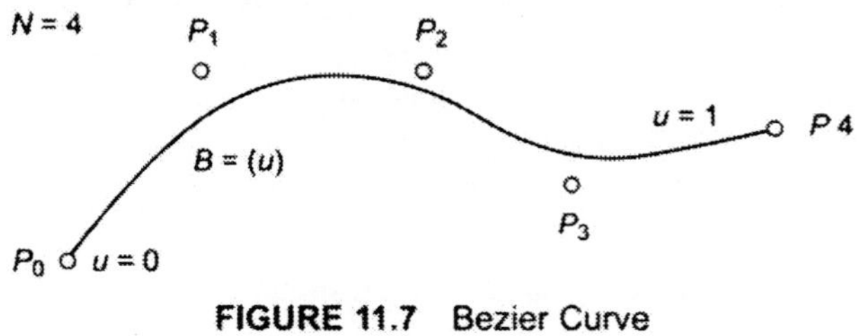

FIGURE 11.7 Bezier Curve

Properties of Bezier Curve

(1) Degree of polynomial blending function and thus Bezier curve is one less than number of control points.

(2) Bezier curve always passes through first control point P_o and last control point P_n irrespective of intermediate points ($P_1, P_2, \ldots P_{n-i}$).

(3) Beizer blending functions are all positive and their sum is always equal to 1 i.e.,

$$\sum_{i=0}^{n} B_{i,n}(t) = 1 \text{ and for } n = 3 \text{ we have } \sum_{i=0}^{3} B_{i,3}(t) = 1$$

(4) Bezier curve always lies with convex hull of the control points.

(5) First derivatives of the Bezier curve at the end points can be calculated from control points coordinates as

$$P'(0) = -np_0 + np_1$$
$$P'(1) = -np_{n-1} + np_n$$

(6) Bezier curve can be translated and rotated by performing these operations on the control points.

Undesirable Properties of Bezier Curves are

(1) Numerical instability for large numbers of control points.
(2) Moving a single control point changes the global shape of the curve.

Points to Remember

- The curve, in general, does not pass through any of the control points except the first and last. From the formula $B(0) = P_o$ and $B(1) = P_N$.
- The curve is always contained within the convex hull of the control points, it never oscillates wildly away from the control points.
- If there is only one control point P_o, *i.e.*, $N = 0$ then $\mathbf{B}(u) = P_o$ for all u.
- If there are only two control points P_o and P_1, *i.e.*, $N = 1$ then the formula reduces to a line segment between the two control points.

$$B(u) = \sum_{k=0}^{1} pk \frac{1}{k!(1-k)!} u^k (1-u)^{1-k} = p0 + u(p1 - p0)$$

the term

$$\frac{N!}{K!(N-K)!} u^K (1-u)^{N-K}$$

is called a blending function since it blends the control points to form the Bezier curve.

- The blending function is always a polynomial one degree less than the number of control points. Thus, 3 control points result in a parabola, 4 control points a cubic curve, etc.
- Closed curves can be generated by making the last control point the same as the first control point. First order continuity can be achieved by ensuring the tangent between the first two points and the last two points are the same.
- Adding multiple control points at a single position in space will add more weight to that point "pulling" the Bezier curve towards it.

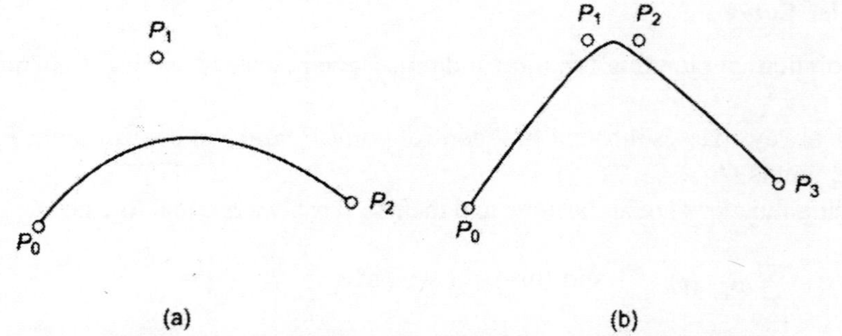

FIGURE 11.8 Effect on Shape of Curve to Add More Weight

- As the number of control points increases it is necessary to have higher order polynomials and possibly higher factorials. It is common therefore to piece together small sections of Bezier curves to form a longer curve. This also helps control local conditions; normally changing the position of one control point will affect the whole curve. Of course, since the curve starts and ends at the first and last control point it is easy to physically match the sections. It is also possible to match the first derivative since the tangent at the ends is along the line between the two points at the end. Second order continuity is generally not possible.

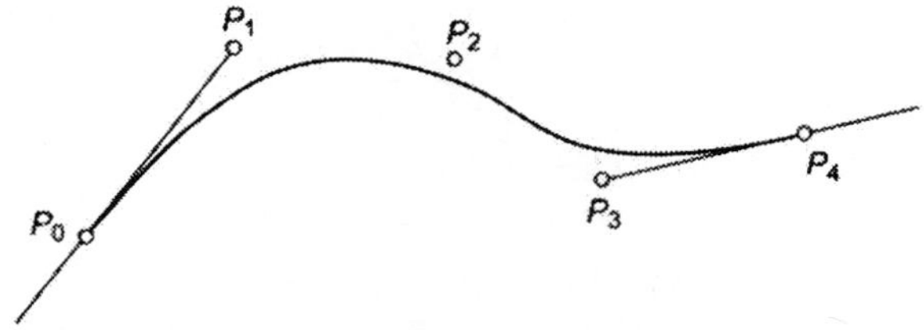

FIGURE 11.9 Role of Control Point Nearest to the End Points

- Except for the redundant cases of 2 control points (straight line), it is generally not possible to derive a Bezier curve that is parallel to another Bezier curve.
- A circle cannot be exactly represented with a Bezier curve.
- It isn't possible to create a Bezier curve that is parallel to another, except in the trivial cases of coincident parallel curves or straight line Bezier curves.
- Special case, 3 control points

$$B(u) = P_o * (1 - u)^2 + P_1 * 2 * u(1 - u) + P_2 u^2$$

- Special case, 4 control points

$$B(u) = P_o * (1 - u)^3 + P_1 * 3 * u * (1 - u)^2 + P_2 * 3 * u^2 * (1 - u) + P_3 * u^3$$

- A generalization of the Bezier curve is the B-Spline.

Bezier curves have wide applications because they are easy to compute and very stable. There are similar formulations which are also called Bezier curves which behave

Special Cases

Case I: Linear Bezier spline

Linear Bezier spline is obtained by *linear interpolation* between two *control points* P_o, P_1 $(n = l)$.

$$P(t) = (1\text{-}t)P_0 + tP_1, \quad 0 <= t <= 1$$

Case II: Quadratic Bezier spline

Quadratic Bezier spline is obtained by *deCasteljau algorithm* as a linear interpolation between linear interpolation between control points P_o, P_1, P_2 $(n = 2)$.

$$P_o^{\,1} = (1\text{-}t)P_o + tP_1, \quad P_1^{\,1} = (1\text{-}t)P_, + tP_2,$$

$$P(t) = (1\text{-}t)P_o^{\,1} + tP_1^{\,1} = (1\text{-}t)[(1\text{-}t)P_0 + tP_1] + t[(1\text{-}t)P_1 + tP_2]$$
$$= (1\text{-}t)^2 P_o + 2(1\text{-}t)\,tP_1 + t^2 P_2,$$

$$P(t) = \sum\nolimits_{i=0,2} B_i^{\,2}(t)P_i$$

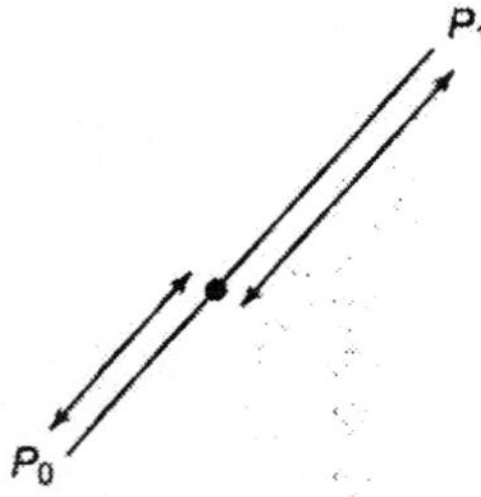

FIGURE 11.10

where, $B_i^n(t)$ are Bernstein polynomials (see below).

Case III: Cubic Bezier Curve

Cubic Bezier spline is obtained by interpolation between four control points P_o, P_1, P_2, P_3 $(n = 3)$.

We will discuss in detail Cubic Bezier curve.

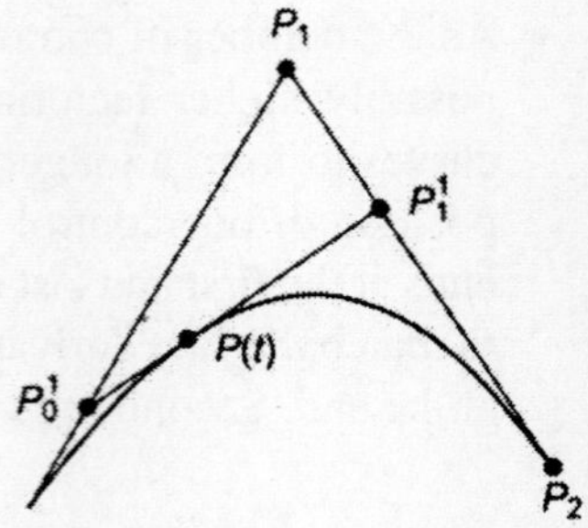

FIGURE 11.11

$$P(t) = \sum_{i=0}^{3} P_i B_{i,3}(t) \quad 0 \le t \le 1$$

$$P(t) = P_0 B_{0,3}(t) + P_1 B_{1,3}(t) + P_2 B_{2,3}(t) + P_3 B_{3,3}(t)$$

Where,

$$B_{0,3}(t) = C(3,0)\, t^0 (1-t)^3 = (1-t)^3$$
$$B_{1,3}(t) = C(3,1)\, t^1 (1-t)^2 = 3t(1-t)^2$$
$$B_{2,3}(t) = C(3,2)\, t^2 (1-t)^1 = 3t^2(1-t)^1$$
$$B_{3,3}(t) = C(3,3\, t^3 (1-t)^O = t^3$$

Therefore,

$$P(t) = P_o (1-t)^3 + P_1 3t(1-t)^2 + P_2 3t^2 (1-t)^1 + P_3 t^3 (1-t)^0$$
$$P(t) = (-t^3 + 3t^2 - 3t + 1)P_O + (3t^3 - 6t^2 + 3t)P_1 + (-3t^3 + 3t^2)\, P_2 + t^3 P_3 \tag{11.2}$$

Expression 11.2 can be translated into the matrix form i.e., as

$$P(t) = [F]\,[B]$$

where, Basis function matrix $[F] = [\, B_{0,3}(t)\; B_{1,3}(\text{t})\; B_{2,3}(\text{t})\; \text{B}_{3,3}(t)\,]$

$$\text{Bezier geometry matrix } [B] = \begin{bmatrix} P0 \\ P1 \\ P2 \\ P3 \end{bmatrix}$$

If $\quad T = [t^3 \;\; t^2 \;\; t \;\; 1]$

$$\text{and the Bezier basis matrix } [M] = \begin{bmatrix} -1 & 3 & -3 & 1 \\ 3 & -6 & 3 & 0 \\ -3 & 3 & 0 & 0 \\ 1 & 0 & 0 & 0 \end{bmatrix}$$

then $\quad [F] = [T][M]$

Cubic Bezier curve in matrix form is

$$P(t) = [t^3\, t^2\, \text{t}\; 1] \begin{bmatrix} -1 & 3 & -3 & 1 \\ 3 & -6 & 3 & 0 \\ -3 & 3 & 0 & 0 \\ 1 & 0 & 0 & 0 \end{bmatrix} \begin{bmatrix} P0 \\ P1 \\ P2 \\ P3 \end{bmatrix}$$

where, P_0, P_1, P_2, P_3 are the four control points.

Figure 11.12 depicts the appearance of cubic Bezier curve for various selection of control points in the *xy* plane (z = 0). However, shape of Bezier curve for same set of four control points varies if the order of the control points his changed.

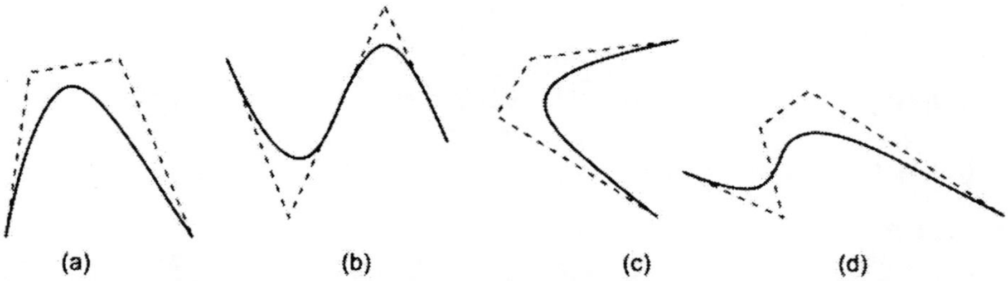

FIGURE 11.12 Cubic Bezier Curve (*xy* plane, *z* = 0) for Different Position of Control Points

If we plot each of the cubic-Bezier blending function $B_{i,3}$ against parameter t for $0 \le t \le 1$ we get as shown in Fig. 11.13.

On careful examining Figure 11.13 we note that

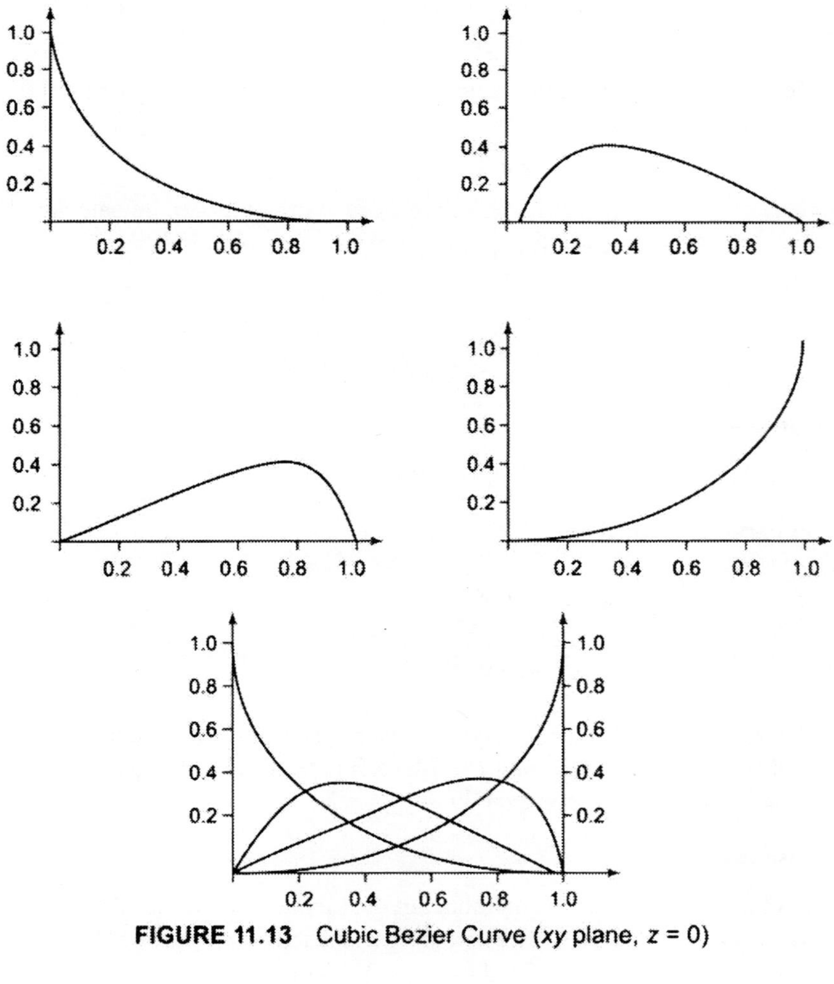

FIGURE 11.13 Cubic Bezier Curve (*xy* plane, *z* = 0)

All the Bezier functions have value > = 0 in the range $0 \leq t \leq 1$

Sum of the Bezier functions is equal to unity i.e.,

$$\sum_{i=0}^{3} B_{i,3}(t) = 1$$

All the curves always lie completely within the convex hull of the control points.

11.3.2 Tangents on Bezier Curve

Equation of cubic Bezier curve is

$$P(t) = (-t^3 + 3t^2 - 3t + 1)P_0 + (3t^3 - 6t^2 + 3t)P_1 + (-3t^3 + 3t^2)P_2 + t^3 P_3$$

The value of parametric tangent vector is obtained by differentiating $P(t)$ at any point t and given by:

$$P'(t) = (-3t^2 + 6t - 3)P_0 + (9t^2 - 12t + 3)P_1 + (-9t^2 + 6t)P_2 + 3t^2 P_3$$

$$P'(t)_{(t=0)} = 3(P_1 - P_0)$$

$$P'(t)_{(t=1)} = 3(P_3 - P_2)$$

$$P''(0) = 6(P_0 - 2P_1 + P_2)$$

$$P''(1) = 6(P_3 - 2P_2 + P_1)$$

In general, Bezier curve of degree n, the parametric first derivatives at the end points are given by

$$P'(0) = n(P1 - P0)$$

$$P'(1) = n(Pn - Pn - 1)$$

Second derivatives of the nth degree Bezier curve at the end points can be calculated as

$$P''(0) = n(n-1)(P_0 - 2P_1 + P_2)$$

$$= n(n-1)(P_2 - P_1) - (P_1 - P_0)$$

$$P''(1) = n(n-1)(Pn - 2P_{n-1} + P_{n-2})$$

$$= n(n-1)(P_{n-2} - Pn - 1) - (P_{n-1} - P_n)$$

11.3.3 Rational Bezier Curve

Definition

A "rational" Bezier curve is defined by

$$C(t) = \frac{\sum_{i=0}^{x} B_{i,P}(t)\, W_i\, \mathbf{P_i}}{\sum_{i=0}^{x} B_{i,P}(t)\, W_i},$$

where, P is the order, $B_{i,p}$ are the Bernstein polynomials, Pi are control points, and the weight W_i of Pi is the last ordinate of the homogeneous point Pi. These curves are closed under perspective transformations, and can represent conic sections exactly.

11.3.4 Bezier Surface

The Bezier surface is formed as the cartesian product of the blending functions of two orthogonal Bezier curves. The simplest way to construct a Bezier surface is as the tensor product of Bezier curves. A tensor product Bezier surface of order $n + 1$ is defined by $(n + 1)^2$ control points. It is called a Bezier patch.

$$B(u,v) = \sum_{i=0}^{Ni}\sum_{j=0}^{Nj} P_{i,j} \frac{Ni!}{i!(Ni-i)!} u^i (1-u)^{Ni-i} \frac{Nj!}{j!(Nj-j)} v^j (1-v)^{Nj-j}$$

$$0 \le u \le 1$$
$$0 \le v \le 1$$

where, $P_{i,j}$ is the i, jth control point. There are N_{i+1} and N_{j+i} control points in the i and j directions, respectively.

You can think about this as moving the control points of one Bezier curve along a set of Bezier curves to sweep out a surface. Continuity across a boundary between two Bezier patches is only guaranteed if each of the Bezier curves across the join obeys the curve continuity conditions.

The corresponding properties of the Bezier curve apply to the Bezier surface.

- The surface does not, in general, pass through the control points except for the corners of the control point grid.
- The surface is contained within the convex hull of the control points.

Along the edges of the grid patch the Bezier surface matches that of a Bezier curve through the control points along that edge.

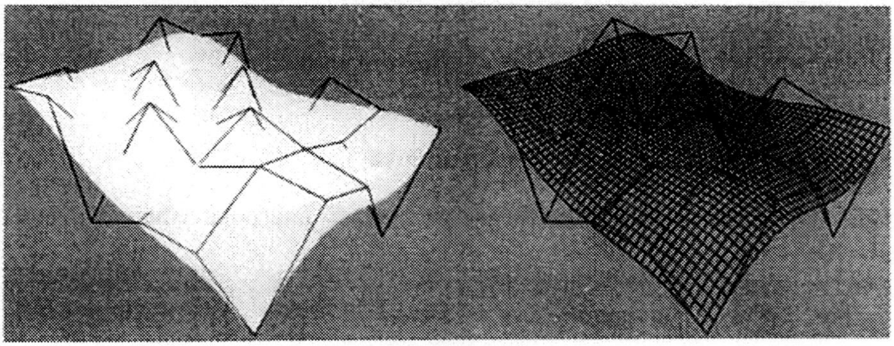

FIGURE 11.14

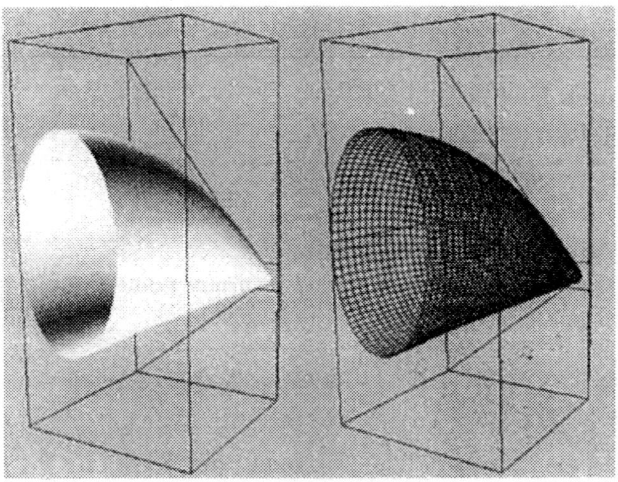

FIGURE 11.15

Closed surfaces can be formed by setting the last control point equal to the first. If the tangents also match between the first two and last two control points, then the closed surface will have first order continuity.

While a cylinder/cone can be formed from a Bezier surface, it is not possible to form a sphere.

11.4 B-SPLINE CURVES AND SURFACES

The name "B-spline" with the "*B*" standing for basis was defined by Sheonberg, in 1967.B-splines curves are widely used in computer aided design and manufacturing and are supported by OpenGL. B-splines are powerful tools for generating curves with many control points and provide advantages over Beizer curves. Furthermore, curve designer has much flexibility in adjusting the curvature of B-spline curve, and B-splines can be designed with sharp bend and even "corners".

B-spline curves are pulled towards the control points in much the same way that a Beizer curve is pulled towards its interior control points.

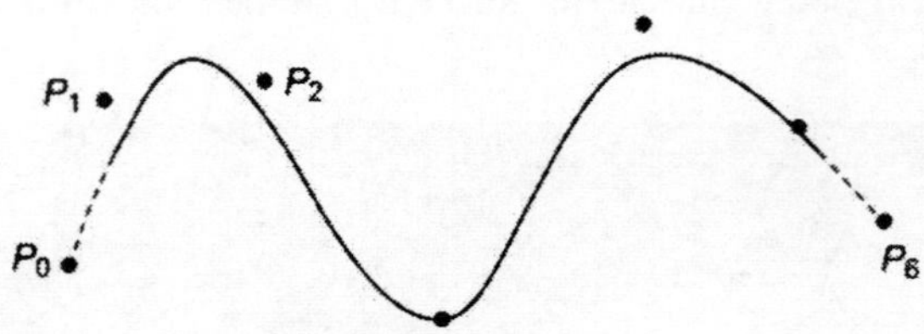

FIGURE 11.16

Unlike Bezier curve, B-spline curves do not necessarily interpolate their first and last control points(Refer to Fig. 11 .16).

A big advantage of B-spline curves over Bezier curves is that they act more flexibly and intuitively with large number of control points.

11.4.1 B-Spline Curves

Definition

Let a vector be known as the knot vector be defined $T = \{t_0, t_1, \ldots, t_m\}$,
where, T is a non-decreasing sequence with $t_i \in [0, 1]$, and define control points $P_0, \ldots, P_n$. Define the degree as

$$p \equiv m - n - 1.$$

The "knots" $'p^{+1}, \ldots, 'm - p - 1$ are called inter-knots.

Considering $P(t)$ as the parametric position vector of any point along the curve, then the general expression for a B-Spline curve of degree $(d - 1)$ is given by,

$$P(t) = \sum_{i=0}^{n} P_i B_{i,d}(t) \quad t_{\min} \le t \le t_{\text{mix}} \text{ and } 2 \le d \le n + 1$$

where, Pi ($i = 0$ to n) are the set of $n + 1$ control points and $Bi,d(t)$ are the $n + 1$ B-Spline blending functions (basis function) defined by the Cox-deBoor recursion formula as,

$$B_{i,d}(t) = \left\{\frac{t - t_i}{t_{i+d-1} - t_i}\right\} B_{i,d-1}(t) + \left\{\frac{t_{i+d} - t_i}{t_{i+d} - t_{i+1}}\right\} B_{i+1,d-1}(t) \quad (11.3)$$

where,

$$B_{i,1}(t) = 1, \text{ if } t_i \leq t \leq t_{i+1}$$

$$B_{i,1} = 0 \quad \text{otherwise}$$

When there are some repeated knots, some of the denominators above may be zero; we adopt the convention that 0/0 =0. Since, $N_{i,k}(u)$ will be identically zero when $u_{i+k} = u_i$, this means that any term with denominator equal to zero may be ignored.

Local control is an important feature of B-spline curves; it allows a designer or an artist to edit one portion of a curve without causing changes to distant parts of the curve.

Properties of B-Splines Curves

(1) The polynomial curve has degree $(d-1)$ and C^{d-2} continuity over the range of u.
(2) For $(n + 1)$ control points, the curve is described with $n + 1$ blending functions.
(3) Each blending function $B_{k,d}$ is defined over the d subintervals of the total range of u, starting of knot value u_k.
(4) The range of parameter u is divided into $n + d$ subintervals by the $n + d + 1$ values specified in the knot vector.
(5) With knot values labeled as $[u_0, u_1, u_2, ..., u_n]$ the resulting B-spline curve is defined only in the interval from knot value u_{d-1} up to knot value u_{n+1}.
(6) Each section of the spline curve is influenced by control points.
(7) Any one control point can affect the shape of at most d curve sections.
(8) A B-spline with no internal knot is a Bezier curve.

11.4.2 Classification of B-Spline Curves

- Uniform
- Non-uniform
- Open uniform

11.4.2.1 Uniform, Periodic B-Splines

A B-Spline curve is called ***uniform B-Spline*** curve if the spacing between knot values is constant.

For example, we can set up a uniform knot vector as

$$[-2.0, -1.5, -1.0, -0.5, 0.0, 0.5, 1.0, 1.5]$$

Normally knot values are normalized to the range between 0 and 1 as in

$$[0.0, 0.1, 0.2, 0.3, 0.4, 0.5, 0.6, 0.7, 0.8, 0.9, 1.0]$$

Uniform B-Splines have ***periodic blending functions***. That is, for a given value of n and d all blending functions have the same shape. In this case equation (11.3) B-Spline blending functions defined by the Cox-deBoor recursion formula becomes:

$$B_{i,d}(u) = B_{i+1,d}(u + \Delta u) = B_{i+2,d}(u + 2u)$$

where, Δu is the interval between adjacent knot values.

Periodic splines are particularly used for generating close certain closed curves.

Now we will consider different cases when knots are uniformly spaced with knot vector equal to [0,1,2, ...ℓ].

Case I

Order $d = 1$ and Degree $k = 0$

In this blending function is defined as

$$B_{i,1}(u) = \begin{cases} 1 \text{ if } i \le u \le i+1 \\ 0 \text{ otherwise} \end{cases}$$

for $\qquad i = 0, 1, \ldots\ldots\ldots \ell - 1$

Case II

Order $d = 2$ and degree $k = 1$

In this case blending function is defined as [From equation (11.3)]

$$B_{i,2}(u) = \frac{u-i}{1} B_{i,1}(u) + \frac{i+2-u}{1} B_{i+1,1}(u)$$

for $\qquad i = 0, 1, \ldots \ell - 2$

In particular to the case $i = 0$, we have

$$B_{0,2}(u) = \frac{u}{1} B_{0,1}(u) + \frac{2-u}{1} B_{1,1}(u)$$

Considering separately the cases $0 \le u < 1$, $1 \le u < 2$, we have

$$B_{0,2}(u) = \begin{cases} u & \text{if } 0 \le u \le 1 \\ 2-u & \text{if } 1 \le u < 2 \\ 0 & \text{otherwise} \end{cases}$$

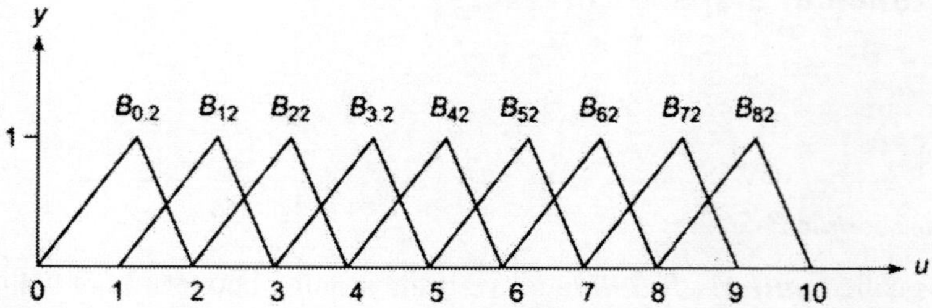

FIGURE 11.17 Periodic Blending Function for a Uniform, Degree one B-Spline

Case III

Order $d = 3$ and degree $k = 2$

In this case blending function is defined as [From equation (11.3)]:

$$B_{i,3}(u) = \frac{u-i}{2} B_{i,2}(u) + \frac{i+3-u}{2} B_{i+1,2}(u)$$

for $\qquad i = 0, 1, \ldots \ell - 3$

In particular to the case $i = 0$, we have

$$B_{0,3}(u) = \frac{u}{2} B_{0,2}(u) + \frac{3-u}{2} B_{1,2}(u)$$

Considering separately the cases $0 \le u < 1, 1 \le u \le 2, 2 \le u < 3$, we have

$$B_{0,3}(u) = \begin{cases} \frac{1}{2}u^2 & \text{if } 0 \le u \le 1 \\ \frac{1}{2}u(2-u) + \frac{1}{2}(3-u)(u-1) = \frac{1}{2}(6u - 2u^2 - 3) & \text{if } 1 \le u < 2 \\ \frac{1}{2}(3-u)^2 & \text{if } 2 \le u < 3 \\ 0 & \text{otherwise} \end{cases}$$

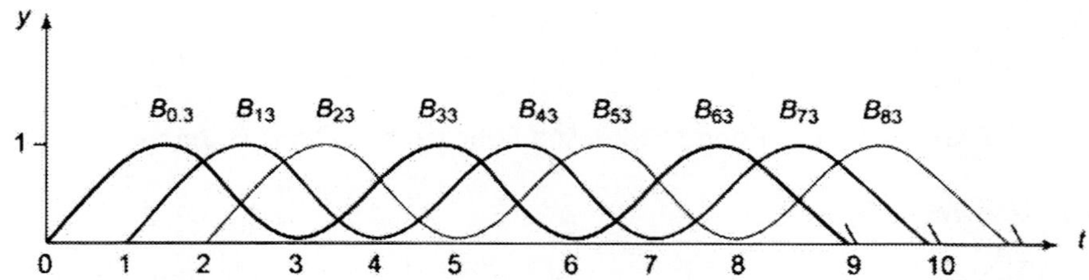

FIGURE 11.18 Periodic Blending Function for a Uniform, Degree Two B-Spline

Case IV

Cubic Periodic B-Spline Curve

As a special for a cubic periodic B-spline curve $d = 4$, then each blending function spans four subintervals of the total range of u; order $d = 4$ and degree $k = 3$.

In this case blending function is defined as [From equation (11.3)]:

$$B_{i,4}(u) = \frac{u-i}{3} B_{i,3}(u) + \frac{i+4-u}{3} B_{i+1,3}(u)$$

for $\qquad i = 0, 1, \ldots . \ell - 4$

If we are to fit the cubic to four control points, then we could use the integer knot vector [0,1,2,3,4,5,6,7] and $i = 0,1,2,3$.

11.4.2.2 Non-uniform B-Splines

A B-splines are called non-uniform B-splines if knot values have unequal spacing or multiple knot values.

For example,

[1,3,5,6,8,9,10]

12[0,0,l,1,3,3]

Such types of B-spline provides increased flexibility in controlling a curve shape. With the unequally spaced intervals in the knot vectors, we can obtain different shapes for the blending functions in different intervals, which can be used to adjust splines shapes. By knot multiplicity, we can produce subtle variations in curve shape and even introduce *discontinuities*.

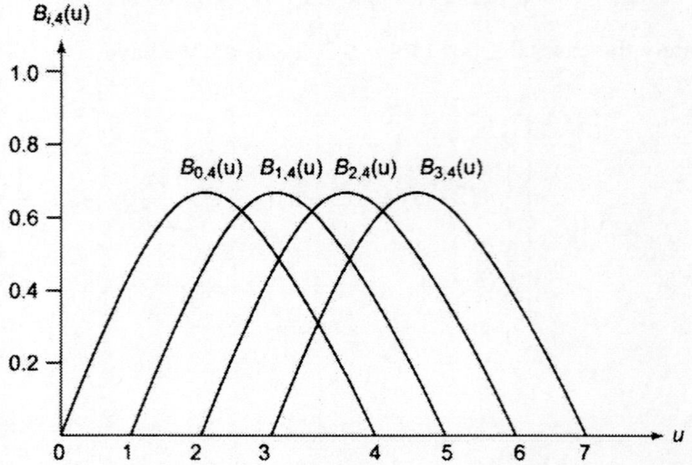

FIGURE 11.19 Periodic Blending Function of a Cubic B-Spline

11.4.2.3 Open Uniform B-Spline

An open uniform B-spline has combined features of uniform B-spline and non-uniform B-spline.

11.4.3 B-Spline Surface

We can create a B-Spline surface using a similar method to the Bezier surface. For B-Spline curves, we used two phantom knots to clamp the ends of the curve. For a surface, we will have phantom knots all around the real knots as shown below for an $M + 1$ by $N + 1$ knot surface.

$$
\begin{array}{l|lllllll|l}
P_{-1,-1} & P_{0,-1} & P_{1,-1} & \cdots & P_{M-1,-1} & P_{M-1} & P_{M+1,-1} \\
\hline
P_{-1,0} & P_{0,0} & P_{1,0} & \cdots & P_{M-1,0} & P_{M,0} & P_{M+1,0} \\
P_{-1,1} & P_{0,1} & P_{1,1} & \cdots & P_{M-1,1} & P_{M,1} & P_{M+1,1} \\
\vdots & \vdots & \vdots & \cdots & \vdots & \vdots & \vdots \\
P_{-1,N-1} & P_{0,N-1} & P_{1,N-1} & \cdots & P_{M-1,N-1} & P_{M,N-1} & P_{M+1,N-1} \\
P_{-1,N} & P_{0,N} & P_{1,N} & \cdots & P_{M-1,N} & P_{M,N} & P_{M+1,N} \\
\hline
P_{-1,N+1} & P_{0,N+1} & P_{1,N+1} & \cdots & P_{M-1,N+1} & P_{0,N+1} & P_{M+1,N+1}
\end{array}
$$

There are two extra rows and two extra columns of knots in parametric space surrounding the real knots. Where we place these knots determines the shape of the surface at the edges. The method described here gives similar results to the method used for Bezier surfaces; that is, the edges of the surface form a B-Spline curve of the edge knots. This means some of the boundary conditions are

$$P_{m,-1} = 2P_{m,0} - P_{m,1}$$
$$P_{m,N+1} = 2P_{m,N} - P_{m,N-1}$$

$$P_{-1,n} = 2P_{0,n} - P_{1,n}$$
$$P_{M+1,n} = 2P_{M,n} - P_{m-1,n}$$

for $0 <= m <= M$ and $0 <= n <= N$. These conditions are essentially the same as the two-dimensional case. They mean the weighting of a sample taken at the boundary $m = 0$ is dependent only on knots along the $m = 0$ boundary (the phantom knots at $m = -1$ balance out the real knots at $m = 1$). The remaining boundary conditions make the surface corners and the corner knots coincide. The coordinate of the corner as set by $P_{0,0}$ (and hence the parametric knot at $\{-1,-1\}$) is

$$P_{0,0} = \frac{4}{9}P_{0,0} + \frac{1}{9}(P_{-1,0} + P_{0,-1} + P_{1,0} + P_{0,1}) + \frac{1}{36}(P_{-1-1} + P_{1,-1} + P_{-1,1} + P_{1,1})$$

$$P_{-1,-1} = 4P_{0,0} - 2P_{1,0} - 2P_{0,1} + P_{1,1}$$

This gives us a surface that interpolates the corner knots and forms B-Spline curves down each side. To explore the B-Spline surface further, see the surface created from a 4 × 4 or a 5 × 5 mesh.

11.4.4 Rational B-Splines

Definition

A B-spline curve is a rational curve if the control points are specified with homogeneous coordinates. Such curves are sometimes also known as non-uniform, rational B-spline (NURBS).

A rational B-spline has 4 tuples (x,y,z,w) as control points, curve $q(u)$ is represented as weighted averages of control points,

$$P(t) = \sum_{i=0}^{n} P_i B_{i,d}(t)$$

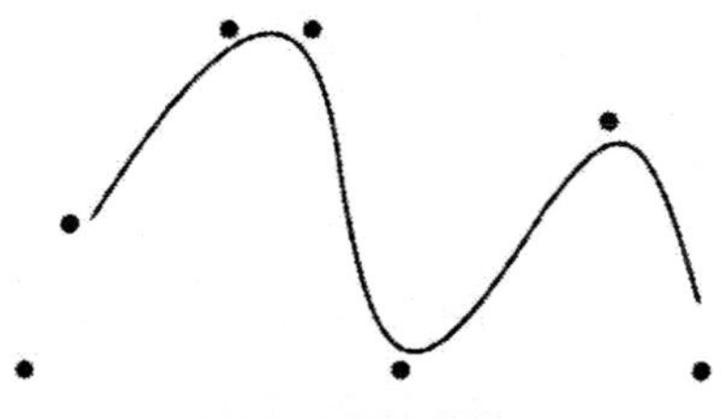

FIGURE 11.20 Rational B-Spline

11.5 BEZIER SPLINE CURVE VS B-SPLINE CURVE

(1) Bezier curves are special cases of B-spline curves.
(2) In Bezier curve change in a portion of a curve causing changes to whole curve. In contrast B-spline has local control over curve. This property allows a designer or artist to edit one portion of a curve without causing changes to the remaining portion of the curve.
(3) Unlike Bezier curve, B-spline curves do not necessarily interpolate their first and last control points.
(4) B-spline curves are more flexible and intuitive than Bezier curves with large number of control points.
(5) Curve designer has much flexibility in adjusting the curvature of B-spline curve than Bezier curves.
(6) B-splines can be designed with sharp bend and even "corners" than Bezier Curves.

SOLVED PROBLEMS

Problem 11.1 Find the cubic Bezier curve with the following control points: $A(0,40)$, $B(40,40)$, $C(60,20)$, $D(60,-10)$?

Solution

Equation of cubic Bezier curve passes through A, B C, D is given by

$$B(t) = [t^3\ t^2\ t\ 1]\begin{bmatrix}-1 & 3 & -3 & 1\\ 3 & -6 & 3 & 0\\ -3 & 3 & 0 & 0\\ 1 & 0 & 0 & 0\end{bmatrix}\begin{bmatrix}0 & 40\\ 40 & 40\\ 60 & 20\\ 60 & -10\end{bmatrix}$$

where $(0 \le t \le 1)$

$$B(t) = [t^3\ t^2\ t\ 1]\begin{bmatrix}0 & 10\\ -60 & -60\\ 120 & 0\\ 0 & 40\end{bmatrix}$$

$$B(t) = [-60t^2 + 120t \quad 10t^3 - 60t^2 + 40]$$

Problem 11.2 Find the cubic B-spline curve with the following control points: $A(0,40)$, $B(40,40)$, $C(60,20)$, $D(60, -10)$?

Solution:

Equation of cubic B-spline curve passes through A, B, C, D is given by

$$B(t) = [t^3\ t^2\ t\ 1]\frac{1}{6}\begin{bmatrix}-1 & 3 & -3 & 1\\ 3 & -6 & 3 & 0\\ -3 & 0 & 3 & 0\\ 1 & 4 & 1 & 0\end{bmatrix}\begin{bmatrix}0 & 40\\ 40 & 40\\ 60 & 20\\ 60 & -10\end{bmatrix}$$

where $(0 \le t \le 1)$

$$= [t^3\ t^2\ t\ 1]\ \frac{1}{6}\begin{bmatrix}0 & 10\\ -60 & -60\\ 180 & -60\\ 220 & 220\end{bmatrix}$$

$$B(t) = [\frac{1}{6}\ (-60t^2 + 180t + 220) \qquad \frac{1}{6}\ (10t^3 - 60t^2 - 60t + 220)]$$

EXERCISES

1. What is a knot?
2. What is the importance of representing a curve in a parametric form?
3. What is a spline? What are the major differences between Bezier curve and B-spline?
4. What is Convex Hull property of Bezier curves?
5. Cubic polynomial curves are more preferred in graphics than any other polynomial curve. Justify.
6. Obtain expression of Bezier curve and B-spline curve.
7. Bezier curve is a special case of B-spline curve. Prove this statement.
8. Define rational Bezier curve and rational B-spline.
9. What is the difference between uniform and non-uniform B-spline?
10. What are the various properties of Bezier curve and B-spline curve?
11. Perform following conversions:

    (a) Bezier curve to B-spline
    (b) B-spline to Bezier curve.

12. Find the equation of Bezier curve which passes through (0,0) and (2,1) and is controlled through points (7,5) and (2,0).
13. Suppose three points on a 2D curve are given by (0,0), (0.5) and (1,0). Find out the equation of the approximated curve using Bezier polynomial.
14. Construct B-spline curve of order 3 and 4 polygon vertices $A(1,1)$, $B(2,3)$, $C(4,3)$ and $D(6,4)$.

12

Animation

12.1 INTRODUCTION

The word *animation* derives from **'animate'** meaning *'to give life to'*. Animations are created from a sequence of images. Each image is slightly changed from the previous one with respect to one or more objects in the image.

Animation is the process of creating movement on the screen with a series of still pictures with the help of 'persistence of vision'. Animation is possible because of biological phenomenon known as persistence of vision. An object seen by human eye remains on retina for a brief time (about 0.1 second) after the viewing. Therefore, a series of images having a small change in position of objects in each time if projected rapidly on the eye, creates a virtual illusion of the movement. A complete screen full image of animation sequence is called **frame.**

Figure 12.1 shows sequence of images of a filled circle with different values of radius when displayed rapidly over one after another gives the illustration of circle moving inside.

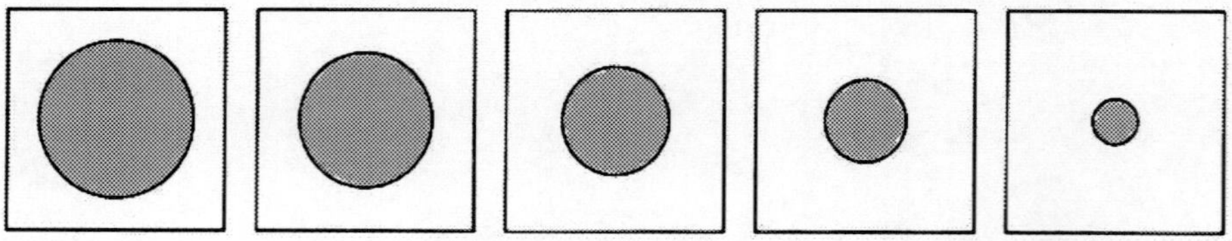

FIGURE 12.1

Animation is based on the way our eye and brain work. If slow sequence of images are presented in front of our eyes, then brain interprets as separate; and if fast sequence of images are presented, then brain starts motion with flickers, then as continuous motion, and, finally, as a distort. The rate of animation should be fast enough to create the perception of continuous motion but slow enough so as not to waste resources. In practice playback rates of 24 to 30 frames per second are normally used.

12.1.1 Why do We See these Images as Moving?

The reason our eyes are tricked into seeing movement can be explained by the 'Persistence of Vision' theory.

The Persistence of Vision Theory

Our brain holds onto an image for a fraction of a second after the image has passed. If the eye sees a series of still images very quickly one picture after another, then the images will appear to move because our eyes cannot deal with fast-moving images -our eyes have been tricked into thinking they have seen movement. We see these many pictures per second!

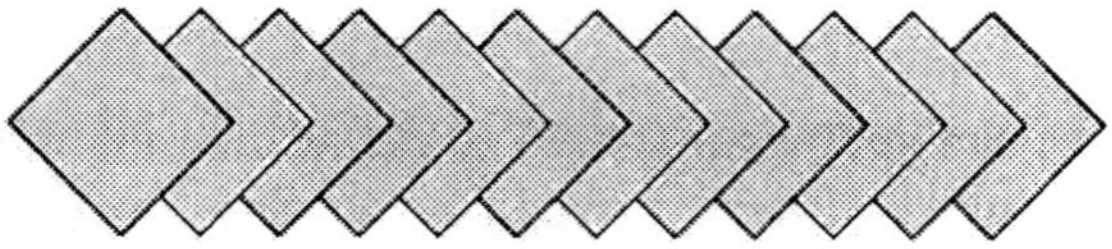

FIGURE 12.2

The Moving Hand Theory

You can do this by waving your hand in front of your eyes very fast. You will seem to see several hands at once. Try doing this in front of a television screen when it is switched on. You will see even more images of your hand because the television is actually flickering. By waving your hand in front of it you make your eyes very confused about what they are actually seeing.

In fact computer graphics has three stages:

First stage: to display a single image consisting of smooth, curved, realistic-looking, surfaces.

Second stage: to create and display an entire animation made of many frames, where each frame is an image.

Third stage: It is related to virtual reality, where the user can interact with animation.

12.2 WHAT IS ANIMATION?

Definition I

Webster define animate as

" *to give life to; to make alive*"

Definition II

Animation is the illusion of motion that is created by displaying a series of images or frames, each one slightly different from the last, over a brief period of time.

Definition III

Animation is the process by which we see still pictures MOVE. Each picture is shot on film one at a time and is shown at the rate of 24 pictures per second making the pictures appear to move.

Definition IV

Animation refers to change in object position with translation or rotation. It could also be involving size or color or transparency variation.

Definition V

Animation is the process (computer algorithms) resulting time-varying visual effects of motion, shape, color, texture, and so on.

12.3 EFFECTS ON PICTURE DURING ANIMATION

In animation, you get moving images when the pictures change in some way. Here are some ways in which pictures can change:

- **Change in size:** Things can get bigger (grow) or get smaller (shrink). Try drawing a balloon. Now draw it again but a little bit bigger. Now draw it getting even bigger. Draw it so that it is so big that it bursts!
- **Change in position:** Imagine the spokes on a bike-wheel moving around as the wheel runs full circle. Draw the wheel five times—each time showing how the spokes on the wheel have moved.
- **Change in angle:** Draw the hands of a clock as time is passing. Each time the hands should show a different angle.
- **Change in speed:** Draw a car parked. Now draw the same car speeding down a road. How could you show the element of speed?
- **Change in colour:** Draw six circles and colour them in, each time showing how the colours are getting darker.
- **Change of shape:** Draw a face that is sad. Now draw three other faces changing the eyes and mouth to make, in four stages, a happy face.

Computer animation can also be generated by changing camera parameter such as position, orientation, and focal length. Computer animation can also be produced by changing lighting effects or other parameters and procedures associated with rendering and illumination.

12.4 CATEGORIES OF ANIMATION

Animation deals with graphics drawn by hand or by animation software. Depending upon the techniques used to create and manage the frame. There are two broad categories of animation.

12.4.1 Cel Animation

Traditional animation sequence is created by two types of artists:

- The lead artists or experts who draw those frames where major changes take place within the sequence, called **key-frames.**
- Assistants draw a number of frames in between the frames, process is called **tweening.**
- Traditional animation is based on key-frames. Traditional animation films are created by hand. Artists draw image on films and each frame is called cel (drawn from celluloid). Hence, named cel animation. As 25 frames need to be displayed to achieve the effect of smooth motion of objects. Even a small sequence of animation requires thousands of cells.

12.4.2 Computer Animation

There are two main categories of computer animation

- **Computer assisted (two-dimensional) animation**
  It is also based on key-frame concepts. The advantage of computer assistant animation is that in-between frames are created by the animation software, instead of junior assistant animator who requires more time to create frames.

Computer animation software simulates the process of traditional cel based animation by placing the animated object. Computer animation programs usually have grid and alignment commands to help animation to correctly register drawing.

It uses the computer to interpolate between two-dimensional shapes. 2D animations are more popular, most cartoons that you watch on television are based on 2D animation technique.

- **Computer-generated (three-dimensional) animation**
  It uses the computer to build three-dimensional objects, to move both camera and objects along their paths, and to stop and take a snapshot at each frame. In this case mathematical model of a 3D object is created to portray its width and height as well as depth. 3D animation is mostly used in computer-aided design (CAD).

  A complete piece of animation is sometimes called **presentation.** It consists of a number of acts, where each act is broken down into several scenes. A scene is made of several slots of sequence of animation, each a succession of animation frames, where there is small change in scene and camera position between consecutive frames.

Thus, the order is: [See Figure 12.3]

12.5 PROBLEMS IN COMPUTER ANIMATION

- How to display on the screen, only parts of the scene that would be seen by an actual camera located at a certain point?
- How to move camera along any desired path and rotate it during the movement so it always points to the centre of intersect?
- How to move the scene along another path and move parts of the scene in different ways?

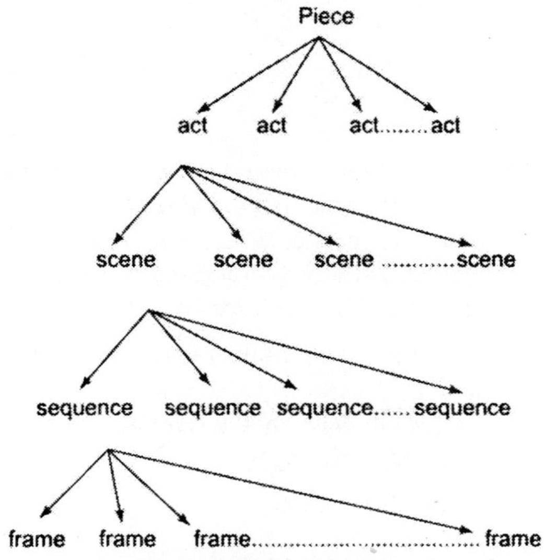

FIGURE 12.3 Piece of Animation

12.6 ANIMATION FUNCTIONS

12.6.1 Zooming

If we fix the window on an object but reduce or increase its size, the object would appear bigger(**zoom in**) or smaller(**zoom out**), respectively.

Reducing the size of window is much like **zooming in** on the object with a camera.

The contents in the window must be stretched to fit into the fixed viewport, so when the window is made smaller, the portion inside becomes more enlarged.

Similarly, increasing the size of window is much like **zooming out** from the object with a camera.

The example in Figure 12.4 points out how changing can produce useful effects. The window is made smaller (about a fixed center).

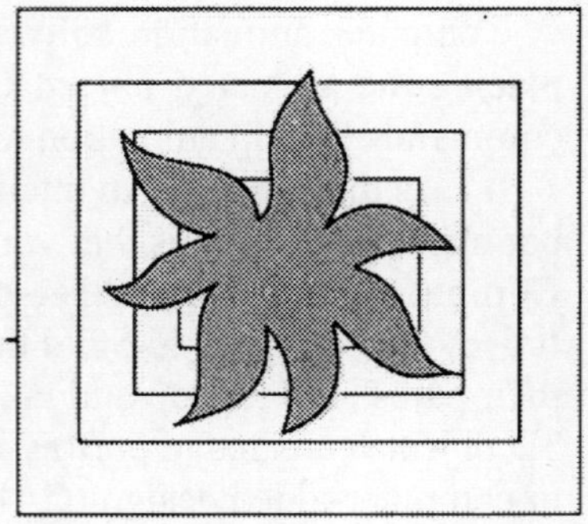

FIGURE 12.4 Zooming in on the Plant

12.6.2 Panning

Panning effects are produced by moving a fixed-size window across the various objects in a scene. In other words, if backward/forward is moved, then object appears to move in opposite direction than backward/forward. Sometimes it is also called **roaming.**

The example in Figure 12.5 illustrates how moon is moving down when backward(sky) is moving upward.

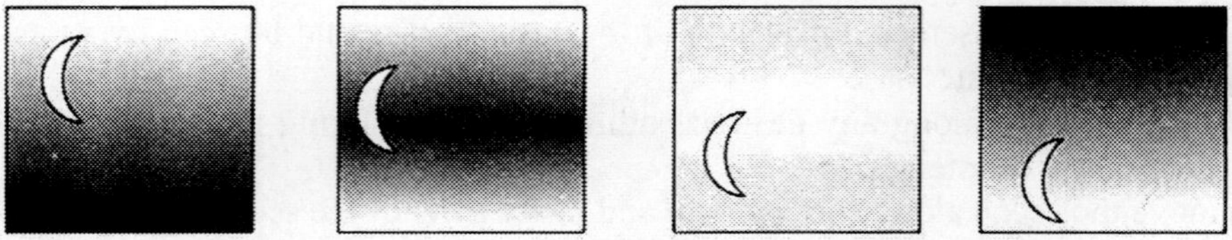

FIGURE 12.5 Effect of Panning, Background is Moved Upward

On an object both zooming and panning functions can be performed simultaneously.

12.6.3 Tweening

Tweening is an interesting animation function. It facilitates us how one figure "tweened" onto other.

It plays important role in film industry. In earlier days an artist has to draw 24 pictures for each second film, because movies display 24 frames per second. With the assistance of computer, however, an artist need draw only the first and final pictures, called key-frames and others are generated automatically.

Traditional animation sequence is created by two types of artists:

- The lead artists or experts who draw those frames where major changes take place within the sequence, called **key-frames.**
- Assistants draw a number of frames in between the frames, process is called **tweening.** It means insert in between other things (in be)tweening.

Figure 12.6 illustrates the motion of filled circle.

12.6.4 Morphing

Transformation of object shapes from one form to another is called **morphing**. Morphing is a shortened form of metamorphosis. It is special type of tween which deals with two different objects. For example, tween between face of one person to another person, cat and tiger, engine oil to tiger, vehicle to tiger.

Morphing is used in TV advertisements, movies, commercials, cartoons, and entertainment, etc.

There are two parts to the morphing algorithm:

Wrap

Wraping is the process of distorting the source image so that it matches with the target image.

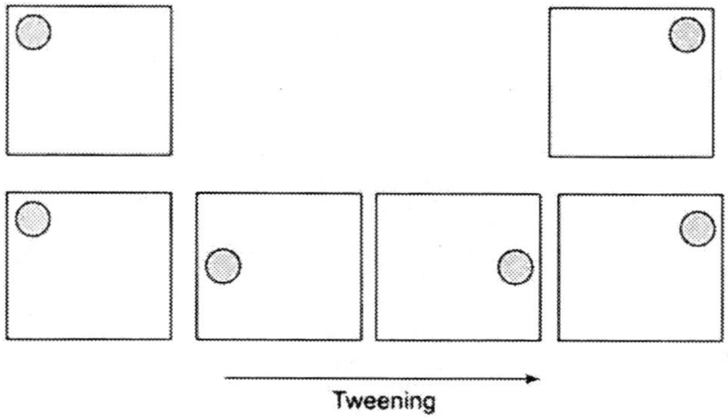

FIGURE 12.6 Effect of Tweening

Dissolve

It creates the sensation of melting the source image into subsequent image frames and finally the target image.

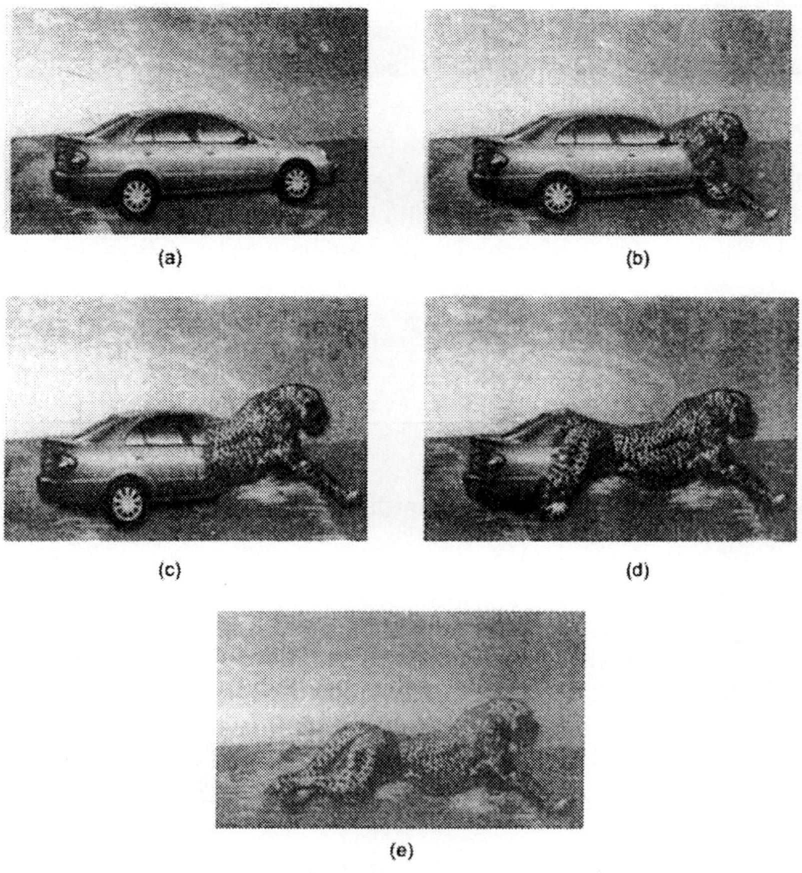

FIGURE 12.7 Morphing

12.6.5 Partial Motion

The term partial motion refers to the movement of parts of an object. Figure 12.8 illustrates the partial motion.

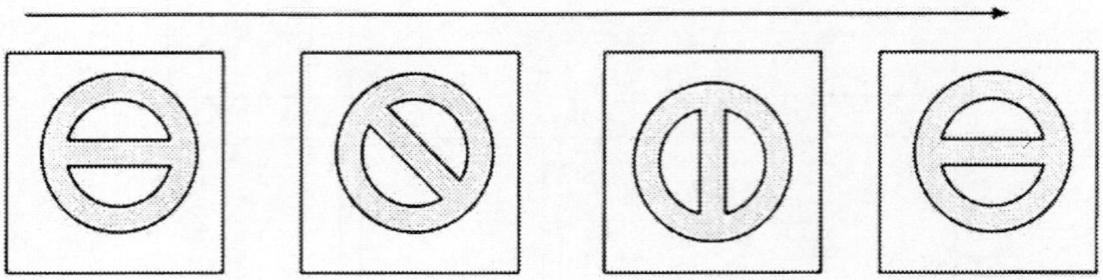

FIGURE 12.8 Effect of No Motion

12.7 ANIMATION TECHNIQUES

There are four basic techniques used in animation. These are:

- Drawn animation
- Cut-out animation
- Model animation or stop motion animation
- Computer animation or computer generated imagery (CGI)

12.7.1 Drawn Animation

This covers any form where one drawing is replaced by another in a sequence. Each drawing is slightly different from the one before. It works the way a flip book does.

These animated films are made up of thousands of drawings which are shown on screen very quickly one after the other.

Advantage

It looks great.

Disadvantage

It takes a very long time to film from start to finish and is expensive needing many animators to complete the work.

12.7.2 Cut-out Animation

This covers any form of animation where cut-out shapes are moved around or replaced by other cut-outs. Flat objects like buttons, matchsticks and string can also be used in this form of animation. Cut-outs can also be laid on top of drawings.

Advantage

It is very quick and easy to do.

Disadvantage

It is difficult to have more than one or two cut-outs moving at the same time. Cut-out animation appears to move in a very stiff and awkward way.

12.7.3 Model Animation or Stop Motion Animation

This involves the filming of puppets or any form of three-dimensional models. The materials used could include plasticine, clay or wire, in fact anything that can be bent or formed into another shape. The puppets are positioned and filmed before being moved ever so slightly and filmed again. These shots are put together as a piece of film and will give the impression of the models moving.

Advantage

Models can be used over and over again and copies made of them to shoot different scenes at the same time so that the filming takes less time.

Disadvantage

This type of animation needs a lot of time and hard work. The makers of 'James and the Giant Peach' were only able to complete 45 seconds of stop-motion animation a week, 10 seconds a day. This was because each puppet had so many joints that needed moving for each frame—the centipede alone had 72.

12.7.4 Computer Animation or Computer Generated Imagery (CGI)

This refers to the drawing of three-dimensional models and sets on the computer. Images can be scanned into the computer using digital photography or made within the computer itself. Human characters can be built from clay whilst sets and furnishings are modeled using design systems similar to architect's drawings. These models are scanned into the computer as wire frame models which are gradually built up into a coloured and textured form which will finally be recorded onto film.

FIGURE 12.9

The wire-frame model (far left) was made on a computer before being built up into the character (left).

12.8 USES OF ANIMATION

- Computer games/CD ROMS creating characters, backgrounds and sound effects.
- Internet: Sound and pictures have to be treated as a form of animation in order to send them through telephone lines.
- Advertising: Animation offers a way of capturing people's attention as it can create fantasy situations.
- Transport: Traffic controllers, who look after the traffic light systems for air and road use animated diagrams to show traffic flow and predict traffic problems.
- Doctors use computer-generated 'virtual' images.

12.9 ANIMATION SOFTWARE

Different types of software are available to create different levels of animation.

Microsoft Power point, CoralDraw and GIF Animator are used for elementary animation.

AutoDesk Animator Studio, Animator Pro, Macromedia Director and Macromedia Flash are used to create sophisticated animation.

3D Studio and Maya are used to create 3D animation.

12.10 ANIMATION FILE FORMATS

Based upon animation software used, there are various animation file formats available as:

DIR for Director Movies

FLI and FLC for AutoDesk and Animator Pro

MAX for Studio Max

GIF for GIF Animator

EXERCISES

1. Define the term animation. Explain the basic principle of animation.
2. An animation consists of frame size 640×480 with 48 bits pixel resolution. Calculate the following:
   (a) Size of frame buffer required
   (b) Bandwidth of system bus to play this animation if frame rate is 30 fps.
   (c) What will be the bandwidth requirement in case of interlacing?
3. Differentiate between traditional animation and computer animation.
4. What is meant by key-framing, tweening, and morphing?
5. Explain briefly the various applications of animations.
6. Explain various animation functions.
7. Explain various animation techniques.

13

Multimedia

13.1 INTRODUCTION

The word multimedia comes from the Latin words ***multus*** which means 'numerous' and media means ***middle*** or ***centre.*** Multimedia may be used as a noun (Multimedia as a new technology field) and as an adjective (a multimedia document). Five senses gifted by god to all human beings:

- Sense of vision
- Sense of hearing
- Sense of smell
- Sense of taste
- Sense of touch

These fives sensory organs enable us to enjoy the reality of nature. In all, the sense of Vision helps us acquire 80% of the knowledge from the world around us, the sense of hearing 15% and other senses, the remaining 5%. Even the knowledge that we gain through reading books is mainly dependent on seeing the text and pictures, other senses are rarely utilized in this process. Figure 13.1 depicts the human perceptions towards various fields.

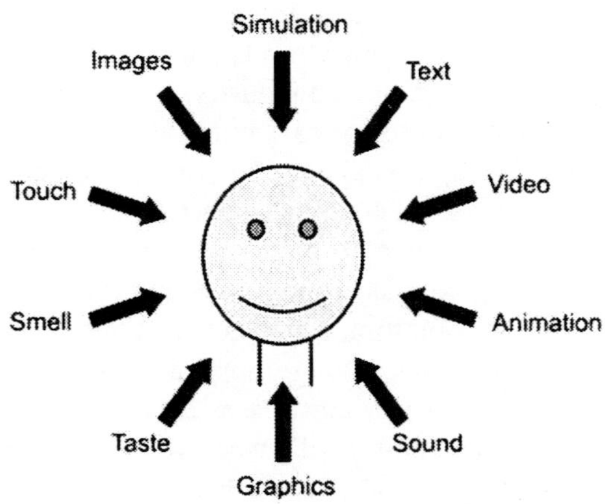

FIGURE 13.1 Human Perception

Newspapers were perhaps the first mass communication medium to employ Multimedia — they used mostly text, graphics, and images.

In 1895, Gugliemo Marconi sent his first wireless radio transmission from Pontecchio, Italy. A few years later (in 1901) he detected radio waves beamed across the Atlantic. Initially invented for telegraph, radio is now a major medium for audio broadcasting.

In 1981, when the first PC came into the market, user could interact with the computer in text mode only, i.e., user could give commands to the computer in the form of text and computer responded with text displayed on its screen as shown in Fig. 13.2(a). After about a year's time, graphics capability was added to machine and hence it became possible to interact with PC through text as well graphics media. Improvement in PC continued, now we have powerful machines that are interfacing with user through variety of media such as text, graphics, animation, sound, and video as shown in Fig. 13.2(b).

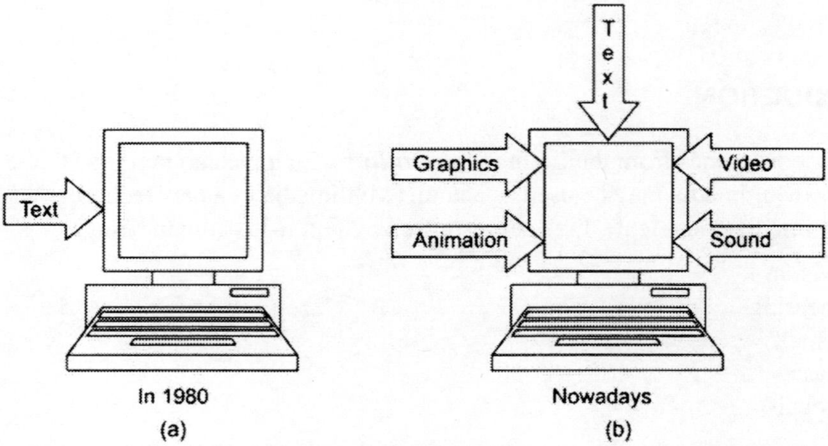

FIGURE 13.2 Man and Machine Interaction

In 1990s, multimedia represented only a combination of text with document images.

Television was the new media for the 20th century. It brings the video and has since changed the world of mass communications.

Multimedia—the combination of text, animated graphics, video and sound—presents information in a way that is more interesting and easier to grasp than text alone. It has been used for education at all levels, job training, games and by the entertainment industry. It is becoming more readily available as the price of personal computers and their accessories decline. Multimedia as a human-computer interface was made possible some half-dozen years ago by the rise of affordable digital technology. Previously, multimedia effects were produced by computer-controlled analog devices, like videocassette recorders, projectors and tape recorders. Digital technology's exponential decline in price and increase in capacity has enabled it to overtake analog technology. The Internet is the breeding ground for multimedia ideas and the delivery vehicle of multimedia objects to a huge audience.

Nowadays, multimedia generally indicates a rich sensory interface between humans and computers or computer-like devices—an interface that in most cases gives the user control over the pace and sequence of the information. We all know multimedia when we see and hear it, yet its precise boundaries elude us. For example, *movies on demand* , in which a viewer can select from a large library of videos and then play, stop, or reposite the tape or change the speed is generally considered multimedia. However, watching the movie on a TV set attached to a videocassette recorder (VCR) with the same abilities to manipulate the play is not considered multimedia. Unfortunately, we have yet to find a definition that satisfies all experts.

Recent multimedia conferences, such as the IEEE International Conference on Multimedia Computing and Systems, ACM Multimedia and Multimedia Computing and Networking, provide a good start for identifying the components of multimedia. The range of multimedia activity is demonstrated in papers on multimedia authoring (i.e., specification of multimedia sequences), user interfaces, navigation (user choices), effectiveness of multimedia in education, distance learning, video conferencing, interactive television, video on demand, virtual reality, digital libraries, indexing and retrieval, and support of collaborative work. The wide range of technologies is evident in papers on disk scheduling, capacity planning, resource management, optimization, networking, switched Ethernet LANs, Asynchronous Transfer Mode (ATM) networking, quality of service in networks, Moving Picture Expert Group (MPEG) encoding, compression, caching, buffering, storage hierarchies, video servers, video file systems, machine classification of video scenes, and Internet audio and video.

Multimedia systems need a delivery system to get the multimedia objects to the user. Magnetic and optical disks were the first media for distribution. The Internet, as well as the Transmission Control Protocol/Internet Protocol (TCP/IP) protocol suite or Net BIOS on isolated or campus LANs, became the next vehicles for distribution. The rich text and graphics capabilities of the World Wide Web browsers are being augmented with animations, video and sound. Internet distribution will be augmented by distribution via satellite, wireless and cable systems.

13.2 WHAT IS MULTIMEDIA?

Multimedia can have many definitions. These include:

Multimedia means that computer information can be represented through audio, video and animation in addition to traditional media (i.e., text, graphics, drawings, images).
A good general definition is:

Multimedia is the field concerned with the computer-controlled integration of text, graphics, drawings, still and moving images (Video), animation, audio and any other media where every type of information can be represented, stored, transmitted and processed digitally.

The *American Heritage Dictionary* defines multimedia as:
"the combined use of several media such as movies, slides, music and lighting, especially for the purpose of education and entertainment".

13.3 MULTIMEDIA SYSTEMS

Borko Furt (1994) defines multimedia system as:
"A multimedia media system consists of three key elements:

- multimedia hardware
- operating system and GUI
- multimedia software development and authoring tools

J. Suterland and L. Litter (1992) introduced a new term as *"**multimedia service**"* on integrating the networking support for multimedia application.

A ***Multimedia System*** is a system capable of processing multimedia data and applications.

A ***Multimedia System*** is characterised by the processing, storage, generation, manipulation and rendition of Multimedia information.

13.3.1 Components of a Multimedia System

A multimedia system may consist of following devices and interfaces along with various software:

- **Media Capture Devices:** These are used for input of various information and data to be processed by multimedia system. The examples are—Video Camera, Video Recorder, Audio Microphone, Keyboards, mice, graphics tablets, 3D input devices, tactile sensors, VR devices, Digitising/Sampling Hardware.
- **Storage Devices** : These devices are used for storing the data of multimedia application in various formats. The examples are— Hard disks, CD-ROMs, Jaz/Zip drives, DVD, *etc*.
- **Communication Networks:** These are used to communicate data between various computer systems such as — Ethernet, Token Ring, FDDI, ATM, Intranets, Internets.
- **Computer Systems:** It is a complete computer system with all basic devices and software such as Multimedia Desktop machines or Multimedia workstations along with all associated hardware and software tools. The examples are— Multimedia Desktop machines, Workstations, MPEG/VIDEO/DSP Hardware.
- **Display and Output Devices:** These are specific and general output devices such as — CD-quality speakers, HDTV, SVGA, Hi-Res monitors, Colour printers, etc.

Hence, various specific devices and modules of a multimedia system may be represented as follows:

CD player, MIDI, Digital camera, Floppy disk drive, Scanner, Multimedia software, Microphone, Video cassette recorder CD-ROM drive, DVD drive, Colour printer, Audio-Video interface.

These devices are in addition to the general to I/O devices.

Multimedia software forms important aspect for a complete multimedia system. These software are used to create multimedia application and effects for text, image, audio and video.

In multimedia technology these software are called Authoring system.

13.3.2 Characteristics of a Multimedia System

A multimedia system has four basic characteristics:

- Multimedia systems must be ***computer controlled.***
- Multimedia systems are ***integrated.***
- The information they handle must be represented ***digitally.***
- The interface to the final presentation of media is usually ***interactive.***

13.3.3 Challenges for Multimedia Systems

Supporting multimedia applications over a computer network renders the application ***distributed.*** This will involve many special computing techniques — discussed later.

Multimedia systems may have to render a variety of media at the same instant — a distinction from normal applications. There is a temporal relationship between many forms of media (*e.g.*, video and audio). There are 2 forms of problems here:

- Sequencing within the media—***Playing frames in correct order/time frame in video.***

- ***Synchronisation*** — inter-media scheduling (*e.g.*, video and audio). Lip synchronisation is clearly important for humans to watch playback of video and audio and even animation and audio. Ever tried watching an out of (lip) sync film for a long time?

The key issues multimedia systems need to deal with here are:

- How to represent and store temporal information.
- How to strictly maintain the temporal relationships on play back/retrieval?
- What processes are involved in the above?

Data has to represented ***digitally*** so many initial source of data needs to be ***digitised*** — translated from analog source to digital representation. This will involve scanning (graphics, still images), sampling (audio/video) although digital cameras now exist for direct scene to digital capture of images and video.

The data is ***large*** several Mb easily for audio and video — therefore storage, transfer (bandwidth) and processing overheads are high. Data compression techniques are very common.

13.3.4 Desirable Features for a Multimedia System

Given the above challenges the following prerequisite features are required and may be called desirable for a multimedia system:

- **Very High Processing Power**: Multimedia system requires high processing speed in the architecture of processor since it needed to deal with large data processing and real time delivery of media.
- **Multimedia Capable File System**: needed to deliver real-time media — *e.g.*, video/audio streaming. Special hardware/software needed *e.g.*, RAID technology.
- **Data Representation/File Formats that Support Multimedia:** Data representations/file formats should be easy to handle yet allow for compression/decompression in real-time.
- **Efficient and High I/O:** Input and output to the file subsystem needs to be efficient and fast. For example, it is required to allow for real-time recording as well as playback of data. *e.g.*, Direct to Disk recording systems.
- **Special Operating System and System Library:** These are required to allow access to file system and process data efficiently and quickly. For example, it may be required to support direct transfers to disk, real-time scheduling, fast interrupt processing, I/O streaming, *etc.*
- **Storage and Memory:** Large storage units (of the order of 50-100 Gb or more) and large memory (50 -100 Mb or more) are required for handling the huge amount of data of a multimedia application.
- **Network Support:** At present trends are moving towards the distributed multimedia application. Hence, various supports in client server model are required in multimedia system.
- **Software Tools:** For creation, capture and processing of media objects, user friendly tools are needed to handle media, design and develop applications, deliver media.

Examples of Prototype Multimedia Systems and Platforms

Education and training

- Computer aided instruction
- Distance and interactive training
- Multimedia Encyclopedias

Operations

- Command and control
- Process control
- CAD/CAM
- Air traffic control
- On-line monitoring
- Multimedia security systems

Public

- Digital libraries
- Electronic museum
- Network kiosk systems (medical, legal, banking, shopping, tourist)

Home

- Video on demand
- Interactive TV
- Home shopping
- Remote home care
- Electronic album
- Personalized electronic journals

Business/Office

- Executive information systems
- Remote consulting systems
- Video conferencing
- Multimedia mail
- Multimedia documents
- Advertising
- Collaborative work
- Electronic publishing

13.4 MULTIMEDIA TECHNOLOGY

A wide variety of technologies contribute to multimedia. Some of the technologies are going through rapid improvement and deployment because of demand for PCs and workstations. As a result, multimedia benefits from lower-cost, better-performance microprocessors, memory chips and disk storage. Other technologies are being developed specifically for multimedia systems. We present here the major technologies relevant to multimedia.

13.4.1 Compression Technology

Compression is a key multimedia technology because it reduces the number of bits needed to represent a multimedia object. At present, compression of motion video reduces the number of bits by a factor of approximately one hundred. Without this enormous factor, we would have to wait many years for storage, logic and memory to become inexpensive enough for uncompressed video data to be used. Compression makes the data not only less expensive to store but also easier to move around.

13.4.2 Video Servers

The role of a multimedia server is to store and deliver multimedia objects, which implies having a mapping from the name of an object to the locations where it is stored. Rotating magnetic disk storage is the preferred medium for storing multimedia objects, with solid-state memory used for buffering. Multimedia servers are based on computer file servers and will benefit from the research being done to improve the performance and reduce the cost of storage, memory and microprocessors. Research to specifically reduce the cost of storing and playing back video files is important. Research is also appropriate to achieve the unique requirement of isochronous delivery of audio and video files because it is a requirement not found in other computer servers.

13.4.3 Networks

Telephone networks dedicate a set of resources that forms a complete path from end to end for the duration of the telephone connection. The dedicated path guarantees that the voice data can be delivered from one end to the other end in a smooth and timely way, but the resources remain dedicated even when there is no talking. In contrast, digital packet networks, for communication between computers, use time-shared resources (links, switches and routers) to send packets through the network. The use of shared resources allows computer networks to be used at high utilization, because even small periods of inactivity can be filled with data from a different user. The high utilization and shared resources create a problem with respect to the timely delivery of video and audio over data networks. Current research centers around reserving resources for time-sensitive data, which will make digital data networks more like telephone voice networks.

13.4.4 Data-transmission Techniques

Modems

Modulator/demodulators, or modems, are used to send digital data over analog channels by means of a carrier signal (sine wave) modulated by changing the frequency, phase, amplitude or some combination of them in order to represent digital data. (The result is still an analog signal.) Modulation is performed at the transmitting end and demodulation at the receiving end. The most common use for modems in a computer environment is to connect two computers over an analog telephone line. Because of the quality of telephone lines, the data rate is commonly limited to 28.8 Kb/s. For transmission of customer analog signals between telephone company central offices, the signals are sampled and converted to "digital form" (actually, still an analog signal) for transmission between offices. Since, the customer voice signal is represented by a stream of digital samples at a fixed rate (64 Kb/s), the data rate that can be achieved over analog telephone lines is limited.

ISDN

Integrated Service Digital Network (ISDN) extends the telephone company digital network by sending the digital form of the signal all the way to the customer. ISDN is organized around 64Kb/s transmission speeds, the speed used for digitized voice. An ISDN line was originally intended to simultaneously transmit a digitized voice signal and a 64Kb/s data stream on a single wire. In practice, two channels are used to produce a 128Kb/s line, which is faster than the 28.8 Kb/s speeds of typical computer modems but not adequate to handle MPEG video.

ADSL

Asymmetric Digital Subscriber Lines (ADSL) extends telephone company twisted-pair wiring to yet greater speeds. The lines are asymmetric, with an outbound data rate of 1.5 Mb/s and an inbound rate of 64 Kb/s. This is suitable for video on demand, home shopping, games, and interactive information systems (collectively known as interactive television), because 1.5 Mb/s is fast enough for compressed digital video, while a much slower "back channel" is needed for control. ADSL uses very high-speed modems at each end to achieve these speeds over twisted-pair wire.

ADSL is a critical technology for the Regional Bell Operating Companies (RBOCs), because it allows them to use the existing twisted-pair infrastructure to deliver high data rates to the home.

13.4.5 Cable Systems

Cable television systems provide analog broadcast signals on a coaxial cable, instead of through the air, with the attendant freedom to use additional frequencies and thus provide a greater number of channels than over-the-air broadcast. The systems are arranged like a branching tree, with "splitters" at the branch points. They also require amplifiers for the outbound signals, to make up for signal loss in the cable. Most modern cable systems use fiber optic cables for the trunk and major branches and use coaxial cable for only the final loop, which services one or two thousand homes. The root of the tree, where the signals originate, is called the *head end.*

Cable Modems

Cable modems are used to modulate digital data, at high data rates, into an analog 6-MHz-bandwidth TV-like signal. These modems can transfer 20 to 40 Mb/s in a frequency bandwidth that would have been occupied by a single analog TV signal, allowing multiple compressed digital TV channels to be multiplexed over a single analog channel. The high data rate may also be used to download programs or World Wide Web content or to play compressed video. Cable modems are critical to cable operators, because it enables them to compete with the RBOCs using ADSL.

Set-top Box

The STB is an appliance that connects a TV set to a cable system, terrestrial broadcast antenna, or satellite broadcast antenna. The STB in most homes has two functions. First, in response to a viewer's request with the remote-control unit, it shifts the frequency of the selected channel to either channel 3 or 4, for input to the TV set. Second, it is used to restrict access and block channels that are not paid for. Addressable STBs respond to orders that come from the head end to block and unblock channels.

13.4.6 Authoring Systems

Multimedia *authoring systems* are used to edit and arrange multimedia objects and to describe their presentation. The authoring package allows the author to specify which objects may be played next. The viewer dynamically chooses among the alternatives. Metadata created during the authoring process is normally saved as a file. At play time, an "execution package" reads the metadata and uses it as a script for the play out.

Authoring systems, as well as systems for gathering information for multimedia presentations (scanning, classifying, indexing and processing images, audio, and video) are very active research areas. Particularly challenging, and also very useful, are techniques that can be applied to compressed data. Entirely new techniques are required, and the human factors involved in the processing of this new data must be understood.

13.5 MULTIMEDIA ARCHITECTURE

In this section, we show how the multimedia technologies are organized in order to create multimedia systems, which in general consists of suitable organizations of clients, application servers and storage servers that communicate through a network. Some multimedia systems are confined to a stand-alone computer system with content stored on hard disks or CD-ROMs. Distributed multimedia systems communicate through a network and use many shared resources, making quality of service very difficult to achieve and resource management very complex.

13.5.1 Single-user Stand-alone Systems

Stand-alone multimedia systems use CD-ROM disks and/or hard disks to hold multimedia objects and the scripting metadata to orchestrate the playout. CD-ROM disks are inexpensive to produce and hold a large amount of digital data; however, the content is static—new content requires creation and physical distribution of new disks for all systems. Decompression is now done by either a special decompression card or a software application that runs on the processor. The technology trend is toward software decompression.

13.5.2 Multi-user Systems

Video Over LAN

Stand-alone multimedia systems can be converted to networked multimedia systems by using client-server remote-file-system technology to enable the multimedia application to access data stored on a server as if the data were on a local storage medium. This is very convenient, because the stand-alone multimedia application does not have to be changed. LAN throughput is the major challenge in these systems. Ethernet LANs can support less than 10 Mb/s, and token rings 16 Mb/s. This translates into six to ten 1.5Mb/s MPEG video streams.

Direct Broadcast Satellite

Direct Broadcast Satellite (DBS), which broadcasts up to 80 channels from a satellite at high power, arrived in 1995 as a major force in the delivery of broadcast video. The high power allows small (18-inch) dishes with line-of-sight to the satellite to capture the signal. MPEG compression is used to get the maximum number of channels out of the bandwidth. The RCA/Hughes service employs two satellites and a backup to provide 160 channels. This large number of channels allows many premium and special-purpose channels as well as the usual free channels. Many more pay-per-view channels can be provided than in conventional cable systems. This allows enhanced pay-per-view, in which the same movie is shown with staggered starting times of half an hour or an hour.

DBS requires a set-top box with much more function than a normal cable STB. The STB contains a demodulator to reconstruct the digital data from the analog satellite broadcast. The MPEG compressed form is decompressed, and a standard TV signal is produced for input to the TV set. The STB uses a telephone modem to periodically verify that the premium channels are still authorized and report on use of the pay-per-view channels so that billing can be done.

Interactive TV and Video to the Home

Interactive TV and video to the home allow viewers to select, interact with and control video play on a TV set in real time. The user might be viewing a conventional movie, doing home shopping or engaging in a network game. The compressed video flowing to the home requires high bandwidth, from 1.5 to 6 Mb/s, while the return path, used for selection and control, requires far lower bandwidth.

Interactive TV architectures are typically three-tiered, in which the client and server tiers interact through an application server. (In three-tier systems, the tier-1 systems are clients, the tier-2 systems are used for application programs, and the tier-3 systems are data servers.) The application tier is used to separate the logic of looking up material in indexes, maintaining the shopping state of a viewer, interacting with credit card servers, and other similar functions from the simple function of delivering multimedia objects.

Internet Over Cable Systems

World Wide Web browsing allows users to see a rich text, video, sound and graphics interface and allows them to access other information by clicking on text or graphics. Web pages are written in HyperText Markup Language (HTML) and use an application communications protocol called HTTP.

Cable TV systems can be used to provide asymmetric Internet access for home computers in ways that are very similar to interactive TV over cable. The data being sent to the client is digitized and broadcast over a prearranged channel over all or part of the cable system. A *cable modem* at the client end tunes to the right channel and demodulates the information being broadcast. It must also filter the information destined for the particular station from the information being sent to other clients.

Video Servers on a LAN

LAN-based multimedia systems go beyond the simple, client-server, remote file system type of video server, to advanced systems that offer a three-tier architecture with clients, application servers and multimedia servers. The application servers provide applications that interact with the client and select the video to be shown. On a company intranet, LAN-based multimedia could be used for just-in-time education, on-line documentation of procedures or video messaging. On the Internet, it could be used for a video product manual, interactive video product support, or Internet commerce. The application server chooses the video to be shown and causes it to be sent to the client.

There are three different ways that the application server can cause playout of the video: by giving the address of the video server and the name of the content to the client, which would then fetch it from the video server; by communicating with the video server and making it send the data to the client; and by communicating with both to set up the relationship.

Video Conferencing

Video conferencing, which will be used on both intranets and the Internet, uses multiple data types, and serves multiple clients in the same conference. Video cameras can be mounted near a PC display to capture the user's picture. In addition to the live video, these systems include shared white boards and show previously prepared visuals.

13.6 TRADE-OFF BETWEEN MULTIMEDIA AND HARDWARE

Multimedia is obviously a fertile ground for both research and the development of new products, because of the breadth of possible usage, the dependency on a wide range of technologies, and the value of reducing cost by improving the technology. Now that the technology has been developed, however, the marketplace will determine future direction. The technology will be used when clear value is found. For example, multimedia is widely used on PCs using CDs to store the content. The CDs are inexpensive to reproduce and the players are standard equipment on most PCs purchased today. The acceptance caused a greater demand for players, which, in turn, caused greater production and further reduced prices.

The computer industry is and an expanding market, for the key hardware technologies that underlie multimedia. These include solid-state memory, logic, microprocessors, modems, switches, and disk storage. The price declines of 30-60% per year that we have seen for several decades will continue into the foreseeable future. As a result, the application of multimedia, which appears expensive now, will become less expensive and more attractive. An exception to this fast rate of improvement is the cost of data communications. Communications depend both on technology with rapidly decreasing cost and on mundane and basically unchanging tasks such as laying cable with the help of a backhoe or stringing cables from poles. The cost of communication is not likely to decline significantly for quite a while.

We feel that multimedia will spread from low-bit-rate to high-bit-rate, and will begin on established intranets first, move to the Internet, and finally be transmitted on broadband connections (ADSL or cable modems) to the home.

13.7 MULTIMEDIA CONTENTS

The content of multimedia can be represented in various ways. Normally, the contents are expressed in terms of multimedia presentation objects or elements such as Text, Image, Graphics, Audio and Vedio. But this is the limited way to describe the functionality and organization of a multimedia, other terms which are used to describe the contents of a multimedia application, may be grouped as follows:

- **Discrete Media or Non-temporal:** These are time-independent media.
  - **Text** : It is basic representation of information in multimedia. The text may me represented in ASCII, HTML, Postscript, PDF, etc.
  - **Graphics:** Although the word graphics and image are used interchangeably in computer science, but it would be better to use graphics as a broad term.
  - **Image:** The image in multimedia may still image or an animated sequence of frames. The image may be a drawing, scanned images, etc.
- **Continuous media or Temporal:** These are time-dependent media.
  - **Audio:** Digital audio or speech is also an important content of multimedia. In an application, the audio may be normal sound, music, speech, structured studio (e.g., MIDI), etc.
  - **Animation:** These are sequence of image frame providing illusion of continuity.
  - **Video:** An animation synchronized with associated audio, is called video. The video may be streaming movie, full motion video or structured video clips different formats.

Multimedia software and other tools are used for creating, processing and organization of multimedia contents. These software may either be bundled into one package or may be provided in independent modules.

13.8 MULTIMEDIA PC

Most of the PCs are IBM compatible but they may or may not be multimedia enabled. To make a PC multimedia enabled some special hardware and software is required. Multimedia Marking Council (MMC) has come out with specifications for multimedia PCs which can assure a quality playback of multimedia productions. These are known as MPC (Multimedia PC) specifications.

Hardware and software requirements of a multimedia PC can be categorized into two classes viz., ***multimedia playback*** and ***multimedia production.***

13.8.1 Multimedia Playback

It usually requires smaller amount of resources, those which are sufficient for viewing an existing multimedia presentation.

13.8.2 Multimedia Production

It usually requires greater and more powerful resources and should fulfil all requirements for designing and developing a multimedia presentation.

Table 13.1 depicts the software and hardware required for multimedia playback and multimedia production.

TABLE 13.1 Software and Hardware for Multimedia PC

S. No		*Multimedia Playback*	*Multimedia Production*
1	Processor	At least Pentium class	At least Pentium II class
2	RAM	Minimum 8 MB is required, although 332 MB is recommended for smoother playback.	Minimum 128 MB with 256 MB recommended.
3	Hard disk	At least 540 MB, have 15 ms access time and should be able to provide 1.5 MB/Sec sustained throughput.	Require huge amount of disk space around 10 GB with 40 GB recommended.
4	VDU	SVGA standard and should be able to support 800 × 600 display mode with true color (16.7 million colors).	SVGA standard and should be able to support 800 × 600 display mode with true color (16.7 million colors). VRAM amount should be at least 4MB with 8MB recommended.
5	CD-ROM	PC should be equipped with CD-ROM drive having speed of at least 4× but higher speeds like 36×, 48× or 52× are also recommended. This may be replaced by a DVD drive.	PC should be equipped with CD ROM drive having speed of at least 4× but higher speeds like 36×, 48× or 52× are also recommended. This may be replaced by a DVD drive. In addition PC should have a CD-writer.

(Contd.)

S. No.		Multimedia Playback	Multimedia Production
6	Sound Card	PC should have a sound card with attached speakers to hear sounds.	PC should have a sound card with attached speakers to hear sounds. In addition for recoding of sound like human speech or environmental sounds, one or more microphones.
7	Input device	Standard 101-keys keyboard and two-button mouse should be presented.	Standard 101-keys keyboard and two-button mouse should be presented. Additional input devices required are scanner, video capture card for converting analog signal to digital signal.
8	Software	Multimedia PC system software should be compatible with Windows 95 or higher, with standard software of playback of media files in standard formats (e.g., Window Media Player).	Multimedia PC system software should be compatible with Windows 95 or higher, with standard software of playback of media files in standard formats (e.g., Window Media Player). Some editing softwares are required to manipulate media components. For example, Adobe photoshope, Coreldraw, Cooledit and Sound Forege.
		Application programs like Web browsers (Internet Explorer), media players (e.g. Quick time, Real media Player), and document reader (Adobe Acrobat Reader, Power point Viewer) might be required to display additional content.	To display Web content web browsers would be required. Examples are: Microsoft Internet Explorer and Netscape Navigator.

A common multimedia may consist of the following hardware besides general hardware:

- Sound blaster
- Video capture hardware
- Compression hardware
- Video conferencing tools
- Inbuilt modem
- Inbuilt network interface

These devices are supported by their driver for communication with CPU. The window based environment for multimedia PC is supported by MCI, TAPI and API for integrating various peripheral devices and communication system.

13.9 APPLICATIONS OF MULTIMEDIA

A *multimedia application* is an application which uses a collection of multiple media sources e.g., text, graphics, images, sound/audio, animation and/or video.

The multimedia is applied now in every walk of life and society. Due to its unlimited power, multimedia, is now widely used in entertainment, business, education, etc. Multimedia applications are primarily existing applications that can be made less expensive or more effective through the use of multimedia technology. In addition, new, speculative applications, like movies on demand, can be created with the technology.
Multimedia applications:

- World Wide Web
- Hypermedia courseware
- Video conferencing
- Video-on-demand
- Interactive TV
- Groupware
- Home shopping
- Games
- Virtual reality
- Digital video editing and production systems
- Multimedia Database systems

Current big applications areas in multimedia include:

World Wide Web — Hypermedia systems — embrace nearly all multimedia technologies and application areas. Ever increasing popularity.

MBone — Multicast Backbone: Equivalent of conventional TV and Radio on the Internet.

Enabling Technologies — developing at a rapid rate to support ever increasing need for Multimedia. Carrier, Switching, Protocol, Application, Coding/Compression, Database, Processing, and System Integration Technologies at the forefront of this.

We present here a few of these applications.

13.9.1 Home Applications

This application further includes various other applications: Video on demand, Networks games, Home shopping.

Video on Demand

Video on demand (VOD) is also called *movies on demand*, is a service that provides movies on an individual basis to television sets in people's homes. The movies are stored in a central server and transmitted through a communication network. A *set-top box* (STB) connected to the communication network converts the digital information to analog and inputs it to the TV set. The viewer uses a remote control device to select a movie and manipulate play through start, stop, rewind, and visual fast forward buttons. The capabilities are very similar to renting a video at a store and playing it on a VCR. The service can provide indices to the movies by title, genre, actors and director. VOD differs from *pay per view* by providing any of the service's movies at any time, instead of requiring that all purchasers of a movie watch its broadcast at the same time. *Enhanced pay per view,* also a broadcast system, shows the same movie at a number of staggered starting times.

Home Shopping

Services to the home that provide video on demand will also provide other, more interactive, home services. Many kinds of goods and services can be sold this way. The services will help the user navigate through the available material to plan vacations, renew driver's licenses, purchase goods, etc.

Networked Games

The same infrastructure that supports home shopping could be used to temporarily download video games with graphic-intensive functionality to the STB, and the games could then be played for a given period of time. Groups of people could play a game together, competing as individuals or working together in teams. Action games would require a very fast, or *low-latency* network.

13.9.2 Business

Real estate agents can easily represent interior and exterior of building along with necessary information like dimension and price. Architects and designers can design blueprints of building and products. This save time and cost and also improve the productivity of product.

13.9.3 Video Conferencing

Currently, most video conferencing is done between two specially set-up rooms. In each room, one or more cameras are used, and the images are displayed on one or more monitors. Text, images and motion video are compressed and sent through telephone lines. Recently, the technology has been expanded to allow more than two sites to participate. Video conferences can also be connected through LANs or the Internet.

13.9.4 Education

One of the chief advantages of such multimedia applications is that the sequence of material presented is dependent upon the student's responses and requests. Multimedia is also used in the classroom to enhance the educational experience and augment the teacher's work. Multimedia for education has begun to employ servers and networks to provide for larger quantities of information and the ability to change it frequently.

Distance Learning

Distance learning is a variation on education in which not all of the students are in the same place during a class. Education takes place through a combination of stored multimedia presentations, live teaching and participation by the students. Distance learning involves aspects of both teaching with multimedia and video conferencing.

e-learning

It is much more effective because it is done right when it is needed. In an industry context, this means that workers can receive training on PCs at their own workplaces at the time of need or of their choosing. This generally implies storing the material on a server and playing it through a wide-area network or LAN.

13.9.5 Virtual Reality

Virtual reality provides a very realistic effect through sight and sound, while allowing the user to interact with the virtual world. Because of the ability of the user to interact with the process, realistic visual effects must be created "on the fly."

13.9.6 Telemedicine

Multimedia and telemedicine can improve the delivery of healthcare in a number of ways. Digital information can be centrally stored, yet simultaneously available at many locations. Physicians can consult with one another using video conference capabilities, where all can see the data and images, thus bringing together experts from a number of places in order to provide better care. Multimedia can also provide targeted education and support for the patient and family.

13.9.7 Engineering Applications

Multimedia is used in designing mechanical, electrical, electronics and mechanical parts through the use of Computer Aided Design (CAD) and Computer Aided Manufacture(CAM) applications. These packages enable users to develop products from various viewpoints, rotate, scale and move parts.

13.10 DATA COMPRESSION

Graphics, Audio, and Video, in its uncompressed form, requires large bandwidth and storage capacity. In multimedia, which consists of the integration of other media, we have to compress these data so that it could be stored in less number of bits and transmit the same amount of data in narrow bandwidth. In multimedia this concept is significant as size of integrated multimedia content is huge and we require some technique for so that multimedia information may be represented in compressed form. ZIP file format is a very common example which provides compression. The areas of compression are divided into two parts, one for computation science where the objective is reduction in the storage space requirement and other communication system where the objective is to reduce the bandwidth requirement for data transmission. Some applications which can be considered both for transmission and storage. For example, the JPEG format not only saves only storage space on the local disk, it also speeds up the delivery of the image over the internet due to its platform independence and compressed format.

13.11 AUTHORING SYSTEM

Multimedia tool may vary from application to application. Therefore, it is the responsibility of multimedia team to select best possible tool, there must be an assessment of time and cost involved in the development process.

A multimedia authoring system is a set of programs, which has preprogrammed, customized and event based element for the development and integration of interactive multimedia components and applications.

Authoring is the process of integrated multimedia development, which is supported by authoring system tools. Authoring tools in multimedia application development provide facilities for organizing and editing basic elements.

Authoring systems are high-level tools for generating programs and components. These are designed to perform these quickly.

13.11.1 Authoring Tools

Authoring Languages (tools) are preferred over programming languages when the application:

- is more display oriented than data oriented
- has a larger number of different screen formats
- needs a lots of effects
- needs to be developed fast

Advantages of authoring tools

- Ability to do fast prototyping
- Ease of expanding the prototype to a full system
- Ease of use
- Built-in multimedia capabilities
- Less need for programming expertise

Disadvantages of authoring tools

- Slow execution
- Poor data handling

Currently, tools such as *Macromedia* and others are used to create multimedia documents.

Examples of Authoring tools

Director, Authorware are the standard authoring system.

Microcosm, Question Mask, Emblaze Creator, Flash, HyperCard, Color Tools, Hyper Studio, IconAuthor, etc. are some authoring tools.

Tasks performed by Multimedia Tools

- Multimedia application enabling software
- Hypermedia
- Multimedia Authoring Tools
- Multimedia databases and retrieval
- System software support for multimedia
- System hardware support for multimedia
- Performance measurement tools for multimedia

13.12 TEXT, HYPERTEXT, HYPERMEDIA

13.12.1 Text

Since its early days, operating systems have provided text based user interface. Even with graphic user interfaces (GUIs), text plays an important role in captioning, menus, and directing user interaction.

Although multimedia products include pictures, audio and video, text is usually the most common data type used to deliver information. Multimedia products use text to:
Provide identification of objects, for example labels for pictures.
Deliver information.
Help the user in navigation of multimedia product.

13.12.2 Hypertext

In a voluminous multimedia product, it is very difficult to access the desired information. Hypertext refers to the text that connects to other documents. These texts are known as *hypertext link, hyperlink, hotlink,* or simply *links.* Hypertext is a text based navigation mechanism to access information in non-linear fashion. In a hypertext systems, keywords are indexed or "markedup". Hypertext is very popular in multimedia and World Wide Web browsers because it allows the interface to link information and user control. A Hyperlink is used to 'jump' to another part of same web page or to load different web page.

Hypertext systems can be used to navigate through large amounts of information. There are two general strategies for hypertext systems.

Indexed Retrieval System

In such a system a list of key words are associated with detailed help topics. Search mechanism is provided to access detailed information associated with any key word.

Linked System

In such a system linkages are established between text elements and various locations in the same document or other document. A linked text is highlighted to differentiate from the rest of the text. When user clicks such highlighted words, he is provided with a jump to a topic related to the word.

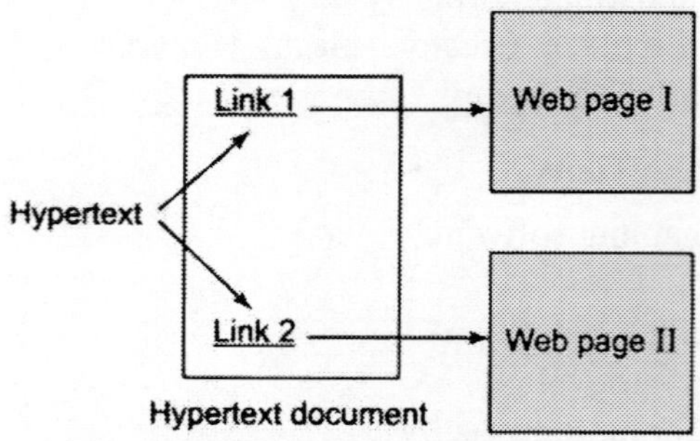

FIGURE 13.3 Hypertext Links

Hyperlinks are the foundation of Web pages and operation on them as it is a means of information retrieval. HTML(Hypertext Markup Language) provide hypertext for the Web and setup hyperlinks.

13.12.3 Hypermedia

A multimedia document provides greater navigational facility with embedded links to other documents. Links in a multimedia document may be explicit or implicit. Explicit links are created by the author. Collections of multimedia documents with explicit links are referred to as ***hypermedia.***

Implicit links are self created links and these are created in between documents with common contents.

Hypermedia documents on the Web can be specified using the Simplified Multimedia Item Language(SMIL) of the World Wide Web Constitution(W3C). SMIL is media neutral; that is; just like HTML, it does not specify the type of the documents that comprise the documents. Figure 13.4 illustrates the relationship between multimedia, hypertext and hypermedia.

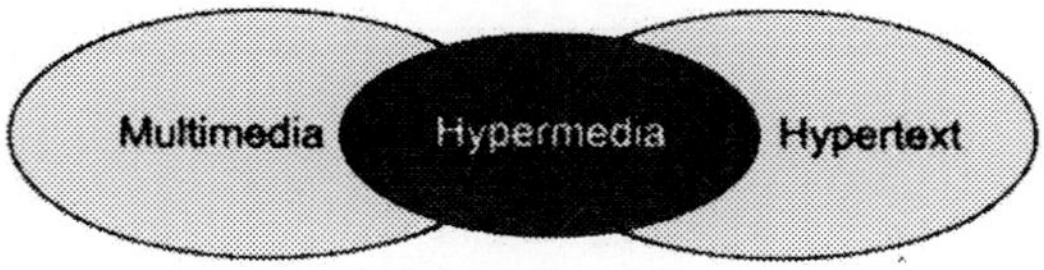

FIGURE 13.4 The Hypertext, Multimedia, Hypermedia Relationship

Hypermedia system is the non-linear links of hypertext systems and the continuous and discrete media of multimedia system. For example, non-linear links consists of text and video data, then this is a hypermedia, multimedia and hypertext system.

EXERCISES

1. Differentiate between
   (a) Image and graphics
   (b) Video and Animation
2. Describe some important applications of multimedia.
3. Discuss different types of software and hardware required for multimedia playback and multimedia production.
4. Define the term multimedia system. Briefly describe the system components of a multimedia system.
5. What is MPC? Explain.
6. What are text, hypertext and hypermedia? Discuss.
7. What are the various multimedia techniques? Explain briefly.
8. What do you mean by authoring system? Differentiate between authoring and programming in multimedia.
9. Explain the importance and role of animation in multimedia application.
10. Explain desirable features of good multimedia system.

14

Color Models

14.1 INTRODUCTION

Color is a very important aspect of computer graphics. Color is the by-product of the spectrum of light, as it is reflected or absorbed, as received by the human eye and processed by the human brain.

14.1.1 Light and Color

Before starting about color models, it is important to know how the human eye and brain turn light into color. Fig. 14.2 depicts the position of visible light in narrow frequency band within the electromagnetic spectrum. A few other frequency bands within this spectrum are also shown.

Monochromatic light is made up of one single pure frequency. In general, we see light made up of multi frequency, is known as multichromatic. Monochromatic light looks to the eye as a pure color, and can never be white or magenta, since it contains only one frequency, the wave of monochromatic light can be *represented* as a **sine,** as shown in Fig. 14.1.

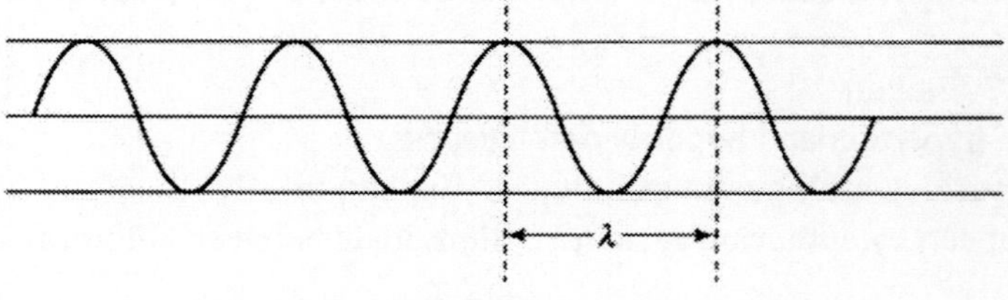

FIGURE 14.1

Brightness of light depends on the height (amplitude) of the sine wave. The width of one period (called lambda denoted as λ) is the wavelength of the light, and is inversely related to the frequency. As illustrated from Fig. 14.2 visible light has wavelengths from around 400 to 700 nm.(1 nm = 10^{-9} meter).

Light itself is an electromagnetic wave. Electromagnetic waves are thus a signal that is made out of one or more frequencies, for example the Electromagnetic waves used by a microwave oven are of very high frequency, while radio waves are very low frequency. The eye is only sensitive to a very narrow band of frequencies, namely, the frequencies between 429 THz and 750 THz (1 THz = 1 TeraHertz - 10^{12} Hz). All other electromagnetic waves can't be seen as shown in Fig. 14.3.

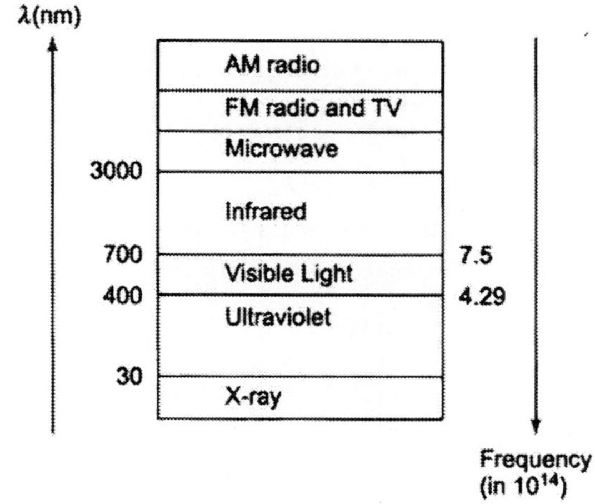

FIGURE 14.2 Electromagnetic Spectrum

Each frequency value within the visible band corresponds to a distinct color. At the low frequency end is a red color and the highest frequency end is a violet color as shown in Fig. 14.3

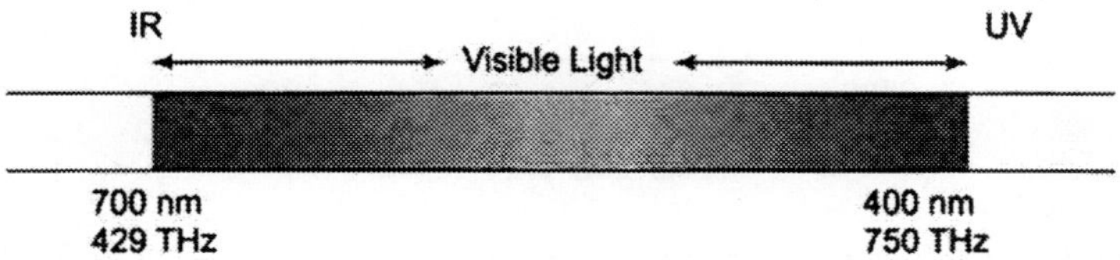

FIGURE 14.3 Color Pattern Corresponding to Electromagnetic Spectrum

This visible spectrum shows all the possible colors that can be made out of monochromatic light. Some light sources, such as lasers and Natrium lights, send out monochromatic light, but in general, light is multichromatic. For example, the sun sends out white light, which is light that contains ALL frequencies! That means the sum of red, yellow, green, blue and violet light looks like white! Physically speaking, it's not white at all, it's the sum of a lot of sine curves, but the human brain makes it look white. Color is thus something psychologically, and not something physical.

14.1.2 Characteristics of Light

Light can be characterized by three terms: saturation, hue and brightness.

Saturation (Purity)

It corresponds to physical property called excitation purity. It refers to how far a color is from white color. It is defined as percentage of luminance allocated to the pure color component i.e.,

$$\text{Saturation} = \frac{\text{Pure color}}{\text{Pure color} + \text{White}}$$

A completely pure color is 100 percent saturated, white light is 0 percent saturated, whereas mixture of pure color and white color have saturations between 0 and 100 percent.

Hue

It distinguishes white color from red, purple, yellow, green, etc. It is the term related to dominan wavelength (or dominant frequency). It is also called the color of the light.

Brightness

It corresponds to the physical property called ***luminance.*** Luminance measure the total energy in th light. It is proportional to the area bounded under the curve (Refer to Fig. 14.4).

$$\text{Luminance} = \text{Area under the curve} = \int_{\lambda} P(\lambda) d\lambda$$

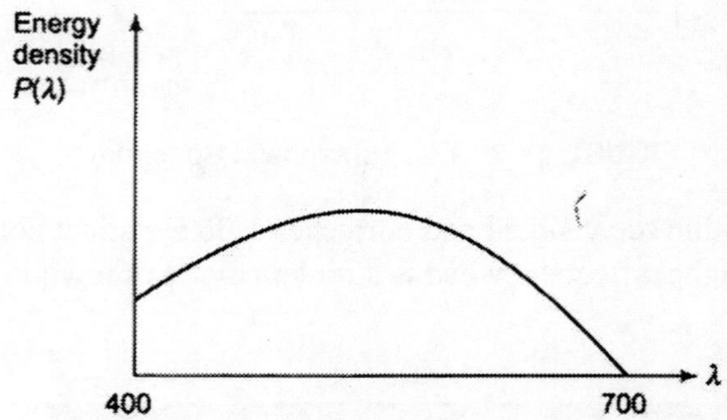

FIGURE 14.4

Higher the luminance, the brighter the light to be observes.
Color gamut determines the dominate wavelength and purity of color (See Section 14.3.2).

Light waves are a sum of many different frequencies, or the sum of many sine curves. Each of thes sine curves has its own frequency, and can have its own amplitude. A **spectrum** shows for each fre quency the amplitude. Here's an example of such a spectrum:

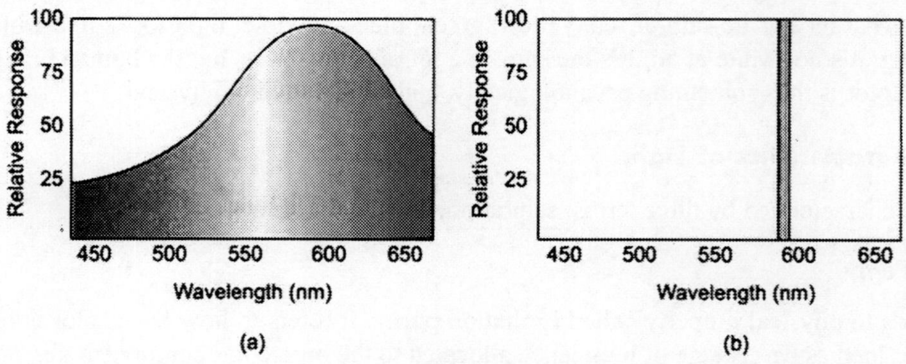

FIGURE 14.5

Fig 14.5(a) illustrates the spectrum of a yellow LED. The top of the spectrum is the Dominant Fre quency, and that is the color our eyes will usually see if light with this spectrum shines on it. If this yellow LED would have been monochromatic, the spectrum would have looked like as shown in Fig. 14.5(b).

Fig 14.6 illustrate the spectrum of white light is as follows (the height of the curve doesn't really matter):

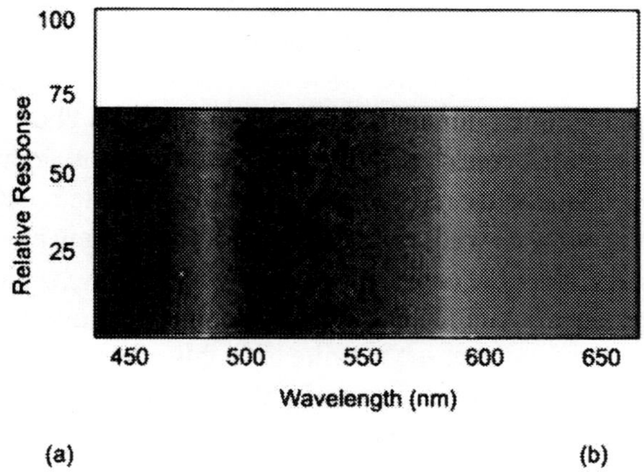

FIGURE 14.6

All frequencies are equally much in the light, only then it looks purely white to the brain. In all other cases, a certain frequency will be dominant and then that frequency will be the color the brain sees.

The spectrum of black light shown in Fig. 14.7.

Indeed, there's no light at all, the amplitude of every frequency is zero. Black is the color the brain gives to the absence of light.

14.1.3 The Eye and Color Perception

This section is about how the eye and the brain distinguish different colors.

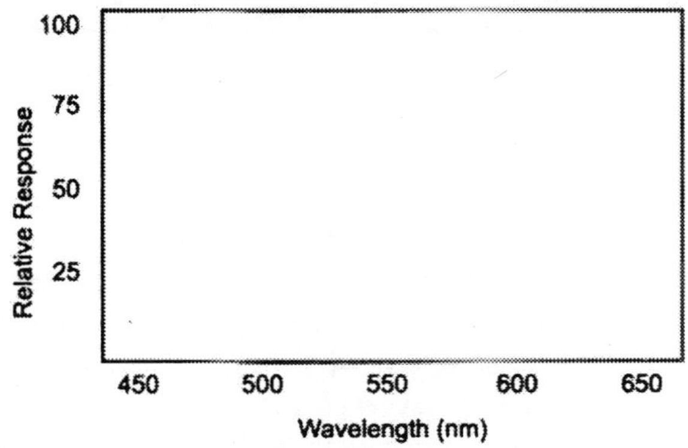

FIGURE 14.7

So light falls on the retina, and on the retina there are two types of cells viz., rods and cones. The rods only detect whether or not light is present, and are important at night. So rods are sensitive to the whole spectrum at once and can't tell what frequency the light has, and thus can't provide any color information. To detect color, you'd need photoreceptors that are sensitive to only a certain frequency.

That's exactly what the cones do?

The eye has three classes of color-sensitive light receptors called *cones,* which respond roughly to red, blue and green light (around 650, 530 and 460 nm, respectively). Such a rod isn't sensitive to a single frequency, they overlap a bit, it's just sensitive mostly to a certain frequency (Refer to fig. 14.4).

For example, yellow has a frequency between red and green. This yellow frequency will excite both the red and green cones a bit, and the human brain converts the signal "both red and green cones are excited" to "yellow". Even the blue cones are still a bit excited by yellow light, but neglegible. If light falls on the eye that has two frequencies: red and green, it will also excite both the red and green cones, so this light will show up as yellow as well, even though it doesn't contain any yellow frequency at all. If blue light falls on the retina, the blue cones are excited very strongly, while the green and red ones will give only a neglectable signal. And the brain turns the signal "mainly the blue cone is excited" to "blue". White light contains **all** frequencies, so if white light falls on the retina, all 3 types of cones are excited, and the brain turns the signal "green, red and blue cones all excited" into "white".

Thanks to God for gifting us with 3 types of cones. Table 14.1 depicts the 8 (2^3) main colors.

TABLE 14.1

Cones			Color	
Blue	*Green*	*Red*		
N	N	N	Black	
N	N	Y	Red	Y: Cone excited
N	Y	N	Green	N: Cone not
N	Y	Y	Yellow	excited
Y	N	N	Blue	
Y	N	Y	Magenta	
Y	N	Y	Cyan	
Y	Y	N	White	

You can, of course, distinguish much more colors than these 8 because each receptor type can have different levels of excitement.

The table explains how the brain creates different "hues" of colors out of the incoming signal, but it also gives a certain brightness to the light, based on how strong the incoming signal is: if it's very strong, the brain indicates it as a very bright red, white, ..., but if it's very weak, it'll be almost black. And then there's also the "saturation" of the color, this is based on the relative difference in strength each color type gives: if the red signal is very strong, but blue and green are also pretty strong, the color will have a low saturation, it's red-grayish or red whitish. If however the red signal would be very strong, and the blue and green signal very weak, a very red color shows up.

Since different spectra can look exactly the same for us, and some animals have different types of color receptors, it's possible that two colors that look same to us, may be two different colors for some animal.

The above process happens on every location of the retina separately, so that a complex two-dimensional image is formed where each location on the image can have it's own color.

Color blindness means one or more of the color types of cones are missing or less sensitive, for example if you miss the red one, you can only see the difference between light that has mainly green and light that has mainly blue. Light with mainly red, will show up as green for such a person, because the green receptors are still more sensitive to red than the blue ones. People who have 2 types of cones missing, and have thus only one type left, see in black and white, because only two main types of signals now exist: "the cone is excited" and "the cone is not excited". Imagine how much more colors a human would be able to see if he had 4 types of color receptors instead of only 3.

14.2 TWO BASIC COLOR APPROACHES

As we have already discussed, the human eye is sensitive to electromagnetic radiation with wavelengths between 400 and 700 nanometers. This radiation is known as ***light.*** The visible spectrum is illustrated in Fig. 14.3. A range of colors can be reproduced by one of two complimentary approaches:

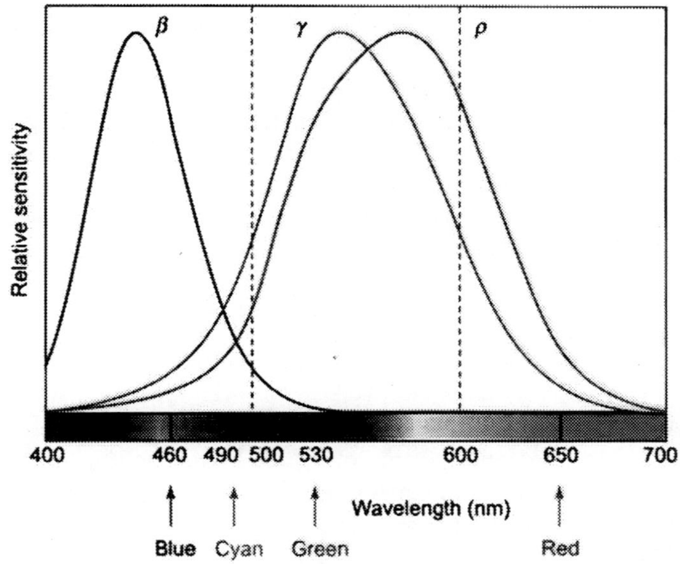

FIGURE 14.8 Human Spectral Sensitivity to Color (Three cones types (p,y,P) correspond to R,G,B)

14.2.1 Additive Colors

Additive colors are created by mixing spectral light in varying combinations. The most common examples of this are television screens and computer monitors, which produce color pixels by firing red, green and blue electron guns at phosphors on the television or monitor screen.

More precisely, additive color is produced by any combination of solid spectral colors that are optically mixed by being placed closely together, or by being presented in very rapid succession. Under these circumstances, two or more colors may be perceived as one color.

The ***additive primary*** colors are red (R), green (G), and blue (B). Adding R and G light makes yellow (Y). Similarly, G + B = cyan (C) and R + B = magenta (M). Combining all three additive primaries in equal amount makes white. Color plate 14.2 (p.323) more precisely defined the color combination of additive primary colors.

14.2.2 Subtractive Colors

Subtractive colors are seen when pigments in an object absorb certain wavelengths of white light while reflecting the rest. We see examples of this all around us. Any colored object, whether natural or man-made, absorbs some wavelengths of light and reflects or transmits others; the wavelengths left in the reflected/transmitted light make up the color we see.

This is the nature of color print production and cyan, magenta and yellow, as used in four-color process printing, are considered to be the subtractive primaries.

The objects may either transmit light (transparencies) or reflect light (paper, for example). The *subtractive primaries* are C, M and Y. Cyan absorbs red; hence C is sometimes called "minus red" (-R). Similarly, M is -G and Y is(-B). Color plate 14.2 more precisely defined the color combination of subtractive primary colors.

The subtractive color model in printing operates not only with CMY(K), but also with spot colors, that is, pre-mixed inks.

Unfortunately, ideal C, Y and M inks don't exist; the subtractive primaries don't entirely remove their compliments (R, B and G). This isn't a problem for film, where light is transmitted through three separate dye layers, but it has important consequences for prints made with ink on reflective media (i.e., paper). Combining C, Y and M usually produces a muddy brown. Black ink or key (K) must be added to the mix to obtain deep black tones. CMYK color is highly ***device dependent***— there are many algorithms for converting RGB to CMYK. Photographic editing should be done in RGB (or related) color spaces. Conversion to CMYK (usually with colors added to extend the printer color gamut) should be left to the printer driver software.

Additive Color vs Subtractive Color

(1) Additive color has primary colors red, green, blue. Subtractive color has primary color cyan, magenta, yellow.
(2) In case of additive color light from independent sources is added.
Whereas in case of subtractive color portion of visible light spectrum are absorbed.
(3) Adding all three additive primaries in equal amounts creates gray or white light. Combining all three subtractive primaries in equal amounts creates gray **or** black.
(4) Each subtractive primary colors removes one of the additive primary colors from the reflected **or** transmitted image. Cyan **(C) removes** red; hence it is known as minus red (-R), Similarly, M is –G and Y is –B.
(5) Additive colors are used to display color. For example, in television screen and color monitors use additive colors.
Subtractive colors are used to print color. For example, ink-jet printers, laser printers use subtractive colors.
(6) Colors perceived in additive colors are the result of **transmitted** light. Colors perceived in subtractive colors are the result of **reflected** light.

You can obtain a wide range of colors, but not *all* the colors the eye can see, by combining RGB light. The *gamut* of colors a device can reproduce depends on the spectrum of the primaries, which can be far from ideal. To complicate matters, the eye's response doesn't correspond *exactly* to R, G and B, as commonly defined (the description above is oversimplified).

14.3 COLOR MODELS

Color models are used to classify colors and to qualify them according to such attributes as hue, saturation, chroma, lightness or brightness. They are further used for matching colors and are valuable resources for anyone working with color in any medium: print, video, or Web.

A color model is an orderly system for creating a whole range of colors from a small set of primary olors. There are two basic types of color models:

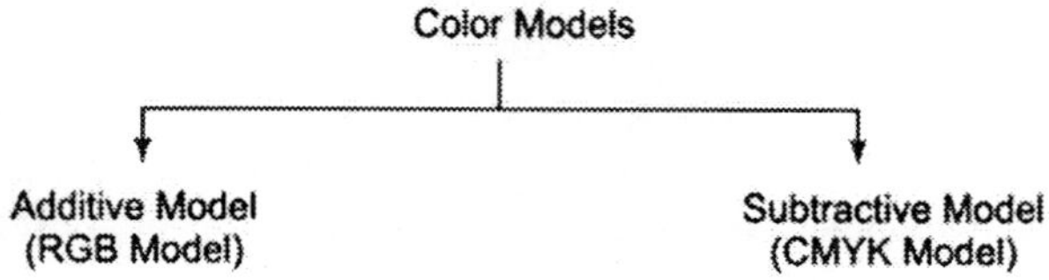

FIGURE 14.9

Additive color models use **light** to display color while subtractive models use printing **inks.** Colors erceived in additive models are the result of **transmitted** light. Colors perceived in subtractive mod-ls are the result of **reflected** light.

dditive vs. Subtractive Color Models

ince, additive color models display color as a result of light being transmitted (added) the total ab-ence of light would be perceived as **black.** Subtractive color models display color as a result of light eing absorbed (subtracted) by the printing inks. As more ink is added, less and less light is reflected. Vhere there is a total absence of ink the resulting light being reflected (from a white surface) would be erceived as **white** as illustrated in figure 14.10.

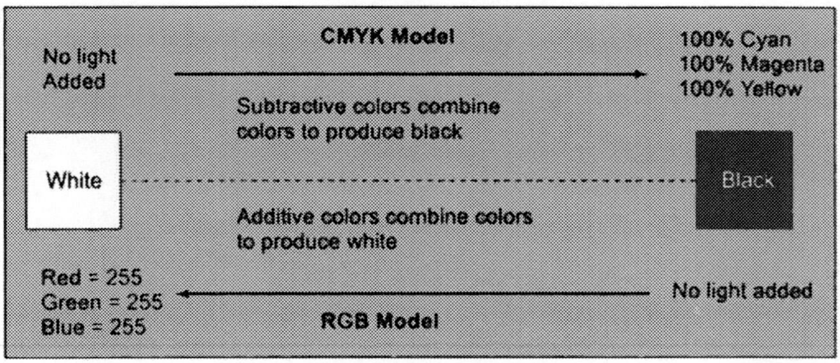

FIGURE 14.10 Comparative Structure of Additive and Subtractive Color Models

14.3.1 Color Gamut and Color "Space"

ach color model has is own gamut (range) of colors that can be displayed or printed. Each color nodel is limited to only a portion of the visible spectrum. Since a color model has a particular range of vailable color or gamut, it is referred to as using a "color space". An image or vector graphic is said to se either the RGB color space or the CMYK color space (or the color space of another color model). ome graphic applications present the user with more than one color model for image editing or illus-ration and it is important to choose the right one for the task.

14.3.2 CIE Chromaticity Diagram

Vhen visible spectrum is plotted on xy plane, then we obtain a tongue-shaped curve as shown by color late 14.1 (page 331). This curve is called **CIE chromaticity diagram.**

The horseshoe line starting at 400 nm on the lower left and wrapping around the top to 700 nm on the right is called the *spectrum locus.* It represents the pure spectral colors— the beautiful, intense colors produced by a prism in clear sunlight. The screen image is but a pale approximation. The straight line connecting the endpoints of the horseshoe is called the *purple boundary.* The full gamut of human vision lies within this figure. The vertical axis gives an approximate indication of the proportion of green; the horizontal axis moves from blue on the left to red on the right.

Point C in the diagram corresponds to the white-light position. The location of white depends on the illuminant color temperature. Some typical values:

Incandescent lamp	2856°K	$x, y = 0.448, 0.407$
Direct sunlight	5335°K	$x, y = 0.336, 0.350$
Overcast sky, D65	6500°K	$x, y = 0.313, 0.329$

The chromaticity diagram is useful for the following:

(1) It helps us to compare color gamut of two different set of primaries.
(2) It helps to identify the complementary colors.
(3) It determines the dominant wavelength of a color. (Refer to fig. 14.11)
(4) It determines the saturation of a color. (Refer to fig. 14.7)

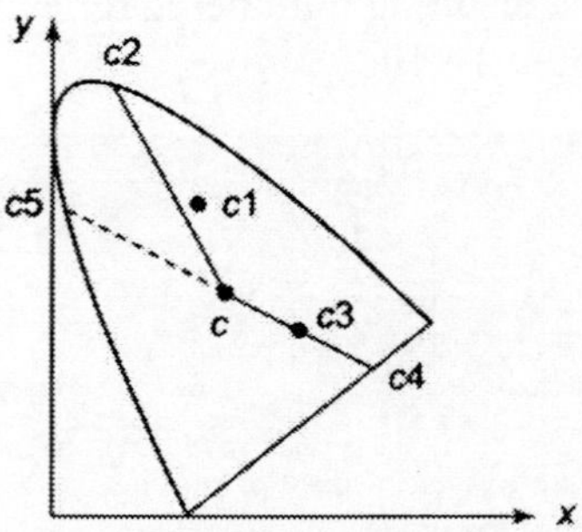

FIGURE 14.11

cc2 line passes through cl and cc4 line passes through c3. Dominant wavelength of color cl = c2

Dominant wavelength of color c3 = complement of c4 = c5 (because color point c3 lies below color point c)

$$\text{Purity of color } c1 = \frac{\text{Distance from c to c1 } (d_{c1})}{\text{Distance from c to c2} (d_{c2})}$$

14.3.3 The RGB Color Model

This color model based upon vision theory. Red, green, and blue are the primary stimuli for human color perception and are the primary additive colors. The RGB color model is the one you will mostly be dealing with in computer graphics. It is also called the ***additive color model,*** because you add three color components together to form any color. The relationship between the colors can be seen in this illustration:

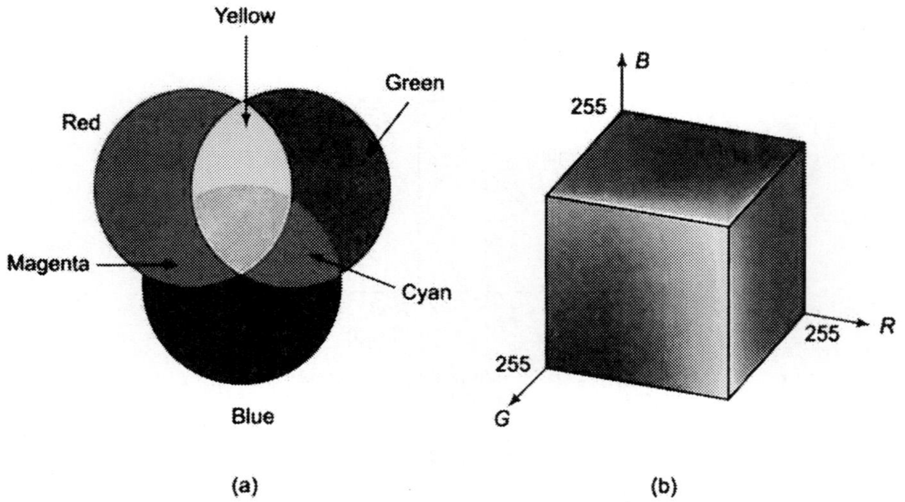

FIGURE 14.12

The RGB color model works exactly like those color receptors of the human eye work: ***the RGB color model describes a color by using three variables: red, green and blue. These variables can be compared to the strength of the signals from the three types of color receptors in the nerves.***

A computer or TV screen works this way too: it has 3 types of cells, red, green and blue, and can make each type brighter or darker independently, exciting the correct receptors of the eye to create the desired color.

If you look with a magnifying glass to a white area of your computer screen, you can see that the color white is actually made out of the three colors red, green and blue. This means the white emitted by a computer screen is different from white sunlight: while white sunlight contains photons of all frequencies (except a few), the computer screen only has three frequencies. The human eye can't see the difference between these two kinds of white.

The combination of red, green, and blue in full intensity makes white. White light is created when all colors of the EM spectrum converge in full intensity. The importance of RGB as a color model is that it relates very closely to the way we perceive color with the $\alpha\,\beta\,\gamma$receptors in our retinas.

RGB is the basic color model used in television or any other medium that projects the color. It is the basic color model on computers and is used for Web graphics, but it cannot be used for print production.

The RGB model forms its gamut from the primary additive colors of red, green and blue, refer to color plate 14.2 (Page 331).

In RGB color, the higher the values of R, G and B, the brighter the color will be, and if R=G=B, the color will be a shade of gray.

RGB color model can represent this model with unit cube defined on R, G and B axes, as shown in Fig. 14.13. The origin represents the black and vertex with coordinates (1,1,1) is white. Vertices of the cube represent the primary colors.

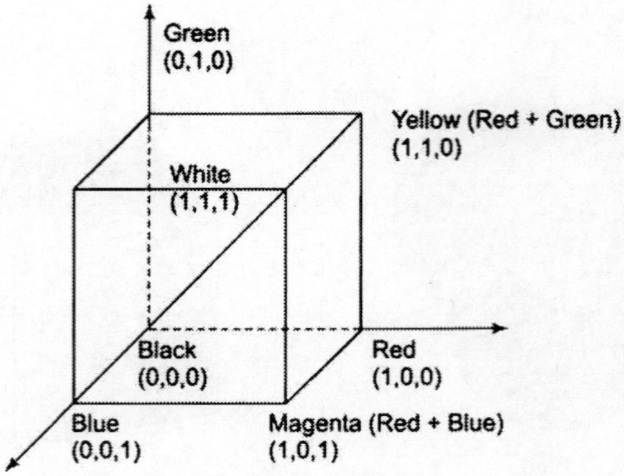

FIGURE 14.13 RGB Color Model

Each color in this model is represented as the triple (R, G, B), where the values of R, G and B lies in the range 0 to 1.

Computers generally display RGB using 24-bit color. In the 24-bit RGB color model there are 256 variations for each of the additive colors of red, green and blue. Therefore, there are 16,777,216 possible colors (256 reds × 256 greens × 256 blues) in the 24-bit RGB color model. In the RGB color model, colors are represented by varying intensities of red, green and blue light. The intensity of each of the red, green and blue components are represented on a scale from 0 to 255 with 0 being the least intensity (no light emitted) to 255 (maximum intensity). 127 is half intensity. This means color 0,0,0 is the darkest black, color 255,0,0 is the brightest red, color 0,255,0 is the brightest green and color 0,0,255 is the brightest blue. 255,255,255 is the brightest white and 127,127,127 is gray. The RGB color model is not very intuitive.

TABLE 14.2 Depicts with Common RGB color Values

R	*G*	*B*	*Hex Value*	*Color*
0	0	0	000000	Black
255	0	0	FF0000	Red
0	255	0	00FF00	Green
0	0	255	0000FF	Blue
255	255	0	FFFF00	Yellow
255	0	255	FF00FF	Magenta

14.3.4 CMY(K) Model or Process Model

CMYK (Cyan, Magenta, Yellow, Key or Ink) is subtractive color model. It based on the theory that colors of an object are seen when pigments in the object absorb certain wavelengths of white light while reflecting the rest.

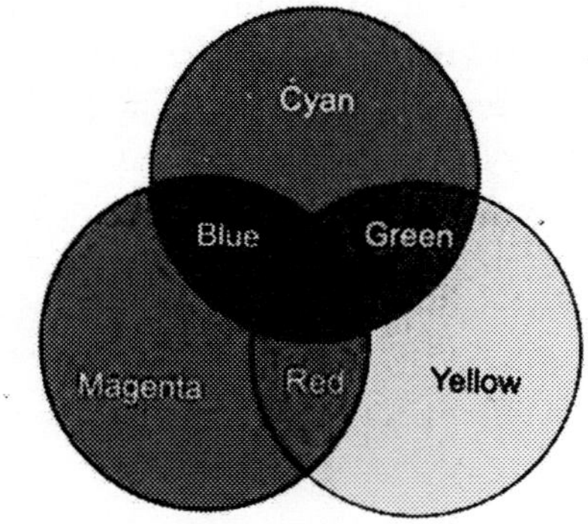

FIGURE 14.14 CMYK Color Model

Just as the primary colors of CMY are the secondary colors of RGB, the primary colors of RGB are the secondary colors of CMY. But as the illustrations show, the colors created by the subtractive model of CMY don't look exactly like the colors created in the additive model of RGB. Particularly, CMY cannot reproduce the brightness of RGB colors. In addition, the CMY gamut is much smaller than the RGB gamut (Refer to color plate 14.4).

In theory, the combination of cyan, magenta and yellow at 100%, create black (all light being absorbed). In practice, however, CMY usually cannot be used alone. Due to imperfections in the inks and other limitations of the process, full and equal absorption of the light isn't possible; thus true black or true grays cannot be created by mixing the inks in equal proportions. When cyan, magenta and yellow inks are combined it forms black—in theory. However, because of the impurities in ink, when cyan, magenta and yellow inks are combined it produces a muddy brown color. Black ink is added to this system to compensate for these impurities. In order to boost grays and shadows, and provide a genuine black, printers resort to adding black ink, indicated as K. Thus the practical application of the CMY color model is the ***four color*** CMYK process.

The CMYK printing method is also known as "four-color process" or simply "process" color. All the colors in the printable portion of the color spectrum can be achieved by overlapping "tints" of cyan, magenta, yellow and black inks. A tint is a screen of tiny dots appearing as a percentage of a solid color. When various tints of the four colors are printed in overlapping patterns it gives the illusion of continuous tones.

Cyan, magenta and yellow correspond roughly to the primary colors in art production: red, blue, and yellow. In the illustration below, you can see the CMY counterpart to the RGB model shown above:

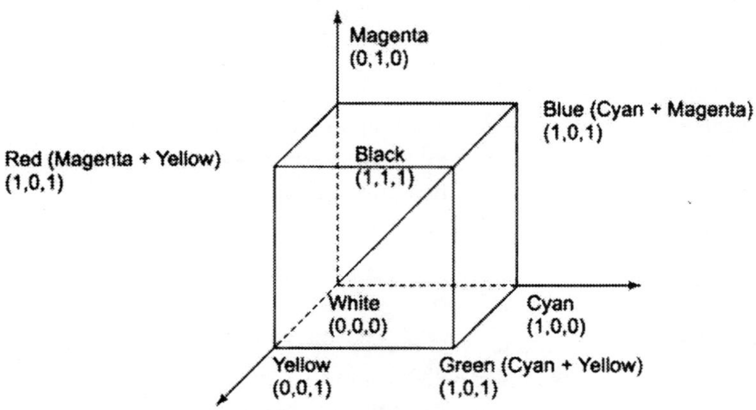

FIGURE 14.15 CMYK Color Model

The CMY model used in printing lays down overlapping layers of varying percentages of transparent cyan, magenta, and yellow inks. Light is transmitted through the inks and reflects off the surface below them (called the substrate). The percentages of CMY ink (which are applied as screens of halftone dots), subtract inverse percentages of RGB from the reflected light so that we see a particular color. This model is sometimes also known as ***process model*** or ***substrate model.***

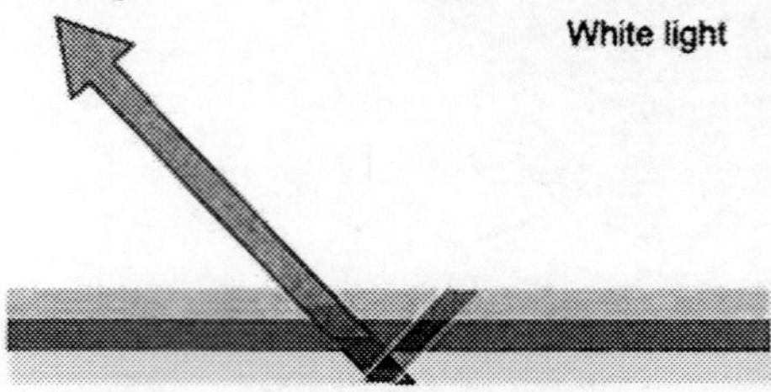

FIGURE 14.16

In the illustration above, a white substrate that reflects 100% of the light is printed with a 17% screen of magenta, a 100% screen of cyan, and an 87% screen of yellow. Magenta subtracts green wavelengths, cyan subtracts red wavelengths, and yellow subtracts blue wavelengths from the light. The reflected light, then, is made up of 0% of the red wavelengths, 44% of the green wavelengths, and 29% of the blue wavelengths.

Relationship between RGB Color Model and CMY Color Model

RGB color model and CMY color model are complement to each other.

$$\begin{bmatrix} C \\ M \\ Y \end{bmatrix} = \begin{bmatrix} 1 \\ 1 \\ 1 \end{bmatrix} - \begin{bmatrix} R \\ G \\ B \end{bmatrix}$$

where, the white is represented in the RGB system as the unit column vector.

$$\begin{bmatrix} R \\ G \\ B \end{bmatrix} = \begin{bmatrix} 1 \\ 1 \\ 1 \end{bmatrix} - \begin{bmatrix} C \\ M \\ Y \end{bmatrix}$$

where, the black is represented in the CMY system as the unit column vector.

Above-mentioned color models none of these models are sensitive to represent color because these are not directly related to intuitive color notations hue, saturation, brightness. Another class of models is introduced such as HSV(HSB), HLS, HVC models.

14.3.5 HSV Color Model

HSV(Hue, Saturation, Value) color model was created in 1978 by Alvy Ray Smith. It is non-linear reformation of RGB color. HSV is the color selection model used most often in illustration and image programs, like Fireworks and Freehand. Color selection is based on these criteria:

With hues along the outer edge at full saturation, and with saturation decreasing as you move to the center of the circle. Value or intensity is adjusted with a brightness bar. Hue is presented as an angle point($0° \le H \le 360°$), while saturation and value are measured as a percentage between 0 and 1.

HSV is one of many color systems that vary the degree of properties of colors to create new colors, rather than using a mixture of the colors themselves. The HSV color model is more intuitive than the RGB and CMY color models. HSV color spaces is device independent.

Figure 14.17 depicts the three-dimensional representation of the HSV model derived from the RGB cube. If we look at the RGB cube along the gray diagonal we can see a hexagon that is the HSV hexcone.

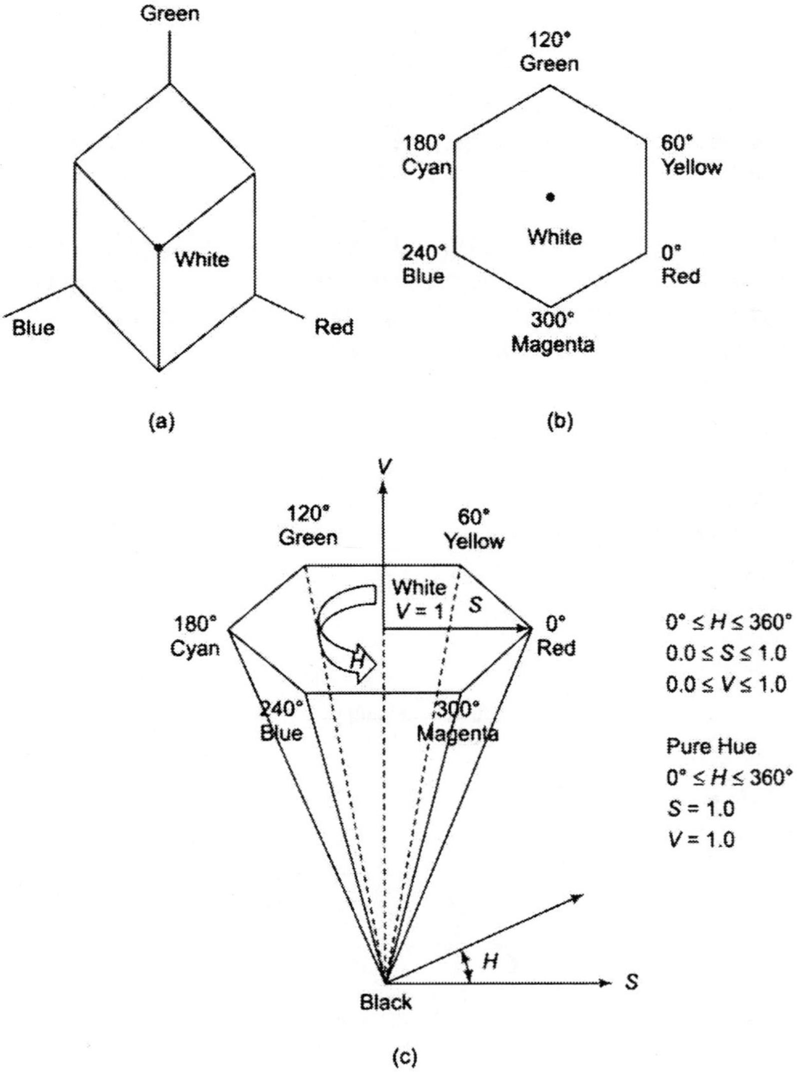

FIGURE 14.17

Three parameter Hue(H), Saturation(S), and Value(V) have the following range of values:

(a) The hue(H) is given by the angle about the vertical axis with red at 0°, yellow at 60°, green at 120°, cyan at 180°, blue at 240° and magenta at 300°. Note that the complementary colors are 180° apart. The complementary colors (red + cyan, blue + yellow, green + magenta) are diagonally opposite.

(b) The vertical axis is called value (V)(0.0< V <1.0). At V=0, we have black, and at V = l, we have white.

(c) The horizontal axis represents saturation(S) (0.0 ≤ S ≤ 1.0). It specifies purity of color and is the ratio of purity of a related hue to its maximum purity at S = "1" and V = l. At S = 0 is the gray scale, that is the diagonal of the RGB cube corresponds to V of the HSV hexcone.

At S = 1 AND V = l, we have pure hue. As S decreases hues are said to be less pure.

The user specifies a color (hue) and then adds white or black. Changing the **saturation** parameter corresponds to adding or subtracting white and changing the **value** parameter corresponds to adding or subtracting black.

Artists start with a "pure color or hue", then add black pigment to produce different *shades*. The more black pigment the darker the *shade*. They add white pigment and get different *tints*. Adding both black and white pigments gives different *tones*. (Refer to fig. 14.18). If we look at the cross-section of the hexcone we can see the analogy with the artists model.

So to choose a color we do the following:

1. Select pure hue (specifies H and sets S = V = 1)
2. To add black decrease V
3. To add white decrease S.
4. To add black and white decrease V and S.

For example: pure blue H = 240°, S = V – 1, dark blue H = 240°, S = 1, V = 0.40, light blue H = 240°, S = .3, V = 1.0

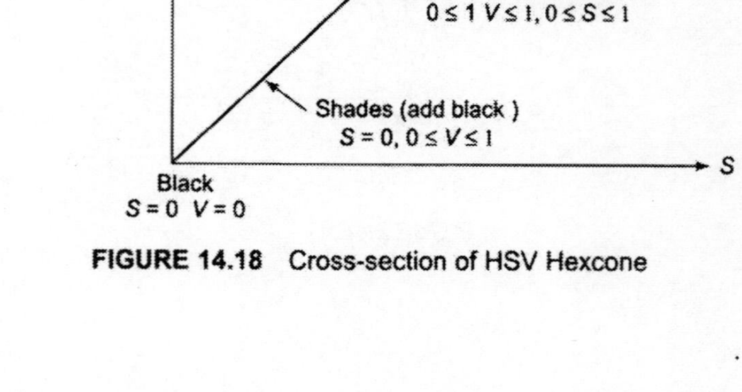

FIGURE 14.18 Cross-section of HSV Hexcone

The human eye can distinguish about 128 different hues, 130 different tints (saturation levels), and from 16 (blue part of spectrum) to 23 (yellow part of spectrum) different shades. So we can distinguish about $128 \times 130 \times 23 = 380{,}000$ colors.

14.3.6 HLS Color Model

HLS(Hue, Lightness, Saturation) is another way to describe intuitive color with 3 parameters. Three colors parameters in this model are called hue(H), (lightness) (L), and saturation(S). HSL is also known by the abbreviations of HLS and HIS, while the L can often refer to luminosity or luminance rather than light. HLS is more intuitive than RGB and CMY color models.

Figure 14.19 depicts the HLS color model. The HLS color model is graphically represented by a double cone or hexcone, this shape resembles a spinning top. The top and bottom ends of the cone, also called apexes, are the colors black and white. In this model, the hue is represented by the angular perimeter. The S part of HSL is graphically viewed by varying distances from the axis, which is the line that is located in the center of the graph in the vertical direction. And finally the distance between the two apexes is what represents the light of the color model. To put this graph, and the one for the similar HSV graph (which is a single cone representation of color model), into perspective both are variations of the well-know RGB color model. HLS color spaces can be device dependent or device independent. Range of parameters and their effect on color specifications is as follows:

(a) Hue specifies the angle about vertical axis($0° \leq H \leq 360°$). In this model blue at H=0°, magenta at H=60°, red at H=120°, yellow at H=180°, green at H=240°, and cyan at H=300°. Note that the complementary colors are 180° apart. The complementary colors(red + cyan, blue + yellow, green + magenta) are diagonally opposite.

(b) The vertical axis is called lightness (L)($0.0 \leq L \leq 1\ ()$). At L=0, we have black , at L=0.5 plane, we have pure hue, and at L=1.0, we have white. Along vertical axis(S=0) we have gray scale.

(c) The horizontal axis represents saturation(S) ($0.0 \leq S \leq 1.0$). It is the measure of the "purity" of a hue. As saturation is decreased, the hue becomes more gray. A saturation value of zero results in a gray-scale value i.e., at S= 0, we have gray scale. It specifies purity of color and is the ratio of purity of a related hue to its maximum purity at S = "l" and L = 0.5.

At S = l and L = 0.5 , we have pure hue. As S decreases hues are said to be less pure.

Likewise HSV model HLS model allows us to change shades, tints, tones in selected color. Thus, lightness is the amount of black or white in a color. Increasing lightness adds white to the hue, decreasing lightness adds black to the hue. Suppose artists start with a "pure color or hue", then add black pigment to produce different *shades.* The more black pigment, the darker the *shade.* Colors are made lighter if we increase the value of L and made darker if we decrease the value of L. They add white pigment and get different *tints.*

Comparison between HSV and HSL Color Models

(a) HSV represents the color model as a single-cone, while the HSL represents color model as a double-cone. Because the HSL model keeps the light and saturation aspects of the color model unique from each other, it tends to be more useful for those wishing to take advantage of these attributes in their work.

(b) The **HSV** goes all the way down to a white, which is not useful to many users of the color model. The HSL color model allows the color to range from a color that is fully saturated to gray.
(c) HSV color model can only range from the desired color to black. On the other hand, light can range from white to black in a HSL model (with the desired color in between). It is obvious that the HSL color model does indeed offer more freedom.

Computer programs that use color model are known to use either the HSL or HSV color models. Some programs will even use both. The most frequently used color model is the HSV. For example, **Apple computers uses** the HSV color model for their color picker, while **Microsoft** uses HSL. And while the simple Paint program provided by Microsoft only uses the HSL color model, more advanced photo editing software such as Adobe Photoshop benefits from using, both color models.

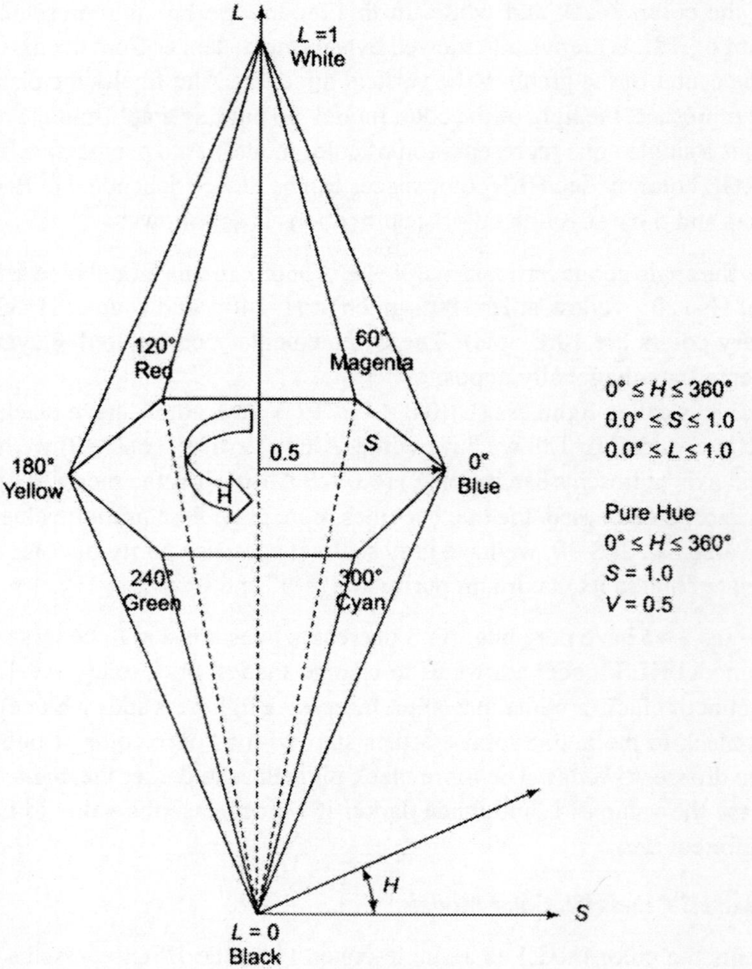

FIGURE 14.19

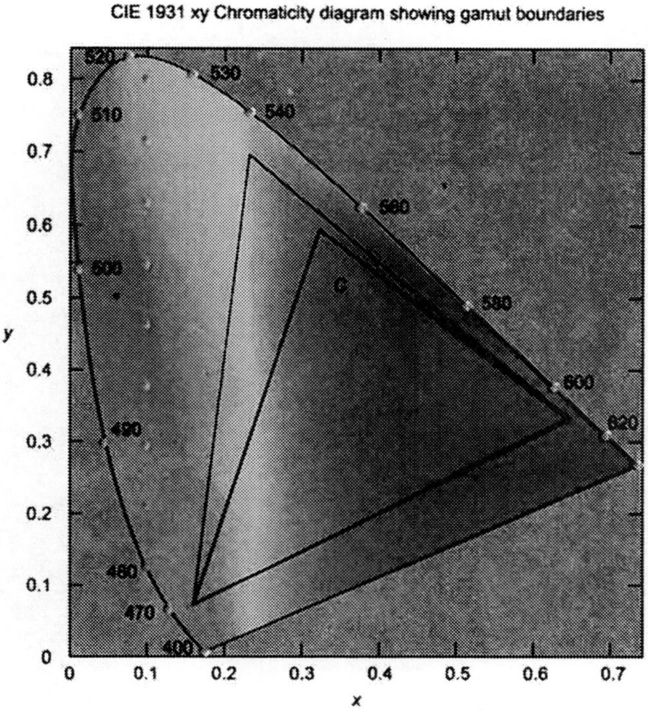

COLOR PLATE 14.1

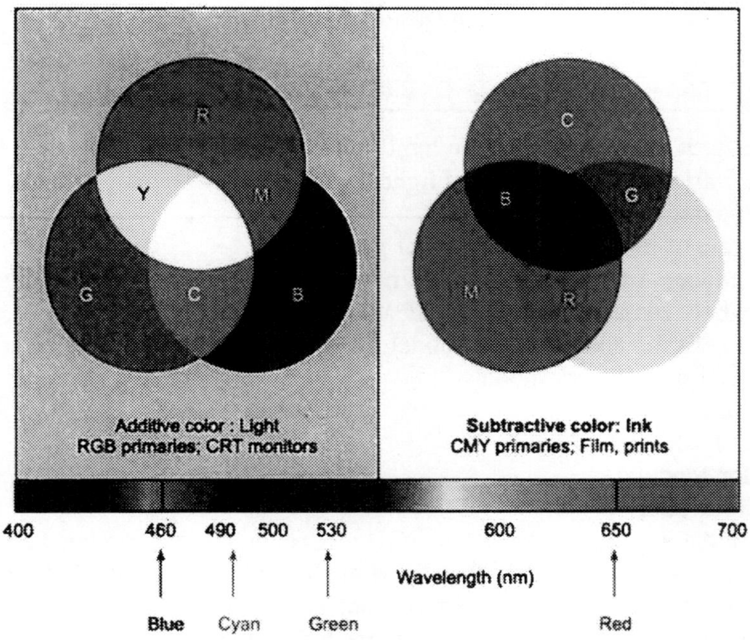

COLOR PLATE 14.2

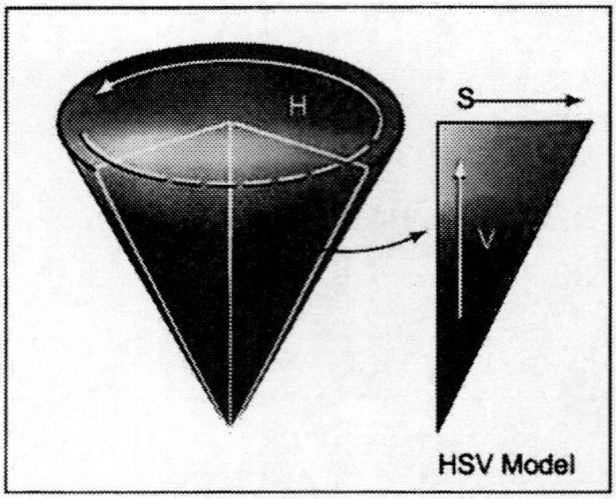

(a) HSV Model

HLS Model

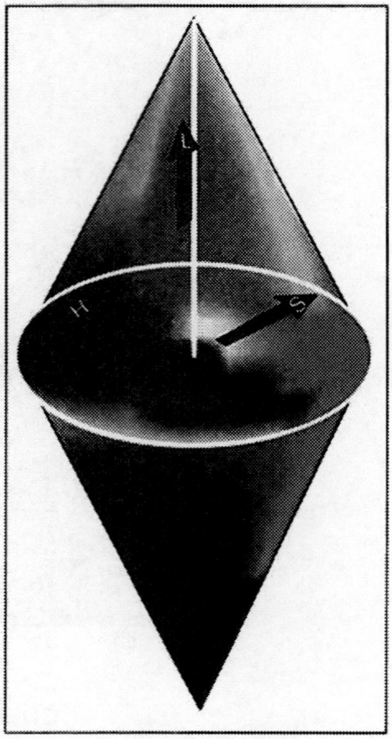

(b) HLS Model

COLOR PLATE 14.3

EXERCISES

1. Differentiate between monochromatic light and multichromatic light.
2. Describe the various characteristics of light.
3. Define color gamut and color space.
4. Explain the role of rods and cons for color prescription.
5. Explain the concept of color blindness. What are the reasons of color blindness?
6. Differentiate between additive colors and subtractive colors.
7. Differentiate between additive color model and subtractive color model.
8. Describe the following color models
   (i) RGB Color Model
   (ii) CMYK Color Model
   (iii) HSV Color Model
   (iv) HLS Color Model
9. Why HSV model is more intuitive than RGB model and CMYK model? Explain.
10. Why HLS model is more intuitive than RGB model and CMYK model? Explain.
11. Explain CIE chromaticity diagram. Hence, specify its importance.
12. Why CMYK model is known as device-dependent? Explain.
13. What is the role of K' in CMYK model?
14. Derive relationship between RGB model and CMYK model.

15

Illumination Models and Shading Models

15.1 INTRODUCTION

Realistic displays of a scene are obtained by generating projections of objects and by applying lighting effects to the visible surfaces. Hidden-surface algorithms enable to identify visible surfaces. Once visible surfaces are identified shading models used to compute the intensities and color for the surfaces in order to improve the realistic image.

Rendering is the process of generating a realistic image from a model, by means of computer programs. Two major techniques are involved in rendering-lighting and shading.

Surface rendering is the process to produce realistic images by setting the surface intensity according to lighting and color conditions in the scene..

Rendering involves two models- illumination models and shading models. Illumination models deals with intensity and color of a point on surface of an object. Shading models deals with intensity and color over surface of an object. The illumination/shading models determine the intensity of light that we should see at given point on the surface of an object. Primary objective of illumination and shading models is to produce a realistic image. Intensity profile of a scene depends on the reflective or refractive properties of the surface and position, power, and the number of light sources present in the environment, orientation of the viewpoint which influences the light and shade of scene.

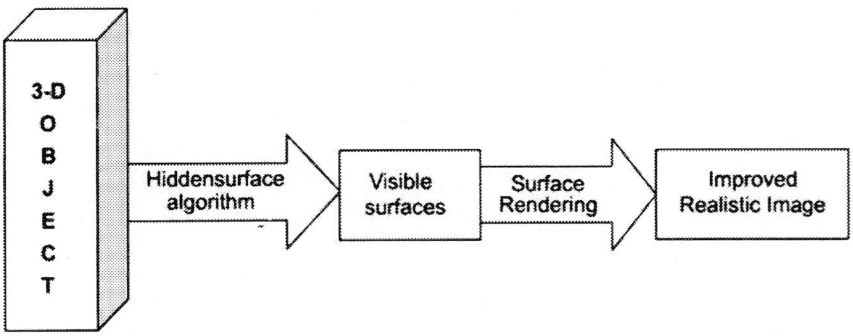

FIGURE 15.1 Impact of Surface Rendering on 3-D object

15.2 LIGHT SOURCES

The source of light that enable us to see an object is called light source. Basically two types of light sources are:

***Point Source*:** Rays from the source follow readily diverging paths from the source position. For example, sun, bulb etc.

***Distributed light source*:** In this case the illumination effects cannot be approximated realistically with take on source, because area of the source is not small compared to the surfaces in the scene. For example, tube light.

15.3 DIRECT AND INDIRECT REFLECTION

An object is visible either by reflected light from surfaces of the object-***direct reflection*** or reflected light from light reflecting surface –***indirect reflection*** as shown in figure 15.2.

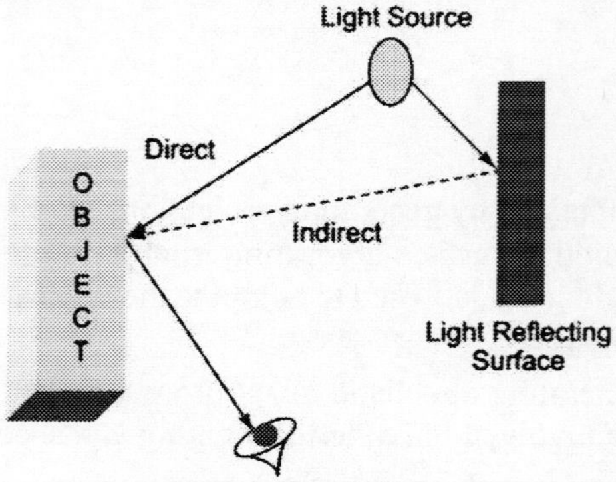

FIGURE 15.2 Object illumination

Total reflected light is the sum of the reflected light from the surfaces of the object and reflected light from light reflecting surface. Thus when an object is not directly illuminated by light source may also be illuminated.

15.4 TYPES OF LIGHT

When light falling on a surface can be –*absorbed*, *reflected*, and *transmitted* as shown in figure 15.3; reflected and transmitted lights make an object visible.

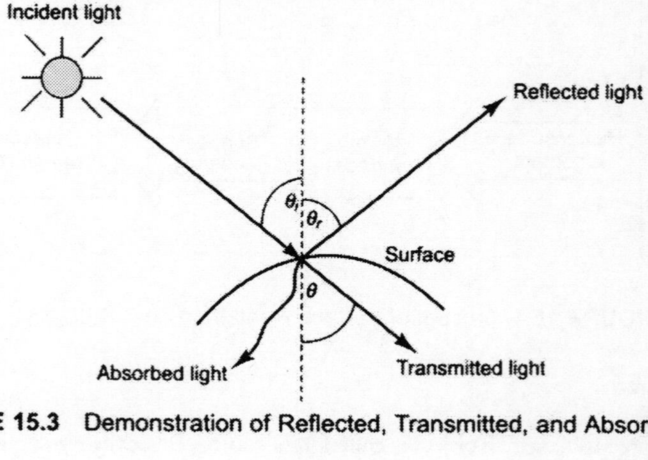

FIGURE 15.3 Demonstration of Reflected, Transmitted, and Absorbed light

The amount of incident light absorbed, reflected, and transmitted by a surface depends on the type of its material.

- Shiny material e.g. mirror reflects more incident light.
- Dull material e.g. paper absorbs more incident light.
- Illuminated transparent surface e.g glass or water reflects as well as transmits some part of the incident light.

The amount of reflected light determines the color and brightness of the object– **subtractive colors**.

15.5 COMPONENTS OF REFLECTED LIGHT

There are three basic light components reflected from a surface:

- Ambient light
- Diffuse light
- Specular light

The character of the light reflected or transmitted depends on

- Composition of the light source
- Direction of the light source
- Geometry of the light source
- The surface orientation
- The surface properties of the object

15.6 ILLUMINATION MODELS

An illumination model is an equation expresses three components –ambient, diffuse, and specular of light reflected from or transmitted (refracted) through a surface.

Illumination Model = Ambient + Diffuse + Specular

15.6.1 Types of Illumination models

***Local Illumination Model*:** These models are local in that they do not consider light from objects in the scene. Only light sources generate light. Light reflected from objects in environment has no effect on other objects. Such types of illumination models express light from single-light, single-surface interaction.

If light arrives straight from the light source then it is known as direct illumination.

In local illumination algorithms only direct lights are taken into account.

***Global Illumination Model*:** Such types of models express light from multiple sources i.e. from direct light source as well as light reflected from objects in environment

If light arrives after interacting with the rest of the scene is known as indirect illumination.

Global illumination model = Direct illumination + Indirect illumination.

In Global Illumination Algorithms both kinds of sources are considered. Ray tracing and radiosity models provide these global lighting effects.

In this chapter we will develop local illumination models that contain some or all of three components -ambient, diffuse, and specular of light.

15.6.2 Ambient Reflected light

Many surfaces that are not lit directly by the light source still we see. They are lit by the light presence in the environment.

A non-directional light, which illuminates all surfaces in the scene and gets reflected uniformally in all directions by each surface, is known as **ambient light**.

Intensity of Ambient reflected light α Ambient Intensity

The ambient illumination equation is

MODEL I

Intensity of Ambient reflected light = Ambient-reflection coefficient x Ambient Intensity

Or

$$I_{\text{ambi}} = k_a I_a$$

Where I_a is ambient light its value is constant for all objects and it is defined once for the entire scene.

k_a is ambient-reflection coefficient which ranges from 0 to 1 i.e. [0,1], it depends upon material of surface.

Ambient light is uniform from all directions, however it may less or more brightly lit an object. Ambient light is not of much interest. Ambient light is independent of the direction and distance of light of source.

15.6.3 Diffuse Reflected Light

Surfaces that are rough or grainy tend to scatter the reflected light in all directions. This scattered light is called diffuse reflected light. Consider illuminating an object by a point light source (L), whose rays radiate uniformly in all directions from a single point, P on the surface of an object as shown in figure 15.4.

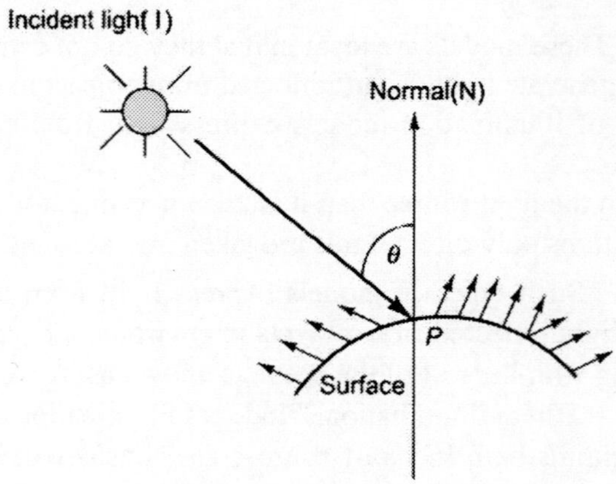

FIGURE 15.4 Diffuse Reflection

The brightness of the object varies from one part to another, depending upon the distance and the direction of the light source. Diffuse light is *reflected*(or *transmitted*) from a point with equal intensity in all directions. *Diffusely reflected* light is typical for dull, matte surfaces such as paper or flat wall paint. *Diffusely refracted* light is typical for frosted glass.

Lambert's Law

This law helps us to calculate the intensity of diffuse light.

Lambert's First Law

The luminance on a surface illuminated by light falling on it perpendicularly from a point source is proportional to the inverse square of the distance between the surface and the source.

$$I \alpha \frac{1}{d^2}$$

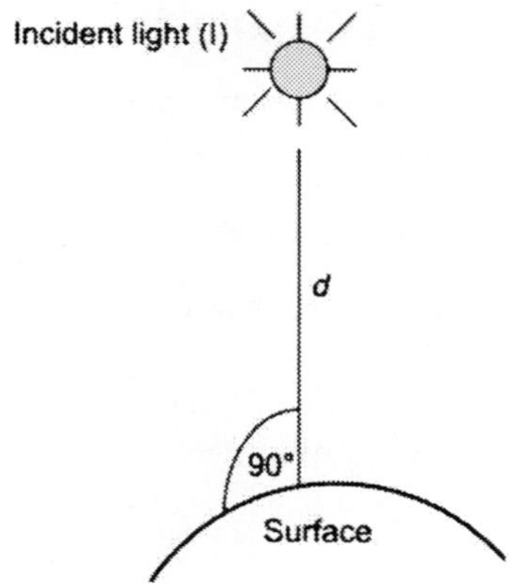

FIGURE 15.5

Lambert's Second Law

If the rays meet the surface at an angle, the luminance is proportional to the cosine of the angle with normal refer to figure 15.6.

Diffuse Illumination Model

Intensity of Diffuse reflected light α Light Source Intensity x Cos(θ)
Thus, for a given light source intensity, the smaller the angle, the higher the reflection.

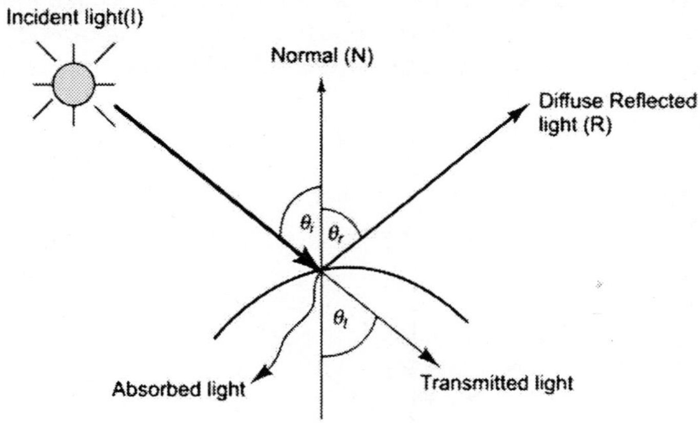

FIGURE 15.6

MODEL II

$$\boxed{\textbf{Intensity of Diffuse reflected light } (I_{\text{diff}}) = k_a\, I \text{ x } \text{Cos}(\theta)}$$

Where $0 \le \theta \le \frac{\pi}{2}$; if θ is negative, the light source is behind the surface.

Assuming that **N** and **L** are unit length vectors, we can write the Cos(θ) as a simple dot product and the diffuse illumination equation becomes

$$I_{diff} = k_a \mathbf{I} \, x \, \overline{N} \bullet \overline{L} \qquad \text{.................. (15.1)}$$

Lambert's Third Law

The luminous intensity of light decreases exponentially with distance as it travels through an absorbing medium.

Intensity Attenuation

Equation 15.1 does not take into account distance of object from light source.
The intensity of more distance surface from light source is lessened. According to Lambert's First Law intensity of light source is inverse square of the distance from surface. Therefore the basic diffuse model should modified to

$$I_{\text{diff}} = \frac{k_a I \times \overline{N} \bullet \overline{L}}{d^2}$$

Where d is the distance from the point light source to the surface.

15.6.4 Specular Reflected Light

Figure 15.3 depicts reflected light distributed uniformly in all directions. In case of an ideal prefect reflector light would be reflected exactly in one direction (the direction of **R**). Since prefect reflector is not possible, so we have specular reflections over a finite of viewing positions around vector **R**.
If $\alpha = 0$, we have perfect reflecting surface(a mirror). An observer locates here sees any specularly reflected light, in other words V and R coincide. Otherwise, we have a specular reflections over a finite of viewing positions around vector **R**. Shiny surfaces have *narrow* specular-reflection range as shown in figure 15.12 , and *dull* surfaces have wider range of specular-reflection range as shown in figure 15.11

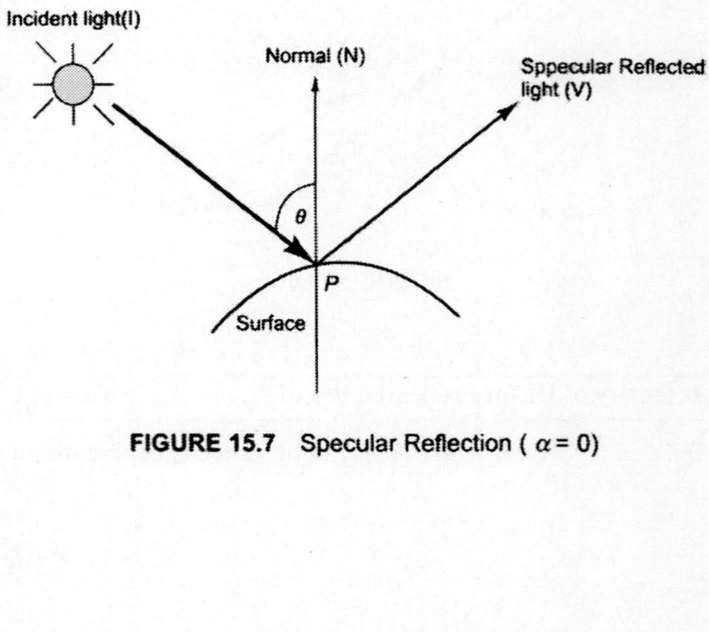

FIGURE 15.7 Specular Reflection ($\alpha = 0$)

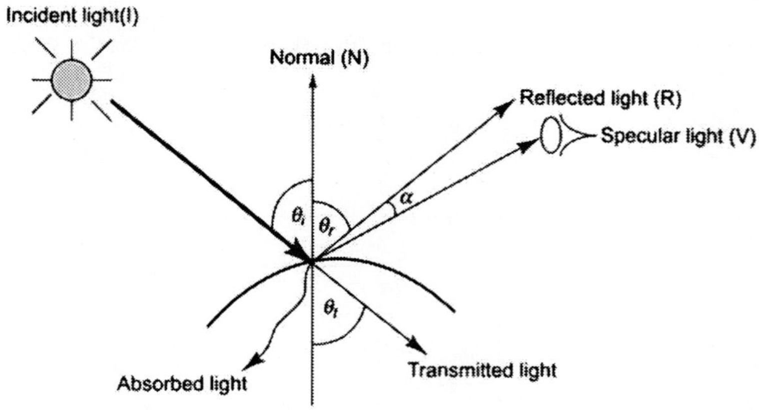

FIGURE 15.8 Specular Reflection

Intensity of Specular reflected light α Light Source Intensity x $\text{Cos}^n(\alpha)$

MODEL III

$$\textbf{Intensity of Specular reflected light } (I_{spec}) = k_s\, I\, x\, \text{Cos}^n(\alpha)$$

$$0 \leq \alpha \leq \frac{\pi}{2}$$

Where value of n depends on type of surface; for, perfect reflector such as mirror, $n = \infty$; very poor reflector $n = 1$; in practice we use $1 \leq n \leq 200$; for rough surface, such as chalk , n would be assigned a value near to 1.

Metals and other shiny surfaces have larger values of n and for nonmetallic surfaces e.g. paper value of n is small. Figure 15.9 illustrates how the function ($\cos^n \alpha$) behaves for different values of n.

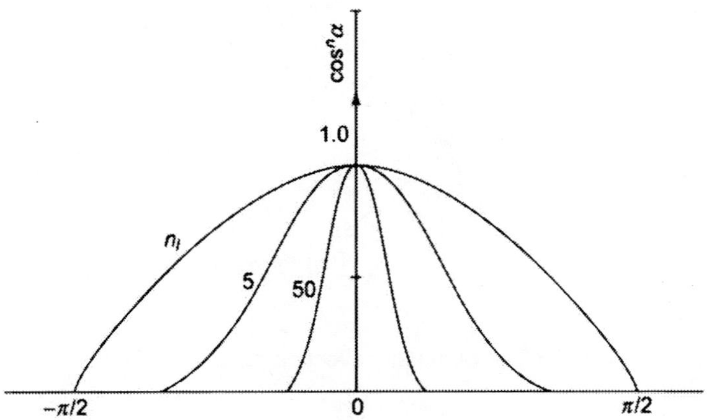

FIGURE 15.9 Fall-off of function ($Cos^n\ \alpha$) with angle for different values of n

Fresnel's Laws of Reflection

According to this law using spectral-reflection function $W(\theta)$,we can write specular-reflection model as

$$I_{spec} = W(\theta).\ I\ x\ Cos^{n}(\alpha)$$

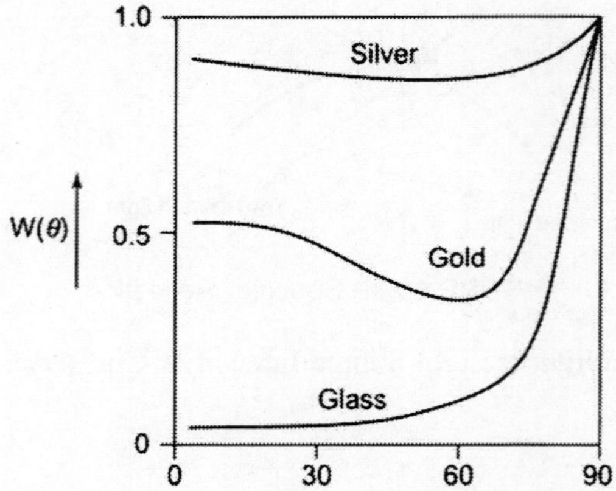

FIGURE 15.10 The Specular reflection co-efficient for a number of materials

Where specular-reflection co-efficient $W(\theta)$ tends to increase with as the angle of incidence increases. At $\theta = 90^0$, $W(\theta) = 1$ and all the incident light is reflected. Figure 15.10 illustrates the variation of specular co-efficient for different materials.

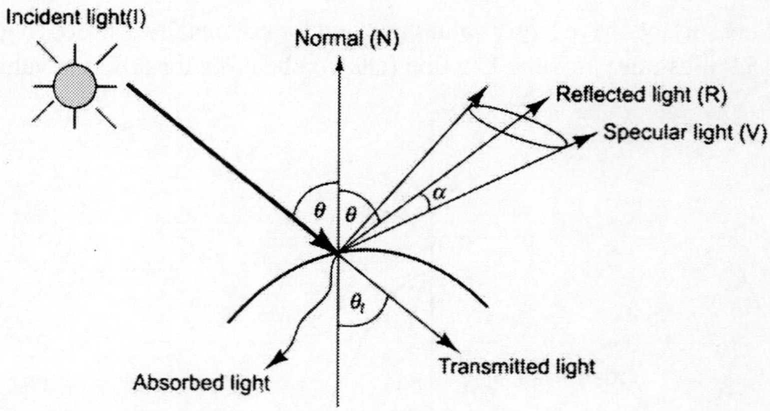

FIGURE 15.11 Specular reflection for Dull surface

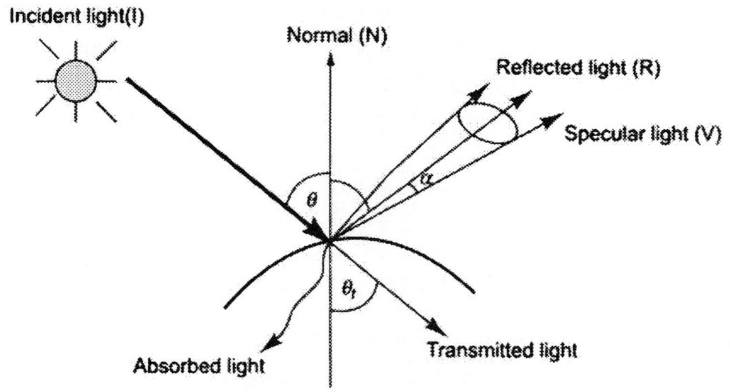

FIGURE 15.12 Specular reflection for Shiny surface

15.6.5 MODEL IV

Phong Model

It was developed by Phong Bui Tuong and also call Phong specular-reflection model or some times Phong illumination model. It is an empirical approach because it based on basic principles of physics. Phong reflection is a local illumination model devised by Bui Tuong Phong and can produce a certain degree of realism in three-dimensional objects by combining three elements - diffuse, specular and ambient lighting for each considered point on a surface. It has several assumptions –

(a) all lights are points
(b) only surface geometry is considered
(c) only local modeling of diffuse and specular exists
(d) specular color is the same as light color
(e) ambient is a global constant.

Phong illumination model is

Intensity of total reflected light = Ambient light + Diffuse light + Specular light

$$I = k_a I_a + k_d I x \text{Cos}(\theta) + k_s I x \text{Cos}^n(\phi)$$

$$I = k_a I_a + k_d I x (\overline{N} \bullet \overline{L}) + k_s I x (\overline{R} \bullet \overline{V})^n$$

For multiple light sources, the effect of light sources is simply additive. For **m** number of light sources, the intensity for monochromic light is given by

$$I = k_a I_a + \sum_{i=1}^{m} \text{Ii} (k_d x (\overline{N} \bullet \overline{L}_i) + ks\, x (\overline{R} \bullet \overline{L}_i)^n$$

Light intensity is in the form of RGB color vector e.g. $I = (I_r, I_g, I_b)$ and each reflection co-efficient are also three dimensional vectors.

15.7 SHADING MODELS

In the last section we have discussed various illumination models to compute the intensity of light at a single point on surface of an object. In this section, we will discuss various models to compute the intensity across a given polygon for surfaces defined by polygon. The shading of a polygon is not constant it is generally approximation value of real surface because the process of shading involves the interpolation of intensities -Gourad shading and interpolation of normal vetors-Phong shading. Figure 15.13 shows division of elliptical surface into number of polygons for implementation of interpolation technique.

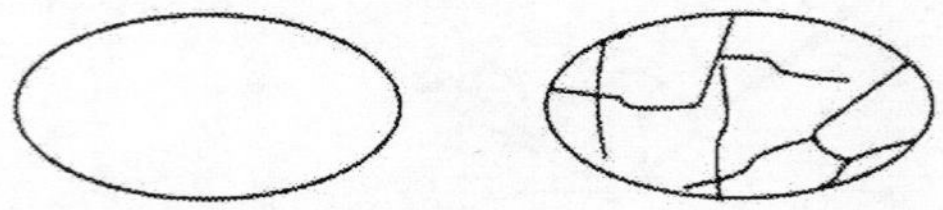

FIGURE 15.13 Division of elliptical surface into polygons for interpolation purpose

Following three basic principles may be used in various shadings:

(a) Compute the shade at all points- It is calculating the surface normal at visible points and applying the desirable illumination model at that point. But this approach is expensive and time consuming.
(b) Compute the shade at the centre and use this to represent the whole polygon—**Flat shading**
(c) Compute shade at key points and interpolate for the rest—**Gouraud shading** and **Phong shading.**

15.7.1 Flat shading

It is the simplest method and most computationally efficient method, also called **constant-intensity shading**.

It is based upon principle that

"Each polygon can be rendered at single intensity value and use this to represent the whole polygon".

Flat shading generally provides accurate renderding for an object if following conditions are true:

- Object is an uniform in shape
- Light sources illuminating the object are sufficiently far from the object
- Viewer's eye sufficiently far from the object

It has number of ambiguities due to following reasons:

(a) Realistic image

It does not produce realistic image

(b) Simultaneous contrast

An area of constant brightness surrounded by a dark area is perceived to be brighter than the same area surrounded by a light area as shown in figure 15.14(a) and 15.14(b).

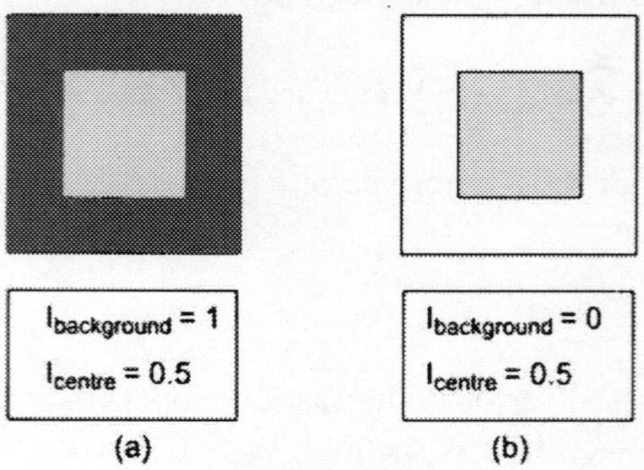

FIGURE 15.14

(c) Mach bending

Brightness perceived by the eye tends to exceed at the boundaries of regions of constant intensity as shown in figure 15.15.

FIGURE 15.15

15.7.2 Gouraud shading or Linearly intensity interpolating

This technique was first presented by Henri Gouraud in 1971. It is based upon principle that

"Firstly illumination model is appleid to find intensity of verices and then to apply the linear interpolation to found the intensity values across the surface"

A polygon surface is rendered using Gouraud shading by carrying out following steps:-

Step 1: Compute the unit normal vector at each vertex **Nv[refer to Figure 15.16(a), 15.16(b),15.16(c)]**

Output $N_A, N_B, N_C, N_D, N_E, N_F$

If plane equations are given then each polygon vertex normal is the average of the surface normal of the all polygons sharing that vertex i.e.

$$N_V = \frac{\sum_{i=1}^{m} N_i}{\left|\sum_{i=1}^{m} N_i\right|}$$

Alternatively, if equation of plane is not given then normal at vertex can be approximated by averaging the cross product of all edges that terminated at the vertex. Using the vertex **v** of figure 15.16(b), the normal vector is

$$Nv = v \bullet v_1\, x\, v \bullet v_2 + v \bullet v_2\, x\, v \bullet v_3 + v \bullet v_3\, x\, v \bullet v_1$$

Step 2: Compute the intensity values at each polygon vertex using illumination model. **[refer to Figure 15.17]**.

Output: $I_A, I_B, I_C, I_D, I_E, I_F$

Step 3: Compute the intensity of surface of the polygon using linear interpolation.

(a) Compute the intensities at points along polygon edges using linear interpolation, as depict in figure 15.18, Q and R be any two points on edges AB and DC respectively of polygon ABCDEF.

Output: I_Q, I_R

$$I_Q = u\, I_A + (1-u)\, I_B$$
$$I_R = v\, I_C + (1-v) I_D$$

$$u = \frac{AQ}{AB} = \frac{y_a - y_q}{y_a - y_b} \quad v = \frac{CR}{CD} = \frac{y_r - y_c}{y_d - y_c}$$

(b) Compute the intensity at all interior points along the scan line using linear interpolation; let us assume an interior point P between Q and R.

Output: I_P

$$I_P = w\, I_Q + (1 - w)\, I_R$$

$$w = \frac{PR}{QR} = \frac{x_r - x_p}{x_r - x_q}$$

Increment calculations are used on steps 3(a) and 3(b) to obtain successive intensities along each edge and to obtain successive intensities along a scan line.

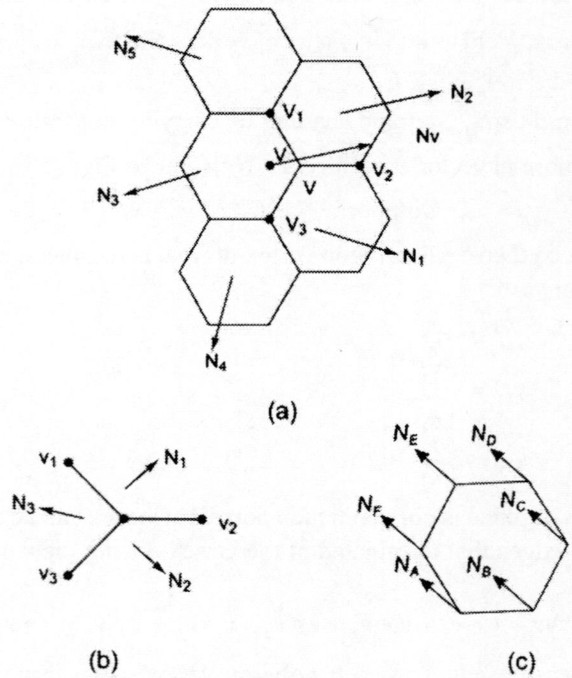

FIGURE 15.16

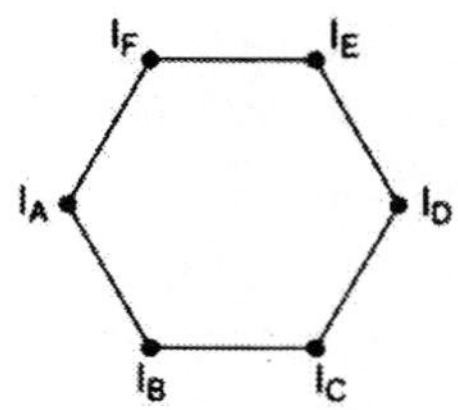

FIGURE 15.17

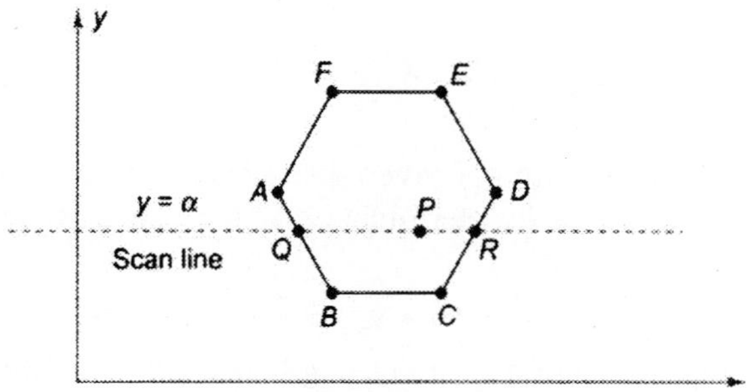

FIGURE 15.18

Gouraud shading can be used with scan line algorithm. Like-wise flat shading linear interpolation may also produce bright or dark intensity streaks, called mach bands to be appear on non-uniform shapes.

15.7.3 Phong shading or Normal-vector interpolation shading

This method was developed by Phong Boi Tuong. It is more realistic than Gouraud shading method. This method removes some of the deficiencies of Gouraud shading method.

It is another approach for rendering. It is based upon principle that

A polygon surface is to interpolate using normal vectors, and then to apply the illumination model to each surface point.

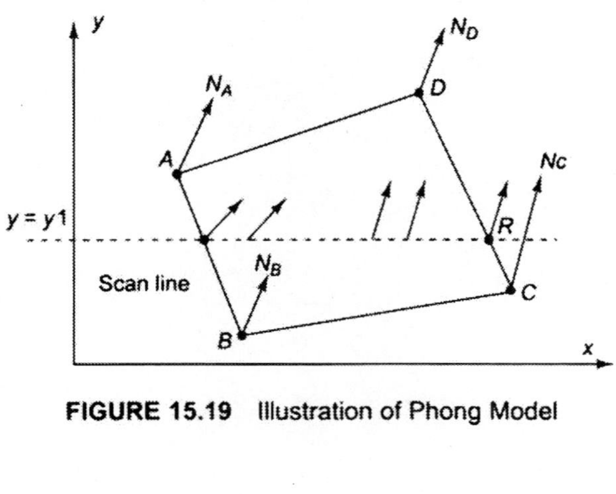

FIGURE 15.19 Illustration of Phong Model

A polygon surface is rendered using Phong shading by carrying out following steps:-

Step 1: Compute the unit normal vector at each polygon vertex **Nv[refer to Figure 15.20(a),15.20(b),15.20(c)].**

Output $N_A, N_B, N_C, N_D, N_E, N_F$

If equation of each polygon vertex is known then polygon vertex is the average of the surface normal of the all polygons sharing that vertex i.e.

$$N_V = \frac{\sum_{i=1}^{m} N_i}{\left|\sum_{i=1}^{m} N_i\right|}$$

Alternatively, if equations of planes are not given then normal at vertex can be approximated by averaging the cross product of all edges that terminating at the vertex. Using the vertex v of figure 15.20(b), the normal vector is

$$Nv = v \bullet v_1 \, x \, v \bullet v_2 + v \bullet v_2 \, x \, v \bullet v_3 + v \bullet v_3 \, x \, v \bullet v_1$$

Step 2: Compute the vector normal over polygon using linearly interpolation of normal vetors **[refer to Figure 15.21].**

(a) Compute normal vectors along edges, let us assume N_Q and N_R be any two normal vectors along the edges respectively over the surface

Output: N_Q, N_R

$$N_Q = u\,N_A + (1-u)\,N_B$$

$$N_R = v\,N_C + (1-v)\,N_D$$

$$u = \frac{AQ}{AB} = \frac{y_a - y_q}{x_a - x_b} \qquad v = \frac{CR}{CD} = \frac{y_r - y_c}{y_d - y_c}$$

(b) Compute normal vectors along scan lines.

Step 3: Compute intensity value at each normal vector along scan line using illumination model **[refer to Figure 15.22].**

Incremental calculations are used on steps 2(*a*) and 2(*b*) to obtain successive normal vectors along edges and normal vectors along scan lines.

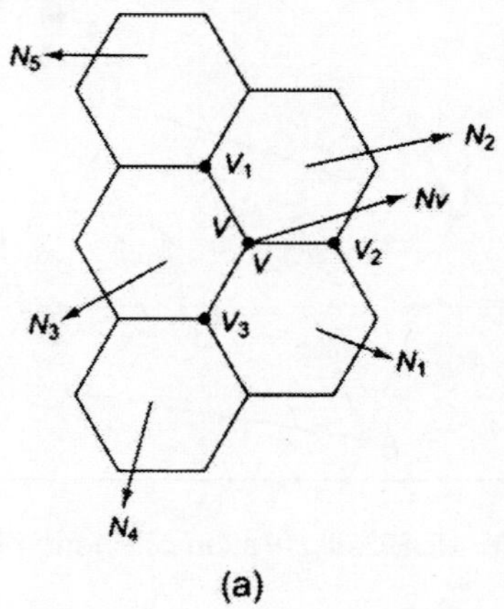

(a)

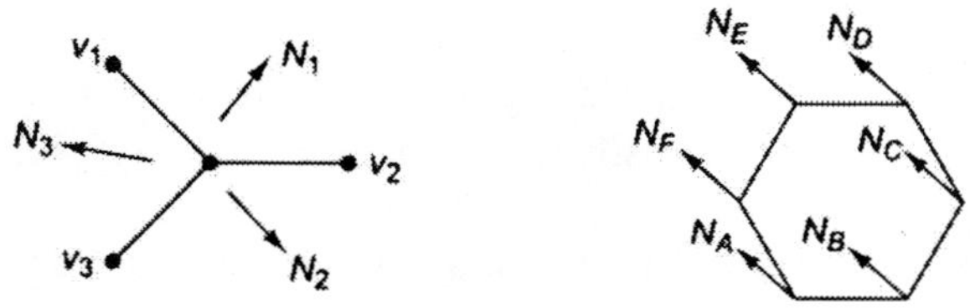

(b) (c)

FIGURE 15.20

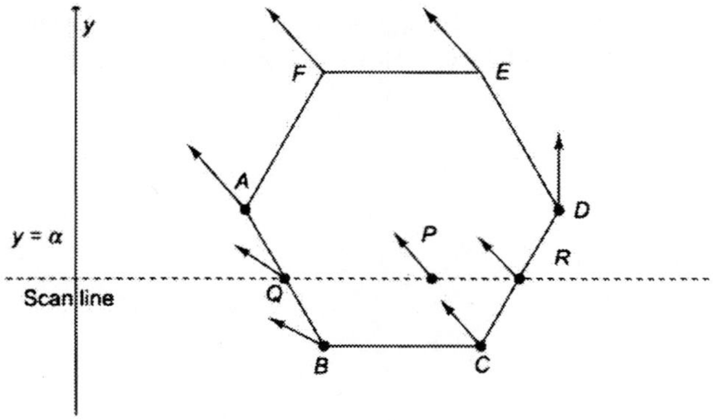

FIGURE 15.21

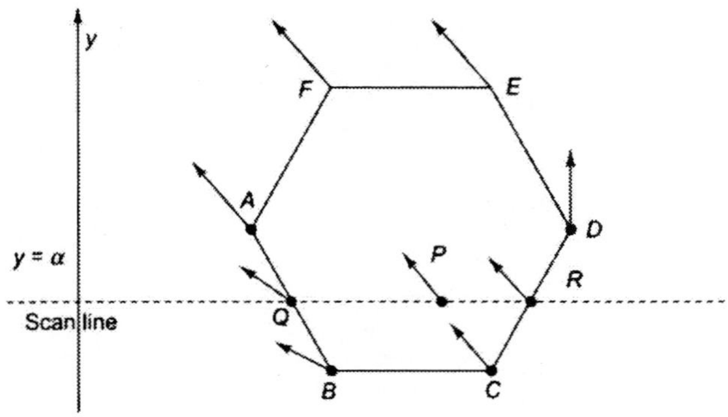

FIGURE 15.22

Phong shading gives better result as compared to Gouraud shading, however it is computational more expensive.

EXERCISES

1. Define the terms Rendering , Surface rendering Ambient reflected light, Diffuse reflected light, Specular reflected light

2. State and explain various Lambert's Laws.
3. Define the term Intensity Attenuation and explain its impact on diffuse reflected light.
4. Derive expressions to measure intensity of Ambient reflected light, Diffuse reflected light, Specular reflected light.
5. Explain trade-off between specular light and angle for different surfaces.
6. State and explain Fresnel's Law of Reflection.
7. Describe in detail Phong Illumination Model. How it can be implemented for RGB light intensity.
8. Define the term Shading. Differentiate between shading and illumination.
9. Differentiate between Flat shading, Gouraud shading, and Phong shading with the help of an example.
10. Describe Gouraud Shading Model and Phong Shading Model. What are the advantages and disadvantages of Phong shading model over Gouraud Model?

16

Segment

16.1 INTRODUCTION

Computer Graphics (CG) applications are now used across a wide range of industries, including the more obvious, such as film and TV, manufacturing and the defense sector. In reality the image on the display screen is often composed of several pictures or items of information. An image contains several views of an object and related information. For example, we may wish to display an internal view of a living room. The plan may contain various objects such as sofa-set, TV, curtain, dining set, and so on. Each object has set of attributes such as size, color, and its position with room. We might wish to see all these objects simultaneous or a single object at a time.

16.1.1 Segmentation

It is process subdivides an image into constitute regions or interest object. The level to which the sub-division is carried depends on the problem being solved.

In computer graphics segmentation refers to the process of partitioning a digital image into multiple segments. The goal of segmentation is to simplify and change the representation of image into something that is more meaningful and easier to analyses.

Segmentation assists texture mapping, shape matching, morphing, multi resolution modeling, mesh editing, compression, animation, etc. The quality of segmentation is often application dependent.

Figure 16.1 shows possible segments of square after segmentations.

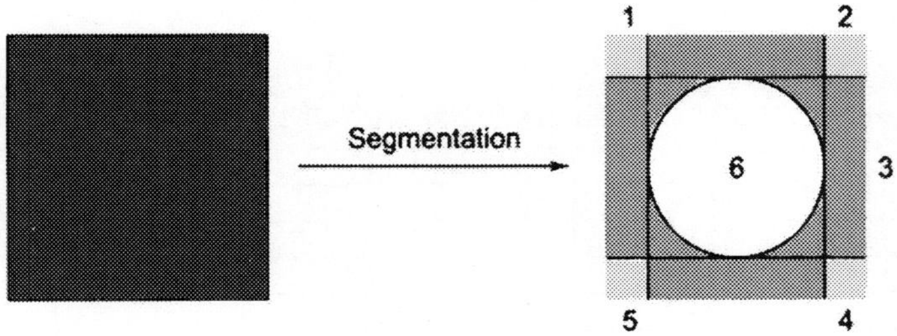

FIGURE 16.1 Segmentation of Square

16.1.2 Segment

The interested objects so formed with the help of segmentation are called segments.

16.1.3 Display File

It is a storage area where the entire image or parts of the image with various attributes in terms of segments are stored.

16.1.4 Segment Table

Display file does not transmit requirements of viewing the image. Due to this, the display structure is modified to reproduce to subpicture.
Segment table contains all relevant information about any segment, e.g. segment name, start position, size, visibility, image transformation parameters such as scaling, rotation, translation, etc. and unique name to access a picture segment and information associated to it.

We use arrays for holding the all properties of segment and segment name is used as index into these arrays. Numbers 1, 2, 3, 4, and so on, in the segment table specify named segment, when there is no any specification of any segment name, then we associate the unnamed segment with table index 0. Figure 16.2 illustrates segment table using arrays.

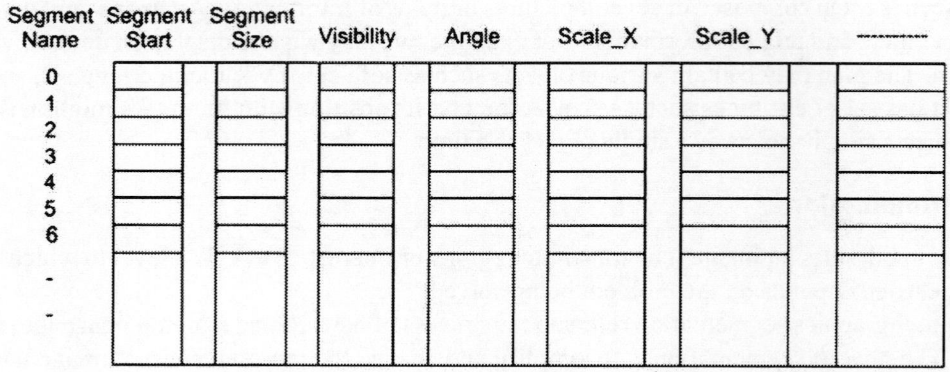

FIGURE 16.2 Representation of Segment Table using Arrays

Linked list may also be used for implementing segment table. Linked list uses the additional field called link or pointer which gives the location of the arrays. Figure 16.3 illustrates segment table using linked list.

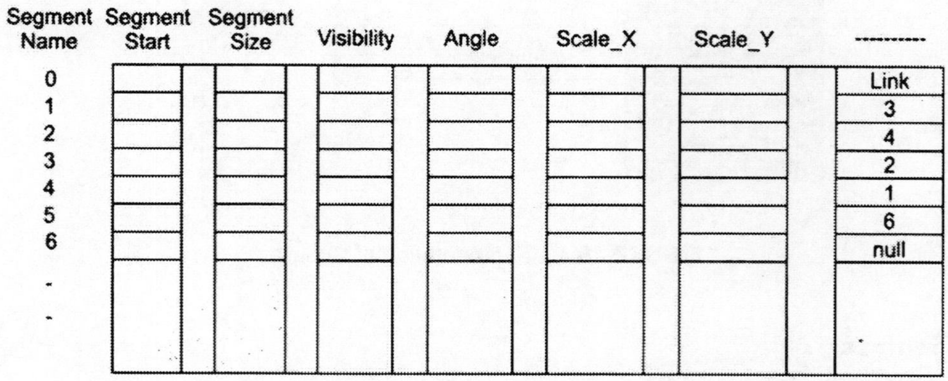

FIGURE 16.3 Representation of Segment Table using Linked List

In case of arrays max number of segments that can be included in the segment table are equal to the size of arrays. But in case of linked list there is no such limit in the max number of segments.

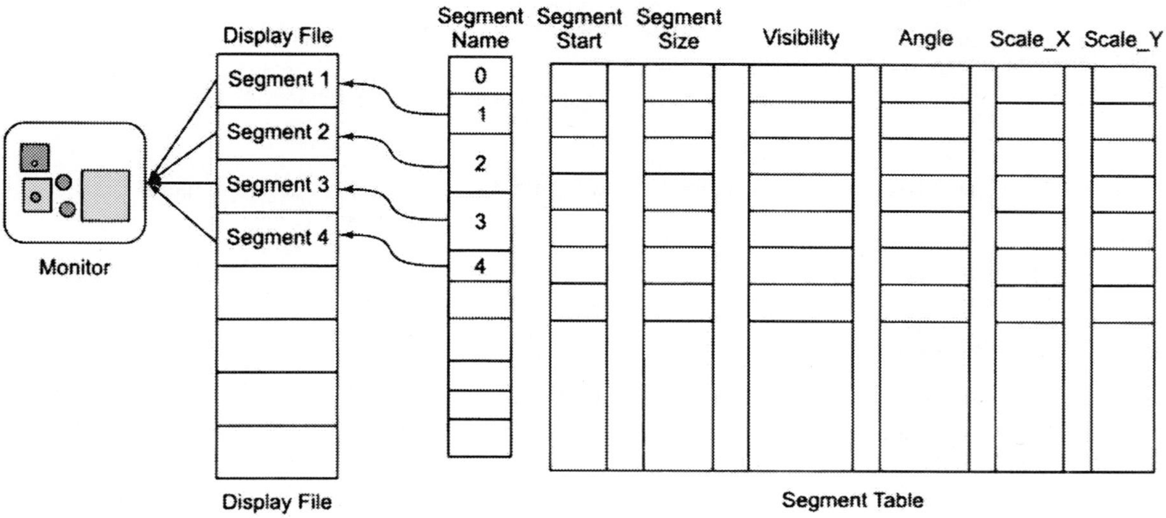

FIGURE 16.4 Illustrates the Process to Display Picture with the Help of Segmented Display File

Advantages of using segmented display file

1. Segmentation helps to assign different set of attributes to different parts of an image.
2. Segmentation makes it easier to modified the picture by changing the segment's attributes.
3. Segmentation allows to organize display files in subpicture structure.
4. Segmentation allows applications of transformations on selective portion of the image.

16.2 FUNCTIONS ON SEGMENTS

We are familiar with operations in sequential files. In such files any operation, i.e. to add a new data or to modify existing data or to delete existing data; we firstly open the file. After completion of these operations the file must be closed. The very similar operations are used for manipulating display file segments. Here, we will discuss following four basic operations:

1. Create Segment
2. Delete Segment
3. Rename Segment
4. Close Segment

16.2.1 Segment Creation

In a segment creation process following sequence of stages are involved:

Stage I

Initially, we have to check whether some other segment is still open. We cannot have more than one segment open at a time because we would not know to which segment we should assign the drawing instructions.

Stage II

Check for the validity of the segment name. We cannot have segment name out of the range of the total number of segments of segment table.

Stage III

Check to see whether there already exist segment under that name, if so we again have an error.

Stage IV

We initialize all the attributes of the segment in the segment table under this segment name.

Stage V

Finally, we indicate that there is now segment open.

Algorithm: Create Segment

```
CREATE_SEGMENT(SEG_NAME,FREE,NUM_OF_SEG,NOW_OPEN,
SEG_START,SEG_SIZE,VISIBILITY, ANGLE,SCALE_X, SCALE_Y,TRANS_X, TRANS_Y)
        Where
        SEG_NAME: Name of the segment
        FREE: Next free display file cell
        NUM_OF_SEG: Size of segment table
        NOW_OPEN: Current open segment
        SEG_START, SEG_SIZE, VISIBILITY, SCALE_X, SCALE_Y, TRANS_X,
        TRANS_Y: Arrays that make up the segment table.
    1 Check
    1.1 Any other segment is open
                IF NOW_OPEN > 0 THEN
                            ERROR 'Segment still open' goto step 4
    1.2 Segment name is not valid
                IF SEG_NAME < 1 OR SEG_NAME > NUM_OF_SEG THEN
                            ERROR 'Invalid Segment Name' goto step 4
    1.3 Segment being created already exist
                IF SEG_SIZE(SEG_NAME)> 0 THEN
                            ERROR 'Segment Already Exist' goto step 4
    2.  Initialize all the arrays in the segment table under this segment name
          SEG_START(SEG_NAME)   ← FREE
          SEG_SIZE(SEG_NAME)    ← 0
          VISIBILITY(SEG_NAME)  ← VISIBILITY(0)
          ANGLE(SEG_NAME)       ← ANGLE(0)
          SCALE_X(SEG_NAME)     ← SCALE_X(0)
          SCALE_Y(SEG_NAME)     ← SCALE_Y(0)
          TRANS_X(SEG_NAME)     ← TRANS_X(0)
          TRANS_Y(SEG_NAME)     ← TRANS_Y(0)
    3.  NOW_OPEN ← SEG_NAME
    4.  RETURN
    5.  END
```

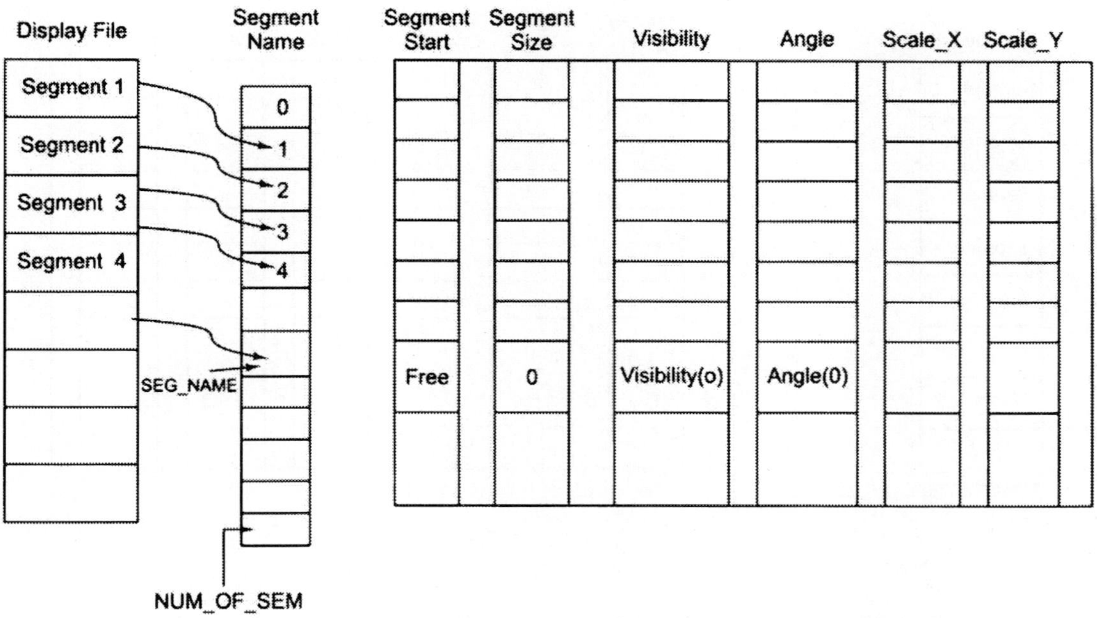

FIGURE 16.5 Segment Creation Process

16.2.2 Deleting the Segment

Segment deletion process involves following sequence of stages:

Stage I

Initially, we have to check whether segment still in use, because open segment if we attempt to delete it return error.

Stage II

Check for the validity of the segment name. We cannot have segment name out of the range of the total number of segments of segment table.

Stage III

Check if segment size is equal to 0. If so, no need to delete the segment only shifting of data below this segment is required.

Stage IV

If segment size is not equal to 0. Then shift the display file elements follow the segment which is to be deleted by its size.

Stage V

Recover the deleted space by resetting the index of the next free instruction.

Stage VI

Adjust the segment table by subtracting the size of the deleted segment from it.

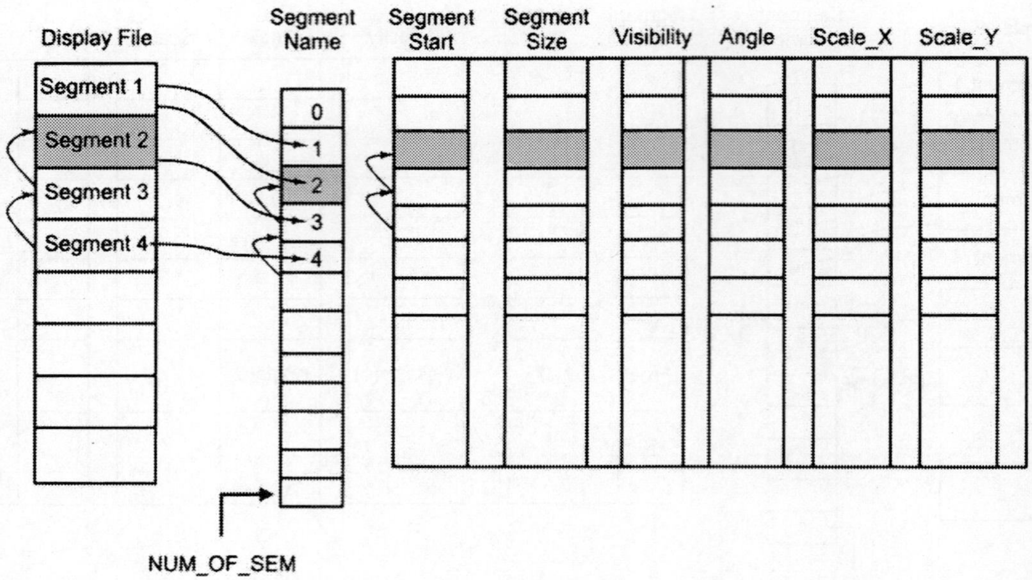

FIGURE 16.6 Segment Deletion Process [Seg_Size(Seg_Name) ≠ 0)]

Algorithm

DELETE_SEGMENT(SEG_NAME, FREE,NUM_OF_SEG, NOW_OPEN, SEG_START, SEG_SIZE, VISIBILITY, SCALE_X, SCALE_Y, TRANS_X, TRANS_Y)

Where
SEG_NAME: Name of the Segment
FREE: Next free display file cell
NUM_OF_SEG: Size of segment table
NOW_OPEN: Current open segment
SEG_START, SEG_SIZE, VISIBILITY, SCALE_X, SCALE_Y, TRANS_X, TRANS_Y: Arrays that make up the segment table.

1. Check
   1.1 Segment is open
       IF SEG_NAME = NOW_OPEN AND SEG_NAME ≠ 0 THEN
           ERROR 'Segment is still open' goto step 7
   1.2 Segment name is not valid
       IF SEG_NAME < 0 OR SEG_NAME > NUM_OF_SEG THEN
           ERROR 'Invalid Segment Name' goto step 7
   1.3 Segment size is Zero
       IF SEG_SIZE(SEG_NAME) = 0 THEN goto step 7
2. Shift display file instructions
   2.1 S_START = SEG_START(SEG_NAME)
   2.2 S_SIZE = SEG_SIZE(SEG_NAME)
   2.3 S_END = S_START + S_SIZE
   2.4 While S_END < FREE

```
begin
    DF_OP(S_START)  ← DF_OP(S_END)
    DF_X(S_START)   ← DF_X(S_END)
    DF_Y(S_START)   ← DF_Y(S_END)
          S_START ← S_START+1
            S_END ← S_END+1
end
```

***/Recover the deleted storage**

3. FREE ← S_START

***/ Update the segment table**

4. FOR I = 0 TO NUM_OF_SEG
   4.1 IF SEG_START(I) > SEG_START(SEG_NAME) THEN
   SEG_START(I) ← SEG_START(I) - SIZE
5. SEG_SIZE(SEG_NAME) ← 0
6. IF VISIBILITY(SEG_NAME) THEN NEW_FRAME
7. RETURN
8. END

16.2.3 Renaming a Segment

This routine is very useful to show an animated image moving on the display. This would be performed by presenting a sequence of images, each with a slightly different. Any image has many segments modifying some segments, we can get new image or we can delete the segment and recreate it with alter segment and show the result. The problem with this is that during the time after the first image is deleted before the second image is completed; only a partially completed image can be seen.

Stage I

Check for the validity of the both segment names. We cannot have segment names out of the range of the total number of segments of segment table.

Stage II

We have to check whether some no segment is still open. We cannot rename any segment open at a time.

Stage III

Check to see whether there already exist segment with new name, if so we again have an error.

Algorithm

RENAME_SEGMENT(SEG_NAME_OLD,SEG_NAME_NEW,NUM_OF_SEG,
SEG_START, , SEG_SIZE, VISIBILITY, SCALE_X,
SCALE_Y, TRANS_X, TRANS_Y)

1. Check

1.1 Validity of the both segments names
IF SEG_NAME_OLD < 1 OR SEG_NAME_NEW <1 OR
SEG_NAME_OLD > NUM_OF_SEG OR SEG_NAME_NEW >
NUM_OF_SEG THEN ERROR 'Invalid Segment Name' goto step 3

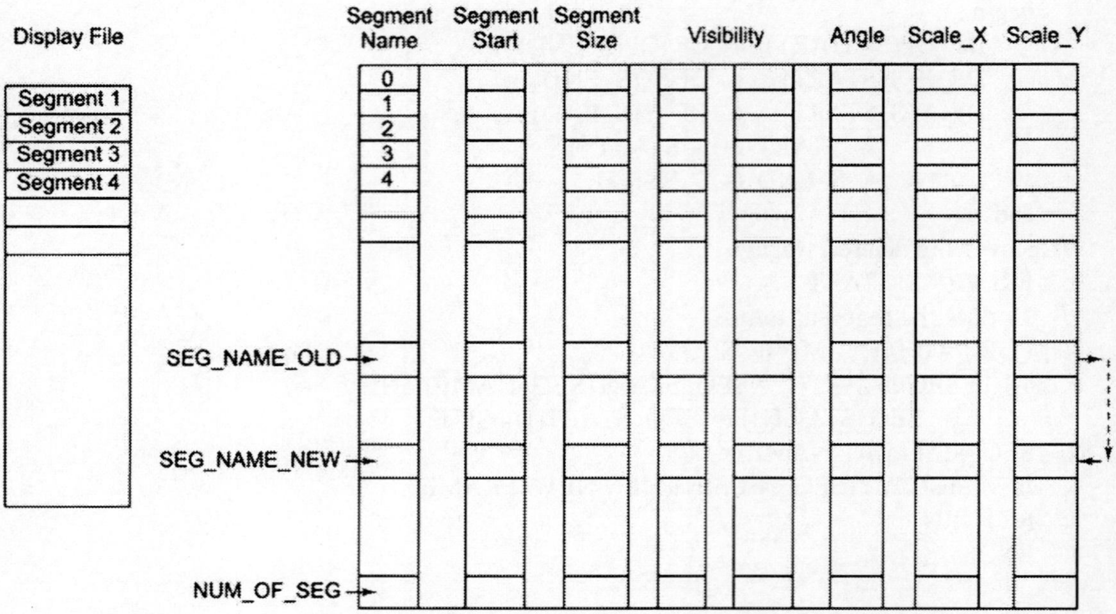

FIGURE 16.7 Segment Renaming Process

1.2 No more segments are open
  IF SEG_NAME_OLD = NOW_OPEN OR
    SEG_NAME_NEW = NOW_OPEN THEN
      ERROR ' Segment Still Open' goto step 3
1.3 Segment already exists
  IF SEG_SIZE(SEG_NAME_NEW) ≠ 0 THEN
    ERROR 'Segment already exists' goto step 3
2. Copy the old segment table entries into new position
  2.1 SEG_START(SEG_NAME_NEW) ← SEG_START(SEG_NAME_OLD)
  2.2 SEG_SIZE(SEG_NAME_NEW) ← SEG_SIZE(SEG_NAME_OLD)
  2.3 VISIBILITY(SEG_NAME_NEW) ← VISIBILITY(SEG_NAME_OLD)
  2.4 SCALE_X(SEG_NAME_NEW) ← SCALE_X(SEG_NAME_OLD)
  2.5 SCALE_Y(SEG_NAME_NEW) ← SCALE_Y(SEG_NAME_OLD)
  2.6 TRANS_X(SEG_NAME_NEW) ← TRANS_X(SEG_NAME_OLD)
  2.7 TRANS_Y(SEG_NAME_NEW) ← TRANS_Y(SEG_NAME_OLD)
3. Delete the OLD Segment
  SEG_SIZE(SEG_NAME_OLD) ← 0
4 RETURN
5 END

16.2.4 Closing a Segment

If we have completed all the operations in any segment then we should close it. Because no any operation can be done on any other segment if a segment is open. If we take any variable while indicates the name of currently open segment, we set the value zero after making it unnamed segment and now there will be two segments just wasting the storage, and therefore we delete one of them.

We have to check whether segment in use, because opened segment cannot be close.

Algorithm

CLOSE_SEGMENT( )

```
1. Check any segment open
   IF NOW_OPEN = 0 THEN RETURN ERROR
                        'No segment open' goto step 4
2. Delete the unnamed segment
   DELETE_SEGMENT(0)
3. Initialize the another unnamed segment
   SEG_START(0) ← FREE
   SEG_SIZE(0)  ← 0
   NOW_OPEN     ← 0
4. RETURN
5. END
```

16.3 METHODS OF REPRESENTATION OF DISPLAY FILE

Display file may be represented in one of following three ways:

1. Array data structure
2. Linked list data structure
3. Paging scheme

16.3.1 Representation of Display File using Array Data Structure

In such type of data structure instructions in display file are stored in sequential manner.

It is one of the simplest way to represent display file since insertion, creation, deletion are easy to perform. When the display file is represented using array, an instruction can be easily deleted from the end of the list. Sometimes deletion may not be efficient. However, if it is desired to delete an instruction from an ith location of the list, then all instructions from $(i + 1)$th location will have to be shifted one step towards up to preserve contiguous locations in the array.

1	Segment 1
2	Segment 2
3	Segment 3
4	Segment 4
5	Segment 5
Unused	

FIGURE 16.8 Representation of Display File using Array

Advantages

1. It is simplest way to represent display file.
2. This structure mirrors logical ordering and physical storage, so address of all elements can be easily calculated from the address of first element.
3. Modification and updation is straightforward

Disadvantages

1. Array is static in nature.
2. Insertion or deletion operation in an array, except from the end, are a costly exercise.

16.3.2 Representation of Display File using Linked List

An alternative data structure is called linked list may be used represent display file. In a linked list the instruction are not stored in a sequence, the new field is added to the instruction this field, called the link of the pointer, gives the location the next instruction. Here, we can step to the instructions by following the chain of link. This is illustrated in Fig. 16.9.

		op	x	y	link
	1	6	2	6	0
Start →	2	4	5	6	4
	3				
	4	2	3	4	6
	5				
	6	1	5	3	1
	7				
	8				

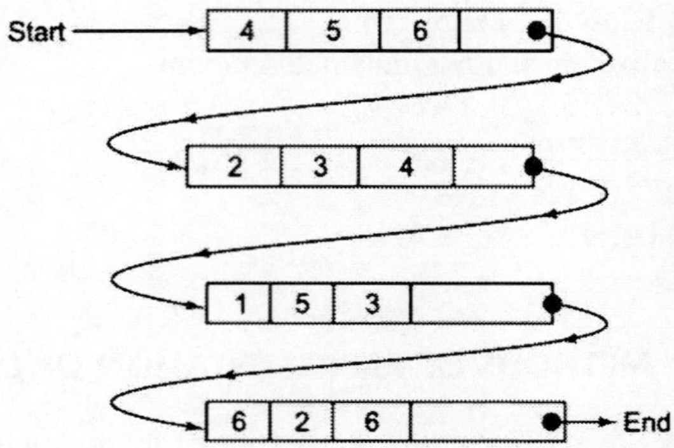

FIGURE 16.9 Representation of Display File using Linked List(Start=2)

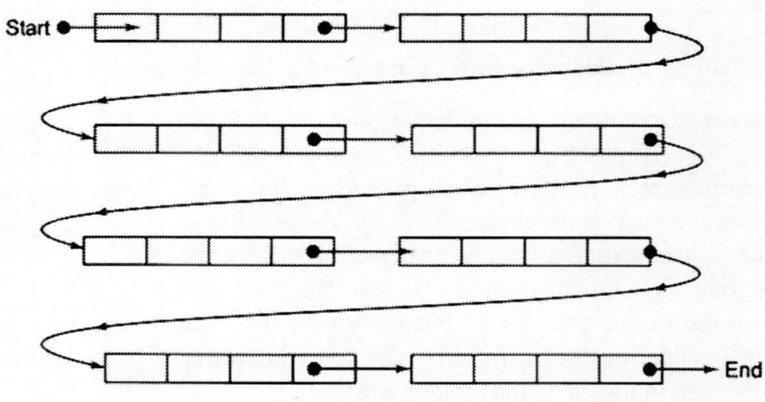

FIGURE 16.10 Original Display File

When we want to add an instruction to a display file, a free cell is obtained from the list, then current instruction operation code and operands are stored, and cell is linked to the display file list as shown in Fig. 16.11. Deletion of cells from a linked list is very easy. To delete a cell, we need only change the pointer which points to this cell so that it points to the successes cell. This is illustrated in Fig. 16.12.

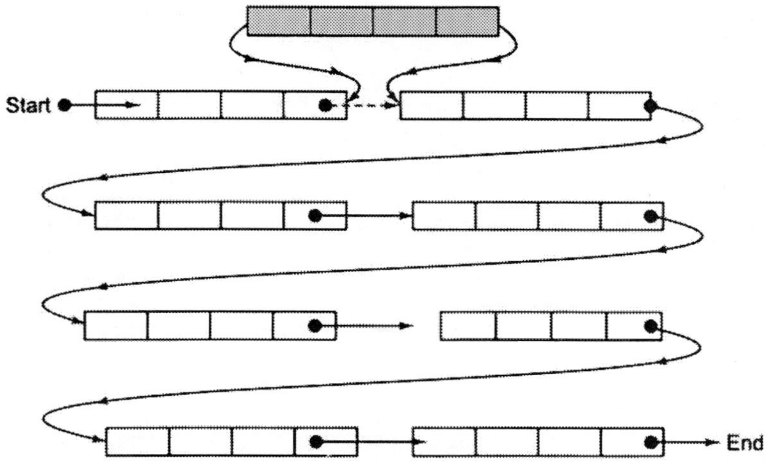

FIGURE 16.11 After Addition of Instruction into Display File

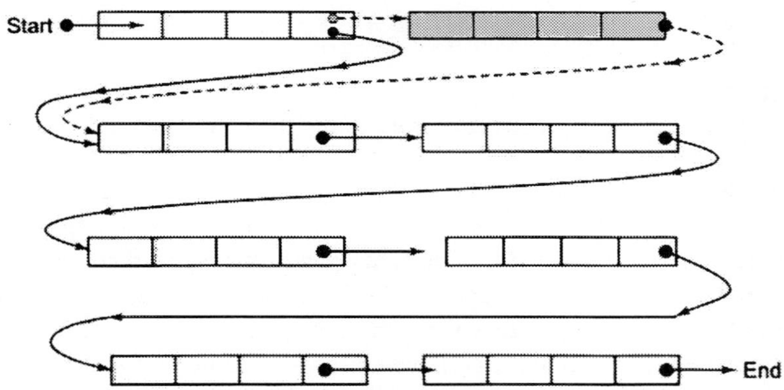

FIGURE 16.12 After Deletion of Instruction from Display File

Advantages of Linked List

1. Deletion and insertion of instruction in display file structure is more simple.
2. It is dynamic in nature.

Disadvantages

1. It requires additional field link, hence more storage space.
2. In such representation logical ordering and physical storage of instructions need not be same.

16.3.3 Display File using Paging Scheme

The paging scheme is combination of array and linked structure. In this method the display file is organized into number of small arrays called pages. The pages are linked to form a linked list of pages, each segment starts at the beginning of a page. If segment ends before the page boundary, the remaining page is not used. In this method, display file instructions can be accessed within a page just as they were accessed in an array. When the end of a page is reached, a link is followed to find the next page. This is illustrated in Fig. 16.13.

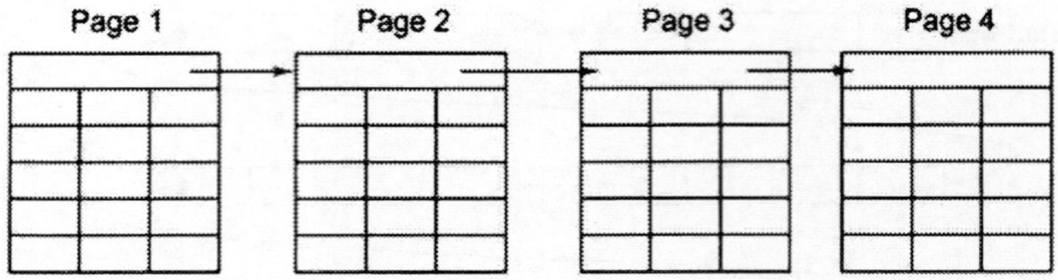

FIGURE 16.13 Representation of Display File using Paging

Advantages

1. It groups number of instructions into pages hence reducing the number of links.
2. It allows deletion of segment by simply altering links.
3. List of unused pages can also be used as new pages.
4. Deleted pages can be reused.

Disadvantages

1. Accessing instructions is bit more complex.
2. The storage space is lost if a segment does not occupy the complete page.

16.4 IMAGE TRANSFORMATION

Computer graphics facilitate various transformations hence we can display pictures with certain alternations if required, for example, we can see image from different angle, we can show particular part of the image, we can change the size of the image, we can translate a picture from one point to another point.

When display an image using segments then these changes can be performed more easily because the graphics image information is stored in different segments and we can apply changes to different segments independently. The changes in the original graphics information are called **image transformations.**

An image transformation is carried out on the contents of the display file. A graphics system may not have individual routines for setting image scale, and rotation. This is because almost every time a scale or rotation is performed a translation is needed. As we give different attributes in segment table for image transformation, e.g. SCALE_X, SCALE_Y for scaling transformation, TRANSLATE_X, TRANSLATE_Y for transformation, and ANGLE for rotation transformation. These are the five factors which are responsible for transforming any image stored in display file.

Algorithm
IMAGE_TRANSFORMATION(SEG_NAME,NUM_OF_SEG,TX,TY,SX,SY,THETA, ANGLE,SCALE_X, SCALE_Y,TRANS_X, TRANS_Y)

Where
SEG_NAME: The segment being transformed.
NUM_OF_SEG: Size of segment table

SX,SY,TX,TY,THETA : New image transformation parameters
SCALE_X, SCALE_Y, TRANS_X, TRANS_Y,ANGLE : Arrays that make up the segment table.

1 Check
1.1 Segment name is not valid
IF SEG_NAME < 1 OR SEG_NAME > NUM_OF_SEG THEN
ERROR 'Invalid Segment Name' goto step 4
2 Perform translation for the segment SEG_NAME
TRANS_X(SEG_NAME) ← TX
TRANS_Y(SEG_NAME) ← TY
3 Perform scaling for the segment SEG_NAME
SCALE_X(SEG_NAME) ← SX
SCALE_Y(SEG_NAME) ← SY
4 Perform rotation for the segment SEG_NAME
ANGLE(SEG_NAME) ← THETA
5 Check the visibility of the SEG_NAME
If VISIBILITY(SEG_NAME) then write NEWFRAME
6 Stop

Figure 16.14 illustrates the phases after performing various transformations on segment 2(triangle)

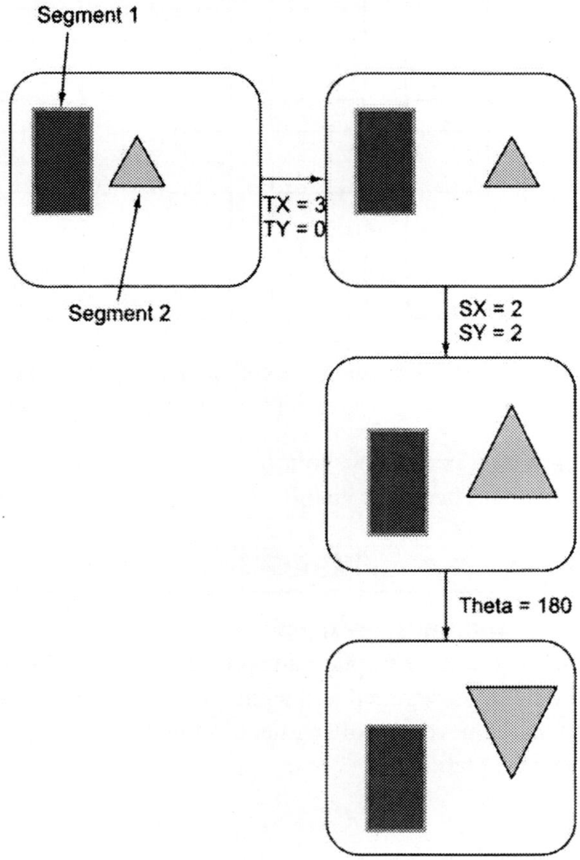

FIGURE 16.14 Stages of Transformation on Segment 2

16.5 POSTING AND UNPOSTING SEGMENTS

If we are interested to display any picture or image on the screen, we have to create segment for various parts of the picture, and we have to set attributes for them. By setting the visible attribute of the segment, we can decide whether to display it or not. For this, we use two additional functions, viz. ***posting*** and ***unposting***.

Posting: Posting is the action of including a segment in the display file; this helps us to make segment visible. When visible attribute of a segment is **"1"** it is included in the action segment list and display file interpreter processes it. Such a segment is called **posted segment**.

Unposting: It is the process to remove the segment from the display file, so that it is no longer visible. When visible attribute of a segment is **"0"** it is not included in the action segment list and display file and interpreter does not process it. Such a segment is called **unposted segment.**

posting (s_name) add segment "s_name" to display file.
unposting(s_name) remove segment "s_name" from display file.

Segment Name	Segment Start	Segment Size	Visibility	Angle	Scale_X	Scale_Y	---------
0							
1							
2			1				
3							
4			0				
5							
6							
. .							

FIGURE 16.15 Representation of Posting and Unposting segment
(Segment with named 2 is posting, Segment with named 4 is unposting)

When we create a new segment it is invisible so it in unposted state. So it is necessary to call post-segment() function before a segment becomes visible.

EXERCISES

1. Describe the segment table with suitable example.
2. How renaming of segment is useful? Explain an application of renaming.
3. Explain the process of deleting a segment and what are the steps required to delete a segment.
4. What is segment? Explain the necessity of segment in the display file?
5. Write a short note on segment table.

6. Discuss the segment table structure and explain various data structures used to implement the segment table.
7. Describe various operations carried out on the segment.
8. Explain the concept of segmentation with suitable example.
9. How removing operation of segment is important for automation?
10. Define the terms posting and unposting segments, segment table, segmentation, display file.
11. Write short note on Image Transformation.

Appendix-1

//PROGRAM TO DRAW A LINE USING SIMPLE DDA METHOD

```
#include<stdio.h>
#include<stdlib.h>
#include<conio.h>
#include<graphics.h>
#include<math.h>
void main()
{
     int gd=DETECT,gm;
     int xs,ys,xe,ye,i,t,length;
     float x,y,x1,y1,xinc,yinc,m;
     initgraph(&gd,&gm,»f:\\tc\\bgi»);
     do //Enter co-ordinates till x co-ordinates are not equal
     {
     printf("\nEnter co-ordinates of end points of line segment\n");
     printf("Starting co-ordinates:");
     scanf("%d%d",&xs,&ys);
     printf("Ending co-ordinates:");
     scanf("%d%d",&xe,&ye);
     printf("X co-ordiantes of end points of line segments are same"),
     printf("\nTry again!");
     }
     while((xe-xs)==0);
     clearviewport();
     setbkcolor(9);
     m=float((ye-ys))/(xe-xs);
     printf(" Required line with slope%f\n",m);
     if(abs(ye-ys)>abs(xe-xs)) //check m<=1 or m >1
     length =abs(ye-ys);
     else
     length = abs(xe-xs);
     xinc=float((xe-xs))/length; // Compute increments in x & y
     yinc=float((ye-ys))/length;
     x=xs;
     y=ys;
     i=1;
     x1=(80.0/640)*xs;
     y1=(25.0/480)*ys+2;
     gotoxy(x1,y1);
     printf("(%d,%d)",xs,ys);
     while(i<=length) //Till end of the line reached
     {
     putpixel(x,y,2);
     x=x+xinc;
     y=y+yinc;
```

```
        i=i+1;
        }
        x1=(80.0/640)*xe;
        y1=(25.0/480)*ye+2;
        gotoxy(x1,y1);
        printf("(%d,%d)\n",xe,ye);
        getch();
    }
//end of the main program
```

//PROGRAM TO DRAW A DHASED LINE USING BRESENAM'S METHOD

```
    #include<stdio.h>
    #include<stdlib.h>
    #include<conio.h>
    #include<graphics.h>
    #include<math.h>
    void main()
    {
        int gd=DETECT,gm;
        int xs,ys,xe,ye,x,y,x1,y1,dy,dx,inc1,inc2,d;
        int xend;
        float m;
        initgraph(&gd,&gm,"f:\\tc\\bgi");
        do //Enter co-ordinates till x co-ordinates are not equal
        {
        printf("\nEnter co-ordinates of end points of line segment\n");
        printf("Starting co-ordinates:");
        scanf("%d%d",&xs,&ys);
        printf("Ending co-ordinates:");
        scanf("%d%d",&xe,&ye);
        dy=ye-ys;
        dx=xe-xs;
        m=float(dy)/dx;
        printf("Either X co-ordiantes of end points of line segments are same\n");
        printf("or Slope of line is>1");
        printf("\nTry again!");
        }
        while((xe-xs)==0|| m>1);
        clearviewport();
        setbkcolor(9);
        inc1=2*dy;
        inc2=2*(dy-dx);
        d=inc1-dx;
        if(dx<0)
         {
              x=xe;
              y=ye;
              xend=xs;
              }
```

```
        else
                {
                x=xs;
                y=ys;
                xend=xe;
                }
        x1=(80.0/getmaxx())*xs;
        y1=(25.0/getmaxy())*ys;
        gotoxy(x1,y1);
        printf("(%d,%d)",xs,ys);
        while(x<=xend) // Till end of line reached
        {
        putpixel(x,y,2);
        if(d>=0)
         {
         y=y+1;
         d=d+inc2;
         }
        else
         d=d+inc1;
        x=x+4;
        }
        x1=(80.0/getmaxx())*xe;
        y1=(25.0/getmaxy())*ye;
        gotoxy(x1,y1);
        printf(«(%d,%d)»,xe,ye);
        getch();
   }
//end of the program
```

//PROGRAM TO DRAW A LINE USING BRESENHAM'S METHOD

```
   #include<stdio.h>
   #include<stdlib.h>
   #include<conio.h>
   #include<graphics.h>
   #include<math.h>
   void main()
   {
        int gd=DETECT,gm;
        int xs,ys,xe,ye,x,y,x1,y1,dy,dx,inc1,inc2,d;
        int xend;
        float m;
        initgraph(&gd,&gm,"f:\\tc\\bgi");
        do //Enter co-ordinates till x co-ordinates are not equal
        {
        printf("\nEnter co-ordinates of end points of line segment\n");
        printf("Starting co-ordinates:");
        scanf("%d%d",&xs,&ys);
```

```
        printf("Ending co-ordinates:");
        scanf("%d%d",&xe,&ye);
        dy=ye-ys;
        dx=xe-xs;
        m=float(dy)/dx;
        printf("Either X co-ordiantes of end points of line segments are same\n");
        printf("or Slope of line is>1");
        printf("\nTry again!");
        }
        while((xe-xs)==0|| m>1);
        clearviewport();
        setbkcolor(9);
        incl=2*dy;
        inc2=2*(dy-dx);
        d=incl-dx;
        if(dx<0)
         {
                x=xe;
                y=ye;
                xend=xs;
                }
        else
                {
                x=xs;
                y=ys;
                xend=xe;
                }
        x1=(80.0/getmaxx())*xs;
        y1=(25.0/getmaxy())*ys;
        gotoxy(x1,y1);
        printf("(%d,%4)",xs,ys);
        while(x<=xend) // Till end of line reached
        {
        putpixel(x,y,2);
        if(d>=0)
         {
         y=y+1; /* Select lower pixel
         d=d+inc2;
         }
        else
         d=d+incl; /* Select upper pixel
        x=x+1;
        }
        x1=(80.0/getmaxx())*xe;
        y1=(25.0/getmaxy())*ye;
        gotoxy(x1,y1);
        printf(«(%d,%d)»,xe,ye);
        getch();
    }
//end of the program
```

/PROGRAM TO DRAW A LINE USING SYMMETRICAL DDA METHOD

```
#include<stdio.h>
#include<stdlib.h>
#include<conio.h>
#include<graphics.h>
#include<math.h>
void main()
{
     int gd=DETECT,gm;
     int xs,ys,xe,ye,x,y,x1,y1,dy,dx,incl,inc2,d;
     int xend;
     initgraph(&gd,&gm,"f:\\tc\\bgi");
     printf("Enter starting co-ordinates:");
     scanf("%d%d",&xs,&ys);
     printf(«Enter ending co-ordinates:»);
     scanf("%d%d",&xe,&ye);
     clearviewport();
     setbkcolor(9);
     dy=ye-ys;
     dx=xe-xs;
     incl=2*dy;
     inc2=2*(dy-dx);
     d=incl-dx;
     if(dx<0)
      {
            x=xe;
            y=ye;
            xend=xs;
            }
     else
            {
            x=xs;
            y=ys;
            xend=xe;
            }
     x1=(80.0/getmaxx())*x;
     y1=(25.0/getmaxy())*y;
     gotoxy(x1,y1);
     printf(«%4d%4d»,x,y);
     while(x<=xend)
     {
     putpixel(x,y,2);
     if(d>=0)
      {
      x=x+1;
      d=d+inc2;
      }
     else
      d=d+incl;
```

```
        y=y+1;
        }
        x1=(80.0/getmaxx())*xe;
        y1=(25.0/getmaxy())*ye;
        gotoxy(x1,y1);
        printf("%4d%4d",xe,ye);
        getch();
    }
//end of program
```

//PROGRAM TO DRAW CIRCLE USING Polynomial METHOD

```
    #include<stdio.h>
    #include<conio.h>
    #include<graphics.h>
    #include<math.h>
    void main()
    {
        int r,h,k;
        float xend,x,y,x1,y1;
        int gd=DETECT,gm;
        initgraph(&gd,&gm,"f:\\tc\\bgi");
        printf("\n enter the center of circle\n");
        scanf("%d%d",&h,&k);
        printf("\n enter the radius of circle");
        scanf("%d",&r);
        xend=r/1.414;
        clearviewport();
        setbkcolor(9);
        x1= (80.0/640)*h;
        y1= (25.0/480)*k;
        printf("(%f,%f)",x1,y1);
        gotoxy(x1,y1);
        printf("(%d,%d)",h,k);
        while(x<=xend)
        {
                y=sqrt(r*r-x*x);
                putpixel(x+h,y+k,4);
                putpixel(y+h,x+k,4);
                putpixel(-y+h,x+k,4);
                putpixel(-x+h,y+k,4);
                putpixel(-x+h,-y+k,4);
                putpixel(-y+h,-x+k,4);
                putpixel(y+h,-x+k,4);
                putpixel(x+h,-y+k,4);
        x++;
        }
        getch();
    }
//end of the main program
```

//PROGRAM TO DRAW CIRCLE USING BRESENHAM'S METHOD

```
#include<stdio.h>
#include<conio.h>
#include<graphics.h>
void main()
{
     int r,x,y,h,k,d;
     int gd=DETECT,gm;
     initgraph(&gd,&gm,"f:\\tc\\bgi");
     printf("\n Enter the center of circle\n");
     scanf("%d%d",&h,&k);
     printf("\n Enter the radius of circle");
     scanf("%d",&r);
     x=0;y=r;
     d=3-2*r;
     clearviewport();
     setbkcolor(9);
     while(x<=y)
     {
            putpixel(x+h,y+k,4);
            putpixel(y+h,x+k,4);
            putpixel(-y+h,x+k,4);
            putpixel(-x+h,y+k,4);
            putpixel(-x+h,-y+k,4);
            putpixel(-y+h,-x+k,4);
            putpixel(y+h,-x+k,4);
            putpixel(x+h,-y+k,4);
            if(d<0)
             d=d+4*x+6;
            else
             {
             d=d+4*(x-y)+10;
             y—;
             }
     x++;
     }
     getch();
}
//end of main program
```

//PROGRAM TO DRAW CIRCLE USING MID POINT METHOD

```
#include<stdio.h>
#include<conio.h>
#include<graphics.h>
void main()
{
     int r,x,y,h,k,d;
     int gd=DETECT,gm;
```

```
	initgraph(&gd,&gm,"f:\\tc\\bgi");
	printf("\n enter the center of circle\n");
	scanf("%d%d",&h,&k);
	printf("\n enter the radius of circle");
	scanf("%d",&r);
	x=0;y=r;
	d=1-r;
	clearviewport();
	setbkcolor(9);
	while(x<=y)
	{
		putpixel(x+h,y+k,4);
		putpixel(y+h,x+k,4);
		putpixel(-y+h,x+k,4);
		putpixel(-x+h,y+k,4);
		putpixel(-x+h,-y+k,4);
		putpixel(-y+h,-x+k,4);
		putpixel(y+h,-x+k,4);
		putpixel(x+h,-y+k,4);
		if(d<0)
		 d=d+2*x+3;
		else
		 {
		 d=d+2*(x-y)+5;
		 y-;
		 }
	x++;
	}
	getch();
  }
//end of main program
```

//PROGRAM TO DRAW CIRCLE USING TRIGNOMETRIC METHOD

```
  #include<stdio.h>
  #include<conio.h>
  #include<graphics.h>
  #include<math.h>
  void main()
  {
	int r,h,k;
	float xend,x,y,temp,thetainc,theta,thetaend,angle;
	int gd=DETECT,gm;
	initgraph(&gd,&gm,"f:\\tc\\bgi");
	printf("\n enter the center of circle\n");
	scanf("%d%d",&h,&k);
	printf("\n enter the radius of circle");
	scanf("%d",&r);
	temp=3.141/180;
	thetainc=1.0/r;
```

```
        theta=0;
        clearviewport();
        setbkcolor(9);
        thetaend=45;
        while(theta<=thetaend)
        {
                angle=temp*theta;
                x=r*cos(angle);
                y=r*sin(angle);
                putpixel(x+h,y+k,4);
                putpixel(y+h,x+k,4);
                putpixel(-y+h,x+k,4);
                putpixel(-x+h,y+k,4);
                putpixel(-x+h,-y+k,4);
                putpixel(-y+h,-x+k,4);
                putpixel(y+h,-x+k,4);
                putpixel(x+h,-y+k,4);
                theta = theta + thetainc;
        }
        getch();
    }
//end of main program
```

//PROGRAM TO DRAW ELLIPSE POLYNOMIAL METHOD

```
    #include<stdio.h>
    #include<conio.h>
    #include<graphics.h>
    #include<math.h>
    void main()
    {
        int h,k,a,b;
        float xend,x,y;
        int gd=DETECT,gm;
        initgraph(&gd,&gm,"f:\\tc\\bgi");
        printf("\n enter the center of ellipse\n");
        scanf("%d%d",&h,&k);
        printf("\n enter the major axis and minor axis of ellipse");
        scanf("%d%d",&a,&b);
        clearviewport();
        setbkcolor(9);
        x=0;
        xend=a;
        while(x<=xend)
        {
                y=b*sqrt(1-(x*x)/(a*a));
                putpixel(x+h,y+k,4);
                putpixel(-x+h,y+k,4);
                putpixel(-x+h,-y+k,4);
                putpixel(x+h,-y+k,4);
```

```
        x++;
        }
        getch();
    }
//end of main program
```

//PROGRAM TO DRAW CIRCLE USING TRIGNOMETRIC METHOD

```
    #include<stdio.h>
    #include<conio.h>
    #include<graphics.h>
    #include<math.h>
    void main()
    {
        int a,b,h,k;
        float xend,x,y,temp,thetainc,theta,thetaend,angle;
        int gd=DETECT,gm;
        initgraph(&gd,&gm,"f:\\tc\\bgi");
        printf("\n enter the center of ellipse\n");
        scanf("%d%d",&h,&k);
        printf("\n enter the major and minor axis of ellipse");
        scanf("%d%d",&a,&b);
        temp=3.141/180;
        thetainc=3.141/(2*a);
        theta=0;
        clearviewport();
        setbkcolor(9);
        thetaend=90;
        while(theta<=thetaend)
        {
                angle=temp*theta;
                x=a*cos(angle);
                y=b*sin(angle);
                putpixel(x+h,y+k,4);
                putpixel(-x+h,y+k,4);
                putpixel(-x+h,-y+k,4);
                putpixel(x+h,-y+k,4);
                theta = theta + thetainc;
        }
        getch();
    }
//end of main program
```

//PROGRAM TO DRAW ELLIPSE USING MID POINT METHOD

```
    #include<stdio.h>
    #include<conio.h>
    #include<graphics.h>
    #include<math.h>
    void main()
```

```
  {
       int x,y,h,k,a,b;
       float d1,d2;
       int gd=DETECT,gm;
       initgraph(&gd,&gm,"f:\\tc\\bgi");
       printf("\n enter the center of ellipse\n");
       scanf("%d%d",&h,&k);
       printf("\n enter the major and minor axis of ellipse");
       scanf("%d%d",&a,&b);
       x=0;y=b;
       clearviewport();
       setbkcolor(9);
       d1=b*b-a*a*b+0.25*a*a;
       while(a*a*(y-0.5)> b*b*(x+1))
       {
       printf(«%d %d»,x,y);
       if(d1<0)
              d1=d1+b*b*(2*x+3);
        else
              {
              d1=d1 + b*b*(2*x+3)+a*a*(-2*y+2);
              y—;
              }
        x++;
        putpixel(x+h,y+k,4);
        putpixel(-x+h,y+k,4);
        putpixel(-x+h,-y+k,4);
        putpixel(x+h,-y+k,4);
       }
   printf(«%d %d»,x,y);
   getch();
  d2 =b*b*(x+0.5)*(x+0.5)+a*a*(y-1.0)*(y-1.0)-(a*b)*(a*b);
//printf("%f",d2);
//     printf(«%d»,y);
       while(y>0)
       {
       if(d2<0)
              {
              d2=d2+b*b*(2*x+2)+a*a*(-2*y+3);
              x++;
              }
        else
              d2=d2 + a*a*(-2*y+3);
        y—;
//      printf(«%d %d\n»,x , y);
        putpixel(x+h,y+k,4);
        putpixel(-x+h,y+k,4);
        putpixel(-x+h,-y+k,4);
        putpixel(x+h,-y+k,4);
       }
```

```
        getch();
    }
//end of main program
```

// PROGRAM FOR ROTATION OF AN ELLIPSE

```
#include<stdio.h>
#include<dos.h>
#include<graphics.h>
void main()
{
int i,j;
int driver=DETECT,mode;
char ch;
initgraph(&driver,&mode,"c:\\tc\\bgi");
ellipse(320,240,0,360,140,70);
for(i=140;i>=0;i-)
{
ellipse(320,240,0,360,i,70);
line(320,0,320,480);
line(0,240,640,240);
delay(50);
cleardevice();
if(i==0)
{
for(j=i;j<=140;j++)
{
ellipse(320,240,0,360,j,70);
line(320,0,320,480);
line(0,240,640,240);
delay(50);
cleardevice();
}
}
}
getch();
}
```

//PROGRAM TO TRANSLATE A CIRCLE ALONG THE SIDES AND //THE DIAGONAL OF A RECTANGLE.

```
#include<stdio.h>
#include<graphics.h>
#include<math.h>
#include<conio.h>
#include<dos.h>
void main()
{
int gd,gm,a;
```

```
gd=DETECT,gm;
initgraph(&gd,&gm,"..\\bgi");
rectangle(100,100,700,700);
while(!kbhit())
{
for(int i=300;i>=100;i–)
{  cleardevice();
        rectangle(100,100,400,300);
        line(100,300,400,100);
        setfillstyle(SOLID_FILL,RED);
        fillellipse(50,i,50,50);
        delay(10);
}
for(int j=100;j<=400;j++)
{
        cleardevice();
        rectangle(100,100,400,300);
        line(100,300,400,100);
        setfillstyle(SOLID_FILL,RED);
        fillellipse(j,50,50,50);
        delay(10);
}
for(a=100;a<=300;a++)
{
        cleardevice();
        rectangle(100,100,400,300);
        line(100,300,400,100);
        setfillstyle(SOLID_FILL,RED);
        fillellipse(450,a,50,50);
        delay(10);
}
for(int b=400;b>=100;b–)
{
        cleardevice();
        rectangle(100,100,400,300);
        line(100,300,400,100);
        setfillstyle(SOLID_FILL,RED);
        fillellipse(b,350,50,50);
        delay(10);
}
line(100,300,400,100);
int x1=100,x2=400,y1=250,y2=50,x,y,xend;
float m,c;
x=x1;
xend=x2;
y=y1;
m=(float)(y2-y1)/(x2-x1);
c=y-m*x1;
while(x<=xend)
{
```

```
        y=m*x+c;
        cleardevice();
        rectangle(100,100,400,300);
        line(100,300,400,100);
        setfillstyle(SOLID_FILL,RED);
        fillellipse(x,y,50,50);
        delay(10);
        x++;
}
}
getch();
}
```

//PROGRAM TO SIMULATE ROTATE THE FAN.

```
#include<stdio.h>
#include<conio.h>
#include<graphics.h>
#include<dos.h>
void main()
{
int i,ch;
int gd=DETECT,gm;
initgraph(&gd,&gm,"f:\\tc\\bgi");
do
{
printf("1: slow");
printf("\n2: medium");
printf("\n3: fast");
printf("\n4:exit");
printf("\nenter the choice");
scanf("%d",&ch);
switch(ch)
{
case 1:{
for(i=0;i<=120;i++)
{
cleardevice();
//line(250,250,250,100);
circle(250,250,20);
setfillstyle(SOLID_FILL,RED);
floodfill(250,250,WHITE);
pieslice(250,250,120+i,130+i,130);
pieslice(250,250,360+i,370+i,130);
pieslice(250,250,240+i,250+i,130);
delay(100);
}
}
break;
```

```
case 2:{
for(i=0;i<=360;i++)
{
cleardevice();
circle(250,250,20);
setfillstyle(SOLID_FILL,RED);
floodfill(250,250,WHITE);
line(258,231,350,100);
line(257,231,349,100);
line(256,231,348,100);
pieslice(250,250,120+i,130+i,130);
pieslice(250,250,360+i,370+i,130);
pieslice(250,250,240+i,250+i,130);
delay(20);
}
}
break;
case 3:{
for(i=0;i<=360;i++)
{
cleardevice();
//line(250,250,250,100);
circle(250,250,20);
setfillstyle(SOLID_FILL,RED);
floodfill(250,250,WHITE);
pieslice(250,250,120+i,130+i,130);
pieslice(250,250,360+i,370+i,130);
pieslice(250,250,240+i,250+i,130);
delay(2);
}
}
}
}while(ch!=4);
getch();
}
```

//PROGRAM TO SHOW SCENCE OF FLYING KITE.

```
#include<graphics.h>
#include<conio.h>
#include<stdio.h>
#include<dos.h>
void main()
{
int i;
int gd=DETECT,gm;
initgraph(&gd,&gm,"f:\\tc\\bgi" );
cleardevice();
setcolor(RED);
for(i=0;i<100;i++)
```

```
{
cleardevice();
line(200+i,200-i,300+i,100-i);
line(200+i,200-i,300+i,300-i);
line(200+i,200-i,300+i,300-i);
line(300+i,300-i,400+i,200-i);
line(300+i,100-i,400+i,200-i);
line(300+i,100-i,300+i,300-i);
line(300+i,300-i,290+i,310-i);
line(200+i,200-i,400+i,200-i);
line(300+i,300-i,310+i,310-i);
line(290+i,310-i,310+i,310-i);
line(300+i,150-i,50+i,400-i);
line(300+i,250-i,50+i,400-i);
circle(300+i,150-i,5);
circle(300+i,250-i,2);
delay(80);
}
cleardevice();
getch();
}
```

//PROGRAM TO ROTATE A LINE ABOUT ITS ONE OF THE //END POINT(MID POINT OF THE SCREEN).

```
#include<stdio.h>
#include<conio.h>
#include<graphics.h>
#include<math.h>
#include<dos.h>
void main()
{
     int r,h,k,i;
     float xend,x,y,x1,y1,x2,y2,th,theta;
     int gd=DETECT,gm;
     initgraph(&gd,&gm,"f:\\tc\\bgi");
     x1=500;y1=380;
     x=getmaxx()/2.0;y=getmaxy()/2.0;
     line(getmaxx()/2,getmaxy()/2,x1,y1);
     th=10; i=1;
     while(!kbhit())
     {
     theta=(3.14/180.0)*th;
     cleardevice();
     x2=x1*cos(theta)-y1*sin(theta) x*cos(theta)+y*sin(theta)+x;
     y2=x1*sin(theta)+y1*cos(theta)-x*sin(theta)-y*cos(theta)+y;
     circle(x,y,20);
     setcolor(i);
     line(x,y,x2,y2);
     th=th+2; i++;
```

```
        delay(400);
        }
        getch();
    }
//end of the main program
```

//PROGRAM TO IMPLEMENT COHEN-SUTHERLAND ALGORITHM

```
#include<stdio.h>
#include<conio.h>
#include<graphics.h>
int bit1[4],bit2[4];
int xmin=150,xmax=350,ymin=100,ymax=250,x1,y1,x2,y2;
void main()
{
int gd=DETECT,gm,i,x1p,y1p,x2p,y2p;
void findcode(int *bit,int x,int y);
void intersect(int b[4],int
b1[4],int*x1p,int*y1p,int*x2p,int*y2p);
initgraph(&gd,&gm,»f:\\tc\\bgi»);
printf(«enter the initial coordinates of the line=>»);
scanf("%d%d",&x1,&y1);
printf("enter the final coordinates of the line=>");
scanf("%d%d",&x2,&y2);
x1p=x1;y1p=y1;x2p=x2;y2p=y2;
findcode(bit1,x1,y1);
findcode(bit2,x2,y2);
for(i=0;i<4;i++)
printf("%d",bit1[i]);
printf("\n");
for(i=0;i<4;i++)
printf("%d",bit2[i]);
printf("\n");
rectangle(xmin,ymin,xmax,ymax);
line(x1,y1,x2,y2);
intersect(bit1,bit2,&x1p,&y1p,&x2p,&y2p);
printf(«%d%d%d%d»,x1p,y1p,x2p,y2p);
getch();
cleardevice();
rectangle(xmin,ymin,xmax,ymax);
line(x1p,y1p,x2p,y2p);
x1=x1p;y1=y1p;x2=x2p;y2=y2p;
bit1[0]=0;bit1[1]=0;bit1[2]=0;bit1[3]=0;
bit2[0]=0;bit2[1]=0;bit2[2]=0;bit2[3]=0;
findcode(bit1,x1,y1);
findcode(bit2,x2,y2);
cleardevice();
for(i=0;i<4;i++)
printf("%d",bit1[i]);
printf("\n");
```

```
for(i=0;i<4;i++)
printf("%d",bit2[i]);
//getch();
intersect(bit1,bit2,&x1p,&y1p,&x2p,&y2p);
rectangle(xmin,ymin,xmax,ymax);
line(x1p,y1p,x2p,y2p);
getch();
}
void findcode(int *bit,int x,int y)
{
  if((y-ymax)>0)*(bit+0)=1;
  if((ymin-y)>0)*(bit+1)=1;
  if((x-xmax)>0)*(bit+2)=1;
   if((xmin-x)>0)*(bit+3)=1;
}
void intersect(int b1[4],int b2[4],int*x1p,int*y1p,int*x2p,int*y2p)
{
  int b3[4],i,t;
void point(int b[4],int **xx,int **yy);
for(i=0;i<4;i++)
b3[i]=b1[i]&b2[i];
for(i=0;i<4;i++)
      printf("%d",b3[i]);
if(b1[0]==0 && b1[1]==0 && b1[2]==0 && b1[3]==0
&& b2[0]==0 &&
b2[1]==0 && b2[2]==0 && b2[3]==0)
{
  printf("\n line is visible");
  return;
}
else if(b3[0]!=0 || b3[2]!=0 || b3[3]!=0)
{
   printf("\n not visible");
   return;
}
else
{
  printf("\n Line is clipping candidate");
  point(b1,&x1p,&y1p);
  point(b2,&x2p,&y2p);
}
}
void point(int b[4],int **xx,int **yy)
{     float t;
  if(b[0]==1)
  {
   t=(ymax-y1)/(float)(y2-y1);
   **xx=x1+t*(x2-x1);
   **yy=ymax;
  }
```

```
    else if(b[1]==1)
    {
     t=(ymin-y1)/(float)(y2-y1);
     **xx=x1+t*(x2-x1);
     **yy=ymin;
    }
    else if(b[2]==1)
    {
     t=(xmax-x1)/(float)(x2-x1);
     **yy=y1+t*(y2-y1);
     **xx=xmax;
    }
    else if(b[3]==1)
    {
     t=(xmin-x1)/(float)(x2-x1);
     **yy=y1+t*(y2-y1);
    **xx=xmin;
    }
}
```

//PROGRAM TO SHOW SCENCE OF SOLAR SYSTEM

```
#include<graphics.h>
#include<stdlib.h>
#include<math.h>
#include<conio.h>
#include<dos.h>
#define pi 3.14
void main()
{
int gd=DETECT,gm,a[9]={40,60,100,120,150,200,220,250,280};
int th[9]={20,40,50,60,30,50,35,50,30},b[9]={15,20,40,60,80,100,120,140,160};
int h=320,k=270,i,r[9]={4,5,10,5,12,6,8,9,12},x,y,j,a1,b1,k1;
void draw(int h,int k,int a[9],int b[9],int th[9],int j,int r[9],int v);
initgraph(&gd,&gm,"f:\\tc\\bgi");
setbkcolor(1);
setcolor(14);
setfillstyle(SOLID_FILL,GREEN);
settextstyle(TRIPLEX_FONT,HORIZ_DIR,5);
rectangle(10,10,630,470);
outtextxy(200,30,"Solar System");
for(i=0;i<500;i++)
    {
    x=random(700);
    y=random(500);
    putpixel(x,y,15);
    }
circle(h,k,4);
floodfill(h,k,14);
for(j=0;j<=360;j++)
```

```
{
draw(h,k,a,b,th,j,r,14);
if(j==360)j=0;
if(kbhit())
break;
delay(20);
draw(h,k,a,b,th,j,r,1);
}
getch();
}
void draw(int h,int k,int a[9],int b[9],int th[9],int j,int r[9],int
v)
  {
int i,x,y;
setcolor(v);
setfillstyle(SOLID_FILL,v);
for(i=0;i<9;i++)
   {
   x=h+a[i]*cos((j+th[i])*pi/180);
   y=k+b[i]*sin((j+th[i])*pi/180);
   circle(x,y,r[i]);
   floodfill(x,y,v);
   ellipse(h,k,0,360,a[i],b[i]);
   if(i==5)
   ellipse(x,y,0,360,r[i]+9,r[i]-4);
  }
}
//end of the main program
```

//PROGRAM TO SHOW A SCENCE OF ECLIPSE

```
#include<stdio.h>
#include<conio.h>
#include<graphics.h>
#include<dos.h>
#include<stdlib.h>
#include<math.h>
#define p 3.14/180
void main()
{
int gd=DETECT,gm,j,i=90,h=200,k=230,r=100,x,y,x1,y1;
initgraph(&gd,&gm,"f:\\tc\\bgi");
cleardevice();
setbkcolor(8);
setcolor(14);
settextstyle(TRIPLEX_FONT,HORIZ_DIR,5);
rectangle(10,10,630,470);
settextstyle(TRIPLEX_FONT,HORIZ_DIR,1);
setfillstyle(SOLID_FILL,14);
```

```
circle(h+300,k,50);
outtextxy(h+300,k-80,"sun");
floodfill(h+300,k,14);
setcolor(10);
setfillstyle(SOLID_FILL,10);
circle(h,k,30);
outtextxy(h,k-60,"earth");
floodfill(h,k,10);
for(j=0;j<1000;j++)
    {
    x=random(700);
    y=random(500);
    putpixel(x,y,15);
   }
while (!kbhit())
   {
   x=h+r*cos(i*p);
   y=k+r*sin(i*p);
   x1=(h-100)+r*cos(i*p);
   y1=k+r*sin(i*p);
   setcolor(0);
   setfillstyle(SOLID_FILL,0);
   ellipse(x1,y1,45,405,50,30);
   floodfill(x1,y1,0);
   setcolor(8);
   setfillstyle(SOLID_FILL,8);
   ellipse(x1,y1,45,405,50,30);
   floodfill(x1,y1,8);
   setcolor(15);
   setfillstyle(SOLID_FILL,15);
   circle(x,y,20);
   outtextxy(x,y+30,"moon");
   floodfill(x,y,15);
   delay(200);
   if(y==k)
    break;
   setcolor(0);
   setfillstyle(SOLID_FILL,0);
   outtextxy(x,y+30,"moon");
   circle(x,y,20);
   floodfill(x,y,0);
   i-;
   setcolor(14);
 }
getch();
}
//End of the main program
```

Appendix-2

Mathematics Related to Computer Graphics

A2.1 CARTESIAN CO-ORDINATE SYSTEM

2-Dimensional

Let *X' OX* and *Y' OY* be co-ordinate axes, and let *P* be any point in the plane. Draw perpendiculars PM and *PN* from *P* on *x*-axis and *y*-axis respectively. Length of the directed line segment OM in the units of scale chosen is called **x-coordinate** or **abscissa** of point P. Similarly length of the directed line segment ON on the same scale is called the **y-coordinate** or **ordinate** of point P.

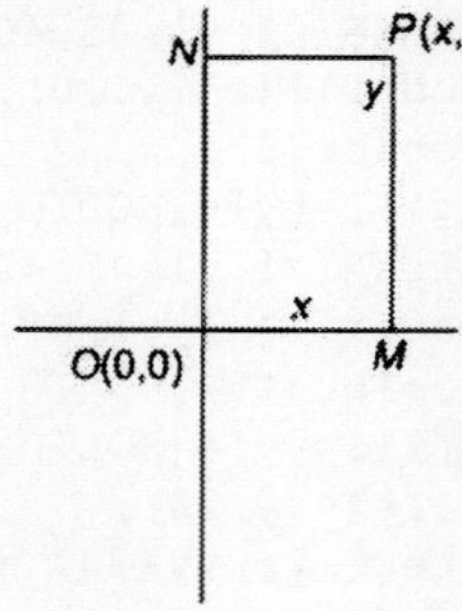

Let $OP = x$ and $ON = y$. Then the point *P* is represented by the ordered pair$(x,\ y)$.

3-Dimensional

In 3-D, another axis normally labeled as z, is added, providing a senses of third dimension of space measurement. To specify a particular point in three dimension co-ordinate system, third co-ordinate z unit (**applicate**) is added, $(x, y,\ z)$ to ordered pair (x, y).

In the three-dimensional Cartesian coordinate system, a point P in the xyz-space is represent by a tuple of three components $(x, y,\ z)$.

x is the signed distance from the *yz*-plane to the point *P*,
y is the signed distance from the *xz*-plane to the point *P*, and
z is the signed distance from the *xy*-plane to the point *P*.

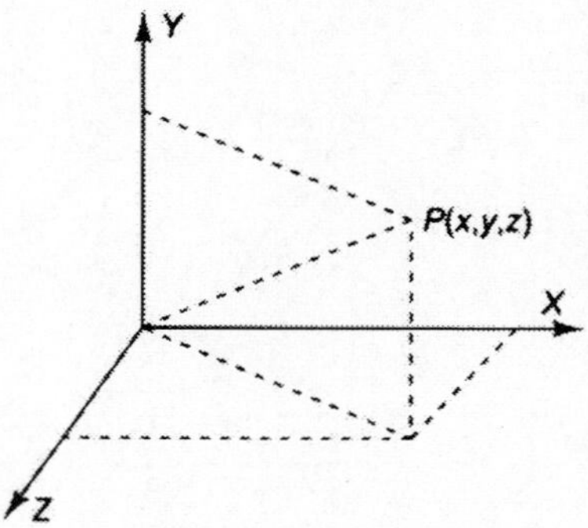

To specify the order of three axis x, y, and z-axis Cartesian co-ordinate system arranged in two possible ways, are called ***right handed system*** and ***left-handed system***.

The right-handed system is universally accepted in the physical sciences, but the left-handed is also still in use.

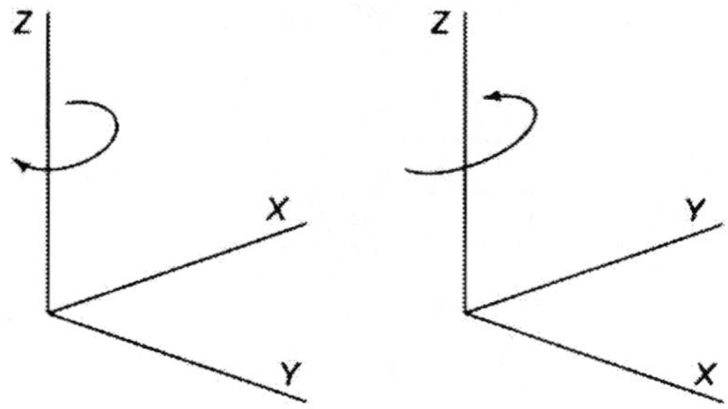

Left-handed system $X \to Y \to Z$ Right-handed system $X \to Y \to Z$

A2.2 POLAR CO-ORDINATE SYSTEM

Let $X'OX$ and $Y'OY$ be co-ordinate axes, and let P be any point in the plane, such that $OP = r$ and $\angle POX = \theta$. Then the point P is represented by the ordered pair(r, θ) and is called polar co-ordinate system.

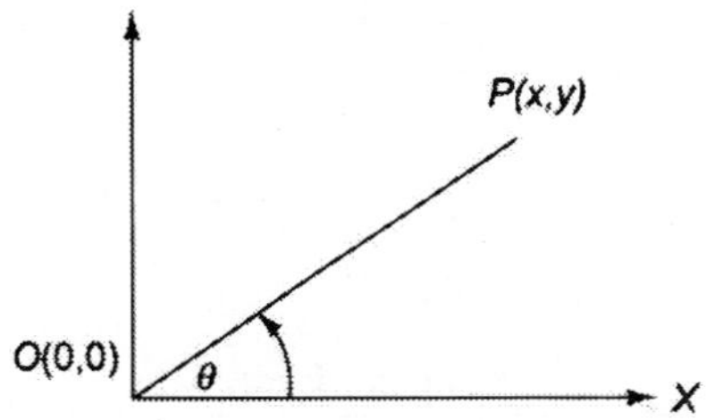

A2.3 RELATIONSHIP BETWEEN CARTESIAN CO-ORDINATE AND POLAR CO-ORDINATE

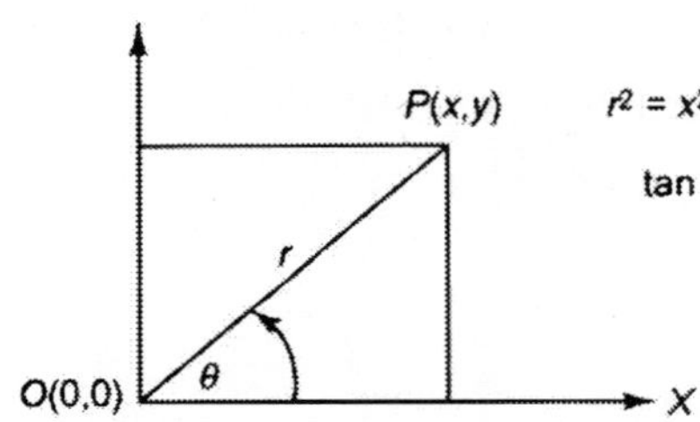

$$r^2 = x^2 + y^2$$

$$\tan\theta = \frac{y}{x}$$

A2.4 QUADRANTS

Let *X'OX* and *Y'OY* be the coordinate axes. We observe that the two axes divide the Euclidian plane into four regions, called the quadrants. The regions *XOY*, *X' OY*, *X' OY'* and *Y'OX* are known as the first, the second, the third, and the fourth quadrant respectively. The line *OX* is called positive x-axis , *OX'* is negative *x*-axis, *OY* as positive *y*-axis and *OY'* negative *y*-axis.

I Quadrants	$x > 0,\ y > 0$
II Quadrants	$x < 0,\ y > 0$
III Quadrants	$x < 0,\ y < 0$
IV Quadrants	$x > 0,\ y < 0$

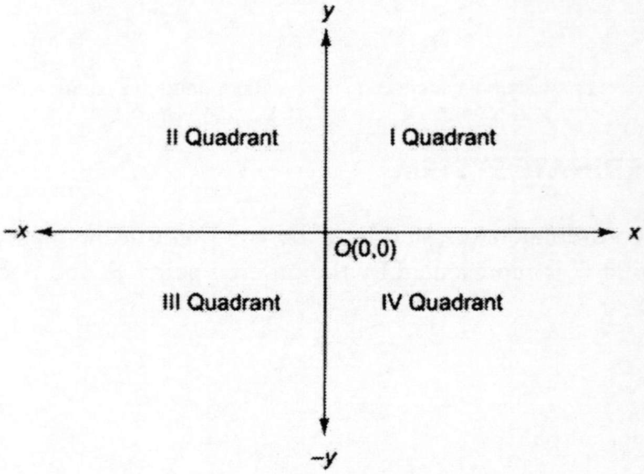

Units of measure for Angle

$$\text{Degree} = \frac{\text{Length of arc}}{\text{Circumference of the circle}} * 360$$

Radian

$$\text{Radian} = \frac{\text{Length of arc cut out by the angle}}{\text{Circle radius}}$$

Note : Circumference of circle $= 2\pi r$ (r = radius of circle)

$$360^0 = 2\pi \text{ radian}$$

$$\text{Degree } (\theta) = \frac{AB}{r} *360$$

$$\text{Radian} = \frac{AB}{r}$$

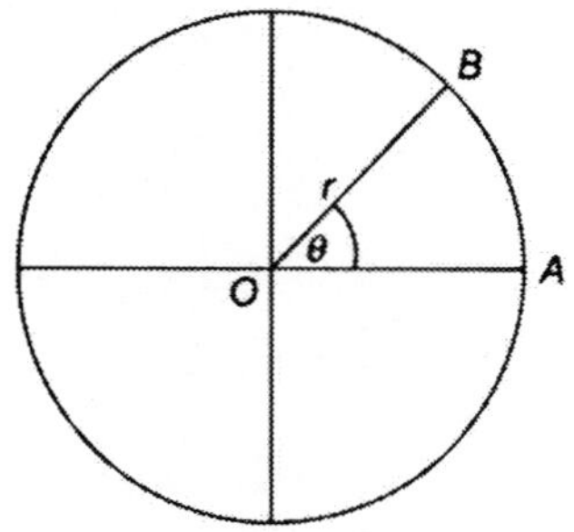

A2.5 DISTANCE BETWEEN TWO POINTS

The distance between two points $P(x1,y1)$ and $Q(x2,y2)$ is given by

$$PQ = \sqrt{(x2-x1)^2 + (y2-y1)^2}$$

In general

Distance between two points =

$$\sqrt{(\text{Difference between x-coordintes })^2 + (\text{Difference between y-coordintes })^2}$$

A2.6 CO-ORDINATE OF A POINT WHICH DIVIDE LINE SEGMENT INTERNALLY

Co-ordinate of a point (x,y) which divide a line segment joining the points $(x1,y1)$ and $(x2,y2)$ internally in the ratio m: n is given by

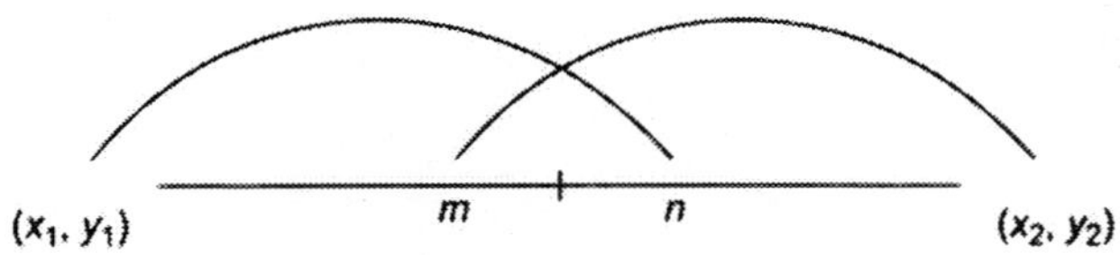

$$x = \frac{mx2 + nx1}{m+n} \quad y = \frac{my2 + ny1}{m+n}$$

A2.7 CO-ORDINATE OF A POINT WHICH DIVIDE LINE SEGMENT EXTERNALLY

Co-ordinate of a point which divide line segment joining the points (x1,y1) and (x2,y2) externally in the ratio m: n is given by

$$x = \frac{mx2 - nx1}{m-n} \quad y = \frac{my2 - ny1}{m-n}$$

A2.8 CO-ORDINATE OF CENTROID OF TRIANGLE

Let $A(x1, y1)$, $B(x2, y2)$ and $C(x3, y3)$ be vertices of a triangle. $M1$, $M2$, and $M3$ are mid- points of the three sides BC, AC, and AB respectively. Point of intersection of line joining $AM1$, $BM2$ and $CM3$ is called centriod (G) of the triangle.

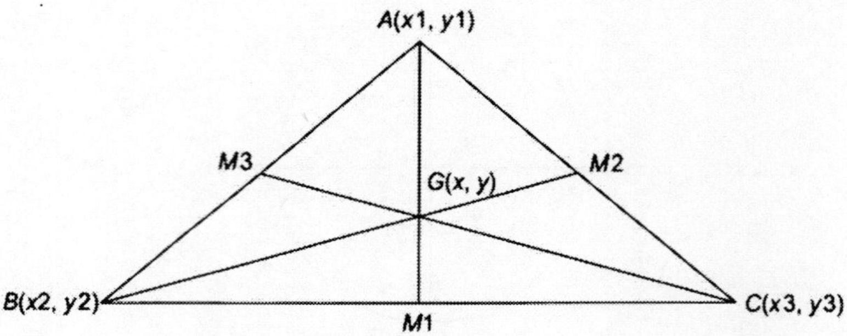

$$x = \frac{x3 + x2 + x1}{3} \qquad y = \frac{y3 + y2 + x1}{3}$$

A2.9 CO-ORDINATE OF IN-CENTRE OF A TRIANGLE

Let $A(x1, y1)$, $B(x2, y2)$ and $C(x3, y3)$ be vertices of a triangle.

AM1 is bisector of angle $\angle BAC$

BM2 is bisector of angle $\angle CBA$

CM3 is bisector of angle $\angle ACB$

then point of intersection of $AM1$, $AM2$ and $AM3$ is called in-centre (I) of the triangle.

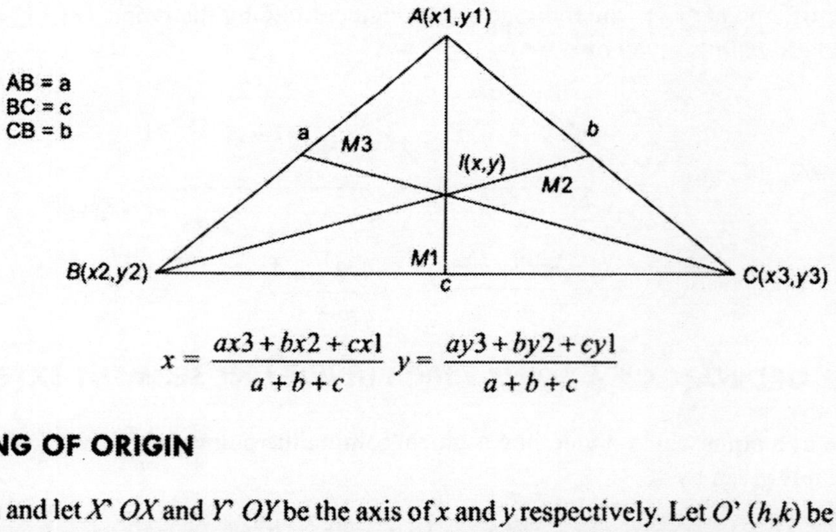

$$x = \frac{ax3 + bx2 + cx1}{a + b + c} \qquad y = \frac{ay3 + by2 + cy1}{a + b + c}$$

A2.10 SHIFTING OF ORIGIN

Let O be the origin and let $X'OX$ and $Y'OY$ be the axis of x and y respectively. Let O' (h,k) be any point in the plane. Let the origin be transferred to O' and $X'O'X$ and $Y'O'Y$ be new co-ordinate axis. Let P be other point in the plane having co-ordinates (x, y) and $(x' y')$ w.r.t. old co-ordinate and new co-ordinate system. Then

$$x = x' + h$$

$$y = y' + k$$

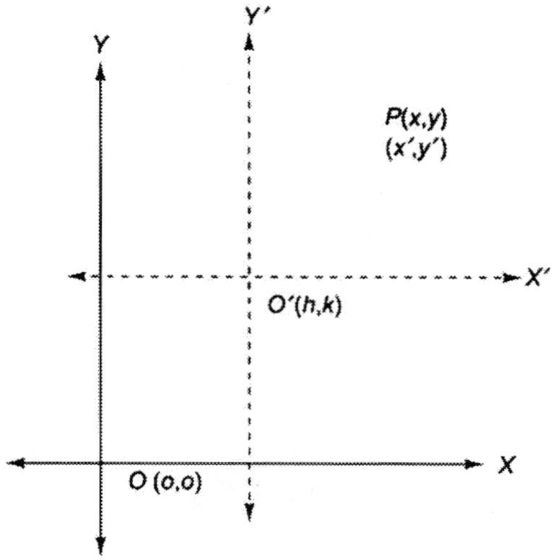

A2.11 SLOPE(GRADIENT) OF A LINE

The trigonometrically tangent of the angle that a line makes with positive direction of the x-axis in anticlockwise is called slope or gradient of the line.
It is generally denoted by m. Thus, $m = \tan\theta$.

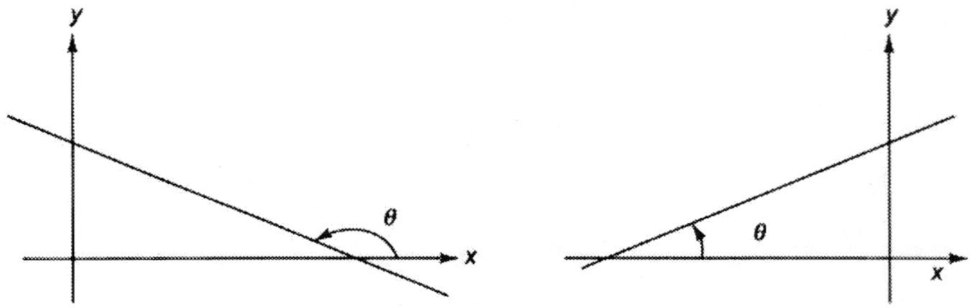

A2.12 DIFFERENT FORMS OF STRAIGHT LINES

A2.12.1 Slope Intercept form of a line

Equation of a line with slope m and intercept c on positive direction of y-axis is

$$y = mx + c.$$

Where $m = \tan\theta$

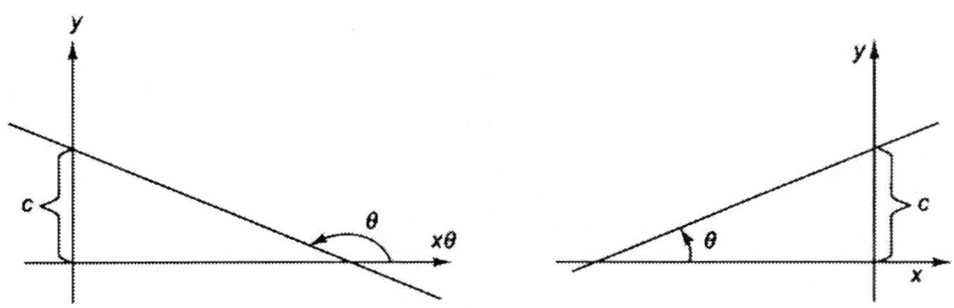

A2.12.2 The point-slope form of a line

Equation of a line passes through a point $(x1, y1)$ and has the slope m is
$y - y1 = m\,(x - x1)$

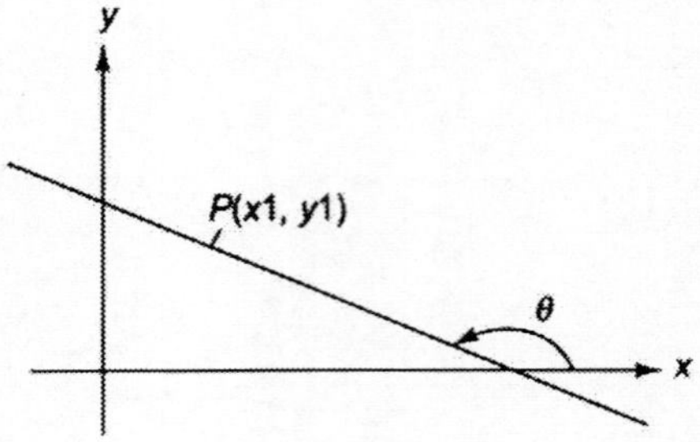

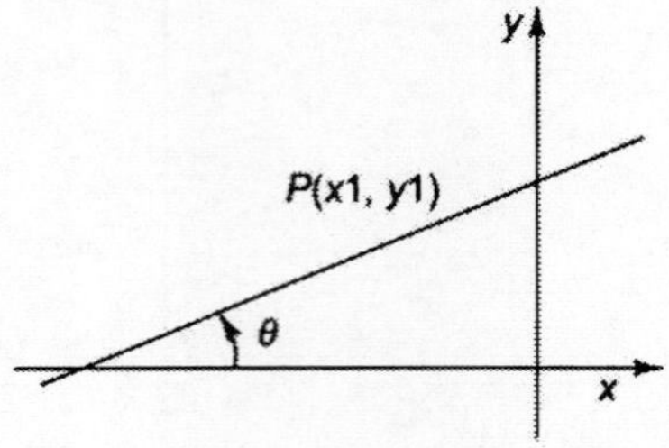

A2.12.3 Two-point form a line

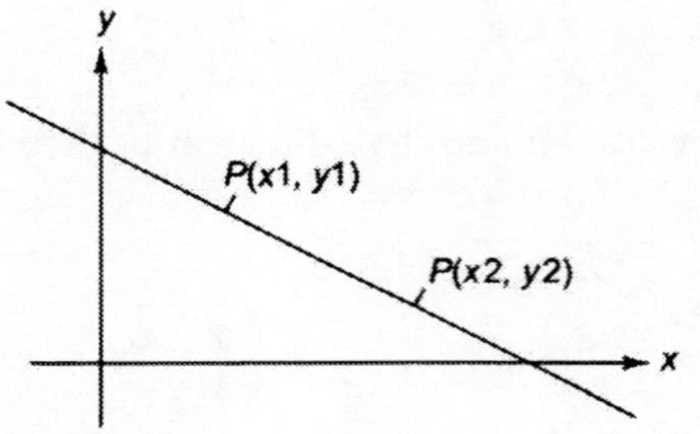

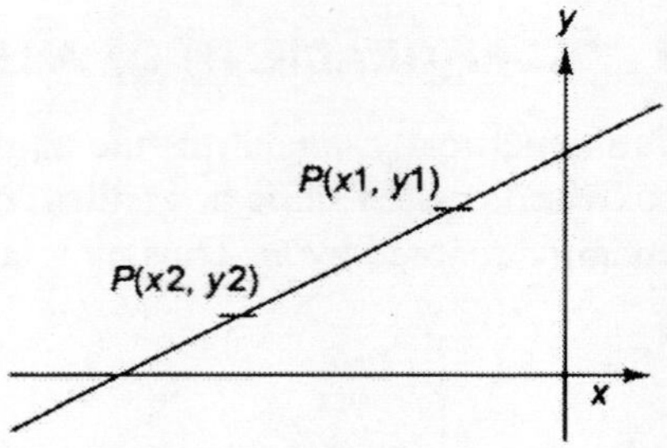

$$y - y1 = \frac{y2 - y1}{x2 - x1}\,(x - x1)$$

A2.12.4 Parametric Equation of a Line

Parametric equation of a line passes through point $A(x1, y1)$ and $B(x2. y2)$ is given by

$$x = x1 + u(x2 - x1)$$
$$y = y1 + u(y2 - y1)$$
$$\text{Where } 0 = u = 1$$

A2.13 PERPENDICULAR DISTANCE OF POINT FROM A LINE

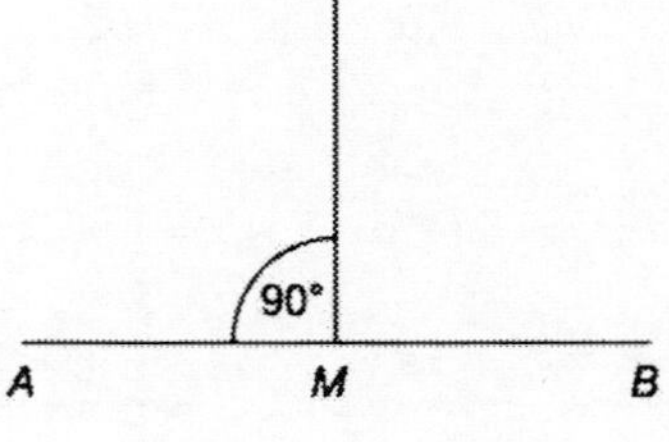

Perpendicular distance PM of a point from a point $P(x1, y1)$ from a line $ax + by + c = 0$ is given by

$$PM = \frac{ax1 + by1 + c}{\sqrt{a^2 + b^2}}$$

A2.14 CIRCLE

A2.14.1 Standard Equation of a circle

Equation of a circle with centre $C(h, k)$ and radius r is given by
$(x - h)^2 + (y - k)^2 = r^2$

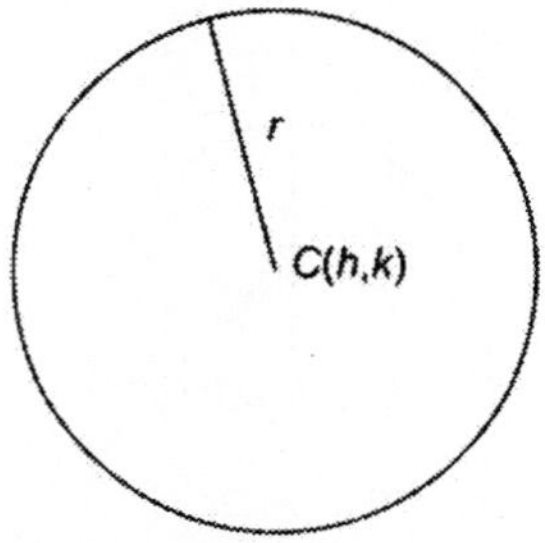

A2.14.2 Equation of circle with centre at O(0, 0) and radius r is given by
$x^2 + y^2 = r^2$

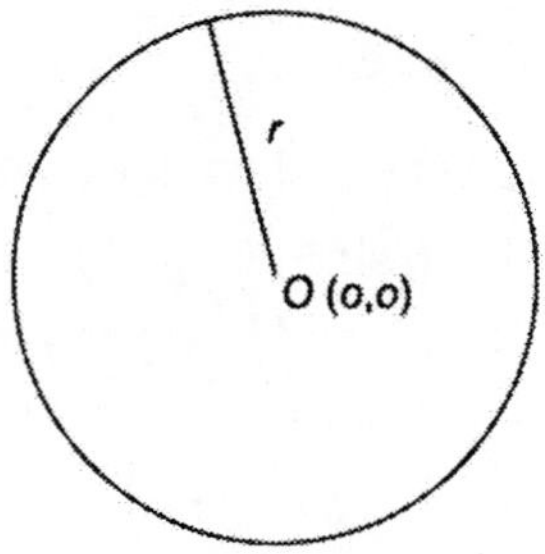

A2.14.2 Parametric Equation of Circle

With centre $C(h. k)$ and radius r

$x = h + r \cos \theta$ $\qquad$ $y = k + r \sin \theta$

With centre $C(0. 0)$ and radius r

$x = r \cos \theta$ $\qquad$ $y = r \sin \theta$

A2.15 ELLIPSE

A2.15.1 Standard Equation of an ellipse

Equation of an ellipse with centre $C(h, k)$ and length of major and minor axis **a** and **b** respectively.

$$\frac{(x - h)^2}{a^2} + \frac{(y - k)^2}{b^2} = 1 \text{ when } a > b$$

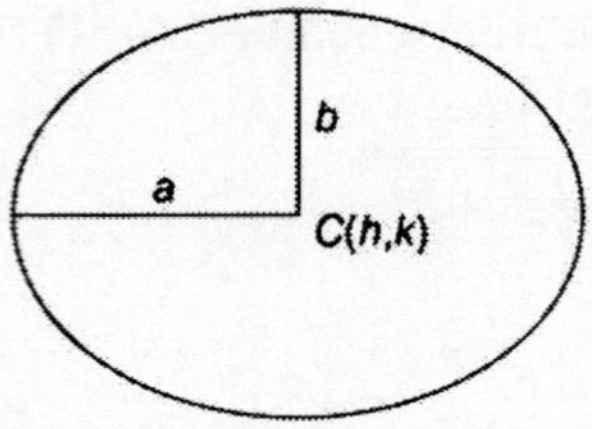

Equation of an ellipse with centre $C(h, k)$ and length of major and minor axis **b** and **a** respectively.

$$\frac{(x-h)^2}{a^2}+\frac{(y-k)^2}{b^2}=1 \quad \text{when } a<b$$

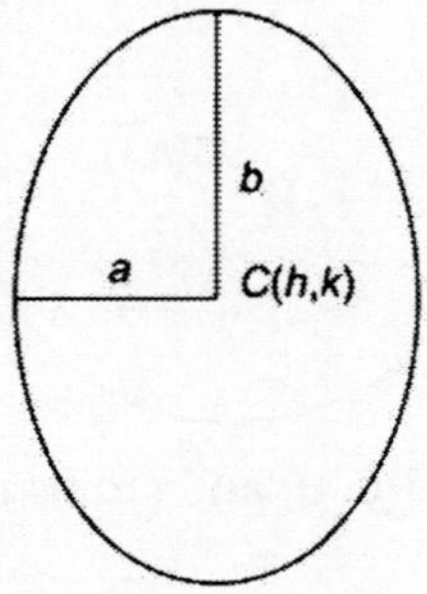

A2.15.2 Parametric Equation of Ellipse

With centre $C(h, k)$ and major and minor axis a and b respectively.

$x = h + a\cos\theta \qquad y = k + b\sin\theta$

With centre $C(0, 0)$ and major and minor axis a and b respectively.

$x = a\cos\theta \qquad y = b\sin\theta$

A2.16 MATRIX

A set of $m \times n$ numbers(real or complex) arranged in the form of a rectangular array of m rows and n columns is called an $m \times n$ matrix.
An $m \times n$ matrix is usually written as:

$$A = \begin{bmatrix} a_{11} & a_{12} & a_{13} & a_{14} & \cdots & a_{1n} \\ a_{21} & a_{22} & a_{23} & a_{24} & \cdots & a_{2n} \\ a_{31} & a_{32} & a_{33} & a_{34} & \cdots & a_{3n} \\ . & . & . & . & & . \\ . & . & . & . & & . \\ a_{m1} & a_{m2} & a_{m3} & a_{m4} & \cdots & a_{mn} \end{bmatrix}$$

$$A = [aij]mxn \quad or \quad A = [aij]$$

A2.16.1 Types of Matrices

S No	Type of Matrix	Description
1	Row Matrix	A matrix having only one row
2	Column matrix	A matrix having only one column
3	Square Matrix	A matrix with number of rows equal to number of columns
4	Diagonal Matrix	A square matrix having all elements equal to zero except diagonal elements.

A2.16.2 Addition of Matrices

Let A , B be two matrices each of order mxn. Then their addition A+B is a matrix of order mxn and is obtained by adding the corresponding elements of A and B.

$A = [aij]$ mxn and $B = [bij]$ mxn then
$A + B = [aij + bij]$ for $i = 1,2..........m$ and $j = 1, 2, ...n.$

Note : Sum of two matrices is defined only when they are of same order.

For example, let

$$A = \begin{bmatrix} a11 & a12 \\ a21 & a22 \end{bmatrix} \qquad B = \begin{bmatrix} b11 & b12 \\ b21 & b22 \end{bmatrix}$$

Here the sum $A + B$ is defined because A and B are of same order.

$$\boldsymbol{A + B} = \begin{bmatrix} a11 + b11 & a12 + b12 \\ a21 + b21 & a22 + b22 \end{bmatrix}$$

NOTE : Matrix addition is commutative
$\boldsymbol{A + B = B + A}$

A2.16.3 Subtraction of matrices

Let A, B be two matrices each of order mxn. Then their subtraction $A - B$ is a matrix of order mxn and is obtained by adding the corresponding elements of A and $(-B)$.

$A = [aij]$ $m \times n$ and $B = [bij]$ mxn then
$A-B= [aij - bij]$ for $i = 1, 2..........m$ and $j = 1, 2, ...n.$

Note: Subtraction of two matrices is defined only when they are of same order.

A2.16.4 Multiplication of Matrices

Let A and B be two matrices of orders mxn and nxp respectively. The product AB of matrices A and B is defined only if the number of columns of A is equal to the number of rows of B. The product AB will be a mxp matrix.

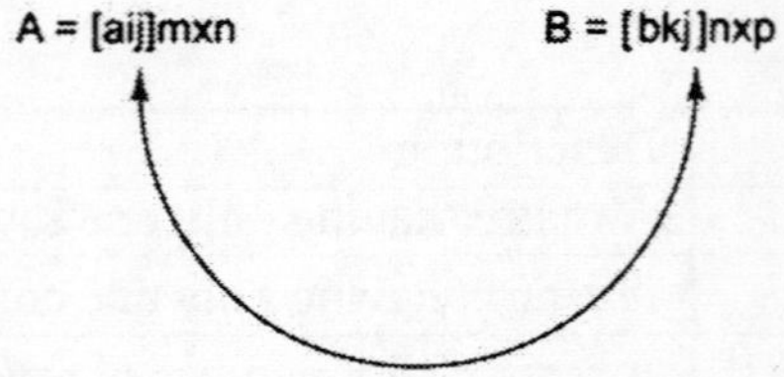

In the product AB, A is called pre-factor of AB, and B is called post-factor of AB.
The ij^{th} element of AB matrix is obtained by adding the products of the elements of the ith row of A by the corresponding elements of the jth columns of B.
For example, let

$$A = \begin{bmatrix} a11 & a12 \\ a21 & a22 \end{bmatrix} \quad B = \begin{bmatrix} b11 & b12 & b13 \\ b21 & b22 & b23 \end{bmatrix}$$

Here the product AB is defined because the no. of columns of A are equal to no. of rows of B.

$$A = \begin{bmatrix} \overrightarrow{a11 \quad a12} \\ a21 \quad a22 \end{bmatrix} \quad B = \begin{bmatrix} b11 & \downarrow & b12 & b13 \\ b21 & & b22 & b23 \end{bmatrix}$$

$$= \begin{bmatrix} a11b11 + a12b21 & a11b12 + a12b22 & a11\,b13 + a12b23 \\ a21b11 + a22b21 & a21b12 + a22b22 & a21b13 + a22b23 \end{bmatrix}$$

To be taken another example, let

$$A = \begin{bmatrix} 6 & 9 \\ 2 & 3 \end{bmatrix} \quad B = \begin{bmatrix} 2 & 6 & 0 \\ 7 & 9 & 8 \end{bmatrix}$$

$$AB = \begin{bmatrix} 6x2+9x7 & 6x6+9x9 & 6x0+9x8 \\ 2x2+3x7 & 2x6+3x9 & 2x0+3x8 \end{bmatrix}$$

$$AB = \begin{bmatrix} 75 & 117 & 72 \\ 25 & 39 & 24 \end{bmatrix}$$

For the above matrices, the product BA is not defined, because no. of columns of B are not equal to no. of rows of A.

Note: Matrix multiplication is not commutative in general.
$AB \neq BA$

A2.17 STRAIGHT LINE IN 3-D

Equation of the straight line XY passes through a given point $A(x1, y1, z1)$ and having the direction cosines $< l, m, n >$

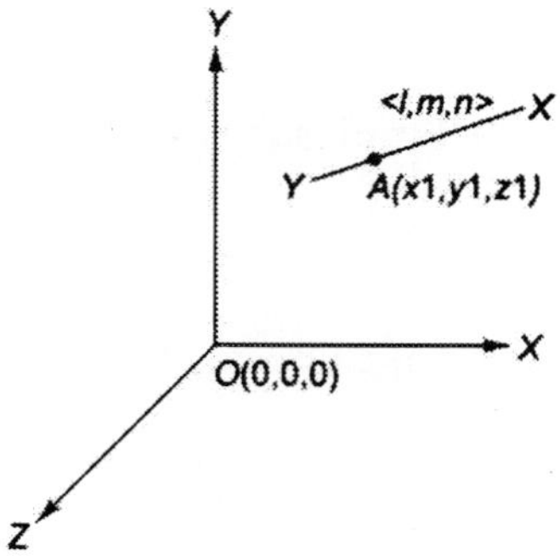

$$\frac{x-x1}{l}=\frac{y-y1}{m}=\frac{z-z1}{n}(=r)\text{say}$$

Thus the co-ordinates of any point at a distance r from $(x1, y1, z1)$ on a line with direction cosines are $<l,m,n>$ are

$$(x1+lr, y1+mr, z1+nr) \qquad \text{..................(A2.1)}$$

By giving different values to **r** , we get all points on the line.
Equations (A2.1) are called parametric equations to straight line.

A2.17.1 Two-point form of Straight line in 3-D

Equation of the straight line *XY* passes trough two points $A(x1, y1, z1)$ and $B(x2, y2, z2)$

$$\frac{x-x1}{x2-x1}=\frac{y-y1}{y2-y1}=\frac{z-z1}{z2-z1}(=r)\text{say}$$

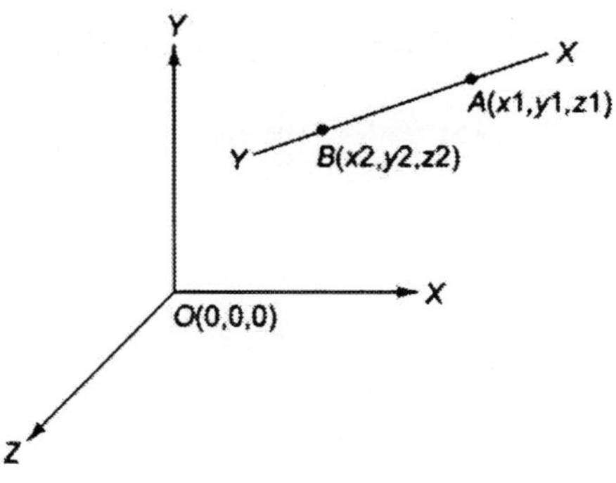

A2.18 GENERAL EQUATION OF 3-D PLANE

$ax + by + cz + d = 0$
where a, b, c are not all equal to zero.

Special Cases

Case I

$a = 0$, the plane is parallel to x-axis.

Case II

$a = b = 0$, the plane is parallel to xy plane.

A2.19 VECTOR

Definition : Vector is defined as segment of a directed line.

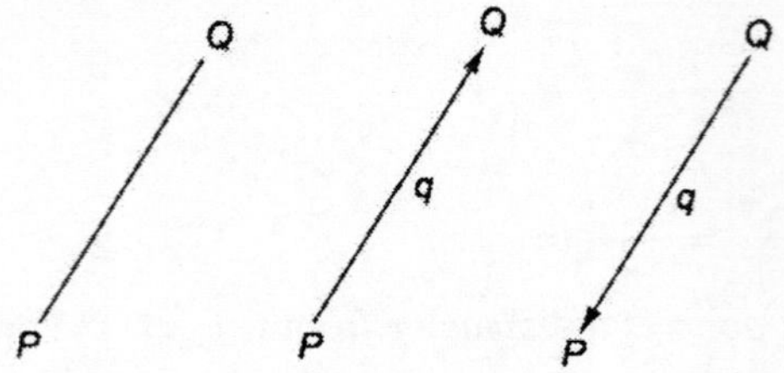

Line PQ or QP (a) Line PQ (b) Line QP (c)

In Fig. (a) , the point P is called the tail, base, start, or origin; point Q is called the head, tip, endpoint, or destination.

Magnitude and direction of a Vector

The distance between initial point P and final point Q of vector **PQ** is called the magnitude of vector **PQ** and is denoted by $|PQ|$ or simply as PQ

The direction of vector PQ is defined from P to Q.
In above cases both vectors **PQ** and **QP** have same magnitude q, but have opposite directions.

Note : **The magnitudes of vectors PQ and QP are equal but directions are not equal.**

A2.19.1 Representation of a Vector in 2-Dimension

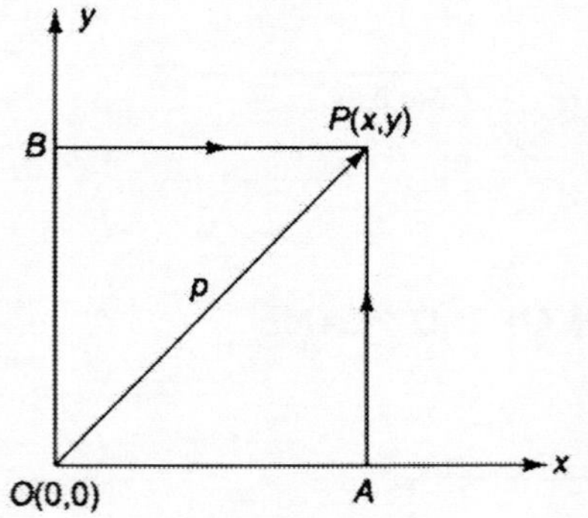

Let $P(x, y)$ be any point in the plane. Let $\hat{i}$ and $\hat{j}$ be unit vectors along OX and OY respectively. These are called basic unit vectors. Then vector **OP** is written as

$$\mathbf{OP} = OA\ \hat{i} + OB\ \hat{j}$$

OA and OB are called components of vector **OP** along x-axis and y-axis respectively.
Magnitude of vector **OP** is

$$p = \sqrt{OA^2 + OB^2}$$

Similarly **KL** be any vector in the plane.

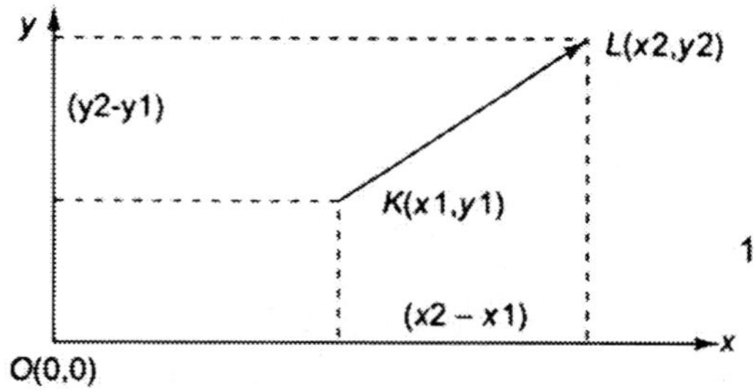

Then

$$\mathbf{KL} = (x2 - x1)\hat{i} + (y2 - y1)\hat{j}$$

A2.19.2 Components of Vector in 3-dimensions

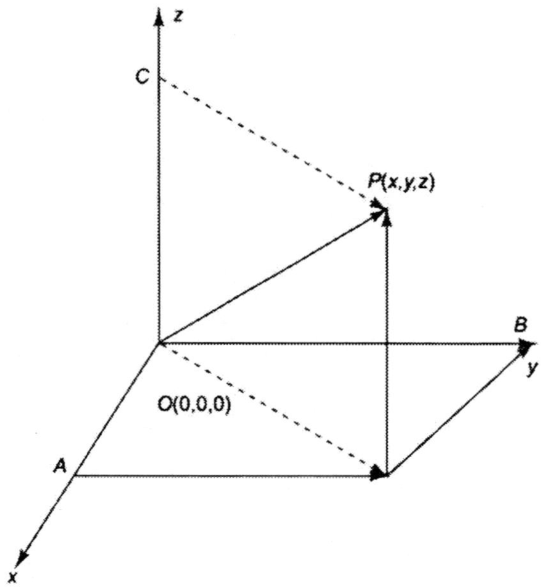

Let $P(x, y, z)$ be any point in the plane. Let $\hat{i}, \hat{j}$ and $\hat{k}$ be unit vectors along OX. OY and OZ respectively. These are called basic unit vectors. Then vector **OP** is written as

$$\mathbf{OP} = OA\ \hat{i} + OB\ \hat{j} + OC\ \hat{k}$$

OA, *OB* and *OC* are called components of vector **OP** along *x*-axis, *y*-axis and *z*-axis respectively.

Magnitude of vector **OP** is = $\sqrt{OA^2 + OB^2 + OC^2}$

Or

Magnitude of vector **OP is** = $\sqrt{x^2 + y^2 + z^2}$

Sometimes magnitude of vector is also written as a 3 – by – 1 or 1 – by 3 matrix

$$\text{Magnitude of vector } \mathbf{OP} = \begin{bmatrix} x \\ y \\ z \end{bmatrix}$$

Or

Magnitude of vector **OP** = $[\, x,\ y,\ z \,]$

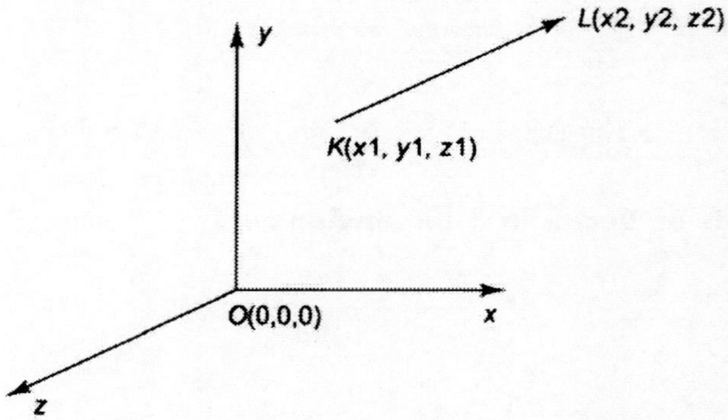

$$\mathbf{KL} = (x2 - x1)\,\hat{i} + (y2 - y1)\,\hat{j} + (z2 - z1)\,\hat{k}$$

Index